Complexity, Fractality and Fractional Dynamics Applied to Science and Engineering

Complexity, Fractality and Fractional Dynamics Applied to Science and Engineering

Guest Editors

Alexandra M. S. F. Galhano
Sergio Adriani David
António Lopes

MDPI

Basel • Beijing • Wuhan • Barcelona • Belgrade • Novi Sad • Cluj • Manchester

Guest Editors
Alexandra M. S. F. Galhano
Faculdade de Ciências Naturais, Engenharias e Tecnologias
Universidade Lusófona
Porto
Portugal

Sergio Adriani David
Faculdade de Zootecnia e Engenharia de Alimentos
University of São Paulo
Pirassununga
Brazil

António Lopes
Faculty of Engineering
University of Porto
Porto
Portugal

Editorial Office
MDPI AG
Grosspeteranlage 5
4052 Basel, Switzerland

This is a reprint of the Special Issue, published open access by the journal *Fractal and Fractional* (ISSN 2504-3110), freely accessible at: https://www.mdpi.com/journal/fractalfract/special_issues/9K10NKTKAW.

For citation purposes, cite each article independently as indicated on the article page online and as indicated below:

Lastname, A.A.; Lastname, B.B. Article Title. *Journal Name* **Year**, *Volume Number*, Page Range.

ISBN 978-3-7258-6290-0 (Hbk)
ISBN 978-3-7258-6291-7 (PDF)
https://doi.org/10.3390/books978-3-7258-6291-7

Contents

Alexandra M. S. F. Galhano, Sergio Adriani David and António M. Lopes
Complexity, Fractality and Fractional Dynamics Applied to Science and Engineering
Reprinted from: *Fractal Fract.* **2025**, *9*, 800, https://doi.org/10.3390/fractalfract9120800 1

Behrouz Parsa Moghaddam, Mahmoud A. Zaky, António Mendes Lopes and Alexandra Galhano
A Fractional Time–Space Stochastic Advection–Diffusion Equation for Modeling Atmospheric Moisture Transport at Ocean–Atmosphere Interfaces
Reprinted from: *Fractal Fract.* **2025**, *9*, 211, https://doi.org/10.3390/fractalfract9040211 5

Marcin Wątorek, Marcin Królczyk, Jarosław Kwapień, Tomasz Stanisz and Stanisław Drożdż
Approaching Multifractal Complexity in Decentralized Cryptocurrency Trading
Reprinted from: *Fractal Fract.* **2024**, *8*, 652, https://doi.org/10.3390/fractalfract8110652 23

M. Mossa Al-Sawalha, Saima Noor, Mohammad Alqudah, Musaad S. Aldhabani and Roman Ullah
Dynamics of the Traveling Wave Solutions of Fractional Date–Jimbo–Kashiwara–Miwa Equation via Riccati–Bernoulli Sub-ODE Method through Bäcklund Transformation
Reprinted from: *Fractal Fract.* **2024**, *8*, 497, https://doi.org/10.3390/fractalfract8090497 41

M. Mossa Al-Sawalha, Saima Noor, Mohammad Alqudah, Musaad S. Aldhabani and Rasool Shah
Formation of Optical Fractals by Chaotic Solitons in Coupled Nonlinear Helmholtz Equations
Reprinted from: *Fractal Fract.* **2024**, *8*, 594, https://doi.org/10.3390/fractalfract8100594 53

Ömer Akgüller, Mehmet Ali Balcı, Larissa Margareta Batrancea and Lucian Gaban
Fractional Transfer Entropy Networks: Short- and Long-Memory Perspectives on Global Stock Market Interactions
Reprinted from: *Fractal Fract.* **2025**, *9*, 69, https://doi.org/10.3390/fractalfract9020069 72

Mohamed Kayid and Mansour Shrahili
Information Properties of Consecutive Systems Using Fractional Generalized Cumulative Residual Entropy
Reprinted from: *Fractal Fract.* **2024**, *8*, 568, https://doi.org/10.3390/fractalfract8100568 107

Liran Wei, Mingzhu Tang, Na Li, Jingwen Deng, Xinpeng Zhou and Haijun Hu
Multifractal-Aware Convolutional Attention Synergistic Network for Carbon Market Price Forecasting
Reprinted from: *Fractal Fract.* **2025**, *9*, 449, https://doi.org/10.3390/fractalfract9070449 124

Haji Ahmed, Faheem Aslam and Paulo Ferreira
Navigating Choppy Waters: Interplay between Financial Stress and Commodity Market Indices
Reprinted from: *Fractal Fract.* **2024**, *8*, 96, https://doi.org/10.3390/fractalfract8020096 149

Katica R. (Stevanović) Hedrih
New Class of Complex Models of Materials with Piezoelectric Properties with Differential Constitutive Relations of Fractional Order: An Overview
Reprinted from: *Fractal Fract.* **2025**, *9*, 170, https://doi.org/10.3390/fractalfract9030170 172

Katica R. (Stevanović) Hedrih and Andjelka N. Hedrih
Rheological Burgers–Faraday Models and Rheological Dynamical Systems with Fractional Derivatives and Their Application in Biomechanics
Reprinted from: *Fractal Fract.* **2024**, *8*, 742, https://doi.org/10.3390/fractalfract8120742 . . . . . **212**

Patricio Venegas-Aravena and Enrique G. Cordaro
The Multiscale Principle in Nature (*Principium luxuriæ*): Linking Multiscale Thermodynamics to Living and Non-Living Complex Systems
Reprinted from: *Fractal Fract.* **2024**, *8*, 35, https://doi.org/10.3390/fractalfract8010035 . . . . . . **245**

fractal and fractional

MDPI

Editorial

Complexity, Fractality and Fractional Dynamics Applied to Science and Engineering

Alexandra M. S. F. Galhano [1], Sergio Adriani David [2] and António M. Lopes [3,*]

1 Faculdade de Ciências Naturais, Engenharias e Tecnologias, Universidade Lusófona do Porto, Rua Augusto Rosa 24, 4000-098 Porto, Portugal; alexandra.galhano@ulusofona.pt
2 Faculdade de Zootecnia e Engenharia de Alimentos da USP, University of São Paulo, Av. Duque de Caxias-Norte, 225, Jardim Elite, Pirassununga 13635-900, SP, Brazil; sergiodavid@usp.br
3 LAETA/INEGI, Faculty of Engineering, University of Porto, Rua Dr. Roberto Frias, 4200-465 Porto, Portugal
* Correspondence: aml@fe.up.pt

Many problems in classical and quantum physics, statistical physics, engineering, biology, psychology, economics, and finance are inherently global rather than merely local, often exhibiting long-range correlations in time and space, memory effects, fractality, and power-law dynamics. Fractional calculus and fractional processes have been widely adopted across these disciplines, emerging as highly effective tools for capturing non-local behaviors and representing long-term memory effects in diverse applied sciences. The fractional paradigm extends beyond calculus to stochastic processes, providing a unified framework to model complex phenomena. Furthermore, big data analysis, organization, retrieval, and modeling have become essential computational approaches for addressing complex, fractal, and fractional dynamics.

This Special Issue, titled "Complexity, Fractality and Fractional Dynamics Applied to Science and Engineering" aims not only to present the state of the art in complex, fractal, and fractional dynamics and their applications but also to explore the potential and broader applicability of these tools in modeling real-world phenomena. It includes 11 manuscripts addressing novel issues and specific topics that illustrate the richness and applicability of fractional calculus. In the follow-up the selected manuscripts are presented in alphabetic order of their titles.

In the paper "A Fractional Time–Space Stochastic Advection–Diffusion Equation for Modeling Atmospheric Moisture Transport at Ocean–Atmosphere Interfaces" [1], the authors propose a one-dimensional fractional time–space stochastic advection–diffusion equation for modeling moisture transport in atmospheric boundary layers over ocean surfaces. Combining fractional calculus, advective transport, and pink-noise stochasticity, the model captures temporal memory, non-local turbulent diffusion, and correlated ocean–atmosphere fluctuations. Using Caputo derivatives, a fractional Laplacian, and a $1/f$ stochastic term, the framework is solved through Fourier–Laplace techniques, yielding closed-form Mittag–Leffler solutions. Applied to a coastal domain, results show that stronger advection expands regions exceeding fog-formation thresholds and that the model reproduces anomalous diffusion and realistic variability with robust numerical performance.

In "Approaching Multifractal Complexity in Decentralized Cryptocurrency Trading" [2], decentralized cryptocurrency trading is studied to uncover potential multifractal features known from mature financial markets. Using tick-by-tick transaction data from Uniswap's Universal Router (June 2023–June 2024) and applying multifractal detrended fluctuation analysis, the study finds signs of emerging multifractality despite lower liquidity relative to centralized exchanges. The multifractal spectra exhibit strong left-sided asymmetry, indicating that large fluctuations dominate the multifractal structure, while small fluctuations behave similar to uncorrelated noise. The results also show that multifractality is more pronounced in transaction volumes than in returns and that large events reveal multifractal cross-correlations between the two indices.

In "Dynamics of the Traveling Wave Solutions of Fractional Date–Jimbo–Kashiwara–Miwa Equation via Riccati–Bernoulli Sub-ODE Method through Bäcklund Transformation" [3], the wave solutions of the time–space fractional Date–Jimbo–Kashiwara–Miwa (DJKM) equation are obtained using Riccati–Bernoulli sub-ODE method through Bäcklund transformation. The regular dynamical wave solutions of the DJKM equation encompass trigonometric, hyperbolic, and rational functions. These solutions are graphically classified into compacton kink solitary wave solutions, kink soliton wave solutions, and anti-kink soliton wave solutions. To explore the impact of the fractional parameter on those solutions, 2D plots are adopted, while 3D plots are applied to present solutions involving integer-order derivatives.

In their work "Formation of Optical Fractals by Chaotic Solitons in Coupled Nonlinear Helmholtz Equations" [4], the authors construct and examine self-similarity of optical solitons by employing the Riccati modified extended simple equation method (RMESEM) within the framework of non-integrable coupled nonlinear Helmholtz equations (CNHEs). Initially, a complex transformation is used to convert the model into a single nonlinear ordinary differential equation from which hyperbolic, exponential, rational, trigonometric, and rational hyperbolic solutions are produced. Several 3D, contour, and 2D maps are provided, highlighting the behavior of some optical solitons and demonstrating that, under certain conditions, acquired optical solitons lead to the generation of optical fractals. The suggested RMESEM offers important insights into the dynamics of CNHEs and suggests possible applications in the management of nonlinear models.

The paper "Fractional Transfer Entropy Networks: Short-and Long-Memory Perspectives on Global Stock Market Interactions" [5], introduces fractional transfer entropy (FTE), a framework that incorporates fractional calculus into transfer entropy to capture both short-run volatility and long-run dependencies in global stock markets. By tuning memory parameters, FTE reveals how varying temporal emphases reshape directional information networks among major financial indices. Results show that short-memory settings produce fast-adapting but shock-sensitive networks, balanced memory yields more stable structures, and long-memory configurations highlight persistent historical ties. FTE is shown to offer a versatile tool for assessing stability, contagion risk, and the interplay between short-term signals and long-term market structure.

In the work "Information Properties of Consecutive Systems Using Fractional Generalized Cumulative Residual Entropy" [6], the authors investigate information properties of consecutive k-out-of-n:G systems using fractional generalized cumulative residual entropy. They derive a formula for computing this entropy for the system's lifetime and examine its preservation properties under established stochastic orders, also providing useful bounds. To support practical implementation, they propose two nonparametric estimators for the fractional generalized cumulative residual entropy, whose efficiency and performance are demonstrated through both simulated and real datasets.

In "Multifractal-Aware Convolutional Attention Synergistic Network for Carbon Market Price Forecasting" [7], the challenge of accurately predicting carbon market prices is tackled by developing a multifractal-aware deep learning model, MF-Transformer-DEC. Recognizing that traditional methods struggle to capture the multifractal nature of carbon price dynamics, the study introduces a multi-scale convolution module, a fractal attention mechanism, and a dynamic error correction component to better represent scale-invariant structures, nonlinear fluctuations, and uncertainty. Applied to carbon price data from Shanghai and Guangdong, the model is shown to achieve high predictive accuracy, revealing the benefit of integrating fractal theory with AI.

The manuscript "Navigating Choppy Waters: Interplay between Financial Stress and Commodity Market Indices" [8], analyzes how financial stress interacts with major commodity markets by examining the nonlinear and multifractal cross-correlations between the financial stress index (FSI) and four key commodity indices. Using daily data from 2016 to 2023 and applying multifractal detrended cross-correlation analysis, the study identifies strong multifractal behavior and power-law cross-correlations, indicating that significant changes in financial stress tend to coincide with shifts in commodity prices. The findings offer valuable insights for investors and policymakers concerned with market stability and risk transmission.

In "New Class of Complex Models of Materials with Piezoelectric Properties with Differential Constitutive Relations of Fractional Order: An Overview" [9], a new class of fractional rheological models for elastoviscous and viscoelastic materials with piezoelectric properties is reviewed. By introducing two new fractional elements, namely a generalized Newton fluid element and a Faraday elastic element with polarization, the authors develop seven complex models governed by fractional-order constitutive relations. These models describe ideal materials with combined mechanical and piezoelectric behavior and provide a theoretical basis for future research, including applications in energy harvesting.

In their paper "Rheological Burgers–Faraday Models and Rheological Dynamical Systems with Fractional Derivatives and Their Application in Biomechanics" [10], the authors introduce two fractional Burgers–Faraday rheological models and their corresponding dynamical systems, capturing the coupled mechanical and piezoelectric behavior of materials via Kelvin–Voigt–Faraday and Maxwell–Faraday elements. The models feature fractional-order constitutive relations and two internal degrees of freedom, with different element configurations producing either fractional-type oscillations or creeping/pulsating responses under periodic forcing. These systems provide a basis for modeling biomaterials that combine viscoelastic or viscoplastic behavior with piezoelectric properties.

In the paper "The Multiscale Principle in Nature (Principium luxuriæ): Linking Multiscale Thermodynamics to Tiving and Non-living Complex Systems" [11], the authors explore a unifying physical principle behind the widespread occurrence of fractals, proposing a multiscale thermodynamic framework in which fractal and power-law patterns arise as mechanisms for dissipating excess energy across scales. In this view, the thermodynamic fractal dimension reflects how efficiently a system releases energy at microscopic versus macroscopic levels. The paper examines diverse physical, astrophysical, biological, and social systems to show that many can be reinterpreted through the "Principium luxuriæ", suggesting that it may underlie the emergence of fractals in complex systems.

The Guest Editors hope that the selected papers will help scholars and researchers to push forward the progress in complexity, fractality, and fractional dynamics applied to science and engineering.

Acknowledgments: We express our thanks to the authors of the above contributions, and to the journal Fractal and Fractional and MDPI for their support during this work.

Conflicts of Interest: The authors declare no conflict of interest.

References

1. Moghaddam, B.P.; Zaky, M.A.; Lopes, A.M.; Galhano, A. A Fractional Time–Space Stochastic Advection–Diffusion Equation for Modeling Atmospheric Moisture Transport at Ocean–Atmosphere Interfaces. *Fractal Fract.* **2025**, *9*, 211. [CrossRef]
2. Wątorek, M.; Królczyk, M.; Kwapień, J.; Stanisz, T.; Drożdż, S. Approaching Multifractal Complexity in Decentralized Cryptocurrency Trading. *Fractal Fract.* **2024**, *8*, 652. [CrossRef]

3. Al-Sawalha, M.M.; Noor, S.; Alqudah, M.; Aldhabani, M.S.; Ullah, R. Dynamics of the Traveling Wave Solutions of Fractional Date–Jimbo–Kashiwara–Miwa Equation via Riccati–Bernoulli Sub-ODE Method through Bäcklund Transformation. *Fractal Fract.* **2024**, *8*, 497. [CrossRef]
4. Al-Sawalha, M.M.; Noor, S.; Alqudah, M.; Aldhabani, M.S.; Shah, R. Formation of Optical Fractals by Chaotic Solitons in Coupled Nonlinear Helmholtz Equations. *Fractal Fract.* **2024**, *8*, 594. [CrossRef]
5. Akgüller, Ö.; Balcı, M.A.; Batrancea, L.M.; Gaban, L. Fractional Transfer Entropy Networks: Short-and Long-Memory Perspectives on Global Stock Market Interactions. *Fractal Fract.* **2025**, *9*, 69. [CrossRef]
6. Kayid, M.; Shrahili, M. Information Properties of Consecutive Systems Using Fractional Generalized Cumulative Residual Entropy. *Fractal Fract.* **2024**, *8*, 568. [CrossRef]
7. Wei, L.; Tang, M.; Li, N.; Deng, J.; Zhou, X.; Hu, H. Multifractal-Aware Convolutional Attention Synergistic Network for Carbon Market Price Forecasting. *Fractal Fract.* **2025**, *9*, 449. [CrossRef]
8. Ahmed, H.; Aslam, F.; Ferreira, P. Navigating Choppy Waters: Interplay between Financial Stress and Commodity Market Indices. *Fractal Fract.* **2024**, *8*, 96. [CrossRef]
9. Hedrih, K.R. New Class of Complex Models of Materials with Piezoelectric Properties with Differential Constitutive Relations of Fractional Order: An Overview. *Fractal Fract.* **2025**, *9*, 170. [CrossRef]
10. Hedrih, K.R.; Hedrih, A.N. Rheological Burgers–Faraday Models and Rheological Dynamical Systems with Fractional Derivatives and Their Application in Biomechanics. *Fractal Fract.* **2024**, *8*, 742. [CrossRef]
11. Venegas-Aravena, P.; Cordaro, E.G. The Multiscale Principle in Nature (*Principium luxuriæ*): Linking Multiscale Thermodynamics to Tiving and Non-living Complex Systems. *Fractal Fract.* **2024**, *8*, 35. [CrossRef]

fractal and fractional

MDPI

Article

A Fractional Time–Space Stochastic Advection–Diffusion Equation for Modeling Atmospheric Moisture Transport at Ocean–Atmosphere Interfaces

Behrouz Parsa Moghaddam [1], Mahmoud A. Zaky [2], António Mendes Lopes [3] and Alexandra Galhano [4,*]

[1] Department of Mathematics, La.C., Islamic Azad University, Lahijan P.O. Box 44169-39515, Iran; bparsa@iau.ac.ir
[2] Department of Mathematics and Statistics, College of Science, Imam Mohammad Ibn Saud Islamic University (IMSIU), Riyadh 11566, Saudi Arabia; mibrahimm@imamu.edu.sa
[3] LAETA/INEGI, Faculty of Engineering, University of Porto, Rua Dr. Roberto Frias, 4200-465 Porto, Portugal; aml@fe.up.pt
[4] Faculdade de Ciências Naturais, Engenharias e Tecnologias, Universidade Lusófona-CUP, Rua Augusto Rosa 24, 4000-098 Porto, Portugal
* Correspondence: alexandra.galhano@ulusofona.pt

Abstract: This study introduces a novel one-dimensional Fractional Time–Space Stochastic Advection–Diffusion Equation that revolutionizes the modeling of moisture transport within atmospheric boundary layers adjacent to oceanic surfaces. By synthesizing fractional calculus, advective transport mechanisms, and pink noise stochasticity, the proposed model captures the intricate interplay between temporal memory effects, non-local turbulent diffusion, and the correlated-fluctuations characteristic of complex ocean–atmosphere interactions. The framework employs the Caputo fractional derivative to represent temporal persistence and the fractional Laplacian to model non-local turbulent diffusion, and incorporates a stochastic term with a $1/f$ power spectral density to simulate environmental variability. An efficient numerical solution methodology is derived utilizing complementary Fourier and Laplace transforms, which elegantly converts spatial fractional operators into algebraic expressions and yields closed-form solutions via Mittag–Leffler functions. This method's application to a benchmark coastal domain demonstrates that stronger advection significantly increases the spatial extent of conditions exceeding fog formation thresholds, revealing advection's critical role in moisture transport dynamics. Numerical simulations demonstrate the model's capacity to reproduce both anomalous diffusion phenomena and realistic stochastic variability, while convergence analysis confirms the numerical scheme's robustness against varying noise intensities. This integrated fractional stochastic framework substantially advances atmospheric moisture modeling capabilities, with direct applications to meteorological forecasting, coastal climate assessment, and environmental engineering.

Keywords: fractional calculus; advection–diffusion; stochastic modeling; pink noise; atmospheric moisture; ocean–atmosphere interface; Fourier transform; Laplace transform; Mittag–Leffler function; numerical simulation

MSC: 35R11; 60H10; 76R50; 86A10; 65M70

1. Introduction

The Advection–Diffusion Equation (ADE) stands as a cornerstone mathematical framework that elegantly describes the transport phenomena of substances in fluid flows. This powerful equation captures the dual physical processes of advection—the transport of materials by bulk fluid motion—and diffusion—the spreading of particles due to random molecular movements [1,2]. Its versatility and broad applicability have made it indispensable across numerous scientific and engineering disciplines.

In environmental engineering, the ADE serves as the foundation for modeling pollutant dispersion in atmospheric and aquatic systems. Researchers have developed sophisticated analytical solutions using methods like separation of variables and the Generalized Integral Laplace Transform Technique (GILTT) to simulate how contaminants spread through different environmental media [3]. These models prove crucial for predicting air quality, assessing water pollution, and designing effective remediation strategies.

The equation's utility extends deeply into fluid dynamics, where it illuminates complex processes such as sediment transport in rivers and coastal environments. Stochastic interpretations of the ADE have enhanced our understanding of the statistical properties of particle movement in these systems [4], providing valuable insights for river management and coastal protection initiatives.

Hydrogeologists rely on the ADE to track contaminant migration through groundwater systems, while chemical engineers apply it to optimize reaction processes in industrial settings [5]. The medical field has adopted variants of the equation to model drug delivery and distribution within biological systems.

Recent mathematical innovations have expanded the ADE's applicability to scenarios involving time-dependent velocity fields and anisotropic diffusion [6]. Numerical methods like the Du-Fort–Frankel approach have enabled solutions to real-world problems in irregular domains that were previously intractable [7]. These advancements continue to broaden the equation's reach across scientific disciplines.

The ADE thus represents not merely a mathematical construct but a powerful conceptual tool that bridges theoretical understanding and practical application across the natural and engineered worlds [8], demonstrating the profound unity underlying seemingly disparate physical phenomena.

The ADE is a fundamental mathematical model used extensively in environmental engineering to describe the transport and dispersion of substances within various media. In water bodies, it models the spread of pollutants such as dissolved salts, chemicals, and bacteria in rivers, lakes, and coastal environments, with applications including the simulation of pollutant propagation in Guaíba Lake, Brazil, to assist local water treatment and sewage disposal authorities [9–11]. For groundwater systems, the equation is essential for understanding the movement of contaminants like phosphorus and other solutes through aquifers, where its nonlinear variant, Richard's equation, proves particularly valuable for simulating water content in unsaturated porous media [12–14]. In air pollution modeling, the ADE predicts the dispersion of atmospheric pollutants, aiding in the assessment of industrial emissions and natural disaster impacts on air quality, with techniques like the Advection–Diffusion Multilayer Method (ADMM) offering accurate semi-analytical solutions [15]. The equation also supports soil contamination studies by modeling the movement of contaminants through soil, including non-classical phenomena like superdiffusion, which informs effective remediation strategies [13]. In hydrology, it facilitates the modeling of water transfer and tracer spread in water bodies, notably in the study of high-velocity pollutant transport in heterogeneous aquifers [16]. Additionally, the ADE contributes to the design and operation of sedimentation basins and hindered-settling columns for separating contaminants from soil, enhancing soil classification and remediation efforts [17,18]. Finally, the development of numerical and analytical solutions, such as the lattice Boltzmann method and the Generalized Integral Transform Technique (GITT), enables the ADE to address complex environmental systems, providing critical validation for transport models and optimizing engineering processes [13,19]. These diverse applications highlight the ADE's versatility and its critical role in tackling environmental engineering challenges. The modeling of complex transport phenomena has been significantly advanced by recent developments in fractional stochastic partial differential equations (PDEs), as comprehensively reviewed by Moghaddam et al. [20]. Their state-of-the-art survey explores numerical techniques and practical applications of fractional stochastic PDEs, emphasizing their ability to capture anomalous diffusion and randomness in systems with symmetry-breaking characteristics. This work underscores the growing importance of integrating fractional calculus with stochastic processes, providing a robust foundation for addressing real-world challenges in diverse fields such as environmental modeling and geophysical dynamics. Building on these insights, our study extends the application of such frameworks to atmospheric moisture transport at ocean–atmosphere interfaces, introducing a novel Fractional Time–Space Stochastic Advection–Diffusion equation tailored to this context.

Our research introduces a novel one-dimensional Fractional Time–Space Stochastic Advection–Diffusion Equation (FTSADE) that characterizes moisture transport processes within an atmospheric layer adjacent to oceanic surfaces. This mathematical framework delineates specific humidity variations along a horizontal transect, employing fractional calculus principles, advective transport mechanisms, and pink noise stochasticity to represent the sophisticated interplay between temporal memory effects, turbulent phenomena, and random fluctuations arising from ocean–atmosphere coupling.

The governing equation adopts an "Atmospheric Moisture Transport" paradigm, with each mathematical component corresponding to a distinct physical mechanism:

$$\underbrace{{}^{c}\partial_t^{\alpha} q(x,t)}_{\substack{\text{Memory Effects} \\ \text{(Temporal Persistence)}}} + \underbrace{\kappa_{\beta}(-\Delta)^{\beta/2} q(x,t)}_{\substack{\text{Maritime-Induced} \\ \text{Turbulent Mixing}}} + \underbrace{v\frac{\partial q(x,t)}{\partial x}}_{\substack{\text{Advection by} \\ \text{Marine Winds}}} = \underbrace{\sigma\eta(x,t).}_{\substack{\text{Correlated Noise} \\ \text{(Ocean–Air Interface)}}} \tag{1}$$

The specific humidity function $q(x,t)$ is defined over the spatial domain $x \in [c, c+L]$ and temporal domain $t > 0$, with fractional parameter constraints $0 < \alpha \leq 1$ and $0 < \beta \leq 2$.

The model incorporates boundary specifications through the initial condition $q(x,0) = q_0(x)$ for $x \in [c, c+L]$ and periodic boundary condition $q(c,t) = q(c+L,t)$, which encapsulates the cyclical nature of moisture exchange processes.

Each term in Equation (1) represents distinct physical phenomena. The Caputo fractional temporal derivative term ${}^{c}\partial_t^{\alpha} q$ captures moisture memory effects through temporal persistence. The fractional Laplacian term $\kappa_{\beta}(-\Delta)^{\beta/2} q$ represents non-local turbulent diffusion processes driven by oceanic influences. The advection term $v\frac{\partial q}{\partial x}$ accounts for directional moisture transport by marine winds with velocity v measured in m/s. The stochastic forcing term $\sigma\eta(x,t)$ introduces correlated fluctuations at the ocean–air interface.

The model employs several physically meaningful parameters. The specific humidity $q(x,t)$, measured in kg/kg, represents the mass ratio of water vapor to total air mass—a dimensionless metric particularly appropriate for atmospheric moisture content characterization, as it remains invariant to changes in pressure and temperature commonly experienced in oceanic boundary layers. This formulation provides advantages over volumetric concentration measures (kg/m^3) by ensuring consistency across vertical atmospheric profiles.

The diffusivity coefficient κ_{β} quantifies turbulent dispersion rates along the horizontal domain. The fractional diffusion exponent β modulates diffusion behavior: values approaching zero indicate super-diffusive regimes characterized by rapid mixing, while values near 2 correspond to sub-diffusive processes with hindered spreading rates. Wind velocity v represents the mean horizontal air motion driving advective transport. The noise amplitude σ scales the correlated stochastic perturbations $\eta(x,t)$, which exhibit power spectral density proportional to $1/f$, capturing temporally coherent moisture fluctuations.

This one-dimensional framework successfully integrates fractional diffusion mechanics, advective transport, and correlated stochastic processes, with $q(x,t)$, measured in kg/kg, providing a robust representation of moisture dynamics in oceanic atmospheric contexts.

The Caputo fractional derivative is mathematically expressed as

$$\underbrace{{}^{c}\partial_t^{\alpha} q(x,t)}_{\substack{\text{Memory Effects}\\ \text{(Temporal Persistence)}}} = \frac{1}{\Gamma(1-\alpha)} \int_0^t \frac{\partial q(x,\tau)}{\partial \tau} \frac{1}{(t-\tau)^{\alpha}} \, d\tau, \quad 0 < \alpha < 1. \tag{2}$$

This integral formulation encapsulates temporal memory by applying diminishing weights to historical system states, effectively modeling the gradual dissipation of moisture memory in turbulent atmospheric conditions.

The one-dimensional fractional Laplacian operator is defined through

$$\underbrace{\kappa_\beta(-\Delta)^{\beta/2} q(x,t)}_{\substack{\text{Maritime-Induced}\\ \text{Turbulent Mixing}}} = \kappa_\beta \left(-\frac{1}{2\cos(\pi\beta/2)} \left({}_cD_x^{\beta} q(x,t) + {}_xD_{c+L}^{\beta} q(x,t) \right) \right), \tag{3}$$

where the Riemann–Liouville fractional derivatives are given by

$${}_cD_x^{\beta} q(x,t) = \frac{1}{\Gamma(n-\beta)} \frac{d^n}{dx^n} \int_c^x (x-\xi)^{n-\beta-1} q(\xi,t) \, d\xi, \tag{4}$$

$${}_xD_{c+L}^{\beta} q(x,t) = \frac{(-1)^n}{\Gamma(n-\beta)} \frac{d^n}{dx^n} \int_x^{c+L} (\xi-x)^{n-\beta-1} q(\xi,t) \, d\xi, \tag{5}$$

with $n = \lceil \beta \rceil$ and $0 < \beta < 2$. This non-local differential operator facilitates long-range spatial correlations in moisture distribution, effectively simulating ocean-influenced turbulent transport phenomena.

The stochastic forcing function is characterized by

$$\underbrace{\sigma\eta(x,t)}_{\substack{\text{Correlated Noise}\\ \text{(Ocean–Air Interface)}}} \qquad \text{with power spectral density} \propto \frac{1}{f}. \tag{6}$$

The $1/f$ spectral distribution distinguishes pink noise from uncorrelated white noise by accentuating low-frequency components, thereby capturing persistent fluctuation patterns characteristic of ocean–atmosphere interactions.

Pink noise, also known as $1/f$ noise or flicker noise, is a signal distinguished by a power spectral density that is inversely proportional to its frequency, mathematically expressed as $S(f) \propto 1/f$. This relationship results in a power density decrease of 3 dB per octave or 10 dB per decade, creating a balanced sound that feels less harsh than white noise, which maintains a flat spectral density ($S(f) \propto$ constant) [21]. Compared to brown noise, where the spectral density follows $S(f) \propto 1/f^2$, pink noise offers a more even distribution across octaves, resembling natural phenomena like rainfall or rustling leaves, which contributes to its soothing quality.

When juxtaposed with other noise types, pink noise's characteristics shine through. White noise, with its uniform power across frequencies, produces a consistent hiss that can feel sharp, while brown noise's steeper $1/f^2$ profile yields a deeper, rumbling tone [22]. Pink noise, striking a middle ground, is widely applied in sound masking, audio testing, and relaxation practices due to its balanced frequency distribution [23]. In the context of moisture transfer near an ocean's atmospheric layer, though not directly cited, ambient noise studies—including those with pink noise-like patterns—help analyze environmental factors such as wind speed and wave activity, indirectly informing moisture dynamics [24]. This suggests pink noise could play a supplementary role in understanding atmospheric–ocean interactions.

The proposed one-dimensional FTSADE framework, incorporating fractional calculus and pink noise stochasticity, presents an innovative approach to modeling moisture transport dynamics at ocean–atmosphere interfaces, building upon established mathematical principles in fractional differential equations. The FTSADE is a powerful mathematical tool that enhances traditional advection–diffusion models by integrating fractional derivatives and stochastic elements, making it ideal for capturing anomalous diffusion in systems with memory or heavy-tailed behaviors. Research has demonstrated that numerical schemes leveraging fractional derivatives, such as those explored by Néel, offer high accuracy and stability in modeling these complex dynamics [8]. Similarly, advancements in stochastic methods, like those developed by Smith, have introduced compact finite difference techniques to address equations perturbed by white noise, achieving results consistent with analytical solutions [25]. Recent progress by Jones has further expanded the field, employing decomposition methods to derive explicit solutions for both linear and nonlinear variants, broadening the equation's applicability [26]. Practically, this framework excels in modeling phenomena such as heat propagation in heterogeneous media and stochastic processes in engineering, as highlighted by Brown's work on real-world diffusion scenarios [27], significantly advancing our grasp of intricate physical systems.

This paper is structured to provide a comprehensive exploration of the FTSADE and its application to moisture transport in oceanic atmospheric layers. The introduction establishes the significance of the ADE across various disciplines and introduces the novel FTSADE framework, setting the stage for a detailed analysis. The subsequent sections systematically build upon this foundation: Section 2 outlines the implementation of Fourier and Laplace transforms to solve the FTSADE (1) analytically, leveraging spectral methods for computational efficiency. Section 3 details numerical simulation techniques and practical simplifications, offering a robust methodology for implementation in MATLAB. Section 4 presents a benchmark problem of moisture transfer near an ocean coastline, with detailed simulation results and visualizations that demonstrate the model's efficacy across varying advection velocities and noise impacts. Finally, Section 5 presents a numerical convergence analysis, validating the scheme's accuracy and stability under stochastic forcing, followed by conclusions that synthesize our findings and outline future research directions. This logical progression—from theoretical development to practical application and validation—ensures a cohesive and thorough investigation of the FTSADE's capabilities in modeling complex environmental dynamics.

2. Implementation of Fourier and Laplace Transform for FTSADE

This section presents a comprehensive methodology for numerically solving the FTSADE (1) through the combined application of Fourier and Laplace transform techniques. The approach leverages spectral methods to efficiently handle spatial derivatives while addressing the computational challenges inherent in fractional calculus. By transforming the original equation into Fourier space, we convert complex spatial fractional operators into algebraic expressions, significantly simplifying the mathematical treatment. Subsequently, applying the Laplace transform to the resulting system facilitates the analytical representation of fractional time derivatives, ultimately yielding closed-form solutions involving Mittag–Leffler functions. This dual-transform methodology provides both theoretical insights and practical computational advantages, enabling the accurate simulation of anomalous diffusion processes characterized by non-local effects and heavy-tailed distributions that conventional integer-order models cannot adequately capture. This approach aligns with recent advancements in numerical methods for fractional stochastic equations, such as the L1-FFT hybrid framework proposed by Moniri et al. [28], which integrates finite difference approximations with spectral techniques for enhanced computational efficiency.

We begin by applying fast Fourier transform (FFT) to each term in Equation (1) with respect to the spatial variable x. The FFT of the Caputo fractional time derivative maintains its form:

$$\mathcal{F}_x[{}^c\partial_t^\alpha q(x,t)] = {}^c\, \partial_t^\alpha \hat{q}(k,t),$$

where $\hat{q}(k,t) = \mathcal{F}_x\{q(x,t)\}$ represents the FFT of $q(x,t)$ with respect to x, and k denotes the wavenumber.

For the fractional Laplacian term, FFT yields

$$\mathcal{F}_x[(-\Delta)^{\beta/2} q(x,t)] = |k|^\beta \hat{q}(k,t),$$

with $|k|$ indicating the wavenumber magnitude, utilizing the Riesz fractional Laplacian property in Fourier space.

The advection term's FFT (in one dimension with scalar velocity v) is

$$\mathcal{F}_x\left[v\frac{\partial q(x,t)}{\partial x}\right] = ivk\,\hat{q}(k,t),$$

where $i = \sqrt{-1}$ represents the imaginary unit and v is the constant advection velocity. For the pink noise term $\eta(x,t)$, which is spatially uncorrelated, FFT is denoted as $\hat{\eta}(k,t) = \mathcal{F}_x\{\eta(x,t)\}$.

Applying FFT to both sides of the original equation yields

$$\mathcal{F}_x[{}^c\partial_t^\alpha q(x,t)] = \mathcal{F}_x\left[-\kappa_\beta(-\Delta)^{\beta/2} q(x,t) - v\frac{\partial q(x,t)}{\partial x} + \sigma\eta(x,t)\right].$$

Substituting each transformed term provides

$${}^c\partial_t^\alpha \hat{q}(k,t) + \kappa_\beta |k|^\beta \hat{q}(k,t) + ivk\,\hat{q}(k,t) = \sigma\hat{\eta}(k,t).$$

Rearranging this equation gives

$${}^c\partial_t^\alpha \hat{q}(k,t) + \left(\kappa_\beta |k|^\beta + ivk\right)\hat{q}(k,t) = \sigma\hat{\eta}(k,t), \tag{7}$$

where, $a_k = \kappa_\beta |k|^\beta + ivk$ encapsulates the combined effects of fractional diffusion and advection in Fourier space, with $|k|$ as the wavenumber magnitude.

This equation represents a linear fractional ordinary differential equation for each wavenumber k. To solve it, we utilize the Laplace transform, which is particularly effective for fractional calculus problems. Let $\mathcal{L}\{\hat{q}(k,t)\} = \tilde{q}(k,s)$, where s is the Laplace variable. The Laplace transform of the Caputo fractional derivative is

$$\mathcal{L}\{{}^c\partial_t^\alpha \hat{q}(k,t)\} = s^\alpha \tilde{q}(k,s) - s^{\alpha-1}\hat{q}(k,0),$$

where $\hat{q}(k,0) = \mathcal{F}_x\{q(x,0)\}$ represents the initial condition in Fourier space. Applying the Laplace transform to Equation (7) gives

$$s^\alpha \tilde{q}(k,s) - s^{\alpha-1}\hat{q}(k,0) + a_k\tilde{q}(k,s) = \sigma\tilde{\eta}(k,s), \tag{8}$$

with $\tilde{\eta}(k,s) = \mathcal{L}\{\hat{\eta}(k,t)\}$ representing the noise term's Laplace transform. Rearranging Equation (8) gives

$$\tilde{q}(k,s)(s^{\alpha} + a_k) = s^{\alpha-1}\hat{q}(k,0) + \sigma\tilde{\eta}(k,s).$$

The equation in the Laplace domain is expressed as

$$\tilde{q}(k,s) = \frac{s^{\alpha-1}\hat{q}(k,0) + \sigma\tilde{\eta}(k,s)}{s^{\alpha} + a_k}. \tag{9}$$

To determine $\hat{q}(k,t)$, we need to calculate the inverse Laplace transform of $\tilde{q}(k,s)$. The resulting solution consists of homogeneous and particular components:

According to Podlubny [29], the inverse Laplace transform of the homogeneous term is

$$\mathcal{L}^{-1}\left\{\frac{s^{\alpha-1}}{s^{\alpha} + a_k}\right\} = E_{\alpha}(-a_k t^{\alpha}),$$

where $E_{\alpha}(z) = E_{\alpha,1}(z)$ is the one-parameter Mittag–Leffler function, which generalizes the exponential function for fractional derivatives. For this particular term, applying the inverse Laplace transform yields a convolution integral:

$$\mathcal{L}^{-1}\left\{\frac{\tilde{\eta}(k,s)}{s^{\alpha} + a_k}\right\} = \int_0^t (t-\tau)^{\alpha-1} E_{\alpha,\alpha}(-a_k(t-\tau)^{\alpha})\hat{\eta}(k,\tau)\,d\tau.$$

Combining these components, the solution in Fourier space becomes

$$\hat{q}(k,t) = E_{\alpha}(-a_k t^{\alpha})\hat{q}(k,0) + \sigma\int_0^t (t-\tau)^{\alpha-1} E_{\alpha,\alpha}(-a_k(t-\tau)^{\alpha})\hat{\eta}(k,\tau)\,d\tau. \tag{10}$$

The solution in physical space, $q(x,t)$, is then obtained by applying inverse Fourier transform:

$$q(x,t) = \mathcal{F}^{-1}\{\hat{q}(k,t)\}. \tag{11}$$

3. Numerical Simulations and Results

Within this section, we present a range of stochastic functional integral equations to elucidate the practical significance of our results. These examples not only serve to highlight the applicability of our findings, but also provide a concrete demonstration of the broader implications and utility of the results in various contexts. The computational experiments were carried out utilizing MATLAB R2019a on a machine equipped with an Intel (R) Core (TM) i3-8145U CPU operating at 2.30 GHz.

The direct computation of the Mittag–Leffler function E_{α} and the convolution integral in Equation (10) is computationally intensive. We therefore employ these practical simplifications:

- **Spatial Discretization**: We discretize the domain $[0, L]$ into N_x points with spacing $dx = L/(N_x - 1)$. FFT is calculated using MATLAB's `fft` function, with wavenumbers $k = (2\pi/L) \cdot [0 : (N_x/2 - 1), -N_x/2 : -1]$.
- **Time Discretization**: The temporal domain $[0, T]$ is divided into N_t intervals with step size $dt = T/(N_t - 1)$, and the solution advances through these steps iteratively.

- **Mittag–Leffler Approximation**: For computational efficiency, we approximate $E_\alpha(-a_k t^\alpha) \approx \exp(-a_k t^\alpha)$, which is valid when $a_k t^\alpha$ is small or α approaches 1. This simplifies the homogeneous solution to

$$\hat{q}_{\text{hom}}(k,t) = \exp(-a_k t^\alpha)\hat{q}(k,0).$$

- **Noise Convolution**: We approximate the convolution integral using a discrete sum over previous time points:

$$\hat{q}_{\text{inhom}}(k,t_n) = \sigma \sum_{m=1}^{n} (t_n - t_m)^{\alpha-1} E_{\alpha,\alpha}(-a_k(t_n - t_m)^\alpha)\hat{\eta}(k,t_m)\,dt,$$

  This is implemented iteratively, accumulating noise contributions at each time step.
- **Pink Noise Generation**: We generate $\eta(x,t)$ as pink noise by applying a $1/\sqrt{|k|}$ filter to white noise in Fourier space, then transforming it back via inverse FFT. This produces a $1/f$ power spectral density, consistent with atmospheric phenomena.
- **Random Seed Initialization**: To ensure reproducibility of the stochastic simulations, we set the random seed in MATLAB using the command `rng(456, 'twister')`, employing the Mersenne Twister algorithm for consistent noise generation across runs.
- **Inverse FFT**: At each time step, we transform $\hat{q}(k,t_n)$ back to $q(x,t_n)$ using MATLAB's `ifft` function, extracting the real part to ensure physical meaningfulness.

The numerical scheme balances computational efficiency with accuracy by leveraging spectral methods for spatial derivatives and simplified time-stepping for fractional dynamics. While FFT ensures exponential spatial convergence in deterministic cases, the Mittag–Leffler approximation and discrete convolution introduce minor inaccuracies for computational tractability. This trade-off is evident in the convergence analysis (Section 4.3), where high accuracy is maintained under low noise ($\sigma = 0.00$), but efficiency gains reduce precision as noise amplitude increases.

The MATLAB implementation initializes spatial coordinates $x = \text{linspace}(0, L, N_x)$, time points $t = \text{linspace}(0, T, N_t)$, and an initial condition $q_0(x)$. We precompute the coefficient $a_k = \kappa_\beta |k|^\beta + ivk$ and update the solution as follows:

$$\hat{q}(k,t_{n+1}) = \exp(-a_k t_n^\alpha)\hat{q}(k,0) + \hat{q}_{\text{inhom}}(k,t_n).$$

This approach balances accuracy with computational efficiency, leveraging spectral methods for spatial derivatives while using a simplified time-stepping scheme for fractional dynamics and stochastic forcing.

4. Moisture Transfer in an Atmospheric Layer near an Ocean

We apply the FTSADE (1) to model moisture transfer in a horizontal atmospheric layer near an ocean coastline, a scenario relevant to meteorological applications such as fog prediction or localized precipitation. The spatial domain extends from the coast at $x = 0$ m to $x = 5000$ m (5 km inland), over a temporal domain of 7200 s (2 h). Here, $q(x,t)$ represents relative humidity (0–100%), with an initial condition of $C_0(x) = 50 + 40e^{-x/1000}$, yielding 90% humidity at the coast and a value approaching 50% inland. Periodic boundary conditions, $q(0,t) = q(5000,t)$, are imposed for simplicity, approximating cyclic influences.

The model parameters reflect atmospheric dynamics: the temporal fractional order $\alpha = 0.85$ captures turbulent mixing delays, the spatial fractional order $\beta = 1.6$ represents anomalous diffusion due to atmospheric eddies, the diffusion coefficient $\kappa_\beta = 15\,\text{m}^\beta/\text{s}^\alpha$ drives rapid moisture spread, and advection velocity v varies between 0, 1.5, and 3 m/s to simulate calm to windy conditions. A stochastic term $\sigma\eta(x,t)$, with $\sigma = 0.05$ and $\eta(x,t)$ as pink noise ($1/f$ spectrum), introduces realistic fluctuations from local variability, such as uneven evaporation or turbulence.

The simulation, implemented in MATLAB (see Algorithm 1) discretizes the domain with $N_x = 256$ spatial points and $N_t = 1024$ time points, ensuring stability and resolution. Pink noise is generated by filtering white noise with a $1/\sqrt{|k|}$ factor in Fourier space, mimicking natural atmospheric processes. We aim to assess how moisture propagates inland under advection, fractional diffusion, and stochastic forcing, particularly whether inland humidity exceeds 80%—a fog formation threshold.

Algorithm 1 Numerical Solution of FTSADE (1) using FFT and Laplace Transform

Input: $\alpha, \beta, \kappa_\beta, v, \sigma, L, T, N_x, N_t$
Output: $q(x,t)$ for all x and t
Set $x = \text{linspace}(0, L, N_x)$, $t = \text{linspace}(0, T, N_t)$, $\Delta t = T/(N_t - 1)$
Define $q(x,0) = 50 + 40\exp(-x/1000)$, compute $\hat{q}(k,0) = \mathcal{F}\{q(x,0)\}$
Set $k = (2\pi/L) \cdot [0 : (N_x/2 - 1), -N_x/2 : -1]$, $a_k = \kappa_\beta |k|^\beta + ivk$
Initialize $\hat{q}_{\text{inhom}}(k, t_0) = 0$
for $n = 1$ to N_t **do**
    Generate pink noise $\eta(x, t_n)$, compute $\hat{\eta}(k, t_n) = \mathcal{F}\{\eta(x, t_n)\}$
    Compute $\hat{q}_{\text{hom}}(k, t_n) = E_\alpha(-a_k t_n^\alpha)\hat{q}(k, 0)$
    Calculate $\hat{q}_{\text{inhom}}(k, t_n) = \sigma \sum_{m=1}^{n} (t_n - t_m)^{\alpha-1} E_{\alpha,\alpha}(-a_k (t_n - t_m)^\alpha)\hat{\eta}(k, t_m)\Delta t$
    Set $\hat{q}(k, t_n) = \hat{q}_{\text{hom}}(k, t_n) + \hat{q}_{\text{inhom}}(k, t_n)$
    Compute $q(x, t_n) = \text{real}(\mathcal{F}^{-1}\{\hat{q}(k, t_n)\})$
end for
Return: $q(x,t)$

4.1. Simulation Results

For $v = 0\,\text{m/s}$, moisture spreads solely via fractional diffusion ($\beta = 1.6$), reaching a maximum inland humidity (beyond 1000 m) of 63.16% at $t = 7200\,\text{s}$, with no penetration beyond 80%. With $v = 1.5\,\text{m/s}$, advection enhances transport, yielding a maximum of 64.40% but still with no penetration distance where $C \geq 80\%$. For $v = 3\,\text{m/s}$, the maximum rises to 63.93%, also with no penetration distance reaching the 80% threshold. These results highlight advection's role in moisture transport, amplified by fractional diffusion and modulated by pink noise, though their influence appears less pronounced than in previous models.

The standard deviation due to pink noise varies spatially: for $v = 0\,\text{m/s}$, it is 0.5534 at $x = 0$, 0.5755 at $x = 2500\,\text{m}$, and 0.5918 at $x = 5000\,\text{m}$. For $v = 1.5\,\text{m/s}$, the values are 0.9137, 0.7061, and 0.7417, respectively. For $v = 3\,\text{m/s}$, the values are 1.0399, 0.7220, and 0.7004. This indicates a complex spatial relationship between noise impact and velocity, with higher velocities showing greater variability near the source but more complex patterns inland. The spectral analysis shows power spectral density slopes of approximately -1.50, -1.55, and -1.49 for $v = 0, 1.5, 3\,\text{m/s}$, respectively, closely matching the expected behavior of pink noise (slope ≈ -1) interacting with the fractional dynamics of the system.

4.2. Visualization and Analysis

The following figures illustrate the moisture dynamics and noise effects, ordered to progress from an overview to detailed insights:

Figure 1 provides a detailed analysis for $v = 3\,\text{m/s}$. Subfigure (a) depicts $q(x,t)$ as a 3D surface, emphasizing temporal and spatial trends of high humidity near the coast that decreases further inland, modulated by noise-induced variability. Subfigure (b) plots spatial profiles at $t = 0, 1800, 3600, 5400, 7200\,\text{s}$, illustrating advection-driven shifts and noise fluctuations, with humidity exceeding 80% up to 2242 m by the end.

Figure 2 displays heatmaps of $q(x,t)$ for $v = 0, 1.5, 3\,\text{m/s}$, showing moisture evolution over space and time. For $v = 0$, diffusion dominates, spreading moisture gradually. Increasing v accelerates inland transport, with $v = 3\,\text{m/s}$ showing significant penetration. The color gradients (parula colormap) highlight humidity levels, with the colorbar indicating percentages. Figure 3 presents the power spectrum analysis. Subfigure (a) confirms the pink noise's $1/f$ characteristic (slope ≈ -1) against a reference line, validating its generation. Subfigure (b) shows the signal power distribution across frequencies, with steeper slopes for higher v, reflecting advection's smoothing effect. Subfigure (c) plots the noise-to-signal ratio (%), peaking at low frequencies and decreasing, illustrating noise's localized impact.

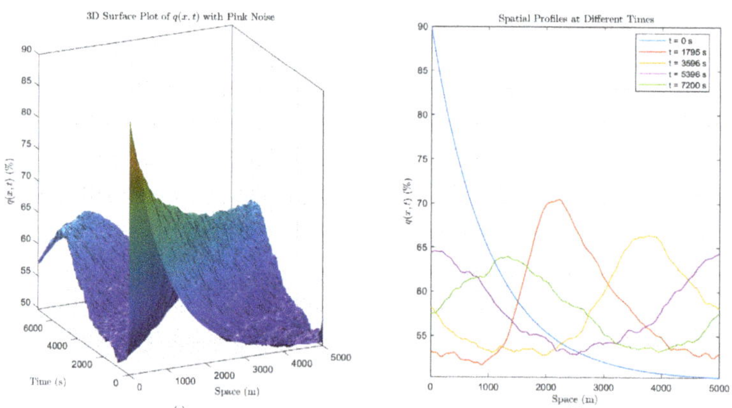

Figure 1. Detailed analysis for $v = 3\,\text{m/s}$. (**a**) Three-dimensional surface plot of $q(x,t)$ with pink noise. (**b**) Spatial profiles at $t = 0, 1800, 3600, 5400, 7200\,\text{s}$, showing advection and noise effects.

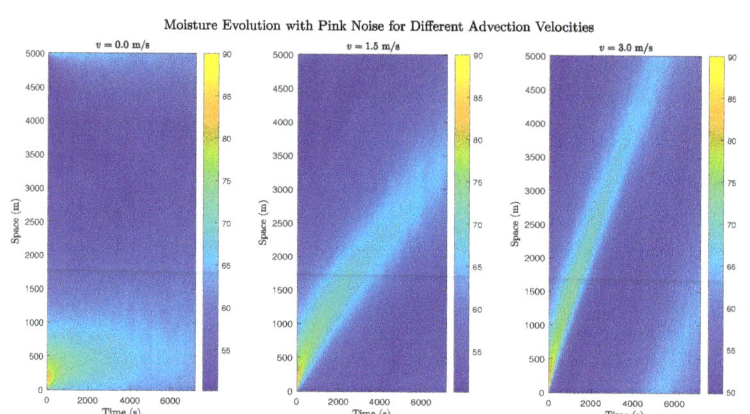

Figure 2. Moisture evolution heatmaps for $v = 0$, 1.5, $3\,\text{m/s}$, showing $q(x,t)$ over space and time with pink noise. (**a**) $v = 0\,\text{m/s}$, (**b**) $v = 1.5\,\text{m/s}$, (**c**) $v = 3\,\text{m/s}$. Higher advection velocities enhance inland transport.

Figure 4 quantifies the noise effects. Subfigure (a) tracks temporal evolution at x = 0, 1250, 2500, 3750, 5000 m for $v = 3\,\text{m/s}$, revealing noise-driven oscillations around the deterministic trend. Subfigure (b) displays the spatial standard deviation, increasing inland due to cumulative noise. Subfigure (c) plots the gradient magnitude $|\nabla q|$ at $t = 7200\,\text{s}$, showing sharper gradients near the coast, softened by advection and noise inland.

Figure 5 compares white and pink noise. Subfigure (a) shows time series samples, with pink noise exhibiting larger low-frequency fluctuations. Subfigure (b) confirms white noise's flat PSD and pink noise's $1/f$ decay in log–log plots, justifying its meteorological relevance.

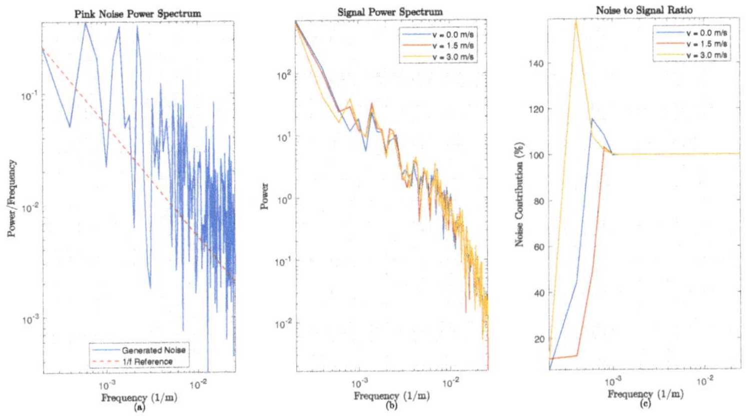

Figure 3. Power spectrum analysis. (**a**) Pink noise spectrum with $1/f$ reference. (**b**) Signal spectrum for all velocities. (**c**) Noise-to-signal ratio (%), showing noise impact across frequencies.

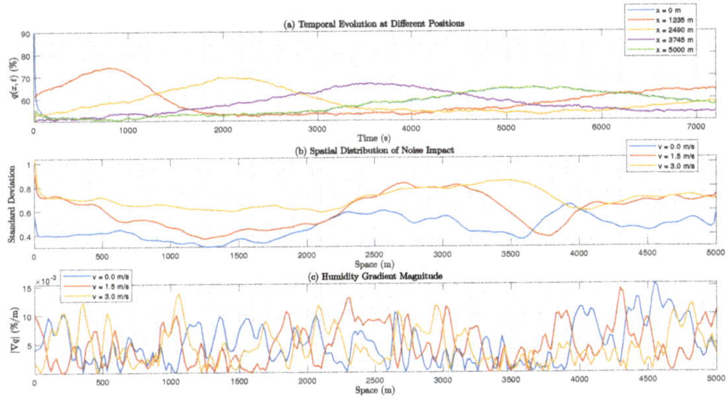

Figure 4. Noise impact analysis. (**a**) Temporal evolution at $x = 0, 1250, 2500, 3750, 5000\,\text{m}$ for $v = 3\,\text{m/s}$. (**b**) Spatial standard deviation due to noise. (**c**) Gradient magnitude of final profiles.

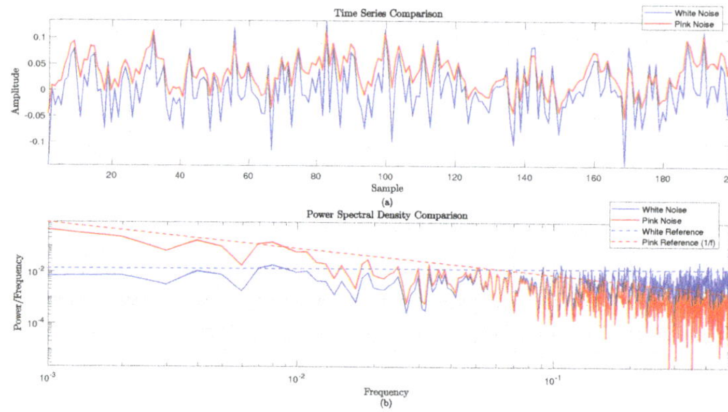

Figure 5. White vs. pink noise comparison. (**a**) Time series samples. (**b**) Power spectral density, comparing flat (white) and $1/f$ (pink) spectra.

Figure 6 isolates the pink noise effects for $v = 3\,\mathrm{m/s}$. Subfigure (a) shows the deterministic solution with smooth advection–diffusion. Subfigure (b) includes pink noise, adding realistic variability. Subfigure (c) presents the difference, highlighting noise's spatial–temporal impact, which is stronger inland.

These visualizations collectively demonstrate the FTSADE (1)'s ability to capture coastal moisture dynamics, with advection enhancing penetration, fractional diffusion accelerating spread, and pink noise introducing realistic variability. Adjusting α, β, or v allows tailoring to diverse atmospheric conditions, supporting applications in weather forecasting.

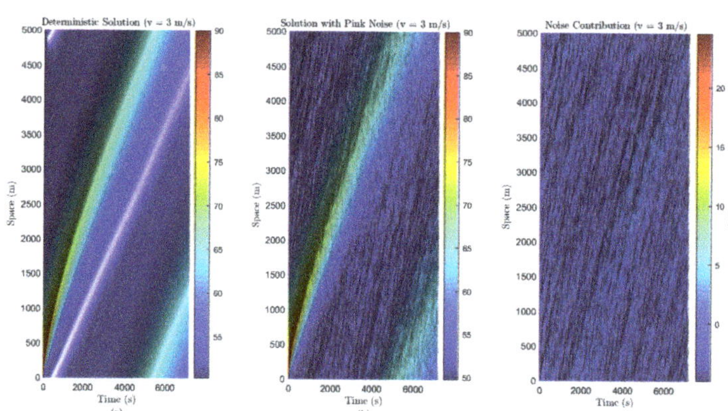

Figure 6. Pink noise effects for $v = 3\,\mathrm{m/s}$. (**a**) Deterministic solution. (**b**) Solution with pink noise. (**c**) Noise contribution difference.

Figure 7 illustrates the influence of the temporal fractional order α on the relative humidity distribution over a 5000-meter domain from the ocean. The parameter α varies from 0.15 to 0.95, with fixed $\beta = 1.6$ and wind velocity $v = 1.5\,\mathrm{m/s}$. The initial condition (black dashed line) shows humidity decreasing from 90% at $x = 0$ to approximately 50% inland. Each curve, colored according to the colorbar, represents a different α. Higher α values result in smoother profiles, approaching classical diffusion.

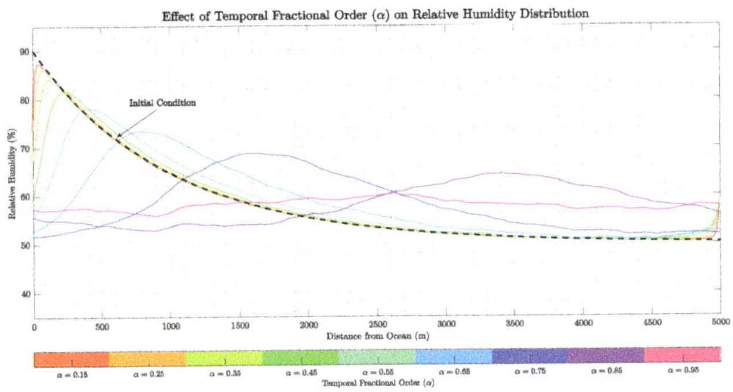

Figure 7. Effect of temporal fractional order (α) on relative humidity distribution. Colorbar indicates α values from 0.15 to 0.95.

4.3. Effect of Spatial Diffusion Exponent

Figure 8 shows the effect of the spatial diffusion exponent β, ranging from 1.3 to 1.9, with fixed $\alpha = 0.85$ and $v = 1.5\,\text{m/s}$. The initial condition is identical to that in the previous figure. Each curve corresponds to a β value, as indicated by the colorbar. Lower β values enhance super-diffusion, producing sharper gradients near the ocean, while higher β values yield more gradual humidity decay.

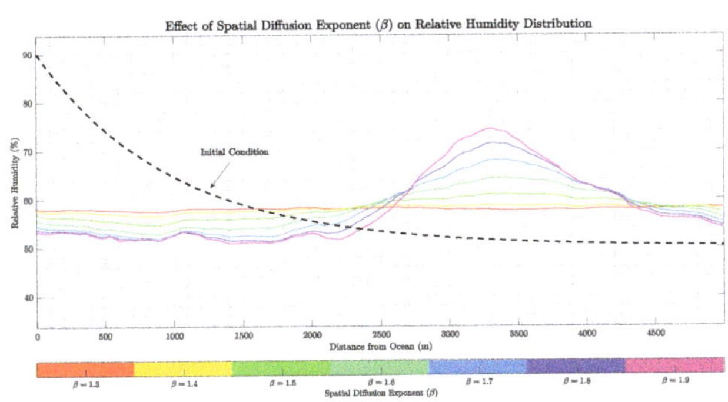

Figure 8. Effect of spatial diffusion exponent (β) on relative humidity distribution. The colorbar indicates β values from 1.3 to 1.9.

4.4. Numerical Convergence Analysis

To evaluate the accuracy and convergence properties of our numerical scheme for the fractional diffusion–advection equation, we conducted a systematic convergence study. The scheme utilizes spectral differentiation in space, implemented via FFT, and a direct integration method for the fractional time derivative. The convergence analysis adhered to the following procedure Algorithm 2:

Algorithm 2 Convergence Analysis Methodology

Step 1: Reference Solution
Establish a reference solution of elevated resolution to serve as a benchmark.
Compute the solution with spatial discretization $N_x = 2^{10}$ (1024) grid points and temporal discretization $N_t = 2^{11}$ (2048) time steps, ensuring sufficient fidelity for comparative purposes.
Step 2: Spatial Convergence Analysis
Fix the temporal resolution at $N_t = 2048$ time steps.
for $N_x = 2^7, 2^8, 2^9$ (128, 256, 512) grid points **do**
    Compute the numerical solution with the current spatial resolution.
    Quantify the relative L^2 error by comparing the solution to an interpolated version of the reference solution.
end for
Step 3: Temporal Convergence Analysis
Fix the spatial resolution at $N_x = 1024$ grid points.
for $N_t = 2^8, 2^9, 2^{10}$ (256, 512, 1024) time steps **do**
    Compute the numerical solution with the current temporal resolution.
    Calculate the relative L^2 error with respect to the reference solution.
end for
Step 4: Determination of Convergence Rates
Perform logarithmic regression analysis in log-log space to derive empirical convergence rates.
Use the functional relationship:

$$\log(E) = p \cdot \log(h) + C, \tag{12}$$

where E denotes the relative error, h represents the discretization step size (spatial or temporal), p signifies the order of convergence, and C is a constant offset.

The results of this convergence analysis are presented in Figure 9 for the fractional ADE with stochastic forcing at noise amplitudes of $\sigma = 0.00$, $\sigma = 0.05$, and $\sigma = 0.20$. The analysis reveals distinct convergence behaviors for spatial and temporal discretizations, modulated by the presence and strength of stochastic forcing.

In the deterministic case ($\sigma = 0.00$), both the spatial and temporal convergence rates exceed typical expectations, underscoring the scheme's effectiveness for smooth, noise-free problems. However, as the noise amplitude increases, the convergence rates degrade significantly below the theoretical predictions, particularly at $\sigma = 0.05$. This degradation indicates numerical challenges in accurately capturing stochastic effects. Notably, spatial refinement proves more effective than temporal refinement for reducing errors, especially under high-noise conditions ($\sigma = 0.20$). These findings offer practical guidance for computational resource allocation in simulations of atmospheric moisture transport with stochastic forcing.

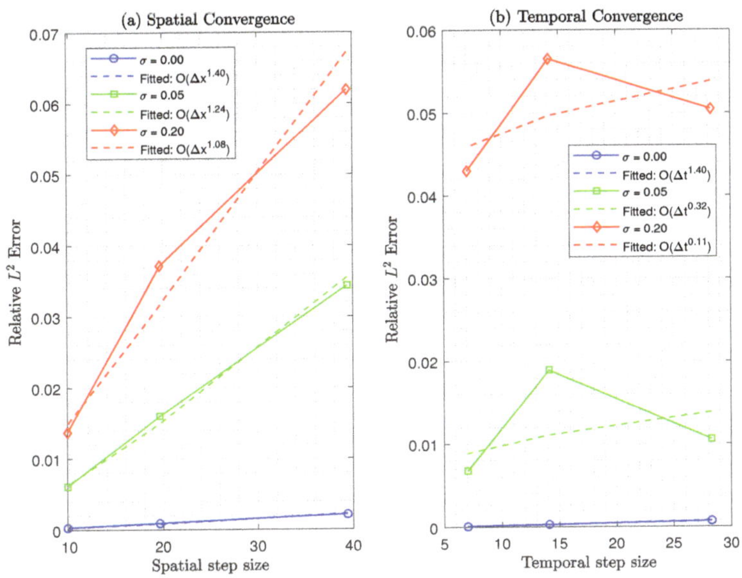

Figure 9. Convergence analysis for the fractional diffusion–advection equation with noise amplitudes of $\sigma = 0.00$, $\sigma = 0.05$, and $\sigma = 0.20$. (**a**) Spatial convergence and (**b**) temporal convergence, plotted on a log–log scale. Solid lines with markers (blue circles, green squares, and red diamonds) depict numerical results for each σ, while dashed lines of corresponding colors represent fitted power-law convergence rates.

Unlike classical diffusion models ($\alpha = 1$, $\beta = 2$), which exhibit exponential spatial convergence and $\mathcal{O}(\Delta t^2)$ temporal convergence, our fractional model's convergence rates reflect the non-local nature of fractional operators and the influence of stochastic effects. The observed degradation in convergence with increasing noise amplitude contrasts sharply with deterministic classical models, highlighting the distinct numerical challenges posed by fractional stochastic systems.

Table 1 summarizes the numerical performance of the FTSADE (1) solution, computed using FFT and the direct integration method. It reports the relative L^2 errors, CPU times, and convergence orders for noise amplitudes of $\sigma = 0.00$, $\sigma = 0.05$, and $\sigma = 0.20$, as derived from the comprehensive convergence study presented above.

Table 1. Numerical performance of the FTSADE (1) solution for different noise amplitudes (σ) and grid sizes.

σ	N_x	N_t	Relative L_2 Error	CPU Time (s)	Convergence Order	
					Spatial	Temporal
ine 0.00	512	256	2.9668×10^{-4}	79.65	1.4043	–
	256	1024	1.0032×10^{-4}	31.93	–	1.4036
0.05	512	256	6.0714×10^{-3}	83.58	1.2432	–
	256	1024	6.7851×10^{-3}	34.35	–	0.3169
0.20	512	256	1.3707×10^{-2}	77.75	1.0828	–
	256	1024	4.2983×10^{-2}	32.82	–	0.1148

5. Results and Discussion

Comprehensive simulations over a coastal domain revealed profound insights into moisture transport dynamics: advection velocity emerges as the dominant factor governing inland humidity penetration, with higher wind speeds significantly extending the reach of elevated humidity levels beyond fog formation thresholds. The fractional parameters α and β provide powerful mechanisms for fine-tuning model behavior, with decreasing α amplifying memory effects and lower β values intensifying super-diffusive characteristics, offering unprecedented flexibility for calibration to site-specific atmospheric conditions.

The incorporation of pink noise with its characteristic $1/f$ spectrum introduces realistic low-frequency variability, essential for accurate environmental modeling, confirmed through spectral analysis that revealed slopes closely aligning with the theoretical expectations across all advection scenarios. A rigorous convergence analysis demonstrated the numerical scheme's exceptional accuracy under deterministic conditions, achieving high spatial and temporal convergence rates, though these rates declined under elevated noise conditions. This finding yields an important computational guideline: spatial grid refinement offers substantially greater error reduction than temporal refinement in stochastically forced simulations.

6. Conclusions

This study developed and validated a one-dimensional FTSADE that fundamentally advances the modeling of moisture transport in near-surface atmospheric layers over oceanic boundaries. By integrating fractional calculus with advective dynamics and pink noise stochasticity, the proposed framework successfully captures three critical phenomena that conventional integer-order models fail to represent adequately: long-range temporal dependencies, non-local turbulent mixing, and correlated environmental fluctuations. The mathematical architecture—combining Caputo fractional derivatives, fractional Laplacian operators, and $1/f$ stochastic forcing—provides a theoretically rigorous yet computationally tractable approach to simulating anomalous diffusion processes in atmospheric systems.

The innovative numerical solution methodology, leveraging combined Fourier–Laplace transformations, demonstrates exceptional efficiency by reducing complex fractional operators to algebraic expressions and enabling closed-form solutions via Mittag–Leffler functions. Enhanced by an optimized convolution approximation for stochastic components, this approach strikes an optimal balance between computational feasibility and physical accuracy.

The FTSADE framework represents a significant advancement in atmospheric moisture transport modeling, bridging sophisticated mathematical theory with practical meteorological applications. Its demonstrated capacity to simulate critical phenomena such as coastal fog formation and localized precipitation establishes its value for environmental engineering, hydrological forecasting, and meteorological prediction. Future research directions include multi-dimensional extensions, the implementation of variable wind fields, and the exploration of alternative noise profiles to further enhance real-world applicability. This study lays a robust foundation for the broader adoption of fractional stochastic models in geophysical sciences, revealing their exceptional potential to elucidate and predict the complex transport processes that govern our natural environment.

Author Contributions: B.P.M. performed the formal analysis, developed the methodology, contributed to software development, managed project administration, conducted the investigations, and participated in the writing—review and editing; M.A.Z. handled the visualization and validation and contributed to the writing—review and editing; A.M.L. led project administration, contributed to the conceptualization, and participated in the writing—review and editing; A.G. provided supervision and contributed to the writing—review and editing. All authors have read and agreed to the published version of the manuscript.

Funding: This work was supported and funded by the Deanship of Scientific Research at Imam Mohammad Ibn Saud Islamic University (IMSIU) (grant number IMSIU-DDRSP2502).

Data Availability Statement: Data sharing is not applicable to this article as no datasets were generated or analyzed during the current study. The data are contained within the article.

Conflicts of Interest: The authors declare no conflicts of interest.

References

1. Sun, Y.; Jayaraman, A.S.; Chirikjian, G.S. Approximate solutions of the advection-diffusion equation for spatially variable flows. *Phys. Fluids* **2022**, *34*, 036601 . [CrossRef]
2. Cushman-Roisin, B.; Beckers, J.-M. Transport and Fate. *Int. Geophys.* **2011**, *100*, 129–214 . [CrossRef]
3. Quadros, R.S.; Gonçalves, G.A.; Buske, D.; Weymar, G.J. An analytical methodology to air pollution modelling in atmosphere. In *Defect and Diffusion Forum*; Trans Tech Publications Ltd.: Stafa-Zurich, Switzerland, 2019; Volume 396, pp. 91–98. [CrossRef]
4. Ancey, C.; Bohorquez, P.; Heyman, J. Stochastic interpretation of the advection-diffusion equation and its relevance to bed load transport. *J. Geophys. Res. Earth Surf.* **2015**, *120*, 2529–2551. [CrossRef]
5. Huang, B.; Hua, H.; Han, H.; Liu, S. Characteristics of advection-diffusion-Langmuir adsorption processes in two-dimensional plane Poiseuille flows. *Phys. Fluids* **2023**, *35*, 013310. [CrossRef]
6. Hernandez-Coronado, H.; Coronado, M.; Del-Castillo-Negrete, D. On the anisotropic advection-diffusion equation with time dependent coefficients. *Rev. Mex. Fis.* **2017**, *63*, 23–33. Available online: https://impact.ornl.gov/en/publications/on-the-anisotropic-advection-diffusion-equation-with-time-dep (accessed on 26 March 2025).
7. Hutomo, G.D.; Kusuma, J.; Ribal, A.; Aris, N. Numerical solution of 2-d advection-diffusion equation with variable coefficient using Du-Fort Frankel method. *J. Phys. Conf. Ser.* **2019**, *1218*, 012032. [CrossRef]
8. Néel, M.-C. Determining the time elapsed since sudden localized impulse given to fractional advection diffusion equation. In *Theory and Applications of Non-integer Order Systems* ; Lecture Notes in Electrical Engineering; Springer: Cham, Switzerland, 2017; Volume 407, pp. 241–251. . [CrossRef]
9. Dhawan, S.; Kapoor, S.; Kumar, S. Numerical method for advection diffusion equation using FEM and B-splines. *J. Comput. Sci.* **2012**, *3*, 429–437. [CrossRef]
10. Cho, Y.-S. A numerical study on the spread of a pollutant in a coastal environment. *Energy Sources Part A* **2012**, *34*, 1743–1752. [CrossRef]
11. Zabadal, J.R.; Poffal, C.A.; Leite, S.B. Closed form solutions for water pollution problems-II. *Lat. Am. J. Solids Struct.* **2006**, *3*, 159–171. Available online: https://www.lajss.org/index.php/LAJSS/article/view/110 (accessed on 26 March 2025).
12. Carlotto, T.; da Silva, R.V.; Grzybowski, J.M.V. GPGPU-accelerated environmental modelling based on the 2D advection-reaction-diffusion equation. *Environ. Model. Softw.* **2019**, *117*, 76–86. [CrossRef]
13. Zhou, J.G.; Haygarth, P.M.; Withers, P.J.A.; Villamizar Velez, M.L. Lattice Boltzmann method for the fractional advection-diffusion equation. *Phys. Rev. E* **2016**, *93*, 043302. [CrossRef]
14. Nasseri, M.; Daneshbod, Y.; Pirouz, M.D.; Shirzad, A. New analytical solution to water content simulation in porous media. *J. Irrig. Drain. Eng.* **2012**, *138*, 776–785. [CrossRef]
15. Costa, C.P.; Pérez-Fernández, L.D.; Rui, K.; Bravo-Castillero, J. Combining the ADMM and mathematical homogenization for atmospherical pollutant dispersion modeling. *Rev. Bras. Meteorol.* **2018**, *33*, 287–296. [CrossRef]
16. Wang, X.; Qian, J.; Ma, H.; Sun, H. Prediction of post-Darcy flow based on the spatial non-local distribution of hydraulic gradient: Preliminary assessment of wastewater management. *Chemosphere* **2023**, *336*, 139221. [CrossRef]
17. Naser, G.; Karney, B.W.; Salehi, A.A. Two-dimensional simulation model of sediment removal and flow in rectangular sedimentation basin. *J. Environ. Eng.* **2005**, *131*, 1740–1749 . [CrossRef]
18. Kim, B.H.; Klima, M.S. Simulation of Hindered-Settling Column Separations for Soil Remediation. *J. Environ. Sci. Health A* **2004**, *39*, 13–33 . [CrossRef]
19. Mashhadgarme, N.; Mazaheri, M.; Mohammad Vali Samani, J. An analytical solution to two-dimensional unsteady pollutant transport equation with arbitrary initial condition and source term in the open channels. *J. Earth Space Phys.* **2021**, *47*, 175–190 . [CrossRef]
20. Moghaddam, B.P.; Babaei, A.; Dabiri, A.; Galhano, A. Fractional Stochastic Partial Differential Equations: Numerical Advances and Practical Applications—A State of the Art Review. *Symmetry* **2024**, *16*, 563. [CrossRef]
21. Yang, M.; De Coensel, B.; Kang, J. Presence of $1/f$ noise in the temporal structure of psychoacoustic parameters of natural and urban sounds. *J. Acoust. Soc. Am.* **2015**, *138*, 916–927 . [CrossRef]

22. Lu, S.-Y.; Huang, Y.-H.; Lin, K.-Y. Spectral content (colour) of noise exposure affects work efficiency. *Noise Health* **2020**, *22*, 19–27 . [CrossRef]
23. Medellin-Serafin, A.E.; Moumtadi, F. Binaural sound stimulation at pink noise frequencies to reduce sleep consolidation time and its effects on bispectral index (BIS). In Proceedings of the 2022 Global Medical Engineering Physics Exchanges/ Pan American Health Care Exchanges (GMEPE/PAHCE), Panama City, Panama, 21–26 March 2022; Volume 2022, pp. 1–6 . [CrossRef]
24. Siderius, M.; Buckingham, M.J. Thirty years of progress in applications and modeling of ocean ambient noise. *AIP Conf. Proc.* **2012**, *1495*, 34–47. [CrossRef]
25. Smith, J.R. Stochastic compact finite difference methods for fractional advection-diffusion equations. *Adv. Comput. Math.* **2020**, *46*, 45–67 . [CrossRef]
26. Jones, L.K. Nonlinear fractional reaction-diffusion equations via decomposition techniques. *J. Appl. Math. Phys.* **2023**, *11*, 123–145. [CrossRef]
27. Brown, T.H. Modeling anomalous diffusion in heterogeneous media with fractional stochastic equations. *Phys. Rev. Appl.* **2021**, *15*, 034021. [CrossRef]
28. Moniri, Z.; Babaei, A.; Moghaddam, B.P. Robust Numerical Framework for Simulating 2D Fractional Time-Space Stochastic Diffusion Equation Driven by Spatio-Temporal Noise: L1-FFT Hybrid Approach. *Commun. Nonlinear Sci. Numer. Simul.* **2025**, in press.
29. Podlubny, I. *Fractional Differential Equations: An Introduction to Fractional Derivatives, Fractional Differential Equations, to Methods of Their Solution and Some of Their Applications*, 1st ed.; Academic Press: San Diego, CA, USA, 1998; ISBN 978-0-12-558840-9 (hardback); 978-0-08-053198-4 (eBook).

fractal and fractional

Article

Approaching Multifractal Complexity in Decentralized Cryptocurrency Trading

Marcin Wątorek [1,2], Marcin Królczyk [1], Jarosław Kwapień [3], Tomasz Stanisz [3] and Stanisław Drożdż [1,3,*]

1 Faculty of Computer Science and Telecommunications, Cracow University of Technology, 31-155 Kraków, Poland; marcin.watorek@pk.edu.pl (M.W.); m.krolczyk66@gmail.com (M.K.)
2 Adapt Centre, School of Computing, Dublin City University, D09 Y074 Dublin, Ireland
3 Complex Systems Theory Department, Institute of Nuclear Physics, Polish Academy of Sciences, 31-342 Kraków, Poland; tomasz.stanisz@ifj.edu.pl (T.S.)
* Correspondence: stanislaw.drozdz@ifj.edu.pl

Abstract: Multifractality is a concept that helps compactly grasp the most essential features of financial dynamics. In its fully developed form, this concept applies to essentially all mature financial markets and even to more liquid cryptocurrencies traded on centralized exchanges. A new element that adds complexity to cryptocurrency markets is the possibility of decentralized trading. Based on the extracted tick-by-tick transaction data from the Universal Router contract of the Uniswap decentralized exchange, from 6 June 2023 to 30 June 2024, the present study using multifractal detrended fluctuation analysis (MFDFA) shows that even though liquidity on these new exchanges is still much lower compared to centralized exchanges, convincing traces of multifractality are already emerging in this new trading as well. The resulting multifractal spectra are, however, strongly left-side asymmetric, which indicates that this multifractality comes primarily from large fluctuations, and small ones are more of the uncorrelated noise type. What is particularly interesting here is the fact that multifractality is more developed for time series representing transaction volumes than rates of return. On the level of these larger events, a trace of multifractal cross-correlations between the two characteristics is also observed.

Keywords: complex systems; multifractality; fluctuations; financial markets; blockchain technology; cryptocurrencies; decentralized trading

1. Introduction

There are two basic types of exchanges on the cryptocurrency market: centralized (CEX) [1] and decentralized (DEX) [2,3]. CEX exchanges operate very similarly to exchanges in traditional financial markets—their main task is to act as an intermediary between buyers and sellers. The entire exchange infrastructure is completely controlled by a single entity, often a private company that decides which elements of the system are publicly available and which should be hidden from ordinary users. The main source of earnings for such exchanges is transaction fees. They are efficient, easy to use, have high liquidity, allow one to exchange fiat money for cryptocurrencies and vice versa, and have well-developed customer service. However, their very nature carries a number of threats: a potential hacker attack on the exchange or the dishonesty of its owners may result in a complete loss of funds by its customers [4–6]. For this reason, these exchanges often require their users to complete KYC/AML procedures [7]. Currently, the most popular exchanges of this type are Binance, Coinbase Exchange, Kraken, Bybit, Kucoin, OKX, and Bitstamp [8].

In turn, DEX exchanges enable trading without the participation of intermediaries. Their architecture is significantly different from that of centralized exchanges because the entire infrastructure is controlled by the community. A front-end server is usually open-source code that can be run by anyone. The contract code is fully available for viewing as well. DEX trading is based on Decentralized Finance (DeFi)—smart contracts, which are computer programs that are executed without human supervision on a blockchain network like, e.g., Ethereum, which is the most popular one, by using cryptographically signed transactions [9]. They are concluded only when both parties consent and meet the requirements specified in the contract. Thanks to smart contracts on DEX exchanges, users can trade cryptocurrencies, make loans, and multiply funds through crypto deposits, among others. The advantage of DEX-type exchanges is also the possibility to trade a larger number of tokens, including less popular ones, that are not available on CEX-type exchanges. The decentralized cryptocurrency exchanges are characterized by a high degree of anonymity because implementing the KYC/AML verification is impossible due to the distributed architecture. Their biggest disadvantages include conscious or unconscious errors, exposure to attacks on smart contracts, the lack of customer support, difficult operation, and often low liquidity and a low trading volume on trading pairs [2,3,10]. The most popular DEX exchanges in 2024 include Uniswap, Radydium, Curve, PancakeSwap, SushiSwap dYdX, Balancer, Orca, and Jupiter [11]. In addition to Ethereum, currently popular platforms supporting the operation of smart contracts and DEX are Solana, Tron, BNB Chain, Arbitrum, Base, Avalanche, Sui, Polygon, and Optimism [12].

A key component of the architecture of decentralized cryptocurrency exchanges is the pricing mechanism, based on which three types of DEXs can be distinguished [13]:

(1) The Automated Market Makers (AMMs), whose task is to determine the appropriate price of assets, are based on smart contracts and liquidity pools (see below) [2,14,15]. They are currently the most popular ones.
(2) The exchanges using order books do not have liquidity pools and, in order to determine the price of assets, the traders' orders are matched directly like on the traditional exchanges [16]. There are two types of ledgers: the on-chain one that uses blockchain to process data and the off-chain one that uses solutions based on centralization to process transactions [17]. However, both types use blockchain networks to store data.
(3) The DEX aggregators, in which the pricing mechanism involves aggregating asset liquidity from many different protocols [18]. Data from many exchanges are concentrated in one place, which allows users to conduct much more profitable trading operations. These exchanges mainly focus on solving the biggest problems of DEXs, which include low liquidity, inflated cryptocurrency trading prices, long waiting times for the execution of transactions at the price specified by a user, and high prices for service fees.

Liquidity pools are used only in the exchanges based on the AMM protocol [14,15]. They are a set of funds (DeFi tokens) locked in a smart contract. They are obtained from liquidity providers (i.e., people who deposit their own funds into a pool to enable others to trade) and used by the contract to support decentralized trading. The reward for providing liquidity is receiving remuneration, most often in the form of tokens of a given pool. The remuneration source is most often the transaction fees, which are collected from traders in a given pool.

There are numerous studies that analyzed CEX trading properties [19–21]. In particular, the microstructure of the market [22], the use of machine learning in trading [23], the role of Binance exchange in volatility transmission [24], and the impact of BTC future contracts on the market [25] were studied. Exchange rates on CEX were analyzed from many perspectives [26], including noise occurrence [27], optimal trading strategies [28], and portfolio construction [29,30]. A multifractal detrended fluctuation analysis (MFDFA) was also applied to study BTC [31–34] and ETH [35–38] price changes on CEX exchanges. On the other hand, there is a limited amount of such studies for DEX exchanges. There are articles that analyze trading properties from the technical point of view [39–41], wash trading occurrences [42–44], and arbitrage and maximal extractable value (MEV) possibilities [45–48], but there are almost none that analyze the price and volume fluctuation characteristics on DEX, probably due to the decentralized character of the data. This article covers this unexplored area by systematically analyzing price change properties on DEX exchanges by advanced methods like MFDFA.

To achieve our research goal, this study focuses on transaction data extracted from the Universal Router contract [49] of the Uniswap DEX [50], which is currently the largest DEX exchange in terms of trading volume and number of available tokens [8]. It is an automated liquidity protocol based on the AMM. Originally, Uniswap operated only on the Ethereum network, but currently, it also operates on Arbitrum, Optimism, Polygon, Base, BNB Chain, Avalanche, Celo, Blast, ZKsync, and Zora [51]. Despite operating on many networks, the exchange is mainly associated with the Ethereum blockchain, and most of its community is concentrated there. Until April 2024, there were four versions of the exchange: Uniswap v1, Uniswap v2 [52], Uniswap v3 [53], and the developer version of Uniswap v4 (the full rollout of v4 has been scheduled to take place in the third quarter of 2024) [54].

There are two basic types of contracts on Uniswap: (1) Factory contracts—the so-called base contracts, on top of which other contracts that support the exchange of specific tokens are created. The contract task is also to manage the mapping between the contract address of a given token and the address of its exchange contract. (2) Exchange contracts executing the exchange of a token—these are contracts that exchange the token assigned to them [55].

To enable transactions on a given token, it is necessary to perform the following steps: (1) the contract representing a given token must be implemented on the Ethereum network, (2) a trade contract for a given token on the Uniswap exchange has to be created through the Factory contract, and (3) this dedicated contract can be used to execute its exchange transactions. In the first version of the exchange, the possibility of creating the token pools was limited as it was possible to create exchange pairs only for the native cryptocurrency Ether (ETH). Currently, however, there are contracts that enable the creation of pools that carry out, for example, a direct exchange of two ERC-20 tokens [56].

The Universal Router contract [49] is currently one of the most important contracts on Uniswap. Within a single transaction on the network, this contract can support multiple exchanges of ERC-20 tokens on Uniswap v2 and v3, as well as the trading of NFT tokens in multiple markets. The mechanism of combining multiple operations into one transaction offers exchange users great flexibility. It allows one, among other things, to optimize token exchange costs—instead of exchanging funds using one low-liquidity pool, a user can, for example, exchange part of their funds on Uniswap v2 and part on Uniswap v3, thus avoiding an unfavorable exchange rate.

The main research question of this article is to investigate to what extent, despite the existing differences in trading methods, the fluctuation characteristics on the most liquid DEX exchange, Uniswap, are similar to those observed on Binance, which is currently the largest CEX exchange. In Section 2.1, the characteristics of the log returns and volume distributions will be compared. The next step will be to check the existence of long-range correlations in the time series of interest rates and volume, which will allow for a comparison of the characteristics of multifractal patterns in time series from both types of exchanges in Section 3.1. Finally, the multifractal properties of the correlation between volatility and volume will be investigated in Section 3.2.

2. Data and Methodology

2.1. Data Specification

In this study, transactions executed via the Uniswap Universal Router in the most liquid pools are analyzed, specifically ETH/USDT on Uniswap version 2 (USDT Uv2), ETH/USDT on Uniswap v3 with 0.3% commission (USDT Uv3_0.3), ETH/USDT on Uniswap v3 with 0.05% commission (USDT Uv3_0.05), ETH/USDC on Uniswap v2 (USDC Uv2), ETH/USDC on Uniswap v3 with 0.3% commission (USDC Uv3_0.3), and ETH/USDC on Uniswap v3 with 0.05% commission (USDC Uv3_0.05) [57]. The tick-by-tick transaction data cover the period from 6 June 2023 to 30 June 2024. For Uniswap v3 pools, the percentage indicates the fee for the respective pool, whereas for Uniswap v2, the fee is consistently 0.3%. Uniswap versions 2 and 3 also differ in trading mechanisms. Uniswap v3 introduces concentrated liquidity, allowing liquidity providers to specify the price range within which they provide liquidity [53]. As a result, each liquidity position may be different and is represented by an NFT token [58]. Version 3 also includes range orders, enabling orders to be placed within a custom price range above or below the current pool price [53]. This mechanism can result in transactions with very low volumes and prices that deviate significantly from those on other exchanges. As such, transactions with volumes below 0.01 USD were excluded from the dataset.

The distinction between liquidity pools with varying commission rates is evident in the distribution of log returns, measured at the highest sampling frequency, $\Delta t = 12$ s, which corresponds to Ethereum's block validation time [59]. Figure 1 demonstrates that, in addition to the usual concentration of log returns around zero, common in financial time series [60–63], notable values of $R_{\Delta t=12\text{ s}} = 0.006$ and $R_{\Delta t=12\text{ s}} = 0.001$ appear for pools with 0.3% (Uv2 and Uv3) and 0.05% (Uv3) commissions, respectively. This can be attributed to the smallest possible price change (twice the commission rate) at which arbitrage transactions (buying and selling) are profitable [45].

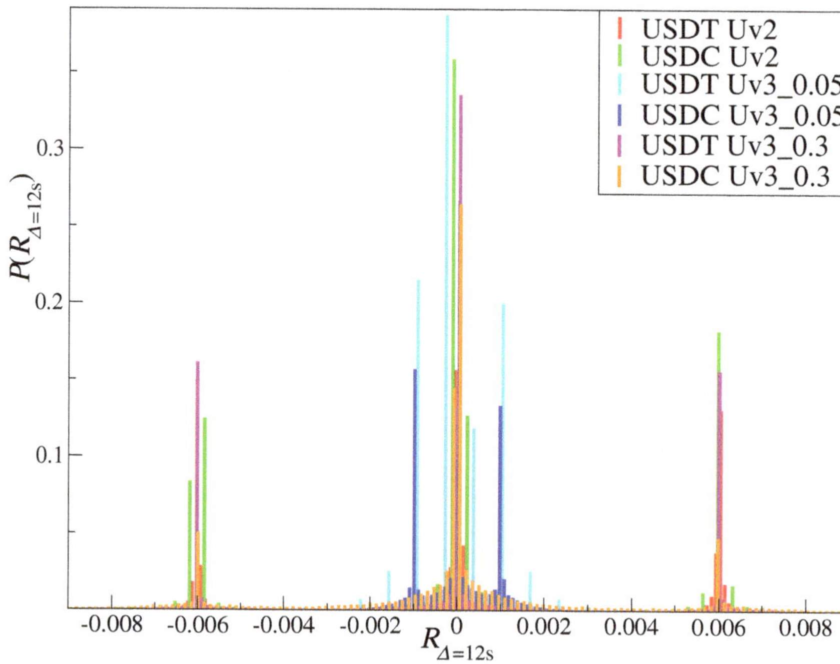

Figure 1. The probability distribution (histogram) of the exchange rates ETH/USDT and ETH/USDC log returns $R_{\Delta t=12\text{ s}}$ on Uniswap liquidity pools—versions 2 and 3 with different trading commissions: 0.3% (USDT Uv3_0.3, USDC Uv3_03, USDT Uv2, and USDC Uv2) and 0.05% (USDT Uv3_0.05 and USDC Uv3_0.05).

To benchmark the time series characteristics from the decentralized exchange Uniswap, exchange rates for ETH/USDT and ETH/USDC from the most liquid centralized exchange, Binance [64], were also included in the dataset.

The basic characteristics of the time series analyzed in this study are presented in Table 1. Notably, the average transaction volume $\langle V \rangle$ is higher on Uniswap than on Binance. Additionally, the maximum observed transaction volume $V_{\max}$ is comparable between the two exchanges. However, the average volume over 5 min intervals $\langle V_{\Delta t=5\text{ min}} \rangle$ is significantly higher for the ETH/USDT exchange rate on Binance. This difference can be attributed to the lower number of transactions N on Uniswap compared to Binance. Another important observation is that Uniswap has a significantly lower trading frequency, with the lowest time between transactions $\delta t = 45$ s on USDT Uv2 compared to $\delta t = 0.11$ s for USDT on Binance.

Table 1. Basic statistics of the ETH exchange rate time series considered in this study: total number of transactions N, the average inter-transaction time δt, the average transaction volume value per transaction $\langle V \rangle$, the highest volume value $V_{\max}$, the average volume value in a measurement interval $\langle V_{\Delta t} \rangle$, and the fraction of zero log returns $\%0R_{\Delta t}$ for Δt = 5 min.

Name	N	$\langle \delta t \rangle$ [s]	$\langle V \rangle$ [USD]	$V_{\max}$ [USD]	$\langle V_{\Delta t} \rangle$ [USD]	$\%0R_{\Delta t}$
USDC Uv3_0.3	37,457	900.26	9903	2,358,376	3298	0.785
USDC Uv3_0.05	765,399	47.01	11,227	7,751,943	76,419	0.006
USDC Uv2	503,569	66.97	1856	1,254,394	8310	0.049
USDT Uv3_0.3	151,003	223.33	3390	3,878,300	4553	0.388
USDT Uv3_0.05	704,276	49.62	5331	2,875,000	33,395	0.009
USDT Uv2	748,919	45.14	1843	1,084,474	11,378	0.028
USDT Binance	297,688,280	0.11	1185	9,739,140	2,955,093	0
USDC Binance	10,343,176	3.31	73	4,265,360	72,643	0.003

To ensure the analysis remains comparable and to avoid an excessive number of zero returns that could distort a more advanced multifractal analysis, the tick-by-tick data were aggregated into a 5 min time series. Additionally, due to the significantly longer inter-transaction time for Uv3 with a 0.3% commission ($\delta t > 200$ s), the time series from these liquidity pools were combined with those from Uv3 with a 0.05% commission. Following this procedure, 6 time series of log returns $R_{\Delta t=5\text{ min}}$ and volume $V_{\Delta t=5\text{ min}}$ were obtained for ETH in USDT and USDC on Uniswap v2, Uniswap v3, and Binance: USDT Uv3, USDT Uv2, USDC Uv3, USDC Uv2, USDT Binance, and USDC Binance. Figure 2 presents the complementary cumulative distribution functions (CCDFs) of these time series.

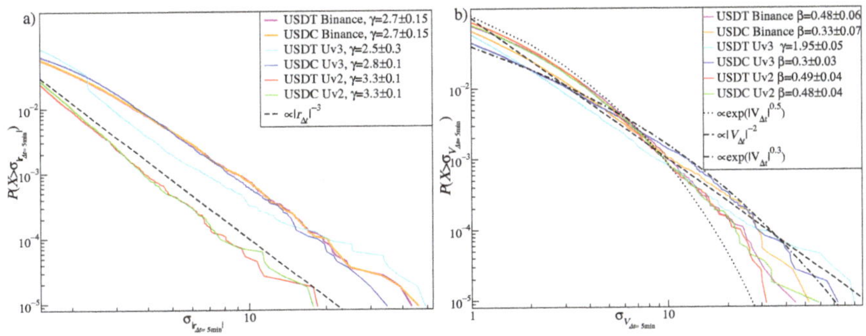

Figure 2. Complementary cumulative distribution functions for (**a**) absolute log returns $|R_{\Delta t=5\text{ min}}|$ and (**b**) volume $V_{\Delta t=5\text{ min}}$ of ETH expressed in USDT and USDC on Binance and Uniswap. The estimated exponent, γ with standard error, is shown in the insets.

It is a well-established stylized fact that return distributions in financial time series exhibit fat tails [65–67]. This has been documented many times for stock markets [60,61,68], Forex [63,69], cryptocurrencies [70,71] and even for the most liquid NFT collections [72–74]. The heavy tails typically manifest as a power-law decay in the complementary cumulative distribution function (CCDF), expressed as $P(X > \sigma) \sim \sigma^{-\gamma}$, where σ represents the estimated standard deviation. For high-frequency data, the power-law exponent often approaches a value of 3, i.e., $\gamma \approx 3$ [75]. This so-called inverse cubic power law for return distributions has been observed not only in traditional financial markets [61,62,76] but also in the cryptocurrency market [77–79].

As shown in Figure 2a, this pattern is also evident in the normalized absolute log returns on the decentralized Uniswap exchange. Interestingly, the tails are fatter, and thus the value of γ is lower for Uniswap v3 compared to Uniswap v2. This can be attributed to the more flexible trading mechanism in Uniswap v3, which allows users to set orders within a custom price range above or below the current price. Combined with the ability to provide concentrated liquidity, this results in trades occurring at prices significantly different from those on other exchanges, as observed on 12 March 2024 in the Uv3 ETH/USDT liquidity pool, where the exchange rate reached approximately 4800 [80]. The γ exponent values for Binance exchange rates fall between those observed for the two Uniswap versions.

Another well-known stylized fact that is observed in mature financial markets is that the volume distributions often exhibit fatter tails than the return distributions [81,82]. In the stock markets, a simple relationship has been proposed between the exponents for volume and log returns, where $\gamma_V = \gamma_R/2$ [83,84]. However, this relationship is more sophisticated for the cryptocurrencies [85,86], where the CCDFs of the normalized volume for the most liquid cryptocurrencies like BTC and ETH are better described by a stretched exponential function $f(x) \sim \exp(x^{\beta})$ [87]. This finding is supported by the more recent data analyzed in this study. For the CCDF of the normalized volume of the most liquid pair on Binance, ETH/USDT, the best fit is $\beta \approx 0.48$ (see Figure 2b). A slightly fatter tail, and thus a lower β, is observed for ETH/USDC on Binance.

The observed trend of thicker tails for Uniswap v3 compared to Uniswap v2, as seen in the normalized absolute log returns, also holds for the CCDFs of the normalized volume, as shown in Figure 2b. The heaviest tail, characterized by a power-law decay, is seen in the ETH/USDT pair traded on Uniswap v3, with $\gamma \approx 1.95$. The second heaviest tail is also found for ETH/USDC on Uniswap v3, though its best fit is a stretched exponential function with $\beta \approx 0.3$. In contrast, the CCDFs of the normalized volume for ETH/USDT and ETH/USDC traded on Uniswap v2 show thinner tails, with the best fit being $\beta \approx 0.49$.

A more detailed examination of the relationship between price and volume on decentralized exchanges, particularly the concept of price impact [88,89], will be explored in a separate, more specialized article.

The measure used to identify linear correlations in a time series is the autocorrelation function (ACF), defined as

$$A(x, \Delta i) = \frac{1/T \sum_{i=1}^{T} [x(i) - \langle x(i) \rangle_i][x(i + \Delta i) - \langle x(i) \rangle_i]}{\sigma_x^2}, \quad (1)$$

where σ_x is the estimated standard deviation of the time series $x(i)$, $\langle \cdot \rangle$ represents the estimated mean, and Δi is the time lag in terms of data points, which can be related to the time as $\tau = \Delta i \Delta t$. For financial time series of log returns, the ACF shows a typical pattern: it quickly drops to zero when analyzing the sign of the returns [63,66] but decays slowly, following a power law, when considering the absolute values [90–92]. The same behavior is observed in the case of the normalized absolute log returns on Uniswap, where the ACF follows a power-law decay, as shown in Figure 3a.

The strongest autocorrelation, similar to that seen on Binance, occurs in the exchange rates traded on Uniswap v3. In contrast, the ACF of the normalized absolute log returns for Uniswap v2 is significantly weaker, with $A_{r_{\mathrm{Uv3}}}(\tau = 1) \approx 0.3$ compared to $A_{r_{\mathrm{Uv2}}}(\tau = 1) \approx 0.06$.

The behavior of the ACF for the normalized volume differs from that of log returns (Figure 3b). While a power-law decay is also observed, the weakest autocorrelations are found in Uniswap v3, with $A_{V_{\mathrm{Uv3}}}(\tau = 1) \approx 0.25$. For Uniswap v2, the autocorrelations are slightly stronger, with $A_{V_{\mathrm{Uv2}}}(\tau = 1) \approx 0.35$ for ETH/USDC and $A_{V_{\mathrm{Uv2}}}(\tau = 1) \approx 0.45$ for ETH/USDT. Even for a larger τ, the ACF in Uniswap v2 remains higher than that observed on Binance, where the largest values of the ACF occur for $\tau < 20$, with $A_V(\tau = 1) \approx 0.56$ for ETH/USDC and $A_V(\tau = 1) \approx 0.7$ for ETH/USDT.

The strength and rate of decay of the ACF discussed here influence the scaling of the fluctuation functions, as temporal correlations are a key source of multifractality [93]. This topic will be explored in detail in the following sections.

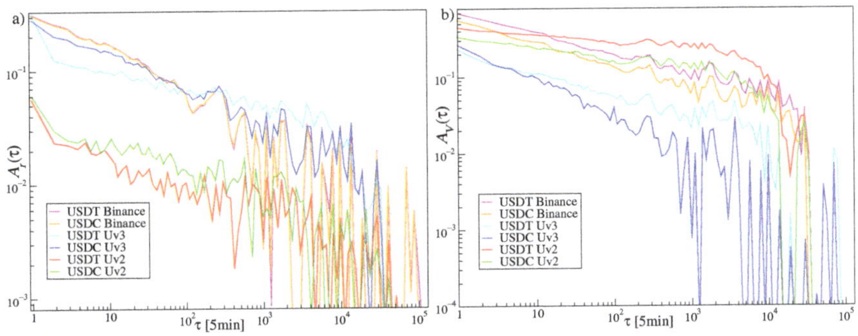

Figure 3. Autocorrelation function for (**a**) absolute log returns $|R_{\Delta t=5\text{ min}}|$ and (**b**) volume $V_{\Delta t=5\text{ min}}$ of ETH expressed in USDT and USDC on Binance and Uniswap exchanges.

2.2. Multifractal Formalism

Multifractality is a well-documented characteristic observed in financial time series [94–96]. It has also been reported in cryptocurrencies traded on centralized exchanges (CEX) such as Binance [97,98]. The primary objective of this article is to investigate the presence of multifractal effects in the time series of log returns and trading volume from a decentralized exchange like Uniswap and to examine whether correlations between volatility (expressed by absolute log returns) and trading volume exist and exhibit multifractality. To test these hypotheses, the multifractal cross-correlation analysis methodology (MFCCA) is applied [99]. This approach is a consistent generalization of the detrended cross-correlation analysis (DCCA) introduced by [100] and expanded by [101]. The methodology builds upon multifractal detrended fluctuation analysis [102] (MFDFA), itself an extension of the widely used detrended fluctuation analysis [103] (DFA).

The MFCCA methodology enables a quantitative assessment of both the scaling properties of individual time series and the degree of multifractal cross-correlation between any two time series. The procedure for multifractal cross-correlation analysis involves the following steps. Two time series, $\{x(i)\}_{i=1,\dots,T}$ and $\{y(i)\}_{i=1,\dots,T}$, each of length T, are divided into M_s segments of length s, starting from the opposite ends. The time series is then integrated and, within each segment ν, a least-square-fitted polynomial trend is removed by using the following equations:

$$X_\nu(s,i) = \sum_{j=1}^{i} x(\nu s + j) - P^{(m)}_{X,s,\nu}(i), \tag{2}$$

$$Y_\nu(s,i) = \sum_{j=1}^{i} y(\nu s + j) - P^{(m)}_{Y,s,\nu}(i), \tag{3}$$

where $P^{(m)}$ represents polynomials of order m. The polynomial order of $m = 2$ is chosen due to its proven efficacy in financial time series analysis [104]. Following this detrending process, a total of $2M_s$ segments with detrended signals are obtained. Variance and covariance for each segment ν are then calculated as follows:

$$f^2_{ZZ}(s,\nu) = \frac{1}{s} \sum_{i=1}^{s} (Z_\nu(s,i))^2, \tag{4}$$

$$f^2_{XY}(s,\nu) = \frac{1}{s} \sum_{i=1}^{s} X_\nu(s,i) \times Y_\nu(s,i), \tag{5}$$

where Z represents either X or Y. These quantities are used to compute a family of fluctuation functions:

$$F_{ZZ}(q,s) = \left\{ \frac{1}{2M_s} \sum_{\nu=0}^{2M_s-1} \left[f_{ZZ}^2(s,\nu) \right]^{q/2} \right\}^{1/q}, \tag{6}$$

$$F_{XY}(q,s) = \left\{ \frac{1}{2M_s} \sum_{\nu=0}^{2M_s-1} \text{sign}\left[f_{XY}^2(s,\nu) \right] \left| f_{XY}^2(s,\nu) \right|^{q/2} \right\}^{1/q}, \tag{7}$$

where the sign function, $\text{sign}\left[f_{XY}^2(s,\nu) \right]$, ensures the consistency of the results across different values of q.

Multifractal cross-correlation is expected to reveal itself through a power-law relationship in the scaling behavior of the qth-order covariance function $F_{XY}(q,s)$. If it is negative for all s, the $-F_{XY}(q,s)$ is taken. The following relationship is obtained:

$$F_{XY}(q,s) \sim s^{\lambda(q)}, \tag{8}$$

where $\lambda(q)$ is an exponent that quantitatively describes the fractal characteristics of the cross-correlations. In the case of monofractal cross-correlation, $\lambda(q)$ is independent of q, while a q-dependence of $\lambda(q)$ indicates the presence of multifractal cross-correlations.

F_{ZZ} describes the scaling properties of a single time series through the following relationship:

$$F_{ZZ}(q,s) \sim s^{h(q)}, \tag{9}$$

where $h(q)$ represents the generalized Hurst exponent [105]. If $h(q)$ remains constant, the time series is considered monofractal, with $h(q=2) = H$, where H is the standard Hurst exponent, a measure of the persistence or memory of the time series [106]. When $h(q)$ varies with q, the series exhibits a multifractal structure. The corresponding singularity spectrum $f(\alpha)$, which provides further insight into the multifractal nature [107], can be computed using the following relations [102]:

$$\alpha = h(q) + q\frac{dh(q)}{dq}, \quad f(\alpha) = q(\alpha - h(q)) + 1, \tag{10}$$

where α is the singularity (or Hölder) exponent and $f(\alpha)$ is the multifractal spectrum.

This methodology also enables the introduction of the q-dependent detrended cross-correlation coefficient $\rho(q,s)$, as proposed by [108], which filters out the strength of cross-correlations that vary with fluctuation size:

$$\rho_{XY}(q,s) = \frac{F_{XY}(q,s)}{\sqrt{F_{XX}(q,s)F_{YY}(q,s)}}. \tag{11}$$

For $q = 2$, this definition can be interpreted as a detrended version of the Pearson cross-correlation coefficient C [109]. In this context, the parameter q acts as a filter: for $q < 2$, small fluctuations have more influence on $\rho(q,s)$, while for $q > 2$, large fluctuations dominate. This allows the method to selectively emphasize different ranges of fluctuation size contributing to the observed correlations. The filtering capability of $\rho(q,s)$ offers an advantage over the conventional methods since cross-correlations in the real-world time series are typically not uniformly distributed across fluctuations of varying magnitudes [110]. Moreover, $\rho(q,s)$ can be applied to quantify cross-correlations even between the time series that do not exhibit multifractal properties.

3. Results

3.1. Multifractal Properties of Returns R *and Volume* V *Time Series*

It is shown in Figure 3 that the autocorrelation function for the absolute log return and volume time series exhibit a power-law decay. The presence of long memory, indicated by this power-law decay, is associated with the occurrence of nonlinear correlations, which are the source of multifractality in time series [93,111,112]. Therefore, multifractal effects are expected to be present in the analyzed time series. However, the individual ones differ in the strength and persistence of the autocorrelation, which impacts the fluctuation functions $F(q,s)$ calculated using Equation (6) and presented in Figure 4 for log returns and Figure 5 for volume.

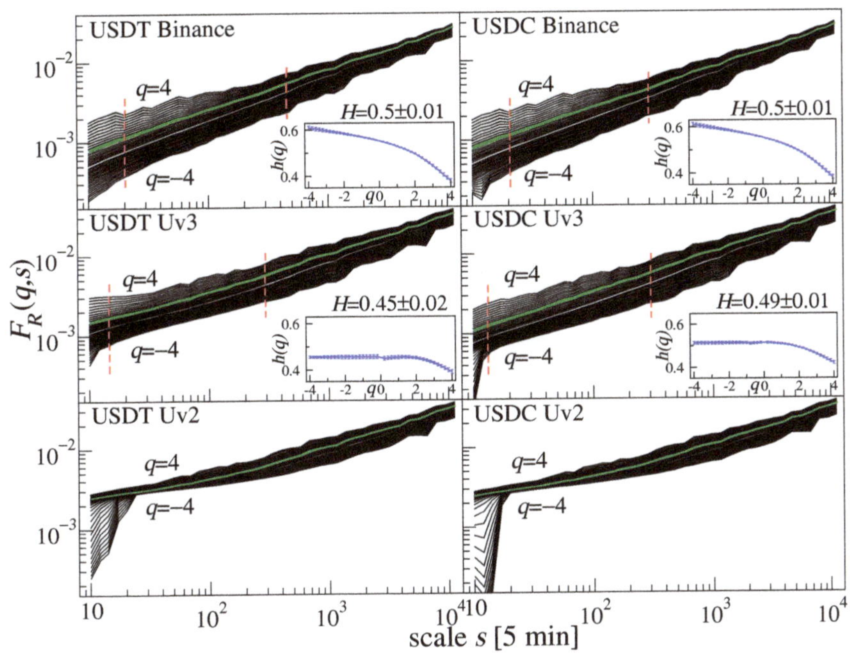

Figure 4. Fluctuation functions $F_{RR}(q,s)$ with the range of $q \in [-4,4]$ ($\Delta q = 0.2$) calculated for ETH/USDT and ETH/USDC log returns $R_{\Delta t=5\text{ min}}$ from Binance (**top**), Uniswap v3 (**middle**), and Uniswap v2 (**bottom**). (Main) Thick green lines represent $F(q=2,s)$, from the slope of which the Hurst exponent H is estimated together with its standard error. Vertical red dashed lines indicate a scale range, where the family of $F_{RR}(q,s)$ exhibits a power-law dependence for different values of q. (Insets) The generalized Hurst exponent $h(q)$ is estimated from the scaling of $F_{RR}(q,s)$. Error bars represent the standard error of linear regression.

For log returns, the best scaling quality was observed for the exchange rates from Binance (the upper panels in Figure 4). This result is expected, given the behavior of the ACF in Figure 3 and the significantly higher liquidity on the Binance pairs compared to the Uniswap ones. Based on the scaling range shown in Figure 4, the generalized Hurst exponent was estimated using Equation (9), with the results displayed in the inset of Figure 4 (the upper panels). The clear dependence of $h(q)$ across the full range of q indicates that the log return time series for ETH/USDT and ETH/USDC are multifractal. This finding aligns with previous studies on older datasets for the most liquid BTC and ETH exchange rates [31–33,35]. The estimated Hurst exponent values, $H = h(2)$, are close to 0.5, which is typical for mature financial markets [113–117].

A slightly weaker scaling of $F_{RR}(q,s)$ is observed for log returns from Uniswap v3 (the middle panels in Figure 4). In this case, $h(q)$ is dependent on q only for $q > 0$, which corresponds to medium and large fluctuations. Combined with $H < 0.5$, this behavior suggests the characteristics typical of immature markets [118–123], where multifractality is observed primarily for large fluctuations, while small, noisy fluctuations tend to be monofractal.

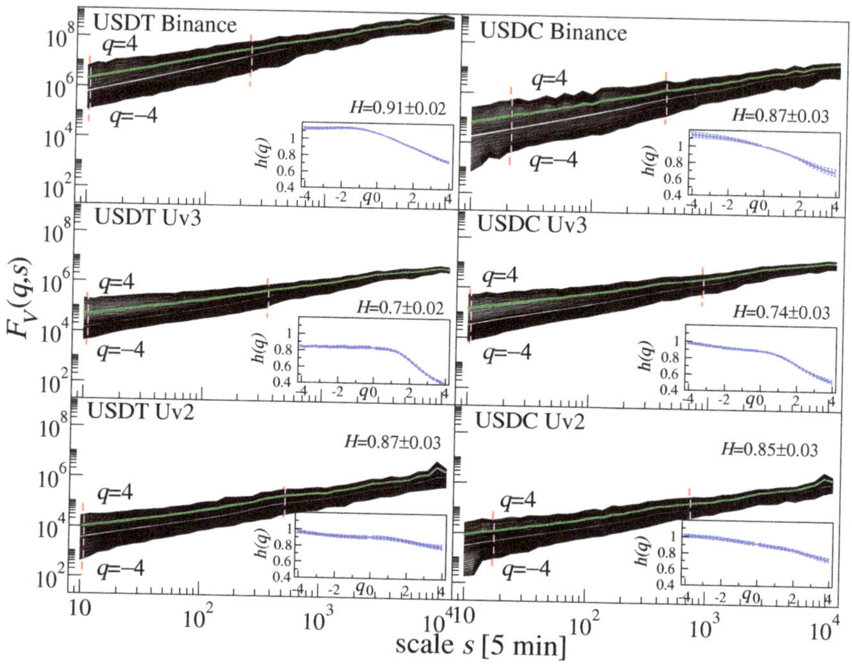

Figure 5. $F_{VV}(q,s)$ obtained in the same way as in Figure 4 but for volume $V_{\Delta t=5\text{ min}}$.

For the log return time series from Uniswap v2 (the middle panels in Figure 4), the scaling quality is so poor that it is not possible to clearly determine the Hurst exponent due to the presence of two distinct scaling regimes in the fluctuation function. This behavior is directly linked to the very weak autocorrelations observed in Figure 3. A potential reason for the weak autocorrelations and poor scaling of fluctuations in the Uniswap v2 log returns could be the trading mechanism, which does not allow setting orders at arbitrary prices in advance. Instead, trading is only possible by submitting a request to the pool at the current price [52].

The scaling quality of the fluctuation functions is better in the case of the volume time series. As is seen in Figure 5, the scaling of $F_{VV}(q,s)$ is sufficient to determine $h(q)$ for all the time series analyzed. Unlike the log returns, there is no significant difference between the $F_{VV}(q,s)$ scaling for volume from Binance and both versions of Uniswap. Interestingly, the Hurst exponent for volume is higher for Uniswap v2 ($H \approx 0.86$) compared to Uniswap v3 ($H \approx 0.72$), which is consistent with the stronger autocorrelations observed for Uv2 in Figure 3.

A natural feature of the volume time series is the higher Hurst exponent compared to log returns because volume is unsigned. The insets of Figure 5 show that the dependence of $h(q)$ on q is evident for all the volume time series, which indicates their multifractal nature. This dependence is particularly pronounced for $q > 0$, highlighting a more developed multifractality in large fluctuations of the volume time series.

This behavior of $h(q)$ is directly reflected in the multifractal spectra shown in Figure 6, which are derived by using Equation (10). In most cases, a left-sided asymmetry of $f(\alpha)$ is observed, with the left arm stretched relative to the right one. This suggests a richer multifractality in the large fluctuations. Such a left-sided asymmetry in the singularity spectrum is commonly seen in financial time series, where small fluctuations often represent noise, while medium and large ones convey meaningful information [77,95,124].

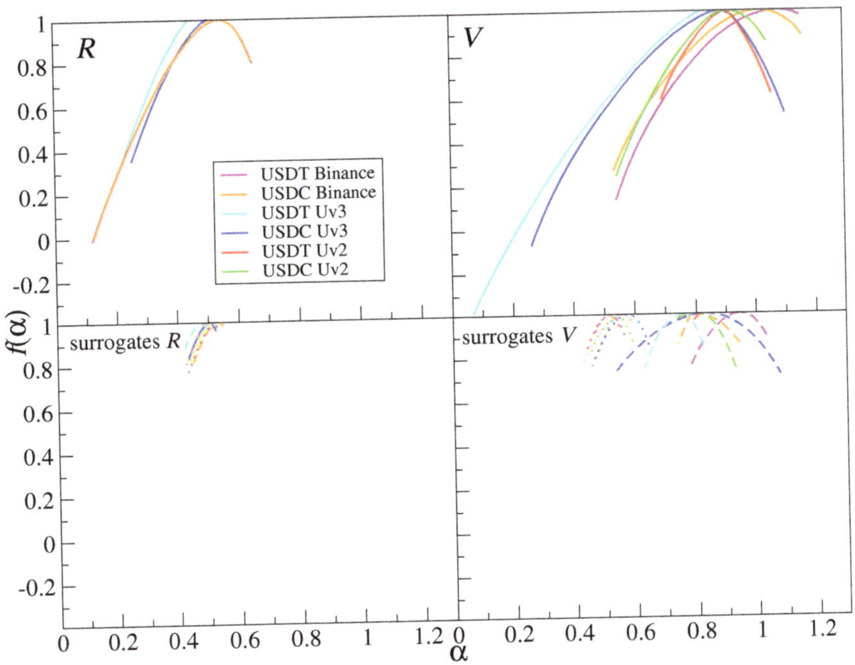

Figure 6. Multifractal spectra $f(\alpha)$ calculated for ETH/USDT and ETH/USDC log returns $R_{\Delta t=5\text{ min}}$ **(left panels)** and volume values $V_{\Delta t=5\text{ min}}$ **(right panels)** from Binance, Uniswap v3, and Uniswap v2 in the range $q \in [-4:4]$ and $\Delta q = 0.2$. The original time series (**top**) are compared with their shuffled surrogates marked with dotted lines and the Fourier surrogates marked with dashed lines (**bottom**).

For log returns (Figure 6, left side), the most developed multifractal spectrum is observed for time series from Binance, which confirms previous findings [26,98]. In the case of Uniswap v3 log returns, only the left arm of the spectrum is present, and it is shorter than that of Binance, indicating that only large fluctuations exhibit multifractality. For Uniswap v2 log returns, the multifractal spectrum could not be determined due to the poor scaling of the fluctuation function $F_{RR}(q,s)$. This suggests that Uniswap, particularly in its version 2, was not yet a mature market from a multifractal perspective. However, in version 3, which was launched later, the appearance of the left arm of the multifractal spectrum may signal a more advanced stage of market development.

Interestingly, for the volume time series (Figure 6, right panels), the longest left arm of $f(\alpha)$ is observed for ETH/USDT from Uniswap v3. In the case of ETH/USDC on Uniswap v3, both arms are well developed. The significant stretching of the left arm for ETH/USDT on Uniswap v3 can be explained by (1) the heavy tails of the corresponding CCDF, where ETH/USDT Uv3 have the heaviest tails (Figure 2b) with $\gamma \approx 1.95$, a value which causes instability in the Lévy sense, and (2) a slow convergence to the normal distribution [76]. Additionally, Uniswap v2 also displays multifractality, though $f(\alpha)$ is narrower here than that of ETH/USDC on Uv3. The singularity spectra obtained from the Binance time series show a left-side asymmetry and are comparable to those from Uniswap v2. However, the ones for Binance are shifted to the right, indicating higher values of the Hurst exponent, as previously shown in Figure 5. The smaller differences between Binance and Uniswap in the multifractal characteristics of volume may stem from the fact that, as shown in the basic statistics in Table 1, Uniswap has a higher transaction volume per trade, despite its slower trading if compared to Binance.

To assess the statistical significance of the observed multifractal effects in the analyzed time series, two types of surrogate time series were generated: the Fourier surrogates [125] and the randomly shuffled surrogates [126]. As can be seen in the lower panels of Figure 6, the multiscale characteristics of the original time series nearly vanish when considering either of the surrogate types. In the case of the Fourier surrogates, nonlinear correlations are eliminated by randomizing the Fourier phases of the original data, leaving only linear correlations intact. As a result, the multifractal spectra $f(\alpha)$ are narrow and shifted to the right for volume since $H > 0.5$ for the original time series. For the shuffled surrogates, both the linear and nonlinear correlations are destroyed, though the log return distributions are preserved. Consequently, $f(\alpha)$ is narrow and centered around $\alpha = 0.5$, which corresponds to an uncorrelated time series ($H = 0.5$). It should be noted that the slightly wider spectra for the Uv3 volume are a numerical artifact caused by the heavy tails in the corresponding CCDFs (for more details, see Refs. [76,127–129]).

3.2. Correlations Between Volatility $|R|$ and Volume V

Another well-documented phenomenon in the mature financial markets is the correlation between volatility (the absolute log return volume [130–132], which has also been observed recently in the most liquid cryptocurrencies [86]). In this study, the MFCCA methodology will be applied to explore the extent to which volatility and volume are correlated on Uniswap, where the trading mechanisms differ from those on the traditional centralized exchanges. These differences in trading mechanisms have led to distortions in some of the time series characteristics discussed above.

The fluctuation functions $F_{|R|V}(q,s)$, representing correlations between volatility $|R|$ and volume V, calculated by using Equation (7), are shown in Figure 7. Similar to the Binance time series (Figure 7, the top panels), Uniswap also exhibits scaling in the fluctuation functions $F_{|R|V}(q,s)$ but only for $q > 0$, which means that the correlations are present mainly in the medium and large fluctuations. However, the scaling for Uniswap is poorer and begins at higher values of q (around $q = 0.6$). This scaling allows for the estimation of λ using Equation (8) and its comparison with the average generalized Hurst exponents for $|R|$ and V defined as $h_{|R|V}(q) = (h_R(q) + h_V(q))/2$ [133]—see the insets of Figure 7. The dependence of λ on q is evident, indicating that the correlation between volatility and volume is multifractal. However, in the case of Uniswap, the difference between $\lambda(q)$ and $h_{|R|V}(q)$ is much larger, signaling weaker cross-correlations [134]. This is further reflected in the behavior of the detrended cross-correlation coefficient $\rho(q,s)$ (calculated by using Equation (11)), which is shown for $q = 2$ in Figure 8. For $q = 2$ and $s = 10$, the coefficient is significantly lower for Uniswap ($\rho(q,s) < 0.1$) compared to Binance ($\rho(q,s) = 0.52$ in the case of ETH/USDT and $\rho(q,s) = 0.37$ in the case of ETH/USDC, particularly at small time scales. In both exchanges, $\rho(q,s)$ increases with time scale s, which is in agreement with the related phenomenon observed in the traditional financial markets [26,134,135]. However, this increase occurs more rapidly in the time series from Uniswap as $\rho(q,s)$ for Binance plateaus around $s = 400$, reaching above 0.8.

The strongest correlation in Figure 8 is observed for the most liquid ETH/USDT pair traded on Binance, while the weakest correlations are seen in Uniswap v2. This, combined with a poorer scaling of $F_{|R|V}(q,s)$ for Uniswap, highlights the differences between Uniswap and Binance in terms of the volatility–volume cross-correlations. Uniswap appears to be a less developed market in this respect, possibly due to its different trading mechanisms and the fact that transactions on Uniswap occur less frequently but with higher average volumes per transaction than on Binance.

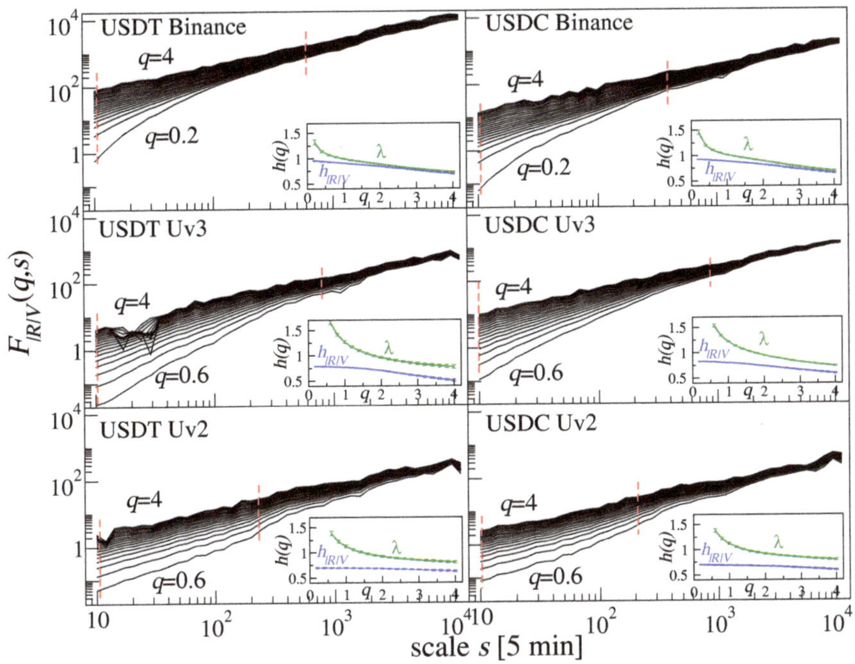

Figure 7. (Main) Fluctuation functions $F_{|R|V}(q, s)$ for $q > 0$ with $\Delta q = 0.2$ calculated for volatility $|R_{\Delta 5=5\text{ min}}|$ and volume $|V_{\Delta 5=5\text{ min}}|$ representing time series from Binance (**top**), Uniswap version 3 (Uv3, **middle**), and version 2 (Uv2, **bottom**). (Insets) The scaling exponent $\lambda(q)$ (green line) and the average generalized Hurst exponent $h_{|R|V}(q)$ (blue line) are estimated from the range of scales marked with the dashed lines. Error bars represent the standard error of linear regression.

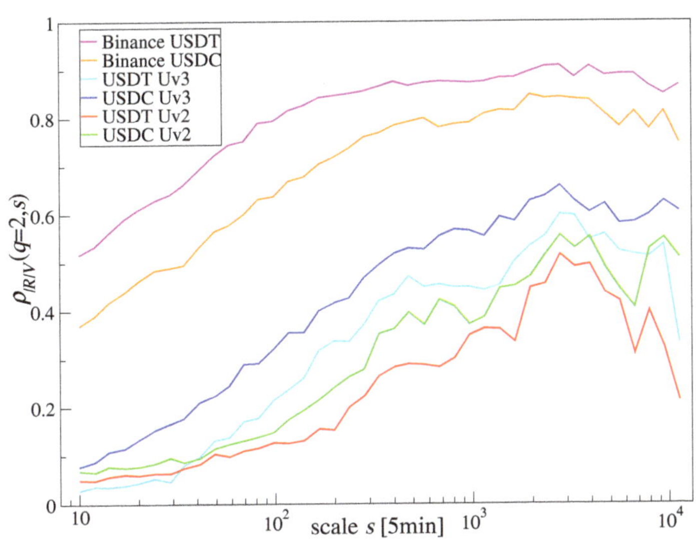

Figure 8. The detrended cross-correlation coefficient $\rho(q, s)$, $q = 2$, calculated for volatility $|R_{\Delta 5=5\text{ min}}|$ and volume $|V_{\Delta 5=5\text{ min}}|$ time series of ETH/USDT and ETH/USDC traded on Binance, Uniswap version 3 (Uv3), and version 2 (Uv2).

4. Conclusions

Despite the different trading mechanisms on the decentralized exchange Uniswap, many of the characteristics of log returns and volume are already similar to those observed on centralized exchanges like Binance. However, several differences remain. The log returns from Uniswap are characterized by weaker autocorrelations, especially for Uniswap version 2, which results in a lack of scaling in the fluctuation function for Uv2 and poor scaling for Uv3. In Uv3, only large fluctuations exhibit a multifractal nature. On the other hand, no significant difference is observed in the volume characteristics between Binance and Uniswap. The cross-correlations between volatility (absolute log returns) and volume are much weaker on Uniswap. These differences may reflect both the lower maturity level of Uniswap and its unique trading mechanism, where fewer transactions occur but with higher volumes. This newly emerging volatility–volume correspondence on DEX is an intriguing effect from the perspective of the functioning of the financial markets and should definitely become a subject of immediate, more specific, systematic research. The obtained results may help investors adapt their investment strategies used on more common CEX exchanges to different trading conditions and price-fluctuation properties that occur on DEX exchanges.

One of the limitations of this study is the fact that the data were obtained only from the Uniswap liquidity pools. Even though it is currently the most liquid DEX exchange, there may exist some specificities on other exchanges. From the investor and arbitrageur perspective, an interesting observation is the significantly higher occurrence of the log returns around the commission-related values. An investigation of this phenomenon on a larger number of liquidity pools and trading protocols will be carried out in the future.

Author Contributions: Conceptualization, M.W. and S.D.; methodology, M.W., M.K., J.K., and T.S.; software, M.W. and M.K.; validation, M.W., T.S., and S.D.; formal analysis, M.W., M.K., and J.K.; investigation, M.W. and M.K.; resources, M.W. and M.K.; data curation, M.W. and M.K.; writing—original draft preparation, M.W., M.K., J.K., and S.D.; writing—review and editing, M.W., M.K., T.S., and S.D.; visualization, M.W. and M.K.; supervision, M.W. and S.D.; project administration, M.W. and S.D.; funding acquisition, M.W. All authors have read and agreed to the published version of the manuscript.

Funding: This research was funded in part by the National Science Centre, Poland, grant number 2023/07/X/ST6/01569.

Data Availability Statement: Data are freely available on the public Ethereum blockchain and on the Binance platform.

Conflicts of Interest: The authors declare no conflicts of interest.

References

1. Bonneau, J.; Miller, A.; Clark, J.; Narayanan, A.; Kroll, J.A.; Felten, E.W. Research Perspectives and Challenges for Bitcoin and Cryptocurrencies. 2015. Available online: https://citeseerx.ist.psu.edu/document?repid=rep1&type=pdf&doi=88a603ffe828c503b6818410bdb3dae435f90ebe (accessed on 25 September 2024).
2. Mohan, V. Automated market makers and decentralized exchanges: A DeFi primer. *Financ. Innov.* **2022**, *8*, 20. [CrossRef]
3. Xu, J.; Paruch, K.; Cousaert, S.; Feng, Y. Sok: Decentralized exchanges (DEX) with automated market maker (AMM) protocols. *ACM Comput. Surv.* **2023**, *55*, 1–50. [CrossRef]
4. Feder, A.; Gandal, N.; Hamrick, J.T.; Moore, T. The impact of DDoS and other security shocks on Bitcoin currency exchanges: Evidence from Mt. Gox. *J. Cybersecur.* **2018**, *3*, 137–144. [CrossRef]
5. Vidal-Tomas, D.; Briola, A.; Aste, T. FTX's downfall and Binance's consolidation: The fragility of centralised digital finance. *Phys. A* **2023**, *625*, 129044. [CrossRef]
6. Hägele, S. Centralized exchanges vs. decentralized exchanges in cryptocurrency markets: A systematic literature review. *Electron. Mark.* **2024**, *34*, 33. [CrossRef]
7. Moreno, S.M.; Seigneur, J.M.; Gotzev, G. A survey of KYC/AML for cryptocurrencies transactions. In *Handbook of Research on Cyber Crime and Information Privacy*; IGI Global: Hershey, PA, USA, 2021; pp. 21–42.
8. CoinMarketCap. Available online: https://coinmarketcap.com (accessed on 25 September 2024).
9. Zheng, Z.; Xie, S.; Dai, H.N.; Chen, W.; Chen, X.; Weng, J.; Imran, M. An overview on smart contracts: Challenges, advances and platforms. *Future Gener. Comput. Syst.* **2020**, *105*, 475–491. [CrossRef]

10. Aspris, A.; Foley, S.; Svec, J.; Wang, L. Decentralized exchanges: The "wild west" of cryptocurrency trading. *Int. Rev. Financ. Anal.* **2021**, *77*, 101845. [CrossRef]
11. Coin Gecko. Available online: https://www.coingecko.com/en/exchanges/decentralized (accessed on 25 September 2024).
12. DeFiLlama. Available online: https://defillama.com/chains (accessed on 25 September 2024).
13. Shah, K.; Lathiya, D.; Lukhi, N.; Parmar, K.; Sanghvi, H. A systematic review of decentralized finance protocols. *Int. J. Intell. Netw.* **2023**, *4*, 171–181. [CrossRef]
14. Bartoletti, M.; Chiang, J.H.Y.; Lluch-Lafuente, A. A theory of automated market makers in DeFi. *Log. Methods Comput. Sci.* **2022**, *18*, 12. [CrossRef]
15. Brönnimann, W.; Egloff, P.; Krabichler, T. Automated market makers and their implications for liquidity providers. *Digit. Financ.* **2024**, *6*, 573–604. [CrossRef]
16. Platt, M.; Pierangeli, F.; Livan, G.; Righi, S. Facilitating the Decentralised Exchange of Cryptocurrencies in an Order-Driven Market. In Proceedings of the 2020 2nd Conference on Blockchain Research & Applications for Innovative Networks and Services (BRAINS), Paris, France, 28–30 September 2020; pp. 30–34.
17. Warren, W.; Bandeali, A. *0x: An Open Protocol for Decentralized Exchange on the Ethereum Blockchain*; 2017; Technical report. Available online: https://cryptopapers.info/0x/ (accessed on 6 November 2024).
18. Takemiya, M. ALT: Aggregate Liquidity Technology. In Proceedings of the 2023 IEEE International Conference on Blockchain and Cryptocurrency (ICBC), Dubai, United Arab Emirates, 1–5 May 2023; pp. 1–6.
19. Corbet, S.; Lucey, B.; Urquhart, A.; Yarovaya, L. Cryptocurrencies as a financial asset: A systematic analysis. *Int. Rev. Financ. Anal.* **2019**, *62*, 182–199. [CrossRef]
20. Makarov, I.; Schoar, A. Trading and arbitrage in cryptocurrency markets. *J. Financ. Econ.* **2020**, *135*, 293–319. [CrossRef]
21. Fang, F.; Ventre, C.; Basios, M.; Kanthan, L.; Martinez-Rego, D.; Wu, F.; Li, L. Cryptocurrency trading: A comprehensive survey. *Financ. Innov.* **2022**, *8*, 13. [CrossRef]
22. Aleti, S.; Mizrach, B. Bitcoin spot and futures market microstructure. *J. Futur. Mark.* **2021**, *41*, 194–225. [CrossRef]
23. Koker, T.E.; Koutmos, D. Cryptocurrency Trading Using Machine Learning. *J. Risk Financ. Manag.* **2020**, *13*, 178. [CrossRef]
24. Carol Alexander, D.F.H.; Kaeck, A. The Role of Binance in Bitcoin Volatility Transmission. *Appl. Math. Financ.* **2022**, *29*, 1–32. [CrossRef]
25. Fassas, A.P.; Papadamou, S.; Koulis, A. Price discovery in bitcoin futures. *Res. Int. Bus. Financ.* **2020**, *52*, 101116. [CrossRef]
26. Wątorek, M.; Drożdż, S.; Kwapień, J.J.; Minati, L.; Oświęcimka, P.; Stanuszek, M. Multiscale characteristics of the emerging global cryptocurrency market. *Phys. Rep.* **2021**, *901*, 1–82. [CrossRef]
27. Dimpfl, T.; Peter, F.J. Nothing but noise? Price discovery across cryptocurrency exchanges. *J. Financ. Mark.* **2021**, *54*, 100584. [CrossRef]
28. James, N. Evolutionary correlation, regime switching, spectral dynamics and optimal trading strategies for cryptocurrencies and equities. *Phys. D* **2022**, *434*, 133262. [CrossRef]
29. James, N.; Menzies, M. Collective Dynamics, Diversification and Optimal Portfolio Construction for Cryptocurrencies. *Entropy* **2023**, *25*, 931. [CrossRef] [PubMed]
30. Nguyen, A.P.N.; Mai, T.T.; Bezbradica, M.; Crane, M. Volatility and returns connectedness in cryptocurrency markets: Insights from graph-based methods. *Phys. A* **2023**, *632*, 129349. [CrossRef]
31. Takaishi, T. Statistical properties and multifractality of Bitcoin. *Phys. A* **2018**, *506*, 507–519. [CrossRef]
32. da Silva Filho, A.C.; Maganini, N.D.; de Almeida, E.F. Multifractal analysis of Bitcoin market. *Phys. A* **2018**, *512*, 954–967. [CrossRef]
33. Stavroyiannis, S.; Babalos, V.; Bekiros, S.; Lahmiri, S.; Uddin, G.S. The high frequency multifractal properties of Bitcoin. *Phys. A* **2019**, *520*, 62–71. [CrossRef]
34. Takaishi, T.; Adachi, T. Market efficiency, liquidity, and multifractality of Bitcoin: A dynamic study. *Asia-Pac. Financ. Mark.* **2020**, *27*, 145–154. [CrossRef]
35. Mensi, W.; Lee, Y.J.; Al-Yahyaee, K.H.; Sensoy, A.; Yoon, S.M. Intraday downward/upward multifractality and long memory in Bitcoin and Ethereum markets: An asymmetric multifractal detrended fluctuation analysis. *Financ. Res. Lett.* **2019**, *31*, 19–25. [CrossRef]
36. Han, Q.; Wu, J.; Zheng, Z. Long-range dependence, multi-fractality and volume-return causality of ether market. *Chaos* **2020**, *30*, 011101. [CrossRef]
37. Kakinaka, S.; Umeno, K. Cryptocurrency market efficiency in short- and long-term horizons during COVID-19: An asymmetric multifractal analysis approach. *Financ. Res. Lett.* **2022**, *46*, 102319. [CrossRef]
38. Ali, H.; Aftab, M.; Aslam, F.; Ferreira, P. Inner Multifractal Dynamics in the Jumps of Cryptocurrency and Forex Markets. *Fractal Fract.* **2024**, *8*, 571. [CrossRef]
39. Capponi, A.; Jia, R. The adoption of blockchain-based decentralized exchanges. *arXiv* **2021**, arXiv:2103.08842.
40. Lo, Y.C.; Medda, F. Uniswap and the Emergence of the Decentralized Exchange. *J. Financ. Mark. Infrastruct.* **2021**, *10*, 1–25.
41. Alexander, C.; Chen, X.; Deng, J.; Fu, Q. Impacts of Protocol Updates on Uniswap Decentralized Crypto Exchanges. 2023. Available online: https://ssrn.com/abstract=4495589 (accessed on 25 September 2024).
42. Victor, F.; Weintraud, A.M. Detecting and quantifying wash trading on decentralized cryptocurrency exchanges. In Proceedings of the Web Conference 2021, Virtual, 19–23 April 2021; pp. 23–32.

43. Gan, R.; Wang, L.; Ruan, X.; Lin, X. Understanding Flash-Loan-based Wash Trading. In Proceedings of the 4th ACM Conference on Advances in Financial Technologies, Cambridge, MA, USA, 19–21 September 2022; pp. 74–88.
44. Gan, R.; Wang, L.; Xue, L.; Lin, X. Exposing Stealthy Wash Trading on Automated Market Maker Exchanges. *ACM Trans. Internet Technol.* **2024**, *24*, 1–30. [CrossRef]
45. Wang, Y.; Chen, Y.; Deng, S.; Wattenhofer, R. Cyclic Arbitrage in Decentralized Exchange Markets. In Proceedings of the WWW '22: Companion Proceedings of the Web Conference 2022, Virtual, 25–29 April 2022.
46. Adams, A.; Chan, B.Y.; Markovich, S.; Wan, X. Don't Let MEV Slip: The Costs of Swapping on the Uniswap Protocol. *arXiv* **2023**, arXiv:2309.13648.
47. Capponi, A.; Jia, R.; Yu, S. Price Discovery on Decentralized Exchanges. Available online: https://ssrn.com/abstract=4236993 (accessed on 25 September 2024).
48. Hansson, M. Price Discovery in Constant Product Markets. Available online: https://ssrn.com/abstract=4582649. (accessed on 25 September 2024).
49. Uniswap's Universal Router for NFT and ERC20 Swapping. 2024. Available online: https://github.com/Uniswap/universal-router (accessed on 25 September 2024).
50. Uniswap DEX. Available online: https://app.uniswap.org (accessed on 25 September 2024).
51. Networks on Uniswap. Available online: https://support.uniswap.org/hc/en-us/articles/14569415293325-Networks-on-Uniswap (accessed on 25 September 2024).
52. Uniswap V2. Available online: https://docs.uniswap.org/contracts/v2/concepts/protocol-overview/how-uniswap-works (accessed on 25 September 2024).
53. Uniswap V3. Available online: https://blog.uniswap.org/uniswap-v3/ (accessed on 25 September 2024).
54. Uniswap V4. Available online: https://docs.uniswap.org/contracts/v4/overview (accessed on 25 September 2024).
55. The Developers Guide to Uniswap. Available online: https://blog.oceanprotocol.com/the-developers-guide-to-uniswap-48fcf6e9ee1e. (accessed on 25 September 2024).
56. Bauer, D.P. ERC-20: Fungible Tokens. In *Getting Started with Ethereum: A Step-by-Step Guide to Becoming a Blockchain Developer*; Springer: Berlin/Heidelberg, Germany, 2022; pp. 17–48.
57. Uniswap Pools. Available online: https://app.uniswap.org/explore/pools/ (accessed on 25 September 2024).
58. Liquidity in Uv3 Postion as a NFT. Available online: https://app.uniswap.org/nfts/collection/0xc36442b4a4522e871399cd717abdd847ab11fe88 (accessed on 25 September 2024).
59. Ethereum Block Time. Available online: https://ethereum.org/en/developers/docs/blocks/ (accessed on 25 September 2024).
60. Mantegna, R.N.; Stanley, H.E. Scaling behaviour in the dynamics of an economic index. *Nature* **1995**, *376*, 46–49. [CrossRef]
61. Gopikrishnan, P.; Plerou, V.; Nunes Amaral, L.A.; Meyer, M.; Stanley, H.E. Scaling of the distribution of fluctuations of financial market indices. *Phys. Rev. E* **1999**, *60*, 5305–5316. [CrossRef] [PubMed]
62. Plerou, V.; Gopikrishnan, P.; Rosenow, B.; Nunes Amaral, L.A.; Stanley, H.E. Universal and nonuniversal properties of cross correlations in financial time series. *Phys. Rev. Lett.* **1999**, *83*, 1471–1474. [CrossRef]
63. Ausloos, M. Statistical physics in foreign exchange currency and stock markets. *Phys. A* **2000**, *285*, 48–65. [CrossRef]
64. Binance. Available online: https://www.binance.com/ (accessed on 25 September 2024).
65. Mandelbrot, B. The Variation of Certain Speculative Prices. *J. Bus.* **1963**, *36*, 394–419. [CrossRef]
66. Cont, R. Empirical properties of asset returns: Stylized facts and statistical issues. *Quant. Financ.* **2001**, *1*, 223–236. [CrossRef]
67. Dhesi, G.; Shakeel, B.; Ausloos, M. Modelling and forecasting the kurtosis and returns distributions of financial markets: Irrational fractional Brownian motion model approach. *Ann. Oper. Res.* **2021**, *299*, 1397–1410. [CrossRef]
68. Drożdż, S.; Forczek, M.; Kwapień, J.; Oświęcimka, P.; Rak, R. Stock market return distributions: From past to present. *Phys. A* **2007**, *383*, 59–64. [CrossRef]
69. Gębarowski, R.; Oświęcimka, P.; Wątorek, M.; Drożdż, S. Detecting correlations and triangular arbitrage opportunities in the Forex by means of multifractal detrended cross-correlations analysis. *Nonlinear Dyn.* **2019**, *98*, 2349–2364. [CrossRef]
70. Begušić, S.; Kostanjčar, Z.; Eugene Stanley, H.; Podobnik, B. Scaling properties of extreme price fluctuations in Bitcoin markets. *Phys. A* **2018**, *510*, 400–406. [CrossRef]
71. James, N.; Menzies, M.; Chan, J. Changes to the extreme and erratic behaviour of cryptocurrencies during COVID-19. *Phys. A* **2021**, *565*, 125581. [CrossRef]
72. Ghosh, B.; Bouri, E.; Wee, J.B.; Zulfiqar, N. Return and volatility properties: Stylized facts from the universe of cryptocurrencies and NFTs. *Res. Int. Bus. Financ.* **2023**, *65*, 101945. [CrossRef]
73. Szydło, P.; Wątorek, M.; Kwapień, J.; Drożdż, S. Characteristics of price related fluctuations in non-fungible token (NFT) market. *Chaos* **2024**, *34*, 013108. [CrossRef]
74. Wątorek, M.; Szydło, P.; Kwapień, J.; Drożdż, S. Correlations versus noise in the NFT market. *Chaos* **2024**, *34*, 073112. [CrossRef]
75. Wątorek, M.; Kwapień, J.; Drożdż, S. Financial return distributions: Past, present, and COVID-19. *Entropy* **2021**, *23*, 884. [CrossRef]
76. Drożdż, S.; Kwapień, J.; Oświęcimka, P.; Rak, R. The foreign exchange market: Return distributions, multifractality, anomalous multifractality and the Epps effect. *New J. Phys.* **2010**, *12*, 105003. [CrossRef]
77. Drożdż, S.; Gębarowski, R.; Minati, L.; Oświęcimka, P.; Wątorek, M. Bitcoin market route to maturity? Evidence from return fluctuations, temporal correlations and multiscaling effects. *Chaos* **2018**, *28*, 071101. [CrossRef] [PubMed]

78. Drożdż, S.; Minati, L.; Oświęcimka, P.; Stanuszek, M.; Wątorek, M. Signatures of the crypto-currency market decoupling from the Forex. *Future Internet* **2019**, *11*, 154. [CrossRef]
79. Drożdż, S.; Kwapień, J.; Oświęcimka, P.; Stanisz, T.; Wątorek, M. Complexity in economic and social systems: Cryptocurrency market at around COVID-19. *Entropy* **2020**, *22*, 1043. [CrossRef]
80. Record Transaction on ETH/USDT Uniswap v3 Liquidity Pool. Available online: https://etherscan.io/tx/0x28bcfb342781641e84ab5ea821e4d2e3ecfdd0852e22460e1c64b33bcc698ae0 (accessed on 25 September 2024).
81. Rak, R.; Drożdż, S.; Kwapień, J.; Oświęcimka, P. Stock returns versus trading volume: Is the correspondence more general? *Acta Phys. Pol. B* **2013**, *44*, 2035–2050. [CrossRef]
82. Yamani, E. Return–volume nexus in financial markets: A survey of research. *Res. Int. Bus. Financ.* **2023**, *65*, 101910. [CrossRef]
83. Gabaix, X.; Gopikrishnan, P.; Plerou, V.; Stanley, H.E. A theory of power-law distributions in financial market fluctuations. *Nature* **2003**, *423*, 267–270. [CrossRef]
84. Plerou, V.; Gopikrishnan, P.; Gabaix, X.; Stanley, H.E. On the origin of power-law fluctuations in stock prices. *Quant. Financ.* **2004**, *4*, 11–15. [CrossRef]
85. Naeem, M.; Saleem, K.; Ahmed, S.; Muhammad, N.; Mustafa, F. Extreme return-volume relationship in cryptocurrencies: Tail dependence analysis. *Cogent Econ. Financ.* **2020**, *8*, 1834175. [CrossRef]
86. Drożdż, S.; Kwapień, J.; Wątorek, M. What is mature and what is still emerging in the cryptocurrency market? *Entropy* **2023**, *25*, 772. [CrossRef]
87. Laherrère, J.; Sornette, D. Stretched exponential distributions in nature and economy: "fat tails" with characteristic scales. *Eur. Phys. J. B* **1998**, *2*, 525–539. [CrossRef]
88. Bouchaud, J.P. Price impact. In *Encyclopedia of Quantitative Finance*; Cambridge University Press: Cambridge, MA, USA, 2010; pp. 1–6.
89. Wilinski, M.; Cui, W.; Brabazon, A.; Hamill, P. An analysis of price impact functions of individual trades on the London stock exchange. *Quant. Financ.* **2015**, *15*, 1727–1735. [CrossRef]
90. Kutner, R.; Świtała, F. Remarks on the possible universal mechanism of the non-linear long-term autocorrelations in financial time-series. *Phys. A* **2004**, *344*, 244–251. [CrossRef]
91. Rak, R.; Drożdż, S.; Kwapień, J. Nonextensive statistical features of the Polish stock market fluctuations. *Phys. A* **2007**, *374*, 315–324. [CrossRef]
92. Klamut, J.; Gubiec, T. Continuous time random walk with correlated waiting times. The crucial role of inter-trade times in volatility clustering. *Entropy* **2021**, *23*, 1576. [CrossRef]
93. Kwapień, J.; Blasiak, P.; Drożdż, S.; Oświęcimka, P. Genuine multifractality in time series is due to temporal correlations. *Phys. Rev. E* **2023**, *107*, 034139. [CrossRef]
94. Ausloos, M.; Ivanova, K. Multifractal nature of stock exchange prices. *Comput. Phys. Commun.* **2002**, *147*, 582–585. [CrossRef]
95. Jiang, Z.Q.; Xie, W.J.; Zhou, W.X.; Sornette, D. Multifractal analysis of financial markets: A review. *Rep. Prog. Phys.* **2019**, *82*, 125901. [CrossRef] [PubMed]
96. Kutner, R.; Ausloos, M.; Grech, D.; Matteo, T.D.; Schinckus, C.; Stanley, H.E. Econophysics and sociophysics: Their milestones & challenges. *Phys. A* **2019**, *516*, 240–253.
97. Kwapień, J.; Wątorek, M.; Bezbradica, M.; Crane, M.; Tan Mai, T.; Drożdż, S. Analysis of inter-transaction time fluctuations in the cryptocurrency market. *Chaos* **2022**, *32*, 083142. [CrossRef]
98. Wątorek, M.; Kwapień, J.; Drożdż, S. Multifractal cross-correlations of bitcoin and ether trading characteristics in the post-COVID-19 time. *Future Internet* **2022**, *14*, 215. [CrossRef]
99. Oświęcimka, P.; Drożdż, S.; Forczek, M.; Jadach, S.; Kwapień, J. Detrended cross-correlation analysis consistently extended to multifractality. *Phys. Rev. E* **2014**, *89*, 023305. [CrossRef] [PubMed]
100. Podobnik, B.; Stanley, H.E. Detrended cross-correlation analysis: A new method for analyzing two nonstationary time series. *Phys. Rev. Lett.* **2008**, *100*, 084102. [CrossRef] [PubMed]
101. Zhou, W.X. Multifractal detrended cross-correlation analysis for two nonstationary signals. *Phys. Rev. E* **2008**, *77*, 066211. [CrossRef]
102. Kantelhardt, J.W.; Zschiegner, S.A.; Koscielny-Bunde, E.; Havlin, S.; Bunde, A.; Stanley, H.E. Multifractal detrended fluctuation analysis of nonstationary time series. *Phys. A* **2002**, *316*, 87–114. [CrossRef]
103. Peng, C.K.; Buldyrev, S.V.; Havlin, S.; Simons, M.; Stanley, H.E.; Goldberger, A.L. Mosaic organization of DNA nucleotides. *Phys. Rev. E* **1994**, *49*, 1685–1689. [CrossRef] [PubMed]
104. Oświęcimka, P.; Drożdż, S.; Kwapień, J.; Górski, A. Effect of detrending on multifractal characteristics. *Acta Phys. Pol. A* **2013**, *123*, 597–603. [CrossRef]
105. Barabasi, A.L.; Vicsek, T. Multifractality of self-affine fractals. *Phys. Rev. A* **1991**, *44*, 2730–2733. [CrossRef] [PubMed]
106. Hurst, H.E. Long-term storage capacity of reservoirs. *Trans. Am. Soc. Civ. Eng.* **1951**, *116*, 770–799. [CrossRef]
107. Halsey, T.C.; Jensen, M.H.; Kadanoff, L.P.; Procaccia, I.; Shraimant, B.I. Fractal measures and their singularities: The characterization of strange sets. *Phys. Rev. A* **1986**, *33*, 1141–1151. [CrossRef]
108. Kwapień, J.; Oświęcimka, P.; Drożdż, S. Detrended fluctuation analysis made flexible to detect range of cross-correlated fluctuations. *Phys. Rev. E* **2015**, *92*, 052815. [CrossRef] [PubMed]
109. Zebende, G. DCCA cross-correlation coefficient: Quantifying level of cross-correlation. *Phys. A* **2011**, *390*, 614–618. [CrossRef]

110. Kwapień, J.; Oświęcimka, P.; Forczek, M.; Drożdż, S. Minimum spanning tree filtering of correlations for varying time scales and size of fluctuations. *Phys. Rev. E* **2017**, *95*, 052313. [CrossRef] [PubMed]
111. Drożdż, S.; Kwapień, J.; Oświęcimka, P.; Rak, R. Quantitative features of multifractal subtleties in time-series. *EPL (Europhys. Lett.)* **2010**, *88*, 60003. [CrossRef]
112. Zhou, W.X. The components of empirical multifractality in financial returns. *EPL (Europhys. Lett.)* **2009**, *88*, 28004. [CrossRef]
113. Carbone, A.; Castelli, G.; Stanley, H. Time-dependent Hurst exponent in financial time series. *Phys. A* **2004**, *344*, 267–271. [CrossRef]
114. Grech, D.; Mazur, Z. Can one make any crash prediction in finance using the local Hurst exponent idea? *Phys. A* **2004**, *336*, 133–145. [CrossRef]
115. Garcin, M. Estimation of time-dependent Hurst exponents with variational smoothing and application to forecasting foreign exchange rates. *Phys. A* **2017**, *483*, 462–479. [CrossRef]
116. Matos, J.A.; Gama, S.M.; Ruskin, H.J.; Sharkasi, A.A.; Crane, M. Time and scale Hurst exponent analysis for financial markets. *Phys. A* **2008**, *387*, 3910–3915. [CrossRef]
117. Drożdż, S.; Kowalski, R.; Oświęcimka, P.; Rak, R.; Gębarowski, R. Dynamical variety of shapes in financial multifractality. *Complexity* **2018**, *2018*, 7015721. [CrossRef]
118. Matteo, T.D.; Aste, T.; Dacorogna, M.M. Long-term memories of developed and emerging markets: Using the scaling analysis to characterize their stage of development. *J. Bank. Financ.* **2005**, *29*, 827–851. [CrossRef]
119. Cajueiro, D.O.; Tabak, B.M. Testing for predictability in equity returns for European transition markets. *Econ. Syst.* **2006**, *30*, 56–78. [CrossRef]
120. James, N. Dynamics, behaviours, and anomaly persistence in cryptocurrencies and equities surrounding COVID-19. *Phys. A* **2021**, *570*, 125831. [CrossRef]
121. James, N.; Menzies, M. Collective correlations, dynamics, and behavioural inconsistencies of the cryptocurrency market over time. *Nonlinear Dyn.* **2022**, *107*, 4001–4017. [CrossRef]
122. Ammy-Driss, A.; Garcin, M. Efficiency of the financial markets during the COVID-19 crisis: Time-varying parameters of fractional stable dynamics. *Phys. A* **2023**, *609*, 128335. [CrossRef]
123. Brouty, X.; Garcin, M. Fractal properties, information theory, and market efficiency. *Chaos Solitons Fractals* **2024**, *180*, 114543. [CrossRef]
124. Drożdż, S.; Oświęcimka, P. Detecting and interpreting distortions in hierarchical organization of complex time series. *Phys. Rev. E* **2015**, *91*, 030902. [CrossRef]
125. Schreiber, T.; Schmitz, A. Surrogate time series. *Phys. D* **2000**, *142*, 346–382. [CrossRef]
126. Theiler, J.; Prichard, D. Constrained-realization Monte-Carlo method for hypothesis testing. *Phys. D* **1996**, *94*, 221–235. [CrossRef]
127. Grech, D.; Pamuła, G. On the multifractal effects generated by monofractal signals. *Phys. A* **2013**, *392*, 5845–5864. [CrossRef]
128. Zhou, W.X. Finite-size effect and the components of multifractality in financial volatility. *Chaos Solitons Fractals* **2012**, *45*, 147–155. [CrossRef]
129. Rak, R.; Grech, D. Quantitative approach to multifractality induced by correlations and broad distribution of data. *Phys. A* **2018**, *508*, 48–66. [CrossRef]
130. Gillemot, L.; Farmer, J.D.; Lillo, F. There's more to volatility than volume. *Quant. Financ.* **2006**, *6*, 371–384. [CrossRef]
131. Podobnik, B.; Horvatic, D.; Petersen, A.M.; Stanley, H.E. Cross-correlations between volume change and price change. *Proc. Natl. Acad. Sci. USA* **2009**, *106*, 22079–22084. [CrossRef]
132. Rak, R.; Drożdż, S.; Kwapień, J.; Oświęcimka, P. Detrended cross-correlations between returns, volatility, trading activity, and volume traded for the stock market companies. *EPL (Europhys. Lett.)* **2015**, *112*, 48001. [CrossRef]
133. Arianos, S.; Carbone, A. Cross-correlation of long-range correlated series. *J. Stat. Mech.* **2009**, *2009*, P03037. [CrossRef]
134. Wątorek, M.; Drożdż, S.; Oświęcimka, P.; Stanuszek, M. Multifractal cross-correlations between the world oil and other financial markets in 2012–2017. *Energy Econ.* **2019**, *81*, 874–885. [CrossRef]
135. Zhao, L.; Li, W.; Fenu, A.; Podobnik, B.; Wang, Y.; Stanley, H.E. The q-dependent detrended cross-correlation analysis of stock market. *J. Stat. Mech. Theory Exp.* **2018**, *2018*, 023402. [CrossRef]

fractal and fractional

MDPI

Article

Dynamics of the Traveling Wave Solutions of Fractional Date–Jimbo–Kashiwara–Miwa Equation via Riccati–Bernoulli Sub-ODE Method through Bäcklund Transformation

M. Mossa Al-Sawalha [1], Saima Noor [2,3,*], Mohammad Alqudah [4], Musaad S. Aldhabani [5] and Roman Ullah [6,*]

1 Department of Mathematics, College of Science, University of Ha'il, Ha'il 2440, Saudi Arabia; m.alswalha@uoh.edu.sa
2 Department of Basic Sciences, General Administration of Preparatory Year, King Faisal University, P.O. Box 400, Al Ahsa 31982, Saudi Arabia
3 Department of Mathematics and Statistics, College of Science, King Faisal University, P.O. Box 400, Al Ahsa 31982, Saudi Arabia
4 Department of Basic Sciences, School of Electrical Engineering & Information Technology, German Jordanian University, Amman 11180, Jordan; mohammad.qudah@gju.edu.jo
5 Department of Mathematics, Faculty of Science, University of Tabuk, P.O. Box 741, Tabuk 71491, Saudi Arabia; maldhabani@ut.edu.sa
6 Department of General Studies, Higher Colleges of Technology, Dubai Women Campus, Dubai 16062, United Arab Emirates
* Correspondence: snoor@kfu.edu.sa (S.N.); romanullah@yahoo.com or rullah@hct.ac.ae (R.U.)

Abstract: The dynamical wave solutions of the time–space fractional Date–Jimbo–Kashiwara–Miwa (DJKM) equation have been obtained in this article using an innovative and efficient technique including the Riccati–Bernoulli sub-ODE method through Bäcklund transformation. Fractional-order derivatives enter into play for their novel contribution to the enhancement of the characterization of dynamic waves while providing better modeling ability compared to integer types of derivatives. The solutions of the above-mentioned time–space fractional Date–Jimbo–Kashiwara–Miwa equation have tremendous importance in numerous scientific scenarios. The regular dynamical wave solutions of the aforementioned equation encompass three fundamental functions: trigonometric, hyperbolic, and rational functions will be among the topics covered. These solutions are graphically classified into three categories: compacton kink solitary wave solutions, kink soliton wave solutions and anti-kink soliton wave solutions. In addition, to explore the impact of the fractional parameter (α) on those solutions, $2D$ plots are utilized, while $3D$ plots are applied to present the solutions involving the integer-order derivatives.

Keywords: fractional Date–Jimbo–Kashiwara–Miwa (DJKM) equation; Bäcklund transformation; nonlinear differential equations; exact solutions

1. Introduction

It is established that fractional-order derivatives provide a remarkable way of describing the wave dynamics because of more flexibility in terms of frequency and phase responses than the integer ones, which do not consider the memory and hereditary nature of the wave systems adequately. With the use of fractional derivatives, it becomes possible to also take into consideration non-locality interactions and anomalous diffusion, thus improving the precision in wave dynamics and propagation. This approach enhances the capacity to give and analyze details of wave complex structures, making the application of this approach key to enhancing the understanding of complex structures. A wide range of phenomena can be described by partial differential equations that are referred to as quasi-linear or nonlinear evolution equations (NLEEs). These are mathematical equations that are dependent on space and time, and they can practically replicate virtually all the phenomena in the natural world, mainly in the science and engineering industries. For depicting the phenomena in the various sectors of science like engineering, solid-state physics, plasma physics, applied physics, applied mathematics, plasma waves, fluid mechanics, quantum mechanics, electrodynamics, magnetohydrodynamics, turbulence, biology, fiberoptics, chemistry, chemical physics, astrophysics, theory of relativity, cosmology and medical science, it becomes relevant to look for exact solutions of NLEEs [1–5]. Numerous researchers have developed various methods to obtain exact solutions for NLEEs. These include the lie group method, the $exp(-\phi(x))$-expansion method, the extended direct algebraic method, the variational iteration method, the unified method, the (G'/G^2)–expansion method, the sine–gordon expansion method, the tanh–coth method, the homotopy analysis method, the auxiliary ordinary differential equation method, and the tanh function method [6–10]. Moreover, applications of fractional calculus (FC) have increased extensively in different branches of science and engineering. It has been used to model and predict many high-order algorithms and nonlinear mechanics of physics and applied electromagnetism and engineering or anomalous diffusion, chemical kinetics, viscoelasticity, and electrochemistry, and so on [11–16]. The application of fractional calculus has been on the rise in these fields in the last few decades. Many algorithms have been proposed for handling nonlinear FDEs, which implies the significance and versatility of FC in expanding the existing understanding and capacity for analyzing and modeling systems [17–19]. As evident from the above discussion, the improvement of techniques regarding the FDEs has enabled researchers to solve the problems which were previously beyond the scope of any theoretical and computational tool, leading to numerous new insights and ideas in various scientific and engineering fields. One of the most interesting and intricate cases of usage of fractional calculus is related to the solution of various partial differential equations using different types of fractional derivatives that are both numerical and analytical [20–24].

The Kadomtsev–Petviashil (KP) equation is one of the essential equations for solitons and is crucial for the connection between mathematics and physics. The Date–Jimbo–Kashiwara–Miwa (DJKM) equation, a member of the KP hierarchy equations, can be expressed as follows [25,26]:

$$D_y^{\alpha}\left(D_x^{3\alpha}f\right)+4D_y^{\alpha}\left(D_x^{2\alpha}f\right)D_x^{\alpha}f+\left(2D_x^{3\alpha}f\right)D_y^{\alpha}f+6D_y^{\alpha}(D_x^{\alpha}f)\left(D_x^{2\alpha}f\right)-\lambda\left(D_y^{3\alpha}f\right)-2\gamma D_t^{\alpha}\left(D_x^{2\alpha}f\right)=0. \tag{1}$$

Here, the notation $f(x,y,t)$ is used for the wave amplitude, with (t) being the time variable. According to the said parameter, the parameter $(0<\alpha\leq 1)$ refers to the fractal dimensions related to the time (t) and the spatial coordinates (x,y). Further, the operator integrating α-derivatives of powers agree exactly with the idea of conformable fractional derivatives [17].

$$D_{\Theta}^{\alpha}M(\Theta)=\lim_{i\to 0}\frac{M(i(\Theta)^{i-\alpha}-M(\theta))}{i},\quad 0<\alpha\leq 1. \tag{2}$$

$$\begin{cases} D_{\Theta}^{\alpha}\Theta^{m}=m\Theta^{m-\alpha}. \\ D_{\Theta}^{\alpha}(m_1\eta(\Theta)\pm m_2t(\Theta))=m_1D_{\Theta}^{\alpha}(\eta(\Theta))\pm m_2D_{\Theta}^{\alpha}(t(\Theta)). \\ D_{\Theta}^{\alpha}[f\circ g]=\Theta^{1-\alpha}g(\Theta)D_{\Theta}^{\alpha}f(g(\Theta)). \end{cases} \tag{3}$$

The (DJKM) equation describes long water waves using frequency dispersion and nonlinear restoring forces that are considered to be weak. This equation has been analyzed with the help of a number of powerful methods among which it is possible to mention the Hirota bilinear method [25], the extended transformed rational function method [27], and the Wronskian and Grammian techniques [28]. Wazwaz [26] proved that this equation is Painleve integrable and obtained several soliton solutions of the (2+1)-dimensional DJKM equation. In this work, the method of Ricatti–Bernoulli sub–ODE will be used to obtain analytical solutions for the (DJKM) equation. This will be accomplished by using the proposed approach [29–31] and the Bäcklund transformation with respect to nonlinear wave effects. This paper is structured as follows:

In Section 2, a brief description of the used methods is provided. Section 3 indicates the actual solutions of the fractional (DJKM) equation. Section 4 focuses on results and discussion and providing graphical illustrations. In the last section, Section 5, the conclusion of our work is provided.

2. Algorithm

Consider the nonlinear partial differential equation of the following form:

$$p_1(U, D_t^{\alpha}(U), D_{x_1}^{\alpha}(U), D_{x_2}^{\alpha}(U), UD_{x_1}^{\alpha}(U), \ldots) = 0, \qquad 0 < \alpha \leq 1, \tag{4}$$

where $U = U(t, x_1, x_2, x_3, \ldots, x_k)$ is an unknown function and p_1 is a polynomial in U and its partial derivatives. We use the wave transformation to translate Equation (4) into an ordinary differential equation (ODE) of the following form:

$$V(\Phi) = v(t, x_1, x_2, x_3, \ldots, x_k), \qquad \Phi = a\frac{t^{\alpha}}{\alpha} + b\frac{x_1^{\alpha}}{\alpha} + c\frac{x_2^{\alpha}}{\alpha} + \ldots, +\omega\frac{x_k^{\alpha}}{\alpha}, \tag{5}$$

where (ω) is the traveling wave velocity and (a), (b), are constants. It follows that Equation (4) becomes an ordinary differential equation:

$$p_2(V, V'(\Phi), V''(\Phi), VV'(\Phi), \ldots) = 0, \tag{6}$$

Equation (6), a wave solution, is expressed as a finite series using the proposed approach:

$$G(\Phi) = \sum_{i=-n}^{n} k_i g(\Phi)^i, \tag{7}$$

In this work, focus is made on the change of $g = g(\Phi)$ as described through the Bäcklund transformation. The Bäcklund transformation can be used as a tool when solving nonlinear differential equations. Specifically, the function (g) as a function of (Φ) is articulated through the following Bäcklund transformation framework:

$$g(\Phi) = \frac{-\rho Y_2 + Y_1 Z(\Phi)}{Y_1 + Y_2 Z(\Phi)}, \tag{8}$$

where (ρ) , (Y_1) , and (Y_2) are constants such that $Y_2 \neq 0$ and $Z = Z(\Phi)$ represent a solution to the generalized Ricatti equation:

$$\frac{dZ}{d\Phi} = \rho + Z(\Phi)^2. \tag{9}$$

The Ricatti Equation (9) possess the following general solutions [32].

$$\begin{aligned}
Z(\Phi) &= \begin{cases} -\sqrt{-\rho}\tanh(\sqrt{-\rho}\Phi), & \text{as } \rho < 0, \\ -\sqrt{-\rho}\coth(\sqrt{-\rho}\Phi), & \text{as } \rho < 0, \end{cases} \\
Z(\Phi) &= -\frac{1}{\Phi}, \quad \text{as } \rho = 0, \\
Z(\Phi) &= \begin{cases} \sqrt{\rho}\tan(\sqrt{\rho}\Phi), & \text{as } \rho > 0, \\ -\sqrt{\rho}\cot(\sqrt{\rho}\Phi), & \text{as } \rho > 0. \end{cases}
\end{aligned} \tag{10}$$

The next step is to obtain the positive integer (n) in our assumed solution by comparing the orders of derivative terms and nonlinear terms for ordinary differential equations. Plug the proposed solution and convert this into a system of algebraic equations and set the coefficients of $Z(\Phi)$ to zero. Then, we plugged the constants (k_i), (ω), and (ρ) we obtained earlier into that algebraic equation which is derived from expansion of functions and solved them in Maple. Consequently, we obtained a set of exact solutions for Equation (4).

3. Problem Execution

This section deals with a new a new algorithm in order to solve the space–time fractional (DJKM) equation, which describes long waves affected by frequency dispersion and weak nonlinear restoring forces. Here, one of the principal aims is to obtain an analytic soliton solution for this fractional partial differential equation (PDE). This is an evaluation of $f(x,y,t)$ at a retarded time (t) due to the propagation in (x). In order to carry this out, we need the wave transformation which transforms Equation (1) into an ordinary differential equation (ODE), making it easier for us deal with them analytically.

$$f(x,y,t) = F(\Phi), \quad \text{where} \quad \Phi = \frac{px^{\alpha}}{\alpha} + \frac{qy^{\alpha}}{\alpha} - \frac{\omega t^{\alpha}}{\alpha}. \tag{11}$$

where (p), (q), and (ω) are constants. Applying the above wave transformation, we convert Equation (1) into a nonlinear ordinary differential equation (ODE):

$$6p^3q\left(\frac{d^2F}{d\Phi^2}\right)^2 - q^3\lambda\left(\frac{d^3F}{d\Phi^3}\right) + 2p^2\omega\gamma\left(\frac{d^3F}{d\Phi^3}\right) + 6p^3q\left(\frac{d^3F}{d\Phi^3}\right)\left(\frac{dF}{d\Phi}\right) + p^4q\left(\frac{d^5F}{d\Phi^5}\right) = 0. \tag{12}$$

Now, after integrating Equation (12) and keeping the constant of integration zero for simplicity, we have

$$-q^3\lambda\left(\frac{d^2F}{d\Phi^2}\right) + 2p^2\omega\gamma\left(\frac{d^2F}{d\Phi^2}\right) + 6p^3q\left(\frac{d^2F}{d\Phi^2}\right)\left(\frac{dF}{d\Phi}\right) + p^4q\left(\frac{d^4F}{d\Phi^4}\right) = 0. \tag{13}$$

Balancing (F'''') and $F'F''$, we obtain N = 1 [33]. Substituting Equation (7) with Equation (9) into Equation (13) and then collecting the coefficients of $Z(\Phi)^i$ yields the following system:

$$\begin{aligned}
&24\,p^4qk_1Y_2^{10}\rho^{10} + 12\,p^3qk_1^2Y_2^{10}\rho^{10} = 0,\\
&40\,p^4qk_1Y_2^{10}\rho^9 - 2\,q^3\lambda\,k_1Y_2^{10}\rho^8 + 24\,p^3qk_1^2Y_2^{10}\rho^9 + 4\,p^2\omega\,\gamma\,k_1Y_2^{10}\rho^8 - 12\,p^3qk_{-1}Y_2^{10}\rho^8k_1 = 0,\\
&-2\,q^3\lambda\,k_1Y_2^{10}\rho^7 + 16\,p^4qk_1Y_2^{10}\rho^8 + 12\,p^3qk_1^2Y_2^{10}\rho^8 + 4\,p^2\omega\,\gamma\,k_1Y_2^{10}\rho^7 - 12\,p^3qk_{-1}Y_2^{10}\rho^7k_1 = 0,\\
&-2\,q^3\lambda\,k_{-1}Y_2^{10}\rho^5 + 16\,p^4qk_{-1}Y_2^{10}\rho^6 - 12\,p^3qk_{-1}^2Y_2^{10}\rho^5 + 12\,p^3qk_{-1}Y_2^{10}\rho^6k_1 + 4\,p^2\omega\,\gamma\,k_{-1}Y_2^{10}\rho^5 = 0,\\
&40\,p^4qk_{-1}Y_2^{10}\rho^5 - 24\,p^3qk_{-1}^2Y_2^{10}\rho^4 - 2\,q^3\lambda\,k_{-1}Y_2^{10}\rho^4 + 12\,p^3qk_{-1}Y_2^{10}k_1\rho^5 + 4\,p^2\omega\,\gamma\,k_{-1}Y_2^{10}\rho^4 = 0,\\
&24\,p^4qk_{-1}Y_2^{10}\rho^4 - 12\,p^3qk_{-1}^2Y_2^{10}\rho^3 = 0.
\end{aligned} \tag{14}$$

This give us the algebraic equations by setting $Z(\Phi) = 0$. The solutions of this system of algebraic equations obtained from Maple are below:

Set:1

$$k_0 = k_0, k_1 = 0, k_{-1} = 1/2\,\frac{-q^3\lambda + 2\,p^2\omega\,\gamma}{p^3q}, \rho = 1/4\,\frac{-q^3\lambda + 2\,p^2\omega\,\gamma}{p^4q}, \omega = \omega, p = p, q = q. \tag{15}$$

Set:2

$$k_0 = k_0, k_1 = -2\,p, k_{-1} = 0, \rho = 1/4\,\frac{-q^3\lambda + 2\,p^2\omega\,\gamma}{p^4q}, \omega = \omega, p = p, q = q. \tag{16}$$

Set:3

$$k_0 = k_0, k_1 = -2\,p, k_{-1} = 1/8\,\frac{-q^3\lambda + 2\,p^2\omega\,\gamma}{p^3q}, \rho = 1/16\,\frac{-q^3\lambda + 2\,p^2\omega\,\gamma}{p^4q}, \omega = \omega, p = p, q = q. \tag{17}$$

3.1. Solution Set 1

For Equation (1), we obtain the following set of solutions (when $\rho < 0$), and for this, we consider set 1.

$$f_1(x,y,t) = 1/2\left(-q^3\lambda + 2\,p^2\omega\,\gamma\right)\left(\Upsilon_1 - 1/2\,\Upsilon_2\sqrt{-\frac{-q^3\lambda + 2\,p^2\omega\,\gamma}{p^4q}}\tanh\left(1/2\sqrt{-\frac{-q^3\lambda + 2\,p^2\omega\,\gamma}{p^4q}}\Phi\right)\right)$$
$$p^{-3}q^{-1}\left(-1/4\,\frac{(-q^3\lambda + 2\,p^2\omega\,\gamma)\Upsilon_2}{p^4q} - 1/2\,\Upsilon_1\sqrt{-\frac{-q^3\lambda + 2\,p^2\omega\,\gamma}{p^4q}}\tanh\left(1/2\sqrt{-\frac{-q^3\lambda + 2\,p^2\omega\,\gamma}{p^4q}}\Phi\right)\right)^{-1} + k_0. \tag{18}$$

or

$$f_2(x,y,t) = 1/2\left(-q^3\lambda + 2\,p^2\omega\,\gamma\right)\left(\Upsilon_1 - 1/2\,\Upsilon_2\sqrt{-\frac{-q^3\lambda + 2\,p^2\omega\,\gamma}{p^4q}}\coth\left(1/2\sqrt{-\frac{-q^3\lambda + 2\,p^2\omega\,\gamma}{p^4q}}\Phi\right)\right)$$
$$p^{-3}q^{-1}\left(-1/4\,\frac{(-q^3\lambda + 2\,p^2\omega\,\gamma)\Upsilon_2}{p^4q} - 1/2\,\Upsilon_1\sqrt{-\frac{-q^3\lambda + 2\,p^2\omega\,\gamma}{p^4q}}\coth\left(1/2\sqrt{-\frac{-q^3\lambda + 2\,p^2\omega\,\gamma}{p^4q}}\Phi\right)\right)^{-1} + k_0. \tag{19}$$

3.2. Solution Set 2

For Equation (1), we obtain the following set of solutions (when $\rho > 0$), and for this, we consider set 1.

$$f_3(x,y,t) = 1/2\left(-q^3\lambda + 2\,p^2\omega\,\gamma\right)\left(\Upsilon_1 + 1/2\,\Upsilon_2\sqrt{\frac{-q^3\lambda + 2\,p^2\omega\,\gamma}{p^4q}}\tan\left(1/2\sqrt{\frac{-q^3\lambda + 2\,p^2\omega\,\gamma}{p^4q}}\Phi\right)\right)$$
$$p^{-3}q^{-1}\left(-1/4\,\frac{(-q^3\lambda + 2\,p^2\omega\,\gamma)\Upsilon_2}{p^4q} + 1/2\,\Upsilon_1\sqrt{\frac{-q^3\lambda + 2\,p^2\omega\,\gamma}{p^4q}}\tan\left(1/2\sqrt{\frac{-q^3\lambda + 2\,p^2\omega\,\gamma}{p^4q}}\Phi\right)\right)^{-1} + k_0. \tag{20}$$

or

$$f_4(x,y,t) = 1/2\left(-q^3\lambda + 2\,p^2\omega\,\gamma\right)\left(\Upsilon_1 - 1/2\,\Upsilon_2\sqrt{\frac{-q^3\lambda + 2\,p^2\omega\,\gamma}{p^4q}}\cot\left(1/2\sqrt{\frac{-q^3\lambda + 2\,p^2\omega\,\gamma}{p^4q}}\Phi\right)\right)$$
$$p^{-3}q^{-1}\left(-1/4\,\frac{(-q^3\lambda + 2\,p^2\omega\,\gamma)\Upsilon_2}{p^4q} - 1/2\,\Upsilon_1\sqrt{\frac{-q^3\lambda + 2\,p^2\omega\,\gamma}{p^4q}}\cot\left(1/2\sqrt{\frac{-q^3\lambda + 2\,p^2\omega\,\gamma}{p^4q}}\Phi\right)\right)^{-1} + k_0. \tag{21}$$

3.3. Solution Set 3

For Equation (1), we obtain the following set of solutions (when $\rho = 0$), and for this, we consider set 1.

$$f_5(x,y,t) = 1/2\left(-q^3\lambda + 2\,p^2\omega\,\gamma\right)\left(\Upsilon_1 - \frac{\Upsilon_2}{\Phi}\right)p^{-3}q^{-1}\left(-1/4\,\frac{(-q^3\lambda + 2\,p^2\omega\,\gamma)\Upsilon_2}{p^4q} - \frac{\Upsilon_1}{\Phi}\right)^{-1} + k_0. \tag{22}$$

where, $\Phi = \frac{px^\alpha}{\alpha} + \frac{qy^\alpha}{\alpha} - \frac{\omega t^\alpha}{\alpha}$.

3.4. Solution Set 4

For Equation (1), we obtain the following set of solutions (when $\rho < 0$), and for this, we consider set 2.

$$f_6(x,y,t) = k_0 - 2\,p\left(-1/4\,\frac{(-q^3\lambda + 2\,p^2\omega\,\gamma)\Upsilon_2}{p^4q} - 1/2\,\Upsilon_1\sqrt{-\frac{-q^3\lambda + 2\,p^2\omega\,\gamma}{p^4q}}\tanh\left(1/2\sqrt{-\frac{-q^3\lambda + 2\,p^2\omega\,\gamma}{p^4q}}\Phi\right)\right)$$
$$\left(\Upsilon_1 - 1/2\,\Upsilon_2\sqrt{-\frac{-q^3\lambda + 2\,p^2\omega\,\gamma}{p^4q}}\tanh\left(1/2\sqrt{-\frac{-q^3\lambda + 2\,p^2\omega\,\gamma}{p^4q}}\Phi\right)\right)^{-1}. \tag{23}$$

or

$$f_7(x,y,t) = k_0 - 2\,p\left(-1/4\,\frac{(-q^3\lambda+2\,p^2\omega\,\gamma)\Upsilon_2}{p^4q} - 1/2\,\Upsilon_1\sqrt{-\frac{-q^3\lambda+2\,p^2\omega\,\gamma}{p^4q}}\coth\left(1/2\sqrt{-\frac{-q^3\lambda+2\,p^2\omega\,\gamma}{p^4q}}\Phi\right)\right)\left(\Upsilon_1 - 1/2\,\Upsilon_2\sqrt{-\frac{-q^3\lambda+2\,p^2\omega\,\gamma}{p^4q}}\coth\left(1/2\sqrt{-\frac{-q^3\lambda+2\,p^2\omega\,\gamma}{p^4q}}\Phi\right)\right)^{-1}. \quad (24)$$

3.5. Solution Set 5

For Equation (1), we obtain the following set of solutions (when $\rho > 0$), and for this, we consider set 2.

$$f_8(x,y,t) = k_0 - 2\,p\left(-1/4\,\frac{(-q^3\lambda+2\,p^2\omega\,\gamma)\Upsilon_2}{p^4q} + 1/2\,\Upsilon_1\sqrt{\frac{-q^3\lambda+2\,p^2\omega\,\gamma}{p^4q}}\tan\left(1/2\sqrt{\frac{-q^3\lambda+2\,p^2\omega\,\gamma}{p^4q}}\Phi\right)\right)\left(\Upsilon_1 + 1/2\,\Upsilon_2\sqrt{\frac{-q^3\lambda+2\,p^2\omega\,\gamma}{p^4q}}\tan\left(1/2\sqrt{\frac{-q^3\lambda+2\,p^2\omega\,\gamma}{p^4q}}\Phi\right)\right)^{-1}. \quad (25)$$

or

$$f_9(x,y,t) = k_0 - 2\,p\left(-1/4\,\frac{(-q^3\lambda+2\,p^2\omega\,\gamma)\Upsilon_2}{p^4q} - 1/2\,\Upsilon_1\sqrt{\frac{-q^3\lambda+2\,p^2\omega\,\gamma}{p^4q}}\cot\left(1/2\sqrt{\frac{-q^3\lambda+2\,p^2\omega\,\gamma}{p^4q}}\Phi\right)\right)\left(\Upsilon_1 - 1/2\,\Upsilon_2\sqrt{\frac{-q^3\lambda+2\,p^2\omega\,\gamma}{p^4q}}\cot\left(1/2\sqrt{\frac{-q^3\lambda+2\,p^2\omega\,\gamma}{p^4q}}\Phi\right)\right)^{-1}. \quad (26)$$

3.6. Solution Set 6

For Equation (1), we obtain the following set of solutions (when ($\rho = 0$), and for this, we consider set 2.

$$f_{10}(x,y,t) = k_0 - 2\,p\left(-1/4\,\frac{(-q^3\lambda+2\,p^2\omega\,\gamma)\Upsilon_2}{p^4q} - \frac{\Upsilon_1}{\Phi}\right)\left(\Upsilon_1 - \frac{\Upsilon_2}{\Phi}\right)^{-1}. \quad (27)$$

where, $\Phi = \frac{px^\alpha}{\alpha} + \frac{qy^\alpha}{\alpha} - \frac{\omega t^\alpha}{\alpha}$.

3.7. Solution Set 7

For Equation (1), we obtain the following set of solutions (when $\rho < 0$), and for this, we consider set 3.

$$f_{11}(x,y,t) = 1/8\,\frac{(-q^3\lambda+2\,p^2\omega\,\gamma)(\Upsilon_1 - \Upsilon_2\sqrt{-\rho}\tanh(\sqrt{-\rho}\Phi))}{p^3q(-\rho\,\Upsilon_2 - \Upsilon_1\sqrt{-\rho}\tanh(\sqrt{-\rho}\Phi))} + k_0 - 2\,\frac{p(-\rho\,\Upsilon_2 - \Upsilon_1\sqrt{-\rho}\tanh(\sqrt{-\rho}\Phi))}{\Upsilon_1 - \Upsilon_2\sqrt{-\rho}\tanh(\sqrt{-\rho}\Phi)}. \quad (28)$$

or

$$f_{12}(x,y,t) = 1/8\,\frac{(-q^3\lambda+2\,p^2\omega\,\gamma)(\Upsilon_1 - \Upsilon_2\sqrt{-\rho}\coth(\sqrt{-\rho}\Phi))}{p^3q(-\rho\,\Upsilon_2 - \Upsilon_1\sqrt{-\rho}\coth(\sqrt{-\rho}\Phi))} + k_0 - 2\,\frac{p(-\rho\,\Upsilon_2 - \Upsilon_1\sqrt{-\rho}\coth(\sqrt{-\rho}\Phi))}{\Upsilon_1 - \Upsilon_2\sqrt{-\rho}\coth(\sqrt{-\rho}\Phi)}. \quad (29)$$

3.8. Solution Set 8

For Equation (1), we obtain the following set of solutions (when $\rho > 0$), and for this, we consider set 3.

$$f_{13}(x,y,t) = 1/8\,\frac{(-q^3\lambda+2\,p^2\omega\,\gamma)(\Upsilon_1 + \Upsilon_2\sqrt{\rho}\tan(\sqrt{\rho}\Phi))}{p^3q(-\rho\,\Upsilon_2 + \Upsilon_1\sqrt{\rho}\tan(\sqrt{\rho}\Phi))} + k_0 - 2\,\frac{p(-\rho\,\Upsilon_2 + \Upsilon_1\sqrt{\rho}\tan(\sqrt{\rho}\Phi))}{\Upsilon_1 + \Upsilon_2\sqrt{\rho}\tan(\sqrt{\rho}\Phi)}. \quad (30)$$

or

$$f_{14}(x,y,t) = 1/8\,\frac{(-q^3\lambda + 2\,p^2\omega\,\gamma)(\Upsilon_1 - \Upsilon_2\sqrt{\rho}\cot(\sqrt{\rho}\Phi))}{p^3q(-\rho\,\Upsilon_2 - \Upsilon_1\sqrt{\rho}\cot(\sqrt{\rho}\Phi))} + k_0 - 2\,\frac{p(-\rho\,\Upsilon_2 - \Upsilon_1\sqrt{\rho}\cot(\sqrt{\rho}\Phi))}{\Upsilon_1 - \Upsilon_2\sqrt{\rho}\cot(\sqrt{\rho}\Phi)}. \quad (31)$$

3.9. Solution Set 9

For Equation (1), we obtain the following set of solutions (when $\rho = 0$), and for this, we consider set 3.

$$f_{15}(x,y,t) = 1/8\left(-q^3\lambda + 2\,p^2\omega\,\gamma\right)\left(\Upsilon_1 - \frac{\Upsilon_2}{\Phi}\right)p^{-3}q^{-1}\left(-\rho\,\Upsilon_2 - \frac{\Upsilon_1}{\Phi}\right)^{-1} + k_0 - 2\,p\left(-\rho\,\Upsilon_2 - \frac{\Upsilon_1}{\Phi}\right)\left(\Upsilon_1 - \frac{\Upsilon_2}{\Phi}\right)^{-1}. \quad (32)$$

where $\rho = 1/16\,\frac{-q^3\lambda+2\,p^2\omega\,\gamma}{p^4q}$ and $\Phi = \frac{px^\alpha}{\alpha} + \frac{qy^\alpha}{\alpha} - \frac{\omega t^\alpha}{\alpha}$.

4. Results and Discussion

Further in the given section, we explore the spatial visualization of the wave solutions derived from the fractional (DJKM) equation. The types of solutions which are identified are trigonometric, hyperbolic and rational solutions as observed from the 3*D* and 2*D* Figures 1–6 for the parameter values $p = 0.5$, $q = 0.2$, $\lambda = 0.01$, $\omega = 0.1$, $\Upsilon_1 = 0.001$, $\Upsilon_2 = 0.01$, $y = 0.2$ and $\gamma = 0.1$.

Figure 1 shows the anti-kink wave solution. However, it can clearly be seen that as the fractional order is small, wave propagation characteristics change drastically. The amplitude of the solution is significantly huge in the medium in which the wave travels. The study shows how minor differences in the parameter of the fractional-order derivative cause different wave characteristics. This is important in the area such as fluid dynamics where innovative methods of propagating waves must be achieved. The solutions suggested show high amplitudes, which means that the interactions occurring in the medium are strong, and these characteristics may be required to explain certain actions or processes in different scientific disciplines.

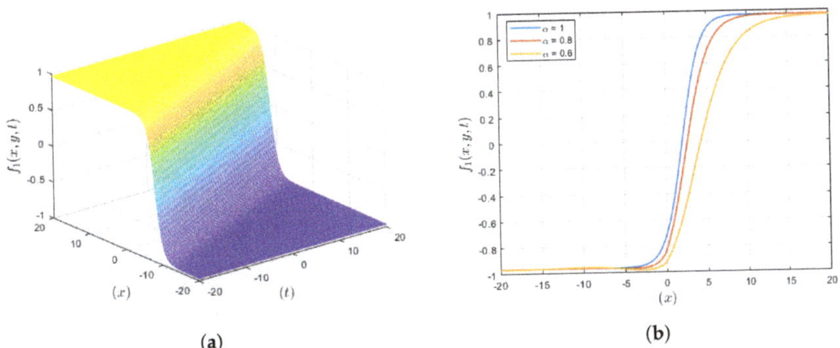

Figure 1. Analyzing the influence of the derivative parameter (α) for both the fractional and integer order of the solution (f_1). (**a**) Three-dimensional (3D) depiction for the solution (f_1) for integer-order derivative parameter (α). (**b**) Two-dimensional (2D) depiction for the solution (f_1) for fractional-order derivative parameter (α).

The compacton kink wave solution of the solution (f_4) is portrayed in Figure 2, which presents the effects of the used fractional order of the derivatives. Hence, the analysis of the 2*D* plot reveals that the amplitude of the wave is highly affected by the use of the fractional-order parameter that implies great changes in wave behavior. The illustration for integer-order derivatives in 3*D* has a localized high amplitude wavelet form and keeps within a finite area of space while oscillating. These plots suggest that fractional derivatives result in significantly higher and higher amplitude oscillations in contrast to integer-order derivatives, which is quite important in fluid dynamics, chemical kinetics and biological morphogenesis applications.

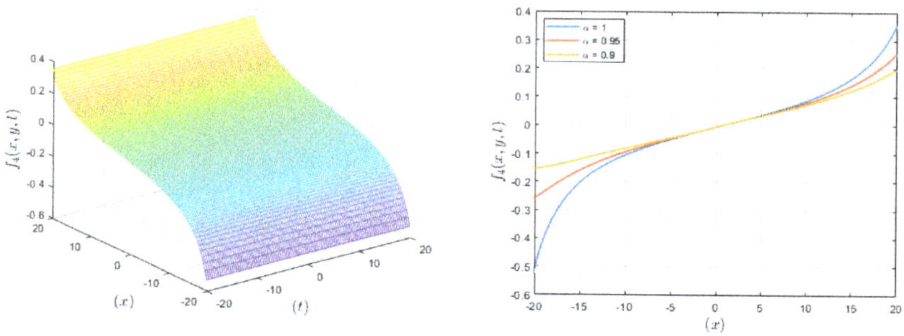

(a) (b)

Figure 2. Analyzing the influence of the derivative parameter (α) for both the fractional and integer order of the solution (f_4). (**a**) Three-dimensional (3D) depiction for the solution (f_4) for integer-order derivative parameter (α). (**b**) Two-dimensional (2D) depiction for the solution (f_4) for fractional-order derivative parameter (α).

The graphical representation of the anti-kink wave solution (f_6) is depicted in Figure 3, where it is revealed that compared to the integer order, the fractional order gives a more localized waveform. If the virtue involves fractional derivatives, then the $2D$ plot reflects more confined waves, while in case of integer-order derivatives, the $3D$ plot illustrates less confined structures. This improved localization is useful for applications that demand a specific manipulation of the wave as in the case of drug delivery or optic fiber communications, hence increasing the probability of the accomplishment of the intended goal through the management of waves.

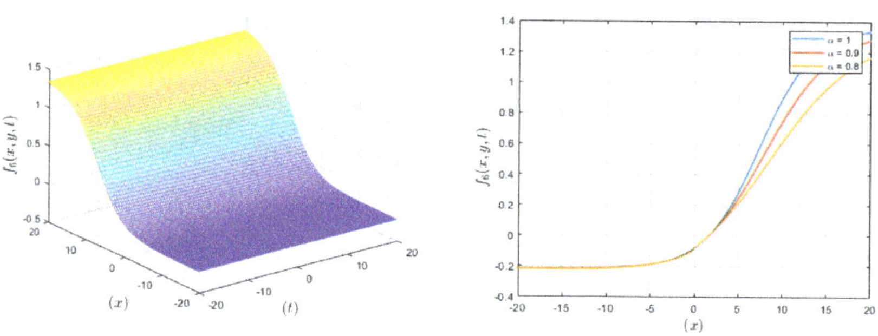

(a) (b)

Figure 3. Analyzing the influence of the derivative parameter (α) for both the fractional and integer order of the solution (f_6). (**a**) Three-dimensional (3D) depiction for the solution (f_6) for integer-order derivative parameter (α). (**b**) Two-dimensional (2D) depiction for the solution (f_6) for fractional-order derivative parameter (α).

Figure 4 illustrates how any changes to the parameter (α), which is dependent on a fractional order, are concentrated at anti-kink waves as opposed to when the parameter (α) depends on an integer order. Plot $2D$ demonstrates that fractional derivatives give a more bound and narrow wavefront, and the third plot for integer-order derivatives reveals a broader wave front. This behavior can be rationalized in terms of long water waves where problems of frequency dispersion and nonlinear restoring forces are recognized as weak. Whereas localizations improve the description of the wave propagation, describing long water waves under these circumstances, fractional derivatives are of extreme value. The use of fractional derivatives is important when it comes to tuning the position of waves in order to model and predict the behavior of waves in situations where both dispersion as well as weak nonlinearity are important.

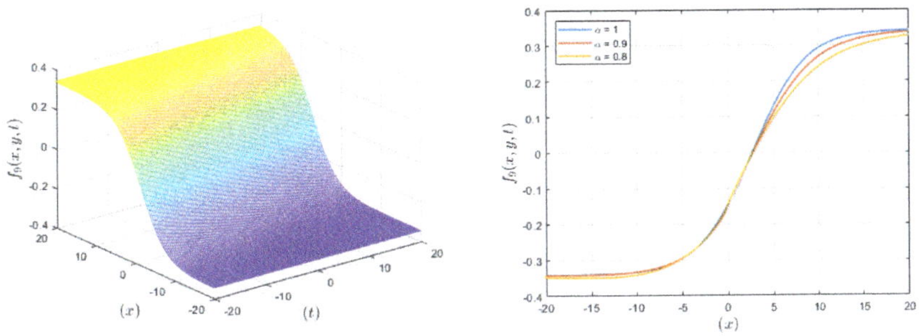

(a) **(b)**

Figure 4. Analyzing the influence of the derivative parameter (α) for both the fractional and integer order of the solution (f_9). (**a**) Three-dimensional (3D) depiction for the solution (f_9) for integer-order derivative parameter (α). (**b**) Two-dimensional (2D) depiction for the solution (f_9) for fractional-order derivative parameter (α).

The kink wave solution (f_{13}) is presented in Figure 5 to depict that the wave amplitude is higher in the fractional-order derivatives than in the integer-order derivatives. From the $2D$ plot, it can be observed that when increasing fractional-order parameters, the resulting wave amplitudes are much higher than the original wave amplitudes. The node $3D$ portrayal of the integer-order derivative looks like it possesses a lesser surge than the one depicted for the fractional-order solutions. This greater amplitude with fractional derivatives means a higher energy of wave propagation, which is beneficial in cases where more energy is to be transferred, such as that which is necessary in fluid dynamics and high-energy wave interactions involving models. The possibility of obtaining larger amplitudes in comparison with fractional-order derivatives gives a powerful tool for the improvement and management of waves in different scientific and engineering fields.

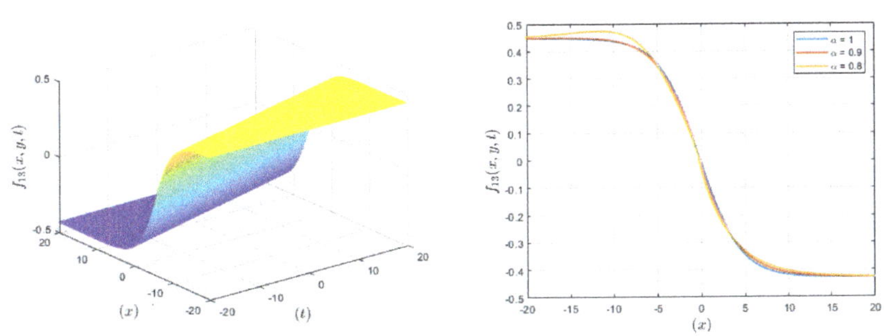

(a) **(b)**

Figure 5. Analyzing the influence of the derivative parameter (α) for both the fractional and integer order of the solution (f_{13}). (**a**) Three-dimensional (3D) depiction for the solution (f_{13}) for integer-order derivative parameter (α). (**b**) Two-dimensional (2D) depiction for the solution (f_{13}) for fractional-order derivative parameter (α).

The anti-kink wave solution (f_{15}) is presented in Figure 6 where the amplitude of the wave is larger with fractional-order derivatives as compared to the integer order. As can be seen in the $2D$ plot, decreasing the fractional-order parameter results in much higher wave amplitudes. When regarding the $3D$ scenario, the integer-order derivative solution bears lower amplitudes compared with the corresponding fractional-order solution, which indicates much more outstanding and higher amplitudes of waveforms. Such behavior implies that while fractional-order derivatives magnify the intensity of the waves to which they are applied, they are more powerful and energetic. This characteristic is highly beneficial for instances where a greater energy of the waves is needed for the interaction with a substance or material such as in the flow dynamics of fluids. The idea of attaining bigger amplitudes with the help of fractional derivatives gives a flexible means for controlling the oscillatory response in a plethora of science and engineering fields.

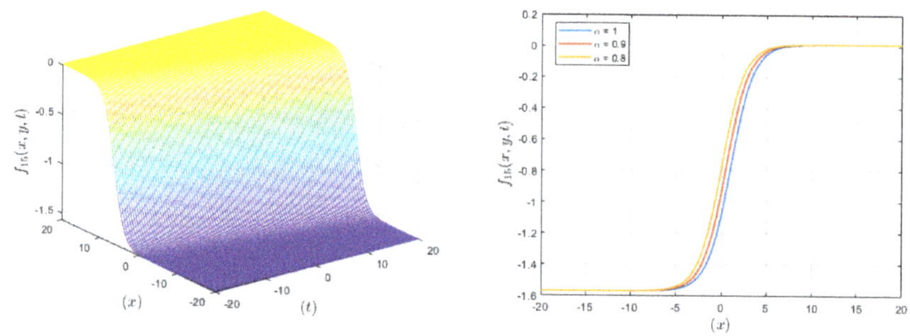

(**a**) (**b**)

Figure 6. Analyzing the influence of the derivative parameter (α) for both the fractional and integer order of the solution (f_{15}). (**a**) Three-dimensional (3D) depiction for the solution (f_{15}) for integer-order derivative parameter (α). (**b**) Two-dimensional (2D) depiction for the solution (f_{15}) for fractional-order derivative parameter (α).

5. Conclusions

In this study, we were able to obtain dynamical wave solutions of the time–space fractional (DJKM) equation using an exciting and very efficient method called Riccati–Bernoulli sub-ODE method through Bäcklund transformation. Indeed, the method used in the paper allowed us to construct different solitary wave solutions such as compacton kink, kink soliton, and anti-kink soliton solutions. From the analysis, it was shown that the fractional-order derivatives give better wave amplitude and localization compared with the integer-order derivatives. These discoveries are significant especially in cases such as application in fluid dynamics, chemical kinetics, and biological morphogenesis where the characteristics of the waves need to be controlled. With the enhanced higher amplitude and better localization, the fractional-order derivatives are useful in enhancing wave behavior in different scientific and engineering fields. In the future, nonlinear dependencies of the electro-osmotic flow through viscoelastic fluids will be investigated as well as comparing the obtained results with experimental data. In conclusion, the present paper shows that fractional-order derivatives play a critical role in wave solutions for providing ways to improve the characterization of dynamic waves in various systems.

Author Contributions: Conceptualization, M.M.A.-S.; Data curation, M.M.A.-S.; Formal analysis, S.N.; Resources, M.M.A.-S.; Investigation, S.N.; Project administration, S.N.; Validation, M.A.; Software, M.A.; Validation, M.A.; Visualization, M.S.A.; Validation, M.S.A.; Visualization, R.U.; Resources, R.U.; Project administration, R.U.; Writing—review & editing, M.S.A. All authors have read and agreed to the published version of the manuscript.

Funding: This work was supported by the Deanship of Scientific Research, Vice Presidency for Graduate Studies and Scientific Research, King Faisal University, Saudi Arabia (KFU241592).

Data Availability Statement: No new data were created or analyzed in this study. Data sharing is not applicable to this article.

Acknowledgments: This work was supported by the Deanship of Scientific Research, Vice Presidency for Graduate Studies and Scientific Research, King Faisal University, Saudi Arabia (KFU241592).

Conflicts of Interest: The authors declare no conflicts of interest.

References

1. Wang, M.L.; Zhou, Y.B.; Li, Z.B. Application of a homogeneous balance method to exact solutions of nonlinear equations in mathematical physics. *Phys. Lett. A* **1996**, *216*, 67–75. [CrossRef]
2. Fan, E.; Zhang, H. A note on the homogeneous balance method. *Phys. Lett. A* **1998**, *246*, 403–406. [CrossRef]
3. Mahak, N.; Akram, G. Exact solitary wave solutions of the (1+1)-dimensional Fokas-Lenells equation. *Optik* **2020**, *208*, 1–9. [CrossRef]
4. Rezazadeh, H.; Manafian, J.; Khodadad, F.S.; Nazari, F. Traveling wave solutions for density dependent conformable fractional diffusion-reaction equation by the first integral method and the improved tan $(\phi(x)/2)$-expansion method. *Opt. Quantum Electron.* **2018**, *50*, 1–15. [CrossRef]
5. Lu, D. Jacobi elliptic function solutions for two variant Boussinesq equations. *Chaos Soliton Fractals* **2005**, *24*, 1373–1385. [CrossRef]
6. Jafari, H.; Kadkhoda, N.; Baleanu, D. Fractional Lie group method of the time-fractional Boussinesq equation. *Nonlinear Dyn.* **2015**, *81*, 1569–1574. [CrossRef]
7. Raza, N.; Aslam, M.R.; Rezazadeh, H. Analytical study of resonant optical solitons with variable coefficients in Kerr and non-Kerrlaw media. *Opt. Quantum Electron.* **2019**, *51*, 59. [CrossRef]
8. Gao, W.; Rezazadeh, H.; Pinar, Z.; Baskonus, H.M.; Sarwar, S.; Yel, G. Novel explicit solutions for the nonlinear Zoomeron equation by using newly extended direct algebraic technique. *Opt. Quantum Electron.* **2020**, *52*, 1–13. [CrossRef]
9. Abdel-Gawad, H.I.; Osman, M.S. On the Variational Approach for Analyzing the Stability of Solutions of Evolution Equations. *Kyungpook Math. J.* **2013**, *53*, 661–680. [CrossRef]
10. Abdel-Gawad, H.I.; Osman, M. On shallow water waves in a medium with time-dependent dispersion and nonlinearity coefficients. *J. Adv. Res.* **2014**, *6*, 593–599. [CrossRef]
11. Ali, M.N.; Osman, M.S.; Husnine, S.M. On the analytical solutions of conformable time-fractional extended Zakharov-Kuznetsov equation through (G'/G^2)-expansion method and the modified Kudryashov method. *SeMA J.* **2019**, *76*, 15–25. [CrossRef]
12. Ali, K.K.; Osman, M.; Abdel-Aty, M. New optical solitary wave solutions of Fokas-Lenells equation in optical fiber via Sine-Gordon expansion method. *Alex. Eng. J.* **2020**, *59*, 1191–1196. [CrossRef]
13. Kumar, A.; Pankaj, R.D. Tanh–coth scheme for traveling wave solutions for Nonlinear Wave Interaction model. *J. Egypt. Math. Soc.* **2015**, *23*, 282–285. [CrossRef]
14. Domairry, G.; Mohsenzadeh, A.; Famouri, M. The application of homotopy analysis method to solve nonlinear differential equation governing Jeffery–Hamel flow. *Commun. Nonlinear Sci. Numer. Simul.* **2009**, *14*, 85–95. [CrossRef]
15. Zhang, Z.Y. Exact traveling wave solutions of the perturbed Klein-Gordon equation with quadratic nonlinearity in (1+1)-dimension. Part I: Without local inductance and dissipation effect. *Turk. J. Phys.* **2013**, *37*, 259–267. [CrossRef]
16. Fan, E. Extended tanh-function method and its applications to nonlinear equations. *Phys. Lett. A* **2000**, *277*, 212–218. [CrossRef]
17. Sarikaya, M.Z.; Budak, H.; Usta, H. On generalized the conformable fractional calculus. *TWMS J. Appl. Eng. Math.* **2019**, *9*, 792–799.
18. Akbar, M.A.; Ali, N.H.M.; Islam, M.T. Multiple closed form solutions to some fractional order nonlinear evolution equations in physics and plasma physics. *AIMS Math.* **2019**, *4*, 397–411. [CrossRef]
19. Liu, T. Exact solutions to time-fractional fifth order KdV equation by trial equation method based on symmetry. *Symmetry* **2019**, *11*, 742. [CrossRef]
20. Alshammari, S.; Al-Sawalha, M.M.; Shah, R. Approximate analytical methods for a fractional-order nonlinear system of Jaulent–Miodek equation with energy-dependent Schrodinger potential. *Fractal Fract.* **2023**, *7*, 140. [CrossRef]
21. Alderremy, A.A.; Shah, R.; Iqbal, N.; Aly, S.; Nonlaopon, K. Fractional series solution construction for nonlinear fractional reaction-diffusion Brusselator model utilizing Laplace residual power series. *Symmetry* **2022**, *14*, 1944. [CrossRef]
22. Yasmin, H.; Alshehry, A.S.; Ganie, A.H.; Mahnashi, A.M. Perturbed Gerdjikov–Ivanov equation: Soliton solutions via Backlund transformation. *Optik* **2024**, *298*, 171576. [CrossRef]
23. Elsayed, E.M.; Nonlaopon, K. The Analysis of the Fractional-Order Navier-Stokes Equations by a Novel Approach. *J. Funct. Spaces* **2022**, *2022*, 8979447. [CrossRef]
24. Alqhtani, M.; Saad, K.M.; Weera, W.; Hamanah, W.M. Analysis of the fractional-order local Poisson equation in fractal porous media. *Symmetry* **2022**, *14*, 1323. [CrossRef]
25. Hajar, F.I.; Hasan, B.; Choonkil, P.; Osman, M.S. M-lump, N-soliton solutions, and the collision phenomena for the (2+1)-dimensional Date–Jimbo–Kashiwara-Miwa equation. *Results Phys.* **2020**, *19*, 103329.
26. Wazwaz, A.M. A (2+1)–dimensional time–dependent Date–Jimbo–Kashiwara–Miwa equation: Painleve integrability and multiple soliton solutions. *Comput. Math. Appl.* **2020**, *79*, 1145–1149. [CrossRef]
27. Adem, A.R.; Yildirim, Y.; Yasar, E. Complexiton solutions and soliton solutions: (2+1)–dimensional Date–Jimbo–Kashiwara–Miwa equation. *Pramana* **2019**, *92*, 1–12. [CrossRef]
28. Yuan, Y.Q.; Tian, B.; Sun, W.R.; Chai, J.; Liu, L. Wronskian and Grammian solutions for a (2+1)-dimensional Date–Jimbo–Kashiwara–Miwa equation. *Comp. Math. Appl. Int. J.* **2017**, *74*, 873–879. [CrossRef]
29. Abdelrahman, M.A.E.; Sohaly, M.A. Solitary waves for the modified Korteweg-de Vries equation in deterministic case and random case. *J. Phys. Math.* **2017**, *8*, 214. [CrossRef]

30. Abdelrahman, M.A.E.; Sohaly, M.A. Solitary waves for the nonlinear Schrödinger problem with the probability distribution function in the stochastic input case. *Eur. Phys. J. Plus* **2017**, *132*, 339. [CrossRef]
31. Yang, X.F.; Deng, Z.C.; Wei, Y. A Riccati-Bernoulli sub-ODE method for nonlinear partial differential equations and its application. *Adv. Differ. Equ.* **2015**, *1*, 117–133. [CrossRef]
32. Lu, D.; Shi, Q. New Jacobi elliptic functions solutions for the combined KdV-mKdV equation. *Int. J. Nonlinear Sci.* **2010**, *10*, 320–325.
33. Zhang, Y. Solving STO and KD equations with modified Riemann-Liouville derivative using improved (G/G')-expansion function method. *Int. J. Appl. Math.* **2015**, *45*, 16–22.

fractal and fractional

Article

Formation of Optical Fractals by Chaotic Solitons in Coupled Nonlinear Helmholtz Equations

M. Mossa Al-Sawalha [1], Saima Noor [2,3,*], Mohammad Alqudah [4], Musaad S. Aldhabani [5] and Rasool Shah [6,*]

1 Department of Mathematics, College of Science, University of Ha'il, Ha'il 55476, Saudi Arabia; m.alswalha@uoh.edu.sa
2 Department of Basic Sciences, General Administration of Preparatory Year, King Faisal University, P.O. Box 400, Al Ahsa 31982, Saudi Arabia
3 Department of Mathematics and Statistics, College of Science, King Faisal University, P.O. Box 400, Al Ahsa 31982, Saudi Arabia
4 Department of Basic Sciences, School of Electrical Engineering & Information Technology, German Jordanian University, Amman 11180, Jordan; mohammad.qudah@gju.edu.jo
5 Department of Mathematics, Faculty of Science, University of Tabuk, P.O. Box 741, Tabuk 71491, Saudi Arabia; maldhabani@ut.edu.sa
6 Department of Computer Science and Mathematics, Lebanese American University, Beirut P.O. Box 13-5053, Lebanon
* Correspondence: snoor@kfu.edu.sa (S.N.); rasoolshah@awkum.edu.pk (R.S.)

Abstract: In the present research work, we construct and examine the self-similarity of optical solitons by employing the Riccati Modified Extended Simple Equation Method (RMESEM) within the framework of non-integrable Coupled Nonlinear Helmholtz Equations (CNHEs). This system models the transmission of optical solitons and coupled wave packets in nonlinear optical fibers and describes transverse effects in nonlinear fiber optics. Initially, a complex transformation is used to convert the model into a single Nonlinear Ordinary Differential Equation (NODE), from which hyperbolic, exponential, rational, trigonometric, and rational hyperbolic solutions are produced. In order to better understand the physical dynamics, we offer several 3D, contour, and 2D illustrations for the independent selections of physical parameter values. These illustrations highlight the graphic behaviour of some optical solitons and demonstrate that, under certain constraint conditions, acquired optical solitons lose their stability when they approach an axis and display periodic-axial perturbations, which lead to the generation of optical fractals. As a framework, the generated optical solitons have several useful applications in the field of telecommunications. Furthermore, our suggested RMESEM demonstrates its use by broadening the spectrum of optical soliton solutions, offering important insights into the dynamics of the CNHEs, and suggesting possible applications in the management of nonlinear models.

Keywords: coupled nonlinear Helmholtz equations; nonlinear partial differential equations; Riccati modified extended simple equation method; optical soliton; fractals; axial and periodic perturbation

1. Introduction

Nonlinear Differential Equations (NDEs) particularly Nonlinear Partial Differential Equations (NPDEs) have important applications in various fields of science such as stochastic Schrödinger equations in spontaneous emissions or thermal fluctuations [1], nonlinear Maccari's systems in plasma physics and hydrodynamics [2], the Navier Stokes equation in fluid [3], Higgs equations in particle physics [4], the Duffing equations in oscillatory motions [5], and Kairat equations in optics [6]. Several numerical and analytical approaches have been developed by researchers to explore the underpinning nature of NPDEs. However, there are several challenges associated with solving NPDEs. These obstacles include the potential for numerous or no solutions, sensitivity to the initial conditions, nonlinearity-related complexity, and difficulty in precisely determining the solution. By offering important insights into the dynamics of nonlinear models, exact solutions of NPDEs in contrast with numerical solutions, particularly the calculation of travelling wave and soliton solutions, are crucial to the study of soliton theory. Numerous useful approaches have been established to obtain soliton solutions for understanding the physical behaviour of these nonlinear models, which aid engineers and other experts as well as provide knowledge about physical issues and their applications. Giving precise soliton solutions for NPDEs with symbolic computer tools like Matlab, Maple, Mathematica, and others that simplify intricate algebraic calculations has garnered more attention in recent years. The literature has several analytical techniques for locating novel soliton solutions, including the Khater method [7], the Sine–Gordon method [8], the Riccati–Bernoulli Sub-ODE method [9], the (G'/G) -expansion method [10–13], the exp-function method [14], the Sardar sub-equation method [15], the Kudryashov method [16], the Poincaré-Lighthill-Kuo method [17], Hirota's bilinear method [18], the extended direct algebraic method [19,20], and the modified simple equation method [21,22], among others. It is also essential to recognize that these methods may have drawbacks and limits (like the seven common errors) [23,24], even though these approaches greatly advance our comprehension of soliton dynamics and help us to relate them to the theories that explain phenomena. Additionally, many of these methods depend on the Riccati equation [25]. Since the Riccati equation has solitary solutions, such techniques are useful in the study of soliton phenomena in nonlinear models [26].

Contemporary advances in soliton theory have led to fascinating new fields of study in the subject of mathematics, particularly, fractal soliton theory, which examines the intricate connection between solitons and fractals [27–29]. A stable, confined wave packet exhibiting both solitonic and fractal geometry is called a fractal soliton. Fractal solitons are solitons with uneven boundaries that exhibit self-replication and intricate geometrical structures at various scales while maintaining a steady speed. The relationship between soliton dynamics and fractal geometry provides fresh insights into nonlinear phenomena in physics, engineering, as well as biological frameworks [30–32]. Therefore, the theory of fractal solitons has many real-world applications in several domains. For instance, fractal solitons are useful in chaos theory because of their special characteristics, which aids in comprehending the dynamics and resilience of chaotic systems. The research on fractal solitons has become a hot issue in modern mathematics, and as it continues to develop, it is anticipated to encourage creative approaches and solutions in both practical and theoretical mathematics.

In this study, a robust and efficient analytical technique namely RMESEM is applied to address CNHEs in order to discover and explore a unique array of optical soliton solutions for them. The RMESEM is one of the most significant simple and effective algebraic procedures among the previously discussed analytical methods for generating soliton solutions to NPDEs. The strategic RMESEM reduces the problem to a set of nonlinear algebraic equations by transforming NPDEs into NODEs using a wave transformation and then assuming a series form solution. Novel families of soliton solutions, including exponential, rational, hyperbolic, and trigonometric functions, are obtained after solving the resulting system by employing the Maple tool. A single, sustainable wave packet that travels across a medium without changing its speed is known as a soliton. Since soliton solutions for NPDEs provide greater depth and granularity than traditional solutions, they continue to be important from an academic standpoint. They are useful because they maintain their innate durability and endurance in a variety of scientific and technical domains.

The aim of this research is to examine optical soliton propagation in CNHEs, which is a crucial Schrödinger-class model for altering the phase and amplitude modulation of continuous waves, as well as for modeling the growing miniaturization of plasmonics and photonic devices. Physically, this system models the transmission of optical solitons and coupled wave packets in nonlinear optical fibers and describes transverse effects in nonlinear fiber optics [33]. This model is expressed as the given coupled NPDEs [34]:

$$\begin{aligned} &iw_t + \varphi w_{tt} + \frac{1}{2}w_{xx} + \kappa_1\left|w^2\right|w + \kappa_2\left|z^2\right|w = 0, \\ &iz_t + \varphi z_{tt} + \frac{1}{2}z_{xx} + \kappa_1\left|w^2\right|z + \kappa_2\left|z^2\right|z = 0, \end{aligned} \tag{1}$$

where $i = \sqrt{-1}$, $w = w(x,t)$, and $z = z(x,t)$ represent envelope fields, while the subscripts x and t indicate the transverse and longitudinal coordinates correspondingly. In Equation (1), the second terms φw_{tt} and φz_{tt} are corresponded to Helmholtz nonparaxiality, while the coefficient $\varphi(>0)$ symbolizes the parameter of nonparaxial, and κ_1 and κ_2 are the coefficients of nonlinearity that might potentially be included into the model itself with slight modifications. Moreover, the coefficients κ_1 and κ_2 are kept in (1) to deal with different nonlinearities namely, focusing nonlinearity $(\kappa_1, \kappa_2 > 0)$ and mixed (focusing–defocusing) nonlinearity $(\kappa_1 > 0, \kappa_2 < 0$ or $\kappa_1 < 0, \kappa_2 > 0)$ and defocusing nonlinearity $(\kappa_1, \kappa_2 < 0)$. This model leads (1) to a Helmholtz–Manakov system for $\kappa_1 = \kappa_2 = \pm 1$.

Many other scholars have addressed the targeted CNHEs using various analytical and numerical approaches before this research project. For instance, Tamilselvan et al. employed the ansatz approach to derive a class of elliptic wave solutions of CNHEs in terms of the Jacobi elliptic functions that characterize non-paraxial ultra-broad beam propagation in nonlinear Kerr-like media. They also examined the limiting forms of these solutions, particularly hyperbolic solutions [35]. Singh et al. employed the $\exp(-\Phi(\varepsilon))$-expansion technique in [36] to derive travelling wave solutions for non-integrable CNHEs that were organised as trigonometric, rational, and hyperbolic functions. Similarly, Alsaud et al. used the generalized (G'/G)-expansion approach to obtain certain optical solitons for CNHEs and then provided an analysis of modulation instability based on the obtained optical solitons [34]. Finally, in the framework of a cubic CNHE, Saha et al. in [37] examined the presence and stability characteristics of anti-dark and chirped grey solitary waves.

It is obvious from the literature that scholars have previously investigated solitonic phenomena in CNHEs, but no study has been conducted to examine and evaluate the formation of optical fractals resulting from chaotic perturbations in solitons within the context of the aimed model. This observation points to a substantial gap in the corpus of existing research. Our research, which employs the suggested RMESEM technique, closes this gap by offering an in-depth and novel analysis of the model's fractal solitonic phenomena. To do this, we generate and analyze novel optical solitons in the form of exponential, hyperbolic, trigonometric, and rational solutions for the non-integrable CNHEs using the RMESEM. We also provide several 3D, 2D, and contour visuals of acquired optical solitons to illustrate their dynamical behaviours, which reveal that, when acquired optical solitons approach an axis, they become unsustainable under specific constraint circumstances and exhibit periodic-axial disturbances, resulting in the formation of optical fractals. There may be several practical uses for the produced optical solitons in the telecom industry.

The rest of the paperwork is arranged as follows: Section 2 provides an explanation of the RMESEM's analytical procedures. Section 3 addresses the CNHEs in order to produce new optical soliton solutions. Section 4 provides visual representations of the perturbed behaviour of the produced optical solitons. Section 5 provides the conclusion, and the Appendix A contains the details about wave functions.

2. The Methodology of RMESEM

Numerous analytical techniques have been developed in the literature to investigate soliton occurrences in nonlinear models [21–35]. However, in this study, we use the RMESEM to construct and examine optical soliton solutions for targeted CNHEs. This section outlines the efficient RMESEM's operational mechanism. Suppose the NPDE of the form [6]:

$$A(\mathfrak{z}, \mathfrak{z}_t, \mathfrak{z}_{t_1}, \mathfrak{z}_{t_2}, \mathfrak{z}\mathfrak{z}_{t_1}, \ldots) = 0, \tag{2}$$

where $\mathfrak{z} = \mathfrak{z}(t, t_1, t_2, t_3, \ldots, t_r)$.

To solve (2), the following steps are performed:

1. Initially, we execute the variable-form complex transformation $\mathfrak{z}(t, t_1, t_2, t_3, \ldots, t_r) = \mathfrak{S}(\chi)$, which can be defined in multiple ways. Using this transformation, the following NODE is obtained from (2):

$$B(\mathfrak{S}, \mathfrak{S}'\mathfrak{S}, \mathfrak{S}', \ldots) = 0, \tag{3}$$

where $\mathfrak{S}' = \frac{d\mathfrak{S}}{d\chi}$. Occasionally, we integrate (3) to coerce the NODE to adhere to the homogenous balancing criterion.

2. Next, the ensuing finite series-based solution for the NODE in (3) is proposed using the solution of the extended Riccati–NODE:

$$\mathfrak{S}(\chi) = \sum_{j=0}^{P} c_j \left(\frac{Q'(\chi)}{Q(\chi)} \right)^j + \sum_{j=0}^{P-1} d_j \left(\frac{Q'(\chi)}{Q(\chi)} \right)^j \cdot \left(\frac{1}{Q(\chi)} \right). \tag{4}$$

Here, $Q(\chi)$ denotes the solution to the resulting extended Riccati–NODE, and the variables $c_j (j = 0, \ldots, P)$ and $d_j (j = 0, \ldots, P-1)$ represent the unknown constants that need to be discovered.

$$Q'(\chi) = \rho + \varrho Q(\chi) + \sigma (Q(\chi))^2, \tag{5}$$

where ρ, ϱ and σ are constants.

3. By homogeneously balancing the largest nonlinear term and the highest-order derivative in Equation (3), we can accomplish the positive integer P required in Equation (4).

4. Then, when (4) is incorporated into (3) or in the equation that results from the integration of (3), all of the terms with the same powers of $Q(\chi)$ are collected, which results in the formation of an equation in terms of $Q(\chi)$. An algebraic system of equations describing the variables $c_j (j = 0, ..., P)$ and $d_j (j = 0, ..., P-1)$ with additional associated parameters may be obtained by setting the coefficients in the resultant equation to zero.

5. The resultant system of nonlinear algebraic equations is analytically solved using Maple.

6. Finally, we compute and insert the unknown values along with $Q(\chi)$ (the Equation (5)'s solution) in Equation (4) to obtain analytical soliton solutions for (2). We may obtain multiple clusters of soliton solutions by using the general solution of (5). These clusters are shown as follows: (see Table 1).

Table 1. The particular solutions $Q(\chi)$ of the Riccati equation in (5) and the formation of $\left(\frac{Q'(\chi)}{Q(\chi)}\right)$, where $z_1, z_2 \in R$, $v = \varrho^2 - 4\sigma\rho$, and $\theta = \cosh\left(\frac{1}{4}\sqrt{v}\chi\right)\sinh\left(\frac{1}{4}\sqrt{v}\chi\right)$.

S. No.	Cluster	Constraint(s)	$Q(\chi)$	$\left(\frac{Q'(\chi)}{Q(\chi)}\right)$
1	Trigonometric Solutions	$v < 0, \quad \sigma \neq 0$	$-\frac{\varrho}{2\sigma} + \frac{\sqrt{-v}\tan\left(\frac{1}{2}\sqrt{-v}\chi\right)}{2\sigma}$, $-\frac{\varrho}{2\sigma} - \frac{\sqrt{-v}\cot\left(\frac{1}{2}\sqrt{-v}\chi\right)}{2\sigma}$, $-\frac{\varrho}{2\sigma} + \frac{\sqrt{-v}\left(\tan\left(\sqrt{-v}\chi\right)+\left(\sec\left(\sqrt{-v}\chi\right)\right)\right)}{2\sigma}$, $-\frac{\varrho}{2\sigma} + \frac{\sqrt{-v}\left(\tan\left(\sqrt{-v}\chi\right)-\left(\sec\left(\sqrt{-v}\chi\right)\right)\right)}{2\sigma}$.	$-\frac{1}{2}\frac{v\left(1+\left(\tan\left(\frac{1}{2}\sqrt{-v}\chi\right)\right)^2\right)}{-\varrho+\sqrt{-v}\tan\left(\frac{1}{2}\sqrt{-v}\chi\right)}$, $\frac{1}{2}\frac{\left(1+\left(\cot\left(\frac{1}{2}\sqrt{-v}\chi\right)\right)^2\right)v}{\varrho+\sqrt{-v}\cot\left(\frac{1}{2}\sqrt{-v}\chi\right)}$, $\frac{-v\left(1+\sin\left(\sqrt{-v}\chi\right)\right)\sec\left(\sqrt{-v}\chi\right)}{-\varrho\cos\left(\sqrt{-v}\chi\right)+\sqrt{-v}\sin\left(\sqrt{-v}\chi\right)+\sqrt{-v}}$, $\frac{v\left(\sin\left(\sqrt{-v}\chi\right)-1\right)\sec\left(\sqrt{-v}\chi\right)}{-\varrho\cos\left(\sqrt{-v}\chi\right)+\sqrt{-v}\sin\left(\sqrt{-v}\chi\right)-\sqrt{-v}}$.

Table 1. *Cont.*

S. No.	Cluster	Constraint(s)	$Q(\chi)$	$\left(\frac{Q'(\chi)}{Q(\chi)}\right)$
2	Hyperbolic Solutions	$\upsilon > 0, \quad \sigma \neq 0$	$-\frac{\varrho}{2\sigma} - \frac{\sqrt{\upsilon}\tanh\left(\frac{1}{2}\sqrt{\upsilon}\chi\right)}{2\sigma}$, $-\frac{\varrho}{2\sigma} - \frac{\sqrt{\upsilon}\left(\tanh\left(\sqrt{\upsilon}\chi\right)+i\left(\operatorname{sech}\left(\sqrt{\upsilon}\chi\right)\right)\right)}{2\sigma}$, $-\frac{\varrho}{2\sigma} - \frac{\sqrt{\upsilon}\left(\tanh\left(\sqrt{\upsilon}\chi\right)-i\left(\operatorname{sech}\left(\sqrt{\upsilon}\chi\right)\right)\right)}{2\sigma}$, $-\frac{\varrho}{2\sigma} - \frac{\sqrt{\upsilon}\left(\coth\left(\sqrt{\upsilon}\chi\right)+\left(\operatorname{csch}\left(\sqrt{\upsilon}\chi\right)\right)\right)}{2\sigma}$.	$-\frac{1}{2}\frac{\left(-1+\left(\tanh\left(\frac{1}{2}\sqrt{\upsilon}\chi\right)\right)^2\right)\upsilon}{\varrho+\sqrt{\upsilon}\tanh\left(\frac{1}{2}\sqrt{\upsilon}\chi\right)}$, $-\frac{\upsilon\left(-1+i\sinh\left(\sqrt{\upsilon}\chi\right)\right)}{\cosh\left(\sqrt{\upsilon}\chi\right)\left(\varrho\cosh\left(\sqrt{\upsilon}\chi\right)+\sqrt{\upsilon}\sinh\left(\sqrt{\upsilon}\chi\right)+i\sqrt{\upsilon}\right)}$, $-\frac{\upsilon\left(1+i\sinh\left(\sqrt{\upsilon}\chi\right)\right)}{\cosh\left(\sqrt{\upsilon}\chi\right)\left(-\varrho\cosh\left(\sqrt{\upsilon}\chi\right)-\sqrt{\upsilon}\sinh\left(\sqrt{\upsilon}\chi\right)+i\sqrt{\upsilon}\right)}$, $-\frac{1}{4}\frac{\upsilon\left(2\left(\cosh\left(\frac{1}{4}\sqrt{\upsilon}\chi\right)\right)^2-1\right)}{\theta\left(-2\varrho\theta+\sqrt{\upsilon}\right)}$.
3	Rational Solutions	$\upsilon = 0$ $\upsilon = 0, \& \varrho = \sigma = 0$ $\upsilon = 0, \& \varrho = \rho = 0$	$-2\frac{\rho(\varrho\chi+2)}{\varrho^2\chi}$, $\chi\rho$, $-\frac{1}{\chi\sigma}$.	$-2\frac{1}{\chi(\varrho\chi+2)}$, $\frac{1}{\chi}$, $-\frac{1}{\chi}$.
4	Exponential Solutions	$\sigma = 0, \& \varrho = \mu$, $\rho = b\mu$ $\rho = 0, \& \varrho = \mu$, $\sigma = b\mu$	$e^{\mu\chi} - b$, $\frac{e^{\mu\chi}}{1-be^{\mu\chi}}$.	$\frac{\mu e^{\mu\chi}}{e^{\mu\chi}-b}$, $-\frac{\mu}{-1+be^{\mu\chi}}$.
5	Rational-Hyperbolic Solutions	$\rho = 0, \& \varrho \neq 0$, $\sigma \neq 0$	$-\frac{\varrho z_1}{\sigma(\cosh(\varrho\chi)-\sinh(\varrho\chi)+z_2)}$, $-\frac{\varrho(\cosh(\varrho\chi)+\sinh(\varrho\chi))}{\sigma(\cosh(\varrho\chi)+\sinh(\varrho\chi)+z_2)}$.	$\frac{\varrho(\sinh(\varrho\chi)-\cosh(\varrho\chi))}{-\cosh(\varrho\chi)+\sinh(\varrho\chi)-z_2}$, $\frac{\varrho z_2}{\cosh(\varrho\chi)+\sinh(\varrho\chi)+z_2}$.

3. Establishing Optical Soliton Solutions for CNHEs

In this study, we present optical soliton solutions for Equation (1) by utilizing the suggested RMESEM. We start with the complex wave transformation that is as follows:

$$\begin{aligned} w(x,t) &= e^{\vartheta i}W(\chi), \quad z(x,t) = e^{\vartheta i}Z(\chi), \\ \chi &= (k_3x - k_3k_4t), \quad \vartheta = (-k_1x + k_2t + \nu). \end{aligned} \tag{6}$$

After substituting (6) in (1) and separating the imaginary and real parts, we obtain

$$\begin{aligned} &(-{k_3}^2 - 2\varphi{k_3}^2{k_4}^2)W'' + ({k_1}^2 + 2k_2 + 2\varphi{k_2}^2)W + (-2\kappa_1W^3 - 2\kappa_2WZ^2) = 0, \\ &(2k_1k_3 + 2k_3k_4 + 4\varphi k_2k_3k_4)W' = 0, \end{aligned} \tag{7}$$

from Equation (1)'s real part, whereas its imaginary part produces

$$\begin{aligned} &(-{k_3}^2 - 2\varphi{k_3}^2{k_4}^2)Z'' + ({k_1}^2 + 2k_2 + 2\varphi{k_2}^2)Z + (-2\kappa_1W^2Z - 2\kappa_2Z^3) = 0, \\ &(2k_1k_3 + 2k_3k_4 + 4\varphi k_2k_3k_4)Z' = 0. \end{aligned} \tag{8}$$

When (8) undergoes transformation via $Z = \beta W$, we mitigate the entire system to a single NODE whenever β is set to 1; alternatively, the system fails to be solved using the RMESEM. The resultant NODE is given as

$$\Pi_1 W + \Pi_2 W'' + \Pi_3 W^3 = 0, \tag{9}$$

in conjunction with the constraint condition from imaginary part:

$$k_4 = \frac{-k_1}{1 + 2\varphi k_2}. \tag{10}$$

Additionally, in (9),

$$\begin{aligned} \Pi_1 &= (k_1{}^2 + 2k_2 + 2\varphi k_2{}^2), \\ \Pi_2 &= (-k_3{}^2 - 2\varphi k_3{}^2 k_4{}^2), \\ \Pi_3 &= (-2(\kappa_1 + \kappa_2)). \end{aligned}$$

Utilizing (9) to determine the homogeneous balancing principle within $W''(\chi)$ and $W^3(\chi)$, $P = 1$ is recommended. Inputting $P = 1$ into (4) yields the following series solution for Equation (9):

$$W(\chi) = \sum_{j=0}^{1} c_j \left(\frac{Q'(\chi)}{Q(\chi)} \right)^j + d_0 \left(\frac{1}{Q(\chi)} \right). \tag{11}$$

By inserting (11) into (9) and collecting every single term with the same power of $Q(\chi)$, an expression in $Q(\chi)$ is obtained. By setting the coefficients in the resultant equation to zero, a system of nonlinear algebraic equations is produced. Using Maple to solve the resulting problem, the following three (3) cases of solutions are found:
Case 1:

$$\begin{aligned} &c_1 = 0, c_0 = \frac{1}{2}\frac{d_0 \varrho}{\rho}, d_0 = d_0, k_1 = \frac{1}{2}\sqrt{-8 k_3{}^2 \rho\, \sigma - 8\, \varphi\, k_2{}^2 - 8\, k_2 - 2\, k_3{}^2 \varrho^2 (2\, \varphi\, k_2 + 1)}\,\Upsilon, k_3 = k_3, \\ &\kappa_1 = \frac{4\, d_0{}^2 \kappa_2 \varphi^2 k_2{}^2 + 4\, d_0{}^2 \kappa_2 \varphi\, k_2 + k_3{}^2 \varphi\, \varrho^2 d_0{}^2 \kappa_2 + k_3{}^2 \rho^2 + d_0{}^2 \kappa_2 - 4\, k_3{}^2 \varphi\, \rho\, \sigma\, d_0{}^2 \kappa_2}{d_0{}^2}\Upsilon^2, \kappa_2 = \kappa_2. \end{aligned} \tag{12}$$

Case 2:

$$c_1 = c_1, c_0 = c_0, d_0 = d_0, k_1 = -\sqrt{-2\, \varphi\, k_2{}^2 - 2\, k_2}, k_3 = 0, \kappa_1 = -\kappa_2, \kappa_2 = \kappa_2. \tag{13}$$

Case 3:

$$\begin{aligned} &c_1 = c_1, c_0 = -\frac{1}{2} c_1 \varrho, d_0 = -c_1 \rho, k_1 = \frac{1}{2}\sqrt{-8 k_3{}^2 \rho\, \sigma - 8\, \varphi\, k_2{}^2 - 8\, k_2 - 2\, k_3{}^2 \varrho^2 (2\, \varphi\, k_2 + 1)}\,\Upsilon, k_3 = k_3, \\ &\kappa_1 = -\frac{-4\, \kappa_2 c_1{}^2 \varphi^2 k_2{}^2 - 4\, \kappa_2 c_1{}^2 \varphi\, k_2 - k_3{}^2 \varphi\, \varrho^2 \kappa_2 c_1{}^2 - k_3{}^2 - \kappa_2 c_1{}^2 + 4\, k_3{}^2 \varphi\, \rho\, \sigma\, \kappa_2 c_1{}^2}{c_1{}^2}\Upsilon^2, \kappa_2 = \kappa_2. \end{aligned} \tag{14}$$

Case 4:

$$\begin{aligned} &c_1 = \Upsilon k_3, c_0 = -\frac{1}{2} k_3 \varrho\, \Upsilon, d_0 = -\rho\, k_3 \Upsilon, k_3 = k_3, \kappa_1 = \kappa_1, \kappa_2 = \kappa_2 \\ &k_1 = \frac{1}{2}\sqrt{-8 k_3{}^2 \rho\, \sigma - 8\, \varphi\, k_2{}^2 - 8\, k_2 - 2\, k_3{}^2 \varrho^2 (2\, \varphi\, k_2 + 1)}\,\Upsilon. \end{aligned} \tag{15}$$

where $\Upsilon := \frac{1}{\sqrt{(\kappa_1 + \kappa_2)\left(-k_3{}^2 \varphi\, \varrho^2 - 1 - 4\, \varphi\, k_2 - 4\, \varphi^2 k_2{}^2 + 4\, k_3{}^2 \varphi\, \rho\, \sigma\right)}}$.

We build the subsequent novel clusters of optical soliton solutions for (1) by assuming Case 1 and employing (6) and (11) together with the corresponding solution of (5):
Cluster 1.1: For $\upsilon < 0$ and $\sigma \neq 0$,

$$w_{1,1}(t,x) = z_{1,1}(t,x) = e^{\vartheta i}\left(\frac{1}{2}\frac{d_0\varrho}{\rho} + d_0\left(-\frac{1}{2}\frac{\varrho}{\sigma} + \frac{1}{2}\frac{\sqrt{-\upsilon}\tan\left(\frac{1}{2}\sqrt{-\upsilon}\chi\right)}{\sigma}\right)^{-1}\right), \tag{16}$$

$$w_{1,2}(t,x) = z_{1,2}(t,x) = e^{\vartheta i}\left(\frac{1}{2}\frac{d_0\varrho}{\rho} + d_0\left(-\frac{1}{2}\frac{\varrho}{\sigma} - \frac{1}{2}\frac{\sqrt{-\upsilon}\cot\left(\frac{1}{2}\sqrt{-\upsilon}\chi\right)}{\sigma}\right)^{-1}\right), \tag{17}$$

$$w_{1,3}(t,x) = z_{1,3}(t,x) = e^{\vartheta i}\left(\frac{1}{2}\frac{d_0\varrho}{\rho} + d_0\left(-\frac{1}{2}\frac{\varrho}{\sigma} + \frac{1}{2}\frac{\sqrt{-\upsilon}(\tan(\sqrt{-\upsilon}\chi) + \sec(\sqrt{-\upsilon}\chi))}{\sigma}\right)^{-1}\right), \tag{18}$$

and

$$w_{1,4}(t,x) = z_{1,4}(t,x) = e^{\vartheta i}\left(\frac{1}{2}\frac{d_0\varrho}{\rho} + d_0\left(-\frac{1}{2}\frac{\varrho}{\sigma} + \frac{1}{2}\frac{\sqrt{-\upsilon}(\tan(\sqrt{-\upsilon}\chi) - \sec(\sqrt{-\upsilon}\chi))}{\sigma}\right)^{-1}\right). \tag{19}$$

Cluster 1.2: For $\upsilon > 0$ and $\sigma \neq 0$,

$$w_{1,5}(t,x) = z_{1,5}(t,x) = e^{\vartheta i}\left(\frac{1}{2}\frac{d_0\varrho}{\rho} + d_0\left(-\frac{1}{2}\frac{\varrho}{\sigma} - \frac{1}{2}\frac{\sqrt{\upsilon}\tanh\left(\frac{1}{2}\sqrt{\upsilon}\chi\right)}{\sigma}\right)^{-1}\right), \tag{20}$$

$$w_{1,6}(t,x) = z_{1,6}(t,x) = e^{\vartheta i}\left(\frac{1}{2}\frac{d_0\varrho}{\rho} + d_0\left(-\frac{1}{2}\frac{\varrho}{\sigma} - \frac{1}{2}\frac{\sqrt{\upsilon}(\tanh(\sqrt{\upsilon}\chi) + i\operatorname{sech}(\sqrt{\upsilon}\chi))}{\sigma}\right)^{-1}\right), \tag{21}$$

$$w_{1,7}(t,x) = z_{1,7}(t,x) = e^{\vartheta i}\left(\frac{1}{2}\frac{d_0\varrho}{\rho} + d_0\left(-\frac{1}{2}\frac{\varrho}{\sigma} - \frac{1}{2}\frac{\sqrt{\upsilon}(\tanh(\sqrt{\upsilon}\chi) - i\operatorname{sech}(\sqrt{\upsilon}\chi))}{\sigma}\right)^{-1}\right), \tag{22}$$

and

$$w_{1,8}(t,x) = z_{1,8}(t,x) = e^{\vartheta i}\left(\frac{1}{2}\frac{d_0\varrho}{\rho} + d_0\left(-\frac{1}{2}\frac{\varrho}{\sigma} - \frac{1}{4}\frac{\sqrt{\upsilon}\left(\tanh\left(\frac{1}{4}\sqrt{\upsilon}\chi\right) - \coth\left(\frac{1}{4}\sqrt{\upsilon}\chi\right)\right)}{\sigma}\right)^{-1}\right). \tag{23}$$

Cluster 1.3: For $\upsilon = 0$ and $\varrho \neq 0$,

$$w_{1,9}(t,x) = z_{1,9}(t,x) = e^{\vartheta i}\left(\frac{1}{2}\frac{d_0\varrho}{\rho} - \frac{1}{2}\frac{d_0\varrho^2\chi}{\rho(\varrho\chi + 2)}\right). \tag{24}$$

Cluster 1.4: For $\upsilon = 0$, when $\varrho = \sigma = 0$,

$$w_{1,10}(t,x) = z_{1,10}(t,x) = e^{\vartheta i}\left(\frac{d_0}{\rho\chi}\right). \tag{25}$$

Cluster 1.5: For $\varrho = \mu$, $\rho = b\mu (b \neq 0)$, and $\sigma = 0$,

$$w_{1,11}(t,x) = z_{1,11}(t,x) = e^{\vartheta i}\left(\frac{1}{2}\frac{d_0\mu}{\rho} + \frac{d_0}{e^{\mu\chi} - b}\right). \tag{26}$$

We build the subsequent novel clusters of optical soliton solutions for (1) by presuming Case 2 and employing (6) and (11) together with the corresponding solution of (5):
Cluster 2.1: For $\upsilon < 0$ and $\sigma \neq 0$,

$$w_{2,1}(t,x) = z_{2,1}(t,x) = e^{\vartheta i}\left(c_0 - \frac{1}{2}\frac{c_1\upsilon\left(1+\left(\tan\left(\frac{1}{2}\sqrt{-\upsilon}\chi\right)\right)^2\right)}{-\varrho+\sqrt{-\upsilon}\tan\left(\frac{1}{2}\sqrt{-\upsilon}\chi\right)} + \frac{d_0}{\left(-\frac{1}{2}\frac{\varrho}{\sigma}+\frac{1}{2}\frac{\sqrt{-\upsilon}\tan\left(\frac{1}{2}\sqrt{-\upsilon}\chi\right)}{\sigma}\right)}\right), \tag{27}$$

$$\begin{aligned} w_{2,2}(t,x) = z_{2,2}(t,x) = & e^{\vartheta i}\left(c_0 - \frac{c_1\upsilon\left(1+\sin\left(\sqrt{-\upsilon}\chi\right)\right)}{\cos\left(\sqrt{-\upsilon}\chi\right)\left(-\varrho\cos\left(\sqrt{-\upsilon}\chi\right)+\sqrt{-\upsilon}\sin\left(\sqrt{-\upsilon}\chi\right)+\sqrt{-\upsilon}\right)}\right. \\ & \left. + d_0\left(-\frac{1}{2}\frac{\varrho}{\sigma}+\frac{1}{2}\frac{\sqrt{-\upsilon}\left(\tan\left(\sqrt{-\upsilon}\chi\right)+\sec\left(\sqrt{-\upsilon}\chi\right)\right)}{\sigma}\right)^{-1}\right), \end{aligned} \tag{28}$$

and

$$\begin{aligned} w_{2,3}(t,x) = z_{2,3}(t,x) = & e^{\vartheta i}\left(c_0 + \frac{c_1\upsilon\left(\sin\left(\sqrt{-\upsilon}\chi\right)-1\right)}{\cos\left(\sqrt{-\upsilon}\chi\right)\left(-\varrho\cos\left(\sqrt{-\upsilon}\chi\right)+\sqrt{-\upsilon}\sin\left(\sqrt{-\upsilon}\chi\right)-\sqrt{-\upsilon}\right)}\right. \\ & \left. + d_0\left(-\frac{1}{2}\frac{\varrho}{\sigma}+\frac{1}{2}\frac{\sqrt{-\upsilon}\left(\tan\left(\sqrt{-\upsilon}\chi\right)-\sec\left(\sqrt{-\upsilon}\chi\right)\right)}{\sigma}\right)^{-1}\right). \end{aligned} \tag{29}$$

Cluster 2.2: For $\upsilon > 0$ and $\sigma \neq 0$,

$$w_{2,4}(t,x) = z_{2,4}(t,x) = e^{\vartheta i}\left(c_0 - \frac{1}{2}\frac{c_1\upsilon\left(-1+\left(\tanh\left(\frac{1}{2}\sqrt{\upsilon}\chi\right)\right)^2\right)}{\varrho+\sqrt{\upsilon}\tanh\left(\frac{1}{2}\sqrt{\upsilon}\chi\right)} + \frac{d_0}{\left(-\frac{1}{2}\frac{\varrho}{\sigma}-\frac{1}{2}\frac{\sqrt{\upsilon}\tanh\left(\frac{1}{2}\sqrt{\upsilon}\chi\right)}{\sigma}\right)}\right), \tag{30}$$

$$\begin{aligned} w_{2,5}(t,x) = z_{2,5}(t,x) = & e^{\vartheta i}\left(c_0 - \frac{c_1\upsilon\left(-1+i\sinh\left(\sqrt{\upsilon}\chi\right)\right)}{\cosh\left(\sqrt{\upsilon}\chi\right)\left(\varrho\cosh\left(\sqrt{\upsilon}\chi\right)+\sqrt{\upsilon}\sinh\left(\sqrt{\upsilon}\chi\right)+i\sqrt{\upsilon}\right)}\right. \\ & \left. + d_0\left(-\frac{1}{2}\frac{\varrho}{\sigma}-\frac{1}{2}\frac{\sqrt{\upsilon}\left(\tanh\left(\sqrt{\upsilon}\chi\right)+i\operatorname{sech}\left(\sqrt{\upsilon}\chi\right)\right)}{\sigma}\right)^{-1}\right), \end{aligned} \tag{31}$$

$$\begin{aligned} w_{2,6}(t,x) = z_{2,6}(t,x) = & e^{\vartheta i}\left(c_0 - \frac{c_1\upsilon\left(1+i\sinh\left(\sqrt{\upsilon}\chi\right)\right)}{\cosh\left(\sqrt{\upsilon}\chi\right)\left(-\varrho\cosh\left(\sqrt{\upsilon}\chi\right)-\sqrt{\upsilon}\sinh\left(\sqrt{\upsilon}\chi\right)+i\sqrt{\upsilon}\right)}\right. \\ & \left. + d_0\left(-\frac{1}{2}\frac{\varrho}{\sigma}-\frac{1}{2}\frac{\sqrt{\upsilon}\left(\tanh\left(\sqrt{\upsilon}\chi\right)-i\operatorname{sech}\left(\sqrt{\upsilon}\chi\right)\right)}{\sigma}\right)^{-1}\right), \end{aligned} \tag{32}$$

Cluster 2.3: For $\varrho = \mu, \rho = b\mu (b \neq 0)$, and $\sigma = 0$,

$$w_{2,7}(t,x) = z_{2,7}(t,x) = e^{\vartheta i}\left(c_0 + \frac{c_1\mu\,\mathrm{e}^{\mu\chi}}{\mathrm{e}^{\mu\chi}-b} + \frac{d_0}{\mathrm{e}^{\mu\chi}-b}\right). \tag{33}$$

Cluster 2.4: For $\varrho = \mu, \sigma = b\mu (b \neq 0)$, and $\rho = 0$,

$$w_{2,8}(t,x) = z_{2,8}(t,x) = e^{\vartheta i}\left(c_0 - \frac{c_1\mu}{-1+b\mathrm{e}^{\mu\chi}} + \frac{d_0(1-b\mathrm{e}^{\mu\chi})}{\mathrm{e}^{\mu\chi}}\right). \tag{34}$$

Cluster 2.5: For $\rho = 0, \sigma \neq 0$, and $\varrho \neq 0$,

$$w_{2,9}(t,x) = z_{2,9}(t,x) = e^{\vartheta i}\left(c_0 + \frac{c_1\varrho\,(\sinh(\varrho\,\chi) - \cosh(\varrho\,\chi))}{-\cosh(\varrho\,\chi) + \sinh(\varrho\,\chi) - z_2} - \frac{d_0\sigma\,(\cosh(\varrho\,\chi) - \sinh(\varrho\,\chi) + z_2)}{z_1\varrho}\right), \quad (35)$$

and

$$w_{2,10}(t,x) = z_{2,10}(t,x) = e^{\vartheta i}\left(c_0 + \frac{c_1\varrho\,z_2}{\cosh(\varrho\,\chi) + \sinh(\varrho\,\chi) + z_2} - \frac{d_0\sigma\,(\cosh(\varrho\,\chi) + \sinh(\varrho\,\chi) + z_2)}{\varrho\,(\cosh(\varrho\,\chi) + \sinh(\varrho\,\chi))}\right). \quad (36)$$

We build the subsequent novel clusters of optical soliton solutions for (1) by presuming Case 3 and employing (6) and (11) together with the corresponding solution of (5):

Cluster 3.1: For $\upsilon < 0$ and $\sigma \neq 0$,

$$w_{3,1}(t,x) = z_{3,1}(t,x) = e^{\vartheta i}\left(-\frac{1}{2}c_1\varrho - \frac{1}{2}\frac{c_1\upsilon\left(1 + \left(\tan\left(\frac{1}{2}\sqrt{-\upsilon}\chi\right)\right)^2\right)}{-\varrho + \sqrt{-\upsilon}\tan\left(\frac{1}{2}\sqrt{-\upsilon}\chi\right)} - \frac{c_1\rho}{\left(-\frac{1}{2}\frac{\varrho}{\sigma} + \frac{1}{2}\frac{\sqrt{-\upsilon}\tan\left(\frac{1}{2}\sqrt{-\upsilon}\chi\right)}{\sigma}\right)}\right), \quad (37)$$

$$w_{3,2}(t,x) = z_{3,2}(t,x) = e^{\vartheta i}\left(-\frac{1}{2}c_1\varrho + \frac{1}{2}\frac{c_1\upsilon\left(1 + \left(\cot\left(\frac{1}{2}\sqrt{-\upsilon}\chi\right)\right)^2\right)}{\varrho + \sqrt{-\upsilon}\cot\left(\frac{1}{2}\sqrt{-\upsilon}\chi\right)} - \frac{c_1\rho}{\left(-\frac{1}{2}\frac{\varrho}{\sigma} - \frac{1}{2}\frac{\sqrt{-\upsilon}\cot\left(\frac{1}{2}\sqrt{-\upsilon}\chi\right)}{\sigma}\right)}\right), \quad (38)$$

$$\begin{aligned} w_{3,3}(t,x) = z_{3,3}(t,x) =& e^{\vartheta i}\left(-\frac{1}{2}c_1\varrho - \frac{c_1\upsilon\,(1 + \sin(\sqrt{-\upsilon}\chi))}{\cos(\sqrt{-\upsilon}\chi)\,(-\varrho\,\cos(\sqrt{-\upsilon}\chi) + \sqrt{-\upsilon}\sin(\sqrt{-\upsilon}\chi) + \sqrt{-\upsilon})}\right. \\ &\left. - c_1\rho\left(-\frac{1}{2}\frac{\varrho}{\sigma} + \frac{1}{2}\frac{\sqrt{-\upsilon}(\tan(\sqrt{-\upsilon}\chi) + \sec(\sqrt{-\upsilon}\chi))}{\sigma}\right)^{-1}\right), \end{aligned} \quad (39)$$

and

$$\begin{aligned} w_{3,4}(t,x) = z_{3,4}(t,x) =& e^{\vartheta i}\left(-\frac{1}{2}c_1\varrho + \frac{c_1\upsilon\,(\sin(\sqrt{-\upsilon}\chi) - 1)}{\cos(\sqrt{-\upsilon}\chi)\,(-\varrho\,\cos(\sqrt{-\upsilon}\chi) + \sqrt{-\upsilon}\sin(\sqrt{-\upsilon}\chi) - \sqrt{-\upsilon})}\right. \\ &\left. - c_1\rho\left(-\frac{1}{2}\frac{\varrho}{\sigma} + \frac{1}{2}\frac{\sqrt{-\upsilon}(\tan(\sqrt{-\upsilon}\chi) - \sec(\sqrt{-\upsilon}\chi))}{\sigma}\right)^{-1}\right). \end{aligned} \quad (40)$$

Cluster 3.2: For $\upsilon > 0$ and $\sigma \neq 0$,

$$w_{3,5}(t,x) = z_{3,5}(t,x) = e^{\vartheta i}\left(-\frac{1}{2}c_1\varrho - \frac{1}{2}\frac{c_1\upsilon\left(-1 + \left(\tanh\left(\frac{1}{2}\sqrt{\upsilon}\chi\right)\right)^2\right)}{\varrho + \sqrt{\upsilon}\tanh\left(\frac{1}{2}\sqrt{\upsilon}\chi\right)} - \frac{c_1\rho}{\left(-\frac{1}{2}\frac{\varrho}{\sigma} - \frac{1}{2}\frac{\sqrt{\upsilon}\tanh\left(\frac{1}{2}\sqrt{\upsilon}\chi\right)}{\sigma}\right)}\right), \quad (41)$$

$$\begin{aligned} w_{3,6}(t,x) = z_{3,6}(t,x) =& e^{\vartheta i}\left(-\frac{1}{2}c_1\varrho - \frac{c_1\upsilon\,(-1 + i\sinh(\sqrt{\upsilon}\chi))}{\cosh(\sqrt{\upsilon}\chi)\,(\varrho\,\cosh(\sqrt{\upsilon}\chi) + \sqrt{\upsilon}\sinh(\sqrt{\upsilon}\chi) + i\sqrt{\upsilon})}\right. \\ &\left. - c_1\rho\left(-\frac{1}{2}\frac{\varrho}{\sigma} - \frac{1}{2}\frac{\sqrt{\upsilon}(\tanh(\sqrt{\upsilon}\chi) + i\,\mathrm{sech}(\sqrt{\upsilon}\chi))}{\sigma}\right)^{-1}\right), \end{aligned} \quad (42)$$

$$w_{3,7}(t,x) = z_{3,7}(t,x) = e^{\vartheta i}\Bigg(-\frac{1}{2}c_1\varrho - \frac{c_1 v\,(1+i\sinh(\sqrt{v}\chi))}{\cosh(\sqrt{v}\chi)(-\varrho\cosh(\sqrt{v}\chi) - \sqrt{v}\sinh(\sqrt{v}\chi) + i\sqrt{v})} - c_1\rho\left(-\frac{1}{2}\frac{\varrho}{\sigma} - \frac{1}{2}\frac{\sqrt{v}(\tanh(\sqrt{v}\chi) - i\,\text{sech}(\sqrt{v}\chi))}{\sigma}\right)^{-1}\Bigg), \tag{43}$$

and

$$w_{3,8}(t,x) = z_{3,8}(t,x) = e^{\vartheta i}\Bigg(-\frac{1}{2}c_1\varrho - \frac{1}{4}\frac{c_1 v\left(2\left(\cosh\left(\frac{1}{4}\sqrt{v}\chi\right)\right)^2 - 1\right)}{\theta(-2\varrho\theta + \sqrt{v})} - c_1\rho\left(-\frac{1}{2}\frac{\varrho}{\sigma} - \frac{1}{4}\frac{\sqrt{v}\left(\tanh\left(\frac{1}{4}\sqrt{v}\chi\right) - \coth\left(\frac{1}{4}\sqrt{v}\chi\right)\right)}{\sigma}\right)^{-1}\Bigg). \tag{44}$$

Cluster 3.3: For $v = 0$ and $\varrho \neq 0$,

$$w_{3,9}(t,x) = z_{3,9}(t,x) = e^{\vartheta i}\left(-\frac{1}{2}c_1\varrho - 2\frac{c_1}{\chi(\varrho\chi + 2)} + \frac{1}{2}\frac{c_1\varrho^2\chi}{\varrho\chi + 2}\right). \tag{45}$$

Cluster 3.4: For $v = 0$, when $\varrho = \rho = 0$,

$$w_{3,10}(t,x) = z_{3,10}(t,x) = -e^{\vartheta i}\left(\frac{c_1}{\chi}\right). \tag{46}$$

Cluster 3.5: For $\varrho = \mu$, $\rho = b\mu(b \neq 0)$, and $\sigma = 0$,

$$w_{3,11}(t,x) = z_{3,11}(t,x) = e^{\vartheta i}\left(-\frac{1}{2}c_1\mu + \frac{c_1\mu\, e^{\mu\chi}}{e^{\mu\chi} - b} - \frac{c_1 b\mu}{e^{\mu\chi} - b}\right). \tag{47}$$

Cluster 3.6: For $\varrho = \mu$, $\sigma = b\mu(b \neq 0)$, and $\rho = 0$,

$$w_{3,12}(t,x) = z_{3,12}(t,x) = e^{\vartheta i}\left(-\frac{1}{2}c_1\mu - \frac{c_1\mu}{-1 + be^{\mu\chi}}\right). \tag{48}$$

Cluster 3.7: For $\rho = 0$, $\sigma \neq 0$, and $\varrho \neq 0$,

$$w_{3,13}(t,x) = z_{3,13}(t,x) = e^{\vartheta i}\left(-\frac{1}{2}c_1\varrho + \frac{c_1\varrho\,(\sinh(\varrho\chi) - \cosh(\varrho\chi))}{-\cosh(\varrho\chi) + \sinh(\varrho\chi) - z_2}\right), \tag{49}$$

and

$$w_{3,14}(t,x) = z_{3,14}(t,x) = e^{\vartheta i}\left(-\frac{1}{2}c_1\varrho + \frac{c_1\varrho\, z_2}{\cosh(\varrho\chi) + \sinh(\varrho\chi) + z_2}\right). \tag{50}$$

We build the subsequent novel clusters of optical soliton solutions for (1) by presuming Case 4 and employing (6) and (11) together with the corresponding solution of (5):
Cluster 4.1: For $v < 0$ $\sigma \neq 0$,

$$w_{4,1}(t,x) = z_{4,1}(t,x) = e^{\vartheta i}\left(\frac{-k_3\varrho\,\Upsilon}{2} - \frac{\Upsilon k_3 v\left(1 + \left(\tan\left(\frac{1}{2}\sqrt{-v}\chi\right)\right)^2\right)}{2(-\varrho + \sqrt{-v}\tan\left(\frac{1}{2}\sqrt{-v}\chi\right))} - \frac{\rho k_3 \Upsilon}{\left(-\frac{1}{2}\frac{\varrho}{\sigma} + \frac{1}{2}\frac{\sqrt{-v}\tan\left(\frac{1}{2}\sqrt{-v}\chi\right)}{\sigma}\right)}\right), \tag{51}$$

$$w_{4,2}(t,x) = z_{4,2}(t,x) = e^{\vartheta i}\left(\frac{-k_3\varrho\,\Upsilon}{2} + \frac{\Upsilon\,k_3 v\left(1+\left(\cot\left(\frac{1}{2}\sqrt{-v}\chi\right)\right)^2\right)}{2(\varrho+\sqrt{-v}\cot\left(\frac{1}{2}\sqrt{-v}\chi\right))} - \frac{\rho\,k_3\Upsilon}{\left(-\frac{1}{2}\frac{\varrho}{\sigma}-\frac{1}{2}\frac{\sqrt{-v}\cot\left(\frac{1}{2}\sqrt{-v}\chi\right)}{\sigma}\right)}\right), \tag{52}$$

$$\begin{aligned} w_{4,3}(t,x) = z_{4,3}(t,x) =& e^{\vartheta i}\Bigg(\frac{-k_3\varrho\,\Upsilon}{2} - \frac{\Upsilon\,k_3 v\,(1+\sin(\sqrt{-v}\chi))}{\cos(\sqrt{-v}\chi)(-\varrho\,\cos(\sqrt{-v}\chi)+\sqrt{-v}\sin(\sqrt{-v}\chi)+\sqrt{-v})} \\ & -\rho\,k_3\Upsilon\left(-\frac{1}{2}\frac{\varrho}{\sigma}+\frac{1}{2}\frac{\sqrt{-v}(\tan(\sqrt{-v}\chi)+\sec(\sqrt{-v}\chi))}{\sigma}\right)^{-1}\Bigg), \end{aligned} \tag{53}$$

and

$$\begin{aligned} w_{4,4}(t,x) = z_{4,4}(t,x) =& e^{\vartheta i}\Bigg(\frac{-k_3\varrho\,\Upsilon}{2} + \frac{\Upsilon\,k_3 v\,(\sin(\sqrt{-v}\chi)-1)}{\cos(\sqrt{-v}\chi)(-\varrho\,\cos(\sqrt{-v}\chi)+\sqrt{-v}\sin(\sqrt{-v}\chi)-\sqrt{-v})} \\ & -\rho\,k_3\Upsilon\left(-\frac{1}{2}\frac{\varrho}{\sigma}+\frac{1}{2}\frac{\sqrt{-v}(\tan(\sqrt{-v}\chi)-\sec(\sqrt{-v}\chi))}{\sigma}\right)^{-1}\Bigg). \end{aligned} \tag{54}$$

Cluster 4.2: For $v > 0$ and $\sigma \neq 0$,

$$w_{4,5}(t,x) = z_{4,5}(t,x) = e^{\vartheta i}\left(\frac{-k_3\varrho\,\Upsilon}{2} - \frac{\Upsilon\,k_3 v\left(-1+\left(\tanh\left(\frac{1}{2}\sqrt{v}\chi\right)\right)^2\right)}{2(\varrho+\sqrt{v}\tanh\left(\frac{1}{2}\sqrt{v}\chi\right))} - \frac{\rho\,k_3\Upsilon}{\left(-\frac{1}{2}\frac{\varrho}{\sigma}-\frac{1}{2}\frac{\sqrt{v}\tanh\left(\frac{1}{2}\sqrt{v}\chi\right)}{\sigma}\right)}\right), \tag{55}$$

$$\begin{aligned} w_{4,6}(t,x) = z_{4,6}(t,x) =& e^{\vartheta i}\Bigg(\frac{-k_3\varrho\,\Upsilon}{2} - \frac{\Upsilon\,k_3 v\,(-1+i\sinh(\sqrt{v}\chi))}{\cosh(\sqrt{v}\chi)(\varrho\,\cosh(\sqrt{v}\chi)+\sqrt{v}\sinh(\sqrt{v}\chi)+i\sqrt{v})} \\ & -\rho\,k_3\Upsilon\left(-\frac{1}{2}\frac{\varrho}{\sigma}-\frac{1}{2}\frac{\sqrt{v}(\tanh(\sqrt{v}\chi)+i\mathrm{sech}(\sqrt{v}\chi))}{\sigma}\right)^{-1}\Bigg), \end{aligned} \tag{56}$$

$$\begin{aligned} w_{4,7}(t,x) = z_{4,7}(t,x) =& e^{\vartheta i}\Bigg(\frac{-k_3\varrho\,\Upsilon}{2} + \frac{\Upsilon\,k_3 v\,(1+i\sinh(\sqrt{v}\chi))}{\cosh(\sqrt{v}\chi)(\varrho\,\cosh(\sqrt{v}\chi)+\sqrt{v}\sinh(\sqrt{v}\chi)-i\sqrt{v})} \\ & -\rho\,k_3\Upsilon\left(-\frac{1}{2}\frac{\varrho}{\sigma}-\frac{1}{2}\frac{\sqrt{v}(\tanh(\sqrt{v}\chi)-i\mathrm{sech}(\sqrt{v}\chi))}{\sigma}\right)^{-1}\Bigg), \end{aligned} \tag{57}$$

and

$$\begin{aligned} w_{4,8}(t,x) = z_{4,8}(t,x) =& e^{\vartheta i}\Bigg(\frac{-k_3\varrho\,\Upsilon}{2} - \frac{1}{4}\frac{\Upsilon\,k_3 v\left(2\left(\cosh\left(\frac{1}{4}\sqrt{v}\chi\right)\right)^2-1\right)}{\theta(-2\,\varrho\,\theta+\sqrt{v})} \\ & -\rho\,k_3\Upsilon\left(-\frac{1}{2}\frac{\varrho}{\sigma}-\frac{1}{4}\frac{\sqrt{v}\left(\tanh\left(\frac{1}{4}\sqrt{v}\chi\right)-\coth\left(\frac{1}{4}\sqrt{v}\chi\right)\right)}{\sigma}\right)^{-1}\Bigg). \end{aligned} \tag{58}$$

Cluster 4.3: For $v = 0$ and $\varrho \neq 0$,

$$w_{4,9}(t,x) = z_{4,9}(t,x) = e^{\vartheta i}\left(\frac{-k_3\varrho\,\Upsilon}{2} - 2\frac{\Upsilon\,k_3}{\chi\,(\varrho\,\chi+2)} + \frac{1}{2}\frac{\Upsilon\,k_3\varrho^2\chi}{\varrho\,\chi+2}\right). \tag{59}$$

Cluster 4.4: For $v = 0$, when $\varrho = \rho = 0$,

$$w_{4,10}(t,x) = z_{4,10}(t,x) = -e^{\vartheta i}\left(-\frac{k_3}{\sqrt{(\kappa_1+\kappa_2)\left(-1-4\,\varphi\,k_2-4\,\varphi^2{k_2}^2\right)\chi}}\right). \tag{60}$$

Cluster 4.5: For $\varrho = \mu$, $\rho = b\mu(b \neq 0)$, and $\sigma = 0$,

$$w_{4,11}(t,x) = z_{4,11}(t,x) = e^{\vartheta i}\left(\frac{1}{2}\frac{k_3\mu}{\sqrt{-(\kappa_1+\kappa_2)\left({k_3}^2\varphi\,\mu^2+1+4\,\varphi\,k_2+4\,\varphi^2{k_2}^2\right)}}\right). \tag{61}$$

Cluster 4.6: For $\varrho = \mu$, $\sigma = b\mu(b \neq 0)$, and $\rho = 0$,

$$w_{4,12}(t,x) = z_{4,12}(t,x) = e^{\vartheta i}\left(-\frac{1}{2}\frac{k_3\mu\,(1+be^{\mu\chi})}{\sqrt{-(\kappa_1+\kappa_2)\left({k_3}^2\varphi\,\mu^2+1+4\,\varphi\,k_2+4\,\varphi^2{k_2}^2\right)(-1+be^{\mu\chi})}}\right). \tag{62}$$

Cluster 4.7: For $\rho = 0$, $\sigma \neq 0$, and $\varrho \neq 0$,

$$w_{4,13}(t,x) = z_{4,13}(t,x) = \frac{k_3\varrho\,(-\cosh(\varrho\,\chi)+\sinh(\varrho\,\chi)+z_2)e^{\vartheta i}}{2\sqrt{-(\kappa_1+\kappa_2)\left({k_3}^2\varphi\,\varrho^2+1+4\,\varphi\,k_2+4\,\varphi^2{k_2}^2\right)(-\cosh(\varrho\,\chi)+\sinh(\varrho\,\chi)-z_2)}}, \tag{63}$$

and

$$w_{4,14}(t,x) = z_{4,14}(t,x) = \frac{-k_3\varrho\,(\cosh(\varrho\,\chi)+\sinh(\varrho\,\chi)-z_2)e^{\vartheta i}}{2\sqrt{-(\kappa_1+\kappa_2)\left({k_3}^2\varphi\,\varrho^2+1+4\,\varphi\,k_2+4\,\varphi^2{k_2}^2\right)(\cosh(\varrho\,\chi)+\sinh(\varrho\,\chi)+z_2)}}. \tag{64}$$

4. Discussion and Graphs

In this section of the study, we discuss various optical wave forms that were found in the model. We were able to extract and vividly exhibit optical solitons' wave patterns in 3D, contour, and 2D formats using RMESEMs. Our comprehension of the dynamics of optical pulse theory in optical fibers may be greatly advanced by the developed optical soliton solutions. Additionally, the optical solitons in the context of CNHEs were shown to visually illustrate how certain limitation conditions cause them to lose stability as they approach an axis, exhibiting periodic axial disturbances and ultimately forming optical fractals. This periodic behaviour of the soliton may also be attributed to the formation of a Duffing equation as stated in (9) from the CNHEs, after the implementation of a complex transformation since a Duffing equation possesses periodic solutions [38]. An optical soliton, as found in the context of CNHEs, is a self-sustaining waveform that travels through fiber optic media without changing its speed and shape. These waves are renowned for their capacity to rebuild and stabilize themselves following a collision with other waves of a similar nature. Nevertheless, our analysis showed that the presence of external forces and the dispersion of nonlinearity cause axial and periodic disturbances in the generated solitons which results in the formation of optical fractals because this chaotic perturbation induces instabilities in the soliton. However, in some of our solitons, the fractal shape has also formed due to the soliton interaction (particularly with singular lumps) and self similarities. Singularities can arise in the setting of CNHEs because of the nonlinear interplay and complex parameter dependencies inside the non-integrable system, especially when periodic and axial perturbations affect the optical solitons. Singular points or localized spikes in the solution may result from these perturbations, which have the potential to destabilize the optical soliton. Furthermore, our proposed RMESEM demonstrates its usefulness by broadening the spectrum of optical soliton solutions, offering important insights into the dynamics of the CNHEs, and suggesting possible applications in the management of nonlinear models. Figure 1, the (**a**) 3D graph, (**b**) contour graph, and (**c**) 2D graph (when $x = 10$) represent the optical soliton solution $u_{1,5}(t,x)$ articulated in (20) for $\rho := 4, \varrho := 5, \sigma := 1, \varphi := 0.25 \times 10^{-2}, k_2 := 0.45 \times 10^{-1}, k_3 := 0.2 \times 10^{-1}, \nu := 2, d_0 := 1$. In this depiction, the optical fractal is formed due to the chaotic axial perturbation. Figure 2, the (**a**) 3D graph, (**b**) contour graph, and (**c**) 2D graph (when $x = 1$) represent the optical soliton solution $u_{1,9}(t,x)$ articulated in (24) for $\rho := 1, \varrho := 2, \sigma := 1, \varphi := 0.15 \times 10^{-2}$, $k_2 := 0.235, k_3 := 0.124, \nu := 1, d_0 := 3$. In this depiction, the optical fractal is formed due to the periodic axial perturbation. Figure 3, the (**a**) 3D graph, (**b**) contour graph, and (**c**) 2D graph (when $x = 1.5$) represent the optical soliton solution $u_{1,11}(t,x)$ articulated in (26) for $\rho := 6, \varrho := 3, \sigma := 0, \varphi := 0.95 \times 10^{-3}, k_2 := 0.445, k_3 := 0.66, \nu := 4, d_0 := 1, b := 2, \mu := 3$. In this depiction, the optical fractal is formed due to the chaotic periodic axial perturbation. Figure 4, the (**a**) 3D graph, (**b**) contour graph, and (**c**) 2D graph (when $x = 3$) represent the optical soliton solution $u_{2,4}(t,x)$ articulated in (30) for $\rho := 2, \varrho := 10, \sigma := 8$, $\varphi := 0.15 \times 10^{-2}, k_3 := 0, k_2 := 1.5, \nu := 1, c_2 := 1, c_0 := 2, d_0 := 1$. In this depiction, the optical fractal is formed due to the periodic axial perturbation. Figure 5, the (**a**) 3D graph, (**b**) contour graph, and (**c**) 2D graph (when $x = 5$) represent the optical soliton solution $u_{2,8}(t,x)$ articulated in (34) for $\rho := 0, \varrho := 1, \sigma := -2, \varphi := 0.75 \times 10^{-2}, k_3 := 0, k_2 := 1$, $\nu := 2, c_2 := 2, c_0 := 3, d_0 := 1, \mu := 1, b := -2$. In this depiction, the optical fractal is formed due to the periodic axial perturbation. Figure 6, the (**a**) 3D graph, (**b**) contour graph, and (**c**) 2D graph (when $t = 0$) represent the optical soliton solution $u_{3,1}(t,x)$ articulated in (37) for $\rho := 1, \varrho := 1, \sigma := 4, \varphi := 0.1 \times 10^{-3}, k_3 := 0.685, k_2 := 0.115, \nu := 1, c_2 := 2$. In this depiction, the optical fractal is formed due to the chaotic bi-axial perturbation. Figure 7, the (**a**) 3D graph, (**b**) contour graph, and (**c**) 2D graph (when $x = 1$) represent the optical soliton solution $u_{3,5}(t,x)$ articulated in (41) for $\rho := 1, \varrho := 10, \sigma := 9$, $\varphi := 0.35 \times 10^{-2}, k_3 := 1, k_2 := 1, \nu := 2, c_2 := 1$. In this depiction, the optical fractal is formed due to the periodic axial perturbation. Figure 8, the (**a**) 3D graph, (**b**) contour graph, and (**c**) 2D graph (when $x = -1$) represent the optical soliton solution $u_{3,13}(t,x)$ articulated in (49) for $\rho := 0, \varrho := 2, \sigma := 5, \varphi := 0.22 \times 10^{-2}, k_3 := 2, k_2 := 1, \nu := 4, c_2 := 3, z_2 := 1$. In this depiction, the optical fractal is formed due to the chaotic axial perturbation.

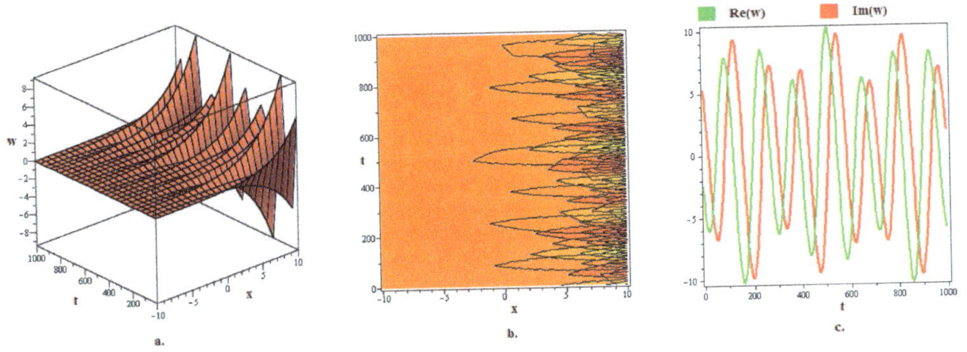

Figure 1. The (**a**) 3D graph, (**b**) contour graph, and (**c**) 2D graph (when $x = 10$) represent the optical soliton solution $u_{1,5}(t,x)$ articulated in (20) for $\rho := 4, \varrho := 5, \sigma := 1, \varphi := 0.25 \times 10^{-2}$, $k_2 := 0.45 \times 10^{-1}, k_3 := 0.2 \times 10^{-1}, \nu := 2, d_0 := 1$. In this depiction, the optical fractal is formed due to the chaotic axial perturbation.

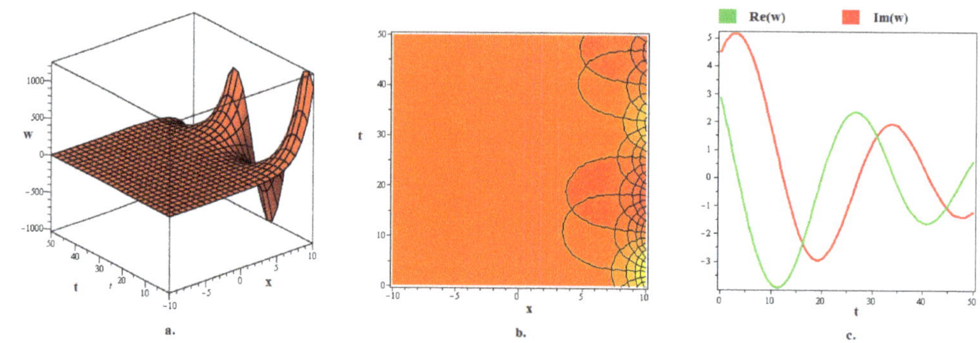

Figure 2. The (**a**) 3D graph, (**b**) contour graph, and (**c**) 2D graph (when $x = 1$) represent the optical soliton solution $u_{1,9}(t,x)$ articulated in (24) for $\rho := 1, \varrho := 2, \sigma := 1, \varphi := 0.15 \times 10^{-2}$, $k_2 := 0.235, k_3 := 0.124, \nu := 1, d_0 := 3$. In this depiction, the optical fractal is formed due to the periodic axial perturbation.

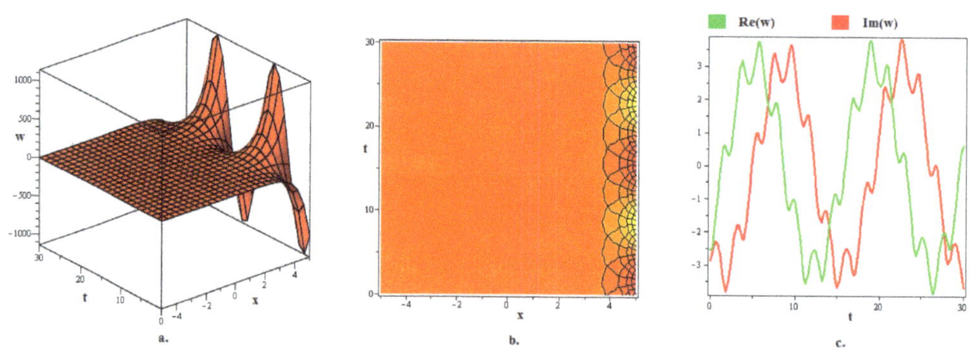

Figure 3. The (**a**) 3D graph, (**b**) contour graph, and (**c**) 2D graph (when $x = 1.5$) represent the optical soliton solution $u_{1,11}(t,x)$ articulated in (26) for $\rho := 6, \varrho := 3, \sigma := 0, \varphi := 0.95 \times 10^{-3}, k_2 := 0.445$, $k_3 := 0.66, \nu := 4, d_0 := 1, b := 2, \mu := 3$. In this depiction, the optical fractal is formed due to the chaotic periodic axial perturbation.

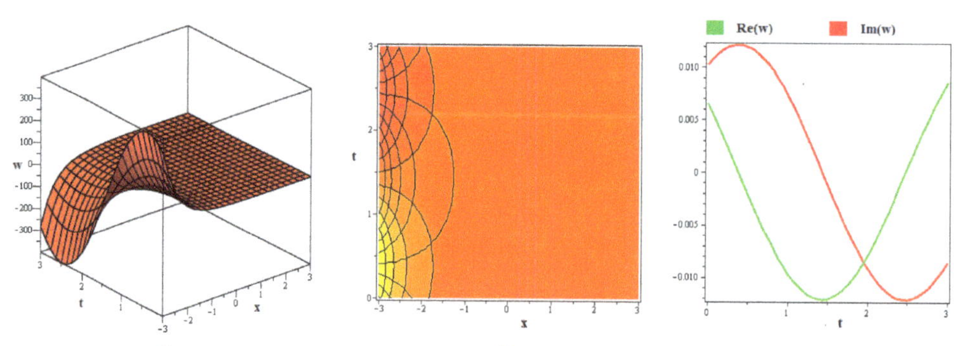

Figure 4. The (**a**) 3D graph, (**b**) contour graph, and (**c**) 2D graph (when $x = 3$) represent the optical soliton solution $u_{2,4}(t,x)$ articulated in (30) for $\rho := 2, \varrho := 10, \sigma := 8, \varphi := 0.15 \times 10^{-2}, k_3 := 0$, $k_2 := 1.5, \nu := 1, c_2 := 1, c_0 := 2, d_0 := 1$. In this depiction, the optical fractal is formed due to the periodic axial perturbation.

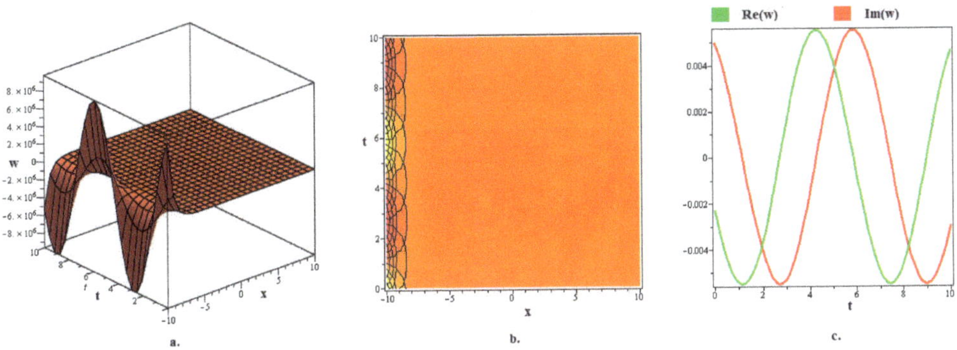

Figure 5. The (**a**) 3D graph, (**b**) contour graph, and (**c**) 2D graph (when $x = 5$) represent the optical soliton solution $u_{2,8}(t,x)$ articulated in (34) for $\rho := 0, \varrho := 1, \sigma := -2, \varphi := 0.75 \times 10^{-2}, k_3 := 0, k_2 := 1, \nu := 2, c_2 := 2, c_0 := 3, d_0 := 1, \mu := 1, b := -2$. In this depiction, the optical fractal is formed due to the periodic axial perturbation.

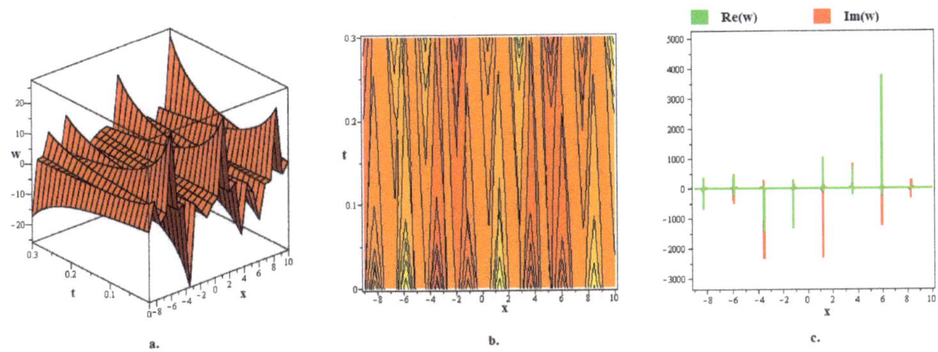

Figure 6. The (**a**) 3D graph, (**b**) contour graph, and (**c**) 2D graph (when $t = 0$) represent the optical soliton solution $u_{3,1}(t,x)$ articulated in (37) for $\rho := 1, \varrho := 1, \sigma := 4, \varphi := 0.1 \times 10^{-3}, k_3 := 0.685, k_2 := 0.115, \nu := 1, c_2 := 2$. In this depiction, the optical fractal is formed due to the chaotic bi-axial perturbation.

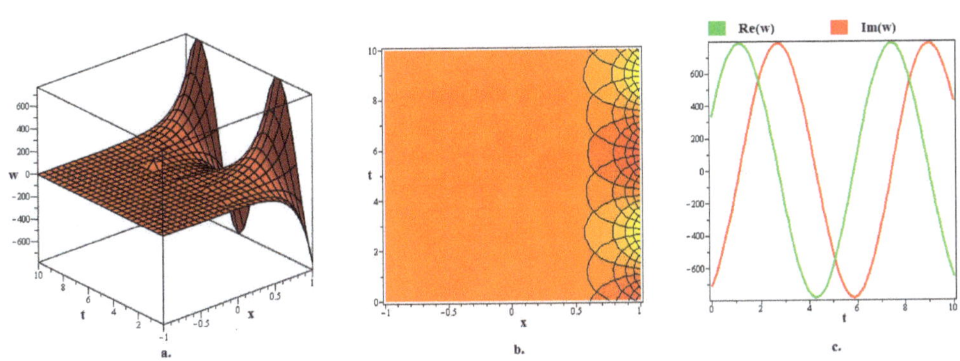

Figure 7. The (**a**) 3D graph, (**b**) contour graph, and (**c**) 2D graph (when $x = 1$) represent the optical soliton solution $u_{3,5}(t,x)$ articulated in (41) for $\rho := 1, \varrho := 10, \sigma := 9, \varphi := 0.35 \times 10^{-2}, k_3 := 1, k_2 := 1, \nu := 2, c_2 := 1$. In this depiction, the optical fractal is formed due to the periodic axial perturbation.

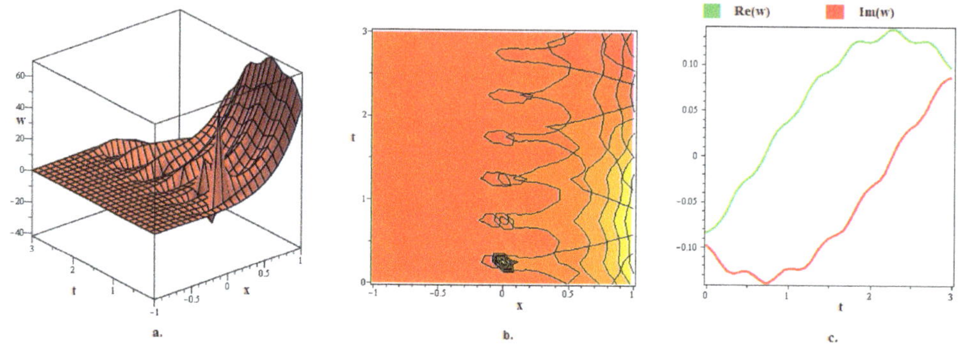

Figure 8. The (**a**) 3D graph, (**b**) contour graph, and (**c**) 2D graph (when $x = -1$) represent the optical soliton solution $u_{3,13}(t,x)$ articulated in (49) for $\rho := 0, \varrho := 2, \sigma := 5, \varphi := 0.22 \times 10^{-2}$, $k_3 := 2, k_2 := 1, \nu := 4, c_2 := 3, z_2 := 1$. In this depiction, the optical fractal is formed due to the chaotic axial perturbation.

Figure 9, the (**a**) 3D graph, (**b**) contour graph, and (**c**) 2D graph (when $x = 0$) represent the optical soliton solution $u_{4,9}(t,x)$ articulated in (59) for $\rho := 4, \varrho := 4, \sigma := 1$, $\varphi := 0.15 \times 10^{-2}, k_3 := 2, k_2 := 1, \nu := 2, c_2 := 3, z_2 := 5, \kappa_2 := 1, \kappa_2 := 4$. In this depiction, the optical fractal is formed due to the chaotic axial perturbation of the optical lump. Figure 10, the (**a**) 3D graph, (**b**) contour graph, and (**c**) 2D graph (when $x = 0$) represent the optical soliton solution $u_{4,14}(t,x)$ articulated in (64) for $\rho := 0, \varrho := 1, \sigma := 3$, $\varphi := 0.45 \times 10^{-2}, k_3 := 3, k_2 := 2, \nu := 5, c_2 := 1, z_2 := 4, \kappa_2 := 2, \kappa_2 := 1$. In this depiction, the optical fractal is formed due to the chaotic axial perturbation of the singular lump.

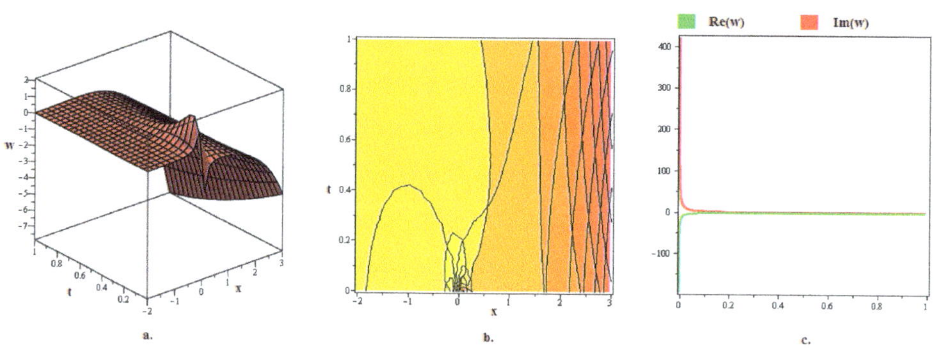

Figure 9. The (**a**) 3D graph, (**b**) contour graph, and (**c**) 2D graph (when $x = 0$) represent the optical soliton solution $u_{4,9}(t,x)$ articulated in (59) for $\rho := 4, \varrho := 4, \sigma := 1, \varphi := 0.15 \times 10^{-2}, k_3 := 2$, $k_2 := 1, \nu := 2, c_2 := 3, z_2 := 5, \kappa_2 := 1, \kappa_2 := 4$. In this depiction, the optical fractal is formed due to the chaotic axial perturbation of the optical lump.

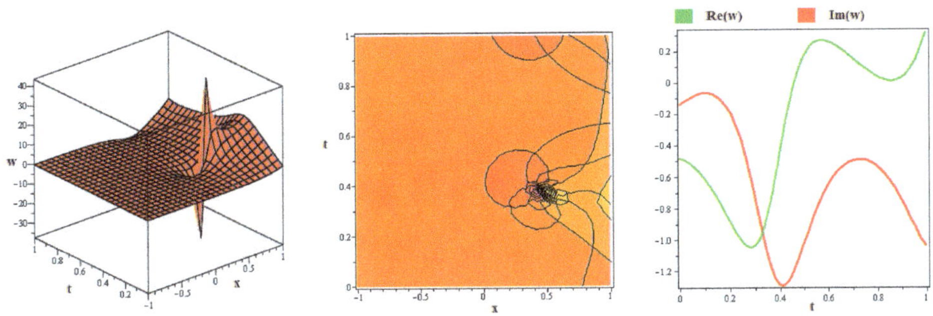

a. b. c.

Figure 10. The (**a**) 3D graph, (**b**) contour graph, and (**c**) 2D graph (when $x = 0$) represent the optical soliton solution $u_{4,14}(t, x)$ articulated in (64) for $\rho := 0, \varrho := 1, \sigma := 3, \varphi := 0.45 \times 10^{-2}, k_3 := 3, k_2 := 2, \nu := 5, c_2 := 1, z_2 := 4, \kappa_2 := 2, \kappa_2 := 1$. In this depiction, the optical fractal is formed due to the chaotic axial perturbation of the singular lump.

5. Conclusions

In this work, we used the effective RMESEM to create and analyze novel optical soliton solutions for CNHEs in the form of exponential, rational, trigonometric, hyperbolic, and rational hyperbolic functions. We also offered some 3D, contour, and 2D plots for the free selections of the physical parameters to more clearly show the propagating behaviours of the produced optical solitons. These visuals reveal that, when acquired optical solitons approach an axis, they lose stability under specific constraint conditions and exhibit periodic axial perturbations, resulting in the formation of optical fractals. There are several practical uses for the produced optical solitons in the fields of optics. Moreover, our hired RMESEM also proves its efficacy by expanding the range of optical soliton solutions, providing valuable insights into the CNHE dynamics, and indicating potential uses in addressing nonlinear models. While the RMESEM has significantly improved our understanding of soliton dynamics and their relationship to the models under investigation, it is important to acknowledge the limitations of this method; particularly, this method fails when the greatest derivative and nonlinear term are not balanced homogeneously. Notwithstanding this limitation, the present investigation demonstrates that the methodology employed in this work is extremely dependable, transferable, and productive for nonlinear problems in a variety of natural science domains. Moreover, the future goal of this investigation is to delve into the sensitiveness of fractal solitons, the incorporation and impact of the fractional derivatives on fractal solitons, and the calculation of scaling factors of fractal theory.

Author Contributions: Conceptualization, M.M.A.-S.; Data curation, M.M.A.-S.; Formal analysis, S.N.; Resources, M.M.A.-S.; Investigation, S.N.; Project administration, S.N.; Validation, M.A.; Software, M.A.; Validation, M.A.; Visualization, M.S.A.; Validation, M.S.A.; Visualization, R.S.; Resources, R.S.; Project administration, R.S.; Writing-review & editing, M.S.A. All authors have read and agreed to the published version of the manuscript.

Funding: This work was supported by the Deanship of Scientific Research, Vice Presidency for Graduate Studies and Scientific Research, King Faisal University, Saudi Arabia (KFU242030).

Data Availability Statement: No new data were created or analyzed in this study. Data sharing is not applicable to this article.

Acknowledgments: The authors thank the support from the Deanship of Scientific Research, Vice Presidency for Graduate Studies and Scientific Research, King Faisal University, Saudi Arabia.

Conflicts of Interest: The authors declare no conflict of interest.

Appendix A

For every set of solutions, ϑ and χ have different values depending on the free parameter values found in Equations (12)–(15), i.e.,

1. For the Solutions of Case 1, Case 3, and Case 4:

For optical soliton solutions articulated in (16)–(26), (37)–(50) and (51)–(64), we have

$$\chi = (k_3 x + \frac{k_1 k_3}{1 + 2\varphi k_2} t), \quad \vartheta = (-k_1 x + k_2 t + \nu), \tag{A1}$$

where

$$k_1 = \frac{1}{2}\sqrt{-8{k_3}^2 \rho\, \sigma - 8\,\varphi\, {k_2}^2 - 8\, k_2 - 2\,{k_3}^2 \varrho^2 (2\,\varphi\, k_2 + 1)\Upsilon}. \tag{A2}$$

2. For the Solutions of Case 2: For optical soliton solutions articulated in (27)–(36),

$$\chi = 0, \quad \vartheta = (-k_1 x + k_2 t + \nu), \tag{A3}$$

where

$$k_1 = -\sqrt{-2\,\varphi\, {k_2}^2 - 2\, k_2}. \tag{A4}$$

References

1. Abdelrahman, M.A.; Mohammed, W.W.; Alesemi, M.; Albosaily, S. The effect of multiplicative noise on the exact solutions of nonlinear Schŕdinger equation. *AIMS Math.* **2021**, *6*, 2970–2980. [CrossRef]
2. Alomair, R.A.; Hassan, S.Z.; Abdelrahman, M.A. A new structure of solutions to the coupled nonlinear Maccari's systems in plasma physics. *AIMS Math.* **2020**, *7*, 8588–8606. [CrossRef]
3. Navier, C.L. *Navier Stokes Equation*; Chez Carilian-Goeury: Paris, France, 1838.
4. Hafez, M.G.; Alam, M.N.; Akbar, M.A. Traveling wave solutions for some important coupled nonlinear physical models via the coupled Higgs equation and the Maccari system. *J. King Saud-Univ.-Sci.* **2015**, *27*, 105–112. [CrossRef]
5. El-Naggar, A.M.; Ismail, G.M. Analytical solution of strongly nonlinear Duffing oscillators. *Alex. Eng. J.* **2016**, *55*, 1581–1585. [CrossRef]
6. Xiao, Y.; Barak, S.; Hleili, M.; Shah, K. Exploring the dynamical behaviour of optical solitons in integrable kairat-II and kairat-X equations. *Phys. Scr.* **2024**, *99*, 095261. [CrossRef]
7. Ali, R.; Barak, S.; Altalbe, A. Analytical study of soliton dynamics in the realm of fractional extended shallow water wave equations. *Phys. Scr.* **2024**, *99*, 065235. [CrossRef]
8. Akbar, M.A.; Akinyemi, L.; Yao, S.W.; Jhangeer, A.; Rezazadeh, H.; Khater, M.M.; Ahmad, H.; Mustafa Inc. Soliton solutions to the Boussinesq equation through sine-Gordon method and Kudryashov method. *Results Phys.* **2021**, *25*, 104228. [CrossRef]
9. Yang, X.F.; Deng, Z.C.; Wei, Y. A Riccati-Bernoulli sub-ODE method for nonlinear partial differential equations and its application. *Adv. Differ. Equ.* **2015**, *2015*, 117. [CrossRef]
10. Khan, H.; Barak, S.; Kumam, P.; Arif, M. Analytical solutions of fractional Klein-Gordon and gas dynamics equations, via the (G'/G)-expansion method. *Symmetry* **2019**, *11*, 566. [CrossRef]
11. Khan, H.; Baleanu, D.; Kumam, P.; Al-Zaidy, J.F. Families of travelling waves solutions for fractional-order extended shallow water wave equations, using an innovative analytical method. *IEEE Access* **2019**, *7*, 107523–107532. [CrossRef]
12. Hammad, M.M.A.; Shah, R.; Alotaibi, B.M.; Alotiby, M.; Tiofack, C.G.L.; Alrowaily, A.W.; El-Tantawy, S.A. On the modified versions of $(\frac{G'}{G})$-expansion technique for analyzing the fractional coupled Higgs system. *AIP Adv.* **2013**, *13*, 105131. [CrossRef]
13. Ali, R.; Tag-eldin, E. A comparative analysis of generalized and extended $(\frac{G'}{G})$-Expansion methods for travelling wave solutions of fractional Maccari's system with complex structure. *Alex. Eng. J.* **2023**, *79*, 508–530. [CrossRef]
14. He, J.H.; Wu, X.H. Exp-function method for nonlinear wave equations. *Chaos Solitons Fractals* **2006**, *30*, 700–708. [CrossRef]
15. Cinar, M.; Secer, A.; Ozisik, M.; Bayram, M. Derivation of optical solitons of dimensionless Fokas-Lenells equation with perturbation term using Sardar sub-equation method. *Opt. Quantum Electron.* **2022**, *54*, 402. [CrossRef]
16. Barman, H.K.; Islam, M.E.; Akbar, M.A. A study on the compatibility of the generalized Kudryashov method to determine wave solutions. *Propuls. Power Res.* **2021**, *10*, 95–105. [CrossRef]
17. Shi-qiang, D. Poincare-Lighthill-Kuo method and symbolic computation. *Appl. Math. Mech.* **2001**, *22*, 261–269. [CrossRef]
18. Hietarinta, J. Introduction to the Hirota bilinear method. In *Integrability of Nonlinear Systems, Proceedings of the CIMPA School Pondicherry University, India, 8–26 January 1996*; Springer: Berlin/Heidelberg, Germany, 2007; pp. 95–103.
19. Bilal, M.; Iqbal, J.; Ali, R.; Awwad, F.A.; Alsmail, E.A. Exploring Families of Solitary Wave Solutions for the Fractional Coupled Higgs System Using Modified Extended Direct Algebraic Method. *Fractal Fract.* **2023**, *7*, 653. [CrossRef]

20. Ald, ani, M.; Altherwi, A.A.; Abushaega, M.M. Propagation patterns of dromion and other solitons in nonlinear Phi-Four (ϕ^4) equation. *AIMS Math.* **2024**, *9*, 19786–19811. [CrossRef]
21. Mirzazadeh, M. Modified simple equation method and its applications to nonlinear partial differential equations. *Inf. Sci. Lett.* **2014**, *3*, 1. [CrossRef]
22. Zayed, E.M.E.; Al-Nowehy, A.G. The Modified Simple Equation Method, the Exp-Function Method, and the Method of Soliton Ansatz for Solving the Long-Short Wave Resonance Equations. *Z. Naturforschung A* **2016**, *71*, 103–112. [CrossRef]
23. Kudryashov, N.A. Seven common errors in finding exact solutions of nonlinear differential equations. *Commun. Nonlinear Sci. Numer. Simul.* **2009**, *14*, 3507–3529. [CrossRef]
24. Navickas, Z.; Ragulskis, M. Comments on "A new algorithm for automatic computation of solitary wave solutions to nonlinear partial differential equations based on the Exp-function method". *Appl. Math. Comput.* **2014**, *243*, 419–425. [CrossRef]
25. Antonova, A.O.; Kudryashov, N.A. Generalization of the simplest equation method for nonlinear non-autonomous differential equations. *Commun. Nonlinear Sci. Numer. Simul.* **2014**, *19*, 4037–4041. [CrossRef]
26. Navickas, Z.; Marcinkevicius, R.; Telksniene, I.; Telksnys, T.; Ragulskis, M. Structural stability of the hepatitis C model with the proliferation of infected and uninfected hepatocytes. *Math. Comput. Model. Dyn. Syst.* **2024**, *30*, 51–72. [CrossRef]
27. Martin-Vergara, F.; Rus, F.; Villatoro, F.R. Fractal structure of the soliton scattering for the graphene superlattice equation. *Chaos Solitons Fractals* **2021**, *151*, 111281. [CrossRef]
28. Wang, K. A new fractal model for the soliton motion in a microgravity space. *Int. J. Numer. Methods Heat Fluid Flow* **2021**, *31*, 442–451. [CrossRef]
29. Zheng, C.L. Coherent soliton structures with chaotic and fractal behaviors in a generalized (2+ 1)-dimensional Korteweg de-Vries system. *Chin. J. Phys.* **2003**, *41*, 442–455.
30. Bunde, A.; Havlin, S. (Eds.). *Fractals in Science*; Springer: Berlin/Heidelberg, Germany, 2013.
31. Stanley, H.E. Fractal landscapes in physics and biology. *Phys. Stat. Mech. Its Appl.* **1992**, *186*, 1–32. [CrossRef]
32. Bizzarri, M.; Giuliani, A.; Cucina, A.; D'Anselmi, F.; Soto, A.M.; Sonnenschein, C. Fractal analysis in a systems biology approach to cancer. In *Seminars in Cancer Biology*; Academic Press: Cambridge, MA, USA, 2011; Volume 21, pp. 175–182.
33. Abraham, N.B.; Firth, W.J. Overview of transverse effects in nonlinear-optical systems. *JOSA B* **1990**, *7*, 951–962. [CrossRef]
34. Alsaud, H.; Youssoufa, M.; Inc, M.; Inan, I.E.; Bicer, H. Some optical solitons and modulation instability analysis of (3+ 1)-dimensional nonlinear Schrdinger and coupled nonlinear Helmholtz equations. *Opt. Quantum Electron.* **2024**, *56*, 1138. [CrossRef]
35. Tamilselvan, K.; Kanna, T.; Khare, A. Nonparaxial elliptic waves and solitary waves in coupled nonlinear Helmholtz equations. *Commun. Nonlinear Sci. Numer. Simul.* **2016**, *39*, 134–148. [CrossRef]
36. Singh, S.; Kaur, L.; Sakthivel, R.; Murugesan, K. Computing solitary wave solutions of coupled nonlinear Hirota and Helmholtz equations. *Phys. Stat. Mech. Its Appl.* **2020**, *560*, 125114. [CrossRef]
37. Saha, N.; Roy, B.; Khare, A. Coupled Helmholtz equations: Chirped solitary waves. *Chaos Interdiscip. J. Nonlinear Sci.* **2021**, *31*, 113104. [CrossRef] [PubMed]
38. Yamaguti, M.; Yoshihara, H.; Niahida, T. Periodic solutions of Duffing equation. *CiNii J.* **1988**, *673*, 80–95.

fractal and fractional

MDPI

Article

Fractional Transfer Entropy Networks: Short- and Long-Memory Perspectives on Global Stock Market Interactions

Ömer Akgüller [1], Mehmet Ali Balcı [1,*], Larissa Margareta Batrancea [2] and Lucian Gaban [3,*]

[1] Deparment of Mathematics, Faculty of Science, Muğla Sıtkı Koçman University, 48000 Muğla, Turkey; oakguller@mu.edu.tr

[2] Department of Business, Babeş-Bolyai University, 7 Horea Street, 400174 Cluj-Napoca, Romania; larissa.batrancea@ubbcluj.ro

[3] Faculty of Economics, "1 Decembrie 1918" University of Alba Iulia, 510009 Alba Iulia, Romania

* Correspondence: mehmetalibalci@mu.edu.tr (M.A.B.); lucian.gaban@uab.ro (L.G.)

Abstract: This study addresses the challenge of capturing both short-run volatility and long-run dependencies in global stock markets by introducing fractional transfer entropy (FTE), a new framework that embeds fractional calculus into transfer entropy. FTE allows analysts to tune memory parameters and thus observe how different temporal emphases reshape the network of directional information flows among major financial indices. Empirical evidence reveals that when short-memory effects dominate, markets swiftly incorporate recent news, creating networks that adapt quickly but remain vulnerable to transient shocks. In contrast, balanced memory parameters yield a more stable equilibrium, blending immediate reactions with persistent structural ties. Under long-memory configurations, historically entrenched relationships prevail, enabling established market leaders to remain central despite ongoing fluctuations. These findings demonstrate that FTE uncovers nuanced dynamics overlooked by methods focusing solely on either current events or deep-rooted patterns. Although the method relies on price returns and does not differentiate specific shock types, it offers a versatile tool for investors, policymakers, and researchers to gauge financial stability, evaluate contagion risk, and better understand how ephemeral signals and historical legacies jointly govern global market connectivity.

Keywords: fractional calculus; transfer entropy; financial networks; network communities; global markets

1. Introduction

Understanding global stock market interactions requires a methodology that can simultaneously capture both rapid responses to emerging shocks and more persistent influences shaped by historical patterns and institutional ties. Many standard approaches focus on either near-instantaneous changes or deep-rooted relationships, but rarely do they integrate these two facets cohesively. Transfer entropy has proven useful for measuring directional information flows among financial time series, as it detects how past values of one process help predict the future of another in a model-free manner. However, conventional transfer entropy methods generally adopt a fixed-lag perspective, where historical data are either equally weighted or follow a narrow range of lags. In reality, stock markets do not uniformly "forget" their past; some rely heavily on distant fundamentals and investor memories, while others react quickly to new policy decisions or macroeconomic announcements.

https://doi.org/10.3390/fractalfract9020069

To address this gap, we propose fractional transfer entropy (FTE), which merges the flexibility of fractional calculus with the original transfer entropy framework. The incorporation of fractional derivatives allows for continuous control over how past information is treated, shifting from a predominantly short-memory setting to a strongly persistent one. By fine-tuning this fractional parameter, FTE illuminates how certain markets preserve long-standing cross-border capital flow patterns or historically established hierarchies, while others respond mostly to fresh signals such as economic data releases, geopolitical shifts, or company-specific events. This balance of short- and long-memory factors helps capture the essential duality of global finance, where markets are never exclusively forward-looking or backward-looking, but operate across a continuum of temporal influences.

In line with previous studies on international stock markets (e.g., refs. [1–4], the core motivation here is to reveal the deeper connectivity that often hides behind surface-level fluctuations. Even if short-term volatility plays a prominent role in daily trading decisions, persistent ties rooted in trade agreements, supply chains, shared investor bases, and historical crises continue to guide investment flows. Conversely, methods that emphasize only structural inertia may overlook how swiftly significant news can ripple through financial hubs and reconfigure the network of global market interactions (refs. [5–7]). By bridging both viewpoints, FTE shows that neither perspective—the immediacy of daily returns nor the depth of historical inertia—adequately reflects the reality of international finance unless they are analyzed together.

This article contributes to a growing body of research on information flow in stock markets, including works that apply Granger causality or traditional transfer entropy [8,9]. While these have uncovered critical insights into directional linkages and contagion, they often assume homogeneity in how the past is remembered. Introducing fractional derivatives addresses this shortfall by enabling a parameterized approach to memory, reflecting the heterogeneous ways that different economies, investor types, or corporate structures might weight prior data. Markets in developed nations with large capital reserves may place greater emphasis on historical credibility and slowly evolving fundamentals, while emerging markets—perhaps more susceptible to daily capital inflows or policy changes—could respond acutely to short-term signals (refs. [10,11]).

Within the FTE framework, we apply fractional differencing to each time series, thereby encoding the degree of memory weighting directly into the underlying data before computing directional information flows. The FTE values then form weighted and directed networks, with the nodes representing stock markets and edges capturing how strongly or weakly information travels under a given memory regime. By exploring distinct parameter configurations, the analysis illustrates how short-memory bias emphasizes highly reactive interconnections, whereas long-memory bias brings to the fore the underlying long-term structures that shape the global financial architecture. Balanced memory parameters, on the other hand, reveal an interplay between current shocks and entrenched relationships.

In applying this approach, we examine how topological features such as node centrality, betweenness, and community detection shift when fractional orders vary. Major markets, like those in the United States or in dominant European and Asian financial centers, frequently remain central hubs, but their influence might wax or wane depending on whether memory weighting privileges well-established historical capital flows or the latest macro announcements. Similarly, emerging markets may exhibit different patterns of integration or isolation when either recent volatility or more extended timelines are prioritized in the analysis. This network-centric perspective sheds light on how risk can propagate and highlights potential sources of resilience or vulnerability in global markets.

Finally, the proposed methodology not only refines the way researchers view cross-market connections today, but also opens possibilities for future inquiry. A broader time horizon, including worldwide shocks like COVID-19 and periods of global financial stress, will enable deeper tests of how short- and long-memory factors interplay when volatility peaks. Extending FTE to higher-level constructs such as community-level or sector-level fractions may also illuminate whether clusters of markets respond uniformly to events or whether divergent regional memories create different contagion patterns. As markets continue to evolve under heightened globalization and algorithmic trading, fractional transfer entropy offers an adaptable lens through which policymakers, investors, and scholars can track shifting structures and dependencies in a world of financial interconnectivity that is neither fully anchored in the past nor wholly captured by the present.

This study is structured as follows: First, Section 2 outlines a comprehensive literature overview. Then, Section 3 outlines the methodology, beginning with the definition and theoretical foundations of fractional transfer entropy, which integrates fractional calculus into the transfer entropy framework to capture both short- and long-term dependencies in financial time series. This section also details the process of forming financial networks from the resulting FTE measures, illustrating how nodes and edges reflect markets and directional information flows. Section 4 presents the results and discussions, starting with a description of the dataset employed, including global stock market indices and their log-return series. Subsequent subsections examine the emerging networks and metric distributions under four distinct parameter settings: $\alpha_X = 0.0$, $\alpha_Y = 0.0$, $\alpha_X = 0.2$, $\alpha_Y = 0.8$; $\alpha_X = 0.5$, $\alpha_Y = 0.5$; and $\alpha_X = 0.8$, $\alpha_Y = 0.2$. Each configuration highlights how varying memory parameters influences global connectivity, market hierarchies, and community structures, and provides an in-depth comparative perspective on the interplay of short-term and long-term factors. Finally, Section 5 offers conclusions, summarizing the key findings, discussing the limitations of the approach, and suggesting avenues for future research based on the insights gained from the fractional transfer entropy analysis of global stock markets.

2. Related Studies

The dynamics of global financial markets have been extensively explored through various methodological approaches, each addressing different aspects of market index interactions, risk transmission, and persistence in price movements. Early research predominantly employed correlation-based measures to evaluate relationships among equities or indices. In refs. [12–14], the authors demonstrated that while correlation measures are straightforward and effective for identifying co-movements, they fall short in capturing the directionality of interactions and accounting for nonlinear dependencies. This limitation hindered deeper analytical insights into the causal mechanisms underlying market behaviors.

Building on these initial findings, subsequent advancements introduced causal inference techniques, with Granger causality emerging as a prominent method. In ref. [15], Granger and Joyeux explored predictive relationships by examining whether past values of one time series could forecast current values of another. This approach marked a significant improvement over correlation-based methods by incorporating temporal precedence and directionality. However, ref. [16] highlighted the inherent limitations of Granger causality, particularly its reliance on linear specifications, which restrict its effectiveness in contexts where financial data exhibit higher-order interactions or structural breaks. These constraints prompted the search for more flexible frameworks capable of capturing the complexities inherent in financial time series.

The introduction of information theory into financial market analysis provided a novel framework for examining market interdependencies. Refs. [17–19] used transfer entropy, a model-free measure that uncovers nonlinear and directional dependencies between systems. These foundational works established transfer entropy as a robust alternative to traditional correlation- and regression-based methods, facilitating the measurement of how one stochastic process influences another. Recognizing its potential, researchers quickly adopted transfer entropy in finance and economics. For instance, in refs. [20,21], studies applied transfer entropy to interbank networks and global stock markets, respectively, demonstrating its superiority in detecting subtle and complex information flow patterns. These applications consistently showed that transfer entropy outperforms simpler metrics in identifying crisis contagion pathways and uncovering leadership structures among major financial hubs.

Despite the successes of transfer entropy, integrating memory effects into the assessment of information flow remains an ongoing challenge. Traditional implementations typically treat past information uniformly, either by considering a limited set of lags or employing a single time-lag approach that assumes equal contribution from all historical data points. Ref. [22] discussed how this uniform treatment overlooks the long-range dependence and variable decay in relevance that characterize financial data, where certain events or macroeconomic conditions continue to influence investor sentiment long after their occurrence. While modifications like partial transfer entropy and multistep transfer entropy introduced additional nuance (refs. [23,24]), they still lacked a systematic and flexible method for weighting historical data across different time horizons.

In response to these limitations, fractional calculus has garnered increasing interest among financial modelers for its ability to describe processes with memory or hereditary properties. Ref. [25] provided a comprehensive overview of fractional derivatives and integrals, highlighting their robustness in modeling persistent or long-memory behavior. Early applications in economics focused on fractional integration to capture long-memory behavior in macroeconomic series (refs. [26–28]). Fractional calculus enables the systematic adjustment of how recent versus distant past observations contribute to a series' present state, thereby bridging the gap between short-term volatility and long-term trends.

Building on these developments, combining fractional calculus with transfer entropy represents a logical progression in modeling information flow within financial markets. Ref. [29] underscored the necessity of capturing memory effects in transfer entropy, particularly given that major global stock markets rarely operate under purely Markovian conditions. Additionally, the versatility of fractional operators in describing memory-induced processes aligns well with the requirements of financial time series analysis. Studies such as refs. [30,31] have begun developing methods that allow transfer entropy to transition smoothly from emphasizing the near past to focusing on deeper historical windows. This approach is particularly relevant in cross-market studies where heterogeneous market structures, varying liquidity levels, and diverse regulatory regimes result in disparities in how quickly and extensively markets incorporate new information.

Advances in network analysis further complement these methodological innovations. The emergence of network-based methods in finance underscores the importance of understanding how individual nodes—representing markets or institutions—interconnect within a global system and how these connections evolve over time. Ref. [32] modeled the structure of stock markets using partial correlations, revealing a core-periphery structure where large, highly liquid markets anchor the system while smaller or less liquid indices occupy the periphery. Later research incorporated causal metrics such as Granger causality and transfer entropy, transforming network links from undirected to directed and providing new insights into contagion and systemic risk (refs. [33–35]). The integration of fractional calculus into this toolkit allows for an even more nuanced understanding, where the memory properties of each node or link are integral to comprehending global market dynamics.

These diverse strands of literature converge in the present study, which introduces FTE as a unified and flexible mechanism for modeling information exchange among global equity markets across different memory horizons. By applying fractional derivatives to time series prior to computing transfer entropy, FTE aligns with previous research advocating for the incorporation of persistent, slowly decaying influences Simultaneously, FTE leverages the network-oriented perspective on financial contagion and interdependence, facilitating the construction of directed graphs that elucidate which markets drive others across both short- and long-range lags. This approach addresses multiple gaps identified in the literature: it extends standard transfer entropy to capture heterogeneous memory effects, employs complex network metrics to examine market hierarchies and modularity

Furthermore, this study provides a framework to re-evaluate established empirical findings in financial economics through a novel lens—one that accounts for the varying half-lives of macroeconomic news, persistent investor sentiment, and the gradual evolution of regional market structures. Whether investigating crisis transmission channels, identifying structural breakpoints in global market integration, or determining which markets exhibit the greatest resilience, FTE offers a pathway to dissect these phenomena with enhanced granularity. In this sense, the current research builds upon and extends a broad spectrum of literature that collectively emphasizes the critical role of memory in shaping cross-market information flows. It resonates with longstanding observations that real-world financial behavior is governed by a balance of immediate volatility and long-running trends—an equilibrium that fractional transfer entropy is uniquely positioned to explore.

3. Methodology

3.1. Fractional Transfer Entropy

The concept of fractional transfer entropy between two time series is introduced here by incorporating fractional calculus and memory kernels. We begin by recalling the classical setting of transfer entropy. Then, we introduce the fractional framework, including integral definitions, memory functions, and the associated fractional derivatives. This approach is subsequently employed to define fractional transfer entropy, and a set of theorems together with their proofs is provided to establish fundamental properties and conceptual significance.

Classical transfer entropy measures directional information flow between two time series. Given two stochastic processes, (X_t) and (Y_t), the transfer entropy from Y to X essentially quantifies how much knowing the past of Y reduces the uncertainty about the future state of X beyond what is already known from the past of X itself. In the standard formulation, the memory or influence from the past is usually considered in discrete, integer-lag steps. However, many real-world socio-economic or physical systems exhibit complex, non-local memory effects that cannot be properly captured by a finite number of discrete lags. Fractional calculus provides a natural mathematical framework to incorporate such long-range dependencies and power law fading memory into the analysis of dynamic processes. To address this need, the fractional transfer entropy is defined by replacing the classical finite-dimensional conditioning sets with fractional memory operators. The new measure captures the influence of one process on another under a generalized memory scenario, where memory decays according to a power law kernel rather than vanishing after a finite lag.

To properly define these memory structures, consider two time-dependent processes, $\{X(t)\}$ and $\{Y(t)\}$. Let $Y(t)$ be an endogenous variable defined by a Volterra integral operator acting on the history of $X(\tau)$ for $\tau \in [0, t]$

$$Y(t) = F_0^t(X(\tau)) := \int_0^t M(t,\tau)X(\tau)d\tau, \tag{1}$$

where $M(t,\tau)$ is the memory function that encodes how past values of X influence the current value of Y. Assuming homogeneity in the time variable allows writing the memory kernel as $M(t,\tau) = M(t-\tau)$. To model power law fading memory, let

$$M_\alpha(t,\tau) = \frac{m}{\Gamma(\alpha)(t-\tau)^{1-\alpha}}, \tag{2}$$

where $\alpha \in (0,1]$ and m is a real constant dependent on α. Substituting this into the Volterra operator yields

$$Y(t) = m(I^\alpha_{0+}X)(t), \tag{3}$$

where I^α_{0+} denotes the Riemann–Liouville fractional integral of order α.

To handle initial conditions more conveniently, one can consider Caputo fractional derivatives. By setting $n = \lfloor \alpha \rfloor + 1$ and using a memory function

$$M_{n-\alpha}(t,\tau) = \frac{a}{\Gamma(n-\alpha)}(t-\tau)^{n-\alpha-1}, \tag{4}$$

one obtains

$$Y(t) = a(D^\alpha_{0+}X)(t), \tag{5}$$

where

$$D^\alpha_{0+}X(t) = \frac{1}{\Gamma(n-\alpha)}\int_0^t \frac{X^{(n)}(\tau)}{(t-\tau)^{\alpha-n+1}}d\tau \tag{6}$$

is the left-sided Caputo fractional derivative of order α.

These operators encapsulate power law and distributed memory effects, making them suitable tools for analyzing complex systems where memory cannot be reduced to a finite set of past values. In the original definition of transfer entropy, let $\{X_t\}$ and $\{Y_t\}$ be discrete-time processes and consider their continuous-valued generalization. The classical transfer entropy from Y to X is

$$T_{Y\to X} = \sum_{x_{t+1},x_t^{(k)},y_t^{(l)}} p(x_{t+1},x_t^{(k)},y_t^{(l)}) \log \frac{p(x_{t+1}|x_t^{(k)},y_t^{(l)})}{p(x_{t+1}|x_t^{(k)})}, \tag{7}$$

where $x_t^{(k)} = (x_t, x_{t-1}, \ldots, x_{t-k+1})$ and similarly for $y_t^{(l)}$. Since this definition relies on a finite number of past values, it cannot directly capture long-memory effects.

To incorporate power law memory, replace finite past lags with fractional derivative-based states. Define the fractional states

$$X_\alpha(t) = D^{\alpha_X}_{0+}X(t), \quad Y_\alpha(t) = D^{\alpha_Y}_{0+}Y(t), \tag{8}$$

where $\alpha_X, \alpha_Y > 0$ and D^α_{0+} is a Caputo fractional derivative. These fractional states encapsulate the entire past of X and Y up to time t with a power law weighting. The fractional transfer entropy (FTE) from Y to X is then defined as

$$T^{(\alpha_X,\alpha_Y)}_{Y\to X} = \mathbb{E}\left[\log \frac{p(X(t+1)|X_\alpha(t),Y_\alpha(t))}{p(X(t+1)|X_\alpha(t))}\right]. \tag{9}$$

In integral form,

$$T^{(\alpha_X,\alpha_Y)}_{Y\to X} = \int p(x(t+1),x_\alpha(t),y_\alpha(t)) \log \frac{p(x(t+1)|x_\alpha(t),y_\alpha(t))}{p(x(t+1)|x_\alpha(t))} dx(t+1)dx_\alpha(t)dy_\alpha(t). \tag{10}$$

By varying α_X and α_Y, it is possible to model short to long-memory ranges.

FTE is non-negativity, i.e., $T^{(\alpha_X,\alpha_Y)}_{Y\to X} \geq 0$. Consider

$$T^{(\alpha_X,\alpha_Y)}_{Y\to X} = \int p(x(t+1), x_\alpha(t), y_\alpha(t)) \log \frac{p(x(t+1)|x_\alpha(t), y_\alpha(t))}{p(x(t+1)|x_\alpha(t))} d\mu. \tag{11}$$

This can be recognized as a Kullback–Leibler divergence

$$T^{(\alpha_X,\alpha_Y)}_{Y\to X} = D_{\mathrm{KL}}(p(x(t+1)|x_\alpha(t), y_\alpha(t)) \| p(x(t+1)|x_\alpha(t))) \tag{12}$$

which is always non-negative. Furthermore, it is zero if and only if $p(x(t+1)|x_\alpha(t), y_\alpha(t)) = p(x(t+1)|x_\alpha(t))$ almost surely, implying no additional information flow from Y to X.

As $\alpha_X, \alpha_Y \to 0$, the fractional transfer entropy reduces to the classical transfer entropy

$$\lim_{\alpha_X,\alpha_Y\to 0} T^{(\alpha_X,\alpha_Y)}_{Y\to X} = T_{Y\to X}. \tag{13}$$

As $\alpha \to 0$, the Caputo fractional derivative $D^\alpha_{0+}X(t)$ approaches $X(t)$ itself, effectively removing long-memory weighting. Thus, $X_\alpha(t) \to X(t)$ and $Y_\alpha(t) \to Y(t)$. In this limit, the conditioning set reverts to finite-lag conditioning, and fractional transfer entropy coincides with the classical definition.

FTE is invariance under linear scaling. If $\tilde{X}(t) = bX(t)$ and $\tilde{Y}(t) = cY(t)$ for non-zero constants b, c, then

$$T^{(\alpha_X,\alpha_Y)}_{\tilde{Y}\to\tilde{X}} = T^{(\alpha_X,\alpha_Y)}_{Y\to X}. \tag{14}$$

Since transfer entropy is based on ratios of conditional probability densities, linear scaling does not change the underlying conditional dependence structure. The densities transform in a way that the logarithmic ratio remains invariant, rendering the fractional transfer entropy scale-invariant.

FTE is also time-invariant under stationarity. If $(X(t), Y(t))$ is a jointly stationary process, then $T^{(\alpha_X,\alpha_Y)}_{Y\to X}$ does not depend on the specific time t. Stationarity implies that the joint distributions involved are invariant with respect to time shifts. Since $T^{(\alpha_X,\alpha_Y)}_{Y\to X}$ is defined through these distributions, it remains constant in time.

These results show that fractional transfer entropy extends the classical notion of information flow between time series to scenarios where the effect of the past does not vanish rapidly but instead follows a heavy-tailed, power law distribution. By incorporating Caputo fractional derivatives or distributed-order derivatives, fractional transfer entropy captures complex memory effects prevalent in socio-economic, biological, and physical systems. For instance, in socio-economic models of labor migration between countries, the memory of agents regarding past economic conditions can be long-lasting and not limited to recent history. The fractional approach ensures that all historical influences are accounted for, weighted according to a power law kernel. The parameter α (or a distribution over α) quantifies how long-range the memory effect is.

The calculation of fractional transfer entropy from empirical time series data requires careful construction of fractional states, estimation of probability distributions, and numerical approximations of the integrals and expectations that define the measure. The process begins with the recorded time series, which typically consist of discrete observations of two processes $X(t)$ and $Y(t)$ at regular time intervals. To incorporate memory of arbitrary length and complexity, fractional calculus operators must be applied to the time series. Given a fractional order $\alpha > 0$, the Caputo fractional derivative $D^\alpha_{0+}X(t)$ can be numerically approximated by discrete convolution-like formulas or by methods that discretize the integral definition of the fractional derivative. Such methods commonly rely on approximating the kernel $(t-\tau)^{-\gamma}$ for some γ depending on α, and employing fractional finite differences.

Although several numerical schemes exist, the essential idea is to approximate $D_{0+}^{\alpha}X(t)$ by combining current and past values of $X(\tau)$ with weights that decrease according to a power law, ensuring that distant past values still influence the present, albeit with diminishing intensity. Once these fractional derivatives are computed for all time points, the resulting transformed time series $X_{\alpha}(t) = D_{0+}^{\alpha_X}X(t)$ and $Y_{\alpha}(t) = D_{0+}^{\alpha_Y}Y(t)$ represent states that are no longer confined to a finite number of past lags but integrate all past history in a continuous and fractional manner.

After constructing $X_{\alpha}(t)$ and $Y_{\alpha}(t)$, the next step involves estimating the joint probability distributions $p(x(t+1), x_{\alpha}(t), y_{\alpha}(t))$ and the conditional distributions $p(x(t+1)|x_{\alpha}(t), y_{\alpha}(t))$ and $p(x(t+1)|x_{\alpha}(t))$. Since fractional transfer entropy involves expectations of logarithms of probability ratios, an accurate and robust method of probability density estimation is required. In practice, one must first discretize the state space or employ non-parametric estimation techniques such as kernel density estimation. For instance, one may define a suitable kernel function and bandwidth parameters to estimate the continuous joint probability density functions from a finite sample of data points $\{(x(t), x_{\alpha}(t), y_{\alpha}(t))\}_{t=1}^{T}$. Another approach is to bin the continuous states into small intervals and approximate probabilities by counting frequencies. While binning provides a straightforward approach, it may lead to coarse approximations and bias if bins are not chosen carefully or if data are limited. Kernel methods typically offer smoother and more flexible density approximations, though they require a thoughtful selection of kernel bandwidths to avoid under- or over-smoothing the underlying distributions. Regardless of the chosen method, the goal is to reliably approximate $p(x(t+1), x_{\alpha}(t), y_{\alpha}(t))$, $p(x(t+1)|x_{\alpha}(t))$, and $p(x(t+1)|x_{\alpha}(t), y_{\alpha}(t))$ as functions of continuous variables.

Once the probability distributions have been estimated, one proceeds to numerically approximate the integral that defines fractional transfer entropy. Conceptually, the expectation of the logarithmic ratio

$$\log \frac{p(x(t+1)|x_{\alpha}(t), y_{\alpha}(t))}{p(x(t+1)|x_{\alpha}(t))} \tag{15}$$

is taken over the joint distribution $p(x(t+1), x_{\alpha}(t), y_{\alpha}(t))$. Since the data are discrete observations, this expectation reduces to a sample-based average or a numerical integration. If a kernel density estimate is employed, the integral can be approximated by summations over the observed data points weighted by their estimated densities, ensuring that the entire support of the joint distribution is covered. The log ratio is computed at each observed triple $(x(t+1), x_{\alpha}(t), y_{\alpha}(t))$, and then an average is taken over the sample. If the sample size is large and the density estimates are accurate, the resulting approximation should converge to the true fractional transfer entropy. A careful analysis of sampling variance and estimation errors is advisable. One may use statistical techniques such as bootstrapping to quantify uncertainty in the fractional transfer entropy estimation, generating multiple surrogate samples from the original dataset to produce confidence intervals.

In certain cases, the parameters α_X and α_Y are chosen a priori based on prior knowledge about the system's memory characteristics. However, it is also conceivable to attempt estimation or model selection techniques to identify the values of α_X and α_Y that best capture the observed dynamics. This might involve comparing fractional transfer entropy values for different fractional orders or employing information criteria to balance model complexity with explanatory power. One could also consider distributed-order derivatives, in which case one must also estimate the weight function $c(\alpha)$ that defines how different fractional orders contribute to the memory kernel. This leads to a more involved estimation procedure requiring either optimization routines or structured assumptions on the form of $c(\alpha)$.

The computational complexity of estimating fractional derivatives and probability densities depends on the length of the time series and the resolution of the chosen discretization. Fractional derivative estimation typically introduces an additional computational overhead because it involves summations over past values at each time point, though efficient algorithms and approximations have been developed. Likewise, probability density estimation, whether bin-based or kernel-based, depends on the sample size and dimensionality of the variable space. Since fractional transfer entropy conditions on potentially infinite memory encoded through fractional derivatives, one must ensure that sufficient data are available to estimate the required distributions reliably. In practice, the dimension of the joint space $(x(t+1), x_\alpha(t), y_\alpha(t))$ remains manageable, but the fractional transformations may introduce smoothness and correlations that must be well understood.

3.2. Financial Network Formation

The process of forming a directed network from worldwide operating stock markets begins by examining the daily closure prices of each market and transforming them into logarithmic returns to ensure both stationarity and proportional comparability. Let $\{S_1, S_2, \ldots, S_N\}$ denote the set of stock markets under consideration. For each market S_i, let $P_i(t)$ be its closure price on day t. The logarithmic return for market S_i at day t is defined as

$$r_i(t) = \log\left(\frac{P_i(t)}{P_i(t-1)}\right). \tag{16}$$

This transformation reduces the influence of non-stationarities and focuses on relative changes, providing a time series $\{r_i(t)\}$ that is more amenable to statistical analysis and suitable for the computation of fractional transfer entropy. Given two such return series, say $\{r_i(t)\}$ and $\{r_j(t)\}$, the previously defined fractional transfer entropy $T_{j\to i}^{(\alpha_X,\alpha_Y)}$ quantifies the directional flow of information from market j to market i, where the memory of the past is encoded through fractional derivatives of order α_X and α_Y.

Once the fractional transfer entropy is computed for all ordered pairs of markets (S_j, S_i), one obtains a complete set of directed, weighted edges. Let $\mathbf{W} = [w_{ij}]$ be the resulting adjacency matrix, where each node corresponds to a stock market and each directed edge from market S_j to market S_i is assigned a weight

$$w_{ij} = T_{j\to i}^{(\alpha_X,\alpha_Y)}. \tag{17}$$

The matrix $\mathbf{W}$ thus encapsulates the complex web of directional relationships inferred from the fractional transfer entropy. To analyze the global structure and dynamics of these interactions, various network metrics are introduced. Consider the degree-based measures first. The out-degree of node i is defined as the sum of the weights of the edges emanating from node i

$$\text{outdeg}(i) = \sum_{j=1}^{N} w_{ij}, \tag{18}$$

while the in-degree of node i is defined as the sum of the weights of the edges incoming to node i

$$\text{indeg}(i) = \sum_{j=1}^{N} w_{ji}. \tag{19}$$

These measures reflect how strongly a particular market influences others (out-degree) and how strongly it is influenced by them (in-degree).

To gain deeper insight into the network's hierarchical structure, one may consider hub and authority scores. In a directed weighted graph, a node serves as a good hub if it points to nodes that are themselves good authorities, and a node is a good authority if it is pointed to by good hubs. Let $\mathbf{H} = [h_i]$ be a vector of hub scores and $\mathbf{A} = [a_i]$ be a vector of authority scores. Their relationship can be expressed as

$$\mathbf{H} = \mathbf{W}\mathbf{A} \quad \text{and} \quad \mathbf{A} = \mathbf{W}^T\mathbf{H}. \tag{20}$$

Solving these equations simultaneously amounts to an eigenvalue problem that determines the relative importance of nodes beyond simple degree counts. Markets with high hub scores can be viewed as global information broadcasters, while those with high authority scores act as key information receivers.

More nuanced topological features can be captured by shortest-path-based centrality measures. Consider the directed weighted graph defined by $\mathbf{W}$. Let $d(i,j)$ represent the shortest path distance from node i to node j. Closeness centrality for node i is defined as

$$C_i = \frac{1}{\sum_{j=1}^{N} d(i,j)}, \tag{21}$$

implying that a node with smaller average distance to all others is more central and can rapidly influence the network. Betweenness centrality focuses on how often a node lies on shortest paths between pairs of other nodes. Let σ_{ij} denote the number of shortest paths from i to j, and let $\sigma_{ij}(k)$ represent the number of those shortest paths passing through node k. The betweenness centrality of node k is given by

$$B_k = \sum_{i,j} \frac{\sigma_{ij}(k)}{\sigma_{ij}}, \tag{22}$$

reflecting the brokerage role of a node. Nodes with high betweenness serve as crucial intermediaries that can facilitate or hinder the flow of information across the network.

In practice, these network metrics help to interpret the intricate interdependencies and hierarchical relationships that characterize global stock markets. A high out-degree or hub score identifies markets functioning as influential sources of information or systemic risk. A high in-degree or authority score reveals markets that aggregate or absorb wide-ranging influences from multiple sources. High closeness centrality points to markets that rapidly integrate signals from other parts of the world, while high betweenness centrality highlights markets acting as key transit points in the information flow. By applying these measures to a fractional-transfer-entropy-derived network constructed from logarithmic return series, it becomes possible to capture not only the direct pairwise influences but also the subtle, memory-dependent patterns of global market interaction. This approach provides a richer characterization of international financial interconnections, enabling a more comprehensive understanding of how shocks propagate, how clusters form, and how certain markets emerge as structurally significant nodes in the worldwide financial landscape.

In the context of network analysis, community detection serves as a pivotal methodology for uncovering the underlying structural organization within complex networks [36–38]. Communities, often referred to as modules or clusters, are subsets of nodes that exhibit a higher density of connections internally compared to their connections with the rest of the network. Mathematically, the identification of such communities can be framed as an optimization problem, wherein the objective is to maximize a quality function that quantifies the strength of the network's division into modules.

A fundamental concept employed in community detection is modularity, denoted as Q, which measures the density of links inside communities compared to links between communities. Formally, modularity is defined as

$$Q = \frac{1}{2m} \sum_{i,j} \left[A_{ij} - \frac{k_i k_j}{2m} \right] \delta(c_i, c_j), \tag{23}$$

where A_{ij} represents the adjacency matrix of the network, where $A_{ij} = 1$ if there is an edge between nodes i and j, and $A_{ij} = 0$ otherwise. The term k_i denotes the degree of node i, and m is the total number of edges in the network. The function $\delta(c_i, c_j)$ is the Kronecker delta, which is equal to 1 if nodes i and j belong to the same community ($c_i = c_j$), and 0 otherwise. The modularity Q thus quantifies the extent to which the actual density of edges within communities exceeds what would be expected in a randomized network with the same degree distribution.

To optimize modularity, the Louvain method is employed, which is a greedy algorithm designed to efficiently partition the network into communities. The algorithm operates iteratively in two main phases: Initially, each node is assigned to its own community. For each node, the algorithm considers the gain in modularity that would result from moving the node to the community of each of its neighbors. The node is then placed in the community that provides the highest positive gain in modularity. This process is repeated for all nodes until no further modularity improvement can be achieved through local moves. After the first phase converges, a new network is constructed where each community identified in the previous phase is represented as a single node. The weights of the edges between these new nodes are determined by the sum of the weights of the edges between the nodes in the corresponding communities. The Louvain method is then recursively applied to this aggregated network. This iterative process continues until no further modularity gains are possible, resulting in a hierarchical structure of communities that optimally partitions the network based on the modularity criterion.

Once the communities are delineated, it becomes imperative to perform statistical analyses to characterize and interpret the properties of these communities. This involves computing descriptive statistics for various network metrics within each community. Let C_k denote the k-th community identified in the network. For each community C_k, we calculate metrics such as the mean, median, and standard deviation of in-degree, out-degree, betweenness centrality, closeness centrality, eigenvector centrality, hub scores, and authority scores of the constituent nodes. Mathematically, for a metric M, the mean within community C_k is given by

$$\mu_M^{C_k} = \frac{1}{|C_k|} \sum_{i \in C_k} M_i. \tag{24}$$

Similarly, the median $\tilde{M}^{C_k}$ and standard deviation $\sigma_M^{C_k}$ are computed to provide insights into the distribution and variability of the metric within the community. These statistical measures facilitate the comparative analysis of communities, enabling the identification of distinctive characteristics and patterns. For instance, a community exhibiting high mean betweenness centrality may indicate a group of nodes that act as critical intermediaries within the network, whereas a community with high eigenvector centrality suggests influential nodes that are connected to other highly influential nodes.

4. Results and Discussions

4.1. Dataset

The dataset used in this study consists of daily financial data spanning from 9 January 2023, to 3 October 2024, a period that offers a focused yet extensive temporal framework for examining the dynamic interactions among global stock markets. This time frame was chosen to capture contemporary market behavior under relatively stable conditions, excluding extreme global shocks such as the COVID-19 pandemic or prior financial crises. By doing so, the analysis isolates the underlying mechanisms of information flow and connectivity without the distortion of extraordinary, one-off events, which may overshadow long-term structural dynamics. The analysis focuses on logarithmic returns derived from daily closing prices, a method that normalizes the data to facilitate comparisons across markets of varying scales. This approach allows for a more precise evaluation of relative price movements, ensuring that scale differences do not bias the assessment of directional information flows and network structures. By selecting this period, the study balances the need for sufficient data to ensure robustness with the objective of understanding market behaviors in a relatively typical economic environment, providing insights into how markets interact under less volatile global conditions.

Prior to conducting the primary analyses, the dataset underwent meticulous preprocessing to ensure its integrity and suitability for subsequent computations. This preprocessing involved the identification and exclusion of any anomalies or inconsistencies within the closing price data, such as missing values or non-positive entries, which could potentially distort the analysis. Ensuring the continuity and reliability of the time series data was paramount, as they underpin the accuracy of the FTE calculations and the resulting network structures. The final curated dataset comprises a comprehensive collection of logarithmic return values for each selected stock market index, providing a nuanced depiction of daily market fluctuations over the specified time frame. These log-differenced values serve as the foundational input for constructing the FTE matrices, which quantify the directional information flow between pairs of markets. By focusing exclusively on the time scale and log returns of daily prices, the analysis maintains a streamlined and consistent approach, enhancing the comparability and interpretability of the results. Descriptive statistics for the log-differenced values, including country names and tickers, are detailed in Table A1.

In this study, we delve into the intricate dynamics of information flow among global stock markets by employing FTE as a pivotal analytical tool. To comprehensively explore the impact of fractional dynamics on information transfer, our analysis is segmented into four distinct scenarios, each characterized by specific fractional derivative orders: $\alpha_X = 0.0$ with $\alpha_Y = 0.0$, $\alpha_X = 0.2$ with $\alpha_Y = 0.8$, $\alpha_X = 0.5$ with $\alpha_Y = 0.5$, and $\alpha_X = 0.8$ with $\alpha_Y = 0.2$.

For each combination of α_X and α_Y, we compute the FTE between pairs of stock markets, subsequently constructing directed networks based on FTE matrices that have been thresholded at the 20th percentile. This thresholding ensures that only the most significant edges, representing the top 80% of FTE values, are retained, thereby encapsulating the strongest directional flows of information. These networks highlight the influential relationships and interdependencies inherent in the global financial landscape. Following network construction, we perform comprehensive community detection to identify clusters of interconnected markets, accompanied by detailed statistical analyses of key network metrics such as in-degree, out-degree, betweenness centrality, closeness centrality, eigenvector centrality, hub scores, and authority scores.

4.2. Results on $\alpha_X = 0.0$ and $\alpha_Y = 0.0$

When $\alpha_X = 0.0$ and $\alpha_Y = 0.0$, the analysis corresponds to a scenario with no fractional memory, so each market's immediate past is weighted uniformly, and distant historical values have negligible influence. Under this "memoryless" setting, the resulting network reveals direct information transfer patterns as they occur from one time step to the next.

Figure 1 presents the ordinary transfer-entropy-based network constructed using memory parameters $\alpha_X = 0.0$ and $\alpha_Y = 0.0$. We shall note here that this case correspondences ordinary transfer entropy.

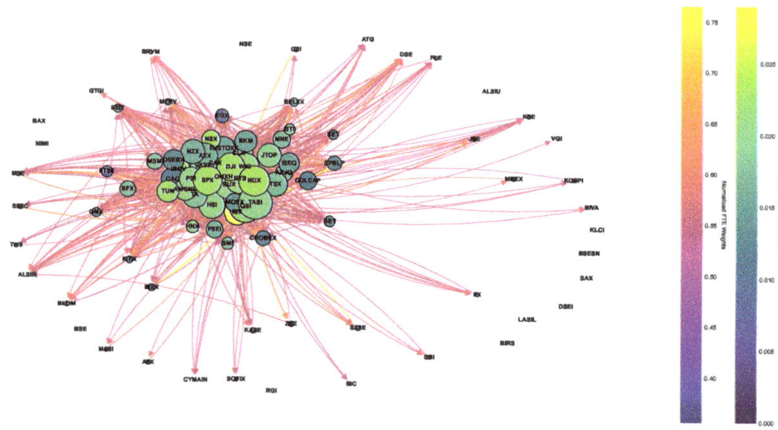

Figure 1. Emerging directed network for $\alpha_X = 0.0$ and $\alpha_Y = 0.0$.

In Figure 1, a heavily interconnected cluster at the center underscores a group of markets whose short-term movements strongly influence each other. Several large stock markets, including those from the United States and leading European indices, exhibit both high in-degree (they receive information flow from many sources) and high out-degree (they also send information to others). This reflects the dominant role of major global markets in shaping short-run price dynamics across regions. Conversely, some markets with sparse connections or negligible in-flows (like BAX or BIRS) indicate localized trading patterns or limited global integration in the immediate past-return sense, as fractional memory is not considered here.

In the "no memory" framework, the Middle Eastern markets such as the Qatar Stock Exchange (QSI) and Saudi Arabia's TASI stand out for considerable out-degree, suggesting strong outward information flow to other indices in short-term horizons. Likewise, markets such as ISX and NDX display a high in-degree, meaning they are recipients of significant immediate information inflows, likely responding quickly to developments in global trading. From a regional perspective, the Americas (e.g., IBOV, TSX, DJIA, SPX) and core European indices (DAX, CAC, Euronext's AEX) appear at or near the center of information transfers, while certain emerging or frontier markets (like those in Africa or smaller Asian exchanges) maintain more peripheral positions. The overall structure illustrates how, without the influence of historical memory, markets with large market capitalization and high liquidity take center stage in dictating short-run price patterns worldwide.

Figure 2 illustrates the distributions of standard network measures for the memoryless setting. Detailed network metrics are presented in Table A2 (Appendix A).

The in-degree and out-degree distributions both exhibit skewed shapes, with a small number of markets exhibiting very high degrees and the majority showing moderate or low connectivity. This underscores the presence of "key influencers" that receive or transmit a disproportionate share of the immediate information flow. Betweenness centrality follows a heavily right-skewed distribution, indicating that only a few indices—such as TASI, TSX, or ISX—act as vital bridges in the network, channeling short-term information between otherwise less-connected nodes. Closeness centrality is relatively more evenly distributed but still shows that certain markets can reach or be reached by others rapidly in terms of path length, fitting with the notion that major global markets are typically only a few steps away from any other market. Eigenvector centrality, which highlights nodes connected to other highly connected nodes, also displays a skewed distribution. Markets like NDX, SPX, and IBOV tend to hold relatively high eigenvector scores, indicating their integral role in the short-run dynamics of global equities. Hub and authority scores underscore these patterns as well: some markets serve as authoritative sources of immediate information, while others function more as hubs redirecting that information. As such, one can glean that in the absence of memory effects, the market network is dominated by a cluster of globally significant exchanges, complemented by pockets of lower-degree or even isolated nodes.

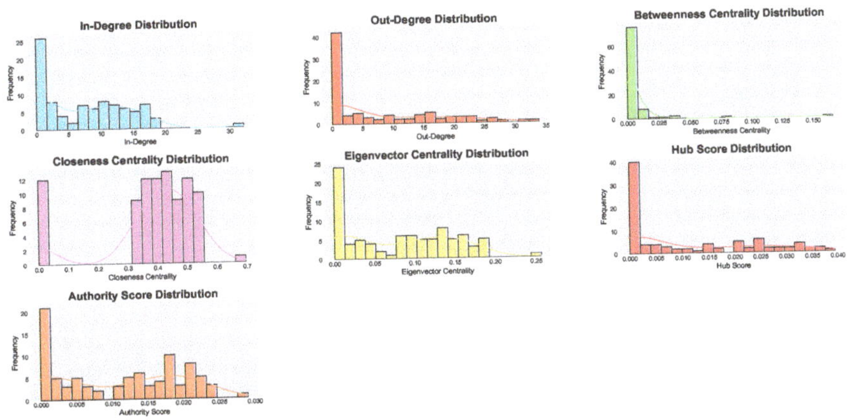

Figure 2. Distributions of network metrics for $\alpha_X = 0.0$ and $\alpha_Y = 0.0$.

Figure 3 reveals the community structure for the same memoryless setting.

The Louvain algorithm detects multiple communities of varying sizes, with two or three large groups often corresponding to major regions or economic alliances, while smaller or isolated communities represent markets that do not share strong short-run informational linkages with any major group. For instance, one large community might predominantly contain established European and North American indices, reflecting their frequent mutual interactions at the daily scale. Another sizable community might combine Latin American markets (e.g., IBOV, MERV, COLCAP) and certain European outliers, indicating either correlated movements or strong capital flows in the short term.

Meanwhile, the presence of small communities or singleton nodes illustrates weaker connections that are overshadowed by larger, more liquid markets. Such nodes might be from smaller frontier economies with limited cross-listings, lower foreign investment, or regulatory barriers, all of which reduce short-run global integration in the absence of historical memory. The community-level centralities—betweenness, closeness, and eigenvector—further reveal which groups act as conduits or integrators of information. Typically, the largest communities, encompassing the global financial hubs, have elevated measures of centrality, signaling their role in unifying or bridging other groups during day-to-day market interactions. By contrast, smaller clusters with lower centralities capture niche regional relationships or markets that remain somewhat detached from the global flow of information when memory effects are not accounted for.

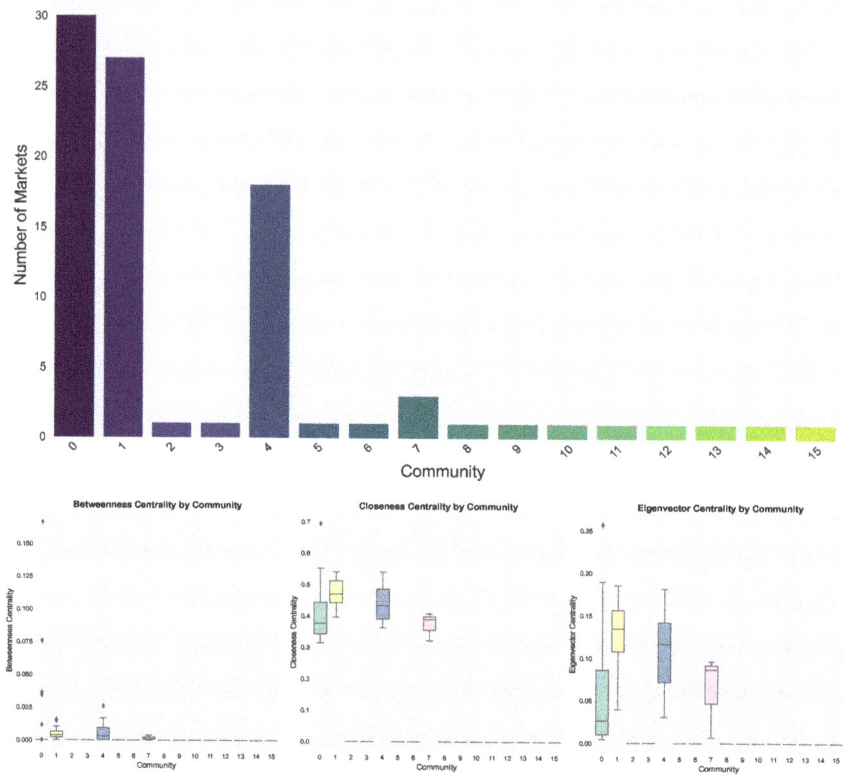

Figure 3. Number of communities detected and community-level centralities for $\alpha_X = 0.0$ and $\alpha_Y = 0.0$.

4.3. Results on $\alpha_X = 0.2$ and $\alpha_Y = 0.8$

Under $\alpha_X = 0.2$ and $\alpha_Y = 0.8$, the target market X places modest weight on its own short-run historical values, while the source market Y emphasizes a much longer memory of its own past. This configuration means that any information flowing from Y to X embeds relatively persistent patterns from Y, whereas X itself relies on a shorter historical window to determine its response. As a result, markets that exhibit long-lasting trends or stable historical influences in Y appear more strongly connected to their counterparts in X.

Figure 4 presents the FTE-based network constructed using memory parameters $\alpha_X = 0.2$ and $\alpha_Y = 0.8$.

Comparing the resulting network, one observes denser connectivity overall, as many nodes show high in-degree and out-degree. This reflects that longer-run influences in Y support more persistent cross-market relationships. From a regional perspective, one still finds major global markets—particularly from North America (e.g., SPX, NDX, TSX, and DJIA), Europe (e.g., DAX, CAC, FTSE), and parts of Asia–Pacific (e.g., HSI, AXJO)—taking on central roles. However, the heavier weighting of historical data in Y tends to amplify the importance of markets whose longer-run performance has proven influential. In the Middle East, TASI and QSI illustrate robust out-degree, suggesting that their extended-memory patterns carry substantial sway in shaping other indices' responses. Meanwhile, several frontier or smaller markets experience augmented in-degrees, reflecting that they respond more noticeably to the persistent signals emanating from larger markets' pasts. Overall, the partial memory for X and extended memory for Y lead to a highly interlinked structure in which historically influential markets exert a steady pull on global price dynamics.

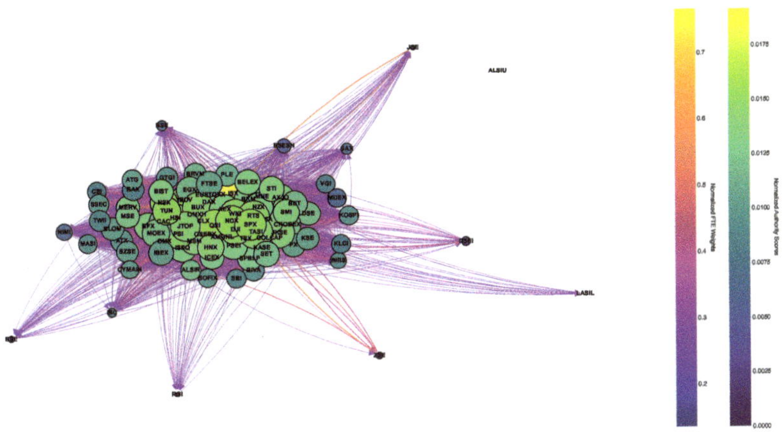

Figure 4. Emerging directed network for $\alpha_X = 0.2$ and $\alpha_Y = 0.8$.

When incorporating a longer memory component on the source side, the distributions of in-degree and out-degree (Figure 5) shift toward higher values for many markets, signifying that most indices become more globally "aware" of each other's persistent trends. Detailed network metrics are presented in Table A3.

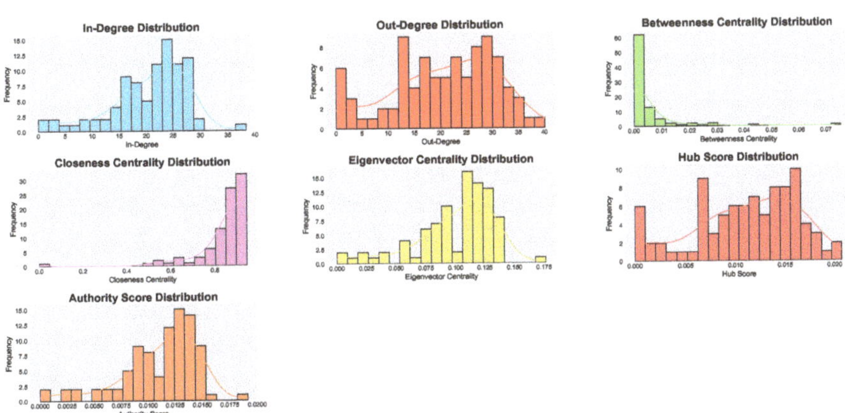

Figure 5. Distributions of network metrics for $\alpha_X = 0.2$ and $\alpha_Y = 0.8$.

A sizable share of nodes is in the 20–30 or even 30+ range for in-degree and out-degree, indicating a more uniformly high level of connectivity. Betweenness centrality remains skewed, with a few nodes—often large or regionally pivotal indices—serving as principal conduits of information. Unlike the memoryless case, however, these bridges reflect a combination of short-run adaptation (through $\alpha_X = 0.2$) and long-run influence ($\alpha_Y = 0.8$), leading to markets that integrate both immediate and historical signals to occupy key network "corridors".

Closeness centrality is, on average, higher for many nodes than in the no-memory setting, suggesting that the longer historical perspective facilitates shorter effective paths among markets. In other words, including persistent sources of influence in Y shortens the distance in the information flow sense. Eigenvector centrality likewise shows that many major global indices—NDX, SPX, IBOV, and others—remain dominant, but with slightly elevated scores that underscore how the system now amplifies historical signals. Hub and authority measures reinforce this pattern: some indices become strong "hubs" for distributing historically grounded information (especially those with high out-degree), while others become "authorities" that aggregate influential past-driven flows from numerous markets.

With partial memory in X and long memory in Y, the Louvain algorithm (Figure 6) detects a handful of sizable communities.

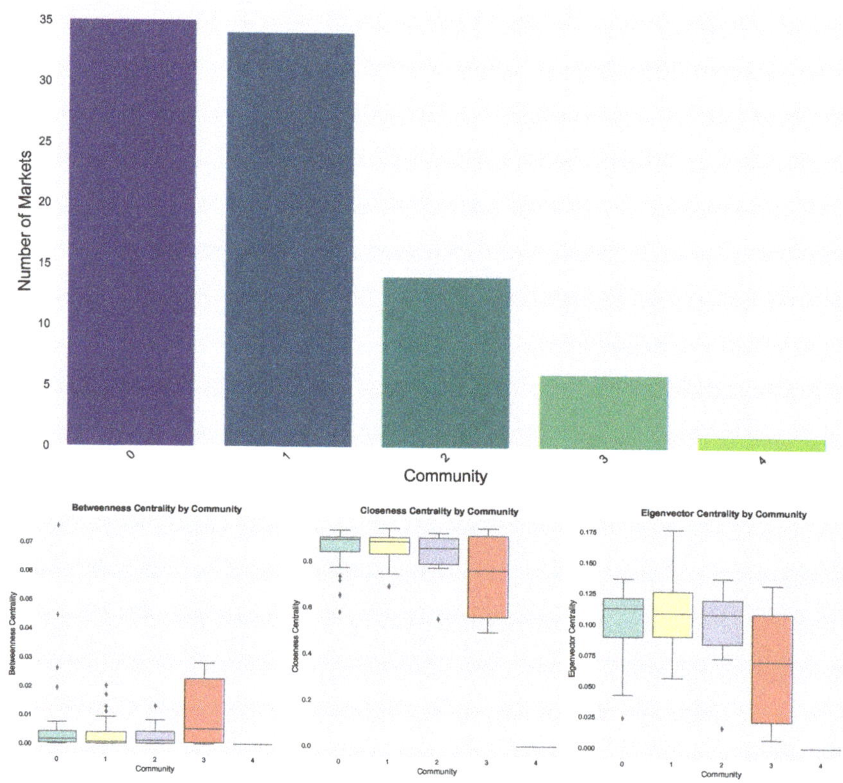

Figure 6. Number of communities detected and community-level centralities for $\alpha_X = 0.2$ and $\alpha_Y = 0.8$.

Two of them are particularly large, each grouping around established financial centers and leading emerging markets whose persistent historical trends form a stable backdrop for price movements. For instance, one community may gather several European and American markets, while another might incorporate Asia–Pacific and select Latin American exchanges that share interlinked long-run dynamics. A third, moderately sized community often contains markets from Eastern Europe or the Middle East that exhibit robust long-memory connections and act as conduits between core and peripheral exchanges. Smaller communities or isolated nodes tend to be those whose local or idiosyncratic patterns (in terms of long memory) fail to resonate strongly with the global cluster.

Regionally, this distribution of communities signals that historical performance in certain areas—like the Middle East's robust growth or Latin America's commodity cycles—can substantially shape how those markets align. Longer-memory effects also enhance connectivity among markets that exhibit stable cyclical or macroeconomic conditions, causing them to cluster even if geographically distant. Conversely, a few frontier markets form smaller clusters, suggesting that while they do respond to broader global trends, their own extended histories may be less influential on the rest of the network. Overall, these communities highlight how partial versus extended memory perspectives interact to form cohesive clusters that reflect both current signals and historically persistent ties across the globe.

4.4. Results on $\alpha_X = 0.5$ and $\alpha_Y = 0.5$

When $\alpha_X = 0.5$ and $\alpha_Y = 0.5$, both the target market X and the source market Y balance short- and long-term historical effects in shaping how information flows. In practical terms, each market's present values weigh its own immediate past and its deeper historical trends on roughly equal footing. As a result, the network that emerges under these equal-memory conditions displays broader connectivity than purely short-memory scenarios (e.g., $\alpha_X = \alpha_Y = 0$) but also tends to be more diffuse than the strong "long-memory" networks where α_X or α_Y was close to 1.

In Figure 7, the core cluster of nodes is sizable, with many indices exhibiting a mix of strong in-degree and out-degree. This reflects how balanced memory parameters encourage information transfer based not only on very recent price changes but also on moderately persistent trends, thus knitting markets together in a more cohesive global fabric.

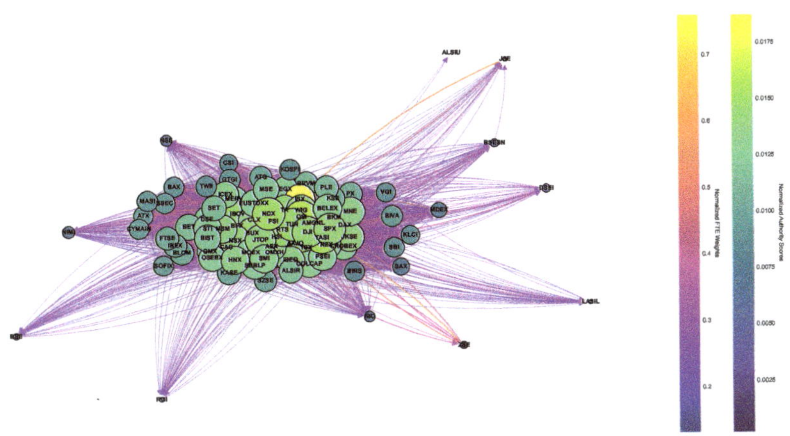

Figure 7. Emerging directed network for $\alpha_X = 0.5$ and $\alpha_Y = 0.5$.

From a regional viewpoint, the well-established North American (SPX, NDX, TSX) and European (DAX, CAC, EUSTOXX) markets remain influential, as they often do, but there is also considerable influence from emerging regions—such as Latin America's IBOV and MERV or the Middle East's TASI and QSI—suggesting that balanced memory permits these markets' historical cycles to be more consistently recognized. The Asia–Pacific region (e.g., HSI, AXJO, JKSE) also displays notable degrees of connectivity, indicating that both their shorter-term fluctuations and medium-term trends feed significantly into global price movements. Overall, this balanced-memory scenario produces a relatively dense, interconnected network that highlights the interplay of immediate shocks and multi-month or even multi-year factors within stock market dynamics.

The in-degree and out-degree distributions (Figure 8) show that many markets cluster around higher values, signifying robust exchanges of information in both directions. Detailed network metrics are presented in Table A4.

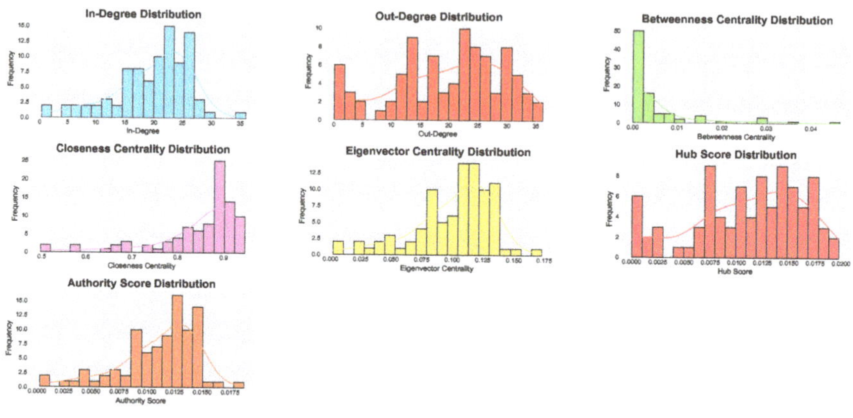

Figure 8. Distributions of network metrics for $\alpha_X = 0.5$ and $\alpha_Y = 0.5$.

The heavier tails in these distributions point to a few standout markets that receive or send a particularly high volume of transfers, reflecting their capacity to integrate both short-run volatility and moderate-term historical signals. Betweenness centrality remains skewed, with nodes like ISX and QSI emerging as potential bridges for inter-regional links, suggesting that their combined short and mid-range memory highlights their role in connecting peripheral or frontier markets to the global system. Closeness centrality, meanwhile, trends higher overall than in the purely short-memory case, as balanced memory shortens effective "distances" in the flow of information: when markets take into account both the immediate past and moderately lagged historical signals, they become more attuned to each other's movements, shrinking the path lengths that define closeness.

Eigenvector centrality also underscores the presence of big global indices as well as influential emerging markets in these networks. Because each market is simultaneously referencing its own medium-range memory and acknowledging other markets' historical paths, the emphasis on connectivity resonates with the idea that large, regionally critical markets can boost the eigenvector scores of their neighbors. Hub and authority scores follow similar logic: markets that consistently send out balanced-memory signals with enough historical momentum, like TASI or NDX, emerge as hubs, while others, especially large receiving markets of these medium-term signals, gain authority. The net effect is a network structure where immediate and historical factors combine to amplify the role of key nodes.

When applying the Louvain algorithm (Figure 9), the network splits into a few sizable communities rather than many small clusters or an overwhelmingly dominant single cluster.

This pattern indicates that, under balanced memory, certain groups of markets share somewhat similar medium-term behavior and respond in parallel to global factors over time. One large community often includes major European and American indices whose mid-term economic cycles and correlated trading habits bind them closely, while another large community may be formed by Asia–Pacific and certain emerging markets that share structural similarities or cyclical patterns. A smaller cluster can sometimes comprise frontier or region-specific indices that, while influenced by the global environment, maintain enough local idiosyncrasies in their medium-range histories to differentiate them from the biggest financial hubs.

Regionally, these communities reflect how balanced memory draws out correlations in markets' moderate historical performance while preserving the impact of shorter-term shocks. Hence, Latin American indices like IBOV and MERV might cluster with other commodity-driven markets if their medium-range trends line up consistently. Simultaneously, some Middle Eastern and Eastern European exchanges can end up either in a separate group or bridging multiple clusters, as they frequently feature specific cyclical elements—energy prices, geopolitical events, or growth surges—that resonate differently with global trends. In sum, the balanced-memory framework not only accentuates major global players but also spotlights intermediate-range commonalities across diverse regions, resulting in clear yet interconnected communities within the network.

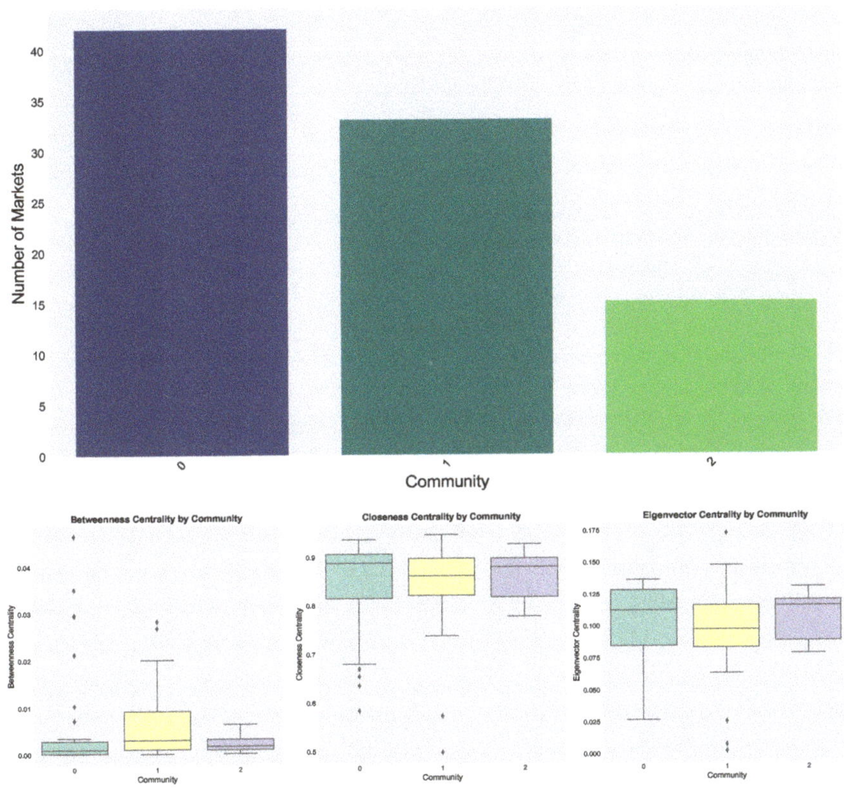

Figure 9. Number of communities detected and community-level centralities for $\alpha_X = 0.5$ and $\alpha_Y = 0.5$.

4.5. Results on $\alpha_X = 0.8$ and $\alpha_Y = 0.2$

When $\alpha_X = 0.8$ and $\alpha_Y = 0.2$, the target market X relies predominantly on its own long historical memory, while the source market Y places more emphasis on its short-run dynamics. In practice, this means that X's reactions to incoming information incorporate deeper, more persistent trends in its own past. Meanwhile, Y contributes relatively immediate signals, reflecting shorter-term fluctuations in its own series. The resulting network, as shown in Figure 10, tends to reveal nodes that adjust gradually given X's heavy historical weighting—yet respond to brief shocks coming from their neighbors.

From a global standpoint, the major stock markets maintain high connectivity in both directions. However, markets whose own past exhibits stable or influential long-run trends stand out for their sizable in-degrees, since many others feed them short-term signals while they incorporate those signals in conjunction with their long memory.

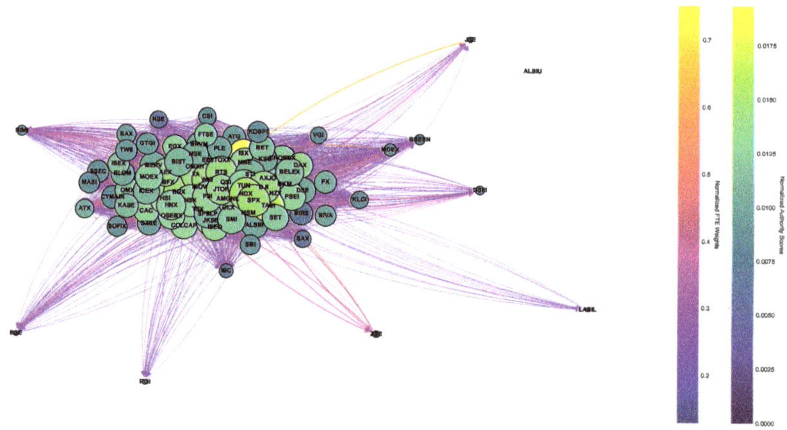

Figure 10. Emerging directed network for $\alpha_X = 0.8$ and $\alpha_Y = 0.2$.

Regionally, large and liquid indices like TASI, QSI, or American benchmarks such as SPX or NDX appear to have both strong receiving and sending roles. Their long-run historical patterns produce stable anchors, yet they still react to shorter-term triggers from source markets that apply relatively little memory. Notably, some frontier or emerging markets in this configuration display moderate to high out-degrees, indicating that, despite their limited reliance on historical patterns, they do send frequent short-term signals to their counterparts. The emphasis on X's long memory also means that if a market has a deep, influential past performance trajectory, it may end up absorbing short-term transmissions from multiple neighbors, thereby revealing strong directional flows from smaller or more volatile source indices.

Under this memory configuration, the in-degree distribution (Figure 11) clusters around moderate to high values, reflecting that many nodes receive inputs from a variety of sources.

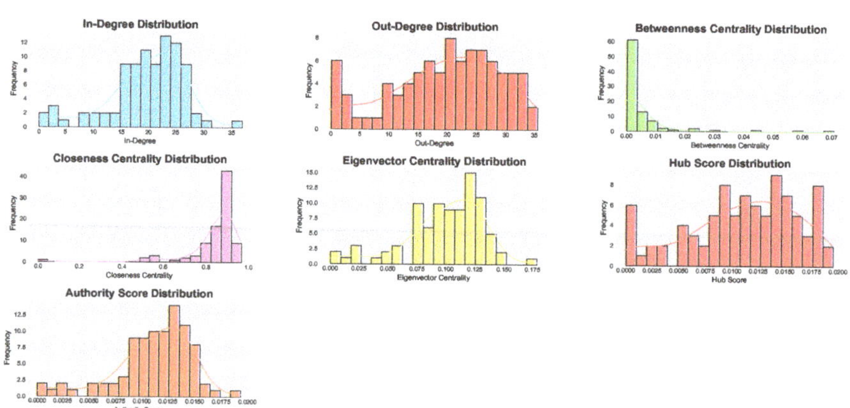

Figure 11. Distributions of network metrics for $\alpha_X = 0.8$ and $\alpha_Y = 0.2$.

Since X weighs its own historical memory heavily, it can still be "open" to receiving numerous short-term signals from different Y markets. The out-degree distribution, meanwhile, shows that some markets—likely those with strong short-run variability—act as persistent senders of immediate signals. Betweenness centrality preserves its right-skewed shape, highlighting particular indices as conduits between localized subgroups. Markets like NSE or SAX may show elevated betweenness because their short-term fluctuations, when passed along, facilitate connections that might otherwise be overlooked if all markets were heavily memory-based.

The closeness centrality distribution tends to be high for a subset of core global markets, revealing their capability to reach or be reached by others relatively quickly, even though they rely on a heavier personal historical memory. Eigenvector centrality underscores the influence of those markets that tie into other prominent nodes—such as major American, European, or Middle Eastern indices. In this environment, authority scores for strongly memory-based target markets can climb if they receive significant short-term signals from numerous neighbors. Conversely, hub scores reveal source markets that continuously emit short-run movements into the broader network, bridging smaller or more peripheral indices with those that depend on historical memory.

When detecting communities (Figure 12), three or four main clusters usually emerge.

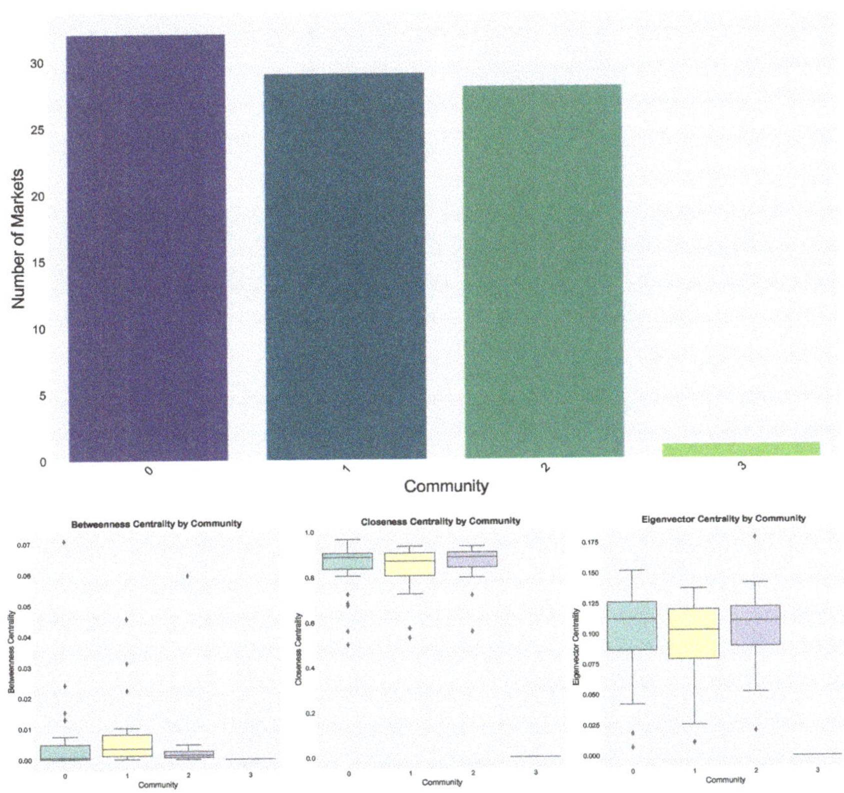

Figure 12. Number of communities detected and community-level centralities for $\alpha_X = 0.8$ and $\alpha_Y = 0.2$.

One large community often includes strongly memory-based indices from major financial centers (like the United States, Western Europe, and the Middle East), where the markets' own persistent pasts lead them to anchor the group. Another comparably sized group may gather emerging or developing markets, which rely more on incoming short-run fluctuations and feed those to larger indices—yet they themselves do not hold extended historical influence in Y. A third community, nearly as large, contains additional mid-tier or frontier markets that reflect specific regional or sectoral patterns, bridging short-term changes from smaller indices to more established markets. Finally, a few outlier or nearly isolated nodes may remain in a separate or trivial community, typically because they do not share substantial short-run correlations with others or possess a historically stable pattern that does not resonate significantly at the global scale.

Regionally, this memory configuration underscores the central role of markets that have well-documented historical performance trends (since α_X is high) and remain attractive to short-run signals from smaller, more volatile neighbors (α_Y is low). In emerging regions, some indices manage to link with the major hubs by sending out frequent short-term signals that these bigger nodes partially absorb. Simultaneously, the major hubs continue to exhibit strong overall connectivity, reflecting the reality that global investment flows respond to short-lived shocks—such as macroeconomic announcements or geopolitical events—even as local indices anchor themselves in their own long-run returns' data.

4.6. Comparative Discussions

The comparative findings across different α_X and α_Y settings consistently underscore that incorporating memory into transfer entropy calculations provides a richer and more nuanced view of global stock market interdependencies compared to a purely memoryless framework. Transfer entropy, a measure rooted in information theory, quantifies the directional information transfer between systems—in this case, stock markets. By integrating memory, the model acknowledges that markets do not operate in isolation at each time step but are influenced by their historical states. This temporal dimension allows for capturing the persistence and evolution of market behaviors over time, offering a more comprehensive understanding of interdependencies.

Under the memoryless condition ($\alpha_X = 0.0$, $\alpha_Y = 0.0$), the resulting networks tend to highlight only immediate, short-lived interactions and place greater emphasis on market shocks that rapidly dissipate. While such a snapshot can be useful for capturing quick information flows, it overlooks the persistent or cyclical patterns that often shape how indices move together over longer horizons. For instance, during economic cycles or in response to prolonged geopolitical events, markets exhibit behaviors that unfold over extended periods. The memoryless approach fails to account for these sustained influences, potentially leading to incomplete or misleading interpretations of market dynamics.

In contrast, once we introduce fractional memory—whether heavily weighted toward the target market X (as when α_X is high and α_Y is low), toward the source market Y, or balanced equally—we witness denser and more interconnected networks. This increased density reflects the cumulative effects of past interactions, allowing for a more intricate web of dependencies. Additionally, shifts in centrality measures emerge, illustrating how certain markets gain prominence in their ability to absorb and emit information over extended time spans. For example, a market with high α_X may act as a persistent influencer, shaping the behavior of other markets through sustained informational flows.

Markets with strong historical trends or stable cyclical behaviors become more prominent because the transfer entropy model now accounts for those longer-run influences, thereby revealing non-trivial relationships that remain hidden under memoryless analysis. These relationships might include enduring economic ties, such as trade partnerships or shared regulatory environments, which influence market movements over time. By capturing these sustained connections, the memory-inclusive approach provides insights into how certain markets consistently drive or respond to global financial trends, offering a deeper layer of analysis than what is possible with a memoryless framework.

This is particularly evident in how betweenness centrality, closeness centrality, and eigenvector centrality evolve from one parameter setting to another. Memory-based configurations illuminate pivotal bridging markets that tie together regions over sustained intervals, while also underscoring the global influence of major financial hubs whose persistent past returns shape the behavior of a host of smaller or emerging exchanges. For instance, a central market identified through betweenness centrality might serve as a critical conduit for information flow between disparate regions, enhancing the overall robustness and resilience of the global market network.

Critically, these findings show that transfer entropy with memory offers a more robust and realistic depiction of global stock market networks. This enhanced depiction allows practitioners to discern both short-run volatility transmission and medium- to long-run structural dependencies that may be driven by macroeconomic factors, regional alliances, or commodity cycles. Such a dual capability is invaluable for risk management, strategic investment planning, and policy formulation, as it provides a multifaceted view of market dynamics that accounts for both immediate and enduring influences.

By integrating fractional derivatives into the state-space representation, the method captures how markets assimilate past data in determining present behavior. Fractional derivatives offer a mathematical framework for modeling memory effects, enabling the transfer entropy measure to account for the weighted influence of historical states. This integration provides a superior lens for identifying key information pathways and systemic drivers, facilitating a more accurate mapping of how information and shocks propagate through the global market network over time.

5. Conclusions

This study has shown that the introduction of fractional derivatives into the transfer entropy framework yields a powerful tool, fractional transfer entropy (FTE), for revealing the multifaceted ways in which global stock markets integrate both short-lived shocks and deeply rooted historical trends. By systematically varying memory parameters, α_X and α_Y, the analysis captures the full continuum of market interactions, from the highly reactive, short-memory regime that emphasizes immediate fluctuations to a balanced scenario blending transient signals with mid-range cycles, culminating in a long-memory-dominated setting where entrenched hierarchies guide capital flows. The results consistently indicate that, in contrast to traditional memoryless approaches, FTE highlights how markets are rarely shaped by instantaneous news alone; instead, they exhibit persistent influences emerging from their own past trajectories or from other markets' structural legacies.

Under short-memory dominance ($\alpha_X = 0.2, \alpha_Y = 0.8$), the networks reflect an environment where prices respond swiftly to fresh headlines, resulting in a more fluid yet fragile tapestry of connections, as momentary policy signals or geopolitical events can quickly redefine relationships. With balanced parameters ($\alpha_X = 0.5, \alpha_Y = 0.5$), one observes a stable interplay that neither neglects the present nor discounts the impact of longer-term patterns, illustrating how established ties and sudden bursts of volatility harmonize to shape global finance. Shifting to a heavier weighting on long memory ($\alpha_X = 0.8, \alpha_Y = 0.2$) reveals a global financial architecture more deeply anchored in historical capital flows and investor sentiment, offering resilience but also reducing the capacity for rapid realignment in response to short-term shocks. These findings imply that tailoring memory parameters offers profound insights into whether markets are driven predominantly by near-term flux or by the cumulative weight of history, thereby underscoring that FTE surpasses memoryless transfer entropy by providing a richer depiction of how each market's past interacts with incoming information from others.

In future research, the time horizon of this methodology can be extended to longer periods that include major worldwide crises—such as COVID-19 or global financial stresses—to test the robustness of FTE under conditions of extreme market turmoil. Moreover, an additional avenue for investigation involves formally defining and analyzing FTE at the community level, which would capture how clusters of markets collectively transmit and absorb both ephemeral and enduring signals. By refining and expanding these approaches, scholars and practitioners can better understand the co-evolution of short-run volatility and structural inertia across multiple regions and asset classes, ultimately enhancing our capacity to anticipate shifts in systemic risk and to design more effective stabilization policies.

Despite these advances, limitations remain. The methodology relies on price returns and the assumption that all price variations are equally informative. It does not discriminate among the types of shocks, nor does it incorporate intangible drivers like investor psychology, cultural ties, or geopolitical nuances that may not register directly in asset prices. Computational complexity and data availability could challenge the approach when examining very large networks, higher fractional orders, or more complex asset classes. Addressing these issues in future work may involve incorporating macroeconomic data, sector-specific fundamentals, or other asset categories, thereby refining the scope of FTE. Exploring adaptive or time-varying memory parameters could also provide a dynamic representation of how market sensitivity and structural inertia evolve across crises or policy regimes. Considering multilayer networks might reveal how global equity markets interact with currencies, bonds, or commodities under different temporal conditions.

The importance of this study lies in its departure from conventional methods that often focus on either short-lived shocks or permanent ties. By combining fractional calculus with transfer entropy, FTE can portray how markets are neither wholly dominated by the past nor entirely tethered to the present. Rather, they navigate a continuum where immediate events and historical legacies jointly steer their behavior. Such a perspective yields a more sophisticated understanding of global financial stability and contagion channels, aiding policymakers, investors, and scholars in anticipating how the interplay of old and new forces will continue to shape the global financial ecosystem.

Author Contributions: Conceptualization, Ö.A., M.A.B., L.M.B. and L.G.; methodology, Ö.A., M.A.B., L.M.B. and L.G.; software, Ö.A. and M.A.B.; validation, Ö.A., M.A.B., L.M.B. and L.G.; formal analysis, Ö.A., M.A.B., L.M.B. and L.G.; investigation, Ö.A., M.A.B., L.M.B. and L.G.; resources, Ö.A., M.A.B., L.M.B. and L.G.; data curation, L.M.B. and L.G.; writing—original draft preparation, Ö.A., M.A.B., L.M.B. and L.G.; writing—review and editing, Ö.A., M.A.B., L.M.B. and L.G.; visualization, Ö.A. and M.A.B.; supervision, M.A.B.; project administration, L.G.; funding acquisition, L.G. All authors have read and agreed to the published version of the manuscript.

Funding: This research received no external funding.

Data Availability Statement: The original contributions presented in this study are included in this article. Further inquiries can be directed to the corresponding authors.

Conflicts of Interest: The authors declare no conflicts of interest.

Appendix A

Table A1. Descriptive statistics for log-return data.

Country	Ticker	Min	Mean	Median	Max	Standard Deviation	Kurtosis	Skewness
Argentina	MERV	−0.1328	0.0049	0.0051	0.2057	0.0323	4.3415	0.0061
Australia	AXJO	−0.0377	0.0003	0.0009	0.0173	0.0071	1.8279	−0.6951
Austria	ATX	−0.0651	0.0002	0.0007	0.0306	0.0091	7.8229	−1.3708
Bahrain	BAX	−0.0107	0.0001	0.0000	0.0370	0.0038	20.7964	2.2684
Bangladesh	DSE	−0.0271	−0.0003	−0.0002	0.0532	0.0074	13.0246	1.5456
Belgium	BFX	−0.0320	0.0002	0.0006	0.0336	0.0082	1.6061	−0.0138
Bosnia Herzegovina	BIRS	−0.0578	0.0002	0.0000	0.0798	0.0104	21.7436	0.9362
Botswana	BSE	−0.0059	0.0005	0.0001	0.0192	0.0016	52.2879	5.3967

Table A1. *Cont.*

Country	Ticker	Min	Mean	Median	Max	Standard Deviation	Kurtosis	Skewness
Brazil	IBOV	−0.0243	0.0004	−0.0001	0.0420	0.0093	0.5846	0.2778
Bulgaria	SOFIX	−0.0420	0.0008	0.0006	0.0306	0.0062	7.6283	−0.5644
Canada	TSX	−0.0232	0.0004	0.0008	0.0283	0.0069	0.9433	−0.2186
Chile	CLX	−0.0349	0.0005	0.0003	0.0289	0.0094	0.6747	−0.1095
China	CSI	−0.0634	−0.0003	0.0000	0.1057	0.0150	8.1915	0.8591
China	SSEC	−0.0272	0.0001	−0.0003	0.0776	0.0093	12.4206	1.8671
China	SZSE	−0.0356	−0.0002	−0.0009	0.1014	0.0129	11.2706	1.9213
Colombia	COLCAP	−0.0392	−0.0001	0.0005	0.0359	0.0096	1.8415	−0.2197
Cote D'Ivoire	BRVM	−0.0403	0.0007	0.0008	0.0308	0.0071	4.8515	−0.1669
Croatia	CROBEX	−0.0279	0.0008	0.0005	0.0167	0.0050	3.6376	−0.5186
Cyprus	CYMAIN	−0.0795	0.0021	0.0009	0.0749	0.0126	9.5252	0.4423
Czech Republic	PX	−0.0426	0.0005	0.0007	0.0181	0.0069	5.5586	−1.2873
Sweden	OMX	−0.0418	0.0004	0.0006	0.0344	0.0087	1.8354	−0.2607
Egypt	EGX	−0.0926	0.0023	0.0043	0.0468	0.0179	5.4877	−1.6185
Estonia	GTGI	−0.0280	−0.0001	−0.0003	0.0214	0.0049	5.2708	−0.1018
Finland	OMXH	−0.0332	−0.0002	−0.0002	0.0241	0.0085	0.4844	−0.1125
France	CAC	−0.0365	0.0002	0.0007	0.0231	0.0084	1.2151	−0.4600
Germany	DAX	−0.0332	0.0006	0.0009	0.0214	0.0079	1.3257	−0.5519
Germany	EUSTOXX	−0.0352	0.0004	0.0008	0.0233	0.0086	1.2117	−0.3938
Greece	ATG	−0.0647	0.0009	0.0012	0.0591	0.0108	5.7976	−0.5201
Hong Kong	HSI	−0.0378	0.0001	−0.0002	0.0601	0.0143	0.5035	0.4554
Hungary	BUX	−0.0317	0.0011	0.0011	0.0296	0.0086	1.6933	−0.3400
Iceland	ICEX	−0.0565	−0.0002	−0.0004	0.0525	0.0107	6.0030	−0.0206
India	BSESN	−0.0591	0.0007	0.0012	0.0333	0.0076	10.0719	−1.0089
India	NIMI	−0.0737	0.0014	0.0026	0.0379	0.0092	12.5656	−1.9128
Indonesia	JKSE	−0.0344	0.0003	0.0005	0.0170	0.0069	1.7150	−0.6322
Iraq	ISX	−0.0949	0.0023	−0.0003	0.1000	0.0203	8.0912	0.8910
Ireland	ISEQ	−0.0374	0.0005	0.0011	0.0379	0.0101	1.4377	−0.3001
Israel	TA	−0.0669	0.0003	0.0008	0.0296	0.0104	3.7900	−0.7261
Jamaica	JSE	−0.1131	−0.0002	−0.0003	0.0984	0.0100	60.0632	−1.0151
Jordan	AMGNL	−0.0228	−0.0002	−0.0001	0.0161	0.0040	3.0863	−0.7068
Kazakhstan	KASE	−0.0255	0.0010	0.0010	0.0215	0.0052	2.5213	−0.2367
Kuwait	BKM	−0.0266	0.0002	0.0003	0.0278	0.0070	1.9506	−0.1487
Latvia	RGI	−0.2256	−0.0006	−0.0002	0.0754	0.0157	101.9888	−7.1920
Lebanon	BLOM	−0.0745	0.0006	0.0000	0.0851	0.0165	5.8583	0.5043
Lithuania	VGI	−0.0264	0.0001	0.0002	0.0117	0.0034	9.2178	−1.2867
Malaysia	KLCI	−0.0474	0.0002	−0.0001	0.0244	0.0055	13.4460	−1.2301
Malta	MSE	−0.0236	0.0001	0.0000	0.0347	0.0059	4.4252	0.3304
Mauritius	MDEX	−0.0173	0.0003	0.0002	0.0143	0.0031	5.3181	0.0873
Mexico	BIVA	−0.0627	−0.0001	0.0000	0.0330	0.0092	5.2621	−0.6090
Mongolia	MNE	−0.0374	0.0006	0.0005	0.0370	0.0094	2.0749	−0.1050
Morocco	MASI	−0.0289	0.0009	0.0007	0.0495	0.0063	10.1469	1.1797
Namibia	NSX	−0.0483	0.0002	0.0002	0.0611	0.0126	2.2692	0.0603
The Netherlands	AEX	−0.0316	0.0005	0.0005	0.0240	0.0077	1.5255	−0.3166
New Zealand	NZX	−0.0153	0.0001	−0.0001	0.0265	0.0057	1.3351	0.5118
Nigeria	NSE	−0.0625	0.0015	0.0004	0.0936	0.0103	19.8051	1.7372
Norway	OSEBX	−0.0381	0.0004	0.0008	0.0246	0.0082	2.3007	−0.6834
Oman	MSM	−0.0259	−0.0001	0.0002	0.0188	0.0047	3.0395	−0.0915
Pakistan	KSE	−0.0419	0.0017	0.0014	0.0574	0.0101	4.2444	0.1777
Palestine	PLE	−0.0418	−0.0007	−0.0005	0.0224	0.0052	13.0132	−1.6202
Peru	SPBLP	−0.0274	0.0007	0.0005	0.0587	0.0086	4.8410	0.5677
The Philippines	PSEI	−0.0298	0.0002	0.0002	0.0351	0.0090	0.4590	−0.0658
Poland	WIG	−0.0342	0.0005	0.0003	0.0472	0.0125	0.5246	0.2487
Portugal	PSI	−0.0281	0.0003	0.0006	0.0344	0.0081	1.1147	−0.2084
Qatar	QSI	−0.0306	−0.0002	0.0001	0.0287	0.0081	1.3649	−0.1109
Romania	BET	−0.0369	0.0008	0.0013	0.0229	0.0068	2.4162	−0.5281
Russia	MOEX	−0.0396	0.0006	0.0011	0.0371	0.0098	1.9100	−0.3111
Russia	RTS	−0.0406	−0.0001	0.0004	0.0352	0.0119	0.6264	−0.1015
Rwanda	ALSIR	−0.0027	0.0001	0.0000	0.0038	0.0006	11.5586	1.3536
Saudi Arabia	TASI	−0.0245	0.0003	0.0005	0.0252	0.0072	0.6871	−0.2204

Table A1. *Cont.*

Country	Ticker	Min	Mean	Median	Max	Standard Deviation	Kurtosis	Skewness
Serbia	BELEX	−0.0299	0.0007	0.0006	0.0264	0.0062	4.1705	−0.0711
Singapore	STI	−0.0416	0.0002	0.0003	0.0197	0.0065	3.6688	−0.5153
Slovakia	SAX	−0.0780	−0.0002	0.0000	0.0415	0.0076	31.3840	−2.5749
Slovenia	SBI	−0.0463	0.0009	0.0006	0.0315	0.0067	6.9273	−0.7276
South Africa	JTOP	−0.0301	0.0002	0.0001	0.0382	0.0099	0.9624	0.1819
South Korea	KOSPI	−0.0946	0.0002	0.0001	0.0513	0.0123	8.4908	−0.9491
Spain	IBEX	−0.0446	0.0006	0.0007	0.0242	0.0086	1.9564	−0.5796
Switzerland	SMI	−0.0365	0.0002	0.0007	0.0285	0.0070	2.2567	−0.4242
Taiwan	TWII	−0.0872	0.0010	0.0014	0.0380	0.0111	11.3302	−1.4818
Tanzania	DSEI	−0.0306	0.0003	0.0000	0.1346	0.0082	163.1680	9.8884
Thailand	SET	−0.0318	−0.0004	−0.0005	0.0280	0.0073	2.0858	0.0248
Tunisia	TUN	−0.0145	0.0005	0.0003	0.0149	0.0035	1.5450	0.2157
Turkey	BIST	−0.0901	0.0013	0.0004	0.0942	0.0198	2.5645	−0.0505
Uganda	ALSIU	−0.2014	−0.0003	−0.0002	0.2025	0.0188	78.3090	−0.0398
The United Kingdom	FTSE	−0.0391	0.0002	0.0005	0.0194	0.0068	3.2779	−0.5784
The United States of America	DJI	−0.0264	0.0005	0.0009	0.0210	0.0069	0.4897	−0.2387
The United States of America	NDX	−0.0372	0.0013	0.0014	0.0350	0.0115	0.2902	−0.1400
The United States of America	SPX	−0.0304	0.0009	0.0009	0.0228	0.0081	0.3962	−0.2604
Venezuela	IBC	−0.1441	0.0036	0.0011	0.1437	0.0207	14.5413	0.9005
Vietnam	HNX	−0.0826	0.0009	0.0025	0.0692	0.0178	4.9780	−0.9771
Zambia	LASIL	−0.1127	0.0018	0.0000	0.1137	0.0117	44.4967	0.3333
Zimbabwe	ZSE	−9.1098	−0.0103	0.0069	0.1074	0.4391	424.9201	−20.6245

Table A2. Statistics for network metrics for $\alpha_X = 0.0$ and $\alpha_Y = 0.0$.

Ticker	In-Degree	Out-Degree	Betweenness Centrality	Closeness Centrality	Eigenvector Centrality	Hub Score	Authority Score	Community
MERV	11.5486	1.0581	0.0001	0.4863	0.1306	0.0018	0.0176	0
AXJO	11.7954	8.62	0.001	0.4349	0.1254	0.0138	0.0177	1
ATX	0.3996	0.4686	0.0	0.3223	0.0055	0.0011	0.0008	0
BAX	0.0	0.0	0.0	0.0	0.0	−0.0	0.0	3
DSE	7.4059	0.0	0.0	0.3877	0.0783	−0.0	0.0106	4
BFX	11.5258	7.4238	0.0004	0.4819	0.1284	0.0121	0.0183	1
BIRS	0.0	0.0	0.0	0.0	−0.0	−0.0	0.0	5
BSE	0.0	0.0	0.0	0.0	0.0	−0.0	0.0	6
IBOV	16.8543	16.0257	0.0069	0.5296	0.1752	0.0249	0.0231	1
SOFIX	0.783	0.3981	0.0	0.3223	0.0071	0.0009	0.0011	7
TSX	13.3499	17.5591	0.0341	0.4953	0.1385	0.0248	0.0178	0
CLX	13.4865	21.871	0.016	0.4908	0.1438	0.0305	0.0196	4
CSI	0.7538	0.5977	0.0	0.3767	0.0116	0.0014	0.0013	0
SSEC	1.9619	0.5435	0.0	0.3905	0.0272	0.0012	0.0035	0
SZSE	1.7436	0.6808	0.0	0.3876	0.025	0.0016	0.003	0
COLCAP	7.7302	9.6775	0.0038	0.4349	0.0937	0.0154	0.0118	1
BRVM	4.5293	0.3696	0.0	0.3715	0.052	0.0005	0.0082	4
CROBEX	7.767	6.5221	0.0037	0.3905	0.0869	0.0102	0.0122	7
CYMAIN	1.8971	0.0	0.0	0.3575	0.024	−0.0	0.0037	0
PX	2.3743	0.3844	0.0	0.3614	0.0291	0.0009	0.0046	0
OMX	7.8908	2.5128	0.0	0.4458	0.0881	0.0045	0.0134	0
EGX	5.3278	5.679	0.0055	0.3715	0.0585	0.0095	0.0079	4
GTGI	0.8455	0.0	0.0	0.3337	0.0108	−0.0	0.0018	0
OMXH	12.3623	22.9772	0.0059	0.4908	0.1382	0.0322	0.0187	1
CAC	7.4486	16.0038	0.0073	0.4421	0.0822	0.024	0.0117	1
DAX	8.7986	14.2726	0.0022	0.4533	0.0974	0.0222	0.0143	1
EUSTOXX	10.0821	15.9324	0.0061	0.4692	0.1073	0.0241	0.0157	1
ATG	2.6789	0.0	0.0	0.367	0.0306	−0.0	0.0047	4
HSI	14.9358	21.1325	0.0115	0.5144	0.1607	0.0286	0.0212	0
BUX	15.6304	25.1031	0.0156	0.5245	0.1582	0.0334	0.0211	1
ICEX	9.6922	1.3431	0.0	0.4533	0.1082	0.0021	0.0144	1
BSESN	0.0	0.0	0.0	0.0	−0.0	−0.0	0.0	9

Table A2. *Cont.*

Ticker	In-Degree	Out-Degree	Betweenness Centrality	Closeness Centrality	Eigenvector Centrality	Hub Score	Authority Score	Community
NIMI	0.0	0.0	0.0	0.0	0.0	−0.0	0.0	10
JKSE	12.975	21.284	0.0045	0.4421	0.1361	0.0301	0.019	4
ISX	32.0838	19.7021	0.1662	0.6947	0.2563	0.0233	0.029	0
ISEQ	9.5023	12.5433	0.002	0.4572	0.1142	0.0199	0.0155	1
TA	13.9757	19.6825	0.0259	0.4999	0.144	0.0266	0.0184	4
JSE	0.5186	0.5255	0.0	0.3689	0.0098	0.0012	0.0007	0
AMGNL	17.4088	14.208	0.0066	0.4612	0.1736	0.0215	0.0217	1
KASE	2.737	0.7833	0.0	0.3992	0.0358	0.0016	0.0049	0
BKM	10.9317	13.7391	0.007	0.4147	0.1137	0.0204	0.0152	4
RGI	0.0	0.0	0.0	0.0	−0.0	−0.0	−0.0	11
BLOM	3.7989	0.7257	0.0	0.4084	0.047	0.0015	0.0062	0
VGI	0.3639	0.0	0.0	0.3201	0.0043	−0.0	0.0008	0
KLCI	0.0	0.0	0.0	0.0	−0.0	−0.0	0.0	12
MSE	8.5736	0.5215	0.0	0.4495	0.0976	0.0012	0.0141	4
MDEX	0.441	0.48	0.0	0.3689	0.0083	0.0011	0.0006	0
BIVA	0.8031	0.0	0.0	0.3378	0.0082	−0.0	0.0011	0
MNE	11.1761	9.0697	0.0001	0.4246	0.1235	0.0145	0.0175	4
MASI	0.8116	0.4858	0.0	0.3302	0.0099	0.0011	0.0014	0
NSX	17.6628	10.7819	0.0147	0.5403	0.185	0.017	0.0236	1
AEX	11.0701	19.747	0.0033	0.4776	0.1209	0.029	0.017	1
NZX	10.7673	17.6174	0.0041	0.4734	0.1199	0.0261	0.0166	4
NSE	0.0	0.0	0.0	0.0	−0.0	−0.0	−0.0	13
OSEBX	7.5291	12.8544	0.001	0.4385	0.0889	0.0204	0.0129	1
MSM	14.22	7.6249	0.0047	0.4421	0.1491	0.0114	0.0187	1
KSE	3.8488	0.3822	0.0	0.3664	0.0431	0.0009	0.0064	0
PLE	3.5629	0.3938	0.0	0.3639	0.0399	0.0006	0.0059	4
SPBLP	8.3807	6.0249	0.0004	0.3992	0.0924	0.0089	0.0128	4
PSEI	10.6868	8.8164	0.0015	0.428	0.1153	0.0145	0.0169	1
WIG	15.5141	23.3888	0.0167	0.5194	0.1627	0.0325	0.0216	4
PSI	14.4183	16.473	0.0049	0.5095	0.1533	0.0252	0.0211	1
QSI	18.4879	30.8259	0.0361	0.5403	0.186	0.0365	0.0225	0
BET	8.5272	3.4532	0.001	0.4084	0.0965	0.0054	0.0137	7
MOEX	8.8544	10.1848	0.0029	0.4084	0.0987	0.0163	0.0141	1
RTS	16.24	26.862	0.011	0.5296	0.1648	0.0355	0.0219	4
ALSIR	7.0304	0.0	0.0	0.437	0.0804	−0.0	0.0105	0
TASI	16.2957	33.8727	0.0757	0.5245	0.1608	0.0394	0.0206	0
BELEX	10.924	1.9507	0.0004	0.4692	0.1228	0.0036	0.0169	4
STI	12.8033	3.7623	0.0032	0.4421	0.1354	0.0056	0.0193	1
SAX	0.0	0.0	0.0	0.0	−0.0	−0.0	−0.0	14
SBI	0.8238	0.3654	0.0	0.3767	0.0125	0.0008	0.0015	0
JTOP	14.6537	16.548	0.0045	0.5144	0.1538	0.0251	0.0205	1
KOSPI	1.168	0.3592	0.0	0.3496	0.0153	0.0005	0.0024	0
IBEX	2.7436	1.4551	0.0	0.4022	0.035	0.0029	0.0049	0
SMI	12.5616	4.4304	0.004	0.4953	0.1344	0.0072	0.0185	1
TWII	1.0924	0.4005	0.0	0.3407	0.0136	0.0006	0.002	0
DSEI	0.0	0.0	0.0	0.0	−0.0	−0.0	−0.0	15
SET	5.8145	2.7128	0.0018	0.4212	0.0703	0.0047	0.0103	4
TUN	16.745	14.1081	0.0103	0.5296	0.1738	0.0216	0.0231	1
BIST	12.4131	1.9188	0.0032	0.4863	0.1349	0.0036	0.0181	1
ALSIU	0.0	0.0	0.0	0.0	−0.0	−0.0	−0.0	8
FTSE	2.9093	3.9813	0.0	0.3963	0.0395	0.0065	0.0056	1
DJI	17.5089	23.4561	0.0101	0.5403	0.1812	0.0322	0.0231	4
NDX	18.5381	27.9864	0.0115	0.5515	0.189	0.0365	0.0236	0
SPX	17.2169	25.8294	0.0083	0.5296	0.1799	0.0346	0.0233	1
IBC	0.7237	0.0	0.0	0.3337	0.0092	−0.0	0.0015	0
HNX	14.9999	4.6347	0.0027	0.5194	0.1613	0.0077	0.0212	1
LASIL	0.0	0.0	0.0	0.0	0.0	−0.0	0.0	2
ZSE	0.5253	0.8521	0.0	0.3147	0.0062	0.0011	0.0012	0

Table A3. Statistics for network metrics for $\alpha_X = 0.2$ and $\alpha_Y = 0.8$.

Ticker	In-Degree	Out-Degree	Betweenness Centrality	Closeness Centrality	Eigenvector Centrality	Hub Score	Authority Score	Community
MERV	23.8295	18.6349	0.0068	0.8952	0.1158	0.0103	0.0129	0
AXJO	24.3806	25.8833	0.0003	0.8859	0.1184	0.0139	0.0131	0
ATX	17.0479	16.9105	0.0042	0.8257	0.0845	0.0093	0.0095	0
BAX	15.4132	16.0068	0.0129	0.8100	0.0747	0.0086	0.0083	1
DSE	23.1006	19.8225	0.0132	0.8952	0.1091	0.0105	0.0120	2
BFX	24.8951	25.5712	0.0027	0.9145	0.1198	0.0137	0.0133	0
BIRS	16.6482	8.8760	0.0043	0.8100	0.0826	0.0052	0.0092	0
BSE	6.0455	1.2635	0.0273	0.6208	0.0319	0.0007	0.0037	3
IBOV	28.5089	29.3099	0.0000	0.9145	0.1367	0.0157	0.0151	0
SOFIX	17.5008	12.0576	0.0083	0.8504	0.0853	0.0069	0.0095	2
TSX	27.0397	30.1651	0.0010	0.9244	0.1285	0.0160	0.0140	2
CLX	26.3866	31.7186	0.0008	0.9244	0.1269	0.0169	0.0140	0
CSI	14.5787	12.5741	0.0040	0.7802	0.0727	0.0072	0.0082	1
SSEC	18.3879	14.6345	0.0093	0.8420	0.0902	0.0080	0.0100	1
SZSE	18.9051	16.3741	0.0029	0.8420	0.0925	0.0090	0.0103	1
COLCAP	23.5117	26.7148	0.0001	0.8952	0.1141	0.0142	0.0126	0
BRVM	20.9988	17.0516	0.0036	0.8768	0.1021	0.0093	0.0114	0
CROBEX	22.6515	25.9519	0.0010	0.8768	0.1096	0.0138	0.0121	2
CYMAIN	18.8448	11.0165	0.0041	0.8590	0.0919	0.0063	0.0102	1
PX	19.5903	19.2708	0.0047	0.8859	0.0950	0.0104	0.0105	0
OMX	22.3633	23.8123	0.0015	0.8768	0.1092	0.0127	0.0122	0
EGX	22.2931	24.2948	0.0005	0.8952	0.1068	0.0128	0.0117	1
GTGI	16.9752	16.3356	0.0061	0.8177	0.0842	0.0089	0.0094	0
OMXH	25.3316	32.6319	0.0000	0.8952	0.1223	0.0174	0.0135	0
CAC	22.5260	28.8532	0.0006	0.8952	0.1091	0.0154	0.0120	0
DAX	22.6741	28.4560	0.0019	0.8768	0.1103	0.0152	0.0123	0
EUSTOXX	23.2623	29.3283	0.0000	0.8859	0.1129	0.0157	0.0126	0
ATG	18.5806	13.9281	0.0018	0.8257	0.0919	0.0078	0.0103	1
HSI	27.0638	30.6681	0.0005	0.9244	0.1293	0.0162	0.0142	0
BUX	26.7524	33.1685	0.0003	0.9047	0.1287	0.0177	0.0142	0
ICEX	23.2367	19.3588	0.0000	0.8590	0.1137	0.0105	0.0126	2
BSESN	8.3664	6.8252	0.0756	0.6492	0.0431	0.0040	0.0051	0
NIMI	10.8230	9.0531	0.0446	0.7147	0.0549	0.0052	0.0064	0
JKSE	26.5356	31.3516	0.0006	0.9145	0.1250	0.0164	0.0138	0
ISX	38.3405	29.7842	0.0001	0.9449	0.1765	0.0154	0.0191	1
ISEQ	23.6559	27.3308	0.0001	0.8952	0.1148	0.0147	0.0127	0
TA	26.9692	31.2581	0.0004	0.9346	0.1277	0.0163	0.0139	0
JSE	8.0761	0.6630	0.0038	0.6542	0.0429	0.0005	0.0049	0
AMGNL	29.3595	28.3843	0.0008	0.9346	0.1387	0.0150	0.0152	1
KASE	18.6595	20.7578	0.0063	0.8177	0.0925	0.0112	0.0104	2
BKM	24.8752	28.1414	0.0010	0.9145	0.1183	0.0149	0.0130	0
RGI	4.6282	0.4645	0.0075	0.5785	0.0241	0.0003	0.0029	0
BLOM	18.9803	17.8871	0.0006	0.8338	0.0936	0.0098	0.0104	1
VGI	15.1949	11.6532	0.0086	0.8177	0.0750	0.0067	0.0084	1
KLCI	14.6070	12.1323	0.0050	0.7802	0.0726	0.0068	0.0082	2
MSE	22.8991	19.6641	0.0000	0.8859	0.1112	0.0107	0.0124	1
MDEX	10.7759	12.1072	0.0202	0.6914	0.0566	0.0069	0.0065	1
BIVA	16.8320	15.4533	0.0046	0.8420	0.0825	0.0086	0.0092	1
MNE	24.9818	26.4698	0.0000	0.9047	0.1208	0.0144	0.0134	1
MASI	16.9303	12.5954	0.0003	0.8177	0.0835	0.0072	0.0094	1
NSX	28.1939	26.8855	0.0000	0.9047	0.1362	0.0143	0.0151	1
AEX	24.2422	31.1113	0.0003	0.8952	0.1176	0.0165	0.0130	0
NZX	24.4019	29.5698	0.0009	0.9145	0.1173	0.0157	0.0129	0
NSE	11.8019	3.5563	0.0171	0.7460	0.0598	0.0022	0.0068	1
OSEBX	22.6118	27.1882	0.0015	0.8768	0.1104	0.0145	0.0122	0
MSM	26.6253	24.9912	0.0008	0.9244	0.1257	0.0131	0.0138	1
KSE	19.4036	17.6855	0.0006	0.8504	0.0949	0.0096	0.0106	1
PLE	20.8457	17.5363	0.0027	0.8768	0.1003	0.0094	0.0111	1
SPBLP	23.3353	20.9547	0.0009	0.8859	0.1132	0.0116	0.0126	1

Table A3. *Cont.*

Ticker	In-Degree	Out-Degree	Betweenness Centrality	Closeness Centrality	Eigenvector Centrality	Hub Score	Authority Score	Community
PSEI	24.1724	26.6070	0.0000	0.9047	0.1158	0.0141	0.0128	1
WIG	27.4338	32.9013	0.0000	0.9244	0.1316	0.0175	0.0145	1
PSI	26.4879	29.3845	0.0000	0.9047	0.1278	0.0156	0.0142	0
QSI	29.9479	37.5390	0.0000	0.9346	0.1411	0.0197	0.0154	1
BET	21.8471	23.1030	0.0022	0.8590	0.1065	0.0123	0.0119	2
MOEX	22.9358	26.1512	0.0023	0.9047	0.1106	0.0140	0.0122	0
RTS	26.9176	34.8737	0.0004	0.9047	0.1300	0.0184	0.0144	0
ALSIR	22.9470	13.9863	0.0282	0.9145	0.1083	0.0076	0.0119	3
TASI	28.2805	40.0989	0.0001	0.9449	0.1316	0.0207	0.0143	3
BELEX	24.7237	21.7411	0.0010	0.9244	0.1189	0.0118	0.0131	1
STI	25.1383	22.0872	0.0011	0.9047	0.1214	0.0120	0.0135	2
SAX	11.7874	4.2767	0.0262	0.7331	0.0602	0.0026	0.0068	0
SBI	15.4441	12.5252	0.0005	0.7593	0.0784	0.0072	0.0089	1
JTOP	26.1592	30.2878	0.0001	0.8952	0.1268	0.0162	0.0140	1
KOSPI	16.6713	12.6579	0.0005	0.7802	0.0839	0.0071	0.0095	2
IBEX	18.2839	21.6307	0.0000	0.8338	0.0904	0.0118	0.0101	1
SMI	25.1071	23.6310	0.0003	0.9047	0.1211	0.0128	0.0134	1
TWII	15.5837	15.6717	0.0014	0.7731	0.0780	0.0087	0.0088	2
DSEI	3.4073	2.6879	0.0014	0.5383	0.0180	0.0016	0.0020	3
SET	22.6547	23.0778	0.0091	0.9047	0.1079	0.0123	0.0120	3
TUN	27.9888	27.6161	0.0003	0.9145	0.1346	0.0147	0.0149	1
BIST	24.4326	21.0539	0.0043	0.9047	0.1185	0.0114	0.0131	1
ALSIU	0.0000	0.0000	0.0000	0.0000	0.0000	0.0000	0.0000	4
FTSE	19.3573	22.5602	0.0018	0.8590	0.0952	0.0122	0.0106	0
DJI	27.5570	32.4339	0.0000	0.9047	0.1333	0.0172	0.0147	2
NDX	28.4418	35.7458	0.0111	0.9145	0.1368	0.0190	0.0151	1
SPX	28.2888	34.3217	0.0000	0.9047	0.1370	0.0182	0.0151	2
IBC	13.9045	2.7609	0.0194	0.7731	0.0701	0.0017	0.0079	0
HNX	26.0851	23.6499	0.0001	0.8952	0.1264	0.0126	0.0140	1
LASIL	3.0893	0.0000	0.0000	0.5507	0.0163	0.0000	0.0020	2
ZSE	1.3142	1.5052	0.0000	0.4944	0.0068	0.0009	0.0008	3

Table A4. Statistics for network metrics for $\alpha_X = 0.5$ and $\alpha_Y = 0.5$.

Ticker	In-Degree	Out-Degree	Betweenness Centrality	Closeness Centrality	Eigenvector Centrality	Hub Score	Authority Score	Community
MERV	21.6735	20.7377	0.0006	0.8879	0.1103	0.0118	0.0122	0
AXJO	22.9346	27.5025	0.0013	0.8879	0.1166	0.0155	0.0129	0
ATX	16.4016	11.7403	0.0033	0.8366	0.0850	0.0069	0.0095	1
BAX	16.3661	12.7732	0.0158	0.8287	0.0831	0.0073	0.0092	1
DSE	22.5531	21.4600	0.0037	0.8970	0.1119	0.0117	0.0123	2
BFX	23.4140	26.3327	0.0009	0.9159	0.1175	0.0146	0.0129	0
BIRS	13.6940	12.7055	0.0024	0.7700	0.0722	0.0075	0.0081	0
BSE	7.5355	1.1379	0.0212	0.6693	0.0409	0.0007	0.0047	0
IBOV	26.1214	30.5404	0.0000	0.8970	0.1321	0.0170	0.0145	0
SOFIX	16.7869	12.5655	0.0008	0.8209	0.0870	0.0075	0.0097	0
TSX	26.7951	28.7579	0.0015	0.9257	0.1327	0.0158	0.0145	0
CLX	24.6730	30.7325	0.0000	0.9064	0.1244	0.0171	0.0137	0
CSI	13.7904	9.9006	0.0149	0.7839	0.0722	0.0060	0.0081	1
SSEC	16.1219	13.3008	0.0019	0.8132	0.0837	0.0079	0.0093	0
SZSE	17.2624	15.0638	0.0057	0.8209	0.0894	0.0088	0.0099	1
COLCAP	23.2209	23.5068	0.0086	0.8879	0.1173	0.0131	0.0129	1
BRVM	19.5480	17.7083	0.0008	0.8701	0.0998	0.0101	0.0111	0
CROBEX	22.9962	24.7361	0.0010	0.8789	0.1160	0.0138	0.0129	2
CYMAIN	16.5913	12.6208	0.0017	0.8209	0.0859	0.0074	0.0096	2
PX	18.9439	17.1518	0.0028	0.8789	0.0965	0.0098	0.0107	2
OMX	21.2751	22.5841	0.0017	0.8789	0.1083	0.0125	0.0120	0
EGX	22.6414	20.4729	0.0046	0.9159	0.1122	0.0114	0.0123	1

Table A4. *Cont.*

Ticker	In-Degree	Out-Degree	Betweenness Centrality	Closeness Centrality	Eigenvector Centrality	Hub Score	Authority Score	Community
GTGI	15.8833	13.8062	0.0010	0.8057	0.0831	0.0080	0.0093	0
OMXH	25.7057	29.4671	0.0026	0.9356	0.1280	0.0163	0.0140	0
CAC	20.9587	22.2982	0.0014	0.8701	0.1068	0.0124	0.0118	0
DAX	21.2860	21.7714	0.0029	0.8789	0.1076	0.0122	0.0119	0
EUSTOXX	21.9408	22.5068	0.0000	0.8789	0.1116	0.0127	0.0123	0
ATG	17.4546	15.4241	0.0031	0.8448	0.0902	0.0089	0.0100	1
HSI	26.3733	30.8581	0.0001	0.9257	0.1318	0.0170	0.0144	0
BUX	26.4539	30.3594	0.0004	0.9064	0.1332	0.0169	0.0146	0
ICEX	23.0480	21.8989	0.0008	0.8789	0.1178	0.0124	0.0130	2
BSESN	9.4030	1.9442	0.0295	0.6961	0.0512	0.0012	0.0059	0
NIMI	9.8285	4.5130	0.0465	0.6961	0.0528	0.0028	0.0061	0
JKSE	25.2926	26.9975	0.0010	0.9159	0.1256	0.0148	0.0139	0
ISX	35.9273	29.0853	0.0156	0.9356	0.1726	0.0157	0.0187	1
ISEQ	24.1730	25.2433	0.0005	0.9159	0.1213	0.0140	0.0133	0
TA	26.2469	28.3277	0.0006	0.9356	0.1299	0.0154	0.0142	0
JSE	4.7414	0.5214	0.0000	0.5840	0.0267	0.0004	0.0030	0
AMGNL	27.4758	33.6387	0.0009	0.9159	0.1365	0.0184	0.0150	0
KASE	17.4170	17.3906	0.0024	0.8132	0.0910	0.0100	0.0102	2
BKM	23.6437	25.0671	0.0006	0.8789	0.1192	0.0139	0.0132	2
RGI	7.3630	0.6471	0.0072	0.6542	0.0400	0.0004	0.0046	0
BLOM	18.7335	18.6220	0.0031	0.8366	0.0961	0.0106	0.0107	0
VGI	15.1833	11.5732	0.0028	0.8132	0.0788	0.0069	0.0088	2
KLCI	15.1369	11.0026	0.0064	0.7910	0.0790	0.0065	0.0088	2
MSE	20.9626	21.2340	0.0004	0.8615	0.1072	0.0119	0.0119	1
MDEX	12.6761	7.2901	0.0200	0.7633	0.0669	0.0045	0.0075	1
BIVA	17.4064	14.1787	0.0092	0.8615	0.0884	0.0081	0.0098	1
MNE	24.0804	26.5257	0.0010	0.8970	0.1220	0.0150	0.0134	2
MASI	16.3155	13.1314	0.0051	0.8531	0.0831	0.0077	0.0092	1
NSX	25.6518	29.3079	0.0003	0.9257	0.1285	0.0163	0.0141	0
AEX	23.9479	26.6351	0.0001	0.8879	0.1214	0.0149	0.0134	2
NZX	23.6362	26.9162	0.0001	0.8970	0.1193	0.0149	0.0131	0
NSE	8.8075	3.8400	0.0296	0.6798	0.0480	0.0025	0.0055	0
OSEBX	22.3079	23.0510	0.0001	0.8879	0.1131	0.0130	0.0125	0
MSM	24.8741	25.2123	0.0000	0.9257	0.1234	0.0140	0.0136	1
KSE	18.9906	17.2953	0.0026	0.8615	0.0972	0.0099	0.0108	1
PLE	20.0077	17.9505	0.0092	0.8701	0.1011	0.0100	0.0112	1
SPBLP	21.5167	23.0141	0.0022	0.8615	0.1105	0.0132	0.0123	1
PSEI	22.9957	24.3512	0.0006	0.8970	0.1162	0.0136	0.0128	1
WIG	25.7607	29.6647	0.0000	0.9159	0.1295	0.0164	0.0142	0
PSI	26.0657	31.9740	0.0000	0.8879	0.1324	0.0176	0.0146	0
QSI	29.9888	36.1823	0.0070	0.9458	0.1477	0.0198	0.0161	1
BET	20.6109	21.7552	0.0034	0.8701	0.1053	0.0121	0.0117	0
MOEX	22.1650	26.3390	0.0019	0.8879	0.1126	0.0147	0.0124	1
RTS	26.4990	34.6342	0.0000	0.9064	0.1337	0.0191	0.0147	0
ALSIR	21.4639	18.5364	0.0158	0.9064	0.1063	0.0102	0.0117	1
TASI	28.5983	32.3290	0.0001	0.9356	0.1395	0.0174	0.0153	1
BELEX	23.0769	25.0070	0.0006	0.8970	0.1165	0.0139	0.0129	2
STI	22.7062	25.2911	0.0001	0.8789	0.1157	0.0142	0.0128	0
SAX	11.8647	9.0764	0.0282	0.7374	0.0631	0.0054	0.0072	1
SBI	14.8968	12.9849	0.0010	0.7769	0.0788	0.0076	0.0089	2
JTOP	25.0044	29.7516	0.0000	0.8970	0.1260	0.0164	0.0139	0
KOSPI	15.0987	13.3327	0.0015	0.7910	0.0787	0.0078	0.0088	1
IBEX	18.2116	17.3332	0.0022	0.8448	0.0943	0.0100	0.0105	1
SMI	23.2862	25.8265	0.0010	0.8970	0.1181	0.0144	0.0130	1
TWII	15.4294	13.8413	0.0024	0.8057	0.0799	0.0081	0.0089	1
DSEI	4.4703	2.2263	0.0114	0.5724	0.0254	0.0014	0.0029	1
SET	21.2021	19.4900	0.0268	0.9064	0.1054	0.0109	0.0116	1
TUN	26.5900	33.2450	0.0000	0.9064	0.1339	0.0183	0.0147	0
BIST	21.2569	22.5329	0.0033	0.8879	0.1077	0.0125	0.0119	0

Table A4. *Cont.*

Ticker	In-Degree	Out-Degree	Betweenness Centrality	Closeness Centrality	Eigenvector Centrality	Hub Score	Authority Score	Community
ALSIU	0.2828	0.0000	0.0000	0.4972	0.0020	0.0000	0.0002	1
FTSE	18.5912	16.7423	0.0027	0.8531	0.0960	0.0096	0.0107	1
DJI	26.0533	30.8819	0.0061	0.9257	0.1303	0.0171	0.0143	2
NDX	27.3363	33.3818	0.0001	0.9159	0.1363	0.0184	0.0149	1
SPX	26.1169	31.2465	0.0059	0.9064	0.1310	0.0172	0.0144	2
IBC	11.2863	3.5411	0.0351	0.7312	0.0608	0.0023	0.0069	0
HNX	24.1829	25.3108	0.0001	0.8970	0.1225	0.0142	0.0135	1
LASIL	6.7435	0.4427	0.0103	0.6351	0.0355	0.0003	0.0041	0
ZSE	1.3203	1.5177	0.0000	0.4972	0.0071	0.0009	0.0008	1

Table A5. Statistics for network metrics for $\alpha_X = 0.8$ and $\alpha_Y = 0.2$.

Ticker	In-Degree	Out-Degree	Betweenness Centrality	Closeness Centrality	Eigenvector Centrality	Hub Score	Authority Score	Community
MERV	18.6612	23.3516	0.0001	0.8615	0.0957	0.0133	0.0106	0
AXJO	22.1005	26.6526	0.0000	0.8879	0.1128	0.0151	0.0125	0
ATX	18.6832	10.7440	0.0073	0.8789	0.0950	0.0065	0.0106	0
BAX	17.1719	11.5777	0.0222	0.8366	0.0870	0.0065	0.0097	1
DSE	19.3751	20.8355	0.0009	0.8531	0.0974	0.0116	0.0107	1
BFX	23.2025	25.0352	0.0004	0.8879	0.1175	0.0141	0.0131	0
BIRS	11.1751	16.2021	0.0026	0.7251	0.0602	0.0094	0.0069	0
BSE	7.8765	0.7155	0.0152	0.6745	0.0421	0.0004	0.0049	0
IBOV	24.6358	34.6936	0.0000	0.9064	0.1256	0.0193	0.0138	0
SOFIX	15.4019	12.5587	0.0005	0.8057	0.0803	0.0076	0.0091	0
TSX	26.7124	28.7383	0.0001	0.8970	0.1338	0.0160	0.0147	0
CLX	25.3397	31.5927	0.0005	0.8879	0.1282	0.0176	0.0142	0
CSI	14.8653	10.0084	0.0041	0.7983	0.0778	0.0060	0.0087	2
SSEC	15.7179	15.4824	0.0059	0.8366	0.0809	0.0090	0.0090	0
SZSE	16.7597	16.2066	0.0045	0.8366	0.0866	0.0095	0.0096	0
COLCAP	23.9271	21.6503	0.0038	0.9159	0.1202	0.0123	0.0132	2
BRVM	18.1098	19.1171	0.0040	0.8701	0.0924	0.0109	0.0103	0
CROBEX	22.0596	20.7987	0.0001	0.8789	0.1112	0.0117	0.0124	1
CYMAIN	15.2388	16.1282	0.0080	0.8209	0.0793	0.0092	0.0089	1
PX	19.0688	15.7232	0.0008	0.8531	0.0976	0.0090	0.0109	2
OMX	21.9815	20.3641	0.0013	0.9064	0.1112	0.0115	0.0123	2
EGX	23.9305	18.2895	0.0020	0.9159	0.1199	0.0103	0.0133	1
GTGI	16.8515	14.7779	0.0050	0.8448	0.0865	0.0086	0.0097	1
OMXH	26.2652	26.2371	0.0000	0.9257	0.1319	0.0148	0.0146	0
CAC	23.4533	19.7628	0.0005	0.9064	0.1186	0.0112	0.0132	0
DAX	25.1330	20.3829	0.0006	0.9159	0.1266	0.0116	0.0140	2
EUSTOXX	24.9512	21.5729	0.0000	0.9064	0.1258	0.0122	0.0140	2
ATG	16.6900	16.0348	0.0029	0.8366	0.0863	0.0093	0.0097	0
HSI	26.2052	29.2287	0.0001	0.9257	0.1316	0.0163	0.0144	0
BUX	26.9795	29.0310	0.0000	0.8970	0.1370	0.0163	0.0151	0
ICEX	19.8475	21.4374	0.0014	0.8615	0.1013	0.0122	0.0113	0
BSESN	11.7270	3.3227	0.0312	0.7566	0.0622	0.0020	0.0071	1
NIMI	14.3055	3.0713	0.0087	0.8057	0.0748	0.0020	0.0084	1
JKSE	24.9107	27.3915	0.0005	0.9257	0.1239	0.0150	0.0137	0
ISX	36.9148	26.5512	0.0000	0.9356	0.1787	0.0145	0.0193	2
ISEQ	24.2110	22.7804	0.0000	0.9159	0.1219	0.0130	0.0135	2
TA	27.0878	28.6748	0.0011	0.9356	0.1344	0.0157	0.0148	1
JSE	3.5677	0.7682	0.0020	0.5578	0.0206	0.0007	0.0023	2
AMGNL	24.5825	33.5486	0.0003	0.8970	0.1239	0.0182	0.0137	0
KASE	20.5240	17.5728	0.0023	0.8879	0.1046	0.0102	0.0117	2
BKM	24.7973	25.7911	0.0011	0.9064	0.1240	0.0143	0.0137	1
RGI	3.2620	0.7075	0.0074	0.5614	0.0183	0.0004	0.0022	0
BLOM	18.6328	18.0156	0.0011	0.8366	0.0959	0.0103	0.0108	0

Table A5. *Cont.*

Ticker	In-Degree	Out-Degree	Betweenness Centrality	Closeness Centrality	Eigenvector Centrality	Hub Score	Authority Score	Community
VGI	14.8793	8.6831	0.0020	0.7910	0.0782	0.0053	0.0088	1
KLCI	14.6003	9.2618	0.0086	0.7910	0.0764	0.0056	0.0086	1
MSE	19.5864	22.9519	0.0001	0.8615	0.1002	0.0130	0.0112	1
MDEX	15.3851	4.9760	0.0026	0.8287	0.0801	0.0032	0.0090	2
BIVA	17.6623	13.5996	0.0047	0.8448	0.0905	0.0078	0.0101	2
MNE	23.9616	26.6835	0.0005	0.9064	0.1216	0.0152	0.0134	1
MASI	14.9479	13.7375	0.0018	0.8057	0.0780	0.0080	0.0087	2
NSX	23.8434	31.6126	0.0001	0.9159	0.1204	0.0178	0.0133	0
AEX	25.5644	24.2483	0.0000	0.9064	0.1294	0.0137	0.0144	2
NZX	24.7918	25.4975	0.0008	0.9257	0.1245	0.0143	0.0137	2
NSE	9.1180	9.1315	0.0707	0.6851	0.0495	0.0055	0.0057	0
OSEBX	23.6326	21.6690	0.0000	0.8970	0.1195	0.0122	0.0133	2
MSM	23.4123	27.2367	0.0032	0.9257	0.1170	0.0149	0.0129	1
KSE	18.6413	18.9022	0.0013	0.8615	0.0959	0.0107	0.0107	2
PLE	18.3393	18.3542	0.0088	0.8531	0.0935	0.0102	0.0104	1
SPBLP	20.1372	24.1959	0.0046	0.8789	0.1033	0.0138	0.0115	1
PSEI	23.2643	23.3254	0.0001	0.8970	0.1176	0.0130	0.0131	2
WIG	26.8636	31.0710	0.0000	0.9159	0.1353	0.0174	0.0150	1
PSI	24.1806	30.0226	0.0015	0.9159	0.1227	0.0168	0.0135	2
QSI	29.3012	35.5651	0.0001	0.9356	0.1460	0.0195	0.0161	0
BET	21.0983	19.8760	0.0057	0.8970	0.1071	0.0113	0.0119	1
MOEX	22.3414	23.2429	0.0000	0.8970	0.1136	0.0133	0.0126	1
RTS	26.3703	32.0433	0.0000	0.9064	0.1338	0.0180	0.0148	1
ALSIR	18.1870	20.8303	0.0240	0.8531	0.0912	0.0114	0.0102	0
TASI	31.2671	31.7303	0.0128	0.9668	0.1517	0.0171	0.0167	0
BELEX	20.9821	24.3344	0.0050	0.8970	0.1067	0.0137	0.0119	1
STI	20.1113	27.2650	0.0034	0.8701	0.1031	0.0153	0.0114	1
SAX	9.7548	9.2577	0.0594	0.7191	0.0524	0.0055	0.0060	2
SBI	15.1354	12.2840	0.0024	0.7983	0.0796	0.0074	0.0089	1
JTOP	25.1785	28.0824	0.0000	0.8970	0.1271	0.0157	0.0141	0
KOSPI	15.0103	13.8115	0.0009	0.8132	0.0777	0.0081	0.0087	2
IBEX	20.9825	15.3125	0.0023	0.8879	0.1067	0.0089	0.0119	2
SMI	21.5195	24.3242	0.0014	0.8789	0.1100	0.0137	0.0123	2
TWII	17.2230	14.2784	0.0028	0.8366	0.0888	0.0083	0.0099	2
DSEI	4.6488	2.3972	0.0101	0.5724	0.0256	0.0015	0.0030	1
SET	22.2820	20.9120	0.0129	0.9064	0.1110	0.0117	0.0123	0
TUN	22.7374	32.8761	0.0006	0.8970	0.1153	0.0182	0.0127	2
BIST	20.1247	24.9178	0.0006	0.8879	0.1027	0.0140	0.0114	2
ALSIU	0.0000	0.0000	0.0000	0.0000	0.0000	0.0000	0.0000	3
FTSE	21.8447	16.7053	0.0026	0.8789	0.1116	0.0096	0.0125	2
DJI	26.5084	32.5869	0.0013	0.9159	0.1332	0.0180	0.0147	1
NDX	28.2602	32.8770	0.0043	0.9159	0.1419	0.0182	0.0157	2
SPX	27.3158	31.8164	0.0055	0.9159	0.1373	0.0177	0.0152	1
IBC	10.7163	6.0304	0.0456	0.7251	0.0575	0.0038	0.0065	1
HNX	22.4021	26.6955	0.0000	0.8970	0.1136	0.0151	0.0126	0
LASIL	1.9165	0.4327	0.0038	0.5306	0.0108	0.0003	0.0013	1
ZSE	1.2550	1.4076	0.0000	0.5030	0.0068	0.0009	0.0007	0

References

1. Ajayi-Nifise, A.O.; Olubusola, O.; Falaiye, T.; Mhlongo, N.Z.; Daraojimba, A.I. A review of US financial reporting scandals and their economic repercussions: Investigating their broader impact and preventative measures. *Financ. Account. Res. J.* **2024**, *6*, 183–201. [CrossRef]
2. Yang, S.; Ding, Y.; Xie, B.; Guo, Y.; Bai, X.; Qian, J.; Gao, Y.; Wang, W.; Ren, J. Advancing Financial Forecasts: A Deep Dive into Memory Attention and Long-Distance Loss in Stock Price Predictions. *Appl. Sci.* **2023**, *13*, 12160. [CrossRef]
3. Shiller, R.J. *Narrative Economics: How Stories Go Viral and Drive Major Economic Events*; Princeton University Press: Princeton, NJ, USA, 2020.

4. Arthur, W.B. Foundations of complexity economics. *Nat. Rev. Phys.* **2021**, *3*, 136–145. [CrossRef] [PubMed]
5. Chen, Y.; Härdle, W.K.; Pigorsch, U. Localized realized volatility modeling. *J. Am. Stat. Assoc.* **2010**, *105*, 1376–1393. [CrossRef]
6. Borup, D.; Jakobsen, J.S. Capturing volatility persistence: A dynamically complete realized EGARCH-MIDAS model. *Quant. Financ.* **2019**, *19*, 1839–1855. [CrossRef]
7. Mensi, W.; Tiwari, A.; Bouri, E.; Roubaud, D.; Al-Yahyaee, K.H. The dependence structure across oil, wheat, and corn: A wavelet-based copula approach using implied volatility indexes. *Energy Econ.* **2017**, *66*, 122–139. [CrossRef]
8. Zhang, R.; Xu, Q.; Wang, S.; Parkinson, S.; Schoeffmann, K. Information Difference of Transfer Entropies between Head Motion and Eye Movement Indicates a Proxy of Driving. *Entropy* **2023**, *26*, 3. [CrossRef] [PubMed]
9. Dong, Y.; Xu, L.; Zheng, J.; Wu, D.; Li, H.; Shao, Y.; Shi, G.; Fu, W. A Hybrid EEG-Based Stress State Classification Model Using Multi-Domain Transfer Entropy and PCANet. *Brain Sci.* **2024**, *14*, 595. [CrossRef] [PubMed]
10. Li, J.; Shang, P.; Zhang, X. Financial time series analysis based on fractional and multiscale permutation entropy. *Commun. Nonlinear Sci. Numer. Simul.* **2019**, *78*, 104880. [CrossRef]
11. Teng, Y.; Shang, P. Transfer entropy coefficient: Quantifying level of information flow between financial time series. *Phys. A Stat. Mech. Its Appl.* **2017**, *469*, 60–70. [CrossRef]
12. Balcı, M.A.; Batrancea, L.M.; Akgüller, Ö.; Nichita, A. Coarse graining on financial correlation networks. *Mathematics* **2022**, *10*, 2118. [CrossRef]
13. Zhou, T.; Ding, R.; Du, Y.; Zhang, Y.; Cheng, S.; Zhang, T. Study on the coupling coordination and spatial correlation effect of green finance and high-quality economic development—evidence from China. *Sustainability* **2022**, *14*, 3137. [CrossRef]
14. Tang, L.; Lu, B.; Tian, T. Spatial correlation network and regional differences for the development of digital economy in China. *Entropy* **2021**, *23*, 1575. [CrossRef] [PubMed]
15. Granger, C.W.; Joyeux, R. An introduction to long-memory time series models and fractional differencing. *J. Time Ser. Anal.* **1980**, *1*, 15–29. [CrossRef]
16. Shojaie, A.; Fox, E.B. Granger causality: A review and recent advances. *Annu. Rev. Stat. Its Appl.* **2022**, *9*, 289–319. [CrossRef] [PubMed]
17. Vicente, R.; Wibral, M.; Lindner, M.; Pipa, G. Transfer entropy—A model-free measure of effective connectivity for the neurosciences. *J. Comput. Neurosci.* **2011**, *30*, 45–67. [CrossRef] [PubMed]
18. Dimpfl, T.; Peter, F.J. Using transfer entropy to measure information flows between financial markets. *Stud. Nonlinear Dyn. Econom.* **2013**, *17*, 85–102. [CrossRef]
19. Smirnov, D.A. Spurious causalities with transfer entropy. *Phys. Rev. E-Nonlinear Soft Matter Phys.* **2013**, *87*, 042917. [CrossRef] [PubMed]
20. Sandoval, L., Jr. Structure of a global network of financial companies based on transfer entropy. *Entropy* **2014**, *16*, 4443–4482. [CrossRef]
21. Hu, C.; Guo, R. Research on Risk Contagion in ESG Industries: An Information Entropy-Based Network Approach. *Entropy* **2024**, *26*, 206. [CrossRef] [PubMed]
22. Ariely, D. Controlling the information flow: Effects on consumers' decision making and preferences. *J. Consum. Res.* **2000**, *27*, 233–248. [CrossRef]
23. Sun, J.; Xiang, J.; Dong, Y.; Wang, B.; Zhou, M.; Ma, J.; Niu, Y. Deep Learning for Epileptic Seizure Detection Using a Causal-Spatio-Temporal Model Based on Transfer Entropy. *Entropy* **2024**, *26*, 853. [CrossRef]
24. Falkowski, M.J.; Domański, P.D. Causality analysis with different probabilistic distributions using transfer entropy. *Appl. Sci.* **2023**, *13*, 5849. [CrossRef]
25. Podlubny, I. *Fractional Differential Equations: An Introduction to Fractional Derivatives, Fractional Differential Equations, to Methods of Their Solution and Some of Their Applications*; Elsevier: Amsterdam, The Netherlands, 1998.
26. Balcı, M.A.; Akgüller, Ö.; Batrancea, L.M.; Nichita, A. The Impact of Turkish Economic News on the Fractality of Borsa Istanbul: A Multidisciplinary Approach. *Fractal Fract.* **2023**, *8*, 32. [CrossRef]
27. Cheow, Y.H.; Ng, K.H.; Phang, C.; Ng, K.H. The application of fractional calculus in economic growth modelling: An approach based on regression analysis. *Heliyon* **2024**, *10*, e35379. [CrossRef]
28. Ali, I.; Khan, S.U. A dynamic competition analysis of stochastic fractional differential equation arising in finance via pseudospectral method. *Mathematics* **2023**, *11*, 1328. [CrossRef]
29. Qiu, L.; Yang, H. Transfer entropy calculation for short time sequences with application to stock markets. *Phys. A Stat. Mech. Its Appl.* **2020**, *559*, 125121. [CrossRef]
30. Zhou, W.; Huang, J.; Wang, M. Multifractal Characteristics and Information Flow Analysis of Stock Markets Based on Multifractal Detrended Cross-Correlation Analysis and Transfer Entropy. *Fractal Fract.* **2024**, *9*, 14. [CrossRef]
31. Caserini, N.A.; Pagnottoni, P. Effective transfer entropy to measure information flows in credit markets. *Stat. Methods Appl.* **2022**, *31*, 729–757. [CrossRef]

32. Kostoska, O.; Mitikj, S.; Jovanovski, P.; Kocarev, L. Core-periphery structure in sectoral international trade networks: A new approach to an old theory. *PLoS ONE* **2020**, *15*, e0229547. [CrossRef]
33. Bonetti, P.; Metelli, A.M.; Restelli, M. Causal feature selection via transfer entropy. In Proceedings of the 2024 International Joint Conference on Neural Networks (IJCNN), Yokohama, Japan, 30 June–5 July 2024; IEEE: Piscataway, NJ, USA, 2024; pp. 1–10.
34. Jizba, P.; Lavička, H.; Tabachová, Z. Causal inference in time series in terms of Rényi transfer entropy. *Entropy* **2022**, *24*, 855. [CrossRef] [PubMed]
35. Jizba, P.; Lavička, H.; Tabachová, Z. Rényi Transfer Entropy Estimators for Financial Time Series. *Eng. Proc.* **2021**, *5*, 33. [CrossRef]
36. Mester, A.; Pop, A.; Mursa, B.E.M.; Greblă, H.; Dioşan, L.; Chira, C. Network analysis based on important node selection and community detection. *Mathematics* **2021**, *9*, 2294. [CrossRef]
37. Trivedi, R.; Patra, S.; Sidqi, Y.; Bowler, B.; Zimmermann, F.; Deconinck, G.; Papaemmanouil, A.; Khadem, S. Community-based microgrids: Literature review and pathways to decarbonise the local electricity network. *Energies* **2022**, *15*, 918. [CrossRef]
38. Sánchez-Arrieta, N.; González, R.A.; Cañabate, A.; Sabate, F. Social capital on social networking sites: A social network perspective. *Sustainability* **2021**, *13*, 5147. [CrossRef]

fractal and fractional

Article

Information Properties of Consecutive Systems Using Fractional Generalized Cumulative Residual Entropy

Mohamed Kayid * and Mansour Shrahili

Department of Statistics and Operations Research, College of Science, King Saud University, P.O. Box 2455, Riyadh 11451, Saudi Arabia; msharahili@ksu.edu.sa
* Correspondence: drkayid@ksu.edu.sa

Abstract: We investigate some information properties of consecutive k-out-of-n:G systems in light of fractional generalized cumulative residual entropy. We firstly derive a formula to compute fractional generalized cumulative residual entropy related to the system's lifetime and explore its preservation properties in terms of established stochastic orders. Additionally, we obtain useful bounds. To aid practical applications, we propose two nonparametric estimators for the fractional generalized cumulative residual entropy in these systems. The efficiency and performance of these estimators are illustrated using simulated and real datasets.

Keywords: consecutive k-out-of-n:G systems; fractional generalized cumulative residual entropy; Shannon entropy; stochastic orders; real data

1. Introduction

Over the past three decades, extensive research has focused on consecutive k-out-of-n systems and their variations. These models have been applied to various engineering contexts, including telecom microwave stations, oil pipelines, vacuum systems in electron accelerators, computer networks, telecommunications, engineering, and integrated circuit design. A consecutive k-out-of-n system can be classified by the arrangement of its components as either linear or circular, and by its functioning principle as either a failure or a good system. A linear consecutive k-out-of-n:G system comprises n independent and identically distributed (i.i.d.) components arranged linearly and is operational if and only if at least k consecutive components are functioning. The consecutive n-out-of-n:G system, which requires all n components to function, is equivalent to a classical series system. In contrast, the 1-out-of-n:G system, which needs at least one operational component, gives a system with parallel structure. Both the consecutive n-out-of-n:G and 1-out-of-n:G systems have been extensively studied in the literature under various assumptions and analytical frameworks. Comprehensive reviews of previous work on the topic are available in Jung and Kim [1], Shen and Zuo [2], Kuo and Zuo [3], Chang et al. [4], Boland and Samaniego [5], and Eryılmaz [6,7], along with their citations.

The derivation of the distribution of the lifetimes of a linear consecutive k-out-of-n:G system is plain in the case where $2k \geq n$. This is because the survival function of the system's lifetime can be formulated in terms of the probability of the union of disjoint events. In this case, the lifetime of each component is represented by the nonnegative random variables $X_1, \ldots, X_n$ having a common probability density function (p.d.f.) $f(x)$, cumulative distribution function (c.d.f.) $F(x)$, and survival (reliability) function $S(x) = P(X > x)$. We denote the system's lifetime by $T_{k|n:G}$. When $2k \geq n$, Eryilmaz [8] showed that the reliability function of the consecutive k-out-of-n:G system can be expressed as

$$S_{k|n:G}(x) = (n-k+1)S^k(x) - (n-k)S^{k+1}(x), \; x > 0. \tag{1}$$

The concept of entropy is an important criterion for measuring the uncertainty of a random event. The Shannon differential entropy is defined by $H(X) = \mathbb{E}[-\log f(X)]$, where "log" means for the natural logarithm, with convention $0 \log 0 = 0$. Various attempts have been made to define possible alternative information measures. To this aim, Rao et al. [9] introduced the concept of the cumulative residual entropy (CRE) as follows:

$$\mathcal{E}(X) = -\int_0^{\infty} S(x) \log S(x) \mathrm{d}x = \int_0^{\infty} S(x) \Lambda(x) \mathrm{d}x, \tag{2}$$

where

$$\Lambda(x) = -\log S(x) = \int_0^{x} \eta(u) \mathrm{d}u, \ x > 0, \tag{3}$$

is the cumulative hazard function and $\eta(u) = f(u)/S(u),\ u > 0$, stands for the hazard rate function where $\eta(u)$ is defined for $u > 0$ such that $S(u) > 0$. In a recent development, Di Crescenzo et al. [10] presented the fractional generalized cumulative residual entropy (FGCRE) as follows:

$$\mathcal{E}_{\alpha}(X) = \frac{1}{\Gamma(\alpha+1)} \int_0^{\infty} S(x)[-\log S(x)]^{\alpha} \mathrm{d}x = \int_0^1 \frac{\psi_{\alpha}(u)}{f(F^{-1}(u))} du, \tag{4}$$

where

$$\psi_{\alpha}(u) = \frac{(1-u)(-\log(1-u))^{\alpha}}{\Gamma(\alpha+1)}, \ 0 \le u \le 1 \tag{5}$$

for all $\alpha \ge 0$, such that $F^{-1}(u) = \inf\{x; F(x) \ge u\}$ denotes the quantile function of $F(x)$. We recall that related results about the FCRE (as a special case of the FGCRE) can be seen in Xiong et al. [11], Alomani and Kayid [12], and Kayid and Shrahili [13]. It is worth noting that if α is a positive integer, it can easily be seen that (4) becomes the measure of generalized CRE established by Psarrakos and Navarro [14].

The study of information properties in reliability systems and order statistics has been explored by several researchers in the literature. For example, Wong and Chen [15] showed that the difference between the average entropy of order statistics and the entropy of data distribution is a constant. They also showed that for symmetric distributions, the entropy of order statistics is symmetric about the median. Ebrahimi et al. [16] explored some properties of the Shannon entropy of the order statistics and showed that the Kullback–Leibler information functions involving order statistics are distribution-free. Toomaj and Doostparatst [17] obtained an expression for the Shannon differential entropy of coherent and mixed systems using the concept of system signature. Moreover, Toomaj and Doostparatst [18] have shown that the Kullback–Leibler information functions involving the lifetime of mixed systems and order statistics as well as the parent distribution are distribution-free. Furthermore, Toomaj et al. [19] leveraged the concept of system signature to analyze the CRE properties of mixed systems. Similarly, Alomani and Kayid [12] employed system signatures to investigate the fractional CRE of coherent systems. For a broader exploration of uncertainty measures in reliability systems, readers can refer to [13,20,21], and the cited references therein. Motivated by the established body of research on information measures in reliability, this paper delves into the uncertainty properties of CRE specifically within the framework of consecutive k-out-of-n systems. By building upon this foundation, we aim to contribute to a deeper understanding of FGCRE properties within this particular system configuration.

This paper is structured as goes after. In Section 2, we introduce a representation of the FGCRE for consecutive k-out-of-n systems with lifetime $T_{k|n:G}$ from a sample drawn from any c.d.f. F. This representation is defined in terms of the FGCRE for consecutive k-out-of-n systems from a sample drawn from the uniform distribution. We then provide an in-depth analysis examining the preservation of stochastic ordering properties for this type of system. In the sequel part, we provide a number of bounds of the FGCRE of consecutive k-out-of-n systems. Several characterization results are achieved in Section 3. In Section 4, we present computational studies to validate and confirm the achieved outcomes. Specifically, we propose two nonparametric estimators for estimating the FGCRE of consecutive systems and demonstrate their application using both real and simulated data, emphasizing the potential practical value of these new estimators. In Section 5, the paper is concluded by presenting some essential points and, further, outlining some possible future investigations.

2. FGCRE of Consecutive k-out-of-n:G System

This section is organized into two key subsections. We first present a useful expression for the FGCRE of the lifetime of the consecutive k-out-of-n:G system. This analytical formulation serves as the foundation for the subsequent in-depth examination of the preservation of stochastic ordering properties inherent to this class of systems. In the second subsection, we establish and provide some useful bounds that offer remarkable utility in situations where the number of the components of the consecutive k-out-of-n:G systems is large.

2.1. Expression and Stochastic Orders

We now find an explicit expression for the FGCRE of the consecutive k-out-of-n:G system with lifetime $T_{k|n:G}$, where the component lifetimes have a common continuous c.d.f. F. To achieve this, we use the probability integral transformation $U_{k|n:G} = F(T_{k|n:G})$. It is known that the corresponding transformations of the system's components, denoted as $U_i = F(X_i)$ for $i = 1, \dots, n$, are independent and identically distributed (i.i.d.) random variables (r.v.s) that follow a uniform distribution on the interval $[0,1]$. Using Equation (1), when $2k \geq n$, the survival function of $U_{k|n:G}$ is given by

$$\overline{G}_{k|n:G}(u) = (n-k+1)(1-u)^k - (n-k)(1-u)^{k+1}, \tag{6}$$

for all $0 < u < 1$. We now give the next theorem.

Theorem 1. *For $2k \geq n$, the FGCRE of $T_{k|n:G}$, can be expressed as follows:*

$$\mathcal{E}_\alpha(T_{k|n:G}) = \int_0^1 \frac{\psi_\alpha(\overline{G}_{k|n:G}(u))}{f(F^{-1}(u))} du, \tag{7}$$

where $\psi_\alpha(x)$ and $\overline{G}_{k|n:G}(u)$ are defined in (5) *and* (6)*, respectively.*

Proof. Applying the transformation $u = F(x)$ and referring to (1) and (4), we obtain

$$\begin{aligned}
\mathcal{E}_\alpha(T_{k|n:G}) &= \frac{1}{\Gamma(\alpha+1)} \int_0^\infty S_{k|n:G}(x)[-\log S_{k|n:G}(x)]^\alpha dx \\
&= \int_0^\infty \psi_\alpha(S_{k|n:G}(x)) dx \\
&= \int_0^\infty \psi_\alpha((n-k+1)S^k(x) - (n-k)S^{k+1}(x)) dx \qquad (8) \\
&= \int_0^1 \frac{\psi_\alpha((n-k+1)(1-u)^k - (n-k)(1-u)^{k+1})}{f(F^{-1}(u))} du \\
&= \int_0^1 \frac{\psi_\alpha(\overline{G}_{k|n:G}(u))}{f(F^{-1}(u))} du, \qquad (9)
\end{aligned}$$

and this completes the proof. □

The following example demonstrates the application of Equation (7) in the consecutive k-out-of-n:G system.

Example 1. *Let us consider a linear consecutive 3-out-of-5:G system as shown in Figure 1 with a lifetime*

$$T_{3|5:G} = \max(\min(X_1, X_2, X_3), \min(X_2, X_3, X_4), \min(, X_3, X_4, X_5)),$$

As illustrated in Figure 1, this system can be regarded as a mixed system with shared components. This concept is explored further in Sections 5 and 6 of the works referenced in [22,23]. Assume further that the lifetimes of the components are i.i.d. following the common Lomax distribution, also known as the Pareto Type II distribution. The p.d.f. of the Lomax distribution is given by

$$f(x) = \frac{2}{\lambda}\left(1 + \frac{x}{\lambda}\right)^{-3}, \ x > 0, \tag{10}$$

where $\lambda > 0$ *denotes the scale parameters. It is clear that* $f(F^{-1}(u)) = \frac{2}{\lambda}(1-u)^{\frac{3}{2}}$ *for all* $0 < u < 1$*. Through algebraic manipulations and recalling (7), we can derive the following expression:*

$$\mathcal{E}_\alpha(T_{3|5:G}) = \frac{\lambda}{2}\int_0^1 \psi_\alpha(\overline{G}_{k|n:G}(u))(1-u)^{-\frac{3}{2}}du. \tag{11}$$

It is clear that the FGCRE is an increasing function of the scale parameter λ *for all* $\alpha \geq 0$*. This means that as the scale parameter* λ *increases, the system's uncertainty concerning the FGCRE increases. Therefore, this gives the significant impact of the Lomax distribution with the scale parameter* λ *on the FGCRE, and, thus, the uncertainty of the system lifetime.*

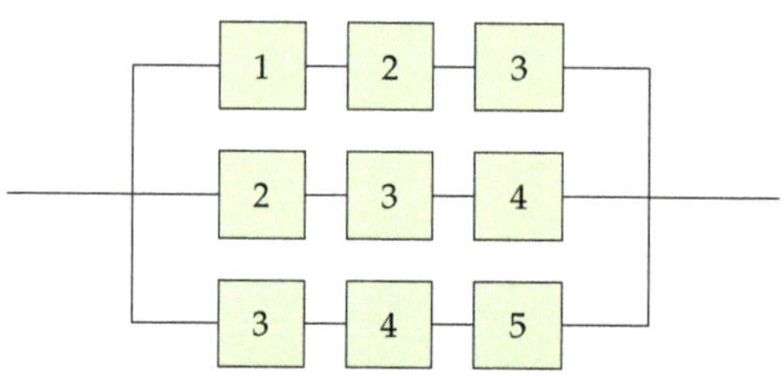

Figure 1. Figure of the linear consecutive 3-out-of-5:G system.

We now demonstrate that the FGCRE of the consecutive k-out-of-n:G systems is preserved under the dispersive and location-independent riskier orders. To begin with, let us review some stochastic orders and aging notion concepts. Hereafter, we denote the set of absolutely continuous nonnegative r.v.s with support $(0, \infty)$ as $\mathfrak{R}_+ = \{X; X \geq 0\}$.

Definition 1. *Let* $X, Y \in \mathfrak{R}_+$ *be r.v.s with pdfs* $f_X(x)$ *and* $f_Y(x)$*, cdfs* $F_X(x)$ *and* $F_Y(x)$*, survival functions* $S_X(x)$ *and* $S_Y(x)$ *and hazard rate orders* $\lambda_X(x) = f_X(x)/S_X(x)$ *and* $\lambda_Y(x) = f_Y(x)/S_Y(x)$*, respectively. Then, we say that*

1. *X has decreasing failure rate (DFR) if* $\lambda_X(x)$ *is decreasing in x;*
2. *X is smaller than Y in the hazard rate order (denoted by* $X \leq_{hr} Y$*) if* $\lambda_X(x) \geq \lambda_Y(x)$ *for all* $x > 0$*;*
3. *X is smaller than Y in the dispersive order (denoted by* $X \leq_d Y$*) if* $F_X^{-1}(v) - F_X^{-1}(u) \leq F_Y^{-1}(v) - F_Y^{-1}(u)$*, for all* $0 < u \leq v < 1$*;*
4. *X is smaller than Y in the location-independent riskier order (denoted by* $X \leq_{lir} Y$*) if* $\int_0^{F_X^{-1}(p)} F_X(x)dx \leq \int_0^{F_Y^{-1}(p)} F_Y(x)dx$*, for all* $p \in (0,1)$*;*

The dispersive $\leq_d$ order was initially explored by Bickel and Lehmann [24] in non-parametric statistics, while the $\leq_{lir}$ order was proposed by Jewitt [25] in expected utility theory and its applications in insurance. We recall that $X \leq_d Y$ is equivalent to

$$f_Y(F_Y^{-1}(v)) \leq f_X(F_X^{-1}(v)), \text{ for all } 0 < v < 1. \tag{12}$$

Additionally, the following implications are well recognized:

$$\text{if } X \leq_{hr} Y \text{ and either } X \text{ or } Y \text{ is DFR} \implies X \leq_d Y \Longrightarrow X \leq_{lir} Y. \tag{13}$$

Since $\psi_\alpha(x) \geq 0$ for all $0 \leq x \leq 1$ and $\alpha \geq 0$, relations (4) and (12) imply that $\mathcal{E}_\alpha(X) \leq \mathcal{E}_\alpha(Y)$ when $X \leq_d Y$. Consequently, from implication (13), we obtain the following corollary.

Corollary 1. *If $X \leq_{hr} Y$ and either X or Y is DFR, then $\mathcal{E}_\alpha(X) \leq \mathcal{E}_\alpha(Y)$ for all $\alpha \geq 0$.*

If Z is an r.v. with c.d.f. H, then the cumulative reversed hazard function is defined as

$$\eta_Z(z) = \int_0^z H(v)dv, \ z > 0. \tag{14}$$

Landsberger and Meilijson [26] showed that

$$X \leq_{lir} Y \Longleftrightarrow \eta_Y^{-1}(z) - \eta_X^{-1}(z) \text{ is increasing in } z > 0, \tag{15}$$

where $\eta^{-1}(z)$ denotes the left continuous version of $\eta(z)$. Here, we present a theorem demonstrating that the FGCRE of a series system with k components is lower than that of a consecutive k-out-of-n:G system, assuming both systems' components exhibit the DFR property.

Theorem 2. *For $2k \geq n$, let $T_{k|n:G}$ be the lifetime of consecutive k-out-of-n:G system having the common p.d.f. $f_X(x)$ and c.d.f. $F_X(x)$. If X is DFR, then $\mathcal{E}_\alpha(X_{1:k}) \leq \mathcal{E}_\alpha(T_{k|n:G})$ for all $\alpha \geq 0$.*

Proof. Since X is DFR, $X_{1:k}$ is also DFR. By applying Theorem 4.5 from Eryılmaz and Navarro [27], we have $X_{1:k} \leq_{hr} T_{k|n:G}$. Therefore, Corollary 1 completes the proof. □

The next theorem outlines the conditions for preserving the dispersive order in consecutive systems. The proof is omitted as it is deemed straightforward.

Theorem 3. *For $2k \geq n$, let $T^X_{k|n:G}$ and $T^Y_{k|n:G}$ be the lifetimes of two consecutive k-out-of-n:G systems having the common pdfs $f_X(x)$ and $f_Y(x)$ and cdfs $F_X(x)$ and $F_Y(x)$, respectively. If $X \leq_d Y$, then $\mathcal{E}_\alpha(T^X_{k|n:G}) \leq \mathcal{E}_\alpha(T^Y_{k|n:G})$ for all $\alpha \geq 0$.*

The following example illustrates the application of Theorem 3.

Example 2. *Consider two consecutive k-out-of-n:G systems with lifetimes $T^X_{k|n:G}$ and $T^Y_{k|n:G}$, respectively. The system $T^X_{k|n:G}$ has i.i.d. component lifetimes $X_1, X_2, \ldots, X_n$, which follow a Makeham distribution with the survival function $S(x) = e^{-x-a(x+e^{-x}-1)}$, where $x > 0$ and $a > 0$. Moreover, the system $T^Y_{k|n:G}$ has i.i.d. component lifetimes $Y_1, Y_2, \ldots, Y_n$ that follow an exponential distribution with the survival function $S_Y(x) = e^{-x}$, $x > 0$. It is clear that $\lambda_X(x) = 1 + a(1 - e^{-x})$ and $\lambda_Y(x) = 1$. Comparing the hazard rate functions shows that $\lambda_X(x) > \lambda_Y(x)$ for $a > 0$, indicating that $X \leq_{hr} Y$. Given that Y has the DFR property, relation (13) leads to $X \leq_d Y$. Consequently, by Corollary 3, we have $\mathcal{E}_\alpha(T^X_{k|n:G}) \leq \mathcal{E}_\alpha(T^Y_{k|n:G})$ for all $\alpha \geq 0$. This indicates that the uncertainty of the system with lifetime $T^X_{k|n:G}$ is less than or equal to that of the system with lifetime $T^Y_{k|n:G}$, according to the FGCRE measure.*

The next theorem outlines the conditions for preserving location-independent riskier orders in the formation of consecutive systems.

Theorem 4. *In the setting of Theorem 3, let* $\phi_{k|n}(t) = (n-k+1)(1-t)^k - (n-k)(1-t)^{k+1}$, $0 < t < 1$. *For* $2k \geq n$, *if* $X \leq_{lir} Y$ *and*

$$\frac{\psi_\alpha(\phi_{k|n}(t))}{t},\ 0 \leq t \leq 1, \tag{16}$$

is a decreasing function of t for all $\alpha \geq 0$, *then* $\mathcal{E}_\alpha(T^X_{k|n:G}) \leq \mathcal{E}_\alpha(T^Y_{k|n:G})$ *for all* $\alpha \geq 0$.

Proof. It is clear that Equation (1) can be represented as $S_{k|n:G}(x) = \phi_{k|n}(F(x))$. From (15), recalling (14), we derive

$$\frac{d}{dz}(\eta_Y^{-1}(z) - \eta_X^{-1}(z)) = \frac{1}{F_Y(\eta_Y^{-1}(z))} - \frac{1}{F_X(\eta_X^{-1}(z))} \geq 0,$$

which implies that

$$F_X(z) \geq F_Y(\eta_Y^{-1}(\eta_X(z))), \tag{17}$$

for all $z > 0$. From relations (1) and (4), we obtain

$$\begin{aligned}
\int_0^\infty \frac{S^X_{k|n:G}(x)[-\log S^X_{k|n:G}(x)]^\alpha}{\Gamma(\alpha+1)}dx &= \int_0^\infty \psi_\alpha(S^X_{k|n:G}(x))dx \\
&= \int_0^\infty \frac{\psi_\alpha(S^X_{k|n:G}(x))}{F_X(x)}F_X(x)\mathrm{d}x \\
&= \int_0^\infty \frac{\psi_\alpha(\phi_{k|n}(F_X(x)))}{F_X(x)}F_X(x)\mathrm{d}x \\
&\leq \int_0^\infty \frac{\psi_\alpha(\phi_{k|n}(F_Y(\eta_Y^{-1}(\eta_X(x)))))}{F_Y(\eta_Y^{-1}(\eta_X(x)))}F_X(x)\mathrm{d}x. \quad (18)
\end{aligned}$$

The inequality arises from Equation (17) and using the fact that $\psi_\alpha(\phi_{k|n}(t))/t$ is a decreasing function of $0 \leq t \leq 1$. Furthermore, by setting $u = \eta_Y^{-1}(\eta_X(x))$, we have

$$dx = \frac{F_Y(u)}{F_X(\eta_X^{-1}(\eta_Y(u)))}du.$$

Upon using this, the last term of (18) reduces to

$$\begin{aligned}
&\int_{\eta_Y^{-1}(\eta_X(0))}^\infty \frac{\psi_\alpha(\phi_{k|n}(F_Y(u)))}{F_Y(u)}\frac{F_X(\eta_X^{-1}(\eta_Y(u)))F_Y(u)}{F_X(\eta_X^{-1}(\eta_Y(u)))}\mathrm{d}u \\
= &\int_{\eta_Y^{-1}(\eta_X(0))}^\infty \psi_\alpha(\phi_{k|n}(F_Y(u)))\mathrm{d}u \\
= &\int_0^\infty \psi_\alpha(S^Y_{k|n:G}(x))dx \\
= &\int_0^\infty \frac{S^Y_{k|n:G}(x)[-\log S^Y_{k|n:G}(x)]^\alpha}{\Gamma(\alpha+1)}dx.
\end{aligned}$$

The final equality in the previous relation follows from the fact that $\eta_Y^{-1}(\eta_X(0)) = 0$, implying that $\mathcal{E}_\alpha(T^X_{k|n:G}) \leq \mathcal{E}_\alpha(T^Y_{k|n:G})$. Hence, the theorem. □

2.2. Some Bounds

Due to the absence of closed-form expressions for the FGCRE of consecutive systems across various distributions and with numerous components, it is essential to employ bounding techniques to estimate the FGCRE of the system's lifetime. Recognizing this challenge, we aim to explore the effectiveness of these bounds in characterizing the FGCRE of consecutive systems. The initial finding establishes a bound on the system's FGCRE based on the common FGCRE of its components.

Theorem 5. *For $2k \geq n$, the FGCRE of $T_{k|n:G}$ are bounded as follows:*

$$\mathfrak{B}_\alpha \mathcal{E}_\alpha(X_1) \leq \mathcal{E}_\alpha(T_{k|n:G}) \leq \mathfrak{D}_\alpha \mathcal{E}_\alpha(X_1),$$

where $\mathfrak{B}_\alpha = \inf_{u\in(0,1)} \frac{\psi_\alpha(\overline{G}_{k|n:G}(u))}{\psi_\alpha(u)}$, $\mathfrak{D}_\alpha = \sup_{u\in(0,1)} \frac{\psi_\alpha(\overline{G}_{k|n:G}(u))}{\psi_\alpha(u)}$.

Proof. The upper bound can be identified from (7) as follows:

$$\begin{aligned}\mathcal{E}_\alpha(T_{k|n:G}) &= \int_0^1 \frac{\psi_\alpha(\overline{G}_{k|n:G}(u))}{f(F^{-1}(u))}du = \int_0^1 \frac{\psi_\alpha(\overline{G}_{k|n:G}(u))}{\psi_\alpha(u)}\frac{\psi_\alpha(u)}{f(F^{-1}(u))}du \\ &\leq \sup_{u\in(0,1)} \frac{\psi_\alpha(\overline{G}_{k|n:G}(u))}{\psi_\alpha(u)} \int_0^1 \frac{\psi_\alpha(u)}{f(F^{-1}(u))}du = \mathfrak{D}_\alpha \mathcal{E}_\alpha(X_1).\end{aligned}$$

The lower bound can be similarly derived. □

The upcoming theorem introduces additional useful bounds based on the extremes of the p.d.f. and the function $\psi_\alpha(u)$.

Theorem 6. *Let $T_{k|n:G}$ be the lifetime of consecutive k-out-of-n:G system having the common pdfs $f_X(x)$ and c.d.f. $F_X(x)$. If S is the support of f, $m = \inf_{x\in S} f(x)$ and $M = \sup_{x\in S} f(x)$ such that $0 < m < M < 1$, then*

$$\frac{\mathcal{E}_\alpha(U_{k|n:G})}{M} \leq \mathcal{E}_\alpha(T_{k|n:G}) \leq \frac{\mathcal{E}_\alpha(U_{k|n:G})}{m}, \tag{19}$$

where $\mathcal{E}_\alpha(U_{k|n:G}) = \int_0^1 \psi_\alpha(\overline{G}_{k|n:G}(u))du$.

Proof. Since $0 < m \leq f(F^{-1}(u)) \leq M < 1,\ 0 < u < 1$, we have

$$\frac{1}{M}\int_0^1 \psi_\alpha(\overline{G}_{k|n:G}(u))du \leq \int_0^1 \frac{\psi_\alpha(\overline{G}_{k|n:G}(u))}{f(F^{-1}(u))}du \leq \frac{1}{m}\int_0^1 \psi_\alpha(\overline{G}_{k|n:G}(u))du.$$

Upon recalling Equation (7), we have the result. □

The term $\mathcal{E}_\alpha(U_{k|n:G})$ denotes the FGCRE of a consecutive k-out-of-n:G system with a uniform distribution on the interval $(0,1)$. The bounds in Equation (19) depend on the extremes of the p.d.f. f. If the lower bound m is zero, an upper bound does not exist. Conversely, if the upper bound M is infinite, a lower bound is absent. The following example illustrates the application of the bounds from Theorems 5 and 6 for a consecutive k-out-of-n:G system.

Example 3. *Consider a linear consecutive 6-out-of-10:G system. The system lifetime, denoted by $T_{6|10:G}$, is defined as the maximum of the minimum values within consecutive blocks of nine components. Specifically, $T_{6|10:G} = \max(X_{[1:6]}, X_{[2:7]}, \ldots, X_{[6:10]})$, where $X_{[j:r]} = \min(X_j, \ldots, X_r)$ for $1 \leq j < r \leq 10$. Assuming an exponential distribution with mean μ, it is easy to see that $m = 0$ and $M = 1/\mu$. Moreover, one can see that $\mathfrak{B}_\alpha = 0$ for all $\alpha \geq 0$. On the other hand, one* *can obtain* $\mathcal{E}_\alpha(X_1) = \mu$ *for all* $\alpha \geq 0$. *Through algebraic manipulations, we can derive the following expression:*

$$\mathcal{E}_\alpha(T_{6|10:G}) = \mu \int_0^1 \frac{\psi_\alpha(\overline{G}_{k|n:G}(u))}{(1-u)} du, \tag{20}$$

for all $\alpha \geq 0$. *It is not easy to come up with an exact expression for the value and given bounds, so we have to use numerical computations. In Table 1, we listed the values of these expressions. The bounds mentioned in Theorem 6 are important, easy, and useful for the application.*

Table 1. The exact value and bounds for $\mathcal{E}_\alpha(T_{6|10:G})$ for different choices of α.

α	$\mathcal{E}_\alpha(T_{6\|10:G})$	$\mathfrak{D}_\alpha \mathcal{E}_\alpha(X_1)$	$\mathcal{E}_\alpha(U_{6\|10:G})/M$
0.1	0.253790μ	1.0717μ	0.203247μ
0.2	0.246750μ	1.1486μ	0.193446μ
0.5	0.230447μ	1.4543μ	0.169647μ
0.8	0.219056μ	1.9115μ	0.151681μ
1.0	0.213247μ	2.3252μ	0.141883μ
1.5	0.202674μ	3.9250μ	0.122404μ
2.0	0.195588μ	6.8618μ	0.107592μ
2.5	0.190529μ	12.3063μ	0.095717μ
3.0	0.186745μ	22.5143μ	0.085853μ

3. Characterization Results

The aim of this section is to present some characterization results using the FGCRE properties of consecutive k-out-of-n:G systems. To start, we need the following lemma which is a direct corollary of the Stone–Weierstrass Theorem (see Aliprantis and Burkinshaw [28]). The given lemma will be used to prove the main results in this subsection.

Lemma 1. *If* ζ *is a continuous function on* $[0,1]$ *such that* $\int_0^1 x^n \zeta(x)dx = 0$ *for all* $n \geq 0$, *then* $\zeta(x) = 0$ *for any* $x \in [0,1]$.

Building upon this foundational result, we can establish that the parent distribution of a lifetime r.v. can be uniquely characterized by the FGCRE of $T_{k|n:G}$, where $\{k_j\}_{j\geq 1}$ is a strictly increasing sequence of positive integers.

Theorem 7. *Let* $T^X_{k|n:G}$ *and* $T^Y_{k|n:G}$ *be lifetimes of two consecutive k-out-of-n:G systems having the common pdfs* $f_X(x)$ *and* $f_Y(x)$ *and cdfs* $F_X(x)$ *and* $F_Y(x)$, *respectively. Then* $F_X(x)$ *and* $F_Y(x)$ *are members of one family of distributions if, and only if, for a fixed n,*

$$\mathcal{E}_\alpha(T^X_{k|n:G}) = \mathcal{E}_\alpha(T^Y_{k|n:G}), \tag{21}$$

for all $2k \geq n$.

Proof. The necessity is trivial; therefore, we need to prove the sufficiency part. First, note that Equation (7) can be rewritten as follows:

$$\begin{aligned}
\mathcal{E}_\alpha(T^X_{k|n:G}) &= \int_0^1 \frac{\psi_\alpha(\overline{G}_{k|n:G}(u))}{f_X(F_X^{-1}(u))} du \\
&= -\int_0^1 (1-u)^{2k-n} \frac{(1-u)^{n-k}((n-k+1)-(n-k)(1-u))\log(\overline{G}_{k|n:G}(u))}{f_X(F_X^{-1}(u))} du \\
&= \int_0^1 z^{2k-n} \frac{\Omega(z)}{f_X(F_X^{-1}(1-z))} dz, \text{ (taking } z = 1-u) \qquad (22)
\end{aligned}$$

where

$$\Omega(z) = -z^{n-k}((n-k+1)-(n-k)z)\log(\overline{G}_{k|n:G}(z)), \qquad (23)$$

such that $\Omega(z) \neq 0$ for all $0 < z < 1$. A similar argument holds for $\mathcal{E}_\alpha(T^Y_{k|n:G})$. From (22), we have

$$\int_0^1 \left[\frac{1}{f_X(F_X^{-1}(1-z))} - \frac{1}{f_Y(F_Y^{-1}(1-z))} \right] z^k \Omega(z) dz = 0.$$

According to Lemma 1, we can conclude that

$$f_X(F_X^{-1}(1-z)) = f_Y(F_Y^{-1}(1-z)), \quad a.e. \quad z \in (0,1),$$

or, equivalently, $f_X(F_X^{-1}(v)) = f_Y(F_Y^{-1}(v))$, $0 < v < 1$. So, it follows that $F_X^{-1}(v) = F_Y^{-1}(v) + d$, where d is a constant. By noting that $\lim_{v \to 0} F_X^{-1}(v) = \lim_{v \to 0} F_Y^{-1}(v) = 0$ for all $v \in (0,1)$, we have $F_X^{-1}(v) = F_Y^{-1}(v)$. This relationship implies that F_X and F_Y are members of one family of distributions. □

Since a consecutive n-out-of-n:G system is a series system (as mentioned before), the next corollary details its characteristics.

Corollary 2. *Under the conditions of Theorem 7, F_X and F_Y are members of one family of distributions if, and only if,*

$$\mathcal{E}_\alpha(T^X_{n|n:G}) = \mathcal{E}_\alpha(T^Y_{n|n:G}),$$

for all $n \geq 1$.

A further characterization is established in the following theorem.

Theorem 8. *In the setting of Theorem 7, F_X and F_Y are members of one family of distributions with a change in the scale if, and only if, for a fixed n,*

$$\frac{\mathcal{E}_\alpha(T^X_{k|n:G})}{\mathcal{E}_\alpha(X)} = \frac{\mathcal{E}_\alpha(T^Y_{k|n:G})}{\mathcal{E}_\alpha(Y)}, \qquad (24)$$

for all $2k \geq n$.

Proof. The necessity is trivial; hence, it remains to prove the sufficiency part. From (22), we can write

$$\frac{\mathcal{E}_\alpha(T^X_{k|n:G})}{\mathcal{E}_\alpha(X)} = \int_0^1 z^{2k-n} \frac{\Omega(z)}{\mathcal{E}_\alpha(X) f_X(F_X^{-1}(1-z))} dz. \qquad (25)$$

A similar argument can be obtained for $\mathcal{E}_\alpha(T^Y_{k|n:G})/\mathcal{E}_\alpha(Y)$. From (24) and (25), we obtain

$$\int_0^1 z^{2k-n} \frac{\Omega(z)}{\mathcal{E}_\alpha(X) f_X(F_X^{-1}(1-z))} dz = \int_0^1 z^{2k-n} \frac{\Omega(z)}{\mathcal{E}_\alpha(Y) f_Y(F_Y^{-1}(1-z))} dz, \qquad (26)$$

where $\Omega(z)$ is defined in (23) such that $\Omega(z) \neq 0$ for all $0 < z < 1$. Let us set $c = \mathcal{E}_\alpha(Y)/\mathcal{E}_\alpha(X)$. Then, (26) can be expressed as

$$\int_0^1 \left[\frac{1}{f_X(F_X^{-1}(1-z))} - \frac{1}{cf_Y(F_Y^{-1}(1-z))}\right] z^{2k-n}\Omega(z)dz = 0.$$

Now, by using similar arguments to Theorem 7, we can complete the proof of the theorem. □

Using Theorem 8, we obtain the following corollary.

Corollary 3. *Under the assumptions given in Theorem 8, F_X and F_Y are members of one family of distributions with a change in the scale if, and only if,*

$$\frac{\mathcal{E}_\alpha(T^X_{n|n:G})}{\mathcal{E}_\alpha(X)} = \frac{\mathcal{E}_\alpha(T^Y_{n|n:G})}{\mathcal{E}_\alpha(Y)},$$

for all $n \geq 1$.

4. Nonparametric Estimation

Hereafter, we present two nonparametric estimators of the FGCRE of consecutive k-out-of-n:G systems. To achieve this, let us consider a sequence of absolutely continuous, nonnegative, i.i.d. r.v.s $X_1, X_2, \ldots, X_N$, where $X_{1:N} \leq X_{2:N} \leq \cdots \leq X_{N:N}$ denote their order statistics. By recalling (7), the FGCRE of $T_{k|n:G}$ can be rewritten as

$$\begin{aligned}\mathcal{E}_\alpha(T_{k|n:G}) &= \int_0^1 \frac{\psi_\alpha(\overline{G}_{k|n:G}(u))}{f(F^{-1}(u))}du = \int_0^1 \psi_\alpha(\overline{G}_{k|n:G}(u))\left[\frac{dF^{-1}(u)}{du}\right]du \\ &= \int_0^1 \psi_\alpha((n-k+1)(1-u)^k - (n-k)(1-u)^{k+1})\left[\frac{dF^{-1}(u)}{du}\right]du, \quad (27)\end{aligned}$$

which holds for $2k \geq n$. Based on (27), we estimate the FGCRE $\mathcal{E}_\alpha(T_{k|n:G})$. This approach uses derivative estimates of the inverse distribution function at the sample points. Following Vasicek [29], we estimate the derivative $\frac{dF^{-1}(u)}{du}$ by approximating it as the slope, defined as

$$\frac{dF^{-1}(u)}{du} = \frac{N(X_{i+m:N} - X_{i-m:N})}{2m},$$

where $X_{i:N} = X_{1:N}$ for $i < 1$ and $X_{i:N} = X_{N:N}$ for $i > N$. In this case, N is the sample size and m is a positive integer referred to as the window size, satisfying $m \leq N/2$. This allows us to obtain the first estimator for $\mathcal{E}_\alpha(T_{k|n:G})$ given by

$$\begin{aligned}\widehat{\mathcal{E}}_{\alpha,1}(T_{k|n:G}) &= \frac{1}{N}\sum_{i=1}^N \psi_\alpha\left(\overline{G}_{k|n:G}\left(\frac{i}{N+1}\right)\right)\left(\frac{N(X_{i+m:N} - X_{i-m:N})}{2m}\right) \\ &= \frac{1}{N}\sum_{i=1}^N \psi_\alpha\left((n-k+1)\left(1-\frac{i}{N+1}\right)^k - (n-k)\left(1-\frac{i}{N+1}\right)^{k+1}\right) \\ &\times \left(\frac{N(X_{i+m:N} - X_{i-m:N})}{2m}\right), \quad (28)\end{aligned}$$

for all $2k \geq n$ and $\alpha \geq 0$. We now introduce the second estimator based on the empirical survival function for the sample corresponding to $S(x)$ as

$$S_N(x) = \sum_{i=1}^{N-1} \frac{N-i}{N} I_{[X_{i:N}, x_{(i+1)}]}, \; x \geq 0,$$

where $I_A(x) = 1$ if $x \in A$. Upon recalling (8), the empirical FGCRE estimator for the consecutive k-out-of-n:G system can be obtained as

$$\begin{aligned} \widehat{\mathcal{E}}_{\alpha,2}(T_{k|n:G}) &= \int_0^\infty \psi_\alpha((n-k+1)S_N^k(x) - (n-k)S_N^{k+1}(x))dx \\ &= \sum_{i=1}^{N-1} \int_{X_{i:N}}^{X_{(i+1)}} \psi_\alpha((n-k+1)S_N^k(x) - (n-k)S_N^{k+1}(x))dx \\ &= \sum_{i=1}^{N-1} \psi_\alpha\left((n-k+1)\left(\frac{N-i}{N}\right)^k - (n-k)\left(\frac{N-i}{N}\right)^{k+1}\right)D_{i+1}, \quad (29) \end{aligned}$$

where $D_{i+1} = X_{i+1:N} - X_{i:N}$, $i = 1, 2, \ldots, N-1$, denotes the sample spacings.

To evaluate the performance of the proposed estimators $\widehat{\mathcal{E}}_{\alpha,1}(T_{k|n:G})$ and $\widehat{\mathcal{E}}_{\alpha,2}(T_{k|n:G})$, we conduct a simulation study with exponential data. We assess the average bias and root mean square error (RMSE) for sample sizes of $N = 20, 30, 40, 50, and 100$ and various values of k and n.

To assess the performance of the proposed estimators $\widehat{\mathcal{E}}_{\alpha,1}(T_{k|n:G})$ and $\widehat{\mathcal{E}}_{\alpha,2}(T_{k|n:G})$, we perform a simulation study by employing exponential data. We evaluate the average bias and root mean square error (RMSE) of both estimators for different sample sizes ($N = 20, 30, 40, 50, 100$), various values of k and n, and α. To specify the value of the smoothing parameter m for a given sample size N, we use the heuristic formula $m = [\sqrt{N} + 0.5]$, where $[x]$ denotes the integer part of x. The simulation involves 5000 iterations, and the results are presented in Tables 2–7. After analyzing the information presented in the given tables, we have derived the following outcomes:

- For all k and n, as the sample size N increases, both bias and RMSE of the estimators decrease.
- For fixed n and N, as the number of consecutive working components k increases, both bias and RMSE of the estimator increase.

Generally, we can conclude that the number of components n and the number of consecutive working components k affect the efficiency of the estimator.

Table 2. The bias and RMSE of the first estimator $\widehat{\mathcal{E}}_{\alpha,1}(T_{k|n:G})$.

$\alpha = 0.1$		$N = 30$		$N = 40$		$N = 50$		$N = 100$	
n	k	Bias	RMSE	Bias	RMSE	Bias	RMSE	Bias	RMSE
5	3	−0.010898	0.105216	−0.009579	0.089654	−0.004854	0.080614	−0.004425	0.057484
	4	−0.012101	0.073296	−0.008686	0.063602	−0.007962	0.056373	−0.002357	0.039808
	5	−0.011342	0.056113	−0.007421	0.048443	−0.007876	0.044139	−0.003220	0.031291
6	3	−0.009440	0.117519	−0.004641	0.098258	−0.004978	0.087909	−0.003282	0.061718
	4	−0.010196	0.081712	−0.008803	0.070134	−0.006333	0.063083	−0.002612	0.045212
	5	−0.011518	0.061810	−0.009172	0.054063	−0.007364	0.048630	−0.003255	0.035013
	6	−0.012929	0.051138	−0.009353	0.044888	−0.006708	0.039548	−0.003365	0.028388
7	4	−0.010966	0.090091	−0.008536	0.077953	−0.005575	0.069248	−0.001896	0.049748
	5	−0.011133	0.069115	−0.008268	0.058999	−0.006836	0.053299	−0.002281	0.037963
	6	−0.012696	0.056204	−0.009115	0.048011	−0.006197	0.043047	−0.003890	0.030458
	7	−0.012264	0.045635	−0.008862	0.041127	−0.006831	0.036810	−0.003554	0.026578
8	4	−0.007320	0.095422	−0.005076	0.081741	−0.005717	0.076165	−0.000826	0.053521
	5	−0.011195	0.075112	−0.008280	0.064280	−0.007420	0.057273	−0.003794	0.040709
	6	−0.011476	0.059650	−0.009077	0.051937	−0.006067	0.046792	−0.004184	0.033449
	7	−0.013114	0.050062	−0.008815	0.043506	−0.006897	0.039713	−0.003551	0.028184
	8	−0.011777	0.042585	−0.009081	0.038260	−0.007125	0.033553	−0.003560	0.024383

Table 3. The bias and RMSE of the first estimator $\widehat{\mathcal{E}}_{\alpha,1}(T_{k|n:G})$.

$\alpha = 1$		$N = 30$		$N = 40$		$N = 50$		$N = 100$	
n	k	**Bias**	**RMSE**	**Bias**	**RMSE**	**Bias**	**RMSE**	**Bias**	**RMSE**
5	3	0.000087	0.087601	0.000872	0.074942	−0.000812	0.066222	−0.000199	0.047229
	4	0.000677	0.061861	0.000951	0.052752	−0.000292	0.048263	−0.000173	0.033817
	5	−0.001023	0.047448	−0.000314	0.041763	0.000521	0.036230	0.000228	0.026700
6	3	0.001409	0.089266	0.000389	0.078280	0.000591	0.069693	0.000525	0.048964
	4	0.000284	0.066270	−0.000330	0.056581	0.000154	0.050492	0.000406	0.036359
	5	0.000046	0.052805	−0.000540	0.045278	0.000055	0.039331	0.000399	0.028064
	6	−0.000570	0.042544	−0.000926	0.037313	−0.000428	0.032658	0.000080	0.023334
7	4	0.000300	0.068752	0.000634	0.060594	0.000478	0.053156	0.000868	0.037872
	5	0.000316	0.055068	−0.000188	0.047579	−0.000385	0.043313	−0.000690	0.030024
	6	−0.001600	0.044820	0.000122	0.038575	−0.000157	0.035549	0.000075	0.024823
	7	−0.000246	0.038482	−0.000109	0.033277	−0.000450	0.029768	−0.000460	0.020956
8	4	0.001810	0.071259	−0.000350	0.061727	−0.001011	0.055154	0.000785	0.039367
	5	−0.000294	0.058607	0.000110	0.049190	−0.000007	0.044643	−0.000307	0.031387
	6	−0.000963	0.048215	−0.000025	0.041604	−0.000243	0.037351	0.000320	0.026658
	7	−0.000449	0.041519	−0.000056	0.034707	−0.000747	0.032291	−0.000337	0.022519
	8	−0.001574	0.035239	−0.000403	0.030317	−0.000894	0.027829	0.000223	0.019494

Table 4. The bias and RMSE of the first estimator $\widehat{\mathcal{E}}_{\alpha,1}(T_{k|n:G})$.

$\alpha = 2$		$N = 30$		$N = 40$		$N = 50$		$N = 100$	
n	k	**Bias**	**RMSE**	**Bias**	**RMSE**	**Bias**	**RMSE**	**Bias**	**RMSE**
5	3	−0.001090	0.086459	0.000815	0.075403	−0.001139	0.066924	−0.000073	0.047757
	4	0.034278	0.070438	0.026845	0.060862	0.024803	0.052971	0.014174	0.035674
	5	0.014319	0.047563	0.010515	0.040428	0.009683	0.035569	0.005089	0.025548
6	3	0.063920	0.126898	0.062550	0.111951	0.060926	0.102074	0.044846	0.071823
	4	0.038461	0.075607	0.033681	0.066047	0.029243	0.057837	0.015990	0.039400
	5	0.018664	0.052510	0.014582	0.044903	0.012534	0.039484	0.005635	0.027945
	6	0.007147	0.039141	0.005249	0.034102	0.004860	0.029907	0.002433	0.022023
7	4	0.041086	0.083484	0.036617	0.070899	0.032951	0.062740	0.018144	0.040586
	5	0.021959	0.055792	0.018673	0.048884	0.014572	0.042988	0.008572	0.028540
	6	0.010251	0.042669	0.008163	0.035800	0.006582	0.032881	0.003422	0.023119
	7	0.003633	0.033836	0.003067	0.029107	0.002643	0.026160	0.002013	0.019432
8	4	0.045197	0.085555	0.038435	0.074035	0.037415	0.065820	0.020444	0.042791
	5	0.024856	0.059893	0.019444	0.050514	0.017341	0.044100	0.008817	0.030109
	6	0.012141	0.044384	0.009642	0.038875	0.008753	0.035025	0.003794	0.024345
	7	0.006040	0.036246	0.002859	0.032057	0.003239	0.028222	0.001896	0.020497
	8	0.001058	0.029722	0.001472	0.026524	0.001431	0.024069	0.000941	0.017894

Table 5. The bias and RMSE of the second estimator $\widehat{\mathcal{E}}_{\alpha,2}(T_{k|n:G})$.

$\alpha = 0.1$		$N = 30$		$N = 40$		$N = 50$		$N = 100$	
n	k	**Bias**	**RMSE**	**Bias**	**RMSE**	**Bias**	**RMSE**	**Bias**	**RMSE**
5	3	−0.010609	0.102546	−0.008270	0.088836	−0.005443	0.080873	−0.002863	0.058167
	4	−0.010304	0.073576	−0.010357	0.063081	−0.006064	0.057594	−0.003082	0.041216
	5	−0.014063	0.057050	−0.009564	0.049681	−0.007636	0.043591	−0.003881	0.031672
6	3	−0.007927	0.114087	−0.005274	0.099831	−0.002167	0.088074	−0.002003	0.062661
	4	−0.010957	0.081463	−0.007744	0.071106	−0.006705	0.065384	−0.003142	0.044996
	5	−0.012472	0.061216	−0.008003	0.054332	−0.006736	0.048667	−0.002746	0.034079
	6	−0.013312	0.049958	−0.008733	0.044566	−0.006949	0.040256	−0.003810	0.028654
7	4	−0.010511	0.090065	−0.008348	0.078439	−0.008723	0.068968	−0.002051	0.048977
	5	−0.012018	0.068814	−0.008633	0.059495	−0.004883	0.053448	−0.004237	0.038646
	6	−0.011984	0.054471	−0.007330	0.048398	−0.006811	0.043351	−0.002883	0.031013
	7	−0.010979	0.045610	−0.009159	0.039701	−0.007405	0.036903	−0.003332	0.026529
8	4	−0.008034	0.097000	−0.004299	0.083309	−0.006195	0.075089	−0.001807	0.052764
	5	−0.010637	0.075050	−0.008024	0.065490	−0.007708	0.058203	−0.003380	0.041227
	6	−0.011068	0.060779	−0.007946	0.052276	−0.006342	0.047288	−0.003544	0.033142
	7	−0.011923	0.049250	−0.007979	0.043511	−0.006613	0.038337	−0.003617	0.027815
	8	−0.012459	0.043427	−0.008960	0.037006	−0.007978	0.034281	−0.003476	0.023718

Table 6. The bias and RMSE of the second estimator $\widehat{\mathcal{E}}_{\alpha,2}(T_{k|n:G})$.

$\alpha = 1$		$N = 30$		$N = 40$		$N = 50$		$N = 100$	
n	k	**Bias**	**RMSE**	**Bias**	**RMSE**	**Bias**	**RMSE**	**Bias**	**RMSE**
5	3	0.000212	0.085861	−0.000383	0.074161	0.000658	0.067124	0.001064	0.046434
	4	0.000873	0.060747	−0.001359	0.053834	−0.001447	0.047587	−0.000068	0.033720
	5	0.000465	0.047697	0.000799	0.041411	−0.000355	0.036525	0.000007	0.026548
6	3	−0.000611	0.090382	−0.000357	0.078913	0.000484	0.069387	0.000170	0.049160
	4	−0.000483	0.067131	0.000767	0.057582	0.000042	0.051330	0.000508	0.035924
	5	−0.000430	0.051884	−0.000213	0.045401	−0.000394	0.040414	−0.000242	0.028758
	6	−0.000387	0.042309	−0.000377	0.037006	−0.000479	0.032480	−0.000493	0.023257
7	4	−0.000453	0.068868	−0.000341	0.060492	−0.000269	0.052825	0.000865	0.037833
	5	0.000392	0.056091	0.000053	0.047779	−0.000847	0.042480	−0.000198	0.030513
	6	−0.000500	0.045534	−0.000440	0.039434	−0.000049	0.035552	−0.000028	0.025303
	7	−0.000535	0.038237	−0.000614	0.033145	−0.000271	0.029834	0.000198	0.021260
8	4	0.001655	0.071870	−0.001471	0.062020	−0.000568	0.056329	0.000196	0.039943
	5	−0.000569	0.056866	−0.000085	0.049564	−0.000235	0.045120	−0.000662	0.031710
	6	−0.000216	0.048526	−0.000433	0.041005	−0.001622	0.037182	−0.000601	0.026537
	7	−0.000753	0.040824	−0.000632	0.035827	−0.000771	0.031846	−0.000160	0.022491
	8	−0.001067	0.035046	−0.000742	0.031062	−0.000528	0.027216	0.000628	0.019584

Table 7. The bias and RMSE of the second estimator $\widehat{\mathcal{E}}_{\alpha,2}(T_{k|n:G})$.

$\alpha = 2$		$N = 30$		$N = 40$		$N = 50$		$N = 100$	
n	k	**Bias**	**RMSE**	**Bias**	**RMSE**	**Bias**	**RMSE**	**Bias**	**RMSE**
5	3	0.001317	0.086416	−0.001661	0.076015	0.001307	0.067851	−0.000699	0.047553
	4	−0.000150	0.060925	−0.000304	0.051711	−0.000440	0.047292	−0.000288	0.033949
	5	−0.000058	0.045216	0.000112	0.040160	0.000627	0.035967	0.000482	0.025006
6	3	0.000443	0.093072	−0.001661	0.080002	−0.001348	0.071543	−0.000287	0.049726
	4	0.000374	0.064174	0.000945	0.055211	0.000121	0.050066	0.000298	0.035013
	5	0.000484	0.050087	−0.000586	0.042798	0.000282	0.038479	0.000650	0.027301
	6	−0.000109	0.040256	−0.000478	0.034969	0.000093	0.031228	−0.000690	0.022026
7	4	−0.000368	0.067255	−0.000452	0.056703	−0.001297	0.051753	−0.000065	0.037156
	5	−0.001662	0.051118	0.000641	0.045238	0.000413	0.040474	0.000762	0.028545
	6	−0.000668	0.042594	−0.000386	0.036797	0.000147	0.032351	−0.000145	0.023491
	7	0.000545	0.035956	−0.000206	0.030602	−0.000309	0.028139	0.000132	0.019843
8	4	−0.000954	0.068949	0.000744	0.059647	−0.000047	0.052899	0.000328	0.038041
	5	−0.000855	0.053399	0.000319	0.047349	−0.000043	0.041896	0.000557	0.029469
	6	0.000340	0.044608	−0.000014	0.038450	0.000239	0.034654	−0.000300	0.024364
	7	0.000250	0.037999	0.000033	0.032327	0.000410	0.029667	−0.000122	0.020663
	8	0.000277	0.033181	0.000718	0.028420	−0.000165	0.025314	−0.000493	0.018187

Real Data Analysis

We apply the given estimator to real data to examine how closely the FGCRE estimators from consecutive k-out-of-n:G systems align with the theoretical entropy value. The dataset consists of 15 observations of time intervals between successive failures of air conditioning equipment in a Boeing 720 as follows: 74, 57, 48, 29, 502, 12, 70, 21, 29, 386, 59, 27, 153, 26, 326. These data are modeled using the exponential distribution with the p.d.f.

$$f(x) = \lambda e^{-\lambda x}, \; x > 0, \lambda > 0.$$

As described by Shanker et al. [30], we analyzed the dataset using the maximum likelihood estimator method to estimate the parameter λ, resulting in $\widehat{\lambda} = 0.00825$. Additionally, we calculated the Kolmogorov–Smirnov statistic, yielding a value of 0.277 and a p-value of 0.1662. These statistics confirm the goodness-of-fit between the observed data and the fitted exponential distribution.

Table 8 provides a comprehensive overview of the k, n, and α combinations analyzed, while Figure 2 visually represents these combinations. The results indicate that there is a close agreement between the theoretical entropy value and its estimation when the number of functioning components approaches half of the total number of components (n). This observation suggests that the accuracy of the entropy estimation is higher when the system operates with approximately half of its components in a working state.

Table 8. Comparison of theoretical values and estimates of FGCRE of $T_{k|6:G}$ based on exponential distribution for successive failures of air conditioning equipment in a Boeing 720.

α	k	$\mathcal{E}_\alpha(T_{k|5:G})$	$\widehat{\mathcal{E}}_{\alpha,1}(T_{k|5:G})$	$\widehat{\mathcal{E}}_{\alpha,2}(T_{k|5:G})$	$\mathcal{E}_\alpha(T_{k|6:G})$	$\widehat{\mathcal{E}}_{\alpha,1}(T_{k|6:G})$	$\widehat{\mathcal{E}}_{\alpha,2}(T_{k|6:G})$
	3	58.669550	44.189875	34.759008	65.757406	53.069440	40.154187
0.1	4	36.091734	19.451760	18.285162	41.569942	24.070849	21.252137
	5	24.242424	9.7693280	11.908400	28.135564	12.383475	13.764174
	6				20.202020	7.084899	9.981658
	3	49.258087	61.173750	44.983267	50.171584	67.051873	50.106795
1.0	4	34.258325	31.454190	20.858847	36.756520	36.672164	23.812712
	5	24.242424	16.107555	11.917905	27.091908	19.911450	13.792459
	6				20.202020	11.297715	9.424714
	3	45.368069	67.425564	61.815013	45.642327	69.309002	66.956682
2.0	4	33.033300	43.046387	29.345655	34.306351	47.652819	33.495064
	5	24.242424	23.884659	14.469465	26.333470	28.707664	17.290249
	6				20.202020	16.436591	10.152834

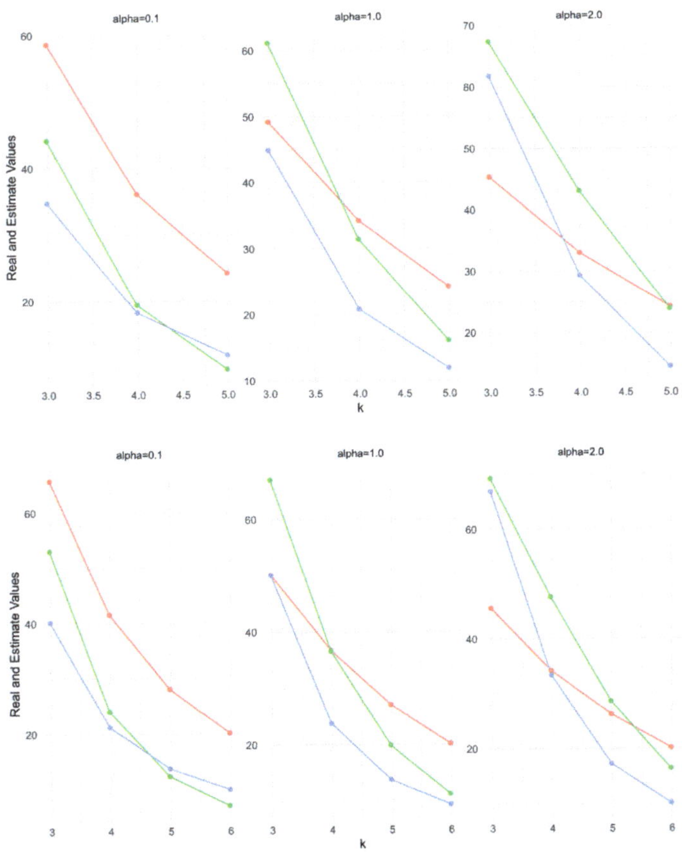

Figure 2. The plot of $\mathcal{E}_\alpha(T_{k|n:G})$ (in red) for $n = 5$ (upper) and $n = 6$ (lower), along with their estimators $\widehat{\mathcal{E}}_{\alpha,1}(T_{k|n:G})$ (in green) and $\widehat{\mathcal{E}}_{\alpha,2}(T_{k|n:G})$ (in blue), as a function of α.

5. Conclusions

In this study, we explored the utilization of the FGCRE concept within consecutive k-out-of-n:G systems. Therefore, it is highlighted that a strong relationship exists between the FGCRE of such systems derived from continuous and uniform distributions. The obtained expression is so useful for the computation of the FGCRE of the system's lifetime. However, deriving closed-form expressions for FGCRE becomes intricate when dealing with systems with large component lifetimes or having complicated reliability functions. To address this challenge, we introduced a set of bounds for the FGCRE of consecutive k-out-of-n:G systems. The given bounds serve as essential resources for researchers to analyze FGCRE behaviors effectively. Moreover, we introduced two nonparametric estimators for consecutive k-out-of-n:G systems, specifically applicable to real-world applications. In summary, this research significantly advances the understanding of FGCRE within consecutive k-out-of-n:G systems. The insights gained from this study can be extended to other information metrics, such as fractional generalized cumulative entropy, cumulative entropy, cumulative residual Tsallis entropy, and cumulative Tsallis entropy.

Author Contributions: Methodology, M.S.; Software, M.S.; Validation, M.S.; Formal analysis, M.S.; Investigation, M.K.; Resources, M.S.; Writing—original draft, M.K.; Writing—review and editing, M.K. and M.S.; Visualization, M.K.; Supervision, M.K.; Project administration, M.S. All authors have read and agreed to the published version of the manuscript.

Funding: This work was supported by Researchers Supporting Project number (RSP2024R464), King Saud University, Riyadh, Saudi Arabia.

Data Availability Statement: The data used to support the findings of this study are included in the article.

Conflicts of Interest: The authors declare no conflict of interest.

References

1. Jung, K.H.; Kim, H. Linear consecutive-k-out-of-n: F system reliability with common-mode forced outages. *Reliab. Eng. Syst. Saf.* **1993**, *41*, 49–55. [CrossRef]
2. Shen, J.; Zuo, M.J. Optimal design of series consecutive-k-out-of-n: G systems. *Reliab. Eng. Syst. Saf.* **1994**, *45*, 277–283. [CrossRef]
3. Kuo, W.; Zuo, M.J. *Optimal Reliability Modeling: Principles and Applications*; John Wiley & Sons: Hoboken, NJ, USA, 2003.
4. In-Hang, C.; Cui, L.; Hwang, F.K. *Reliabilities of Consecutive-k Systems*; Springer Science & Business Media: Berlin, Germany, 2013; Volume 4.
5. Boland, P.J.; Samaniego, F.J. Stochastic ordering results for consecutive k-out-of-n: F systems. *IEEE Trans. Reliab.* **2004**, *53*, 7–10. [CrossRef]
6. Eryılmaz, S. Mixture representations for the reliability of consecutive-k systems. *Math. Comput. Model.* **2010**, *51*, 405–412. [CrossRef]
7. Eryilmaz, S. Conditional lifetimes of consecutive k-out-of-n systems. *IEEE Trans. Reliab.* **2010**, *59*, 178–182. [CrossRef]
8. Eryılmaz, S. Reliability properties of consecutive k-out-of-n systems of arbitrarily dependent components. *Reliab. Eng. Syst. Saf.* **2009**, *94*, 350–356. [CrossRef]
9. Rao, M.; Chen, Y.; Vemuri, B.C.; Wang, F. Cumulative residual entropy: A new measure of information. *IEEE Trans. Inf. Theory* **2004**, *50*, 1220–1228. [CrossRef]
10. Di Crescenzo, A.; Kayal, S.; Meoli, A. Fractional generalized cumulative entropy and its dynamic version. *Commun. Nonlinear Sci. Numer. Simul.* **2021**, *102*, 105899. [CrossRef]
11. Xiong, H.; Shang, P.; Zhang, Y. Fractional cumulative residual entropy. *Commun. Nonlinear Sci. Numer. Simul.* **2019**, *78*, 104879. [CrossRef]
12. Alomani, G.; Kayid, M. Fractional Survival Functional Entropy of Engineering Systems. *Entropy* **2022**, *24*, 1275. [CrossRef]
13. Kayid, M.; Shrahili, M. Some further results on the fractional cumulative entropy. *Entropy* **2022**, *24*, 1037. [CrossRef]
14. Psarrakos, G.; Economou, P. On the generalized cumulative residual entropy weighted distributions. *Commun. Stat.-Theory Methods* **2017**, *46*, 10914–10925. [CrossRef]
15. Wong, K.M.; Chen, S. The entropy of ordered sequences and order statistics. *IEEE Trans. Inf. Theory* **1990**, *36*, 276–284. [CrossRef]
16. Ebrahimi, N.; Soofi, E.S.; Zahedi, H. Information properties of order statistics and spacings. *IEEE Trans. Inf. Theory* **2004**, *50*, 177–183. [CrossRef]
17. Abdolsaeed, T.; Doostparast, M. A note on signature-based expressions for the entropy of mixed r-out-of-n systems. *Nav. Res. Logist. (NRL)* **2014**, *61*, 202–206.

18. Toomaj, A.; Doostparast, M. On the Kullback-Leibler information for mixed systems. *Int. J. Syst. Sci.* **2016**, *47*, 2458–2465. [CrossRef]
19. Toomaj, A.; Zarei, R. Some new results on information properties of mixture distributions. *Filomat* **2017**, *31*, 4225–4230. [CrossRef]
20. Kayid, M.; Alshehri, M.A. Cumulative Residual Entropy of the Residual Lifetime of a Mixed System at the System Level. *Entropy* **2023**, *25*, 1033. [CrossRef]
21. Kayid, M.; Alshehri, M.A. Tsallis entropy for the past lifetime distribution with application. *Axioms* **2023**, *12*, 731. [CrossRef]
22. Parsa, M.; Di Crescenzo, A.; Jabbari, H. Analysis of reliability systems via Gini-type index. *Eur. J. Oper. Res.* **2018**, *264*, 340–353. [CrossRef]
23. Yin, J.; Cui, L. Reliability for consecutive-k-out-of-n: F systems with shared components between adjacent subsystems. *Reliab. Eng. Syst. Safety* **2021**, *210*, 107532. [CrossRef]
24. Bickel, P.J.; Lehmann, E.L. Descriptive statistics for nonparametric models. III. Dispersion. In *Selected Works of EL Lehmann*; Springer: Berlin, Germany, 2011; pp. 499–518.
25. Jewitt, I. Choosing between risky prospects: The characterization of comparative statics results, and location independent risk. *Manag. Sci.* **1989**, *35*, 60–70. [CrossRef]
26. Landsberger, M.; Meilijson, I. The generating process and an extension of Jewitt's location independent risk concept. *Manag. Sci.* **1994**, *40*, 662–669. [CrossRef]
27. Eryılmaz, S.; Navarro, J. Failure rates of consecutive k-out-of-n systems. *J. Korean Stat. Soc.* **2012**, *41*, 1–11. [CrossRef]
28. Aliprantis, C.D.; Burkinshaw, O. *Principles of Real Analysis*; Gulf Professional Publishing: Oxford, UK, 1998.
29. Vasicek, O. A test for normality based on sample entropy. *J. R. Stat. Soc. Ser. B Stat. Methodol.* **1976**, *38*, 54–59. [CrossRef]
30. Shanker, R.; Hagos, F.; Sujatha, S. On modeling of Lifetimes data using exponential and Lindley distributions. *Biom. Biostat. Int. J.* **2015**, *2*, 1–9. [CrossRef]

fractal and fractional

MDPI

Article

Multifractal-Aware Convolutional Attention Synergistic Network for Carbon Market Price Forecasting

Liran Wei [1], Mingzhu Tang [2,*], Na Li [3], Jingwen Deng [1], Xinpeng Zhou [1] and Haijun Hu [4]

1 School of Computer Science and Technology, Changsha University of Science & Technology, Changsha 410114, China; wliran@stu.csust.edu.cn (L.W.); ssscc@stu.csust.edu.cn (J.D.); cyclonezxp@stu.csust.edu.cn (X.Z.)
2 School of Energy and Power Engineering, Changsha University of Science & Technology, Changsha 410114, China
3 School of Economics & Management, Changsha University of Science & Technology, Changsha 410114, China; lina@stu.csust.edu.cn
4 School of Mathematics and Statistics, Changsha University of Science & Technology, Changsha 410114, China; h.hu@csust.edu.cn
* Correspondence: tmz@csust.edu.cn

Abstract: Accurate carbon market price prediction is crucial for promoting a low-carbon economy and sustainable engineering. Traditional models often face challenges in effectively capturing the multifractality inherent in carbon market prices. Inspired by the self-similarity and scale invariance inherent in fractal structures, this study proposes a novel multifractal-aware model, MF-Transformer-DEC, for carbon market price prediction. The multi-scale convolution (MSC) module employs multi-layer dilated convolutions constrained by shared convolution kernel weights to construct a scale-invariant convolutional network. By projecting and reconstructing time series data within a multi-scale fractal space, MSC enhances the model's ability to adapt to complex nonlinear fluctuations while significantly suppressing noise interference. The fractal attention (FA) module calculates similarity matrices within a multi-scale feature space through multi-head attention, adaptively integrating multifractal market dynamics and implicit associations. The dynamic error correction (DEC) module models error commonality through variational autoencoder (VAE), and uncertainty-guided dynamic weighting achieves robust error correction. The proposed model achieved an average R^2 of 0.9777 and 0.9942 for 7-step ahead predictions on the Shanghai and Guangdong carbon price datasets, respectively. This study pioneers the interdisciplinary integration of fractal theory and artificial intelligence methods for complex engineering analysis, enhancing the accuracy of carbon market price prediction. The proposed technical pathway of "multi-scale deconstruction and similarity mining" offers a valuable reference for AI-driven fractal modeling.

Keywords: multifractality; Transformer; dilated convolution; fractal attention; carbon market price prediction; time series

1. Introduction

Transitioning to low-carbon energy is a pivotal strategy to optimize energy consumption structures and promote sustainable development. Carbon emissions trading systems and carbon tax policies are widely recognized as key points for a low-carbon economy [1]. The formation of a carbon market price that meets the supply and demand mechanisms according to the current market situation is the core of the carbon trading market [2]. Therefore, accurate prediction of carbon market price is the core requirement for carbon market participants to optimise their decision-making, and it is also the key technical support to achieve the goal of 'dual-carbon' strategy and the transformation of a low-carbon economy [3]. However, the carbon market price time series in China exhibits characteristics similar to those of financial time series, including overall volatility, heavy tails, and non-normal distribution [4]. Its high nonlinearity and non-stationarity lead to complex price fluctuations, posing significant challenges for accurate carbon price prediction.

Fractal theory has been widely applied in the modeling and structural analysis of complex systems. In financial markets, it is often used to analyze asymmetric and volatile market behaviors, aiding in the identification of nonlinearity and long-memory characteristics in financial time series. Additionally, in tasks such as large language models and image processing, fractal theory is commonly employed to jointly analyze local data and global trends, quantify the self-similarity of language, and perform fractal-based data augmentation. Fractal theory provides theoretical support for understanding complex structures and developing multi-scale analysis algorithms. However, traditional fractal models primarily rely on statistical measures to reveal the nonlinear characteristics, long-memory effects, and scale-invariant structures in multifractal complex systems. Fan et al. [5] used multifractal detrended volatility analysis (MFDFA) to calculate the generalised Hurst exponent h(q), which breaks through the limitations of the qualitative study of the traditional efficient market hypothesis (EMH) and proves the multifractal nature of the carbon market time series. Khurshid et al. [6] applied methods such as Asymmetric Multifractal Detrended Fluctuation Analysis (A-MFDFA) to examine the asymmetric multifractal characteristics and market efficiency of global and Chinese green energy markets. Their study captured the asymmetric multifractal features of price uptrends and downtrends, and constructed a Market Inefficiency Index (MLM) by integrating the Market Deficiency Measure (MDM) and the Hurst exponent, offering a comparative analysis of market dynamics before and after the COVID-19 pandemic. Li and Tian [7] combined the BEAST algorithm with Skewed Multifractal Detrended Cross-Correlation Analysis (MF-DCCA) to detect structural breakpoints in carbon market time series. Their research addressed the limitations of traditional multifractal analysis by accounting for the impact of abrupt changes on the cross-correlation between carbon price and trading volume, and tackled the lack of dynamic efficiency evaluation under pandemic-induced shocks. Ni et al. [8] proposed a stock trend prediction model based on fractal feature selection and Support Vector Machines (SVM). The model measured feature importance using fractal dimensions and employed an Ant Colony Optimization algorithm to select optimal feature subsets, effectively overcoming the limitations of conventional feature selection methods in determining the optimal number of features and handling nonlinear relationships. Liu & Huang et al. [9] use Fractal Brownian Motion (FBM) to effectively portray the long memory and fractal characteristics of the time series, and describe the time-varying volatility of the financial time series through the Generalised Autoregressive Conditional Heteroskedasticity (GARCH) model, which can better adapt to the changes in market structure. Raubitzek and Neubauer [10] proposed a method that integrates fractal interpolation with Long Short-Term Memory (LSTM) neural networks. By using fractal interpolation to dynamically adapt to the complexity characteristics of time series—such as the Hurst exponent—they generated finer-grained sequences that better match the complexity of real-world systems. This approach addresses the poor predictive performance of conventional LSTM models when dealing with insufficient data or highly complex structures. Dandan et al. [11] introduced the Skewed-t distribution—capable of capturing the leptokurtic and skewed features of return series—into the Markov-switching multifractal (MSM) model, forming the Skewed-t-MSM-EVT model to quantify extreme risks in the carbon market. This model overcomes the limitations of traditional approaches that fail to fully account for the multifractal properties of carbon markets and the asymmetry in return distributions. Jin et al. [12] developed a short-term wind speed prediction model that integrates Fractal Dimension (FD), Variational Mode Decomposition (VMD), and Generalized Continued Fraction (GCF). By determining VMD decomposition parameters based on the fractal characteristics of wind speed series, the model solves the ambiguity in parameter selection faced by traditional VMD methods and enhances the ability to capture dynamic wind speed patterns. Alabdulmohsin et al. [13] employed an information-theoretic approach to convert text into bit sequences and used fractal theory to quantify the self-similarity and long-range dependencies of language. This method addresses the incomplete characterization of linguistic structures caused by computational constraints in previous studies, offering a novel perspective for understanding the nature of language and the success of large language models (LLMs). However, traditional econometric models need to go through multiple steps such as distributional assumptions, parameter estimation, and cointegration tests, which makes the modeling process complicated and sensitive to pre-processing. Moreover, traditional econometric models are difficult to capture the nonlinear characteristics and non-stationarity of the carbon market price series due to stringent assumptions [14], and the prediction error is significantly enlarged, especially in the face of sudden market changes. For complex systems, the calculation results of econometric methods are often not intuitive, requiring in-depth research and professional analysis, and the results are difficult to understand and apply.

Deep learning models support end-to-end modeling without manual feature engineering, with powerful nonlinear mapping capability, and support online updating and migration. CNN and its many variants have been widely used in carbon market price time series feature extraction due to their feature extraction advantages, such as parallel computing and local awareness. Transformer, with its core of self-attention mechanism, can effectively capture long-distance dependencies and complex nonlinear features, and has been widely used this year. Wu et al. [15] integrated four different kernels of 1D convolution as a multi-scale extraction module and improved the feature learning ability by designing a dual-stream Transformer module to capture multivariate internal relations and univariate time dependence, respectively. Yin et al. [16] proposed a spatio-temporal multi-dimensional collaborative attention network (TSMA) that, through the temporal attention mechanism, feature attention mechanism, and convolutional block attention module, the features of multi-region information at different spatio-temporal levels are fully extracted, and BIGRU further extracts the time series features and predicts them. Ji et al. [17] (2025) proposed the QRTransformer-MIDAS model, which integrates quantile regression, Transformer architecture, and mixed-frequency modeling. By employing Mixed Data Sampling (MIDAS) regression, the model captures the influence of high-frequency variables on low-frequency carbon prices. It leverages the transformer to model nonlinear dependencies and utilizes kernel density estimation (KDE) for probabilistic forecasting. This approach addresses key limitations of traditional same-frequency models, such as neglecting high-frequency information and relying solely on point forecasts that fail to capture uncertainty in volatility. Zhang et al. [18] implemented a framework that performs multi-scale decomposition and reconstruction of carbon price series via adaptive feature extraction and entropy-based recomposition. The method expands the model's local receptive field through time series patching and applies a two-stage stabilization process to enhance adaptability to non-stationary data. Additionally, a dynamic weighted ensemble algorithm is designed to intelligently assign weights to sub-sequences, overcoming limitations of traditional models related to insufficient feature extraction and sub-sequence weight misallocation.

Due to the multi-scale complexity characteristics of carbon market price time series data, multi-scale decomposition methods are often combined with deep learning methods, which can reduce the data complexity to improve the prediction performance. Current carbon market price prediction models mostly use signal processing methods for multi-scale decomposition. Yue et al. [19] used the Hampel identifier (HI) for outlier processing, time-varying filtering empirical modal decomposition (TVFEMD) for data decomposition and reconstruction, and the Transformer model for multi-step ahead and interval prediction of carbon market price to cope with the nonlinearities, nonsmoothness, and complex fluctuations of the carbon market price series. Smoothness and complex fluctuation problems. Hong et al. [20] proposed a hybrid model combining depth-enhanced frequency-enhanced decomposition transformer (DA-FEDformer), improved complete ensemble empirical modal decomposition with adaptive noise (ICEEMDAN) and multi-model optimised segmentation error correction, which organically integrates the frequency and time domain information and improves the performance of carbon market price prediction. Sun et al. [21] used discrete wavelet transform (DWT), complete ensemble empirical modal decomposition of adaptive noise (CEEMDAN) and singular spectrum analysis (SSA) for hybrid multi-scale decomposition and Transformer model for prediction, which improves the model's fitting and prediction of the data by utilising the carbon market price prediction model with multi-source information and specific data processing methods. Li et al. [22] proposed a dual decomposition ensemble model based on the Sparrow Search Algorithm-optimized Variational Mode Decomposition (SVMD). The model classifies decomposed components using fuzzy entropy, then applies Whale Optimization-enhanced LSTM and Extreme Learning Machine (ELM) for prediction, respectively. Additionally, it introduces Ensemble Empirical Mode Decomposition (EEMD) to further decompose and correct residual error sequences. This approach overcomes issues such as mode mixing and parameter dependency commonly found in traditional decomposition methods. Liu et al. [23] addressed mixed-frequency data by applying frequency alignment and implementing a sub-model selection strategy to match different feature sub-sequences. A multi-objective optimization algorithm is then used to determine integration weights. This method resolves limitations in conventional models that overlook the influence of high-frequency external variables, lack adaptability in sub-sequence model matching, and inadequately optimize ensemble weights. Cai et al. [24] employed the adaptive white-noise-assisted Complete Ensemble Empirical Mode Decomposition with Adaptive Noise (CEEMDAN) to decompose nonlinear and non-stationary carbon price series into structured components such as high-frequency, low-frequency, and trend residuals. Temporal features of each component are then extracted using a TCN-LSTM model to achieve accurate predictions. This approach addresses challenges in capturing complex carbon price fluctuations and reduces the vulnerability of single deep learning models to noise interference. Ma et al. [25] proposed the TCN-LSTM-Self-Attention model for carbon price prediction, which integrates decomposition and a dual-channel attention mechanism. The Temporal Convolutional Network (TCN) is used to extract short-term local features, the LSTM captures long-term dependencies, and self-attention is introduced to enhance the importance of key information. This model effectively overcomes the limitation of traditional methods in jointly modeling short-term volatility and long-term trends. Lu et al. [26] transformed the maximum and minimum carbon prices into central and radius sequences to capture volatility information. Variational Mode Decomposition parameters are optimized using a Differential Evolution Algorithm, and fuzzy entropy is used to reconstruct subsequences. Optimal Multi-Kernel Support Vector Regression (MKSVR) and Exponential Generalized Autoregressive Conditional Heteroskedasticity (EGARCH) models are applied to different sub-sequence types. This method addresses deficiencies in handling interval data volatility, subjective parameter selection in decomposition, and poor adaptability of single kernel functions. Fang et al. [27] developed a carbon price prediction model based on secondary decomposition and BiLSTM. It uses CEEMDAN and VMD to perform a two-stage decomposition of carbon price time series and adopts the Capuchin Optimization Algorithm (COA) to fine-tune BiLSTM parameters such as step size and number of neurons. This framework enables deep feature extraction and model parameter optimization for complex carbon price sequences. Dong et al. [28] employs a multi-wavelet-layered stacked DWNN (Deep Wavelet Neural Network) to achieve more accurate approximation of nonlinear mappings through multi-scale feature extraction.

However, there are still three limitations of existing carbon market price forecasting models.

(1) Most of the existing fractal models are based on traditional statistics and machine learning methods, which struggle to deeply explore multiple fractal characteristics and make predictions. For complex systems, the calculation results of econometric statistical methods are often not intuitive, requiring in-depth research and professional analysis, and the results are difficult to understand and apply practically in prediction tasks. The combination of deep learning models and fractal theory is insufficient, and there is a lack of integration of interdisciplinary methods.
(2) Most of the existing multi-scale prediction methods for carbon market price are based on signal processing, using a fixed way of decomposition, are difficult to co-optimize with downstream models, and lack end-to-end learning, dynamic adaptation, and complex feature modeling capabilities.
(3) Existing forecasting frameworks are difficult to model complex dynamic changes in time series and multiple fractalities well, and there are problems such as gradient disappearance or gradient explosion.

Considering the aforementioned drawbacks and the improvement of carbon market price prediction, this study designs the MF-Transformer-DEC model that contains a multi-scale convolution module, a fractal attention module, and a dynamic error correction module. In addition, to illustrate the superiority of the proposed model, we evaluate it through several experiments. The main contributions of this research are as follows.

(1) A novel multi-scale similarity modeling method MF-Transformer-DEC, is proposed, integrating the self-similarity and scale invariance theories of fractals to build a robust prediction framework with strong feature modeling and mining capabilities. The understanding and prediction ability of complex systems are enhanced.

(2) The multifractal-driven multi-scale convolution (MSC) module introduces a scale-invariant convolutional network, which projects and reconstructs time series data within a multi-scale fractal space, thereby enhancing the model's ability to comprehend multi-scale chaotic sequences. By assigning distinct dilation rates to each convolutional layer, the MSC module efficiently decomposes multi-scale features. Meanwhile, the kernel weights of different dilated convolutions are isomorphic, which ensures the invariance of cross-scale characterization patterns. A meticulously designed convolutional structure endows MSC with a learnable fractal perception capability.

(3) The fractal attention (FA) module computes cross-scale similarity matrices to adaptively capture the potential similar structures in multi-scale feature sequences, enabling the perception of the market's multifractal dynamics. The integration of pooling and nonlinear projection adaptively balances scale-specific patterns, reducing noise sensitivity and enhancing generalization capacity.

(4) The uncertainty-guided dynamic error correction (DEC) module implements a variable autoencoder (VAE) to capture the temporal and distributional characteristics of error sequences, learn the fractal commonality of errors, and finally achieve error correction through uncertainty-guided dynamic weighting. It mitigates the risk of overfitting, often caused by the fixed error weight assignment in traditional error compensation models.

2. Materials and Methods

The carbon market price time series forecasting task aims to construct a model capable of predicting future carbon market price trends based on a given historical time series. The input to the predictive model is a carbon market price time series with a time step length of T, denoted as $X = \{x_1, x_2, \ldots, x_T\}$.

2.1. Overall Architecture

Existing carbon market price prediction frameworks focus on capturing complex temporal dependencies but often suffer from issues such as gradient vanishing or gradient explosion. Moreover, most current methods lack sufficient modeling capability for multi-scale fluctuation patterns and fractal characteristics inherent in carbon market price sequences, neglecting the self-similarity and scale-specific volatility mechanisms across different time horizons in carbon markets, which significantly constrain the model's representational capacity and generalization performance when handling complex price dynamics. To address these challenges, this paper proposes a novel carbon market price forecasting model, MF-Transformer-DEC, which enhances robustness against nonlinear fluctuations. Figure 1 is the overall architecture diagram of the model.

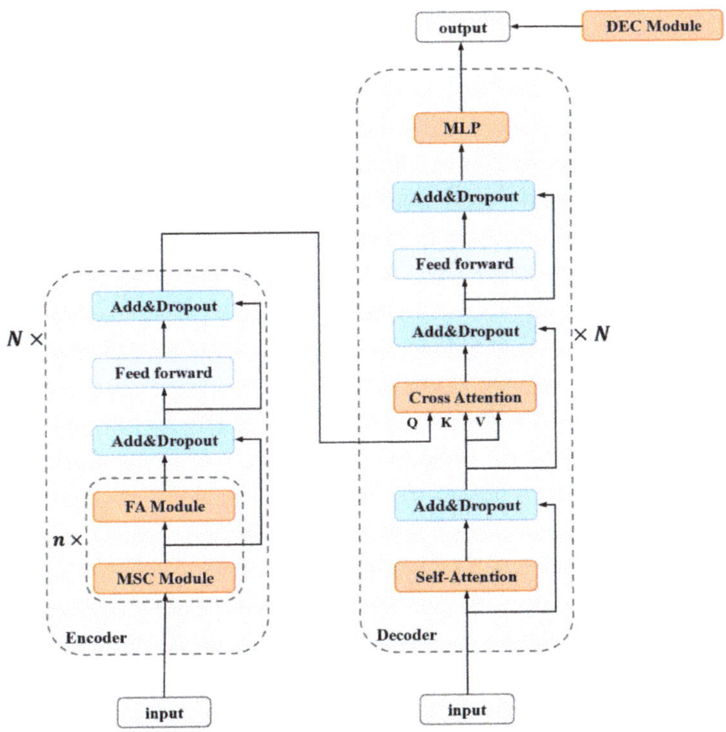

Figure 1. MF-Transformer-DEC schematic diagram.

(1) The MF-Transformer model is constructed based on the MSC module and FA module, combined with transformer architecture, modeling the carbon market price time series and predicting the future trend. This model adopts a Transformer-based encoder-decoder architecture. The encoder processes and encodes the input time series, while the decoder generates predictions through iterative decoding.

(2) The encoder of the MF-Transformer model consists of MSC and FA modules, which decouple and model the multifractal characteristics of carbon market prices. The MSC

module employs multi-layer dilated convolutions to decompose the time series into multi-scale components. The FA module calculates similarity weights between feature sequences at different scales to uncover the underlying multifractal structure of carbon market price series, thereby enhancing the model's perception and understanding capabilities of complex dependency structures.

(3) The decoder of the MF-Transformer model adopts the standard Transformer decoder architecture, comprising self-attention, cross-attention, and feed-forward neural networks. It captures long-range dependencies in carbon market prices and dynamically integrates all extracted features for prediction.

(4) The DEC module is constructed based on the VAE model and an uncertainty-guided dynamic weighting mechanism to capture the latent distribution of error sequences and adaptively fuse the residual correction term with the underlying predicted values.

The MF-Transformer model is constructed by proposing multi-scale convolution, fractal attention, combined with a transformer architecture. And the DEC module is proposed for prediction error correction. The proposed method effectively models and accurately predicts multifractality, non-stationarity, multi-scale properties, and extreme volatility in carbon market price forecasting.

2.2. *Implementation Principle of the MF-Transformer Core Module*

2.2.1. Multi-Scale Convolution (MSC) Module

The carbon market price time series exhibits complex multifractality. However, most existing multi-scale carbon market price prediction methods rely on signal processing techniques and employ fixed decomposition approaches, lacking end-to-end learning capability, dynamic adaptability, and sophisticated feature modeling capacity. To address these limitations, a convolutional network with scale invariance is proposed in the MSC module. The MSC module adopts multiple dilated convolutional layers with varying dilation rates but shared convolutional kernel weights, endowing MSC with a learnable fractal perception capability. Compared with traditional convolution operations, dilated convolution employs interval sampling through hole filling, which expands the receptive field without increasing parameters or computational overhead, resulting in higher convolution efficiency. Figure 2 illustrates the schematic diagram of the multi-scale convolution principle.

The MSC module designs multiple layers of dilated convolutions where different dilated convolutional layers share the same convolutional kernel weights but employ exponentially increasing dilation rates. This creates a multi-layer convolutional structure that maintains identical feature extraction patterns while operating at different temporal scales, thereby projecting and reconstructing time series data within a multi-scale fractal space. Below, we detail the operation of a single dilated convolutional layer.

For a time series $X = \{x_1, x_2, \ldots, x_T\}$, Formula (1) represents the principle of the padding operation, Formula (2) represents the formula for performing dilated convolution with a dilation rate of d on the padded sequence, and Formula (3) represents the formula for applying the activation operation to the convolution output:

$$\widetilde{x}_i = \begin{cases} 0, i < 1 \text{ or } i > T \\ x_i, 1 <= i <= T \end{cases}, \tag{1}$$

$$\{u_t\} = \sum_{n=1}^{N} \omega_n \cdot \widetilde{x}_{t-d\cdot(n-1)} (t = 1, 2, \ldots, T), \tag{2}$$

$$\{z_t\} = \text{RELU}(\{u_t\})(t = 1, 2, \ldots, T), \tag{3}$$

where $\widetilde{x}_i$ represents the result of one time step after the padding operation; $\{u_t\}(t = 1, 2, \ldots, T)$ is the output of the dilated convolution operation with dilation rate d; $\{\omega_1, \omega_2, \ldots, \omega_N\}$ denotes the original convolution kernel weights before dilation; ReLU is the activation layer that introduces nonlinearity, enabling the model to learn complex functional mappings; $\{z_t\}(t = 1, 2, \ldots, T)$ is the output after activation.

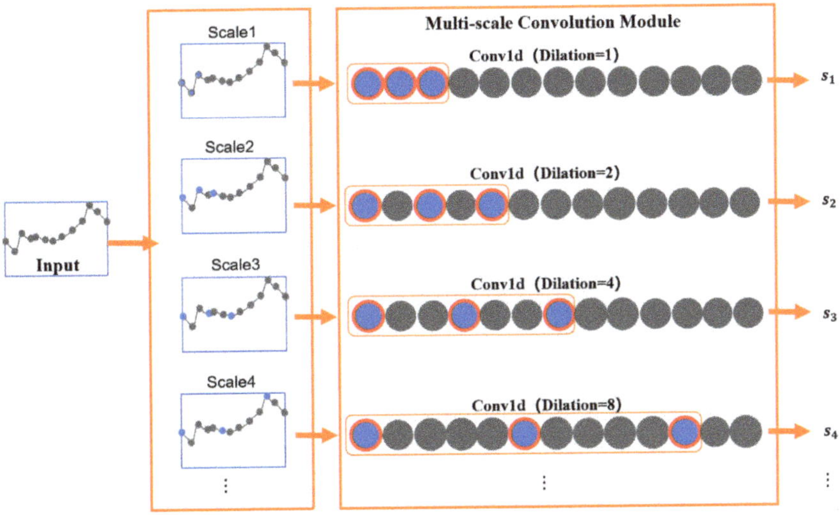

Figure 2. Schematic diagram of multi-scale convolution.

The dilation rates of different dilated convolutional layers vary. To progressively expand the receptive field, we adopt exponentially increasing dilation rates as shown in Formula (4). Different dilation rates correspond to different receptive fields, with the receptive field calculation formula given in Formula (5):

$$d \in \left\{2^0, 2^1, \ldots, 2^{m-1}\right\}, \tag{4}$$

$$\text{Receptive Field} = d \cdot (N - 1) + 1, \tag{5}$$

where 0, 1, . . ., m denotes the exponential order of dilation rate growth; d represents the dilation rate value, which belongs to an exponentially increasing set of dilation rates; N indicates the receptive field size of standard convolution.

2.2.2. Fractal Attention Module (FA)

Carbon market price variations exhibit significant nonlinear dynamic characteristics and prominent non-stationarity, constituting a complex system with implicit multifractality. Existing carbon market price prediction models struggle to effectively capture the intricate temporal dynamics and suffer from issues such as gradient vanishing or explosion. To address this, we propose FA module, which employs multi-head attention to mine similarities across different scales and model multifractality in the data. Figure 3 illustrates the schematic diagram of fractal attention.

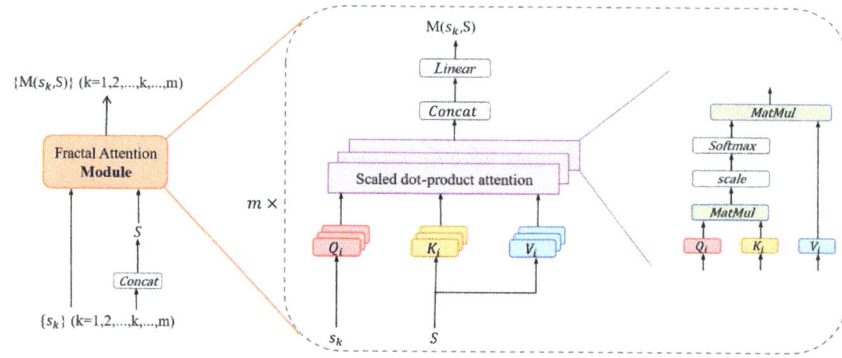

Figure 3. Schematic diagram of fractal attention.

The output of one MSC module is connected to an FA module, where the FA module models latent dependencies in the data by computing similarities between different scales. The calculation of similarity between the k-scale and all scales is illustrated below as an example. Formula (6) is the calculation formula for concatenating all dilated convolution output vectors $s_1, s_2, \ldots, s_k, \ldots, s_m$ to obtain the vector S, containing the feature vectors from all scales. Formula (7) is the calculation formula for the query vector Q_i corresponding to s_k which is the convolution output of scale k, as well as the key vector K_i and value vector V_i corresponding to S, $i \in [1, h]$ represents the i-th attention head. Formula (8) is the calculation formula for the similarity score Score(Q_i,K_i) between the Q_i and the K_i, obtained by the dot product. Formula (9) computes the weighted sum over each position based on the Score(Q_i,K_i) to obtain the output of the attention mechanism Attention(Q_i,K_i,V_i). Formula (10) is the calculation formula for the multi-head attention output M(s_k,S) at s_k on S. Different attention heads focus on different correlation relationships, facilitating comprehensive latent dependency mining.

$$S = \mathrm{Concat}(s_1, s_2, \ldots, s_k, \ldots, s_m, \mathrm{dim} = -1), \tag{6}$$

$$Q_i = s_k \propto_i, \ K_i = S\beta_i, \ V_i = S\gamma_i, \tag{7}$$

$$\mathrm{Score}(Q_i, K_i) = QK_i^{\mathrm{T}}, \tag{8}$$

$$\mathrm{Attention}(Q_i, K_i, V_i) = \mathrm{Softmax}((\frac{\mathrm{Score}(Q, k)}{\sqrt{D_{key}}}))V_i, \tag{9}$$

$$M(s_k, S) = \mathrm{Concat}(\mathrm{Attention}(Q_1, K_1, V_1), \ldots, \mathrm{Attention}(Q_h, K_h, V_h)), \tag{10}$$

Concat(*,dim = −1) denotes concatenation along the last dimension; $\propto_i$, β_i, γ_i are trainable weight matrices D_{key} is the dimension of keys.

By introducing the multi-head attention mechanism, we enable autonomous learning of similarity relationships across multiple scales to model the multifractal market dynamics, thereby enhancing the model's understanding of complex systems and improving prediction accuracy.

2.2.3. MF-Transformer

The MF-Transformer model employs the transformer's encoder-decoder architecture for integrated carbon market price prediction.

The encoder consists of MSC, FA, and other modules to model the multifractality of carbon market price series. Each MSC-FA combination extracts multi-scale similarity features. Multiple such parallel combinations can be configured, with different MSC modules in each combination using distinct convolutional kernel parameters to model time series through varied feature extraction patterns. These different combinations capture diverse feature types, achieving complementary feature learning and enabling comprehensive feature extraction from the time series.

The decoder consists of conventional self-attention, cross-attention, and feed-forward neural networks, featuring high modularity and scalability. The self-attention mechanism captures long-range dependencies within the sequence to enhance model generalization, as shown in Equation (11). The cross-attention dynamically integrates the fractal features extracted by the decoder with the long-range dependencies captured by self-attention, as shown in Equation (12):

$$R_2 = \mathrm{SelfAttention}(X) = M(X, X), \tag{11}$$

$$F = \mathrm{CrossAttention}(R_1, R_2) = M(R_1, R_2), \tag{12}$$

where X is the input time series R_1 represents the encoder's computation results; R_2 denotes the self-attention computation results in the decoder; M(X,X) indicates multi-head attention computation on X; $M(R_1,R_2)$ represents R_1 computes multi-head attention on R_2; F is the output after cross-attention fusion.

Residual connections with dropout are applied to prevent overfitting, followed by ReLU activation, as expressed in the following formula:

$$E = \mathrm{ReLU}(F + \mathrm{Dropout}(F + M(R_1, R_2))), \tag{13}$$

where Dropout denotes the dropout operation; $M(R_1,R_2)$ represents R_1 computes multi-head attention on R_2; ReLU indicates the ReLU activation function operation; E is the final output result.

The feed-forward neural network utilizes the extracted features for prediction. The fused data is flattened and fed into a multi-layer perceptron (MLP), where linear transformation layers map the data to different dimensional spaces. Nonlinear feature transformation is achieved through ReLU activation, ultimately yielding the prediction result. The formula is as follows:

$$\hat{y} = \mathrm{ReLU}(W_2(\mathrm{ReLU}(W_1 \mathrm{Flatten}(E) + b_1)) + b_2), \tag{14}$$

where $\hat{y}$ is the final prediction; W_1 represents the weight matrix from input to hidden layer; W_2 denotes the weight matrix from hidden to output layer; b_1 is the bias term for the hidden layer; b_2 is the bias term for the output layer; ReLU indicates the ReLU nonlinear activation function; Flatten represents the flattening operation.

2.3. *Dynamic Error Correction (DEC) Module*

To enhance the carbon market price prediction model's capability to analyze complex market fluctuations, the DEC module employs a Variational Autoencoder (VAE) to learn the latent distribution of errors and dynamically weights them for error correction in carbon market price sequences.

The VAE captures both temporal and distributional characteristics of error sequences, enabling it to learn the fractal commonality and extract the "de-randomized" core error properties. The VAE models the latent distribution of data through hidden variables and has strong regularization properties that prevent overfitting. Formula (15) is the calculation formula for activating the error sequence ϵ. Formula (16) is the calculation formula for sampling the hidden variable z from a Gaussian distribution using the reparameterization technique. Formula (17) is the calculation formula for activating z. Formula (18) is the calculation formula for prediction output $\hat{\epsilon}$.

$$h_1 = \mathrm{Relu}(W_3\epsilon + b_3), \tag{15}$$

$$z = \mu + \sigma \cdot \epsilon_{noise}, \tag{16}$$

$$h_2 = \mathrm{Relu}(W_4 z + b_4), \tag{17}$$

$$\hat{\epsilon} = W_{out} h_2 + b_{out}, \tag{18}$$

where W_3, W_4 are hidden layer weights; b_3, b_4 are hidden layer bias terms; ReLU denotes the ReLU activation function; μ represents the mean of h_1; σ is the standard deviation of h_1; ϵ_{noise} is noise sampled from standard normal distribution; W_{out} and b_{out} are output layer weight and bias.

Traditional error compensation models using fixed error weights often lead to overfitting risks and struggle to adapt to the non-stationary volatility characteristics of carbon market price series. We utilize standard deviation to quantify uncertainty in error sequences and dynamically adjust the main model's predictions. Formula (19) is the calculation formula for the uncertainty-driven dynamic weighting coefficient α. Formula (20) is the formula for dynamically weighting the error compensation $\hat{\epsilon}$ back into the initial prediction value $\hat{y}$.

$$\alpha = 1/(1 + \sigma), \tag{19}$$

$$\hat{y_c} = \hat{y} + \alpha \cdot \hat{\epsilon}, \tag{20}$$

where σ is the standard deviation of h_1; $\hat{\epsilon}$ denotes the error generated by the VAE model; $\hat{y_c}$ is the final output after error compensation.

Compared with traditional fixed-weight methods, this strategy dynamically adjusts fusion weights based on σ's uncertainty, significantly reducing interference from abnormal fluctuations while enhancing long-term trend fitting capability.

3. Results

This section describes the experimental data, multifractal analysis of carbon market prices, performance metrics, parameter settings, training and prediction process.

3.1. Description of Experimental Data

We construct forecasting tasks based on high-frequency data from China's Shanghai and Guangdong carbon markets. The Shanghai carbon price dataset covers the Shanghai carbon market price series from 19 December 2013 to 30 August 2024, with a total of 1800 carbon price time-point data; the Guangdong carbon price dataset covers the Guangdong carbon market price series from 12 October 2016 to 30 August 2024, with a total of 1845 carbon price time-point data. The Shanghai carbon market price dataset is visualised in Figure 4 below, and the Shanghai carbon market price dataset is visualised in Figure 5 below.

For the Shanghai carbon price dataset, the mean is 43.67 and the median is 40.16. The standard deviation is 17.10, indicating a moderate level of price volatility and suggesting a certain degree of regularity in price fluctuations. The range is 73.47, determined by a maximum value of 77.67 and a minimum value of 4.20, indicating a notable historical fluctuation interval. The skewness is 0.03, showing that the price distribution is nearly symmetric with no significant skew. The kurtosis is −0.30, a negative value suggesting that extremely high and low prices occur less frequently.

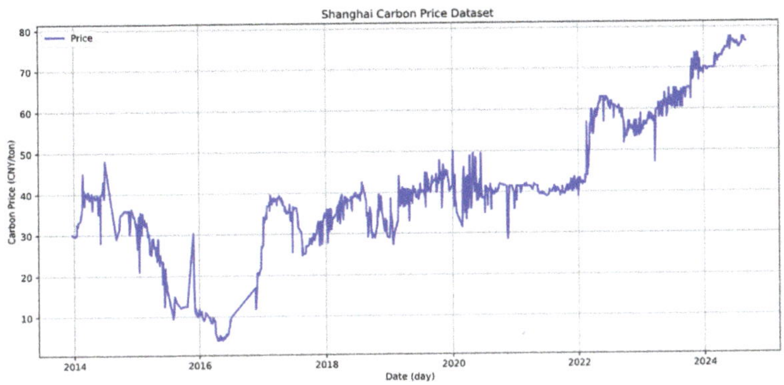

Figure 4. Visualisation of the Shanghai carbon market price dataset.

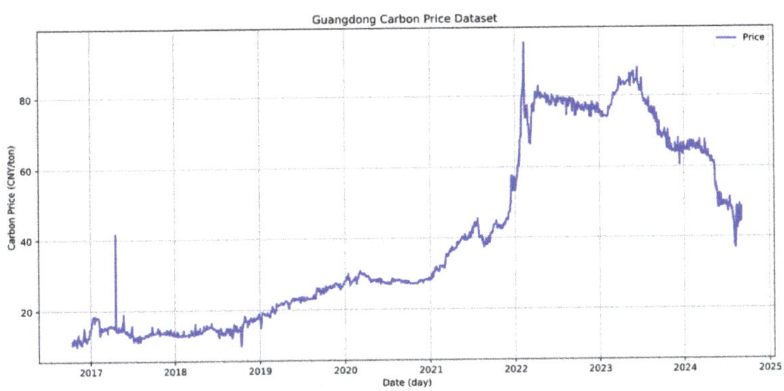

Figure 5. Visualisation of the Guangdong carbon market price dataset.

The statistical characteristics of the Shanghai and Guangdong carbon market price datasets are shown in Table 1. According to the data in the table:

Table 1. Table of Statistical Characteristics of Shanghai Carbon Market Price Dataset and Guangdong Carbon Market Price Dataset.

Statistical Characteristics	Shanghai Carbon Price Dataset	Guangdong Carbon Price Dataset
Mean	43.67	40.35
Median	40.16	28.99
Standard deviation	17.10	24.87
Range	73.47	85.46
Max	77.67	95.26
Min	4.20	9.80
Skewness	0.03	0.51
Kurtosis	−0.30	−1.27

For the Guangdong carbon price dataset, the mean is 40.35 and the median is 28.99, which is significantly lower than the mean, indicating a right-skewed distribution. The standard deviation is 24.87, a relatively large value, reflecting higher price volatility and a less stable market. The range is 85.46, composed of a maximum value of 95.26 and a minimum value of 9.80, indicating a wide historical variation in prices. The skewness is 0.51, a positive value indicating right skewness in the price distribution. The kurtosis is −1.27, also negative, indicating a low frequency of extreme values.

3.2. Multifractal Analysis of Carbon Market Price Series

The carbon market price variation exhibits notable nonlinear dynamical characteristics and pronounced non-stationarity, constituting a complex system with multifractal properties. We employ the Multifractal Detrended Fluctuation Analysis (MFDFA) method from the perspective of mathematical statistical analysis to verify the multifractal characteristics of the carbon market price datasets for Shanghai and Guangdong, thereby demonstrating the practical value of the proposed model.

The following introduction to the MFDFA method is based on the work of Kantelhardt et al. [29]. The specific steps of MFDFA are as follows:

(1) Calculate the dispersion sequence $\{y_i\}$ of the time series $\{x_i\}(i = 1, 2, \ldots, N)$,

$$\{y_i\}= \sum_{k=1}^{i} (x_k - \bar{x}) \ (i = 1,2,\ldots,N), \tag{21}$$

Here $\bar{x}$ represents the mean value,

(2) Divide the sequence $\{y_i\}$ into $N_s = \mathrm{int}(N/s)$ intervals. Each interval contains s data points. When N is not divisible by s, y_i will be a remainder. To avoid losing data, the division process is repeated from the end of the sequence, and ultimately, two equal-length subintervals are obtained, encompassing all the data points in the sequence.

(3) Calculate the mean squared error $F^2(s,v)$. Taking the interval v ($v = 1, 2, \ldots, 2N_s$) as an example, perform k-order polynomial fitting:

$$y_v(i)= a_1 i^k + a_2 i^{k-1} + \ldots + a_{k+1} \ (i = 1,2,\ldots N), \tag{22}$$

For the interval ($v = 1, 2, \ldots, 2N_s$):

$$F^2(s,v) = \frac{1}{s}\sum_{i=1}^{s}\{y[(v-1)s+i] - y_v(i)\}, \tag{23}$$

For the interval ($v = N_s + 1, N_s + 2, \ldots, 2N_s$):

$$F^2(s,v) = \frac{1}{s}\sum_{i=1}^{s}\{y[N-(v-N_s)s+i] - y_v(i)\}, \tag{24}$$

(4) Calculate the q-order fluctuation function F(q,s):

$$F(q,s) = \left\{\frac{1}{2N_s}\sum_{v=1}^{2N_s}\left[F^2(s,v)\right]^{q/2}\right\}^{1/q}, \tag{25}$$

In the formula, q is a non-zero real number, and F(q,s) exhibits a power-law relationship with s.

(5) Calculate the individual generalized Hurst exponent h(q). Take q as a certain value and s as different values, repeat steps (26)–(28), and take the logarithm of F(q,s). Fit the slope of the curve to obtain the generalized h(q) value:

$$\ln F(q,s) = \ln k + h(q)\cdot \ln s, \tag{26}$$

(6) Calculate the generalized Hurst exponent and singularity exponent. Repeat steps (25)–(29) with different values of q to obtain them. Calculate the area and its width according to the following formula:

$$\alpha(q) = h(q) + q\frac{dh(q)}{dq}, \tag{27}$$

$$f(\alpha) = q[\alpha - h(q)] + 1, \tag{28}$$

$$\Delta\alpha = \alpha_{max} - \alpha_{min}, \tag{29}$$

In the formula, α represents the singularity exponent, indicating the growth probability of each sub-interval, and its value is inversely proportional to the singularity; $f(\alpha)$ denotes the multifractal spectrum; $\Delta\alpha$ represents the difference between the maximum and minimum probabilities, and a larger value indicates a more uneven sequence distribution and a stronger fractal intensity.

The multifractal spectrum of the Shanghai and Guangdong carbon market price datasets is shown in Figure 6. It can be concluded that the multifractal spectrum of the Shanghai carbon market price dataset is left-skewed, indicating that short-term fluctuations dominate. On the other hand, the multifractal spectrum of the Guangdong carbon market price dataset is right-skewed, indicating that long-term fluctuations dominate. The calculated value for the multifractal spectrum of the Shanghai carbon market price dataset is $\Delta\alpha = 0.701 > 0$, while that of the Guangdong carbon market price dataset is $\Delta\alpha = 0.786 > 0$, further confirming the multifractal nature of both datasets.

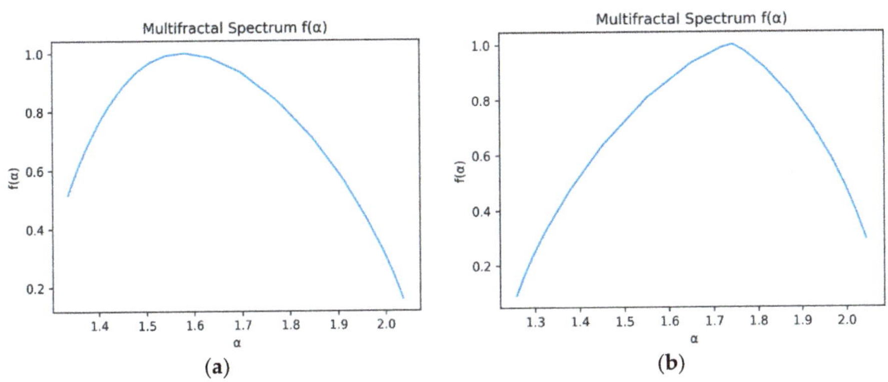

Figure 6. (**a**) Multifractal spectrum of Shanghai carbon market price dataset; (**b**) Multifractal spectrum of Guangdong carbon market price dataset.

3.3. *Performance Metrics*

In this study, mean square residuals (MSE), mean absolute residuals (MAE), and root mean square residuals (RMSE) are selected as the evaluation indices to quantitatively evaluate the model's prediction accuracy and robustness.

MAE is the average of absolute residuals. It is the average value of the absolute difference between the predicted value and the true value, which can intuitively reflect the average level of the prediction residuals. Its calculation formula is:

$$MAE = \frac{1}{n}\sum_{i=1}^{n} |y_i - \hat{y}_i|^2, \tag{30}$$

MSE is the expected value of the square of the difference between the estimated parameter and the true value. It can reflect the overall degree of variation in the predicted residuals. Its calculation formula is:

$$\mathrm{MSE} = \frac{1}{n}\sum_{i=1}^{n}(y_i - \hat{y}_i)^2, \tag{31}$$

RMSE is the square root of the mean square residuals, and its unit is the same as the original data, which can reflect the size of the predicted residuals more intuitively. Its calculation formula is:

$$\mathrm{RMSE} = \sqrt{\frac{1}{n}\sum_{i=1}^{n}(y_i - \hat{y}_i)^2}, \tag{32}$$

R^2 is used as an important indicator for assessing the performance of a regression model, which measures the model's ability to explain the variance of the target variable. The range of values is usually between $(-\infty, 1)$.

$$R^2 = 1 - \frac{\sum_{i=1}^{n}(y_i - \hat{y}_i)^2}{\sum_{i=1}^{n}(y_i - \bar{y})^2}, \tag{33}$$

In the above formula, n is the number of samples that have been validated, is the true value, is the predicted value of the model, is the mean of the actual value; the closer the values of MSE, MAE and RMSE are to 0, the better the predictive performance of the model. The closer the value is to 1, the better the explanatory ability of the model.

3.4. Parameter Settings

In this study, the parameter settings of the model have an important impact on the prediction performance. To ensure the stability and generalisation ability of the model, we optimised the key parameters through experiments and cross-validation. The specific parameter settings are shown in Table 2:

Table 2. Core model hyperparameter settings.

Parameter Category	Parameter Name	Set Value
Model Architecture	dilations	[1, 2, 4, 8]
	kernel_size	3
	num_heads	4
	Dropout	0.1
Training strategy	Optimiser	Adam
	Loss function	MSE
	Batch size	32
	Training rounds (epochs)	60
	Random seed (random state)	42
	Regularisation factor λ_1	1×10^{-4}
	Regularisation factor λ_2	1×10^{-3}

The MSC module in the encoder part of the model uses a kernel size of 3 for the original convolution to extract local and global context information. The num_heads in multi-head attention is set to 4 to enhance the model's ability to perceive features. Also, dropout is set to 0.1 to prevent overfitting.

The standard self-attention and cross-attention mechanisms in the decoder part of the model, num_heads and dropout, are used with settings consistent with the attention mechanism in the decoder.

During training, the Adam optimiser is used with the learning rate set to 1×10^{-3}, the batch size set to 32, and the initial number of training rounds set to 10. The evaluation metrics include MSE, RMSE, MAE, and R^2 to comprehensively measure the model's performance under different error metrics.

To enhance model robustness, a multi-level regularisation strategy is introduced. The L1 regularisation coefficient $\lambda_1 = 1 \times 10^{-4}$ is used to induce sparsity, and the L2 regularisation coefficient $\lambda_2 = 1 \times 10^{-3}$ is used to constrain the smooth variation of the mask function and enhance model stability.

3.5. Training and Prediction Process

The MF-Transformer-DEC's modules work synergistically to achieve high-performance carbon market price prediction. The prediction process is shown in Figure 7. The specific processing steps are as follows:

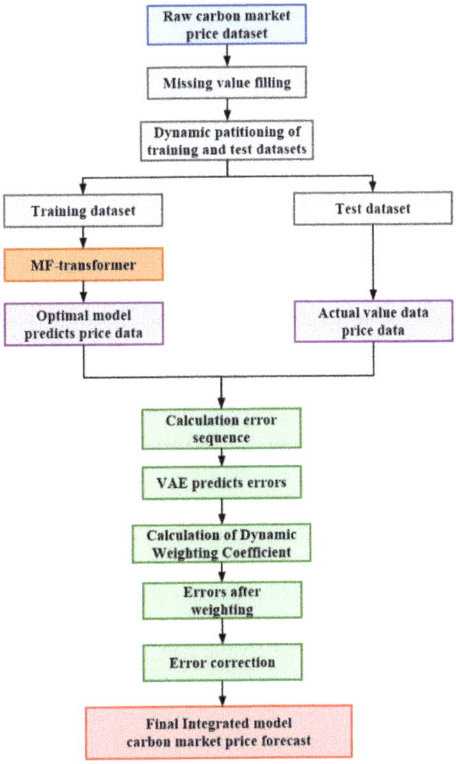

Figure 7. Flowchart of the Prediction Framework.

Step 1: Data Pre-processing: Perform Z-score normalization on the original carbon market price series. Obtain a dataset using the sliding window method, and employ a sliding window technique with a fixed window length of 90 to construct a time series task that predicts the carbon market price trend for the next 7 days using the past 90 days. By defining a window function $W(t) = [x_{t-89}, x_{t-88}, \ldots, x_t]$ that slides continuously along the time axis with a unit stride (Stride=1), a set of observation subsequence samples $\{W(t)\}_{t=90}^{T}$ with strict temporal continuity, a form is formed. The sliding window method not only enhances the availability of training data but also ensures the integrity of sequence information, allowing for flexible construction of multi-step prediction datasets. A training-to-testing split ratio of 0.8:0.2 is adopted for the generated subsequence samples, which ensures sufficient model training while maintaining the effectiveness and comparability of the evaluation. The number of training and testing samples for 1-step, 3-step, and 7-step predictions in the Shanghai and Guangdong carbon market price datasets, which were obtained through the sliding window method and dataset partitioning, is presented in Table 3.

Table 3. Table of training set sample sizes and testing set sample sizes for 1-step, 3-step, and 7-step predictions of the Shanghai carbon market price dataset and the Guangdong carbon market price dataset.

Dataset	Steps	Number of Samples in the Training Set	Number of Samples in the Testing Set
Shanghai carbon price dataset	1-step	1484	371
	3-step	1482	371
	6-step	1479	370
Guangdong carbon price dataset	1-step	1528	382
	3-step	1526	382
	6-step	1523	381
	1-step	1484	371

Step 2: Model Training: Initialize model parameters such as Dropout, and input the training dataset into the model for training.

Step 3: Model Prediction: Input the test dataset into the MF-Transformer model. The model outputs carbon market price prediction data for h time steps $\{\hat{y_1}, \hat{y_2}, \ldots, \hat{y_p}\}$.

Step 4: Residual prediction: Predict the residual sequence $\{\epsilon_1, \epsilon_2, \ldots, \epsilon_p\}$ by inputting it into the VAE model for prediction, serving as the predicted values $\{\hat{\epsilon_1}, \hat{\epsilon_2}, \ldots, \hat{\epsilon_p}\}$ for the carbon market price prediction residuals for h time points.

Step 5: Obtain the final forecast value of the carbon market price. The residual forecast results $\{\hat{\epsilon_1}, \hat{\epsilon_2}, \ldots, \hat{\epsilon_p}\}$ for h time points are used to further optimize the original forecast results $\{\hat{y_1}, \hat{y_2}, \ldots, \hat{y_h}\}$, with the corrected carbon market price serving as the final carbon market price forecast value for the h time points.

4. Experimental Results and Discussion

The fifth part first constructs a multi-step prediction comparison experiment for the MF-Transformer model, then conducts ablation experiments, and finally evaluates the MF-Transformer model after dynamic residual correction. The performance advantages of the proposed model are verified through experiments from multiple aspects.

4.1. Multi-Step Prediction Comparison Experiment

The MF-Transformer proposed in this paper is compared and evaluated with SVR, LSTM, CNN, and Transformer. Based on high-frequency data from the carbon markets in Shanghai and Guangdong, China, a multi-step prediction task is constructed, utilizing carbon market price data from the past 90 time steps to predict future prices at 1, 3, and 7 time steps, respectively. Experimental results show that the MF-Transformer model proposed in this study significantly outperforms traditional methods in multi-dimensional evaluations. Compared to the benchmark models, its prediction accuracy and robustness have been significantly improved, and its key indicators surpass existing methods. The core advantage of this model stems from technological innovation in addressing the complex characteristics of carbon market price series.

The experiment evaluates model performance using four quality metrics (detailed in Section 3.3 Performance Metrics). Mean Absolute Error (MAE) measures the average deviation between predicted and actual values; lower values indicate smaller overall prediction errors. Mean Squared Error (MSE) reflects the stability of the model under extreme conditions; smaller values suggest reduced variance in prediction errors. Root Mean Squared Error (RMSE), the square root of MSE, retains the same unit as the original data, making it easier to interpret the error magnitude; smaller RMSE values indicate better alignment between predicted and actual values. The coefficient of determination (R^2) assesses the proportion of variance in the actual data that is explained by the model; values closer to 1 reflect stronger explanatory power.

The statistical results and visualizations of multi-step carbon price forecasting are presented in Tables 4 and 5 and Figures 8 and 9. The main findings are as follows: (1) The proposed MF-Transformer achieves the best overall performance across all metrics. On the Shanghai carbon price dataset, the average MAE, MSE, RMSE, and R^2 are 0.1081, 0.0231, 0.1517, and 0.9759, respectively. On the Guangdong dataset, the corresponding values are 0.0622, 0.0077, 0.0875, and 0.9925. These results demonstrate the model's strong accuracy, generalization capability, and modeling effectiveness. (2) Deep learning models generally outperform traditional machine learning approaches. Traditional models such as SVR lack the ability to capture sequential dependencies, resulting in R^2 values ranging between 0.88 and 0.91 and MAE values exceeding 0.2. These figures indicate limited capability in capturing complex market dynamics and higher prediction errors. (3) The performance of LSTM and CNN models generally deteriorates as the forecast horizon increases. For instance, in the Guangdong dataset, LSTM's MAE increases from 0.1191 at1-step to 0.1938 at 7-step, and RMSE rises from 0.1520 to 0.2316, highlighting the limitations in long-term forecasting and weak generalization ability. (4) The Transformer model achieves higher prediction accuracy than other baseline models. In the 7-step prediction task on the Guangdong dataset, the Transformer model achieves an RMSE of 0.1564 and an R^2 of 0.9783, clearly outperforming LSTM and CNN, which supports the effectiveness of Transformer-based architectures. (5) MF-Transformer consistently delivers the best performance across all datasets. It maintains R^2 values above 0.97 and RMSE values below 0.15, outperforming other ensemble models. The consistent superiority and stability of MF-Transformer indicate its robustness and strong generalization ability, confirming its structural advantages in carbon price prediction tasks.

Table 4. Evaluation Metrics Table for Multi-Step Forecasting on the Shanghai Carbon Market Price Dataset.

Steps	Experimental Group 1	MAE	MSE	RMSE	R^2
1-step	SVR	0.2395	0.0855	0.2924	0.9108
	LSTM	0.1399	0.0365	0.1911	0.9619
	CNN	0.1680	0.0516	0.2271	0.9462
	Transformer	0.1215	0.0300	0.1732	0.9681
	MF-Transformer	0.1004	0.0204	0.1430	0.9792
3-step	SVR	0.2472	0.0932	0.3054	0.9023
	LSTM	0.1679	0.0572	0.2392	0.9401
	CNN	0.1740	0.0612	0.2473	0.9359
	Transformer	0.1238	0.0374	0.1933	0.9623
	MF-Transformer	0.1086	0.0233	0.1526	0.9755
7-step	SVR	0.2707	0.1168	0.3418	0.8839
	LSTM	0.1852	0.0691	0.2629	0.9313
	CNN	0.1950	0.0711	0.2667	0.9293
	Transformer	0.1332	0.0362	0.1903	0.9621
	MF-Transformer	0.1153	0.0255	0.1596	0.9730

Table 5. Evaluation Metrics Table for Multi-Step Forecasting on the Guangdong Carbon Market Price Dataset.

Steps	Experimental Group 2	MAE	MSE	RMSE	R^2
1-step	SVR	0.2770	0.1050	0.3241	0.9037
	LSTM	0.1191	0.0231	0.1520	0.9788
	CNN	0.0966	0.0255	0.1598	0.9766
	Transformer	0.0745	0.0114	0.1066	0.9898
	MF-Transformer	0.0592	0.0068	0.0822	0.9939
3-step	SVR	0.2692	0.0980	0.3131	0.9077
	LSTM	0.1619	0.0377	0.1941	0.9645
	CNN	0.1824	0.0497	0.2229	0.9532
	Transformer	0.1058	0.0207	0.1440	0.9818
	MF-Transformer	0.0592	0.0068	0.0822	0.9922
7-step	SVR	0.2995	0.1173	0.3426	0.8923
	LSTM	0.1938	0.0536	0.2316	0.9508
	CNN	0.1794	0.0537	0.2318	0.9506
	Transformer	0.1138	0.0245	0.1564	0.9783
	MF-Transformer	0.0683	0.0096	0.0981	0.9914

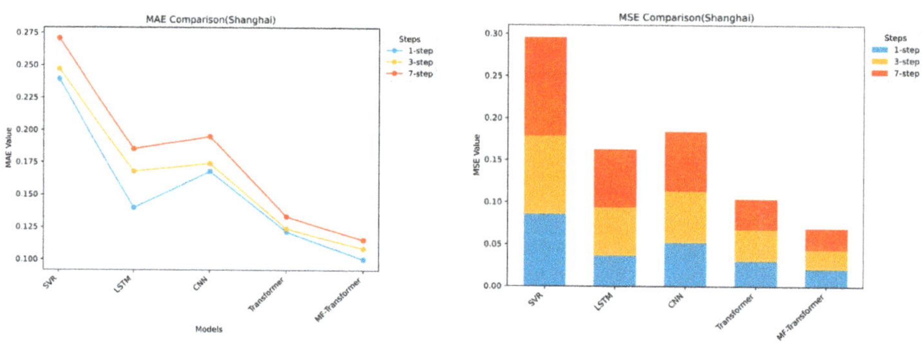

(a) (b)

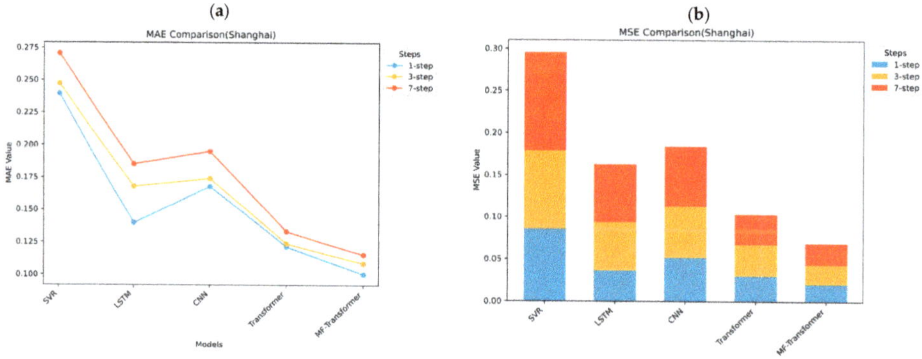

(a) (b)

Figure 8. (**a**) The MAE evaluation metric chart on the Shanghai carbon market price dataset; (**b**) The MSE evaluation metric chart on the Shanghai carbon market price dataset; (**c**) The R^2 evaluation metric chart on the Shanghai carbon market price dataset; (**d**) The RMSE evaluation metric chart on the Shanghai carbon market price dataset.

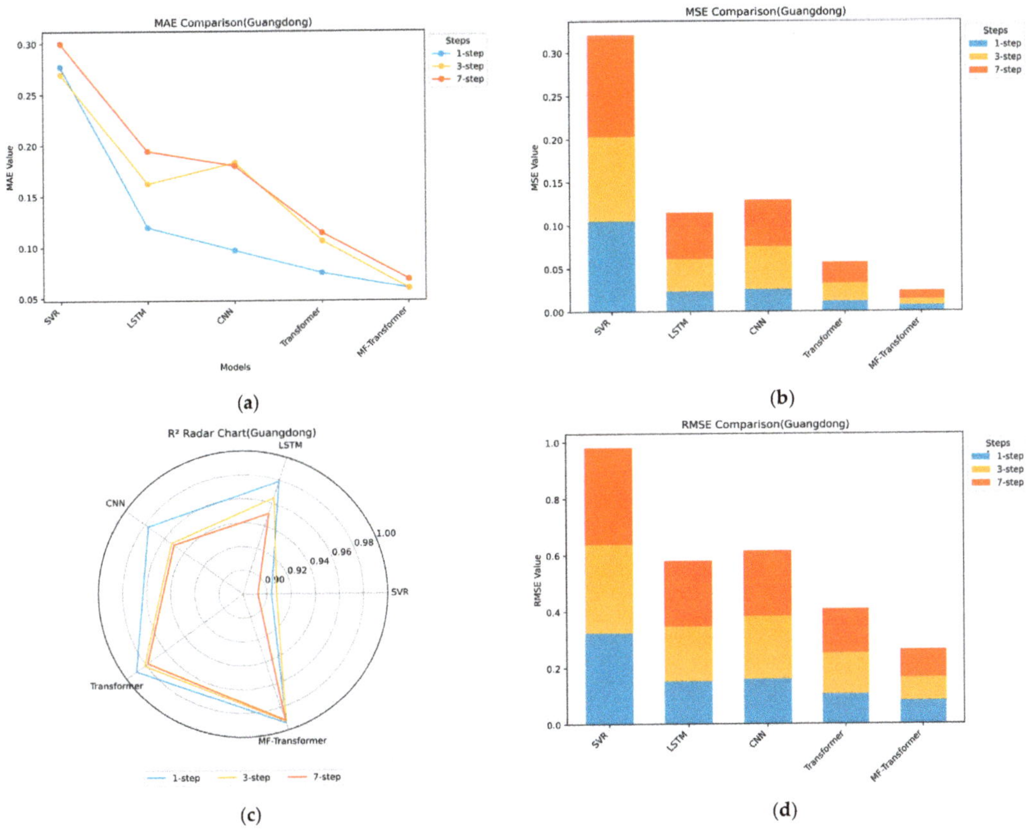

Figure 9. (**a**) The MAE evaluation metric chart on the Guangdong carbon market price dataset; (**b**) The MSE evaluation metric chart on the Guangdong carbon market price dataset; (**c**) The R^2 evaluation metric chart on the Guangdong carbon market price dataset; (**d**) The RMSE evaluation metric chart on the Guangdong carbon market price dataset.

4.2. Ablation Experiment of MF-Transformer

Due to the excellent performance of the proposed method, which is generated by multiple modules, we conducted an ablation study. Since the prediction task of 7 time steps can verify the model's performance on different prediction time scales and ensure the model's generalization ability under multi-step prediction, the ablation experiment was based on the task of predicting carbon market prices for the next 7 time steps. The statistical results of the prediction evaluation metrics are presented in Tables 6 and 7, from which it can be observed that: (1) the proposed model performs the best, indicating that the network architecture of the proposed model excels in carbon market price prediction. (2) The prediction performance of the other three methods declined to varying degrees, indicating that each module of the proposed method plays a positive role and further validates the rationality of the model design. When the MSC module is removed from the proposed model, its performance decreases. On the Shanghai dataset, the MAE increases from 0.1153 to 0.1299, and the R^2 drops from 0.9730 to 0.9653. On the Guangdong dataset, the MAE increases from 0.0683 to 0.1006, and the R^2 decreases to 0.9849. The simultaneous increase in prediction error and decrease in model fit suggest that the MSC module plays a crucial role in capturing temporal scale variations and enhancing the model's fitting ability. Similarly, removing the FA module also leads to increased prediction errors. On the Shanghai dataset, the MAE rises to 0.1286 and the RMSE increases to 0.1740. On the Guangdong dataset, the MAE increases to 0.0909 and the RMSE rises to 0.1191. These results demonstrate that the FA module is essential for modeling the multifractal structure and reducing prediction errors. (3) The single transformer model yields the poorest prediction performance. On the Shanghai and Guangdong datasets, the MAE values are 0.1332 and 0.1138, respectively, and the R^2 values are only 0.9621 and 0.9783. While the proposed ensemble model achieves the highest prediction accuracy on the dataset, it demonstrates the importance of multi-scale complex temporal analysis and similarity modeling in predicting carbon market prices. In summary, the proposed method integrates the aforementioned three modules to ensure high-performance prediction results, further proving that each module plays its own positive role in improving prediction performance.

Table 6. Evaluation Metrics Table for Ablation Experiments on the Shanghai Carbon Market Price Dataset.

Experimental Group 3	MAE	MSE	RMSE	R^2
Single transformer	0.1332	0.0362	0.1903	0.9621
Remove MSC	0.1299	0.0345	0.1857	0.9653
Remove FA	0.1286	0.0303	0.1740	0.9680
MF-Transformer	0.1153	0.0255	0.1596	0.9730

Table 7. Evaluation metric table for ablation experiments on the Guangdong carbon market price dataset.

Experimental Group 4	MAE	MSE	RMSE	R^2
Single transformer	0.1138	0.0245	0.1564	0.9783
Remove MSC	0.1006	0.0170	0.1305	0.9849
Remove FA	0.0909	0.0142	0.1191	0.9868
MF-Transformer	0.0683	0.0096	0.0981	0.9914

4.3. Evaluation Experiment of the DEC Mechanism and Model Stability Analysis

The statistical metrics from 15 repeated experiments of MF-Transformer-DEC on the Shanghai and Guangdong carbon market price datasets were used to evaluate the effectiveness of the DEC mechanism in correcting prediction errors of the MF-Transformer, while also verifying that the model's performance is not due to chance. This eliminates the bias caused by single-run experimental randomness and demonstrates the model's stable and statistically significant performance. Since the 7-step prediction task allows the evaluation of model performance across different forecast horizons, it serves as an effective test of the model's generalization ability under multi-step prediction scenarios. Therefore, the evaluation of the dynamic error correction mechanism was conducted based on the task of forecasting carbon prices over the next 7 time steps.

Table 8 presents the mean and standard deviation of evaluation metrics obtained from 15 runs of MF-Transformer-DEC on the Shanghai and Guangdong datasets. The results show that: (1) Compared with MF-Transformer, MF-Transformer-DEC achieves over a 14% reduction in MAE and MSE on both datasets, indicating smaller prediction errors and higher forecasting accuracy. The R^2 of MF-Transformer-DEC is consistently higher, suggesting an improved ability to capture carbon price trends. These results confirm that the DEC mechanism significantly enhances prediction performance. (2) On the Shanghai dataset, the model achieved very low average MAE, MSE, and RMSE across 15 repeated experiments, with standard deviations all below 0.007, indicating both low prediction error and high consistency. The average R^2 reached 0.9777, meaning the model explains 97.77% of the price variance and demonstrates strong generalization ability. On the

Guangdong dataset, the average MAE was only 0.0485, showing extremely low prediction error. The mean and standard deviation of MSE and RMSE were also low, reflecting high prediction precision. The R^2 reached 0.9942, with minimal standard deviation across 15 runs, indicating that the model accurately captures market fluctuations. (3) Across 15 independent repeated experiments on both datasets, MF-Transformer-DEC consistently achieved excellent average performance and small standard deviations for MAE, MSE, RMSE, and R^2. This confirms the model's high fitting capability and robustness, effectively ruling out the possibility of accidental performance. It demonstrates that the model is stable and reliable.

Table 8. Table of mean and standard deviation of evaluation metrics for MF-Transformer-Dec running 15 times on Shanghai and Guangdong carbon market price datasets.

Experimental Group 5	MAE		MSE		RMSE		R^2		MAE		MSE		RMSE		R^2	
	Mean	Std	Mean	Std	Mean	Std	Mean	Std	Mean	Std	Mean	Std	Mean	Std	Mean	Std
Shanghai Carbon Market Price Dataset	0.0983	0.0064	0.0219	0.0016	0.1478	0.0055	0.9777	0.0016	0.0983	0.0064	0.0219	0.0016	0.1478	0.0055	0.9777	0.0016
Guangdong Carbon Market Price Dataset	0.0485	0.0039	0.0059	0.0005	0.0773	0.0033	0.9942	0.0005	0.0485	0.0039	0.0059	0.0005	0.0773	0.0033	0.9942	0.0005

4.4. Discussion

The proposed MF-Transformer-DEC, through the integration of fractal thinking and architectural innovation, demonstrates significant performance advantages in carbon market price prediction tasks. It breaks through the limitations of traditional methods and existing deep learning structures, providing a new solution and paradigm for complex time series modeling. In three experiments, the average evaluation metrics of MF-Transformer-DEC outperformed all other metrics, exhibiting remarkable advantages and strong modeling capabilities and generalization performance.

In the aspect of multi-scale modeling, MF-Transformer-DEC employs multiple layers of dilated convolutions to capture variation patterns at different temporal scales, enabling fully end-to-end learning. Existing multi-scale modeling approaches often rely on fixed signal processing techniques such as discrete wavelet transform (DWT), variational mode decomposition (VMD), and ensemble empirical mode decomposition (EEMD), which involve complex decomposition procedures and are difficult to unify within a trainable framework. The proposed model addresses these limitations by integrating multi-scale modeling directly within the deep learning architecture, jointly training it with the backbone network. This approach overcomes the separation of decomposition and prediction, non-learnable parameters, and strong dependence on prior assumptions seen in traditional methods, significantly enhancing the model's dynamic adaptability and its ability to represent complex, non-stationary temporal features.

In the aspect of multifractal modeling, MF-Transformer-DEC introduces innovative methods and carefully designed modules to dynamically perceive and effectively model multifractal characteristics using deep learning. Traditional fractal modeling techniques primarily depend on mathematical statistical methods, including multifractal detrended fluctuation analysis (MFDFA), asymmetric MFDFA (A-MFDFA), multifractal detrended cross-correlation analysis (MF-DCCA), fractal dimension calculation, and Hurst exponent estimation. These approaches focus on analysis without predictive capabilities, often involving complex workflows, heavy reliance on data pre-processing, and modular separation that hinders embedding into deep networks. MF-Transformer-DEC overcomes these issues by enabling MSA and FA modules to work synergistically, converting traditional fractal feature extraction from a static, non-trainable, and prediction-decoupled external process into an end-to-end trainable embedded module. This resolves the limitations of non-integrability and non-optimizability in conventional methods. The MSC module is designed as a scale-invariant convolutional network that adaptively extracts fractal features relevant to prediction through learnable convolution kernels. The FA module explicitly models potential multifractal structures in carbon price sequences by computing similarity weights among multi-scale convolution features, enabling cross-scale relational modeling and enhancing the model's understanding of complex fluctuation patterns. This approach effectively improves the model's adaptability to nonlinear features in carbon market price sequences, increasing prediction accuracy and generalization performance, and demonstrates a novel paradigm integrating fractal modeling with deep learning.

In the aspect of modeling long-range dependencies, MF-Transformer-DEC adopts a standard Transformer decoder architecture, comprising self-attention, cross-attention, and feed-forward networks, which provides strong capabilities for capturing global dependencies. In contrast, recurrent structures like LSTM and GRU, although possessing memory mechanisms, depend on sequential state updates, limiting parallelization and suffering from information decay across multiple steps. Such architectures often encounter vanishing gradient and information loss issues when processing long sequences or distant dependencies. The global modeling and parallel processing advantages of the decoder's self-attention enable MF-Transformer-DEC to more accurately capture the propagation of long-distance fluctuations in the carbon market.

In the aspect of residual correction, MF-Transformer-DEC utilizes an uncertainty-guided dynamic weighted fusion strategy to address a common shortcoming in existing research, where prediction residuals are often ignored or treated with static adjustments. Compared with other methods that employ fuzzy entropy combined with EEMD for secondary residual decomposition, support vector regression for residual modeling, or BiLSTM for independent error learning—which, although improving accuracy to some extent, mostly rely on static modeling that neglects temporal variability and uncertainty in errors—MF-Transformer-DEC measures uncertainty of the residual sequence using standard deviation to guide adaptive weighted fusion. This dynamic compensation of prediction errors significantly enhances robustness under abnormal fluctuations and sudden market changes. Moreover, the VAE module employed is simple, with low parameter count, fast forward propagation, and minimal training overhead. Traditional approaches based on fuzzy entropy, differential evolution, or EEMD for secondary residual correction often depend on manual tuning and external algorithms, leading to complexity, limited interpretability, and difficulty in joint optimization within the model.

The proposed MF-Transformer-DEC model consistently delivers excellent results across multiple datasets, demonstrating strong transferability and broad applicability in various carbon market environments. Compared to traditional and existing deep integration models, it significantly reduces errors, facilitating more accurate guidance for policy formulation, market decision-making, and carbon asset management. This provides a solid model foundation for high-quality, deployable carbon market price prediction tasks.

5. Conclusions

This study proposes a Transformer model based on multi-scale convolution and fractal attention, incorporating a variational autoencoder (VAE) to model error distribution. By adaptively integrating the residual correction term with the baseline prediction value, the model enhances its ability to analyze the complex fluctuation characteristics of the energy market. The proposed model flexibly models the multifractality of carbon market prices and performs fusion prediction while introducing an uncertainty-guided dynamic residual prediction mechanism, significantly improving the prediction accuracy of complex carbon market price sequences. Experimental results demonstrate that the proposed model outperforms benchmark models in key metrics such as MAE, RMSE, and R^2, validating the effectiveness of the synergistic interaction between multi-scale extraction, similarity mining, and residual correction.

The primary limitation of this study lies in the insufficient consideration of exogenous variables, such as geographical factors, that may impact carbon market prices. Future research could introduce a dynamic variable selection mechanism to enhance model adaptability. Additionally, exploring the integration of multi-source heterogeneous data (e.g., satellite remote sensing carbon monitoring data) with the existing model represents a promising direction for expanding the model's application scenarios.

Author Contributions: L.W., data collection, methodology, experiments, visualization, and writing—original draft preparation; M.T., data collection, methodology, funding acquisition, project administration, resources, supervision, and proofreading; N.L., writing—review and editing; J.D., visualization, writing—review and editing; X.Z., writing—review and editing; H.H., supervision and proofreading. All authors have read and agreed to the published version of the manuscript.

Funding: This work was supported in part by the National Natural Science Foundation of China (grant no. 62173050), the Natural Science Foundation of Hunan (grant no. 2023JJ30051 and 2023JJ30006), and the Major Scientific and Technological Innovation Platform Project of Hunan Province (grant no. 2024JC1003), the Scientific Research Fund of Hunan Provincial Education Department of China (grant no. 21A0192), and the Energy Conservation and Emission Reduction Hunan University Student Innovation and Entrepreneurship Education Center (grant no. 2020-19).

Data Availability Statement: The data that support the findings of this study are available from the third party https://www.cctd.com.cn/, accessed on 30 August 2024. But restrictions apply to the availability of these data, which were used under licenses for the current study and so are not publicly available.

Acknowledgments: The authors are grateful to the reviewer for comments that improved the paper.

Conflicts of Interest: The authors declare that there are no conflicts of interest regarding the publication of this paper.

Abbreviations

The following abbreviations are used in this manuscript:

MDPI	Multidisciplinary Digital Publishing Institute
MSC	Multi-scale Convolution
FA	Fractal Attention
DEC	Dynamic Error Correction
MAE	Mean Absolute Error
MSE	Mean Square Error
RMSE	Root Mean Square Error
R2	R-Square

References

1. Güney, T. Renewable energy, non-renewable energy and sustainable development. *Int. J. Sustain. Dev. World Ecol.* **2019**, *26*, 389–397. [CrossRef]
2. Zheng, G.; Li, K.; Yue, X.; Zhang, Y. A multifactor hybrid model for carbon price interval prediction based on decomposition—Integration framework. *J. Environ. Manag.* **2024**, *363*, 121273. [CrossRef]
3. Wang, P.; Liu, J.; Tao, Z.; Chen, H. A novel carbon price combination forecasting approach based on multi-source information fusion and hybrid multi-scale decomposition. *Eng. Appl. Artif. Intell.* **2022**, *114*, 105172. [CrossRef]
4. Zhou, K.; Li, Y. Influencing Factors and Fluctuation Characteristics of China's Carbon Emission Trading Price. *Phys. A Stat. Mech. Its Appl.* **2019**, *524*, 459–474. [CrossRef]
5. Fan, X.; Lv, X.; Yin, J.; Tian, L.; Liang, J. Multifractality and Market Efficiency of Carbon Emission Trading Market: Analysis Using the Multifractal Detrended Fluctuation Technique. *Appl. Energy* **2019**, *251*, 113333. [CrossRef]

6. Khurshid, A.; Khan, K.; Cifuentes-Faura, J.; Chen, Y. Asymmetric multifractality: Comparative efficiency analysis of global technological and renewable energy prices using MFDFA and A-MFDFA approaches. *Energy* **2024**, *289*, 130106. [CrossRef]
7. Liu, Z.; Tian, Y. Skewed Multifractal Cross-Correlation between Price and Volume during the COVID-19 Pandemic: Evidence from China and European Carbon Markets. *Appl. Energy* **2024**, *371*, 123716. [CrossRef]
8. Ni, L.; Ni, Z.; Gao, Y. Stock trend prediction based on fractal feature selection and support vector machine. *Expert Syst. Appl.* **2011**, *38*, 5569–5576. [CrossRef]
9. Zhibin, L.; Huang, S. Carbon Option Price Forecasting Based on Modified Fractional Brownian Motion Optimized by GARCH Model in Carbon Emission Trading. *North Am. J. Econ. Financ.* **2021**, *55*, 101307. [CrossRef]
10. Raubitzek, S.; Neubauer, T. A fractal interpolation approach to improve neural network predictions for difficult time series data. *Expert Syst. Appl.* **2021**, *169*, 114474. [CrossRef]
11. Zhu, D.D.; Zhang, C.; Pan, D. Extreme Risk Measurement of Carbon Market Considering Multifractal Characteristics. *J. Syst. Sci. Complex.* **2023**, *36*, 2497–2514. [CrossRef]
12. Jin, J.; Wang, B.; Yu, M.; Li, B. Short-term wind speed prediction based on fractal dimension-variational mode decomposition and general continued fraction. *Chaos Solitons Fractals* **2023**, *173*, 113704. [CrossRef]
13. Alabdulmohsin, I.; Tran, V.Q.; Dehghani, M. Fractal Patterns May Illuminate the Success of Next-Token Prediction. *NeurIPS* **2024**. Available online: https://proceedings.neurips.cc/paper_files/paper/2024/hash/cd004fa45fc1fe5c0218b7801d98d036-Abstract-Conference.html (accessed on 24 June 2025).
14. Jin, Y.; Sharifi, A.; Li, Z.; Chen, S.; Zeng, S.; Zhao, S. Carbon emission prediction models: A review. *Sci. Total Environ.* **2024**, *927*, 172319. [CrossRef]
15. Han, W.; Du, P. Dual-Stream Transformer-Attention Fusion Network for Short-Term Carbon Price Prediction. *Energy* **2024**, *311*, 133374. [CrossRef]
16. Hao, Y.; Yin, Y.; Li, H.; Zhu, J.; Xian, Z.; Tang, Y.; Xiao, L.; Rong, J.; Li, C.; Zhang, H.; et al. Carbon Emissions Trading Price Forecasting Based on Temporal-Spatial Multidimensional Collaborative Attention Network and Segment Imbalance Regression. *Appl. Energy* **2025**, *377*, 124357. [CrossRef]
17. Ji, Y.; Du, T.; Du, P.; Niu, T.; Wang, Z. A novel probabilistic carbon price prediction model: Integrating the transformer framework with mixed-frequency modeling at different quartiles. *Appl. Energy* **2025**, *391*, 125951. [CrossRef]
18. Zhang, X.; Wang, J.; He, X. An Optimal Multi-Scale Ensemble Transformer for Carbon Emission Allowance Price Prediction Based on Time Series Patching and Two-Stage Stabilization. *Energy* **2025**, *328*, 136457. [CrossRef]
19. Yue, W.; Zhong, W.; Xiaoyi, W.; Xinyu, K. Multi-Step-Ahead and Interval Carbon Price Forecasting Using Transformer-Based Hybrid Model. *Environ. Sci. Pollut. Res.* **2023**, *30*, 95692–95719. [CrossRef]
20. Hong, J.-T.; Bai, Y.-L.; Huang, Y.-T.; Chen, Z.-R. Hybrid Carbon Price Forecasting Using a Deep Augmented FED former Model and Multimodel Optimization Piecewise Error Correction. *Expert Syst. Appl.* **2024**, *247*, 123325. [CrossRef]
21. Sun, Q.; Chen, H.; Long, R.; Chen, J. Integrated Prediction of Carbon Price in China Based on Heterogeneous Structural Information and Wall-Value Constraints. *Energy* **2024**, *306*, 132483. [CrossRef]
22. Li, Y.; Zhang, X.; Wang, M. A dual decomposition integration and error correction model for carbon price prediction. *J. Environ. Manag.* **2025**, *374*, 124035. [CrossRef]
23. Liu, J.P.; Wang, J.Q.; Zhao, X.M.; Tao, Z.F. A multi-objective ensemble prediction model for interval-valued carbon price based on mixed-frequency data and sub-model selection. *Energy* **2025**, *326*, 136309. [CrossRef]
24. Cai, X.T.; Yuan, B.; Wu, C. An integrated CEEMDAN and TCN-LSTM deep learning framework for forecasting. *Int. Rev. Financ. Anal.* **2025**, *98*, 103879. [CrossRef]
25. Ma, Z.L.; Wang, C.; Qi, H.; Wood, J. A carbon price prediction model based on decomposition and dual-channel attention network. *Environ. Dev. Sustain.* **2025**, *27*, 125951. [CrossRef]
26. Lu, Y.X.; Wang, J.J.; Li, Q. An interval-valued carbon price prediction model based on improved multi-scale feature selection and optimal multi-kernel support vector regression. *Inf. Sci.* **2025**, *692*, 121651. [CrossRef]
27. Fang, M.; Zhang, Y.L.; Liang, W.; Shi, S.H.; Zhang, J.J. Carbon price prediction research based on CEEMDAN-VMD secondary decomposition and BiLSTM. *Environ. Sci. Pollut. Res.* **2025**, *32*, 8921–8942. [CrossRef]
28. Dong, L.; Jiang, F.; Wang, M.; Li, X. Fuzzy deep wavelet neural network with hybrid learning algorithm: Application to electrical resistivity imaging inversion. *Knowl.-Based Syst.* **2022**, *242*, 108164. [CrossRef]
29. Kantelhardt, J.W.; Zschiegner, S.A.; Koscielny-Bunde, E.; Havlin, S.; Bunde, A.; Stanley, H.E. Multifractal detrended fluctuation analysis of nonstationary time series. *Phys. A* **2002**, *316*, 87–114. [CrossRef]

fractal and fractional

MDPI

Article

Navigating Choppy Waters: Interplay between Financial Stress and Commodity Market Indices

Haji Ahmed [1,2], Faheem Aslam [2,3] and Paulo Ferreira [4,5,6,*]

1 Department of Commerce, Laar Campus Badin, University of Sindh, Jamshoro 76060, Pakistan; ahmed.solangi@usindh.edu.pk
2 Department of Management Sciences, COMSATS University, Park Road, Islamabad 45550, Pakistan; f.aslam@aui.ma
3 School of Business Administration (SBA), Al Akhawayn University, Ifrane 53000, Morocco
4 VALORIZA-Research Center for Endogenous Resource Valorization, 7300-555 Portalegre, Portugal
5 Polytechnic Institute of Portalegre, 7350-092 Portalegre, Portugal
6 Centro de Estudos e Formação Avançada em Gestão e Economia, Instituto de Investigação e Formação Avançada, Universidade de Évora, Largo dos Colegiais 2, 7004-516 Évora, Portugal
* Correspondence: pferreira@ipportalegre.pt

Abstract: Financial stress can have significant implications for individuals, businesses, asset prices and the economy as a whole. This study examines the nonlinear structure and dynamic changes in the multifractal behavior of cross-correlation between the financial stress index (FSI) and four well-known commodity indices, namely Commodity Research Bureau Index (CRBI), Baltic Dry Index (BDI), London Metal Index (LME) and Brent Oil prices (BROIL), using multifractal detrended cross correlation analysis (MFDCCA). For analysis, we utilized daily values of FSI and commodity index prices from 16 June 2016 to 9 July 2023. The following are the most important empirical findings: (I) All of the chosen commodity market indices show cross correlations with the FSI and have notable multifractal characteristics. (II) The presence of power law cross-correlation implies that a noteworthy shift in FSI is likely to coincide with a considerable shift in the commodity indices. (III) The multifractal cross-correlation is highest between FSI and Brent Oil (BROIL) and lowest with LME. (IV) The rolling windows analysis reveals a varying degree of persistency between FSI and commodity markets. The findings of this study have a number of important implications for commodity market investors and policymakers.

Keywords: FSI; financial stress; commodity prices; cross correlation; MFDCCA; econophysics

1. Introduction

Financial stress can have significant implications for individuals, business, and economies. It can harm individuals' physical and mental health, relationships and work, leading to substance abuse and even in some cases to suicide [1–6]. It refers to a discomfort or strain that individuals or entities face due to taking on a high risk or increasing the gap between their obligations and available means [7]. Financial stress also leads to an increased crime rate and damages the social fabric of society [8,9]. It is well documented that financial stress not only impacts on business operations (i.e., staff lay-off, production cut-backs), but also impacts on trading and investment strategies [10–12]. To avoid extreme losses, investors become reluctant to trade and withdraw their investment during periods of high stress and uncertainty. Increased financial stress leads to lower business activity and slows down economic expansion [13,14]. The situation can also precede a trust deficit in the financial system [14,15], which can make it difficult for businesses to borrow and invest funds. It also adversely affects the economy and can lead to a significant decline in consumer spending and investment, which slows down the rhythm of economic growth. It spreads among developed economies through financial, trade, and economic channels, and may extend to emerging economies [16–20], affecting macroeconomic indicators [15,20,21] and causing currency market crises [22,23]. Financial stress can be connected to financial instability through entities' failures [24]. For instance, if the banking system is under stress, banks may be more likely to fail [13,19,25,26]. The situation of loss of trust in the financial system followed by a rise in inflation can make it difficult for borrowers and businesses to access funding [27]. It increases poverty and inequalities, disrupting trade and capital flows and having long-term negative effects on the global economic system. It reduces economic growth, increases unemployment and causes volatility in stock [28] and commodity markets [29].

A growing body of research shows that financial stress affects the performance of stock, cryptocurrency, forex, energy, commodities, and other markets, as well as managerial decisions. Its ups and downs impact asset prices, such as stocks, bonds, gold, oil and cryptocurrencies [30–33]. Past research shows that financial stress affects different classes of economies and main markets, circulating within countries as well as expanding to different economic sectors. The literature reports its spread to various markets and expansion, mainly in financial markets, showing a connection with the foreign exchange market [15,22,34], banking crises [23,26,35] oscillations in equity and bond markets [30,36–39] monetary policy [40,41] and the crypto market [42]. As for commodities, a great amount of research has focused on energy related commodities, Refs. [43–46] revealing a meaningful association with energy markets. There is a dynamic relation with the FSI (Financial Stress Index) and linkages between commodity spot and futures prices through channels of inflation, the demand supply gap and investors searching for a safe haven to mitigate portfolio risk [43,47–50].

Researchers and academics have recently focused more on the commodity market, looking at the relationship between the commodity market and financial stress. Investors in commodities take into account the financial stress that is prevalent in the global economy due to any cause. A large number of studies have focused on the linkage between financial stress and different asset categories and market indices as well as different categories of commodity market future prices such as agriculture, metals and energy [51]. Ordinarily, commodities are far from being a uniform asset class and show a wide range of characteristics. While some commodities, like industrial and precious metals, may be inventoried, others, including energy and livestock products, can only be stored for shorter periods at extremely high costs. In addition, commodities' return distributions differ from conventional assets. Commodity returns typically have positive skews, which reduces downside risk but also produces fat tails [49,52]. Energy commodities show volatile behavior in correlation with financial markets and, in contango times, dependency on their past returns condition capitalizes to prices rising more and falling prices keep falling [53]. In the response of GFC 2008, financialization of commodity markets has enhanced their correlations and diminished the heterogeneity of several key commodities' returns, especially indexed commodities [54]. It is a fact that commodity prices over the decades underwent booms and slumps. Such changes in commodity prices can have disastrous economic and social consequences because many developing nations depend heavily on commodities as their primary source of income [21,55]. Its contagion has not been explored with the composite indices of commodities like CRBI, BDI, LME and BROIL. Financial stress attracted more attention after the recession and inflation episodes in response to the recent catastrophic occurrences of the global financial crises 2007–2009, European credit risk crises 2010–2012, COVID-19 pandemic recession and recovery period shocks [56–58], and the Russian invasion of Ukraine in 2022. There are numerous causes of financial stress but the most important are natural disasters, geopolitical tensions [59,60], structural vulnerabilities [33], economic shocks, and corporate failures [61].

This work differs from previous studies in at least three ways. First, using a Fractal Market Hypothesis framework, it looks at the cross-correlations between the FSI and four commodity market indices, covering the prices of many different commodity returns: the BDI, LME, BROIL, and CRBI. The dynamics of a wide range of significant commodity indexes, which are still subject to scholarly attention, are examined in this paper. Second, it is unknown how the cross-correlation between the commodity markets and the FSI exhibits multifractal behavior. To be more precise, a multifractal measure can be understood broadly mathematically as a fractal measure defined on a fractal domain or set, where multifractality results from the interaction of two families of singularities [62]. We use the econophysics-based MFDCCA, which was first presented by [63], to look into cross correlations between the commodity market indices and the FSI. When it comes to finding nonlinear relationships, which linear approaches frequently fail to reveal, MFDCCA is a better option [64,65]. Thirdly, by applying the rolling windows approach, this study, grounded on the perspective of the commodity market, provides a more thorough understanding of that market's dynamics over time. In particular, the power law cross-correlation between fluctuations in FSI and commodity prices indicates that, rather than the other way around, a major change in the FSI was likely caused by a big shift in commodity market prices. Different degrees of multifractality are discovered, with the FSI BROIL showing the highest levels of multifractal cross-correlation and the FSI and LME showing the lowest. Furthermore, the commodity markets show more dependable persistent cross-correlations for small swings than for major ones. These results will enable regulators and institutional investors to develop efficient investment plans and policies while taking the FSI's fluctuations and alerts into account. To maintain financial stability amid these challenges, policy makers, global economic forums, and regulatory bodies need to adopt a coordinated, comprehensive approach. They must take precautionary measures such as strengthening financial oversight, for instance FSI, and responding promptly to its alerts. Larger buffers should be formed by reducing incentives for higher risk taking and increasing capital and liquidity requirements, as stated by Cardarelli, Elekdag and Lall [27]. Financial stability enables the efficient propagation of financial means within a society, by timely and effective allocation of funds and initiating profitable investment [66].

2. Materials and Methods

We applied the MFDCCA method to explore cross-correlations between FSI and four commodity market composite indices. The daily datasets range from 16 June 2016 to 9 July 2023. The first dataset consists of daily values of FISI retrieved rom the official website of Office of Financial Research (www.financialreseach.gov, accessed on 14 January 2024). The FSI was developed by Office of Financial Research (OFR) to detect the threat of financial crises in advance [18,67]. The index utilizes a unique and flexible methodology using daily data from global financial markets. Analysis of the FSI index covers the period from 2000 to 2018. The paper highlights that the OFR_FSI performs well in identifying systemic financial stress, as demonstrated through a logistic regression framework and the use of government intervention dates as proxies for stress events. Additionally, alerts of increased financial stress, as indicated by the OFR FSI, can help predict decreases in economic activity, as shown by a Granger causality analysis comparing the index with the Chicago Fed National Activity Index. It is used to measure and assess the level of strains and risks in a financial system or economy. It provides signals in advance in order to address adverse events and helps in developing appropriate responses. Ref. [55] argues it is typically positive when the stress level is above average and negative when stress is below average. Additional classifications included in the OFR_FSI are credit, fundings, equity valuation, safe assets, and volatility. It is typically designed by compounding a variety of variables that emulate several facets of the financial system, such as credit spreads, market volatility, bank funding and liquidity [31]. The FSIs are found to be useful in predicting economic and financial outcomes, improving forecasts, and identifying high-stress episodes, particularly OFR-FSI used as global measure of financial stress [31,36,68,69]. They also highlight the non-linear effects of financial stress on several variables. Overall, FSIs play a crucial role in monitoring and managing financial stability and can assist policymakers and researchers in making informed decisions [60,70].

The other data set is commodity market indices including the CRBI, BDI, LME and BROIL. The daily prices (USD) of commodity indices are collected from DataStream. Global commodity market indices are essential for the global economy because they provide useful data, benchmarks, and clues with an impact on numerous types of economic activities around the world. This study focuses mainly on the four global commodity indices. The motivation for selecting these commodity indices is the vast coverage of the different categories of global commodities, for instance energy, agriculture, metals or shipping costs of commodities. The CRBI index weighs 41% for agriculture and 39% for energy commodities. It is one of the most liquid indices representing the global commodity markets and is considered a measure that comprehensively tracks movements in all economic sectors [71]. The effectiveness of a commodity price index as a precursor to inflation is investigated by multiple studies [71,72]. Since 1956, it has kept track of a broad index of commodity prices. BDI covers the cost of main shipping routes, carrying industrial, energy and food commodities. Crises like COVID-19 pandemic lockdowns, trade tensions, recession, and inflation cause fluctuations in the global financial system reflected in BDI, which is considered a world import indicator [73] to gauge economic activity. It is an effective predictor of commodity, stock returns and economic activity [74,75], major currencies' exchange rates [76], industrial production and financial asset prices [77]. LME reflects the prices of the six most liquid industrial base metals: aluminum, copper, zinc, lead, nickel, and tin [78]. Crude oil is one of the oil price benchmarks, being a basic commodity and major influencer of many facets of world policies and economies [79–81]. These commodity indices represent a diverse range of global commodities. The particulars of the commodity data set, their coverage and weights are provided in Table 1. For the execution of MFDCCA, commodity datasets are matched with FSI after performing the data cleaning process. We removed extreme inorganic observations from the FSI for the sake of brevity, as these showed abrupt unnatural negative and positive changes in daily stress changes. We converted the indices into daily changes to determine the cross-correlation between the FSI and certain chosen commodity indices.

Table 1. Commodity Index Weights and Coverage.

Index	Symbol	Coverage	Weights
Commodity Research Bureau Index	CRBI	Basket of 19 Agricultural, Energy and Food commodities	41% to agriculture, 39% to energy, and the remainder to others.
Baltic Dry Index	BDI	Shipping freight rates of coal, iron ore, and other commodities.	40% Capesize, 30% Supramax and Panamax 30% cost on shipping routes carrying coal, grains, iron ore, and other commodities.
London Metal Exchange	LME	Industrial Metals Aluminum, Copper, Zinc, Lead, Nickel and Tin.	The average global production volume and trade liquidity for the previous five years are used to determine the weight of the six metals, i.e., aluminum, copper, zinc, lead, nickel, and tin (42.8%, 31.2%, 14.8% 8.2%, 2% & 1%), respectively.
Brent Oil Price Index	BROIL	Brent Crude spot	Prices per barrel in US dollars.

We transformed the original series into daily changes, aiming to calculate the cross-correlation between them. The daily commodity market returns are calculated by applying the commodity indices' closing price as usual, i.e.,

$$r_{t,j} = \frac{(p_{t,j} - p_{t-1,j})}{p_{t-1,j}} \tag{1}$$

Similarly, Financial stress index FSI's daily changes are calculated as follows.

$$\Delta_{FSI} = \frac{(FSI_{t,j} - FSI_{t-1,j})}{FSI_{t-1,j}} \tag{2}$$

Figure 1 plots the daily index of FSI and plots a graph line for the sample period from 16 July 2016 to 9 July 2023. From July 2016 to February 2020, FSI remained below the average line, except for a single spike in 2018 for a shorter time span. This established that global economies were recovering after the global financial crises of 2008. The policies and structures incorporated to tackle such crises and policies strengthen the confidence of investors and the business community to participate in economic activities and make investment. In the interim, decision-makers focused on developing policies and precautionary steps to avert crises of this nature. The period from 2012 to 2017 is particularly captivating because of the positive bubble in the US currency and the negative bubble in the oil market [82]. Moreover, a short span stress spike cropped up during the last quarter of 2018 due to the US-China trade conflict [42]. Throughout the sample period, the largest stress spikes were observed during the COVID-19 period from the end of the first quarter of 2020 to the end of the second quarter of 2022. On 11 March 2020, the WHO declared COVID-19 as a global pandemic [83], and in April 2020 suggested lockdown. Lockdown caused a sudden rise in financial stress from the beginning of the second quarter of 2020 [84]. With the relaxation of lockdown, financial stress decreased below the average line and financial conditions remained stable from the end of the second quarter of 2020 through the last quarter of 2021 as seen in the graph. The FSI graph line again exhibited a rising trend from February 2022 because of the Ukraine–Russia war [85], Russia invaded Ukraine on 24 February 2022. The stress time span is longer during this period, with the FSI line remaining above the average line from February 2022 to December 2022. For the remaining period till July 2023, the FSI graph remained stable on the average line.

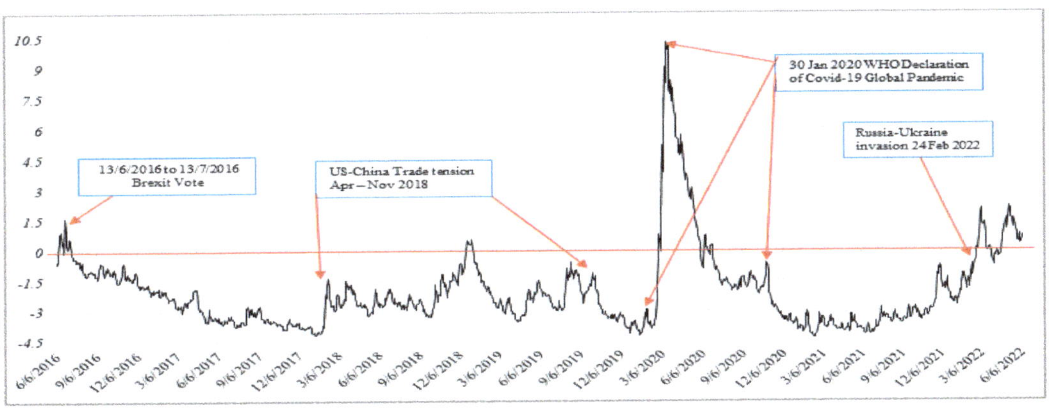

Figure 1. Daily Index values of FSI.

Panel A of Figure 2 shows the CRBI daily values graph on average remains stable with minor variations from June 2016 to March 2020, with a sharp decline from April 2020 to May 2020 and reaching its lowest point in the sample period during the COVID-19 lockdown period. It rises gradually and then sharply from December 2021. Commodity prices have increased significantly as lockdowns around the world have decreased and economies return to a more normal trend. In response to the market recovery period after COVID-19, the CRBI graph touched its highest point in February and March 2022. However, from July 2022 the CRBI graph line shows a gradual declining phase and a sharp decline in March 2022 because of the Russia–Ukraine war. The index line shows that since the start of 2023 commodity prices have dropped 13.02 points, or 4.3%. Compared to pre COVID-19, prices remained elevated till July 2023. Commodity prices will remain high in 2023 due to high energy costs, shortages of agricultural supply brought about by the Russia-Ukraine war, and unfavorable weather patterns.

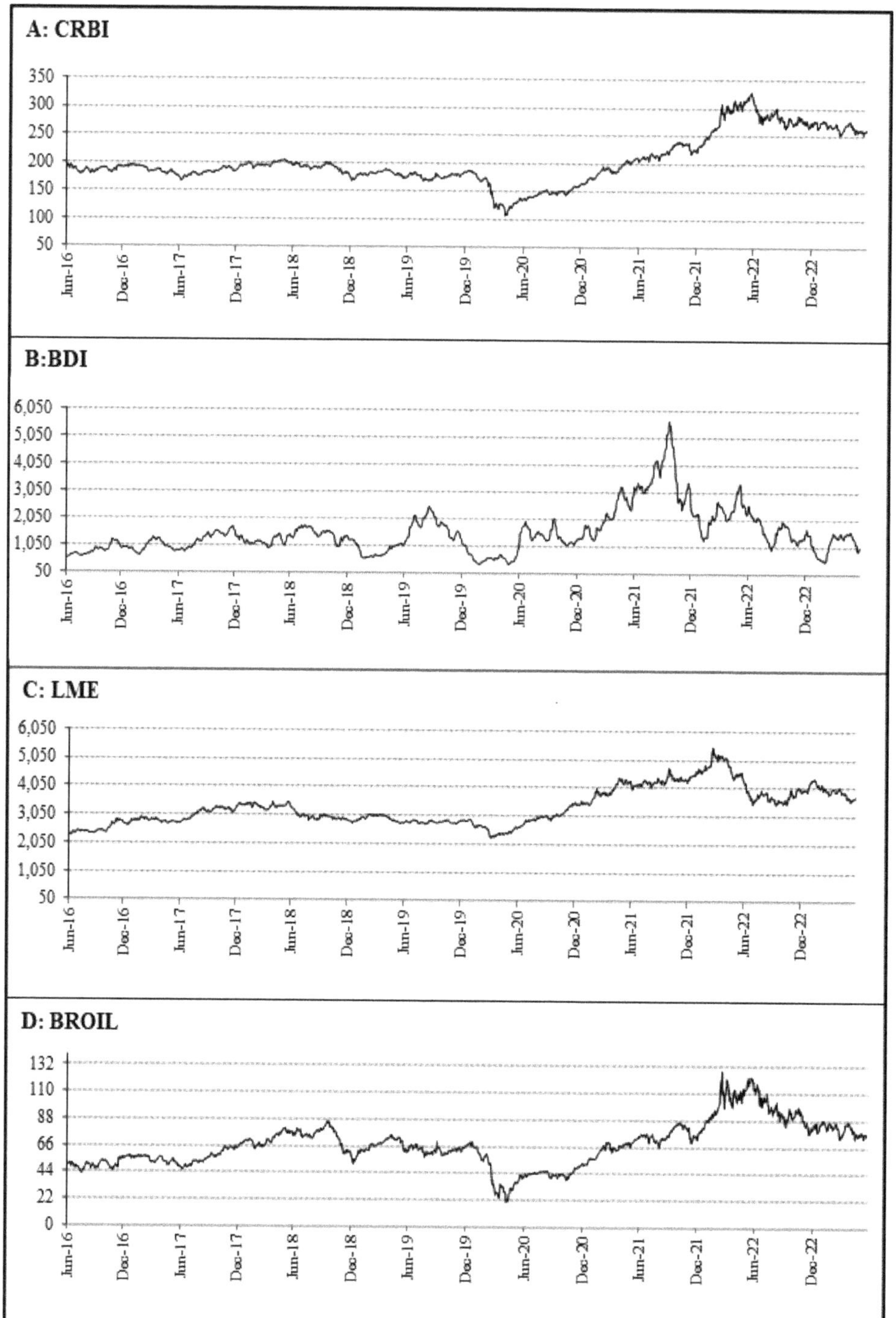

Figure 2. Daily Index values CRBI, BDI, LME & BROIL.

Panel B of Figure 2 shows the daily values of the BDI and shows a downward trend as 2016 got underway amid worries about China's slowing economy, which had an impact on the demand for commodities globally. Lower shipping costs and a drop in the BDI were caused by decreased Chinese imports. Due to an oversupply of ships, the index continued to fall in December 2016 and did so into the first quarter of 2017. As long as commodity prices were high, economies started to increase again in March 2017. By May, it had reached its peak and was therefore quite stable. The BDI's upward trajectory was disrupted once more in December 2017 as trade tensions between the US and China increased concerns about world trade. It was further affected from March 2018 to May 2018 due to the Iranian sanctions. Due to trade concerns, the downward trend persisted until January 2019. The index began to rise once again in February 2019 as trade tensions between the US and China briefly subsided. Downward trends through January 2020 were brought on by Brazilian iron ore extraction and increased shipping costs. The BDI showed very minor variations at the end of the year in December 2019. The COVID-19 pandemic caused a large fall in shipping demand from February 2020, which caused the BDI to decline sharply. From April through June 2020, the BDI reached its lowest point of the year. After the first phase of the COVID-19 crises, lockdowns were relaxed, and an inclining trend started. The multiple COVID-19 pandemic episodes, lockdowns, and corresponding seasonal changes all had an ongoing impact on BDI. It began to rise as the economic recovery got underway but was still below pre-pandemic levels. As global trade and commodity demand started to recover in February 2021, the BDI kept moving upward. Continuous supply chain disruptions led to changes in shipping costs in May 2021. Because of these factors, the BDI reached its peak in October 2021. In 2021, there was a significant demand for several important commodities, including grain, iron ore, and coal. Shipping costs rose significantly because of China's high demand for iron ore. The demand for large quantities of commodities was also influenced by the recovery of the global construction sector and the demand for energy resources. Industrial raw material caused the index to maintain its pre-pandemic level after the boom until January 2022. In February 2022, there were many noticeable seasonal variations, but in March, the Russia–Ukraine war's impact on the closure of shipping lanes caused a spike in shipping expenses. Due to fewer coal imports to Europe and China's slow economic recovery, the BDI showed a severe downward trend from January to February 2023. From March onward, the index returned to its usual threshold, but in the second half of June started to decline again and fell below 1000 points, 13% down in July for the first time in a month due to the diminished shipment of coal and Iron.

Panel C plots the graph line of LME, interestingly showing a similar pattern from the beginning of the sample period, during the US–China trade conflict in 2018, and the COVID-19 crises in 2020, as well as a similar pattern after the COVID-19 recovery period. It was different during the Ukraine–Russia war and showed a sharp declining trend, remaining unstable during the period as compared to CRBI.

Finally, Panel D shows the BROIL throughout the period of our study. The first notable downward trend is from April through June 2016, due to the oversupply of U.S crude oil from 384,000 b/d to 9.2 million b/d, this dent being created by supply pressure on oil prices [86]. This increased the price differential between Brent and WTI while decreasing the demand for Brent crude oil, which serves as the benchmark for the majority of global crude oil trade. Furthermore, in May 2017, OPEC, and its collaborators, including Russia, agreed to extend their production cuts through March 2018. While this was projected to stabilize prices, it also highlighted the ongoing challenges in rebalancing the market. Despite the November 2018 sanctions, the US granted exceptions to eight countries, allowing them to keep importing oil from Iran. This allayed the supply shortfall worries that had raised prices earlier in the year. Oil production in Saudi Arabia, Russia, and the US all reached new highs, outpacing the rate of increase in demand from November through December 2018. The BROIL started an inclining trend due to the supply demand gap and remained stable till February 2020 before the COVID-19 outbreak. The Brent oil price decreased to the lowest ever as the WHO declared the COVID-19 lockdown in March 2020, remaining down throughout COVID-19 because of the crunch in global oil demand. From May 2020 onwards, after the easing of COVID lockdowns, BROIL started a gradual increase, experiencing a recovery period after the longest recession period after COVID-19. March 2022 shows increasing spikes in response to the Ukraine–Russia war because Russia is the second largest oil producer in the world. There was fear of the widening supply demand gap throughout the world. Brent prices gradually returned to their normal prices after June 2022 and remain stable thereafter.

2.1. Multifractal Detrended Cross Correlation Analysis (MFDCCA)

Comprising several nonlinearly interacting elements, the complex systems of physical quantities include ecological, biological, technical, social, and financial variables. It has been demonstrated that these factors display long-range correlations [87]. To uncover the multifractal properties of two cross-correlated non-stationary indicators, Zhou [63] devised multifractal detrended cross-correlation analysis (MFDCCA, alternatively termed MFDXA), a consolidation of the MFDFA and DCCA methods. Since then, DCCA and MFDCCA have been extensively utilized in fields such as finance, chemistry and geophysics [88–91]. Regarding empirical investigation, several studies applied the MFDCCA approach to explore the cross-correlations between two financial time series, for instance efficiency of stock prices, Cryptocurrency prices and economic policy uncertainty, commodity prices and energy market, tourism and supply chain management [92–99].

Zhou [63] states that the following phases summarize the MFDCCA algorithm:

With N denoting the length of the time series, we can calculate the remaining component for the commodity market composite indices and the FSI by taking into account the two times series $\{(x_i)\}$ and $\{(y_i)\}$ of an equal length. $X_{(i)}$ and $Y_{(i)}$ signal profiles are initially put together as follows.

$$X_{(i)} = \sum_{i=1}^{j} (x_i - \overline{x}), \quad i = 1,2,3,\ldots,N, \tag{3}$$

$$Y_{(i)} = \sum_{i=1}^{j} (y_t - \overline{y}), \quad i = 1,2,3,\ldots,N, \tag{4}$$

where the mean values of $\{(x_i)\}$ and $\{(y_i)\}$, respectively, are represented by $\overline{x}$ and $\overline{y}$. The profiles $X_{(i)}$ and $Y_{(i)}$ are divided into $N_s = int\frac{N}{s}$ boxes of the same length s. Even so, as t N might not always be a non-multiple of s, the reserve series of the profile is maintained using the same technique, yielding $2N_s$ without overlapping splits being gained.

Third, we investigate each portion's local pattern $X^v(i)$ and $Y^v(i)$ of each segment and probe the variance for each $v = 1, 2, \ldots, 2N_s$ as:

$$F^2(s,v) = \frac{1}{s}\sum_{i=1}^{s} |X[(v-1)s+i] - X^v(i)| \,.\, |Y[(v-1)s+i] - Y^v(i)| \tag{5}$$

for each divide $v = 1, 2, \ldots, N_s$ and

$$\mathrm{F}^2(\mathrm{s},\mathrm{v}) = \frac{1}{\mathrm{s}}\sum_{\mathrm{j}=1}^{\mathrm{s}} |\mathrm{X}[\mathrm{N}-(\mathrm{v}-\mathrm{N_s})\mathrm{s}+\mathrm{i}] - \mathrm{X^v(i)}|.|\mathrm{Y}[\mathrm{N}-(\mathrm{v}-\mathrm{N_s})\mathrm{s}+\mathrm{i}] - \mathrm{Y^v(i)}| \tag{6}$$

for $v = N_s, \ldots, 2N_s$.

Fourth, we use the following equation to compute the qth sequence variations function.

$$F_{q\,(s)} = \left\{ \frac{1}{2N_s}\sum_{v=1}^{2N_s} \left[F^2(s,\, v)\right]^{q/2} \right\}^{1/q} \tag{7}$$

For any q ≠ 0, while for $q = 0$ it is shown as:

$$F_{0(s)} = exp\left\{\frac{1}{4N_s}\sum_{v=1}^{2N_s} ln\left[F^2(s,v)\right]\right\} \quad (8)$$

Here, with $F_{q(s)}$ being an increasing function of s, we retrieve the conventional DCCA at $q = 2$.

Finally, in order to identify the multi-scaling pattern of the fluctuation, we investigate the log-log plots of $F_q(s)$ against s for each q.

$$F_q(s) \sim s^{H_{xy}(q)} \quad (9)$$

In this case, the scaling exponent $H_{xy}(q)$ denotes the power-law relationship between two non-linear time series, which shows the magnitude of $F_q(s)$ as a function of the scale step s. When there is similarity between the two time series of $\{(x_i)\}$ and $\{(y_i)\}$, MFDCCA indicates a distinctive case of MFDFA.

The long-range cross-correlations of two time series coexisting simultaneously can be characterized using multifractal detrended cross-correlation analysis (MFDCCA) [100]. If a normal stationary time series occurs, the Generalized Hurst Exponent at $H_{xy}(2)$, is comparable to the conventional Hurst exponent h [101]. Moreover, $H_{xy}(2) = 0.5$ shows that there is no cross-correlation between the two series. On the other hand, the presence of cross-correlation between the two time series is persistent at H_{xy} $(2) > 0.5$, indicating positive correlation between the two series. The cross-correlation shows anti-persistence behavior and inverse association, or -ve cross-correlations, where $H_{xy}(2) < 0.52$). We calculated the fluctuation function $F_{xyq}(S)$ with growing scaling order q from $-5\ to + 5$, and scales are selected according to the series length N. The maximum scale is taken as $S_{max} < \frac{N}{5}$ and the maximum range of moment is approximated as |q_max| = |ln N_points| $- 1$

According to ref. [102], the multifractality degree ΔH is defined as follows:

$$\Delta H = H_{max}(q) - H_{min}(q) \quad (10)$$

The ΔH reflects the strength of multifractality. A larger value of ΔH denotes the strongest level of multifractality. Furthermore, with further cross-correlations, the corresponding values of $H_{xy}(q)$ can show the degree of multifractality. Through the Legendre transform, the following can be acquired to calculate the degree of multifractality.

$$\alpha = H(q) + q.H'_{xy}(q) \quad (11)$$

Consequently, the singularity spectrum $f(\alpha)$ can be constructed as follows:

$$f(\alpha) = q(\alpha - H_{xy}(q)) + 1 \quad (12)$$

2.2. Multifractal Indices

2.2.1. The Degree of Multifractality

The multifractal strength can be estimated by the following spectrum width $\Delta\alpha$.

$$\Delta\alpha = \alpha_{max} - \alpha_{min} \quad (13)$$

A larger multifractality is represented by a broader multifractal spectrum.

2.2.2. Degree of Asymmetry (AI)

The asymmetric intensity likewise represented as the skewness of $f(\alpha)$ spectrum, can be acquired as under:

$$AI = \frac{\alpha_{max} - \alpha_0}{\alpha_0 - \alpha_{min}} \quad (14)$$

The fractal exponent, represented by the power law exponent α, is the fractal onset time, quantifies the strength of time-clustering, and delimits the lower bound of significant scaling behavior in the variables [103]. However, the value of α is represented by the α_0, if $f(\alpha)$ is at its maximum. It has three different shapes associated with the values of A, which indicate the asymmetry position as positive-skewed $(AI > 1)$, symmetric $(AI = 1)$, or negative-skewed $(0 < AI < 1)$, according to Freitas et al. [104]. The extreme values of the singularity exponent are represented by the right end point, α_{max} and the left end point, α_{max} which correspond to the minimum and maximum fluctuations of the signal, respectively.

2.2.3. Singularity Parameters

The singularity ratio C is utilized, and it can be computed as the ratio of $\Delta f_{left}(\alpha)$ and $\Delta f_{right}(\alpha)$, evaluated in relation to the maximum fractal dimension $f^{max}[\alpha(q = 0)]$. The singularity ratio index C can be interpreted as a direct measure of truncation, with $C > 1$ denoting the left side of truncation and $C < 1$ denoting the right side. The formula below can be used to calculate the strength in the singularities, which is represented by the proportional ratio $f(\alpha)$ between the widths of the left and right sides.

$$C = \frac{\Delta f_L(\alpha)}{\Delta f_R(\alpha)} = \frac{1 - f_L^{min}(\alpha)}{1 - f_R^{max}(\alpha)} \tag{15}$$

According to Ref. [105], the intensity of the multifractal spectrum and the singularity strength α have an inverse relationship. Furthermore, higher values of h indicate smoother variations because of the weakening of the singularity.

2.2.4. The Hurst Index (H)

According to Ref. [106], the generalized Hurst exponent $h(q = 2)$ is used to determine the Hurst index (H) at second-order. Furthermore, Ref. [107] described a method of classifying different types of processes by identifying the characteristics of $1/f^{\beta}$ noises, which have a Fourier power spectrum scaling element β. Nevertheless, the slope of a linear trend is used to calculate β. In a similar vein, the trend can be either $-1 < \beta < 1$ for fGn, or $1 < \beta < 3$. Furthermore, Ref. [104] claimed that the relationship $\beta = 2 + \tau(2)$ can be used to estimate β. Long-range dependence (LRD) between the non-linear data series is represented by the values of H, which vary from 0.5 to 1. The closer a value is to 1, the higher the periodicity. On the other hand, H values close to zero denote white noise, while $H = 0.5$ denotes uncorrelated data.

3. Empirical Results

3.1. Descriptive Statistics

Table 2 describes the summary statistics of the FSI and Commodity market indices. The mean of the FSI is -0.0012, while for commodity indices LME shows the highest mean value followed by BDI, CRBI and BROIL. BDI exhibits the highest range in all commodity series followed by LME, CRBI, BROIL, and FSI. Range depicts the spread between minimum and maximum returns from the sample time span under study. BDI showed more volatile behavior (S.D = 0.54) followed by LME, CRBI, BROIL, and FSI exhibited the least volatile behavior (S.D = 0.270). FSI is right skewed contrary to the BROIL which is left skewed. CRBI is moderately skewed while the BDI and LME are approximately skewed. The Kurtosis scores determined that aside from LME all the other series exhibit heavy tails as their Kurtosis score is highly positive and more than three. The verification of high kurtosis levels is a common result, meaning the presence of fat tails, a feature related to the Fractal Market Hypothesis. The Jarque–Bera (JB) test of goodness of fit was applied to diagnose the normality of the data series. The findings for all variables are significant at 1% significance. The null hypothesis of the JB test "data is normally distributed", in the light of the above results, is rejected. The Augmented Dicky–Fuller (ADF) test was applied to assess the stationarity of the variables. The ADF test results for all variables are significant at 1% significance. Therefore, the null hypothesis "time series has unit root" is rejected here. It could be inferred that all variables are stationary at I (0) level.

Table 2. Summary Statistics of FSI and Commodity Market Indices.

	FSI	CRBI	BDI	LME	BROIL
Mean	−0.0012	0.0386	0.2649	0.8367	0.0145
Standard Deviation	0.2695	2.3279	54.1240	40.3048	1.6843
Range	5.5010	28.82	594.0	400.0	25.64
Kurtosis	33.5989	6.0868	5.8149	2.9636	11.4127
Skewness	2.8494	−0.7096	0.1125	−0.1907	−1.1543
Jarque-Bera test	1022 ***	1759 ***	370 ***	118 ***	2305 ***
ADF	−11.74 ***	−10.64 ***	−10.31 ***	11.18 ***	−10.641 ***

Note: *** represents 99% significance level.

Figure 3 plots the daily change of the FSI and the commodity indices selected for this study. Daily change pathways show volatility clusters and high volatility. The FSI index daily change shows variation spikes in different time periods. When we plotted temporal changes of the FSI, stress spikes were observed during global stress events in the sample period, i.e., US–China trade tension, COVID-19 pandemic, and the Russian invasion of Ukraine. The highest stress spike observed during the COVID-19 pandemic from early 2020 to mid-2021 which is the steepest in the whole sample period. The Ukraine–Russia war is represented in the graph as the second stressful event, but this event lasts longer than the COVID-19 pandemic. FSI, CRBI, and BROIL exhibited similar patterns and likeness in their volatile periods like trade tensions, COVID-19, and the Ukraine war. BDI and LME exhibited more volatile patterns than the others. From February 2018 to February 2020, a few factors may have contributed to the increased volatility of these indicators, i.e., trade tensions during this period, as trade tension escalated between the US and China, as well as between other major trading partners. This uncertainty and disruption to global trade flows likely contributed to the BDI's volatility. There were several instances of political instability during this period, including Brexit, protests in Hong Kong, and the ongoing conflict in the Middle East. These events may have contributed to the LME's volatility, as investors reacted to the potential impacts of these events on global economic activity. The LME and BDI followed similar patterns in extreme events like COVID-19 from March 2020 and the Russia–Ukraine war from February 2022 onwards.

3.2. Multifractal Detrended Cross Correlation Analysis (MFDCCA)

To compute the cross-correlation between FSI and commodity indices' daily changes, we applied the existing multifractal detrended cross-correlation analysis. We determined the variability function F_{xyq} (S) by increasing scaling order q from −5 to 5 step by step length, in line with the number of observations. Figure 4. plots the log-log movement of F_{xyq} (S) depends on the time span s *(days)* between FSI and commodity indices' daily changes of CRBI (Panel-A), BDI (Panel-B), LME (Panel-C), and BROIL(Panel-D). The lines rising from lowest to the highest relate to subsequent scale orders $F_{xyq}(S)$ for q = −5, q = 0, and q = +5. It is clear that $F_{(xyq(S))}$ is well-shaped and exhibits an increasing trend with the gradual linear rise with the scale s orders, showing there is a power law correlation between FSI and four time series of commodity indices.

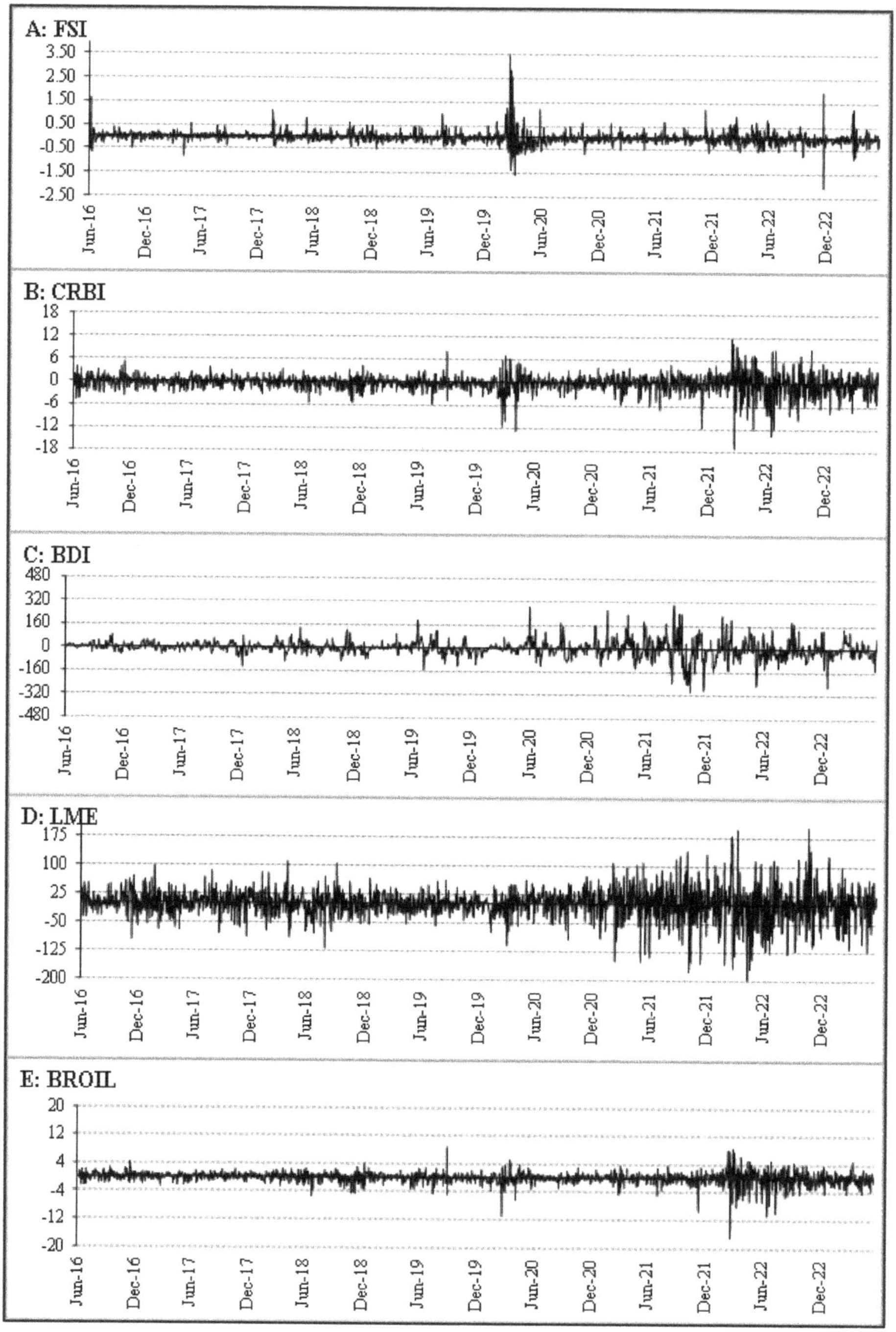

Figure 3. Daily Change of FSI, CRBI, BDI, LME & BROIL.

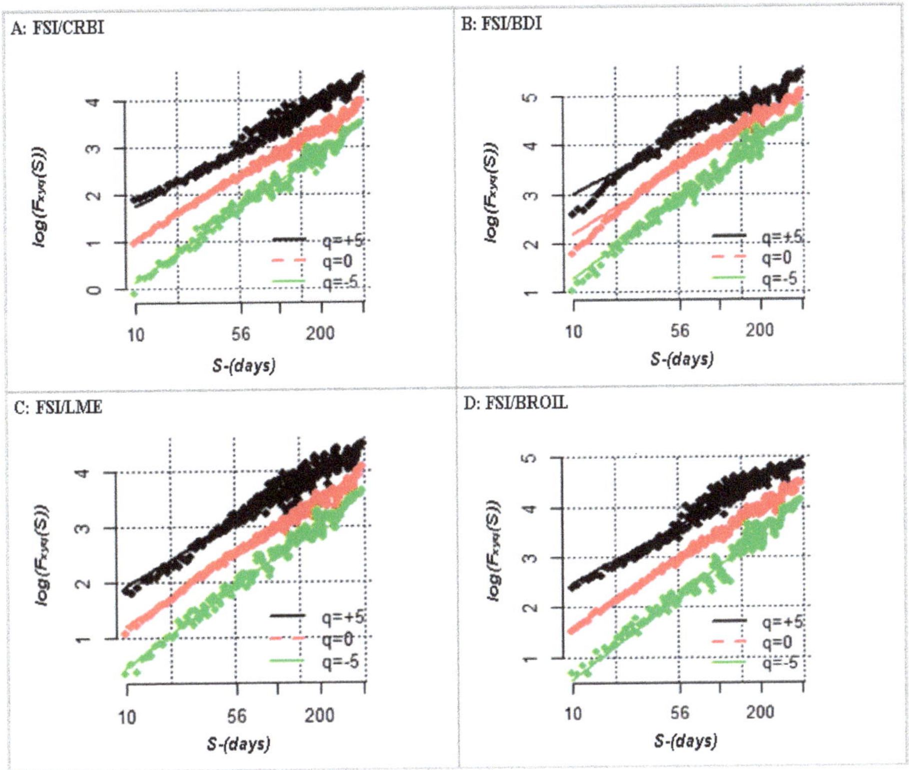

Figure 4. Log-Log plot of Fluctuation functions F_{xyq} (S) versus s for q = [−5, 0, +5].

The result of the Hurst exponent between FSI and commodity market returns shows a declining trend as the order of q increases. As the highest value of $H_{xy}(q)$ for FSI–BROIL reported in (column 5) Table 3, is 0.672 when q = −5, decreases to 0.540 at q = 0 and further declines to 0.472 when q = 5. A similar pattern is observed in the FSI-BDI pair Hurst index, i.e., 0.648, 0.581 and 0.455 at q = −5, q = 0 and q = 5, respectively. The same pattern is followed by the FSI–CRBI pair, the highest Hurst index 0.633 when hq = −5, while 0.543 and 0.507 when hq = 0 and hq = 5, respectively. The lowest Hurst index score is found in the FSI–LME pair, which is 0.612 with the order of q = −5, declining to 0.545 with the order of q = 0 and reaching 0.496 with the order of q = 5. The declining structure is found in the Hurst exponents of all FSI and commodity market index pairs. The declining trend is evidence of multifractality in the time variations in the pairs of FSI and commodity market indices' daily change. The results show that the Hurst exponent scores between FSI and selected commodities' return series behave with a declining trend, as long as the time scale rises. Further, they show that $H_{xy}(q)$ values for $q < 0$ are all greater than the values of $q > 0$, confirmation of the more persistent cross correlation pattern for minor variations than for large variations. Moreover, large variations have week cross-correlation compared to small variations, because $H_{xy}(q)$ for smaller and large variations declines as the order of scaling q rises.

Table 3 further reports the findings of $H_{xy}(q = 2)$, which quantify the level of persistence among the cross correlations of the FSI and commodity market indices' returns. Interestingly, the $H_{xy}(q = 2)$ score for FSI and the commodities CRBI and BROIL is greater than 0.5, which is evidence of the persistent behavior between the FSI and the selected commodity market indices' daily price change.

Table 3. Hurst exponent for FSI and Commodity Market ranging over qε(−5, 5).

Order	FSI-CRBI	FSI-BDI	FSI-LME	FSI-BROIL
−5	0.6335	0.6482	0.6124	0.6717
−4	0.6113	0.6319	0.5952	0.6506
−3	0.5873	0.6128	0.5879	0.6256
−2	0.5639	0.6035	0.5772	0.5968
−1	0.5441	0.5910	0.5596	0.5665
0	0.5437	0.5810	0.5445	0.5397
1	0.5421	0.5694	0.5331	0.5311
2	0.5327	0.5491	0.5234	0.5213
3	0.5193	0.5132	0.5148	0.4919
4	0.5139	0.4775	0.5057	0.4815
5	0.5072	0.4551	0.4964	0.4716

Three different interpretations of these data are offered by the literature. A cross-persistent series is represented by $H_{xy}(2) > 0.5$, and a positive (negative) value of $\Delta_{x_t y_t}$, denotes a significant probability of another positive (negative) value of $\Delta_{x_{t+1} y_{t+1}}$ as claimed by [101]. Refs. [102,108] assert that long-term cross correlation implies that each series has a long memory of both its own past values and the past values of the other series. According to Ref. [109], power-law cross-correlations show that a change in one series will be followed by a change in the other. Considering these ideas, we can claim that a large increment in the FSI is likely to be followed by a large increment in commodity market prices, daily change [109].

BDI High Multifractal Variation when $q = 2$ and $q = 0$ indicates diverse and vibrant relationships with the FSI. Fluctuations in FSI impact shipping demand, and subsequently, BDI in complex ways. Increasing stress can lead to diminished trade and demand for shipping, affecting BDI inversely. However, if stress stems from geopolitical disruptions or tensions in specific trade routes, BDI might benefit from increased demand for alternative routes. Anti-Persistence to March 2021 with FSI is consistent with the hypothesis that higher levels of financial stress predictably affect economic activity negatively and decrease demand for shipping. The Brent Oil shows higher levels at $q > 0$ meaning high sensitivity and wildly reacts against the variations in FSI, implying that, when financial stress increase, in the future it could result in economic slowdown and recession (like, for example, the COVID-19 economic dumping caused a decrease in oil demand). LME and CRBI have a diverse range of commodities and have a mild reactive behavior, compared to the former index, meaning they are affected by multiple factors, just as agricultural commodities in CRBI are affected by seasonal variations or environmental changes. While LME includes industrial base metals, it is also affected by multiple factors beyond the FSI, like technological advancements, industrial demand or geopolitical factors, which weakens the covariations of LME with FSI, compared to the three other commodity indices.

Table 4 reports the summary of the multifractal indices. The Hurst-exponent-average values lie between 0.5 and 0.6, indicating intensity or level of multifractality. However, the values of ΔH are significantly higher than zero, establishing that the cross-correlations between FSI and commodity indices show robust multifractal patterns. A few interesting insights emerge, for instance, a degree of multifractal persistence that varies, with the maximum multifractality in the FSI-BROIL pair (ΔH = 0.2001) followed by FSI-BDI (ΔH = 0.193) then FSI-CRBI (ΔH = 0.126), while FSI-LME (ΔH = 0.125) has the lowest multifractality of the pairs under study. This shows that BROIL and BDI have the highest multifractality cross-correlation, while the LME and CRBI show a similarly low level of multifractality in the cross-correlations with FSI. These results can be confirmed by Figures 4–6, as well as by the results of $\Delta\alpha$ in column 4 of Table 4. Figure 4 represents the association between log(s) and log (F_xyq (S)) for q = −5 (green), q = 0 (red) and q = 5 (black), stretched with time length s for all the pairs of FSI with commodity market indices CRBI, BDI, LME and BROIL. The log–log plots are mapped well and increasing linearly as the scale s increases, meaning that power-law behavior and long-range cross-correlations occur between the FSI and commodity markets. The power-law cross-correlation infers that large variations in commodity market prices move to be complemented by the considerable variations in FSI and vice versa. The higher width here is evidence of more variations, indicating random and heterogeneous distribution, which points to the more unpredictable descriptions of the daily change in commodity market indices.

Table 4. Summary of Multifractality of FSI and Commodity Market Indices.

Pair	Hurst Average	ΔH	Δα	AI	C
FSI-CRBI	0.5545	0.1263	0.2419	3.9688	0.3018
FSI-BDI	0.5666	0.1931	0.3079	1.2845	0.7607
FSI-LME	0.5500	0.1253	0.2313	1.8599	0.5407
FSI-BROIL	0.5589	0.2001	0.3241	2.2047	0.4692

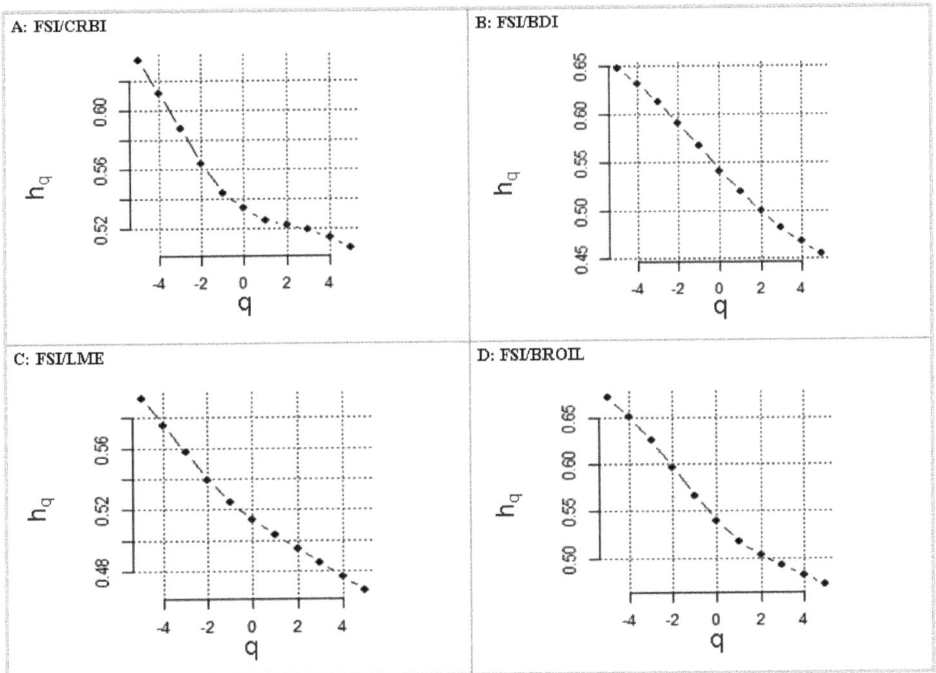

Figure 5. Generalized Hurst exponent H_{xy} dependence on q for q = −5, q = 0, q = 5.

The significant difference from zero spans of the cross-correlations' multifractal progressions corroborates the obvious deviations from the random walk process. Lo's [110] adaptive market hypothesis (AMH) assumptions regarding the role of human psychology and market efficiency is not static, considering time variance across different categories of assets supported by evidence in favor of complex market structures and multifractality in the cross-correlation form [111], which has also been demonstrated in earlier research [112–114].

The degree of asymmetry results is reflected in column 5 of Table 4. The FSI–CRBI pair represented the highest *AI* value (3.968) followed by the FSI-BROIL pair (2.204) and FSI-BDI showed the lowest asymmetry AI value (1.285). Interestingly, all commodity market indices paired with FSI show right skewed cross-correlations. When the value of the $AI > 1$ cross-correlation between the pair is right skewed contrary to the $AI < 1$, is left skewed cross correlations. Additionally, outcomes of the singularity ratio C, a truncation gauge, for almost all the pairs indicate more profound left side tails $(C > 1)$ of the spectrum $f(\alpha)$, suggesting more potent singularities, and the cross-correlation has a multifractal synthesis that is impervious to small-scale local variations [115].

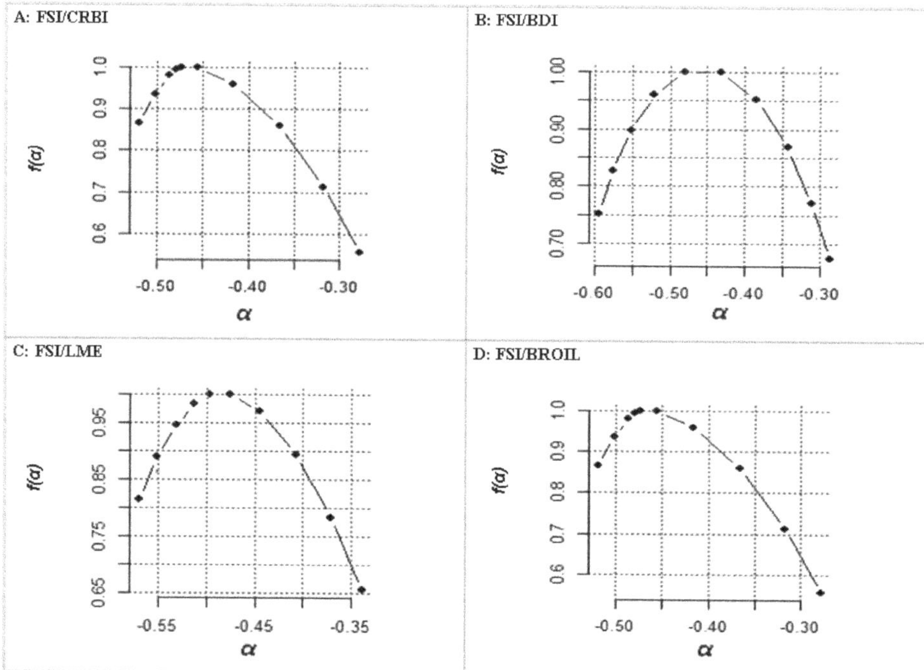

Figure 6. The Multiple Spectra of f(α) vs. α.

The findings of singularity ratio C are reported on the right side of the last column of Table 4, where FSI–BDI is (0.7607) followed by FSI–LME (0.541) then FSI–BROIL (0.469) and the least value of FSI–CRBI (0.302). Interestingly, similar to the findings of (AI), all commodity market indices showed $(C > 1)$, indicating strong singularities and the cross-correlations have a multifractal formation that reacts promptly to local fluctuations even with small variations [115].

Past literature shows that long-range cross-correlations, fat-tails, and intermittency are the main features of multifractality in the commodity markets. Cross-correlation indicates that the indices' oscillations over longer time scales rely heavily on their past behavior rather than being independent of one another. The persistence or anti-persistence trends, loops, or volatility in the indices can lead to long-range correlations. The Hurst exponent, which runs between 0 and 1, can be used to calculate long-range correlations. An approximate Hurst exponent of 0.5 signals an arbitrary process, while an approximate Hurst exponent of 0 or 1 indicates either high persistence or anti-persistence, respectively. Fat-tails indicate the probable occurrence of extreme events (such as sharp price movements or crashes) is higher than would be estimated from a normal distribution in cases of fat-tailed distributions. The assortment of market participants, complicated feedback actions, the existence of outliers or aberrations in the data, or all these factors, can lead to fat-tailed distributions. Kurtosis, a measurement of how peaked or flat a distribution is in comparison to a normal distribution, can be used to identify fat-tailed distributions. A normal distribution is indicated by a Kurtosis that is near to 3, whereas a fat-tailed distribution is indicated by a Kurtosis that is higher than 3. Intermittency describes how the indices' variations fluctuate in intensity throughout a range of time scales rather than being uniform. The multiscale structure of market activity, including the various trading frequencies, methods, and horizons of market participants, can lead to intermittent activity. The scaling exponents, which express how the fluctuations alter with the observation time scale, can be used to quantify intermittentness. A multifractal process is indicated by a changing scaling exponent, whereas a self-similar process is shown by a constant scaling exponent.

In their study of the realized volatility series of the Shanghai Stock Exchange Composite Index (SSEC) and the Shenzhen Stock Exchange Composite Index (SZSEC), Ref. [116] discovered that both indices displayed multifractality. Additionally, they discovered that fat-tailed distributions had some effects on multifractality and that long-range correlations of minor and significant major variations were the primary drivers of multifractality. In order to look into the nonlinear dependency and multifractality in the price-volume associations of China's and the US's agricultural commodities' futures markets, Ref. [117] used multifractal detrended cross-correlation analysis (MFDCCA). They reported that both markets' price-volume interactions demonstrated multifractality, with the main contributors being long-range cross-correlations and fat-tailed distributions.

Ref. [118] explored the multifractal features of financial markets, including commodity markets, employing multifractal analysis techniques and multifractal models. They scrutinized the accumulating proof of multifractality in financial time series across many markets and time periods and argued about its origins. Additionally, they highlighted how multifractal analysis might be used to assess market inefficiencies and improve risk management, along with other applications.

3.3. Rolling Windows Analysis

We use the MFDCCA with the rolling window technique to capture the dynamic changes in the cross-correlation between the FSI and the commodity market indices of CRBI, BDI, LME and BROIL. In Figure 7, Panel-A shows the evolution of the Hurst exponent ($Q = 2$) across a rolling window of 500 trading days, whereas Panel-B shows the daily variations in multifractal strength. It is easily seen that the BDI exponent line remained above the other three commodity pairs and above 0.5 until July 2022, demonstrating a persistent cross-correlation between the daily changes of BDI and FSI. For the other three commodity indices (CRBI, LME and BROIL), the respective Hurst exponents are lower than 0.5 and anti-persistent with FSI before March 2021, known as the COVID-19 pandemic period. Their Hurst exponent value increased intermittently and touched 0.5, remaining there from September to November 2020, which indicates the weakness (or absence) of cross-correlation between FSI commodities CRBI, LME, and BROIL. This implies the weak knowledge of commodity prices about FSI during these months due to uncertainty and on/off episodes of COVID-19 lockdowns after the first pandemic phase. Before and after, the FSI was likely to be negatively followed by CRBI, LME, and BROIL. Interestingly, during the COVID-19 recovery period, from March 2021 to April 2022, these three commodity indices jumped above the threshold of 0.5, remaining above the parameter and showing a strong level of persistence with FSI. This implies that the FSI is negatively followed by commodity prices. After April 2022, all four commodity indices' Hurst exponents dived and crossed the 0.5 threshold, showing persistence with the FSI, meaning that an increase in FSI was followed by the commodity market indices. This flip in the relationship between FSI and commodity market indices happened because of the Russian invasion of Ukraine from February 2022. The BROIL has the highest multifractality based on DH value, whereas LME demonstrates the lowest multifractal cross-correlation with the FSI, which is consistent with the overall results. In general, all commodity indices percentage changes in 2020 exhibit significant multifractality in contrast to slightly lower DH values in the months following March 2022.

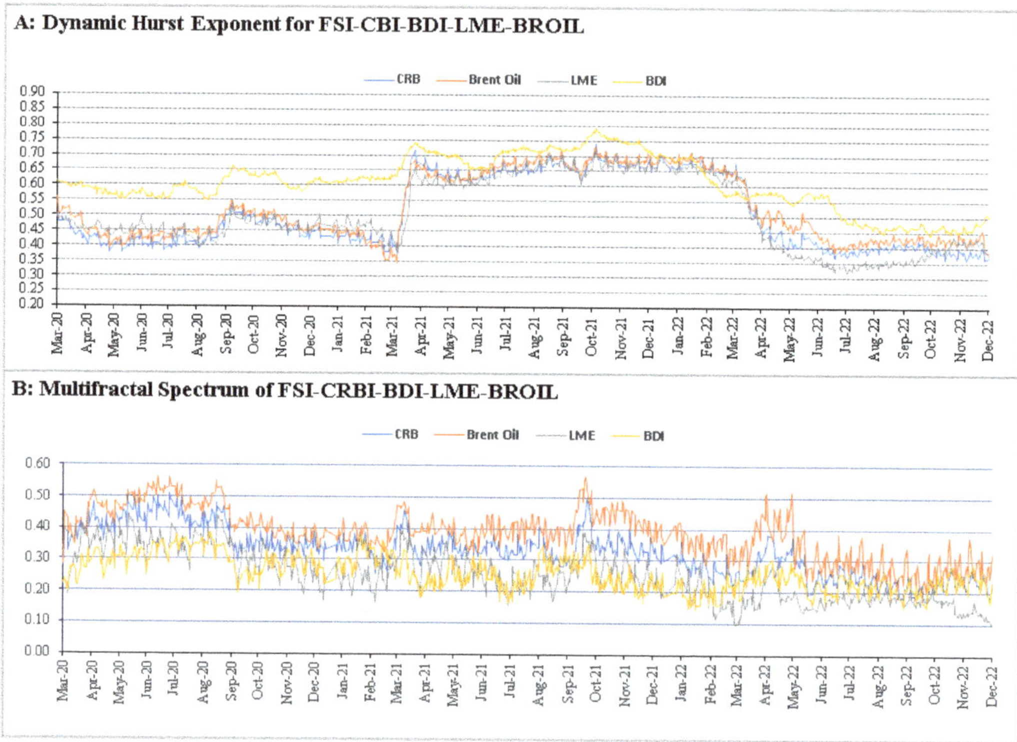

Figure 7. Dynamic Hurst exponents evolution for FSI and Commodity Markets (q = 2 and window = 500).

4. Conclusions

The purpose of this study is to measure the multifractal cross-correlations between the FSI and four commodity market indices, which represent the prices of wide range of commodities: the CRBI, BDI, LME, and BROIL. We used the daily data from June 16, 2016, to June 9, 2023. We used multifractal detrended cross-correlation analysis (MFDCCA) to investigate the dynamic relationships between the returns of the commodity market indices and the financial stress index. This approach is helpful in revealing the long-term memory, persistence, and mysterious behavior of the cross-correlations between financial stress and commodity returns, as well as their complex geometry and multifractality. To summarize, our findings corroborate the existence of cross-correlation by showing a connection between daily fluctuations in the FSI and commodity market indices. The power-law cross-correlation relationship shows that large price fluctuations in the commodity markets are more likely to follow significant fluctuations in the FSI. Additionally, different levels of multifractality are seen; the FSI and BROIL show higher levels of multifractality, whilst the FSI and LME have the lowest multifractal cross-correlation. Furthermore, the consistent persistence in cross-correlation behavior between the FSI and all chosen commodity market indices is confirmed by the Generalized Hurst Exponent. These results imply that financial stress and commodity indices retain a long-term memory of their respective historical lag values in addition to the historical values of the associated variable. One could contend that changes in the FSI are also reflected in the changes in returns of commodity markets. Furthermore, the evidence of long-range cross-correlations implies that past changes in FSI values can improve the predictability of commodity market prices. Additionally, the findings demonstrate that all FSI-commodity pairs' minor fluctuations exhibit more persistent cross-correlation characteristics than do large fluctuations. The pairs show a longer right tail because of the existence of singularities, as multifractal structure in their cross-correlation is sensitive to local fluctuations with small magnitudes and the change in commodities is associated with fluctuations in FSI. Moreover, the quantification of small and big fluctuations by the MFDCCA model reveals an imbalance in the fractal complexity between the oscillations of the commodity market with varying amplitudes and the FSI.

Understanding of cross-correlations for fund managers and investors, in the long run indicates that changes in FSI will have an effect on the returns and volatility of the commodity markets indices in crucial times, in order to adjust portfolios for better diversification. Moreover, recognizing these correlations can help to develop effective hedging strategies. The integration of cross-correlations into risk management models can improve portfolio risk estimation and forecasting accuracy, especially during global turbulence. This means they should remain vigilant, using commodity markets as a safe haven in uncertain periods. Policy-makers, like regulatory bodies and central banks, can benefit from incorporating cross-correlations to calibrate interest rates and implement policy measures effectively, preventing unnecessary propagation of crises and unintended consequences. FSI and commodity markets' cross-correlation provides insight into the regulation and control of the macroeconomy. As a result, to prevent any significant swings in the commodity markets, regulators of these markets must continuously develop regulations that take into account the broader impact on them. Governments can apply understanding of abstracted cross-correlation to devise macroeconomic policy appropriately, to decide tariffs for commodities by foreseeing how financial stress might influence commodity prices, eventually affecting, economic growth, inflation, and trade.

Our research offers a framework for investigating the relationship between financial stress and commodity market returns, as well as a basis for investigating similar content in other global markets. This study is limited to daily data, so in future studies intraday changes in FSI and commodity markets could provide interesting insights. Through intraday data analysis, we would have more pinpoints in the commodity market fluctuations and fine-tuned information that would allow us to explain market dynamics in a more interesting way.

Author Contributions: Conceptualization, H.A. and F.A.; Data curation, F.A. and P.F.; Formal analysis, F.A. and H.A.; Writing—Original draft, H.A. and F.A.; Writing—Review and editing, P.F. and H.A. All authors have read and agreed to the published version of the manuscript.

Funding: This research was funded by Fundação para a Ciência e a Tecnologia (grant UIDB/05064/2020).

Institutional Review Board Statement: Not applicable.

Informed Consent Statement: Not applicable.

Data Availability Statement: The data will be furnished when required.

Conflicts of Interest: The authors declare no conflicts of interest.

References

1. Moore, R.; Mao, Y.; Zhang, J.; Clarke, K. Economic burden of illness in Canada, 1993. *Chronic Dis. Inj. Can.* **1997**, *18*, 1F.
2. Jahoda, M. Economic recession and mental health: Some conceptual issues. *J. Soc. Issues* **1988**, *44*, 13–23. [CrossRef]
3. Huang, R.; Ghose, B.; Tang, S. Effect of financial stress on self-rereported health and quality of life among older adults in five developing countries: A cross sectional analysis of WHO-SAGE survey. *BMC Geriatr.* **2020**, *20*, 288. [CrossRef]
4. Sturgeon, J.A.; Arewasikporn, A.; Okun, M.A.; Davis, M.C.; Ong, A.D.; Zautra, A.J. The psychosocial context of financial stress: Implications for inflammation and psychological health. *Psychosom. Med.* **2016**, *78*, 134. [CrossRef]
5. Taylor, M.; Stevens, G.; Agho, K.; Raphael, B. The impacts of household financial stress, resilience, social support, and other adversities on the psychological distress of Western Sydney parents. *Int. J. Popul. Res.* **2017**, *2017*, 6310683. [CrossRef]
6. Åslund, C.; Larm, P.; Starrin, B.; Nilsson, K.W. The buffering effect of tangible social support on financial stress: Influence on psychological well-being and psychosomatic symptoms in a large sample of the adult general population. *Int. J. Equity Health* **2014**, *13*, 85. [CrossRef]
7. Altman, E.I.; Hotchkiss, E. *Corporate Financial Distress and Bankruptcy*; John Wiley & Sons: New York, NY, USA, 1993; Volume 1998.

8. Davis, C.G.; Mantler, J. *The Consequences of Financial Stress for Individuals, Families, and Society*; Centre for Research on Stress, Coping and Well-Being, Carleton University: Ottawa, ON, Canada, 2004.
9. Frank, C.; Davis, C.G.; Elgar, F.J. Financial strain, social capital, and perceived health during economic recession: A longitudinal survey in rural Canada. *Anxiety Stress Coping* **2014**, *27*, 422–438. [CrossRef] [PubMed]
10. Koh, S.; Durand, R.B.; Dai, L.; Chang, M. Financial distress: Lifecycle and corporate restructuring. *J. Corp. Financ.* **2015**, *33*, 19–33. [CrossRef]
11. Setiany, E. The effect of investment, free cash flow, earnings management, and interest coverage ratio on financial distress. *J. Soc. Sci.* **2021**, *2*, 64–69.
12. Efthyvoulou, G. The impact of financial stress on sectoral productivity. *Econ. Lett.* **2012**, *116*, 240–243. [CrossRef]
13. Cardarelli, R.; Elekdag, S.A.; Lall, S. Financial stress, downturns, and recoveries. *IMF Work. Pap.* **2009**, *2009*, WP/09/100.
14. Ahir, H.; Dell'Ariccia, G.; Furceri, D.; Papageorgiou, C.; Qi, H. Financial Stress and Economic Activity. *IMF Work. Pap.* **2023**, *2023*, WP/23/217.
15. Mundra, S.; Bicchal, M. Asymmetric effects of monetary policy and financial accelerator: Evidence from India. *J. Econ. Asymmetries* **2023**, *27*, e00296. [CrossRef]
16. Apostolakis, G.; Papadopoulos, A.P. Financial stress spillovers in advanced economies. *J. Int. Financ. Mark. Inst. Money* **2014**, *32*, 128–149. [CrossRef]
17. Ishrakieh, L.M.; Dagher, L.; El Hariri, S. A financial stress index for a highly dollarized developing country: The case of Lebanon. *Cent. Bank Rev.* **2020**, *20*, 43–52. [CrossRef]
18. Ilesanmi, K.D.; Tewari, D.D. Financial stress index and economic activity in South Africa: New evidence. *Economies* **2020**, *8*, 110. [CrossRef]
19. Cevik, E.I.; Dibooglu, S.; Kenc, T. Financial stress and economic activity in some emerging Asian economies. *Res. Int. Bus. Financ.* **2016**, *36*, 127–139. [CrossRef]
20. Hubrich, K.; Tetlow, R.J. Financial stress and economic dynamics: The transmission of crises. *J. Monet. Econ.* **2015**, *70*, 100–115. [CrossRef]
21. Apostolakis, G.; Papadopoulos, A.P. Financial stability, monetary stability and growth: A PVAR analysis. *Open Econ. Rev.* **2019**, *30*, 157–178. [CrossRef]
22. Ozcelebi, O. Assessing the impacts of financial stress index of developed countries on the exchange market pressure index of emerging countries. *Int. Rev. Econ. Financ.* **2020**, *70*, 288–302. [CrossRef]
23. Vermeulen, R.; Hoeberichts, M.; Vašíček, B.; Žigraiová, D.; Šmídková, K.; de Haan, J. Financial stress indices and financial crises. *Open Econ. Rev.* **2015**, *26*, 383–406. [CrossRef]
24. Altman, E.I.; Hotchkiss, E. *Corporate Financial Distress and Bankruptcy: Predict and Avoid Bankruptcy, Analyze and Invest in Distressed Debt*; John Wiley & Sons: Hoboken, NJ, USA, 2010; Volume 289.
25. Jadoon, I.A.; Mumtaz, R.; Sheikh, J.; Ayub, U.; Tahir, M. The impact of green growth on financial stability. *J. Financ. Regul. Compliance* **2021**, *29*, 533–560. [CrossRef]
26. Geetha, K.; Suganthi, L.M.; Vasanthi, K.; Kavitha, B. Financial stress testing in US banking sector. *Mater. Today Proc.* **2021**, *37*, 2252–2255. [CrossRef]
27. Cardarelli, R.; Elekdag, S.; Lall, S. Financial stress and economic contractions. *J. Financ. Stab.* **2011**, *7*, 78–97. [CrossRef]
28. Cevik, E.I.; Dibooglu, S.; Kutan, A.M. Measuring financial stress in transition economies. *J. Financ. Stab.* **2013**, *9*, 597–611. [CrossRef]
29. Chen, L.; Verousis, T.; Wang, K.; Zhou, Z. Financial stress and commodity price volatility. *Energy Econ.* **2023**, *125*, 106874. [CrossRef]
30. Xu, Y.; Liang, C.; Wang, J. Financial stress and returns predictability: Fresh evidence from China. *Pac.-Basin Financ. J.* **2023**, *78*, 101980. [CrossRef]
31. Hoque, M.E.; Soo-Wah, L.; Tiwari, A.K.; Akhter, T. Time and frequency domain connectedness and spillover among categorical and regional financial stress, gold and bitcoin market. *Resour. Policy* **2023**, *85*, 103786. [CrossRef]
32. Mezghani, T.; Boujelbène, M.; Boutouria, S. Forecasting the impact of financial stress on hedging between the oil market and GCC financial markets. *Manag. Financ.* **2023**. [CrossRef]
33. Sohag, K.; Kalina, I.; Elsayed, A.H. Financial stress in Russia: Exploring the impact of oil market shocks. *Resour. Policy* **2023**, *86*, 104150. [CrossRef]
34. Adam, T.; Benecká, S.; Matějů, J. Financial stress and its non-linear impact on CEE exchange rates. *J. Financ. Stab.* **2018**, *36*, 346–360. [CrossRef]
35. Apostolakis, G.; Papadopoulos, A.P. Financial stress spillovers across the banking, securities and foreign exchange markets. *J. Financ. Stab.* **2015**, *19*, 1–21. [CrossRef]
36. Li, Y.; Liang, C.; Huynh, T.L.D. Combination forecast based on financial stress categories for global equity market volatility: The evidence during the COVID-19 and the global financial crisis periods. *Appl. Econ.* **2023**, 1–36. [CrossRef]
37. Armah, M.; Bossman, A.; Amewu, G. Information flow between global financial market stress and African equity markets: An EEMD-based transfer entropy analysis. *Heliyon* **2023**, *9*, e13899. [CrossRef]
38. Chau, F.; Deesomsak, R. Does linkage fuel the fire? The transmission of financial stress across the markets. *Int. Rev. Financ. Anal.* **2014**, *36*, 57–70. [CrossRef]

39. Sousa, R.M. Wealth-to-income ratio, government bond yields and financial stress in the Euro Area. *Appl. Econ. Lett.* **2012**, *19*, 1085–1088. [CrossRef]
40. Liang, C.; Hong, Y.; Huynh, L.D.T.; Ma, F. Asymmetric dynamic risk transmission between financial stress and monetary policy uncertainty: Thinking in the post-covid-19 world. *Rev. Quant. Financ. Account.* **2023**, *60*, 1543–1567. [CrossRef]
41. Gomis-Porqueras, P.; Ruprecht, R. *A Financial Stress Index for a Small Open Economy: The Australian Case*; Board of Governors of the Federal Reserve System: Washington, DC, USA, 2023.
42. Zhang, H.; Wang, P. Does Bitcoin or gold react to financial stress alike? Evidence from the US and China. *Int. Rev. Econ. Financ.* **2021**, *71*, 629–648. [CrossRef]
43. Reboredo, J.C.; Uddin, G.S. Do financial stress and policy uncertainty have an impact on the energy and metals markets? A quantile regression approach. *Int. Rev. Econ. Financ.* **2016**, *43*, 284–298. [CrossRef]
44. Miah, M.D.; Shafiullah, M.; Alam, M.S. The effect of financial stress on renewable energy consumption: Evidence from US data. *Environ. Dev. Sustain.* **2023**, 1–24. [CrossRef]
45. Apostolakis, G.N.; Floros, C.; Gkillas, K.; Wohar, M. Financial stress, economic policy uncertainty, and oil price uncertainty. *Energy Econ.* **2021**, *104*, 105686. [CrossRef]
46. Xiang, J.; Chen, H.; Li, L. Oil Price Uncertainty, Financial Distress and Real Economic Activities: Evidence from China. *Pac. -Basin Financ. J.* **2023**, *81*, 102103.
47. Cifarelli, G.; Paladino, G. A dynamic model of hedging and speculation in the commodity futures markets. *J. Financ. Mark.* **2015**, *25*, 1–15. [CrossRef]
48. Chen, Y.-F.; Mu, X. Asymmetric volatility in commodity markets. *J. Commod. Mark.* **2021**, *22*, 100139. [CrossRef]
49. Ghoshray, A. Do international primary commodity prices exhibit asymmetric adjustment? *J. Commod. Mark.* **2019**, *14*, 40–50. [CrossRef]
50. Andreasson, P.; Bekiros, S.; Nguyen, D.K.; Uddin, G.S. Impact of speculation and economic uncertainty on commodity markets. *Int. Rev. Finance. Anal.* **2016**, *43*, 115–127. [CrossRef]
51. Liu, L. Cross-correlations between crude oil and agricultural commodity markets. *Phys. A Stat. Mech. Its Appl.* **2014**, *395*, 293–302. [CrossRef]
52. Bhardwaj, G.; Janardanan, R.; Rouwenhorst, K.G. The first commodity futures index of 1933. *J. Commod. Mark.* **2021**, *23*, 100157. [CrossRef]
53. Aepli, M.D.; Füss, R.; Henriksen, T.E.S.; Paraschiv, F. Modeling the multivariate dynamic dependence structure of commodity futures portfolios. *J. Commod. Mark.* **2017**, *6*, 66–87. [CrossRef]
54. Mulvey, J.M.; Kim, W.C.; Lin, C. Optimizing a portfolio of liquid and illiquid assets. In *Optimal Financial Decision Making under Uncertainty*; Springer: Berlin/Heidelberg, Germany, 2017; pp. 151–175.
55. Monin, P.J. The OFR financial stress index. *Risks* **2019**, *7*, 25. [CrossRef]
56. Robillard, R.; Saad, M.; Edwards, J.; Solomonova, E.; Pennestri, M.-H.; Daros, A.; Veissière, S.P.L.; Quilty, L.; Dion, K.; Nixon, A. Social, financial and psychological stress during an emerging pandemic: Observations from a population survey in the acute phase of COVID-19. *BMJ Open* **2020**, *10*, e043805. [CrossRef]
57. Wan, Y.; Wang, W.; He, S.; Hu, B. How do uncertainties affect the connectedness of global financial markets? Changes during the Russia-Ukraine conflict. *Asia-Pac. J. Account. Econ.* **2023**, 1–28. [CrossRef]
58. Li, Z.-C.; Xie, C.; Zeng, Z.-J.; Wang, G.-J.; Zhang, T. Forecasting global stock market volatilities in an uncertain world. *Int. Rev. Financ. Anal.* **2023**, *85*, 102463. [CrossRef]
59. Adrian, T. Safeguarding Financial Stability amid High Inflation and Geopolitical Risks. Available online: https://www.imf.org/en/Blogs/Articles/2023/04/11/global-financial-system-tested-by-higher-inflation-and-interest-rates (accessed on 14 January 2024).
60. Shahzad, U.; Mohammed, K.S.; Tiwari, S.; Nakonieczny, J.; Nesterowicz, R. Connectedness between geopolitical risk, financial instability indices and precious metals markets: Novel findings from Russia Ukraine conflict perspective. *Resour. Policy* **2023**, *80*, 103190. [CrossRef]
61. Gadanecz, B.; Jayaram, K. Measures of financial stability-a review. *Irving Fish. Comm. Bull.* **2008**, *31*, 365–383.
62. Consolini, G.; De Michelis, P. A Joint Multifractal Approach to Solar Wind Turbulence. *Fractal Fract.* **2023**, *7*, 748. [CrossRef]
63. Zhou, W.-X. Multifractal detrended cross-correlation analysis for two nonstationary signals. *Phys. Rev. E* **2008**, *77*, 066211. [CrossRef]
64. Kojić, M.; Mitić, P.; Minović, J. Gold and Sustainable Stocks in the US and EU: Nonlinear Analysis Based on Multifractal Detrended Cross-Correlation Analysis and Granger Causality. *Fractal Fract.* **2023**, *7*, 738. [CrossRef]
65. Duanzhu, S.; Wang, J.; Jia, C. Hotel Comment Emotion Classification Based on the MF-DFA and Partial Differential Equation Classifier. *Fractal Fract.* **2023**, *7*, 744. [CrossRef]
66. ECB. Financial Stability Review. Available online: https://www.ecb.europa.eu/pub/pdf/fsr/financialstabilityreview201206en.pdf (accessed on 11 October 2023).
67. Gençyürek, A.G. Leading and lagging role between financial stress and crude oil. *Stud. Econ. Financ.* **2023**. [CrossRef]
68. Yan, X.; Bai, J.; Li, X.; Chen, Z. Can dimensional reduction technology make better use of the information of uncertainty indices when predicting volatility of Chinese crude oil futures? *Resour. Policy* **2022**, *75*, 102521. [CrossRef]

69. Bouri, E.; Gupta, R.; Lau, C.K.M.; Roubaud, D.; Wang, S. Bitcoin and global financial stress: A copula-based approach to dependence and causality in the quantiles. *Q. Rev. Econ. Financ.* **2018**, *69*, 297–307. [CrossRef]
70. SARI, S.S. Predicting Financial Stress Index Using Wavelet Transform Artificial Neural Networks. *J. Int. Sci. Res.* **2022**, *7*, 282–296.
71. Bhardwaj, G.; Gorton, G.; Rouwenhorst, G. *Facts and Fantasies About Commodity Futures Ten Years Later*; National Bureau of Economic Research: Cambridge, MA, USA, 2015.
72. Acharya, R.N.; Gentle, P.F.; Paudel, K.P. Examining the CRB index as a leading indicator for US inflation. *Appl. Econ. Lett.* **2010**, *17*, 1493–1496. [CrossRef]
73. Katris, C.; Kavussanos, M.G. Time series forecasting methods for the Baltic dry index. *J. Forecast.* **2021**, *40*, 1540–1565. [CrossRef]
74. Bakshi, G.; Panayotov, G.; Skoulakis, G. *The Baltic Dry Index as a Predictor of Global Stock Returns, Commodity Returns, and Global Economic Activity*; Georgetown University: Washington, DC, USA, 2010.
75. Bildirici, M.E.; Kayıkçı, F.; Onat, I.Ş. Baltic Dry Index as a major economic policy indicator: The relationship with economic growth. *Procedia-Soc. Behav. Sci.* **2015**, *210*, 416–424. [CrossRef]
76. Han, L.; Wan, L.; Xu, Y. Can the Baltic Dry Index predict foreign exchange rates? *Financ. Res. Lett.* **2020**, *32*, 101157. [CrossRef]
77. Apergis, N.; Payne, J.E. New evidence on the information and predictive content of the Baltic Dry Index. *Int. J. Financ. Stud.* **2013**, *1*, 62–80. [CrossRef]
78. Park, J.; Lim, B. Testing efficiency of the London metal exchange: New evidence. *Int. J. Financ. Stud.* **2018**, *6*, 32. [CrossRef]
79. Dedi, V.; Mandilaras, A. Trader positions and the price of oil in the futures market. *Int. Rev. Econ. Financ.* **2022**, *82*, 448–460. [CrossRef]
80. Gao, X.; Li, B.; Liu, R. The relative pricing of WTI and Brent crude oil futures: Expectations or risk premia? *J. Commod. Mark.* **2023**, *30*, 100274. [CrossRef]
81. Naqvi, B.; Mirza, N.; Umar, M.; Rizvi, S.K.A. Shanghai crude oil futures: Returns Independence, volatility asymmetry, and hedging potential. *Energy Econ.* **2023**, *128*, 107110. [CrossRef]
82. Watorek, M.; Drożdż, S.; Oświęcimka, P.; Stanuszek, M. Multifractal cross-correlations between the world oil and other financial markets in 2012–2017. *Energy Econ.* **2019**, *81*, 874–885. [CrossRef]
83. Yarlagadda, H.; Patel, M.A.; Gupta, V.; Bansal, T.; Upadhyay, S.; Shaheen, N.; Jain, R.; Patel, M.; Bansal, T.K. COVID-19 vaccine challenges in developing and developed countries. *Cureus* **2022**, *14*, e23951. [CrossRef]
84. Kasal, S. What are the effects of financial stress on economic activity and government debt? An empirical examination in an emerging economy. *Borsa Istanb. Rev.* **2023**, *23*, 254–267. [CrossRef]
85. IMF. The Outlook is Uncertain Again Amid Financial Sector Turmoil, High Inflation, Ongoing Effects of Russia's Invasion of Ukraine, and Three Years of COVID. Available online: https://www.imf.org/en/Publications/WEO/Issues/2023/04/11/world-economic-outlook-april-2023 (accessed on 13 September 2023).
86. EIA. Today in Energy. Available online: https://www.eia.gov/todayinenergy/detail.php?id=34372 (accessed on 19 September 2023).
87. Aslam, F.; Ali, I.; Amjad, F.; Ali, H.; Irfan, I. On the inner dynamics between Fossil fuels and the carbon market: A combination of seasonal-trend decomposition and multifractal cross-correlation analysis. *Environ. Sci. Pollut. Res.* **2023**, *30*, 25873–25891. [CrossRef]
88. Jiang, Z.-Q.; Zhou, W.-X. Multifractal detrending moving-average cross-correlation analysis. *Phys. Rev. E* **2011**, *84*, 016106. [CrossRef] [PubMed]
89. Xu, W.; Liu, C.; Shi, K.; Liu, Y. Multifractal detrended cross-correlation analysis on NO, NO2 and O3 concentrations at traffic sites. *Phys. A Stat. Mech. Its Appl.* **2018**, *502*, 605–612. [CrossRef]
90. Li, B.-G.; Ling, D.-Y.; Yu, Z.-G. Multifractal temporally weighted detrended partial cross-correlation analysis of two non-stationary time series affected by common external factors. *Phys. A Stat. Mech. Its Appl.* **2021**, *573*, 125920. [CrossRef]
91. Song, J.; Shang, P. Effect of linear and nonlinear filters on multifractal detrended cross-correlation analysis. *Fractals* **2011**, *19*, 443–453. [CrossRef]
92. Devaguptapu, A.; Dash, P. Global commodity prices and inflation expectations. *Int. J. Emerg. Mark.* **2023**, *18*, 1053–1077. [CrossRef]
93. Aslam, F.; Zil-E-Huma; Bibi, R.; Ferreira, P. The Nexus Between Twitter-Based Uncertainty And Cryptocurrencies: A Multifractal Analysis. *Fractals* **2023**, *31*, 2350027. [CrossRef]
94. Aslam, F.; Ferreira, P.; Mohti, W. Investigating efficiency of frontier stock markets using multifractal detrended fluctuation analysis. *Int. J. Emerg. Mark.* **2023**, *18*, 1650–1676. [CrossRef]
95. Daglis, T. The Tourism Industry's Performance During the Years of the COVID-19 Pandemic. *Comput. Econ.* **2023**, 1–17. [CrossRef]
96. Daglis, T. The dynamic relationship of cryptocurrencies with supply chain and logistics stocks–the impact of COVID-19. *J. Econ. Stud.* **2023**, *50*, 840–857. [CrossRef]
97. Zhang, S.; Guo, Y.; Cheng, H.; Zhang, H. Cross-correlations between price and volume in China's crude oil futures market: A study based on multifractal approaches. *Chaos Solitons Fractals* **2021**, *144*, 110642. [CrossRef]
98. Ghazani, M.M.; Khosravi, R. Multifractal detrended cross-correlation analysis on benchmark cryptocurrencies and crude oil prices. *Phys. A Stat. Mech. Its Appl.* **2020**, *560*, 125172. [CrossRef]
99. Anand, B.; Paul, S.; Nair, A.R. Time-varying effects of oil price shocks on financial stress: Evidence from India. *Energy Econ.* **2023**, *122*, 106703. [CrossRef]

100. de la Torre, J.C.; Pavón-Domínguez, P.; Dorronsoro, B.; Galindo, P.L.; Ruiz, P. Multi-Signal Multifractal Detrended Fluctuation Analysis for Uncertain Systems—Application to the Energy Consumption of Software Programs in Microcontrollers. *Fractal Fract.* **2023**, *7*, 794. [CrossRef]
101. Kristoufek, L. Multifractal height cross-correlation analysis: A new method for analyzing long-range cross-correlations. *EPL Europhys. Lett.* **2011**, *95*, 68001. [CrossRef]
102. Yuan, Y.; Zhuang, X.-T.; Jin, X. Measuring multifractality of stock price fluctuation using multifractal detrended fluctuation analysis. *Phys. A Stat. Mech. Its Appl.* **2009**, *388*, 2189–2197. [CrossRef]
103. Telesca, L.; Thai, A.T.; Cao, D.T.; Cao, D.T.; Dinh, Q.V.; Mai, X.B. Fractal and Spectral Analysis of Seismicity in the Lai Chau Area (Vietnam). *Fractal Fract.* **2023**, *7*, 776. [CrossRef]
104. Freitas, D.B.d.; Nepomuceno, M.M.F.; Nepomuceno, M.M.F.; Leão, I.C.; Chagas, M.L.D.; Chagas, M.L.D.; Martins, B.L.C.; Medeiros, J.R.D. New Suns in the Cosmos. IV. The Multifractal Nature of Stellar Magnetic Activity in Kepler Cool Stars. *Astrophys. J.* **2017**, *843*, 103. [CrossRef]
105. Hampson, K.M.; Mallen, E.A. Multifractal nature of ocular aberration dynamics of the human eye. *Biomed. Opt. Express* **2011**, *2*, 464–470. [CrossRef]
106. Hurst, H.E. Long term storage: An experimental study. *J. R. Stat. Soc. Ser. A* **1965**, *129*, 591–593.
107. Seuront, L. *Fractals and Multifractals in Ecology and Aquatic Science*; CRC Press: Boca Raton, FL, USA, 2009.
108. Podobnik, B.; Wang, D.; Horvatic, D.; Grosse, I.; Stanley, H.E. Time-lag cross-correlations in collective phenomena. *Europhys. Lett.* **2010**, *90*, 68001. [CrossRef]
109. Podobnik, B.; Stanley, H.E. Detrended cross-correlation analysis: A new method for analyzing two nonstationary time series. *Phys. Rev. Lett.* **2008**, *100*, 084102. [CrossRef] [PubMed]
110. Lo, A.W. The adaptive markets hypothesis: Market efficiency from an evolutionary perspective. *J. Portf. Manag.* **2004**, *30*, 15–29. [CrossRef]
111. Kristoufek, L.; Vosvrda, M. Measuring capital market efficiency: Global and local correlations structure. *Phys. A Stat. Mech. Its Appl.* **2013**, *392*, 184–193. [CrossRef]
112. Hasan, R.; Salim, M.M. Power law cross-correlations between price change and volume change of Indian stocks. *Phys. A Stat. Mech. Its Appl.* **2017**, *473*, 620–631. [CrossRef]
113. Ferreira, P. Assessing the relationship between dependence and volume in stock markets: A dynamic analysis. *Phys. A Stat. Mech. Its Appl.* **2019**, *516*, 90–97. [CrossRef]
114. Ruan, Q.; Jiang, W.; Ma, G. Cross-correlations between price and volume in Chinese gold markets. *Phys. A Stat. Mech. Its Appl.* **2016**, *451*, 10–22. [CrossRef]
115. Ihlen, E. Introduction to Multifractal Detrended Fluctuation Analysis in Matlab. *Front. Physiol.* **2012**, *3*, 141. [CrossRef]
116. Wang, G.-J.; Xiong, L.; Zhu, Y.; Xie, C.; Foglia, M. Multilayer network analysis of investor sentiment and stock returns. *Res. Int. Bus. Financ.* **2022**, *62*, 101707. [CrossRef]
117. Cao, G.; Han, Y.; Cui, W.; Guo, Y. Multifractal detrended cross-correlations between the CSI 300 index futures and the spot markets based on high-frequency data. *Phys. A Stat. Mech. Its Appl.* **2014**, *414*, 308–320. [CrossRef]
118. Jiang, Y.; Nie, H.; Ruan, W. Time-varying long-term memory in Bitcoin market. *Financ. Res. Lett.* **2018**, *25*, 280–284. [CrossRef]

fractal and fractional

MDPI

Article

New Class of Complex Models of Materials with Piezoelectric Properties with Differential Constitutive Relations of Fractional Order: An Overview

Katica R. (Stevanović) Hedrih [1,2]

[1] Department of Mechanics, Mathematical Institute of Serbian Academy of Science and Arts, ul. Knez Mihailova 36/III, 11000 Belgrade, Serbia; katicah@mi.sanu.ac.rs or katicahedrih@gmail.com
[2] Faculty of Mechanical Engineering, University of Niš, Aleksandra Medvedeva bb, 18000 Nis, Serbia

Abstract: Rheological complex models of various elastoviscous and viscoelastic fractional-type substances with polarized piezoelectric properties are of interest due to the widespread use of viscoelastic–plastic bodies under loading. The word "overview" used in the title means and corresponds to the content of the manuscript and aims to emphasize that it presents an overview of a new class of complex rheological models of the fractional type of ideal elastoviscous, as well as viscoelastic, materials with piezoelectric properties. Two new elementary rheological elements were introduced: a rheological basic Newton's element of ideal fluid fractional type and a basic Faraday element of ideal elastic material with the property of polarization under mechanical loading and piezoelectric properties. By incorporating these newly introduced rheological elements into classical complex rheological models, a new class of complex rheological models of materials with piezoelectric properties described by differential fractional-order constitutive relations was obtained. A set of seven new complex rheological models of materials are presented with appropriate structural formulas. Differential constitutive relations of the fractional order, which contain differential operators of the fractional order, are composed. The seven new complex models describe the properties of ideal new materials, which can be elastoviscous solids or viscoelastic fluids. The purpose of the work is to make a theoretical contribution by introducing, designing, and presenting a new class of rheological complex models with appropriate differential constitutive relations of the fractional order. These theoretical results can be the basis for further scientific and applied research. It is especially important to point out the possibility that these models containing a Faraday element can be used to collect electrical energy for various purposes.

Keywords: new class of rheological complex models of ideal materials of the fractional type with polarization property; ideal fluid; Faraday element with property of polarization; differential constitutive relation fractional order; internal degrees of freedom; energy dissipation; Kelvin–Voigt–Faraday model; Maxwell–Faraday model; Lethersich–Faraday model; Jeffrey–Faraday viscoelastic fluid model; Jeffrey–Faraday-F model; Burgers–Faraday model

1. Introduction

The inspiration for the design and construction of a new class of rheological complex model materials came from a lesson on classic rheological complex models contained in a chapter of the author's university publication on elastodynamics [1], which was used to convey knowledge about rheological complex models to mechanical engineering students.

This new article provides a complete overview of a new class of fractional-type rheological complex material models with piezoelectric properties, providing complete mathematical descriptions and derivations of the fractional order, with all of the details explained for each of the new complex material models.

The author and their coauthors previously researched the dynamics of oscillating certain rheological discrete dynamic systems with one and more degrees of freedom of oscillation, of the fractional type, applying a mathematical description with differential equations of the fractional order. For details, see References [2–5]. It has been shown through new research results on the topic of elements of mathematical phenomenology and analogies of electrical and mechanical oscillators of the fractional type with a finite number of degrees of freedom of oscillation that there are linear and nonlinear modes; for details, see Reference [4].

In our previously published Reference [5], in the introductory part, we pointed to the list of references and their contents, which were inspirational for researchers and helped to achieve the new results shown in that area, as well as those that we will show in this article, so we will not list them here, nor are they included in the present list of references.

In our work in Reference [5], titled "Rheological Burgers–Faraday models and rheological dynamical systems with fractional derivatives and their application in biomechanics", two rheological Burgers–Faraday models and the dynamics of two rheological discrete dynamical systems were created by using, without more detail, two new rheological models: a Kelvin–Voigt–Faraday fractional-type model and a Maxwell–Faraday fractional-type model. The Burgers–Faraday models described, also without more detail, in the paper are new models of the dynamical behavior of materials with coupled fields: mechanical normal stress and axial dilatation and the electric field of polarization through Faraday's element. An analysis of the constitutive relation of differential fractional orders for Burgers–Faraday models is given, in brief.

This new article includes those models, but also with new details of mathematical descriptions and the derivation of differential constitutive relations of the fractional order and determination of their solutions, which were not presented in the previous published article [5]. This completes the presentation and overview of all of the new rheological complex models of the fractional type with piezoelectric properties, which belong to a new class of complex material models with the property of polarization of the piezoelectric elements contained in those models.

We should also mention References [6,7], of which the group of authors' common contribution is given in the mathematical field of fractional calculus with applications in mechanics, particularly vibrations and diffusion processes, as well as wave movements in continuums.

Using the previous definition of the differential operator $\mathrm{D}_t^{\alpha}[\bullet]$ of the fractional order, we introduce an ideal new fluid element, Newton's ideal viscous element, based on the differential constitutive relationship $\sigma_z = \mathbf{E}_{\alpha}\mathrm{D}_t^{\alpha}[\varepsilon_z]$ between the normal stress σ_z and the velocity of axial dilatation $\mathrm{D}_t^{\alpha}[\varepsilon_z]$ (fractional type).

The piezoelectric materials are used for modeling new types of rheological models of materials. It is known that piezoelectric materials have coupled tensors of mechanical and electrical states; for details, see Reference [8]. The relationships between the elements of the tensor of the mechanical stress state and the tensor of the mechanical deformation state in coupling with the tensor of the electrical state of polarization were studied for samples with different direction of polarizations; see Reference [8].

Today, the application of piezoelectric materials is widespread and they are productively used in various fields of technology and medicine, as sensors, actuators, and exciters; see References [3,5].

In addition to the keyword of the fractional type, we will often use the word Faraday, so we provide basic information about the famous scientist Michael Faraday (22 September 1791–25 August 1867).

Faraday was an English bookbinder who became interested in electricity (for details, see References [9,10]). He earned the title of assistant in Davy's laboratory, and at the age of 19, Faraday studied with the renowned chemist Sir Humphry Davy (Sir Humphry Davy, 17 December 1778–Geneva, 29 May 1829), president of the Royal Society, and John Tatum, founder of the Civil Philosophical Society. Then, he began to conduct his own experiments. He was the first to discover that electricity produces an electrical "tension" (electric voltage), which produces an "electrotonic state", or the polarization of matter molecules.

For the formation of complex rheological models of fractional-type materials with piezoelectric properties, we introduced a new rheological element, which we called Faraday's rheological ideal elastic element with polarization ability and piezoelectric properties. This will be discussed in the next chapter.

Therefore, to begin with, we provide a basic short presentation of some publications on rheological complex models of the fractional type, which we will modify by parallel or series coupling with the newly introduced rheological Faraday element—an ideal elastic element with polarization capability [5].

From the published literature, we learned that rheological models are used to describe the models and compositions of building materials, yarns in the textile industry, and biomaterials. Reference [11] shows the use of ultrasonic piezoceramic materials in a practical model of an ultrasonic sprayer design. An auxiliary size distribution model for the ultrasonically produced water droplets was experimentally tested. Reference [11] inspired the author of this paper in the introduction of the new Faraday element. This sprayer design using an ultrasonic oscillator allows the formation of a new design of a fractional-type ultrasonic sprayer with piezoelectric properties in which the concentrator of variable cross-section is a fractional-type rheological element.

The contents of References [12–15] present research on rheological models in civil engineering, from studying rheological models of soft rock matrix creep [16,17] to studying composite and prestressed structures using rheological modals and presenting the corresponding classification of the rheological models used [13].

In his doctoral dissertation [18], entitled "Dynamic Behavior of the Mechanism System—the Working Object of the Weaving Process", the author studied the dynamics and use of several rheological models of textile fibers, with which he demonstrated their use in the textile industry, while in [19], he studied the rheological modeling of yarn elongation.

Reference [20], entitled "Review: Rheological properties of living materials. From cells to tissues", as well as Reference [21], entitled "New rheological problems involving general fractional derivatives with nonsingular power-law kernels", present the applications of rheological models in biomaterials.

The content of [22], entitled "A fractional model for time-variant Non-Newtonian Flow", presents new results and insights into the behavior of certain rheological models: as the author calls them, models of Non-Newtonian Flow. Reference [23] presents the results of the research of the group of authors entitled "A unified rheological model for cells and cellularised materials" and provides insights into the basic models of rheological biomaterials. The group of authors in Reference [24], entitled "Fractional rheology-informed neural networks for data-driven identification of viscoelastic constitutive models", presents new results using fractional rheological models.

The author in Reference [25] presents the results of research and modeling of thermorheological models and thermomechanical systems using fractional-order differentials.

The following conclusions can be drawn from the published literature: First, the majority of published papers on rheological models of ideal materials refer to classical complex rheological models, which are presented in integral form, in one chapter of a university textbook [1] on the Theory of Elasticity. Second, most of the papers on rheological models are regarding applications in construction, on concrete and rock materials, and then in the textile dyeing industry with application to cotton and yarn (see References [18,19]).

The complete and integral theory of the Analytical Dynamics (Mechanics) of Discrete Hereditary Systems is presented in Reference [26], as well as some experiments to determine the kernel of theology for different rheological materials' hereditary properties.

The generalized function of fractional-type dissipation of system energy is presented in Reference [27].

The previously cited Reference [8] contains significant knowledge about the coupled fields of mechanical and piezoelectric states.

The citation and presentation of the contents of the references from the above-mentioned list of references, which were available to the author, provide sufficient evidence of the uniqueness and originality of the author's new scientific results presented in this manuscript. At the same time, the author is free to emphasize that the scientific results presented in this manuscript are the result of spontaneous scientific inspiration and knowledge acquired during the author's more than half a century of dedication to science. In this sense, the list of references is only a description of the contents contained in these published references.

These rheological complex models of materials of the fractional type with piezoelectric polarization properties are suitable for studying the behavior of complex systems such as rheological oscillators or creepers of the fractional type. In addition, the obtained rheological complex models of materials also open possibilities to create numerous new materials whose performance characteristics are primarily based on combinations of their elastic, viscous, viscoelastic, elastoviscous, fractional-type, or even piezoelectric properties.

The theoretical research and scientific results on a new class of rheological complex models of fractional-type materials with piezoelectric properties, which the author presents in this paper, represent, the author emphasizes, the basis and inspiration for applications in real-world technologies, such as materials science, engineering, or biomedical applications. Of course, these results will become the basis for experimentalists to investigate this new class of material models and compile studies of the parameters of each of the theoretical models with the aim of designing technologies for practical applications in engineering and in technologies of biomedical materials with piezoelectric properties.

2. The Purpose of the Work

The purpose of the work is to make a theoretical contribution by introducing, designing, and presenting a new class of rheological materials with piezoelectric properties and corresponding differential constitutive relations.

These theoretical results can be the basis for further scientific and applied research and help provide new contributions to science and applications in various fields of technical and natural sciences, as well as in medicine. It is especially important to point out the possibility that these models containing Faraday's elastic and piezoelectric element, through their polarization and the effect of mechanical loading and deformation, are able to collect electrical energy that can be used for various purposes, for example, for lighting bridges, for spraying fluids in conjunction with ultrasonic sprayers to refresh lawns in parks, or for covering disco club spaces and the like.

The dynamics of the newly introduced class of rheological complex models of fractional-type materials and piezoelectric properties, in this work, is theoretically studied in isothermal conditions, at constant temperature and with fractional-type properties of mechanical energy dissipation.

3. Methodology

In this manuscript, we have outlined the basics of the methodology used to carry out our set of research tasks and to describe and compile differential constitutive relations of the fractional order. Firstly, it is necessary to explain how these differential constitutive equations of the fractional order compiled when the basic elements of the structure of basic and complex rheological models of materials are connected in parallel or in series. Then, by decomposing the complex structure of the model to enable parallel connection of rheological elements, we assumed that the resulting normal stress could be obtained as the sum of the component normal stresses in the rheological elements connected in parallel. From there, we determined the differential constitutive relation of the fractional order with piezoelectric properties.

We also show, by introducing the decomposition of the velocities of axial dilatations of the fractional type, that the resulting axial velocity of the fractional-type dilatations is obtained as the sum of the component axial velocities of the fractional-type axial dilatations of the rheological elements connected in a regular manner in a complex material model. From there, the differential constitutive relation of the fractional order is obtained for the regular rheological models. We see that two approaches and two methods for describing the dynamics of the rheological complex material model and compiling the differential equations of the constitutive relations of the fractional order are used. These two methods are used to analyze the physical properties of rheological complex materials of the fractional type with piezoelectric properties. For the next phase of studying this new rheological complex model's materials, a mathematical description was formulated consisting of one or more differential equations that need to be solved. To solve these differential relations, we used the methods of Laplace transform and inverse Laplace transform. To obtain approximate analytical expressions for the solution of the constitutive relations, we used the expansion in power series of the parameters of the Laplace transforms. We also used the expression for the inverse Laplace transform of the power.

Next, we will provide some basic information about differentiation of the fractional order, as it will be one of the most frequently used terms in this manuscript.

Differentiation of the fractional order, although it first appeared in the scientific communications of Leibniz and the Marquis L'Hospital, has only recently gained wider application in various fields of science and technology, as in References [3,4,28,29]. A brief story about the operators of generalized fractional calculus is presented in [30], while [31] decribe an application of Fractional calculus as an introduction for physicists. Generalized Fractional calculus and applications are in [32]. The analysis of fractional differential equations and fractional equations and models are presented in [33,34]. Numerical methods for Fractional calculus are described in [35,36].

Today, there are different definitions of differentiating a fractional order. For basic knowledge about differentiating a fractional order, it is very useful to read the following articled [37–40], which present the mathematical foundations and some of the applications in continuum mechanics. Publication [41,42] present generalized Mittag-Leffler functions and their properties, which are often used in some transformations of fractional order derivative expressions. For approximate calculations of some expressions with fractional order differentials, it is necessary to use numerical methods, see scientific publications [43–46], which contain some of the new numerical methods. Reference [47] contains results on Summation identities for the Kummer confluent hypergeometric function, which are useful in the application of numerical methods.

Publications [48,49] present the coupled tensors of the piezoelectric material mechanical states and electrical voltage, and their applications in ultrasonic transducers with applications in sprayers and other devices.

For background information on Michael Faraday, see References [50,51].

Articles [16] presents a classification of classical rheological models of materials in civil engineering with corresponding definitions, while

References [17,52,53] present the properties of complex structures, various classical rheological models of their creep, and their applications to civil engineering materials.

It should be noted that rheological models can also be used in the textile industry to describe yarn dynamics. The results of the application of classical linear rheological models to the study of yarn dynamics in the textile industry are given in References [54,55], for example, under the title: "Rheological modeling of yarn elongation" or "Dynamic behavior of the mechanism–Working object system of the weaving process".

In Reference [56], the application of new rheological models of materials to biomaterials is presented, under the title "New rheological problems involving general fractional derivatives with nonsingular power-law kernels".

In this paper, we use Caputo's definition of the derivative of the fractional order over the differential operator of the fractional order, which we denote by $D_t^\alpha[\bullet]$, in the following form:

$$\mathrm{D}_t^\alpha[x(t)] = \frac{d^\alpha x(t)}{dt^\alpha} = x^{(\alpha)}(t) = \frac{1}{\Gamma(1-\alpha)}\frac{d}{dt}\int\limits_0^t \frac{x(\tau)}{(t-\tau)^\alpha}d\tau,\ for\ 0<\alpha\le 1 \tag{1}$$

For example, $\sigma_{z,\alpha} = \mathbf{E}_\alpha \mathrm{D}_t^\alpha[\varepsilon_z]$, in which α is determined as an exponent, in interval $0<\alpha<1$. If in the previous Equation (1), the exponent $\alpha = 1$, then the application of the differential operator $D_t^\alpha[\bullet]$ of the fractional order gives the first-time derivative $\dot{\varepsilon}_z(t)$ of the time function to which it is applied. In terms of the differential operator $D_t^\alpha[\bullet]$ of the fractional order, when its exponent α of the fractional order is formed of rational numbers and is in the interval $0<\alpha\le 1$, including its limit values, it can be useful as a mathematical description in various applications. In the previous definition of the differential operator $D_t^\alpha[\bullet]$ of the fractional order, the special function $\Gamma(1-\alpha)$ represents a special Gamma function, which is defined in the form of an integral (see Reference [57]):

$$\Gamma(1-\alpha) = \int\limits_0^{+\infty} e^{-t}t^{-\alpha}dt,\ 1-\alpha>0 \tag{2}$$

which is a function of the exponent α of the differential operator $D_t^\alpha[\bullet]$ of the fractional order, or in the general case, is a function of the variable x, in the following form:

$$\Gamma(x) = \int\limits_0^{+\infty} e^{-t}t^{x-1}dt,\ x>0\quad \Gamma(x+1) = x\Gamma(x),\ x>0 \tag{3}$$

Let us also mention the important references in which numerical methods for calculating derivatives of the fractional order are shown and explained, such as the following References [58–62].

In this work, we used analytical methods and analytical approaches, but researchers have access to new numerical methods and commercial software that can be used to study the dynamics of rheological complex model materials.

4. New Newton Element and Faraday Element with Polarization Properties

In this part of the paper, we introduce and use two new elementary rheological elements, one of which is the fractional type and the other ideal elastic with piezoelectric properties. These two new elementary rheological elements are the rheological basic Newton element of an ideal fluid, which is fractional type, and the basic Faraday element of an ideal elastic material with coupled mechanical and electrical fields, exhibiting polarization under mechanical loading and piezoelectric properties.

By introducing these newly introduced rheological elements into classical complex rheological models, a new class of complex rheological models of the fractional type with piezoelectric properties was obtained.

In this paper, also, we introduce the following new class of complex rheological fractional-type models with piezoelectric properties: 1*—a complex basic rheological Kelvin–Voigt–Faraday fractional-type model of elastoviscous solid material with piezoelectric properties; 2*—a complex basic rheological Maxwell–Faraday fractional-type model of viscoelastic fluid with piezoelectric properties; 3*—a complex rheological Lethersich–Faraday fractional-type model of viscoelastic fluid with piezoelectric properties; 4*—a complex rheological Jeffrey–Faraday fractional-type model of viscoelastic fluid with piezoelectric properties; 5*—a rheological complex Jeffrey–Faraday-F fractional-type model of an elastoviscous solid body with piezoelectric properties; 6*—a rheological complex Burgers–Faraday fractional-type model of viscoelastic fluid with piezoelectric properties; and 7*—a rheological complex Burgers–Faraday-F fractional-type model of an elastoviscous solid body with piezoelectric properties.

This new element of a Newtonian ideal viscous fluid is of a fractional type. The axial flow of the fractional-type fluid, which is stressed axially, has normal stress σ_z at the points of transverse transitions of the fluid flow and the fractional-type axial dilatation velocity $D_t^{\alpha}[\varepsilon_z]$ of line elements of the fluid is in the axial direction. The constitutive relation is $\sigma_z = \mathbf{E}_{\alpha} D_t^{\alpha}[\varepsilon_z]$ and is in differential-fractional-order form. This differential-fractional-order constitutive relation shows the connection between the normal stress σ_z in the axial flow of the fluid in the cross-section of the fluid flow and the velocity of the fractional-type axial dilatation $D_t^{\alpha}[\varepsilon_z]$ of the linear elements of the fluid in the axial direction of the linear element flow of the fluid. The material constant $\boldsymbol{E}_{\alpha}$ is the viscosity coefficient of the fractional-type fluid and is determined experimentally for each fluid.

The basic dimensions of the measurements are as follows: for normal stress, σ_z, at the cross-sections, fractional-type fluid flow is measured in forces per unit area; for the fractional-type axial velocity $D_t^{\alpha}[\varepsilon_z]$ of dilatation of the line elements in the axial direction of the fractional-type fluid flow, the length increment is given by the total length, and the unit of time depends on the exponent of the order of fractional differentiation, or can be a dimensionless quantity; and for the viscosity coefficient $\boldsymbol{E}_{\alpha}$, it can be given in forces per square of length or surface area, and the unit of time, to a degree, corresponds to the order of fractional differentiation (see Figure 1c).

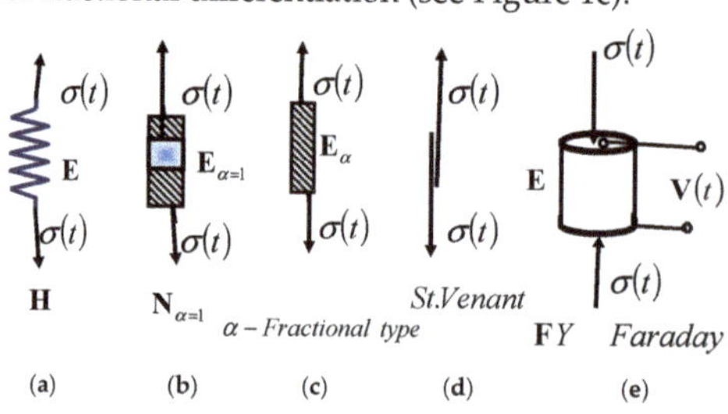

Figure 1. Basic rheological elementary elements: (**a**) Hooke's ideal elastic solid body, (**b**) Newton's element of an ideal linear viscous fluid, and (**d**) Saint Venant's ideal plastic material, as well as (**c**) the new rheological basic Newtonian model of a fractional-type ideal viscous fluid and (**e**) the basic Faraday element with coupled mechanical and electrical fields of an ideal elastic solid material and with piezoelectric properties.

Let us denote by **F***Y* the rheological Faraday element with coupled mechanical and electrical fields of an ideal elastic solid body with polarization under mechanical loading and deformation and exhibiting piezoelectric properties. When a test tube made of this piezoelectric material is subjected to axial normal stress, due to ideal elasticity, axial dilatation occurs, as well as deformation of the crystal lattice of the material, and due to ideal piezoelectricity, axial polarization of the transverse contour surfaces occurs, and electric voltage and dielectric displacement occur.

The normal stress at the points of the cross-sections can be denoted by $\sigma_z(t)$, the axial dilatation of the axial line elements by $\varepsilon_z(t)$, the electric polarization voltage by $\mathbf{V}(t)$, and the dielectric displacements by D. As such, the constitutive relations of the rheological Faraday ideal elastic and ideal piezoelectric elements can be expressed as follows: the relation between the electric polarization voltage and mechanical normal stress is $\mathbf{V}_z(t) = -g\sigma_z(t)$, while the relation between the axial dilatation and the electric polarization voltage is $\varepsilon_z(t) = b\mathbf{V}_z(t)$.

These constitutive relations are linear and provide a connection between the mechanic state of normal stress $\sigma_z(t)$ and axial dilatation $\varepsilon_z(t)$ and the electrical state of electric voltage $\mathbf{V}(t)$ of the electric field of the piezoelectric material. The symbols g, e, and b are the constants of the piezoelectric material, mechanical and electrical, and are determined experimentally. The units $\mathbf{V}[V/m]$, $g[Vm/N]$, and $b[m/V]$ are the units of the ideal elastic and ideal piezoelectric material constants.

In this paper, as we indicated in the Introduction, we will use the derivatives of the fractional-order functions and the fractional-order differential operator in order to describe the constitutive relation of the newly introduced viscous element of the fractional type, which we called the rheological Newton viscous element of the fractional type, with the constitutive relation of the normal stress $\sigma_z(t)$ connection and axial dilatation $\varepsilon_z(t)$, i.e., the rate of axial dilatation of the fractional type in the form $\mathrm{D}_t^{\alpha}[\varepsilon_z]$, where the differential operator of the fractional order is $D_t^{\alpha}[\bullet]$, and the fractional-order differentiation exponent α has values greater than zero and less than or equal to one ($0 < \alpha \leq 1$), in accordance with Equation (1).

New complex rheological models of ideal materials with piezoelectric properties are obtained through parallel or serial linking of new, more complex models of the fractional type with the basic Faraday model with ideal piezoelectric properties.

5. New Class of Complex Rheological Models

We will form two basic complex rheological models of the fractional type with piezoelectric properties by connecting two basic complex rheological models, the Kelvin–Voight or Maxwell model (both fractional type), in parallel, respectively, with Faraday's ideal elastic and piezoelectric material model—or another simple element with piezoelectric properties. The structures of these basic complex models with piezoelectric properties are shown in Figures 2 and 3.

Here, we will study the properties of two new fractional-type complex rheological models with piezoelectric properties: a basic fractional-type complex rheological Kelvin–Voigt–Faraday solid model, an ideal piezoelectric model material, and a basic fractional-type complex rheological Maxwell–Faraday model of a viscoelastic fluid, which is also an ideal piezoelectric model material.

The first model has the parallel connection structure of the basic fractional-type complex rheological Kelvin–Voight solid model in parallel connection with Faraday's ideal piezoelectric model material, as shown in Figures 2a and 3a.

The second one has the series connection structure of the basic complex rheological Maxwell model of a fractional-type viscoelastic fluid material in series connection with Faraday's ideal elastic and piezoelectric material element, as shown in Figures 2b and 3b.

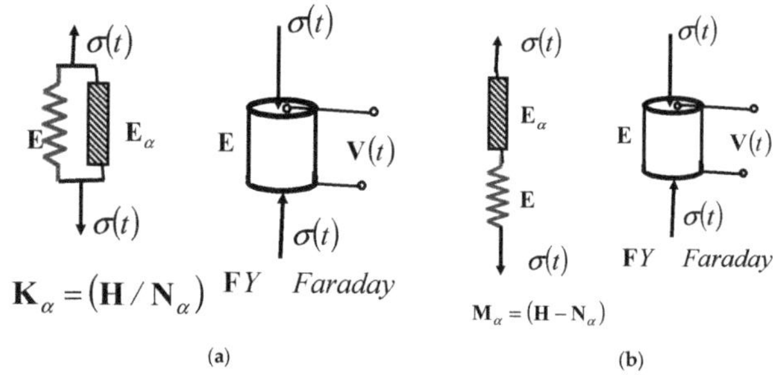

Figure 2. Structure of two basic complex fractional-type rheological models with piezoelectric properties: (**a**) basic complex Kelvin–Voigt model of a solid material with the Faraday element and (**b**) basic complex Maxwell model of a viscoelastic fluid with the Faraday element; these can be connected in parallel or series with Faraday's ideal piezoelectric material element to obtain new rheological complex models.

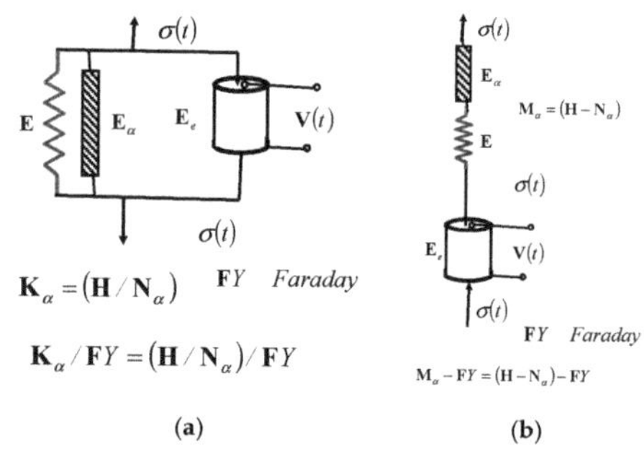

Figure 3. Two new complex fractional-type rheological models with piezo-electric properties: (**a**) parallel connection structure of basic complex Kelvin–Voigt solid material model, in parallel connection with Faraday's element, forming the new complex Kelvin–Voigt–Faraday model of a solid material; (**b**) series connection structure of the basic complex Maxwell model of viscoelastic fluid material, in series connection with Faraday's element, forming the new complex Maxwell–Faraday model of a viscoelastic fluid material.

The constitutive relations of the normal stress σ_z and axial dilatation ε_z, i.e., the velocity of axial dilatation $\mathrm{D}_t^{\alpha}[\varepsilon_z]$ of the fractional type, are given in the following form (see Figure 2 for more details on the model compositions):

$$\sigma_{z,1} = \mathbf{E}\varepsilon_z \ \sigma_{z,\alpha.2} = \mathbf{E}_\alpha \mathrm{D}_t^{\alpha}[\varepsilon_z] \ \ \sigma_{z,12} = \mathbf{E}_e\varepsilon_z \tag{4}$$

$$\mathbf{V}_z(t) = -g\sigma_z(t) \ \ D_z(t) = b\sigma_z(t) \text{ и } D_z(t) = e\varepsilon_z(t) \tag{5}$$

where $D_t^{\alpha}[\bullet]$ is the differential operator of the fractional-order exponent α, determined by Equation (1), where the fractional-order differentiation exponent α has values greater than zero and less than or equal to one ($0 < \alpha \leq 1$).

5.1. New Basic Complex Rheological Kelvin–Voigt–Faraday Model of the Fractional Type with Piezoelectric Properties

The structural formula of the rheological complex Kelvin–Voigt–Faraday fractional-type model with piezoelectric propertied is $\boldsymbol{K}_\alpha/\boldsymbol{FY} = (\boldsymbol{H}/\boldsymbol{N}_\alpha)/\boldsymbol{FY}$.

The resulting normal stress at the ends of the basic rheological complex Kelvin–Voigt–Faraday model, consisting of the basic rheological complex Kelvin–Voigt fractional-type model in parallel with the Faraday ideal elastic and piezoelectric material element, is equal to the sum of the normal stresses of the elements connected in parallel (see Figures 2a, 3a, and 4a,b).

$$\sigma_z = \sigma_{z,} + \sigma_{z.\alpha,2} + \sigma_{z,12} = \mathbf{E}\varepsilon_z + \mathbf{E}_\alpha \mathrm{D}_t^\alpha[\varepsilon_z] + \mathbf{E}_e\varepsilon_z \tag{6}$$

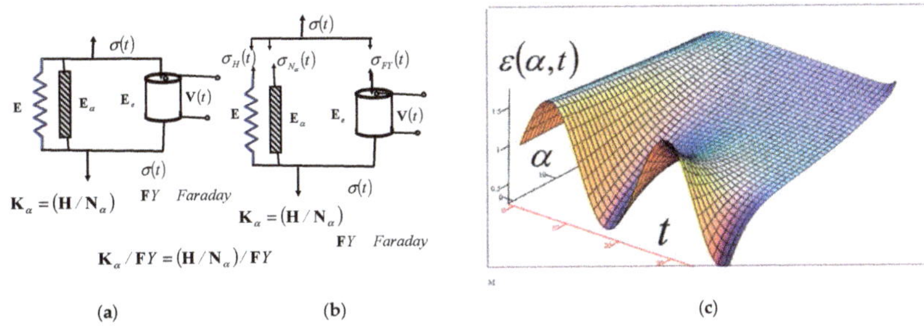

Figure 4. Rheological basic complex Kelvin–Voigt–Faraday fractional-type model with piezoelectric properties: (**a**) structure of the model; (**b**) decomposition of the model; (**c**) subsequent elasticity of the material's surface.

In addition, the electric polarization voltage in Faraday's ideal piezoelectric material element is equal to

$$V_z(t) = -g\sigma_z(t) \tag{7}$$

Equation (6) is a differential constitutive relation of the fractional order and gives the relationship between the normal stress $\sigma_z(t)$ of the fractional-type rheological basic complex Kelvin–Voight–Faraday model with piezoelectric properties and the axial dilatation $\varepsilon_z(t)$, or the axial dilatation rate of the fractional-type material, $\mathrm{D}_t^\alpha[\varepsilon_z]$. It is a constitutive relation of the fractional order, as follows:

$$\varepsilon_z + \frac{\mathbf{E}_\alpha}{\mathbf{E} + \mathbf{E}_e} D_t^\alpha[\varepsilon_z] = \frac{\sigma_z(t)}{\mathbf{E} + \mathbf{E}_e},\ 0 < \alpha \leq 1 \tag{8}$$

The fractional-order differential constitutive relation given in Equation (8) for the rheological basic complex Kelvin–Voigt–Faraday model, a complex rheological material, is in the general form. By applying the Laplace transform $\mathrm{L}\{\cdot\}$ to the previous differential constitutive relation given in Equation (8), we obtain the Laplace transform $\mathrm{L}\{\varepsilon_z(t)\}$ of the axial dilatation of that model as a differential function of the Laplace transform $\mathrm{L}\{\sigma_z(t)\}$ of the normal stress, in the following form:

$$\mathrm{L}\{\varepsilon_z\} = \frac{\mathrm{L}\{\sigma_z(t)\}}{(\mathbf{E} + \mathbf{E}_e)} \cdot \frac{1}{1 + \frac{\mathbf{E}_\alpha}{\mathbf{E} + \mathbf{E}_e} p^\varepsilon} \tag{9}$$

where $\mathrm{L}\{\cdot\}$ is the Laplace operator in the following form:

$$\mathrm{L}\{f(t)\} = \int_0^\infty e^{-pt} f(t)dt \tag{10}$$

This Laplace operator $\mathrm{L}\{\cdot\}$ can be applied to the following expression:

$$\mathrm{L}\{t^n\} = \frac{n!}{p^{n+1}} \tag{11}$$

Equation (9) is the product of two Laplace transforms: one Laplace transform, $L\{\sigma_z(t)\}$, is of the normal stress $\sigma_z(t)$, and the other, $L\{f(t)\} = \frac{1}{1+\frac{\mathbf{E}_\alpha}{\mathbf{E}+\mathbf{E}_e}p^\varepsilon}$, which concluded that these two functions $\sigma_z(t)$ and $f(t)$ are also in convolution with the axial dilatation function $\varepsilon_z(t)$. As such, the following equation can be derived:

$$L\{\varepsilon_z(t)\} = \frac{L\{\sigma_z(t)\}}{(\mathbf{E}+\mathbf{E}_e)} \cdot \frac{1}{1+\frac{\mathbf{E}_\alpha}{\mathbf{E}+\mathbf{E}_e}p^\varepsilon} = \frac{L\{\sigma_z(t)\}}{(\mathbf{E}+\mathbf{E}_e)} \cdot L\{f(t)\} \tag{12}$$

The expression $\frac{\mathbf{E}_\alpha}{\mathbf{E}+\mathbf{E}_e}p^\varepsilon$ is much smaller than one; that is, $\frac{\mathbf{E}_\alpha}{\mathbf{E}+\mathbf{E}_e}p^\varepsilon << 1$. Therefore, we can expand the expression $\frac{1}{1+\frac{\mathbf{E}_\alpha}{\mathbf{E}+\mathbf{E}_e}p^\varepsilon}$ to powers of the order and write it in the following form (see Reference [27]):

$$\frac{1}{1+\dfrac{\mathbf{E}_\alpha}{\mathbf{E}+\mathbf{E}_e}p^\varepsilon} \approx \left\langle 1+1\sum_{k=1}^{\propto}(-1)^k\left(\frac{\mathbf{E}_\alpha}{(\mathbf{E}+\mathbf{E}_e)}\right)^k p^{k\alpha}\right\rangle \tag{13}$$

Next, the inverse Laplace transform of the previous Equation (13) can be obtained in the following form:

$$L^{-1}\left\{\frac{1}{1+\dfrac{\mathbf{E}_\alpha}{\mathbf{E}+\mathbf{E}_e}p^\varepsilon}\right\} \approx L^{-1}\left\{1+\sum_{k=1}^{\propto}(-1)^k\left(\frac{\mathbf{E}_\alpha}{(\mathbf{E}+\mathbf{E}_e)}\right)^k p^{k\alpha}\right\} = \sum_{k=0}^{\propto}(-1)^k\left(\frac{\mathbf{E}_\alpha}{\mathbf{E}+\mathbf{E}_e}\right)^k \frac{t^{(2-\alpha)k}}{\Gamma(2k+1-\alpha k)} \tag{14}$$

Based on the property of the three functions, which are in convolution and for which it is true that

$$\varepsilon_z(t) \approx \frac{\sigma_z(t)}{(\mathbf{E}+\mathbf{E}_e)} * \left\langle \sum_{k=0}^{\propto}(-1)^k\left(\frac{\mathbf{E}_\alpha}{\mathbf{E}+\mathbf{E}_e}\right)^k \frac{t^{(2-\alpha)k}}{\Gamma(2k+1-\alpha k)}\right\rangle, \tag{15}$$

we can write the convolution integral in the following form:

$$\varepsilon_z(t) \approx \frac{1}{(\mathbf{E}+\mathbf{E}_e)}\int_0^t \sigma_z(t-\tau)\left\langle \sum_{k=0}^{\propto}(-1)^k\left(\frac{\mathbf{E}_\alpha}{\mathbf{E}+\mathbf{E}_e}\right)^k \frac{\tau^{(2-\alpha)k}}{\Gamma(2k+1-\alpha k)}\right\rangle d\tau \tag{16}$$

Both Equations (15) and (16), i.e., the convolution integrals, are integral constitutive equations relating the axial dilatation $\varepsilon_z(t)$ and normal stress $\sigma_z(t)$ of the rheological basic complex fractional-type Kelvin–Voigt–Faraday model with piezoelectric polarization properties.

The Faraday element in the complex Kelvin–Voigt–Faraday model of the fractional type, due to deformation, axial dilatation $\varepsilon_z(t)$, and normal stress $\sigma_z(t)$, enters a state of polarization, with its axial dilatation $\varepsilon_z(t)$ calculated using Equation (17), and the electric voltage stored in that element is expressed in the following form:

$$V_z(t) = -g\sigma_z(t) \approx -\frac{g}{(\mathbf{E}+\mathbf{E}_e)}\int_0^t \sigma_z(t-\tau)\left\langle \sum_{k=0}^{\propto}(-1)^k\left(\frac{\mathbf{E}_\alpha}{\mathbf{E}+\mathbf{E}_e}\right)^k \frac{\tau^{(2-\alpha)k}}{\Gamma(2k+1-\alpha k)}\right\rangle d\tau \tag{17}$$

In the resting case of a rheological basic complex Kelvin–Voigt–Faraday fractional-type model in parallel with Faraday's ideal elastic and piezoelectric model of the material at a very slow load change, when we can assume that the fractional-type axial dilatation rate is small and tends to zero ($D_t^\alpha[\varepsilon_z] \to 0$), the material behaves as a basic ideal elastic material, and the normal stress of the material $\sigma_{z\backslash} \to \mathbf{E}\varepsilon_z + \mathbf{E}_e\varepsilon_z$ is almost proportional to the dilatation $\varepsilon_z(t)$:

$$\sigma_z = \sigma_{z,} + \sigma_{z.\alpha,2} + \sigma_{z,12} = \mathbf{E}\varepsilon_z + \mathbf{E}_\alpha D_t^\alpha[\varepsilon_z] + \mathbf{E}_e\varepsilon_z \tag{18}$$

$$D_t^\alpha[\varepsilon_z] \to 0 \;\Rightarrow\; \sigma_{z\backslash} \to \mathbf{E}\varepsilon_z + \mathbf{E}_e\varepsilon_z \tag{19}$$

If the normal stress σ_z at the ends of a rheological basic complex Kelvin–Voigt–Faraday model, in the case where it is in parallel with the Faraday ideal piezoelectric material element, suddenly rises from zero to some finite value, $\sigma_z = \sigma_{z,0} = const$, which remains constant in the following time interval, then we are interested in the behavior of this basic model of the complex material.

If we assume that the normal stress rises suddenly to some value and remains constant $\sigma_{z,0} = const$, then the following can be determined:

$$\mathbf{E}\varepsilon_z + \mathbf{E}_e\varepsilon_z + \mathbf{E}_\alpha D_t^\alpha[\varepsilon_z] = \sigma_{z,0} = const \tag{20}$$

In order to find the time dependence of the axial dilatation $\varepsilon_z(t)$ of the rheological basic complex Kelvin–Voigt–Faraday fractional-type model, in parallel with Faraday's ideal piezoelectric material element, we first apply the Laplace transform to the previous differential fractional-order constitutive equation and obtain the Laplace transform of axial dilatation $\varepsilon_z(t)$ in the following form:

$$\mathrm{L}\{\varepsilon_z\} = \frac{\sigma_{z,0}}{(\mathbf{E}+\mathbf{E}_e)} \cdot \frac{1}{p} \cdot \frac{1}{\left\langle 1 + \frac{\mathbf{E}_\alpha}{(\mathbf{E}+\mathbf{E}_e)} p^\alpha \right\rangle} \tag{21}$$

The solution for the axial dilatation $\varepsilon_z(t)$ as a function of time for the basic complex Kelvin–Voigt–Faraday model, in parallel with Faraday's element, when suddenly subjected to a constant normal stress and held at a constant normal stress $\sigma_z = \sigma_{z,0} = const$, is the inverse Laplace transform $\varepsilon_z(t) = \mathrm{L}^{-1}\mathrm{L}\{\varepsilon_z\}\backslash$ of Equation (21):

$$\varepsilon_z(t) = \mathrm{L}^{-1}\mathrm{L}\{\varepsilon_z\} = \mathrm{L}^{-1}\left\{ \frac{\sigma_{z,0}}{(\mathbf{E}+\mathbf{E}_e)} \cdot \frac{1}{p} \cdot \frac{1}{\left\langle 1 + \frac{\mathbf{E}_\alpha}{(\mathbf{E}+\mathbf{E}_e)} p^\alpha \right\rangle} \right\} \tag{22}$$

Next, it is necessary to determine the approximate analytical expression for the time function $\varepsilon_z(t) = \mathrm{L}^{-1}\mathrm{L}\{\varepsilon_z\}\backslash$ as the inverse Laplace transform of the previous expression and transfer it into the time domain.

As such, it is necessary to develop the expression $\frac{\sigma_{z,0}}{(\mathbf{E}+\mathbf{E}_e)} \cdot \frac{1}{p} \cdot \frac{1}{\left\langle 1 + \frac{\mathbf{E}_\alpha}{(\mathbf{E}+\mathbf{E}_e)} p^\alpha \right\rangle}$ in order by powers of p, which is a complex number, using the formula $\frac{1}{1\pm x} = 1 \mp x + x^2 \mp x^3 + x^4 \mp x^5 + \ldots\ldots\ldots\ldots$ (see References [4,5,57,63]). As such,

$$\frac{\sigma_{z,0}}{(\mathbf{E}+\mathbf{E}_e)} \cdot \frac{1}{p} \cdot \frac{1}{\left\langle 1 + \frac{\mathbf{E}_\alpha}{(\mathbf{E}+\mathbf{E}_e)} p^\alpha \right\rangle} = \frac{\sigma_{z,0}}{(\mathbf{E}+\mathbf{E}_e)} \cdot \frac{1}{p} \cdot \left\langle 1 + \sum_{k=1}^{\infty} (-1)^k \left(\frac{\mathbf{E}_\alpha}{(\mathbf{E}+\mathbf{E}_e)} \right)^k p^{k\alpha-1} \right\rangle$$

The inverse Laplace transform now gives an analytically approximate expression for the time-domain axial dilatation $\varepsilon_z(t)$ for the basic complex rheological Kelvin–Voigt–Faraday fractional-type model with piezoelectric properties, when suddenly subjected to a constant normal stress $\sigma_z = \sigma_{z,0} = const$ and kept under constant normal stress in the following form:

$$\varepsilon_z(t) = \mathrm{L}^{-1}\mathrm{L}\{\varepsilon_z\} = \frac{\sigma_{z,0}}{(\mathbf{E}+\mathbf{E}_e)} \cdot \left\langle 1 + \sum_{k=1}^{\infty} (-1)^k \left(\frac{\mathbf{E}_\alpha}{(\mathbf{E}+\mathbf{E}_e)} \right)^k \frac{t^{(2-\alpha)k+1}}{\Gamma(2k+2-\alpha k)} \right\rangle \tag{23}$$

The dielectric displacement (shift) D, represented as $D_z(t) = b\sigma_z(t)$ and $D_z(t) = e\varepsilon_z(t)$ in the polarized Faraday element included in parallel in the basic complex rheological Kelvin–Voigt–Faraday fractional-type model with piezoelectric properties, can be expressed in the following form:

$$D_z(t) = e\varepsilon_z(t) = e\frac{\sigma_{z,0}}{(\mathbf{E}+\mathbf{E}_e)} \cdot \left\langle 1 + \sum_{k=1}^{\infty} (-1)^k \left(\frac{\mathbf{E}_\alpha}{(\mathbf{E}+\mathbf{E}_e)} \right)^k \frac{t^{(2-\alpha)k+1}}{\Gamma(2k+2-\alpha k)} \right\rangle \quad (24)$$

This model of a complex rheological Kelvin–Voigt–Faraday material of the fractional type with piezoelectric properties, with the parallel connection structure of the basic complex rheological Kelvin–Voight model of a solid elastoviscous fractional-type material in parallel connection with Faraday's ideal piezoelectric material model, possesses the property of post-elasticity, when axial dilatation $\varepsilon_z(t)$ lags behind normal stress $\sigma_z(t)$.

In Figure 4c, the surface of the subsequent elasticity of that basic complex rheological Kelvin–Voigt–Faraday material of the fractional type with piezoelectric properties is presented in a coordinate system with coordinate axes: the elongation of axial dilatation $\varepsilon_z(t)$, the exponent α of fractional-order differentiation, in an interval greater than zero and less than or equal to one ($0 < \alpha \leq 1$), and time.

The rheological complex Kelvin–Voigt–Faraday fractional-type model, with piezoelectric properties has no internal degree of freedom.

5.2. *New Basic Complex Rheological Maxwell–Faraday Model*

We will now further study the properties of a new basic complex rheological model, a fractional-type model with piezoelectric properties that has a series connection structure of the basic complex rheological Maxwell model of a viscoelastic fluid material, a fractional type model, in series connection with a Faraday ideal elastic and piezoelectric model material. As a result, a new rheological basic complex Maxwell–Faraday model, a fractional-type model with piezoelectric properties, is obtained. See Figures 2b and 3b.

Throughout the entire basic complex model with the Hooke ideal elastic element $\mathbf{H}$, the Newton viscous element of the fractional type $\mathbf{N}_\alpha$, and the Faraday ideal elastic and piezoelectric material element, the normal stress $\sigma_z(t)$ in all the regularly connected elements is the same, while the resulting fractional-type dilatation velocity is equal to the sum of the dilatation velocities of the elements $D_t^\alpha[\varepsilon_{z,1}]$, $D_t^\alpha[\varepsilon_{z,e}]$, and $D_t^\alpha[\varepsilon_{z,2}]$ in the order connection. Figure 5b shows the component dilatations of these regularly connected elements of the complex rheological complex basic Maxwell–Faraday model of the fractional type.

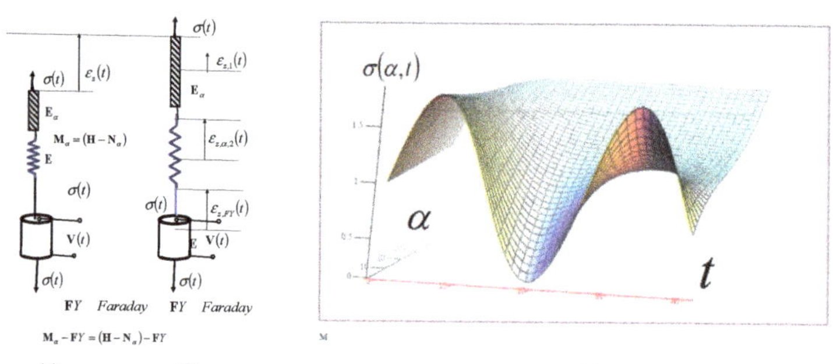

(a) (b) (c)

Figure 5. Rheological basic complex Maxwell–Faraday fractional-type model with piezoelectric properties: (**a**) structure of the model; (**b**) decomposition of the model; (**c**) normal stress relaxation of the model's surface.

Faraday's ideal elastic and piezoelectric material model was added to a rheological basic complex Maxwell's model of the fractional type, whose structural formula is $\boldsymbol{M}_{\alpha} = (\boldsymbol{H} - \boldsymbol{N}_{\alpha})$, to create a new rheological basic complex Maxwell–Faraday model.

When using Hooke's ideal elastic solid element $\boldsymbol{H}$, Newton's fractional-type viscous element $\boldsymbol{N}_{\alpha}$, and Faraday's ideal elastic and piezoelectric material element, throughout the entire basic complex model $\boldsymbol{M}_{\alpha} - \boldsymbol{FY} = (\boldsymbol{H} - \boldsymbol{N}_{\alpha}) - \boldsymbol{FY}$, the velocity of axial dilatation of the fractional type through the entire element is equal to the sum of the axial dilatation velocities of the elements, $\mathrm{D}_t^{\alpha}[\varepsilon_{z,1}]$, $\mathrm{D}_t^{\alpha}[\varepsilon_{z,e}]$, and $\mathrm{D}_t^{\alpha}[\varepsilon_{z,2}]$ in a regular series connection, so in the sum of the axial dilatation rates, we use the dilatation rates of the fractional-type equation $\mathrm{D}_t^{\alpha}[\varepsilon_{z,1}]$. See Figure 5a,b. In Figure 5b, the decomposition of the axial dilatation of the new rheological basic complex Maxwell–Faraday model is presented and component dilatations are visible.

The normal stress is the same throughout the entirety of the new rheological basic complex Maxwell–Faraday model of the fractional type with piezoelectric properties, so we can determine the differential constitutive relations of each basic rheological element in this series connection; as such, the same normal stresses are a function of the resulting dilatation of the model (see Figure 5b):

$$\sigma_{z,1} = \mathbf{E}\varepsilon_z,\ \sigma_{z,\alpha.2} = \mathbf{E}_{\alpha} D_t^{\alpha}[\varepsilon_z],\ \text{and}\ \sigma_{z,12} = \mathbf{E}_e\varepsilon_z \tag{25}$$

The differential constitutive relations between the normal stress σ_z and velocity axial dilatation $\mathrm{D}_t^{\alpha}[\varepsilon_z]$ of the fractional type (see Figure 5b for an illustration of the idea of decomposition by dilatations) of each of the regularly connected elements of the complex structure of the Maxwell–Faraday model are determined by Equation (26), as shown previously.

For Hooke's ideal elastic element, the normal stress is $\sigma_{z,1} = \mathbf{E}\varepsilon_z$ and is linearly related to the dilatation, and the velocity of fractional-type dilatation is a function of the normal stress of the fractional-type equation $\mathrm{D}_t^{\alpha}[\varepsilon_{z.1}] = \frac{1}{\mathbf{E}}\mathrm{D}_t^{\alpha}[\sigma_z]$. For the new ideal viscous Newtonian element of the fractional-type fluid, the normal stress is differentially related by fractional order to the velocity of fractional-order axial dilatation $\sigma_{z,\alpha.2} = \mathbf{E}_{\alpha}\mathrm{D}_t^{\alpha}[\varepsilon_z]$. The velocity of fractional-type axial dilatation is expressed in terms of the normal stress $\mathrm{D}_t^{\alpha}[\varepsilon_{z.2}] = \frac{\sigma_z}{\mathbf{E}_{\alpha}}$. For the ideal elastic Faraday element with piezoelectric properties, the mechanical normal stress is linearly related to the axial dilatation $\sigma_{z,12} = \mathbf{E}_e\varepsilon_z$ and the electrical voltage $\boldsymbol{V}_z(t) = -g\sigma_z(t)$ due to the polarization of the Faraday element by mechanical strain, and also the dielectric displacements $D_z(t) = b\sigma_z(t)$ and $D_z(t) = e\varepsilon_z(t)$ are linearly related to the mechanical normal stress or dilatation. For this Faraday element, the velocity of fractional-type axial dilatation is a function of the velocity of fractional-type normal stress in the form $\mathrm{D}_t^{\alpha}[\varepsilon_{z.e}] = \frac{1}{\mathbf{E}_e}\mathrm{D}_t^{\alpha}[\sigma_z]$.

The electric voltage can be expressed as $\boldsymbol{V}_z(t) = -g\sigma_z(t)$ and the dielectric displacement (shift) as D, $D_z(t) = b\sigma_z(t)$, and $D_z(t) = e\varepsilon_z(t)$ in the polarized Faraday's element included in serial in the basic complex model.

Figure 5a presents the basic complex Maxwell–Faraday model and Figure 5b presents the decomposition into component axial dilatations of rheological elements of the basic complex Maxwell–Faraday model of the fractional type with piezoelectric properties. This figure shows and explains how the differential constitutive relations of the fractional order are constructed.

The resulting velocity of axial dilatation $\mathrm{D}_t^{\alpha}[\varepsilon_z]$ of the basic complex Maxwell–Faraday model of the serial structure is equal to the sum of the component fractional-type axial dilatation velocities of Newton's fractional-type viscous element $\mathrm{D}_t^{\alpha}[\varepsilon_{z,1}]$, of Hooke's ideal elastic element $\mathrm{D}_t^{\alpha}[\varepsilon_{z,2}]$, and of Faraday's ideal elastic element with the property of piezoelectricity, and can be expressed in the following form:

$$\mathrm{D}_t^{\alpha}[\varepsilon_z] = \mathrm{D}_t^{\alpha}[\varepsilon_{z,1}] + \mathrm{D}_t^{\alpha}[\varepsilon_{z,2}] + \mathrm{D}_t^{\alpha}[\varepsilon_{z,e}] \tag{26}$$

As such, $\varepsilon_{z,1} = \frac{\sigma_z}{\mathbf{E}}$ and therefore $D_t^\alpha[\varepsilon_{z.1}] = \frac{1}{\mathbf{E}} D_t^\alpha[\sigma_z]$, $D_t^\alpha[\varepsilon_{z.2}] = \frac{\sigma_z}{\mathbf{E}_\alpha}$, and $\varepsilon_{z,e} = \frac{\sigma_z}{\mathbf{E}_e}$, resulting in $D_t^\alpha[\varepsilon_{z.e}] = \frac{1}{\mathbf{E}_e} D_t^\alpha[\sigma_z]$. Therefore, the sum can be expressed as follows (see Figure 5b):

$$D_t^\alpha[\varepsilon_z] = \frac{1}{\mathbf{E}} D_t^\alpha[\sigma_z] + \frac{\sigma_z}{\mathbf{E}_\alpha} + \frac{1}{\mathbf{E}_e} D_t^\alpha[\sigma_z] \tag{27}$$

Next, based on the previous analysis, it follows that this sum of fractional-type axial dilatations in the rheological basic complex Maxwell–Faraday model is of the following form (see Figure 5b):

$$\left(\frac{1}{\mathbf{E}} + \frac{1}{\mathbf{E}_e}\right) D_t^\alpha[\sigma_z(t)] + \frac{\sigma_z(t)}{\mathbf{E}_\alpha} = \{D_t^\alpha[\varepsilon_z(t)]\} \neq const,\ 0 < \alpha \leq 1 \tag{28}$$

The last inhomogeneous ordinary differential Equation (29) of the fractional order is a differential constitutive relation of the fractional-order exponent α, highlighting the axial dilatation ε_z and normal stress $\sigma_z(t)$ relationship of the rheological basic complex Maxwell–Faraday model of the fractional type with piezoelectric properties.

The last inhomogeneous differential constitutive equation, Equation (29), of fractional-order exponent α can be solved by applying the Laplace transform $L\{\cdot\}$, which gives the following:

$$L\{\sigma_z(t)\} = \mathbf{E}_\alpha L\{\varepsilon_z(t)\} \frac{p^\alpha \backslash p}{\left\langle 1 + \left(\frac{\mathbf{E}_\alpha}{\mathbf{E}_e} + \frac{\mathbf{E}_\alpha}{\mathbf{E}}\right) p^\alpha \right\rangle} \tag{29}$$

Then, expanding in order by powers of the complex parameter, we obtain the following:

$$\frac{p^\alpha}{\left\langle 1 + \left(\frac{\mathbf{E}_\alpha}{\mathbf{E}_e} + \frac{\mathbf{E}_\alpha}{\mathbf{E}}\right) p^\alpha \right\rangle} = p^\alpha \frac{1}{\left\langle 1 + \left(\frac{\mathbf{E}_\alpha}{\mathbf{E}_e} + \frac{\mathbf{E}_\alpha}{\mathbf{E}}\right) p^\alpha \right\rangle} \approx p^\alpha \cdot \left\langle 1 + \sum_{k=1}^{\infty} (-1)^k \left(\frac{\mathbf{E}_\alpha}{\mathbf{E}_e} + \frac{\mathbf{E}_\alpha}{\mathbf{E}}\right)^k p^{k\alpha} \right\rangle \tag{30}$$

Using the property of the three functions being convolved, as well as the relationship between their Laplace transforms and the convolution integral, in a similar way as in [5], we can produce the following convolution integral:

$$\sigma_z(t) = \mathbf{E}_\alpha \int_0^t \varepsilon_z(t-\tau) \left\langle L^{-1}\left\{ p^\alpha + \sum_{k=1}^{\infty} (-1)^k \left(\frac{\mathbf{E}_\alpha}{\mathbf{E}_e} + \frac{\mathbf{E}_\alpha}{\mathbf{E}}\right)^k p^{(k+1)\alpha} \right\} \right\rangle_{t=\tau} d\tau \tag{31}$$

Equation (32), which is the convolution integral, represents an approximate analytical expression of the dependence of the normal stress $\sigma_z(t)$ in the basic complex Maxwell–Faraday model, as a function of the total axial dilatation $\varepsilon_z(t)$ over time, and is also the constitutive integral equation of that model.

If the material in the basic complex Maxwell–Faraday model is suddenly loaded to a certain value of normal stress $\sigma_{z,0}$, it will respond to an elastic deformation, $\varepsilon_{z,0} = \frac{\sigma_{z,0}}{\mathbf{E}+\mathbf{E}_e}$, created instantaneously in Hooke's ideal elastic element and Faraday's piezoelectric element. This is because due to a sudden load added immediately at the beginning of the observation of the behavior of the material of the basic complex Maxwell–Faraday model, flow in the regularly connected modified Newton viscous element, in this case, in the viscous fluid, does not come to the fore. If we prevent the development of axial dilatation, assuming that the velocity of axial dilatation tends to zero, $D_t^\alpha[\varepsilon_z] \to 0$, then the normal stress is a function of time, which needs to be determined.

When the normal stress rate $D_t^\alpha[\sigma_z]$ of the fractional type of the rheological basic complex Maxwell–Faraday model tends to zero, $D_t^\alpha[\sigma_z] \to 0$, then the normal mechanical stress $\sigma_z(t)$ tends to a value proportional to the axial dilatation rate of the fractional type, $\sigma_z \to \mathbf{E}_\alpha D_t^\alpha[\varepsilon_z]$:

$$D_t^\alpha[\sigma_z] \to 0 \;\Rightarrow\; \sigma_z \to \mathbf{E}_\alpha D_t^\alpha[\varepsilon_z] \tag{32}$$

In order to find the dependence of the normal stress $\sigma_z(t)$ on time, when we keep the model of the material of the rheological basic complex Maxwell–Faraday model of the fractional type with piezoelectric properties at some constant velocity of fractional-type axial dilatation, $\left\{D_t^\alpha[\varepsilon_z]_{z,,0}\right\} = const$, the following can be determined:

$$\frac{1}{\mathbf{E}}D_t^\alpha[\sigma_z] + \frac{1}{\mathbf{E}_e}D_t^\alpha[\sigma_z] + \frac{\sigma_z}{\mathbf{E}_\alpha} = \left\{D_t^\alpha[\varepsilon_z]_{z,,0}\right\} = const \tag{33}$$

Then, we apply the Laplace transformation to that fractional-order functional dependence outlined in Equation (34), and after applying the Laplace transformation to the previous differential constitutive relation in Equation (34) for the special case of the state of the model material, we obtain the following:

$$\left(\frac{1}{\mathbf{E}} + \frac{1}{\mathbf{E}_e}\right)D_t^\alpha[\sigma_z] + \frac{\sigma_z}{\mathbf{E}_\alpha} = \left\{D_t^\alpha[\varepsilon_z]_{z,,0}\right\} = const \tag{34}$$

Then, by arranging the Laplace transform to the previous constitutive relation in Equation (35), we obtain $L\{\sigma_z(t)\}$.

$$L\{\sigma_z\} = \mathbf{E}_\alpha\left\{D_t^\alpha[\varepsilon_z]_{z,,0}\right\}\frac{1}{p}\cdot\frac{1}{\left\langle 1 + \left(\frac{\mathbf{E}_\alpha}{\mathbf{E}_e} + \frac{\mathbf{E}_\alpha}{\mathbf{E}}\right)p^\alpha\right\rangle} \tag{35}$$

By solving the obtained relation using $L\{\sigma_z\}$, the Laplace transform of the normal stress as a function of time in the rheological basic complex Maxwell–Faraday model can be given in Equation (36).

Next, it is necessary to determine an approximate analytical solution for the normal stress $\sigma_z(t) = L^{-1}L\{\sigma_z\}$ as a function of time, in a rheological basic complex Maxwell–Faraday model, as the inverse Laplace transformation $\sigma_z(t) = L^{-1}L\{\sigma_z\}$ of the previous Equation (36) and move from the complex domain of the Laplace transformation to the time domain.

To this end, it is necessary to develop the expression $\mathbf{E}_\alpha\left\{D_t^\alpha[\varepsilon_z]_{z,,0}\right\}\frac{1}{p}\cdot\frac{1}{\left\langle 1+\left(\frac{\mathbf{E}_\alpha}{\mathbf{E}_e}+\frac{\mathbf{E}_\alpha}{\mathbf{E}}\right)p^\alpha\right\rangle}$ in order of powers of p, which is a complex number, using the formula $\frac{1}{1\pm x} = 1 \mp x + x^2 \mp x^3 + x^4 \mp x^5 + \ldots\ldots\ldots\ldots$ (see References [4,5,58,63]). Therefore,

$$\mathbf{E}_\alpha\left\{D_t^\alpha[\varepsilon_z]_{z,,0}\right\}\frac{1}{p}\cdot\frac{1}{\left\langle 1 + \left(\frac{\mathbf{E}_\alpha}{\mathbf{E}_e} + \frac{\mathbf{E}_\alpha}{\mathbf{E}}\right)p^\alpha\right\rangle} \approx \mathbf{E}_\alpha\left\{D_t^\alpha[\varepsilon_z]_{z,,0}\right\}\frac{1}{p}\cdot\left\langle 1 + \sum_{k=1}^{\infty}(-1)^k\left(\frac{\mathbf{E}_\alpha}{\mathbf{E}_e} + \frac{\mathbf{E}_\alpha}{\mathbf{E}}p^\alpha\right)^k\right\rangle \tag{36}$$

The inverse Laplace transform $\sigma_z(t) = L^{-1}L\{\sigma_z\}$ of the previous expression $L\{\sigma_z(t)\}$, given in Equation (36), now gives an approximate analytical solution for $\sigma_z(t)$ in the time domain, in a basic complex Maxwell–Faraday model, in the form of a power order by degrees of time, in the following form:

$$\sigma_z(t) = L^{-1}L\{\sigma_z\} \approx \mathbf{E}_\alpha\left\{D_t^\alpha[\varepsilon_z]_{z,,0}\right\}\cdot\left\{1 + \sum_{k=1}^{\infty}(-1)^k\left(\frac{\mathbf{E}_\alpha}{\mathbf{E}_e} + \frac{\mathbf{E}_\alpha}{\mathbf{E}}p\right)^k\frac{t^{(2-\alpha)k+1}}{\Gamma(2k+2-\alpha k)}\right\} \tag{37}$$

The electric voltage polarization field of the Faraday element included serially in the rheological basic complex Maxwell–Faraday model of the fractional type with piezoelectric properties can be determined as follows:

$$\mathbf{V}_z(t) = -g\sigma_z(t) \approx -g\mathbf{E}_\alpha\left\{\mathrm{D}_t^\alpha[\varepsilon_z]_{z,,0}\right\}\cdot\left\{1+\sum_{k=1}^{\infty}(-1)^k\left(\frac{\mathbf{E}_\alpha}{\mathbf{E}_e}+\frac{\mathbf{E}_\alpha}{\mathbf{E}}p\right)^k\frac{t^{(2-\alpha)k+1}}{\Gamma(2k+2-\alpha k)}\right\} \quad (38)$$

And dielectric displacement is in the following form:

$$D_z(t) = b\sigma_z(t) \approx b\mathbf{E}_\alpha\left\{\mathrm{D}_t^\alpha[\varepsilon_z]_{z,,0}\right\}\cdot\left\{1+\sum_{k=1}^{\infty}(-1)^k\left(\frac{\mathbf{E}_\alpha}{\mathbf{E}_e}+\frac{\mathbf{E}_\alpha}{\mathbf{E}}p\right)^k\frac{t^{(2-\alpha)k+1}}{\Gamma(2k+2-\alpha k)}\right\} \quad (39)$$

We can see from the previous solution (38), and from the graph of the relaxation surface of $\sigma_z(t)$, that, in that case, the normal stress $\sigma_z(t)$ will asymptotically decrease and tend to zero, as shown in Figure 5c. The occurrence of a decrease in normal stress $\sigma_z(t)$ with the passage of time at a constant velocity of axial dilatation, $\left\{\mathrm{D}_t^\alpha[\varepsilon_z]_{z,,0}\right\} = const$, is referred to as the normal stress relaxation of the material in the basic complex Maxwell–Faraday model. The studied material of the rheological basic complex fractional-type Maxwell–Faraday model with piezo-electric properties is a viscoelastic fluid of the fractional type with piezoelectric properties and can be used as a model for describing the properties of metals at very high temperatures and with piezoelectric properties.

The new rheological basic complex Maxwell–Faraday model has two internal degrees of freedom.

5.3. New Rheological Complex Lethersich–Faraday Model of a Viscoelastic Material

In this section, we study the new rheological complex Lethersich–Faraday model of an ideal material of the fractional type with piezoelectric properties in two variants: 1*—when Faraday's ideal elastic material with polarization properties is connected in parallel with the rheological Kelvin–Voigt structure, as shown in Figure 6b; and 2*—when Faraday's ideal elastic material with polarization properties is connected in parallel with the rheological Newtonian viscous fluid element, as shown in Figure 6c. In the first case, labeled 1*, the rheological complex Lethersich–Faraday model of an ideal fractional-type material with piezoelectric properties has the properties of a viscoelastic material and has the structural formula $\boldsymbol{L_\alpha/FY = H/N_\alpha/FY - N_\alpha}$. The second case, labeled 2*, is the rheological complex Lethersich–Faraday model of an ideal material, which has the properties of an elastoviscous solid material and has the structural formula $\boldsymbol{L_\alpha/FY = H/N_\alpha - N_\alpha/FY}$.

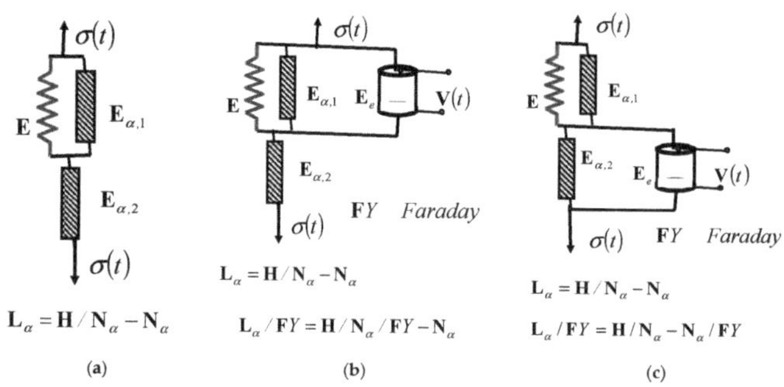

Figure 6. Three new rheological complex Lethersich–Faraday fractional-type models: (**a**) structure of the complex linear Lethersich viscoelastic fluid model; (**b**) structure of the new rheological complex Lethersich–Faraday viscoelastic fluid model; and (**c**) structure of the new rheological complex Lethersich–Faraday's elastoviscous solid model.

In Figure 6, three new rheological complex Lethersich fractional-type models, in two variants, are visible. In Figure 6a, the structure of the new Lethersich viscoelastic fluid material model is presented. Figure 6b shows the structure of the new Lethersich–Faraday model of viscoelastic fluid with polarization properties, with Faraday's element connected in parallel with the Kelvin–Voigt model. Figure 6c shows the structure of the new Lethersich–Faraday-F elastoviscous solid model with polarization properties, with Faraday's element connected in parallel with Newton's viscous fluid element.

5.3.1. The Rheological Complex Linear Lethersich–Faraday Model of an Ideal Material with Piezoelectric Properties

This model contains the following parallel-connected elements: Hooke's element of an ideal elastic material, Newton's linear element of an ideal viscous fluid, and Faraday's ideal elastic and piezoelectric element (which form, in parallel connection, the Kelvin–Voigt–Faraday linear model of an ideal material, with the quality of subsequent ecstaticity). They all form a sequential connection with the linear Newtonian element of an ideal viscous fluid. Let us now denote the specific axial deformations and axial dilatations of the Newtonian elements of an ideal viscous fluid in the rheological basic complex linear Kelvin–Voigt–Faraday model of an ideal solid elastoviscous material with piezoelectric properties by $\varepsilon_{z,N}$ and $\varepsilon_{z,K}$. To establish the total axial dilatation ε_z of this new rheological linear Lethersich–Faraday model of an ideal material with piezoelectric properties, which is serially connected in the Kelvin–Voigt–Faraday model with the Newtonian linear element of an ideal viscous fluid, we calculate the sum of these axial dilatations: $\varepsilon_z = \varepsilon_{z,N} + \varepsilon_{z,K}$.

The constitutive relation between the normal stress at the points of the cross-sections of the test tube and the axial dilatations of the linear elements for the rheological complex Lethersich–Faraday linear model of an ideal material with piezoelectric properties is obtained from the relation of the sum of the component velocities of the axial dilatations in the form $\dot{\varepsilon}_z = \dot{\varepsilon}_{z,N} + \dot{\varepsilon}_{z,K}$. For Newton's model of an ideal linear viscous fluid, the following applies:

$$\dot{\varepsilon}_{z,N} = \frac{\sigma_z}{\boldsymbol{E}_{\alpha=1}} \tag{40}$$

Alternatively, for the rheological basic complex Kelvin–Voigt–Faraday ideal model of an ideal solid body with piezoelectric properties, the sum of the dilatations can be calculated as follows:

$$\sigma_{z,K} = \boldsymbol{E}\varepsilon_{z,K} + \boldsymbol{E}_{\alpha=1}\dot{\varepsilon}_{z,K} + \boldsymbol{E}_e\varepsilon_{z,K} = (\boldsymbol{E} + \boldsymbol{E}_e)\varepsilon_e + \boldsymbol{E}_\alpha\dot{\varepsilon}_{z,K} \;\; \dot{\varepsilon}_{z,N} = \frac{\sigma_z}{\boldsymbol{E}_{\alpha=1}} \tag{41}$$

It follows that the axial dilatation as a function of time can be written in the following form:

$$\varepsilon_{z,K} = e^{-\frac{(\mathbf{E}+\mathbf{E}_e)}{\mathbf{E}_{\alpha=1}}t}\left(\varepsilon_{z,K,o} + \frac{1}{\mathbf{E}_\alpha}\int_0^t e^{\frac{(\mathbf{E}+\mathbf{E}_e)}{\mathbf{E}_\alpha = 1}t}\sigma_{z,K}(t)dt\right) \tag{42}$$

in which $\varepsilon_{z,K,o}$ is the initial axial dilatation of the rheological basic complex Kelvin–Voigt–Faraday ideal linear model of an ideal solid body with piezoelectric properties.

Then, by differentiating in time the previous expression for the axial expansion in Equation (43) of the rheological basic Kelvin–Voigt–Faraday linear model of an ideal body with piezoelectric properties and adding the axial dilatation velocity $\dot{\varepsilon}_{z,N} = \frac{\sigma_z}{\mathbf{E}_\alpha}$ of the Newtonian linear element of an ideal viscous fluid to the axial dilatation velocity $\dot{\varepsilon}_{z.L}$ of the rheological basic Lethersich–Faraday ideal linear material model, we obtain the following expression:

$$\dot{\varepsilon}_{z.L} = \left(\frac{1}{\mathbf{E}_{\alpha=1,b}} + \frac{1}{\mathbf{E}_{\alpha=1,k}}\right)\sigma_z(t) - \frac{(\mathbf{E}+\mathbf{E}_e)}{\mathbf{E}_{\alpha=1}} e^{-\frac{\mathbf{E}}{\mathbf{E}_\alpha = 1}t}\left(\varepsilon_{z,K,o} + \frac{1}{\mathbf{E}_{\alpha=1}}\int_0^t e^{\frac{(\mathbf{E}+\mathbf{E}_e)}{\mathbf{E}_{\alpha=1}}t}\sigma_{z,K}(t)dt\right) \tag{43}$$

Equation (44) represents the differential constitutive relation of the connection between the velocity of axial dilatation and the normal stress of the new rheological complex Lethersich–Faraday linear model of an ideal viscoelastic fluid body with piezoelectric properties.

5.3.2. New Rheological Complex Lethersich–Faraday Model in the Form of Viscoelastic Fluid

The rheological complex fractional-type Lethersich–Faraday model of an ideal material with piezoelectric properties, as shown in Figure 6b, contains the following parallel-connected elements: Hooke's element of an ideal elastic material, Newton's fractional-type element of an ideal viscous fluid, and Faraday's ideal elastic piezoelectric element material (which make up, in parallel connection, a basic fractional-type Kelvin–Voigt–Faraday model of an ideal material with piezoelectric properties and with the quality of subsequent elastity). These elements are in series connection with Newton's element of an ideal fractional-type viscous fluid.

Let us now denote the specific axial deformations and axial expansions of Newton's elements of an ideal viscous fluid in the model presented in Figure 6b and in the rheological complex Lethersich–Faraday model of an ideal fractional-type material with piezoelectric properties by $\varepsilon_{z,N}$ and $\varepsilon_{z,K}$. And for the total axial dilatation ε_z of this Lethersich–Faraday model, which is a series connection of the rheological basic complex Kelvin–Voigt–Faraday model of an ideal fractional-type solid body with piezoelectric properties and Newton's element of an ideal viscous fractional-type fluid, we obtain the sum of these axial expansions and dilatations: $\varepsilon_z = \varepsilon_{z,N} + \varepsilon_{z,K}$.

The differential constitutive relay connection between normal stress and axial dilatations for the rheological complex Lethersich–Faraday model of an ideal fractional-type material with piezoelectric properties is obtained from the relation of the sum of component axial velocities of axial dilatations in the form $\dot{\varepsilon}_{z,L} = \dot{\varepsilon}_{z,N} + \dot{\varepsilon}_{z,K}$, that is, the sum of the fractional-type axial dilatation velocities: $D_t^\alpha[\varepsilon_{z,L}] = D_t^\alpha[\varepsilon_{z,K}] + D_t^\alpha[\varepsilon_{z,N}]$. For Newton's element of an ideal viscous fractional-type fluid, the sum can be calculated as follows:

$$D_t^\alpha[\varepsilon_{z,N}] = \frac{\sigma_z}{\mathbf{E}_\alpha} \tag{44}$$

Meanwhile, for the rheological basic complex fractional-type Kelvin–Voigt–Faraday ideal model of an elastoviscous body with piezoelectric properties, the sum of the normal stresses can be calculated as follows:

$$\sigma_{z,K} = (\mathbf{E}+\mathbf{E}_e)\varepsilon_{z,K} + \mathbf{E}_\alpha D_t^\alpha[\varepsilon_{z,K}] \quad D_t^\alpha[\varepsilon_{z,K}] = \frac{\sigma_z}{\mathbf{E}_\alpha} \tag{45}$$

From this, it follows that the rate of velocity of axial dilatation, of the fractional type, through the rheological basic complex Kelvin–Voigt–Faraday model of an ideal solid material of the fractional type with piezoelectric properties is the solution of an inhomogeneous differential equation of the fractional order, as follows:

$$D_t^\alpha[\varepsilon_{z,K}] + \frac{(\mathbf{E}+\mathbf{E}_e)}{\mathbf{E}_\alpha}\varepsilon_{z,K} = \frac{1}{\mathbf{E}_\alpha}\sigma_{z,K}(t),\ 0 < \alpha \leq 1 \tag{46}$$

Next, let us apply, as in the previous paragraph, the Laplace transform L to the previous inhomogeneous differential equation of the fractional order:

$$\mathrm{L}\{\varepsilon_z\} = \frac{\mathrm{L}\{\sigma_z(t)\}}{(\mathbf{E}+\mathbf{E}_e)} \cdot \frac{1}{1+\frac{\mathbf{E}_\alpha}{\mathbf{E}+\mathbf{E}_e}p^{\varepsilon}} \tag{47}$$

On the right-hand side, we have the product of two Laplace transforms of each function, which can be viewed as two functions, which are in convolution. So, we need to determine the inverse transforms of each of those functions individually: $\frac{1}{\left(1+\frac{\mathbf{E}_\alpha}{(\mathbf{E}+\mathbf{E}_e)}p^{\alpha}\right)}$ and $\mathrm{L}\{\sigma_{z,K}(t)\}$.

The solution of the inhomogeneous differential equation of the fractional order, shown in Equation (47), which describes the axial dilatation through the rheological complex Kelvin–Voigt–Faraday model of an ideal material of the fractional type with piezoelectric properties, is a convolution integral that can be written as follows (see References [64–66]):

$$\varepsilon_{z,K} = \frac{1}{(\mathbf{E}+\mathbf{E}_e)}\int_0^t \sigma_{z,K}(t-\tau)\sum_{k=1}^{\propto}(-1)^k\left(\frac{\mathbf{E}_\alpha}{(\mathbf{E}+\mathbf{E}_e)}\right)^k \frac{\tau^{(2-\alpha)k}}{\Gamma(2k+1-\alpha k)}d\tau,\ 0<\alpha\leq 1 \tag{48}$$

in which $\varepsilon_{z,K,o}$ is the initial axial dilatation of the rheological complex Kelvin–Voigt–Faraday ideal model of an ideal visvoelastic fractional-type fluid body with piezoelectric properties.

Then, by differentiating in time the previous expression of axial dilatation shown in Equation (49) of the rheological basic Kelvin–Voigt–Faraday model of an ideal elastoviscous solid body, as well as adding the axial dilatation velocity $\dot{\varepsilon}_{z,N} = \frac{\sigma_z}{E_\alpha}$ of the elementary Newtonian element of an ideal fractional-type viscous fluid, to obtain the axial dilatation velocity $\dot{\varepsilon}_{z.L}$ of the rheological complex Lethersich–Faraday model of an ideal visclastic fluid material, we obtain the following expression:

$$\mathrm{D}_t^{\alpha}[\varepsilon_{z,L}] = \mathrm{D}_t^{\alpha}[\varepsilon_{z,K}] + \mathrm{D}_t^{\alpha}[\varepsilon_{z,N}]$$

$$\dot{\varepsilon}_{z.L} = \dot{\varepsilon}_{z,K} + \dot{\varepsilon}_{z,N_\alpha}$$

$$\dot{\varepsilon}_{z.L} = \dot{\varepsilon}_{z,K} + \dot{\varepsilon}_{z,N_\alpha} = \frac{1}{(\mathbf{E}+\mathbf{E}_e)}\frac{d}{di}\left\langle \int_0^t \sigma_{z,K}(t-\tau)\sum_{k=1}^{\propto}(-1)^k\left(\frac{\mathbf{E}_\alpha}{(\mathbf{E}+\mathbf{E}_e)}\right)^k \frac{\tau^{(2-\alpha)k}}{\Gamma(2k+1-\alpha k)}d\tau \right\rangle + \dot{\varepsilon}_{z,N_\alpha} \tag{49}$$

$$V_z(t) = -g\sigma_z(t)$$

$$D_z(t) = b\sigma_z(t) \text{ и } D_z(t) = e\varepsilon_z(t)$$

From the structure, shown in Figure 6b, of the rheological complex Lethersich–Faraday model of this ideal viscoelastic fluid material, which is formed by a series connection of the rheological basic Kelvin–Voigt–Faraday elastoviscous solid material and Newton's element of an ideal viscous fluid of the fractional type, and from the properties of the models of these ideal materials that we have identified, the first being subsequent elasticity and the second being normal stress relaxation, it can be seen that the rheological complex Lethersich–Faraday material possesses both properties of subsequent elasticity and stress relaxation and that it is a more complex model of the material than its substructures.

The rheological complex Lethersich–Faraday model of an ideal viscoelastic fluid material belongs to the group of rheological viscoelastic creepers.

The new rheological complex Lethersich–Faraday model has one internal degree of freedom of mobility.

5.4. New Rheological Complex Lethersich–Faraday-F Model of an Elastoviscous Solid Material

As we emphasized in the previous Section 5.3, in Figure 6c, the second model of the new rheological complex Lethersich–Faraday-F model of a fractional-type ideal material with piezoelectric properties has the properties of an elastoviscous solid material and has the structural formula $L_\alpha/FY = H/N_\alpha - N_\alpha/FY$. It consists of a regular connection of the rheological basic Kelvin–Voigt model of a fractional-type elastoviscous solid material and the rheological Newton–Faraday model of a fractional-type elastoviscous solid and piezoelectric material with the ability to polarize under deformation and loading.

This rheological model, the second rheological complex Lethersich–Faraday-F model of an ideal elastoviscous solid material, belongs to a group of rheological elastoviscous oscillators.

The second new rheological complex Lethersich–Faraday-F model of an elastoviscous material has one internal degree of freedom of mobility at the point of regular connection of the substructure.

The constitutive relationship of the second rheological complex Lethersich–Faraday model of a fractional-type elastoviscous solid material with piezoelectric properties is determined by the sum of the fractional-type dilatations of the following component substructures: the rheological basic Kelvin–Voigt model of a fractional-type elastoviscous solid material and the rheological Newton–Faraday model of a fractional-type elastoviscous solid of the piezoelectric polarized material. The normal stress through the entire structure of the rheological complex Lethersich–Faraday model of a fractional-type elastoviscous solid material with piezoelectric properties is the same, which means that the resultant normal stress is also the same in the rheological basic complex Kelvin–Voigt model of a fractional-type elastoviscous solid material and in the rheological Newton–Faraday model of a fractional-type elastoviscous solid with piezoelectric properties.

For the rheological Newton–Faraday model, in which they are measured in parallel, the resulting normal stress should be determined as the sum of the normal stresses in the Newton and Faraday models, as follows:

$$\sigma_{z,\alpha.2} = \mathbf{E}_\alpha \mathrm{D}_t^\alpha[\varepsilon_{z,NF}] \quad \sigma_{z,2} = \mathbf{E}_e \varepsilon_{z,NF} \tag{50}$$

$$\mathrm{D}_t^\alpha[\varepsilon_{z,NF}] = \frac{\sigma_{z,\alpha.2}}{\mathbf{E}_\alpha} \quad \mathrm{D}_t^\alpha[\varepsilon_{z,NF}] = \frac{1}{\mathbf{E}_e \varepsilon}\mathrm{D}_t^\alpha[\sigma_{z,z,NF}] \tag{51}$$

$$\sigma_{z,\alpha,NF} = \sigma_{z,\alpha.2} + \sigma_{z,2} = \mathbf{E}_e \varepsilon_{z,NF} + \mathbf{E}_\alpha \mathrm{D}_t^\alpha[\varepsilon_{z,NF}] \quad \sigma_{z,2} = \mathbf{E}_e \varepsilon_{z,NF} \tag{52}$$

$$\begin{aligned} \sigma_{z,\alpha,NF} &= \sigma_{z,\alpha.2} + \sigma_{z,2} = \mathbf{E}_e \varepsilon_{z,NF} + \mathbf{E}_\alpha \mathrm{D}_t^\alpha[\varepsilon_{z,NF}] = \\ &= \int_0^t \sigma_z(t-\tau)\left\langle \sum_{k=0}^{\infty} (-1)^k \left(\frac{\mathbf{E}_\alpha}{\mathbf{E}_e}\right)^k \frac{\tau^{(2-\alpha)k}}{\Gamma(2k+1-\alpha k)} \right\rangle d\tau \\ \varepsilon_{z,K} &= \frac{1}{(\mathbf{E}+\mathbf{E}_e)}\int_0^t \sigma_{z,K}(t-\tau)\sum_{k=0}^{\infty}(-1)^k\left(\frac{\mathbf{E}_\alpha}{(\mathbf{E}+\mathbf{E}_e)}\right)^k \frac{\tau^{(2-\alpha)k}}{\Gamma(2k+1-\alpha k)} d\tau \end{aligned} \tag{53}$$

5.5. New Rheological Complex Jeffrey–Faraday Model of a Viscoelastic Fluid Material

In this section, we study the new rheological complex Jeffrey–Faraday model of an ideal fractional-type material with piezoelectric properties, in two variants: 1*—when Faraday's ideal elastic material with polarization properties is connected in parallel with Hooke's rheological ideal elastic element, as shown in Figure 7b; and 2*—when Faraday's ideal elastic material with polarization properties is connected in parallel with the Newton rheological elementary fractional-type viscous fluid element or the rheological basic complex Maxwell viscoelastic fluid model, as shown in Figure 7c. The first case, labeled 1*, is the rheological fractional-type complex Jeffrey–Faraday model of an ideal material with piezoelectric properties, which has the properties of a viscoelastic fluid material and has the structural formula $\mathbf{J}_\alpha/FY = \mathbf{N}_{\alpha,1}/(\mathbf{H}/FY - \mathbf{N}_{\alpha,2})$. The second case, labeled 2*, is the rheological fractional-type complex Jeffrey–Faraday model of an ideal material with piezoelectric properties, which has the properties of an elastoviscous solid material and has the structural formula $\mathbf{J}_\alpha/FY = \mathbf{N}_{\alpha,1}/(\mathbf{H} - \mathbf{N}_{\alpha,2})/FY$ or $\mathbf{L}_\alpha/FY = \mathbf{H}/\mathbf{N}_\alpha - \mathbf{N}_\alpha/FY$.

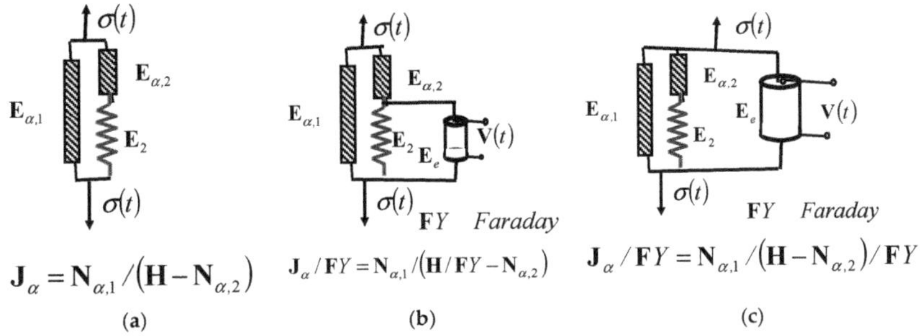

Figure 7. Three new Jeffrey rheological complex fractional-type models: (**a**) new Jeffrey viscoelastic fluid model; (**b**) new Lethersich–Faraday viscoelastic fluid model; (**c**) new Jeffrey–Faraday-F elastoviscous solid model.

In Figure 7, three new rheological complex Jeffrey fractional-type models, in two variants, are visible. In Figure 7a, the structure of the new rheological complex Jeffrey fractional-type viscoelastic fluid material model is presented. Figure 7b shows the structure of the new rheological complex Jeffrey–Faraday fractional-type model of a viscoelastic fluid with piezoelectric properties, with Faraday's piezoelectric element connected in parallel with Hooke's ideal elastic element. Figure 7c shows the new Jeffrey–Faraday elastoviscous solid model, with Faraday's element connected in parallel with Newton's fractional-type viscous fluid element.

5.5.1. The Rheological Complex Linear Jeffrey–Faraday Model of an Ideal Material with Piezoelectric Properties

This model contains Hooke's element of an ideal elastic material and Faraday's ideal elastic and piezoelectric element connected in parallel, and they are in a sequential connection with the linear Newtonian element of an ideal viscous fluid and in parallel connection with another linear Newtonian element of an ideal viscous fluid. Let us now denote the specific axial deformations and axial dilatations of the linear Newtonian elements of an ideal viscous fluid and the rheological Hooke model of an ideal solid element material by $\varepsilon_{z,N}$ and $\varepsilon_{z,K}$. And to obtain the total axial dilatation ε_z of this new rheological linear complex Jeffrey–Faraday model of an ideal viscoelastic model material with piezoelectric properties, we calculate the sum of these axial dilatations as follows: $\varepsilon_z = \varepsilon_{z,N} + \varepsilon_{z,K}$.

The rheological linear complex Jeffrey–Faraday model $\mathbf{J}_\alpha/FY$ of an ideal viscoelastic fluid material with piezoelectric properties, similar to that shown in Figure 7b, contains a parallel connection of Newton's linear element of an ideal viscous fluid and Maxwell's model of an ideal viscoelastic material with a parallel connection to Hooke's ideal elastic model and Faraday's element of an ideal piezoelectric and ideal elastic material, for which there are individually constitutive relations between normal stress and axial dilatation, i.e., axial dilatation velocity, in the following form:

$$\dot{\varepsilon}_{z,N1} = \frac{\sigma_{z,N}}{\mathbf{E}_{\alpha=1,1}} \quad \sigma_{z,N1} = \mathbf{E}_{\alpha=1,1}\dot{\varepsilon}_{z,N1} \tag{54}$$

$$\dot{\varepsilon}_{z,M} = \frac{\dot{\sigma}_{z,M}}{E} + \frac{\dot{\sigma}_{z,M}}{E_e} + \frac{\sigma_{z,M}}{E_{\alpha=1,2}} = \left(\frac{1}{E} + \frac{1}{E_e}\right)\dot{\sigma}_{z,M} + \frac{\sigma_{z,M}}{E_{\alpha=1,2}} = \frac{E + E_e}{EE_e}\dot{\sigma}_{z,M} + \frac{\sigma_{z,M}}{E_{\alpha=1,2}} \quad (55)$$

$$\dot{\sigma}_{z,M} + \frac{\mathbf{EE}_e}{\mathbf{E}_{\alpha=1,2}(\mathbf{E} + \mathbf{E}_e)}\sigma_{z,M} = \frac{\mathbf{EE}_e}{(\mathbf{E} + \mathbf{E}_e)}\dot{\varepsilon}_{z,M} \quad (56)$$

From here, by integrating Equation (57), the following can be determined:

$$\sigma_{z,M} = e^{-\frac{\mathbf{EE}_e}{\mathbf{E}_{\alpha=1,2}(\mathbf{E}+\mathbf{E}_e)}t}\left\langle \sigma_{z,M,o} + \frac{\mathbf{EE}_e}{(\mathbf{E}+\mathbf{E}_e)}\int_0^t \dot{\varepsilon}_{z,M}(t)e^{\frac{\mathbf{EE}_e}{\mathbf{E}_{\alpha=1,2}(\mathbf{E}+\mathbf{E}_e)}t}dt\right\rangle \quad (57)$$

Then, by adding $\sigma_{z,N1}$ and $\sigma_{z,M}$, we obtain the resulting normal stress $\sigma_{z,J}$ in the rheological linear complex Jeffrey–Faraday model $\mathbf{J}_\alpha/\mathbf{F}Y$ of an ideal viscoelastic fluid material with bolariyation under deformation, shaped by piezoelectric properties, in the following form:

$$\sigma_{z,J} = \sigma_{z,N1} + \sigma_{z,M} = \mathbf{E}_{\alpha=1,1}\dot{\varepsilon}_{z,N1} + e^{-\frac{\mathbf{EE}_e}{\mathbf{E}_{\alpha=1,2}(\mathbf{E}+\mathbf{E}_e)}t}\left\langle \sigma_{z,M,o} + \frac{\mathbf{EE}_e}{(\mathbf{E}+\mathbf{E}_e)}\int_0^t \dot{\varepsilon}_{z,M}(t)e^{\frac{\mathbf{EE}_e}{\mathbf{E}_{\alpha=1,2}(\mathbf{E}+\mathbf{E}_e)}t}dt\right\rangle \quad (58)$$

This is measured over the velocity (rate) of axial dilatation as a function of time in the form of Equation (59).

5.5.2. New Rheological Complex Jeffrey–Faraday Model of a Viscoelastic Fluid Material

The new rheological complex Jeffrey–Faraday model $\mathbf{J}_\alpha\mathbf{F}\mathbf{Y}$ of an ideal fractional-type viscoelastic fluid material with piezoelectric properties, as shown in Figure 7b, contains a parallel connection of a Newtonian element of an ideal fractional-type viscous fluid and a new basic complex Maxwell model of an ideal fractional-type viscoelastic material, for which Hooke's ideal elastic element is connected in parallel to Faraday's ideal piezoelectric and ideal elastic material elements, which are individually serially connected.

For the first elementary Newtonian element of an ideal fractional-type viscous fluid, the velocity of axial dilatation can be expressed in the following form:

$$\sigma_{z,N_\alpha,1}(t) = \mathbf{E}_{\alpha,1}\mathrm{D}_t^\alpha[\varepsilon_{z,N_\alpha,1}] \; \mathrm{D}_t^\alpha[\varepsilon_{z,N_\alpha,1}] = \frac{\sigma_{z,N_\alpha,1}(t)}{\mathbf{E}_{\alpha,1}} \quad 0 < \alpha \leq 1 \quad (59)$$

For the second Newtonian element of an ideal fractional-type viscous fluid, in terms of the rate of velocity of fractional-type axial dilatation, the constitutive diferential relation of the element showing the diferential relation between normal stress and velocity rate of axial dilatation, of the fractional order, is in the following form:

$$\sigma_{z,N_\alpha,2}(t) = \mathbf{E}_{\alpha,2}\mathrm{D}_t^\alpha[\varepsilon_{z,N_\alpha,2}] \; \mathrm{D}_t^\alpha[\varepsilon_{z,N_\alpha,2}] = \frac{\sigma_{z,N_\alpha,12}(t)}{\mathbf{E}_{\alpha,2}} \quad 0 < \alpha \leq 1 \quad (60)$$

For Hooke's ideal elastic element connected in parallel in the model with Faraday's ideal piezoelectric and ideal elastic material model, there are individually constitutive relations between normal stress and axial dilatation, i.e., the fractional-type dilatation rate of velocity, which take the following forms:

For Hooke's element,

$$\sigma_{z,H}(t) = \mathbf{E}\varepsilon_{z,H} \; \mathrm{D}_t^\alpha[\varepsilon_{z,H}] = \frac{\mathrm{D}_t^\alpha[\sigma_{z,H}(t)]}{\mathbf{E}} \quad (61)$$

For Faraday's element,

$$\sigma_{z,FY}(t) = \mathbf{E}_e \varepsilon_{z,FY} \ \ \mathrm{D}_t^{\alpha}[\varepsilon_{z,FY}] = \frac{\mathrm{D}_t^{\alpha}[\sigma_{z,FY}(t)]}{\mathbf{E}_e} \tag{62}$$

The rates of velocity of the dilatations of the fractional type of these two parallel-connected elements, Hooke's ideal elastic element and Faraday's elements of the ideal piezoelectric and ideal elastic material model, are equal, so $\varepsilon_{z,H} = \varepsilon_{z,FY}$ and the following equation can be formed:

$$\mathrm{D}_t^{\alpha}[\varepsilon_{z,H}] = \frac{\mathrm{D}_t^{\alpha}[\sigma_{z,H}(t)]}{\mathbf{E}} = \mathrm{D}_t^{\alpha}[\varepsilon_{z,FY}] = \frac{\mathrm{D}_t^{\alpha}[\sigma_{z,FY}(t)]}{\mathbf{E}_e}, \ 0 < \alpha \leq 1 \tag{63}$$

The sum of the normal stresses in parallel elements, i.e., Hooke's ideal elastic element and Faraday's element of the ideal piezoelectric and ideal elastic material, can be expressed in the following form:

$$\sigma_{z,R1}(t) = \sigma_{z,H}(t) + \sigma_{z,FY}(t) = \mathbf{E}\varepsilon_{z,H} + \mathbf{E}_e\varepsilon_{z,FY} = (\mathbf{E} + \mathbf{E}_e)\varepsilon_{z,H} \tag{64}$$

As such, we have determined $\sigma_{z,R1}(t)$ through the entire series connection of the structure of new complex Jeffrey–Faraday model $\mathbf{J}_{\alpha}\mathbf{FY}$ of an ideal viscoelastic fluid material, shown in Figure 7b. The velocity of axial dilatation of Newton's element of viscous fluid, connected in series with the parallel-connected Hooke's ideal elastic element and Faraday's ideal piezoelectric model and ideal elastic material model, can be expressed as follows:

$$\sigma_{z,R1}(t) = \sigma_{z,H}(t) + \sigma_{z,FY}(t) = \mathbf{E}\varepsilon_{z,H} + \mathbf{E}_e\varepsilon_{z,FY} = (\mathbf{E} + \mathbf{E}_e)\varepsilon_{z,H} \tag{65}$$

$$\sigma_{z,N_{\alpha},2}(t) = \mathbf{E}_{\alpha,2}\mathrm{D}_t^{\alpha}[\varepsilon_{z,N_{\alpha},2}] \ \ \mathrm{D}_t^{\alpha}[\varepsilon_{z,N_{\alpha},2}] = \frac{\sigma_{z,N_{\alpha},2}(t)}{\mathbf{E}_{\alpha,2}} \tag{66}$$

$$\mathrm{D}_t^{\alpha}[\varepsilon_{z,N_{\alpha},2}] = \frac{\sigma_{z,N_{\alpha},2}(t)}{\mathbf{E}_{\alpha,2}} = \frac{\sigma_{z,RE}(t)}{\mathbf{E}_{\alpha,2}} = \frac{(\mathbf{E} + \mathbf{E}_e)\varepsilon_{z,H}}{\mathbf{E}_{\alpha,2}}, \ 0 < \alpha \leq 1 \tag{67}$$

Then, the sum of the fractional-type axial dilatation velocity rates of the two parallel elements, Hooke's element and Faraday's elastic material, and Newton's element of an ideal viscous fluid, which is regularly related to them, can be expressed in the following form:

$$\mathrm{D}_t^{\alpha}[\varepsilon_{z,H}] = \frac{\mathrm{D}_t^{\alpha}[\sigma_{z,H}(t)]}{\mathbf{E}} = \mathrm{D}_t^{\alpha}[\varepsilon_{z,FY}] = \frac{\mathrm{D}_t^{\alpha}[\sigma_{z,FY}(t)]}{\mathbf{E}_e} \tag{68}$$

$$\mathrm{D}_t^{\alpha}[\varepsilon_{z,N_{\alpha},2}] = \frac{\sigma_{z,N_{\alpha},2}(t)}{\mathbf{E}_{\alpha,2}} = \frac{\sigma_{z,RE}(t)}{\mathbf{E}_{\alpha,2}} = \frac{(\mathbf{E} + \mathbf{E}_e)\varepsilon_{z,H}}{\mathbf{E}_{\alpha,2}}$$

$$\mathrm{D}_t^{\alpha}[\varepsilon_{z,RRE1}] = \mathrm{D}_t^{\alpha}[\varepsilon_{z,N_{\alpha},2}] + \mathrm{D}_t^{\alpha}[\varepsilon_{z,H}] = \frac{\mathrm{D}_t^{\alpha}[\sigma_{z,H_{\alpha}}(t)]}{\mathbf{E}} + \frac{\sigma_{z,H_{\alpha}}(t)}{\mathbf{E}_{\alpha,2}}, \ 0 < \alpha \leq 1 \tag{69}$$

This value is equal to the axial dilatation velocity of the first Newtonian element of an ideal viscous fluid, which is connected in parallel with them, as shown in Figure 7b:

$$\mathrm{D}_t^{\alpha}[\varepsilon_{z,RRE1}] = \mathrm{D}_t^{\alpha}[\varepsilon_{z,N_{\alpha},2}] + \mathrm{D}_t^{\alpha}[\varepsilon_{z,H}] = \frac{\mathrm{D}_t^{\alpha}[\sigma_{z,H_{\alpha}}(t)]}{\mathbf{E}} + \frac{\sigma_{z,H_{\alpha}}(t)}{\mathbf{E}_{\alpha,2}} \tag{70}$$

We now determine the normal stress in the first Newtonian viscous fluid element, using the previous velocity of axial dilatation, which we determined using the following equation:

$$\mathrm{D}_t^\alpha[\varepsilon_{z,N_\alpha,1}] = \frac{\mathrm{D}_t^\alpha[\sigma_{z,H}(t)]}{\mathbf{E}} + \frac{(\mathbf{E}+\mathbf{E}_e)\varepsilon_{z,H}}{\mathbf{E}_{\alpha,2}}$$

$$\mathrm{D}_t^\alpha[\varepsilon_{z,RRE1}] = \mathrm{D}_t^\alpha[\varepsilon_{z,N_\alpha,2}] + \mathrm{D}_t^\alpha[\varepsilon_{z,H}] = \frac{\mathrm{D}_t^\alpha[\sigma_{z,H_\alpha}(t)]}{\mathbf{E}} + \frac{\sigma_{z,H_\alpha}(t)}{\mathbf{E}_{\alpha,2}}.\ 0 < \alpha \le 1 \tag{71}$$

The normal voltage can be expressed in the following form:

$$\sigma_{z,N_\alpha,1}(t) = \mathbf{E}_{\alpha,1}\mathrm{D}_t^\alpha[\varepsilon_{z,N_\alpha,1}] = \mathbf{E}_{\alpha,1}\left\langle \frac{\mathrm{D}_t^\alpha[\sigma_{z,H}(t)]}{\mathbf{E}} + \frac{\sigma_{z,H}(t)}{\mathbf{E}_{\alpha,2}} \right\rangle, 0 < \alpha \le 1$$

$$\sigma_{z,N_\alpha,1}(t) = \mathbf{E}_{\alpha,1}\left\langle \frac{(\mathbf{E}+\mathbf{E}_e)\mathrm{D}_t^\alpha[\varepsilon_{z,H}(t)]}{\mathbf{E}} + \frac{(\mathbf{E}+\mathbf{E}_e)\varepsilon_{z,H}}{\mathbf{E}_{\alpha,2}} \right\rangle' 0 < \alpha \le 1 \tag{72}$$

Next, we can write a differential constitutive fractional-order relation for the complete rheological complex Jeffrey–Faraday model of an ideal fractional-type viscoelastic fluid material with piezoelectric properties, shown in Figure 7b, which contains a serial connection of a Newtonian element of an ideal fractional-type viscous fluid and a rheological basic complex Maxwell–Faraday model of an ideal fractional-type viscoelastic material with piezoelectric properties, to which Hooke's ideal elastic element is connected in parallel with the element of Faraday's ideal piezoelectric and ideal elastic material model with coupled mechanical and electrical fields.

For all those rheological elements of different material properties, we determined the differential constitutive relations individually, on the basis of which we now write that the resulting normal stress of this model is in the form of the sum of the component normal stresses in the parallel branches of the complex Jeffrey–Faraday model of an ideal viscoelastic fluid material, shown in Figure 7b, in the following form:

$$\sigma_{z,N_\alpha,1}(t) = \mathbf{E}_{\alpha,1}\left\langle \frac{\mathrm{D}_t^\alpha[\sigma_{z,H}(t)]}{\mathbf{E}} + \frac{(\mathbf{E}+\mathbf{E}_e)\varepsilon_{z,H}}{\mathbf{E}_{\alpha,2}} \right\rangle$$

$$\sigma_{z,N_\alpha,1}(t) = \mathbf{E}_{\alpha,1}\left\langle \frac{(\mathbf{E}+\mathbf{E}_e)\mathrm{D}_t^\alpha[\varepsilon_{z,H}(t)]}{\mathbf{E}} + \frac{(\mathbf{E}+\mathbf{E}_e)\varepsilon_{z,H}}{\mathbf{E}_{\alpha,2}} \right\rangle$$

$$\sigma_{z,N_\alpha,1}(t) = \mathbf{E}_{\alpha,1}\mathrm{D}_t^\alpha[\varepsilon_{z,N_\alpha,1}] = \mathbf{E}_{\alpha,1}\left\langle \frac{\mathrm{D}_t^\alpha[\sigma_{z,H}(t)]}{\mathbf{E}} + \frac{\sigma_{z,H}(t)}{\mathbf{E}_{\alpha,2}} \right\rangle$$

$$\sigma_{z,R1}(t) = \sigma_{z,H}(t) + \sigma_{z,FY}(t) = \mathbf{E}\varepsilon_{z,H} + \mathbf{E}_e\varepsilon_{z,FY} = (\mathbf{E}+\mathbf{E}_e)\varepsilon_{z,H}$$

$$\sigma_{z,,J_\alpha FY}(t) = \sigma_{z,R2}(t) = \sigma_{z,H}(t) + \sigma_{z,FY}(t) + \sigma_{z,N_{\alpha,1}}(t),\ 0 < \alpha \le 1 \tag{73}$$

The preceding constitutive relation shown in Equation (74) is in the form of an inhomogeneous differential relation of fractional-order exponent α, where $0 < \alpha \le 1$. From the previous relation, we form an ordinary inhomogeneous fractional differential equation of the following form:

$$\mathrm{D}_t^\alpha[\varepsilon_{z,H}(t)] + \frac{\mathbf{E}}{\mathbf{E}_{\alpha,1}}\left(\frac{\mathbf{E}_{\alpha,1}}{\mathbf{E}} + 1\right)\varepsilon_{z,H}(t) = \frac{\mathbf{E}}{\mathbf{E}_{\alpha,1}(\mathbf{E}+\mathbf{E}_e)}\sigma_{z,,J_\alpha FY}(t),\ 0 < \alpha \le 1 \tag{74}$$

It gives the relation between the dilatation $\varepsilon_{z,H}(t)$ of Hooke's element and the resulting normal stress $\sigma_{z,,J_\alpha FY}(t)$ in the structure of the complex Jeffrey–Faraday model $\mathbf{J}_\alpha\mathbf{FY}$ of an ideal viscoelastic fluid material, shown in Figure 7b, which can also be written in the following form:

$$D_t^{\alpha}[\varepsilon_{z,H}(t)] + \frac{\mathbf{E}}{\mathbf{E}_{\alpha,1}}\left(\frac{\mathbf{E}_{\alpha,1}}{\mathbf{E}}+1\right)\varepsilon_{z,H}(t) = \frac{\mathbf{E}}{\mathbf{E}_{\alpha,1}(\mathbf{E}+\mathbf{E}_e)}\sigma_{z,,J_\alpha FY}(t), 0<\alpha\leq 1$$

$$\frac{\mathbf{E}}{\mathbf{E}_e}D_t^{\alpha}[\varepsilon_{z,FY}(t)] + \frac{\mathbf{E}}{\mathbf{E}_e}\frac{\mathbf{E}}{\mathbf{E}_{\alpha,1}}\left(\frac{\mathbf{E}_{\alpha,1}}{\mathbf{E}}+1\right)\varepsilon_{z,FY}(t) = \frac{\mathbf{E}}{\mathbf{E}_{\alpha,1}(\mathbf{E}+\mathbf{E}_e)}\sigma_{z,,J_\alpha FY}(t) \tag{75}$$

From this, it can be determined that

$$D_t^{\alpha}[\varepsilon_{z,FY}(t)] + \frac{\mathbf{E}}{\mathbf{E}_{\alpha,1}}\left(\frac{\mathbf{E}_{\alpha,1}}{\mathbf{E}}+1\right)\varepsilon_{z,FY}(t) = \frac{1}{(\mathbf{E}+\mathbf{E}_e)}\sigma_{z,,J_\alpha FY}(t),\ 0<\alpha\leq 1 \tag{76}$$

because

$$D_t^{\alpha}[\varepsilon_{z,H}] = \frac{D_t^{\alpha}[\sigma_{z,H}(t)]}{\mathbf{E}} = D_t^{\alpha}[\varepsilon_{z,FY}] = \frac{D_t^{\alpha}[\sigma_{z,FY}(t)]}{\mathbf{E}_e} \tag{77}$$

$$\sigma_{z,H}(t) = \frac{\mathbf{E}}{\mathbf{E}_e}\sigma_{z,FY}(t) \quad \varepsilon_{z,H}(t) = \frac{\mathbf{E}}{\mathbf{E}_e}\varepsilon_{z,FY}(t) \tag{78}$$

in which $\varepsilon_{z,FY}(t)$ is the axial dilatation of the elements. Next, we need to determine the solutions of this inhomogeneous ordinary differential equation of the fractional order which is in the following form, adapted from Equation (77):

$$L\{\varepsilon_{z,FY}(t)\} = \frac{1}{(\mathbf{E}+\mathbf{E}_e)\left\langle p^{\alpha}+\frac{\mathbf{E}}{\mathbf{E}_{\alpha,1}}\left(\frac{\mathbf{E}_{\alpha,1}}{\mathbf{E}}+1\right)\right\rangle}L\{\sigma_{z,,J_\alpha FY}(t)\}$$

Alternatively, it can be transformed as follows:

$$L\{\varepsilon_{z,FY}(t)\} = \frac{\mathbf{E}_{\alpha,1}}{(\mathbf{E}+\mathbf{E}_e)(\mathbf{E}_{\alpha,1}+\mathbf{E})}\frac{1}{\left\langle\frac{\mathbf{E}_{\alpha,1}}{(\mathbf{E}_{\alpha,1}+\mathbf{E})}p^{\alpha}+1\right\rangle}L\{\sigma_{z,,J_\alpha FY}(t)\},\ 0<\alpha\leq 1 \tag{79}$$

Using Equation (77), the inhomogeneous differential equation of fractional-order exponent α is solved by applying the Laplace transform, then developing it in a degrees series and then returning it, with the inverse Laplace transform, as follows:

$$\begin{aligned}&L^{-1}\left\{\left\langle 1+\sum_{k=1}^{\infty}(-1)^k\left(\frac{\mathbf{E}_{\alpha,1}}{(\mathbf{E}_{\alpha,1}+\mathbf{E})}\right)^k p^{\alpha k}\right\rangle\right\} = \\ &= L^{-1}\left\{\left\langle \sum_{k=0}^{\infty}(-1)^k\left(\frac{\mathbf{E}_{\alpha,1}}{(\mathbf{E}_{\alpha,1}+\mathbf{E})}\right)^k p^{\alpha k}\right\rangle\right\} = \sum_{k=0}^{\infty}(-1)^k\left(\frac{\mathbf{E}_{\alpha,1}}{(\mathbf{E}_{\alpha,1}+\mathbf{E})}\right)^k\frac{t^{(2-\alpha)kk}}{\Gamma(2k+1-\alpha k)}\end{aligned} \tag{80}$$

Then, the following can be determined:

$$\varepsilon_{z,FY} = L^{-1}L\{\varepsilon_{z,FY}(t)\} = \frac{\mathbf{E}_{\alpha,1}}{(\mathbf{E}+\mathbf{E}_e)(\mathbf{E}_{\alpha,1}+\mathbf{E})}L^{-1}\left\{\frac{1}{\left\langle\frac{\mathbf{E}_{\alpha,1}}{(\mathbf{E}_{\alpha,1}+\mathbf{E})}p^{\alpha}+1\right\rangle}\right\}L^{-1}L\{\sigma_{z,,J_\alpha FY}(t)\}, 0<\alpha\leq 1$$

$$\begin{gathered}\varepsilon_{z,FY} = \frac{\mathbf{E}_{\alpha,1}}{(\mathbf{E}+\mathbf{E}_e)(\mathbf{E}_{\alpha,1}+\mathbf{E})}\int_0^t\sigma_{z,,J_\alpha FY}(t-\tau)\sum_{k=0}^{\infty}(-1)^k\left(\frac{\mathbf{E}_{\alpha,1}}{(\mathbf{E}_{\alpha,1}+\mathbf{E})}\right)^k\frac{\tau^{(2-\alpha)kk}}{\Gamma(2k+1-\alpha k)}d\tau \\ 0<\alpha\leq 1\end{gathered} \tag{81}$$

At constant axial dilatation of the rheological complex Jeffrey–Faraday model of an ideal viscoelastic fluid material, relaxation of normal stress occurs.

The new rheological complex Jeffrey–Faraday model has one internal degree of freedom of mobility.

5.6. New Rheological Complex Jeffrey–Faraday Model as an Elastoviscous Solid Material

In this section, we study the second variant of the new rheological complex Jeffrey–Faraday-F model of an ideal elastoviscous fractional-type solid material with piezoelectric properties, when Faraday's ideal elastic element with polarization properties is connected in parallel with the rheological fractional-type Newtonian viscous fluid element or the rheological basic complex Maxwell viscoelastic fluid model, as shown in Figure 7c. As we wrote in this case, it is the rheological complex Jeffrey–Faraday model of a fractional-type ideal material with piezoelectric properties, which has the properties of an elastoviscous solid material and has the structural formula $\boldsymbol{J}_{\alpha}/\boldsymbol{FY} = \boldsymbol{N}_{\alpha,1}/(\boldsymbol{H} - \boldsymbol{N}_{\alpha,2})/\boldsymbol{FY}$ or $\boldsymbol{L}_{\alpha}/\boldsymbol{FY} = \boldsymbol{H}/\boldsymbol{N}_{\alpha} - \boldsymbol{N}_{\alpha}/\boldsymbol{FY}$.

The rheological complex Jeffrey–Faraday model of a fractional-type elastoviscous solid and piezoelectric material has the ability to polarize under deformation and loading.

This rheological model, the second rheological complex Jeffrey–Faraday-F model of an ideal elastoviscous solid material, belongs to a group of rheological elastoviscous oscillators.

The second new rheological complex Jeffrey–Faraday-F model has one internal degree of freedom of mobility at the point of regular connection in its substructure.

The constitutive relation of the second rheological complex Jeffrey–Faraday-F model of an elastoviscous solid material is easily determined by the sum of the component normal stresses of two elementary rheological elements connected in parallel in a basic complex model: the Newtonian ideal viscous fluid element and the Faraday element in one rheological basic complex Maxwell model of an elastoviscous fluid, as shown in Figure 7c.

The normal stress through the entire structure of the rheological complex Jeffrey–Faraday-F model of an elastoviscous solid material is the resultant normal stress of the components:

$$\sigma_{z,N_{\alpha},1}(t) = \mathbf{E}_{\alpha,1}\mathrm{D}_t^{\alpha}[\varepsilon_{z,N_{\alpha},1}], \quad \sigma_{z,FY}(t) = \mathbf{E}_e\varepsilon_{z,FY} \tag{82}$$

The normal stress σ_z at the points of the cross-section is the same throughout the entire modified Maxwell model $\mathbf{M}_{\alpha}$, so we can write the constitutive relations of each basic rheological element in this series connection; as such, the normal stresses σ_z in the dilatation function are

$$\sigma_z = \mathbf{E}\varepsilon_{z,1} \tag{83}$$

$$\sigma_{z,\alpha} = \mathbf{E}_{\alpha}\mathrm{D}_t^{\alpha}[\varepsilon_{z.2}] = \sigma_z \tag{84}$$

The velocity rate of axial dilatation of the fractional-type rheological basic complex Maxwell model $\mathrm{D}_t^{\alpha}[\varepsilon_z]$, the fractional-type equal to the sum of the dilatation rates, the fractional-type Newtonian viscous element $\mathrm{D}_t^{\alpha}[\varepsilon_{z,1}]$, and Hooke's ideal elastic element $\mathrm{D}_t^{\alpha}[\varepsilon_{z,2}]$ can be expressed in the following form:

$$\mathrm{D}_t^{\alpha}[\varepsilon_z] = \mathrm{D}_t^{\alpha}[\varepsilon_{z,1}] + \mathrm{D}_t^{\alpha}[\varepsilon_{z,2}] \tag{85}$$

From this, it can be determined that $\varepsilon_{z,1} = \frac{\sigma_z}{\mathbf{E}}$ and therefore $\mathrm{D}_t^{\alpha}[\varepsilon_{z.1}] = \frac{1}{\mathbf{E}}\mathrm{D}_t^{\alpha}[\sigma_z]$ and $\mathrm{D}_t^{\alpha}[\varepsilon_{z.2}] = \frac{\sigma_z}{\mathbf{E}_{\alpha}}$. As such, it follows that a sum (see Figure 7c) can be used for axial dilatation analysis:

$$\mathrm{D}_t^{\alpha}[\varepsilon_z] = \frac{1}{\mathbf{E}}\mathrm{D}_t^{\alpha}[\sigma_z] + \frac{\sigma_z}{\mathbf{E}_{\alpha}} \tag{86}$$

$$\mathrm{L}\{\sigma_z\} = \mathbf{E}_{\alpha}\left\{\mathrm{D}_t^{\alpha}[\varepsilon_z]_{z,,0}\right\} \cdot \frac{1}{p} \cdot \frac{1}{\left\langle 1 + \frac{\mathbf{E}_{\alpha}}{\mathbf{E}}p^{\alpha}\right\rangle}, \; 0 < \alpha \le 1 \tag{87}$$

This model has the property of subsequent elasticity, and the structure model of the rheological complex Jeffrey–Faraday-F model of an elastoviscous solid material in the substructure of the basic complex Maxwell model exhibits normal stress relaxation. The structure of the rheological complex Jeffrey–Faraday-F model of an elastoviscous solid material has the property of subsequent elasticity.

This rheological model, the second rheological complex Jeffrey–Faraday-F model of an ideal elastoviscous solid material, belongs to the group of rheological elastoviscous oscillators.

The second new rheological complex Jeffrey–Faraday model of a fractional-type elastoviscous material with piezoelectric properties has one internal degree of freedom of mobility at the point of regular connection in its substructure.

5.7. New Rheological Complex Burgers–Faraday Model of a Viscoelastic Fluid Material

In this section, we study two new rheological complex Burgers–Faraday $\boldsymbol{B_{Bu,\alpha}FY}$ models of an ideal fractional-type material with piezoelectric properties: 1*—when Faraday's ideal elastic element with polarization properties is connected in parallel with the rheological basic complex Kelvin–Voigt ideal elastoviscous fluid model, as shown in Figure 8b; and 2*— when Faraday's ideal elastic element with polarization properties is connected in parallel with the rheological basic complex Maxwell viscoelastic fluid model, as shown in Figure 8c. The first case, labeled 1*, is the rheological complex Burgers–Faraday model of an ideal material, which has the properties of a viscoelastic fluid material and has the structural formula $\boldsymbol{B_{Bu,\alpha}}/FY = \boldsymbol{K}/FY - M_\alpha$, $\boldsymbol{B_{Bu,\alpha}K}/FY = (\boldsymbol{H}/\boldsymbol{N_\alpha}/FY) - (\boldsymbol{H} - \boldsymbol{N_\alpha})$.

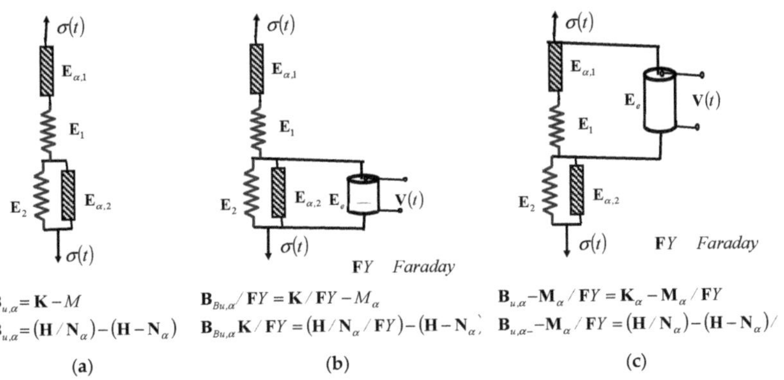

Figure 8. Three new rheological complex Burgers fractional-type models: (**a**) new complex Burgers viscoelastic fluid model; (**b**) new complex Burgers–Faraday fractional-type viscoelastic fluid model with piezoelectric properties; (**c**) new complex Burgers–Faraday-F elastoviscous solid model with piezoelectric properties.

The second case, labeled 2*, is the rheological complex Burgers–Faraday-F model of an ideal material, which has the properties of an elastoviscous solid material and has the structural formula $\boldsymbol{B_{u,\alpha}} - \boldsymbol{M_\alpha}/FY = \boldsymbol{K_\alpha} - \boldsymbol{M_\alpha}/FY, \boldsymbol{B_{u,\alpha-}} - \boldsymbol{M_\alpha}/FY = (\boldsymbol{H}/\boldsymbol{N_\alpha}) - (\boldsymbol{H} - \boldsymbol{N_\alpha})/FY$; see Figure 8c.

In Figure 8, the structures of three new rheological complex Burgers models, one Burgers model as well as two Burgers–Faraday models, are presented. Figure 8a shows a new complex Burgers fractional-type viscoelastic fluid model. Figure 8b shows a new complex Burgers–Faraday viscoelastic fluid material model. In Figure 8c, a new complex Burgers–Faraday-F elastoviscous solid material model is visible.

The second rheological complex Burgers–Faraday model $\boldsymbol{B_{u,\alpha}}FY$ of an ideal viscoelastic fluid material with piezoelectric properties is shown in Figure 8b, and represents a series connection of the rheological basic complex Maxwell viscoelastic fluid model and the rheological basic complex Kelvin–Voight–Faraday elastoviscous solid model (with a piezoelectric element connected in parallel with the Faraday element). Both rheological basic complex models are of the fractional type; one is formed of an ideal viscoelastic fluid and the second of elastoviscous solid materials.

The structural formula of the Burgers–Faraday viscoelastic fluid material is in the form $\boldsymbol{B}_{u,\alpha} - \boldsymbol{K}/\boldsymbol{FY} = \boldsymbol{K}/\boldsymbol{FY} - M_{\alpha}\, \boldsymbol{B}_{u,\alpha}\boldsymbol{K}/\boldsymbol{FY} = (\boldsymbol{H}/\boldsymbol{N}_{\alpha}/\boldsymbol{FY}) - (\boldsymbol{H} - \boldsymbol{N}_{\alpha})$.

The third rheological complex Burgers–Faraday model $\boldsymbol{B}_{u,\alpha}\boldsymbol{F}Y$ of an ideal elastovisous solid material with piezoelectric properties is shown in Figure 8c, and represents a series connection of the rheological basic complex Maxwell–Faraday elastoviscous solid model (with a piezoelectric element connected in parallel with the Faraday element) and the rheological basic complex Kelvin–Voight elastoviscous solid model. Both rheological basic complex models are of the fractional type, and both utilize ideal and different viscoelastic solid material models. The constitutive relations (equations of coupled mechanical normal stress and axial expansions) of this rheological complex material model are now easily determined using the following structural formula: $\boldsymbol{B}_{u,\alpha} - \boldsymbol{M}_{\alpha}/\boldsymbol{FY} = \boldsymbol{K}_{\alpha} - \boldsymbol{M}_{\alpha}/\boldsymbol{FY} \quad \boldsymbol{B}_{u,\alpha-} - \boldsymbol{M}_{\alpha}/\boldsymbol{FY} = (\boldsymbol{H}/\boldsymbol{N}_{\alpha}) - (\boldsymbol{H} - \boldsymbol{N}_{\alpha})/\boldsymbol{FY}$.

5.7.1. New Rheological Complex Burgers–Faraday Linear Model of a Linear Viscoelastic Fluid Material with Piezoelectric Properties

First, we will study the properties of the new rheological complex Burgers–Faraday linear model of a linear viscoelastic fluid material with piezoelectric properties, which has a structure similar and analogous to the structure of the model shown in Figure 8b, in which the Newton elements are linear.

The total axial dilatation of the complex linear-type Burgers–Faraday viscoelastic fluid model $\boldsymbol{B}_{u,\alpha}\boldsymbol{F}Y$ of an ideal material with piezoelectric properties is equal to the sum of the component axial dilatations $\varepsilon_{z,M}$, $\varepsilon_{z,K}$, and $\varepsilon_{z,K}$, of the component substructure, as well as the basic complex Maxwell and Kelvin–Voigt–Faraday models (complex model with Faraday's element connected in parallel). The mechanical normal stress in all of the cross-sections of the component substructures of the basic complex models is the same throughout the entire complex Burgers–Faraday model. Based on this analysis and these derived conclusions, we can determine the following:

$$\varepsilon_{z,Bu} = \varepsilon_{z,M} + \varepsilon_{z,K} + \varepsilon_{z,FY} \tag{88}$$

$$\sigma_{z,K1} = \mathbf{E}_{K}\varepsilon_{z,K} + \mathbf{E}_{\alpha=1,K}\dot{\varepsilon}_{z,K} + \mathbf{E}_{e}\varepsilon_{z,K} \tag{89}$$

$$\dot{\varepsilon}_{z,M} = \frac{\dot{\sigma}_{z,M}}{\boldsymbol{E}_{M}} + \frac{\sigma_{z,M}}{\boldsymbol{E}_{\alpha=1,M}} \tag{90}$$

Let us differentiate the first constitutive relation shown in Equation (89) from the previous system, and replace the terms from the third constitutive equation of the previous system given in Equations (90) and (91); based on that, we can write the following constitutive relation for the complex Burgers–Faraday linear model of an ideal viscoelastic fluid material:

$$\dot{\varepsilon}_{z,Bu} = \dot{\varepsilon}_{z,M} + \dot{\varepsilon}_{z,K} + \dot{\varepsilon}_{z,FY} = \frac{\dot{\sigma}_{z,M}}{\boldsymbol{E}_{M}} + \frac{\sigma_{z,M}}{\boldsymbol{E}_{\alpha=1,M}} + \dot{\varepsilon}_{z,K} + \dot{\varepsilon}_{z,FY} \tag{91}$$

Next, the last constitutive relation shown in Equation (92) can be differentiated once more in time to obtain the following:

$$\dot{\varepsilon}_{z,Bu} = \dot{\varepsilon}_{z,M} + \dot{\varepsilon}_{z,K} + \dot{\varepsilon}_{z,FY} = \frac{\dot{\sigma}_{z,M}}{\boldsymbol{E}_{M}} + \frac{\sigma_{z,M}}{\boldsymbol{E}_{\alpha=1,M}} + \dot{\varepsilon}_{z,K} + \dot{\varepsilon}_{z,FY} \tag{92}$$

$$\ddot{\varepsilon}_{z,Bu} = \frac{\ddot{\sigma}_{z,M}}{E_M} + \frac{\dot{\sigma}_{z,M}}{E_{\alpha=1,M}} + \ddot{\varepsilon}_{z,K1} + \ddot{\varepsilon}_{z,FY} \tag{93}$$

Let us now multiply Equation (90) by $\mathbf{E}_{\alpha=1,M}$ and Equation (94) by $\mathbf{E}_{\alpha=1,M}$ and combine them with $\dot{\sigma}_{z,K} = (\mathbf{E}_K + \mathbf{E}_e)\dot{\varepsilon}_{1z,K} + \mathbf{E}_{\alpha=1,K}\ddot{\varepsilon}_{z,K}$ for the component Kelvin–Voigt–Faraday complex model of an ideal material with piezoelectric properties so that we obtain the following relation:

$$\dot{\sigma}_{z,K} = (\mathbf{E}_K + \mathbf{E}_e)\dot{\varepsilon}_{1z,K} + \mathbf{E}_{\alpha=1,K}\ddot{\varepsilon}_{z,K} \;\; / E_{\alpha=1,M}$$

$$\ddot{\varepsilon}_{z,Bu} = \frac{\ddot{\sigma}_{z,M}}{E_M} + \frac{\dot{\sigma}_{z,M}}{E_{\alpha=1,M}} + \ddot{\varepsilon}_{z,K1} + \ddot{\varepsilon}_{z,FY} \; / (E_K + E_e)$$

$$(E_K + E_e)\ddot{\varepsilon}_{z,Bu} = (E_K + E_e)\frac{\ddot{\sigma}_{z,M}}{E_M} + (E_K + E_e)\frac{\dot{\sigma}_{z,M}}{E_{\alpha=1,M}} + (E_K + E_e)\ddot{\varepsilon}_{z,K1} + (E_K + E_e)\ddot{\varepsilon}_{z,FY} \tag{94}$$

Finally, we obtain the following differential relationship between the mechanical normal stress and the first and third derivatives by time of the axial dilatation in the following form:

$$\ddot{\sigma}_{z,Bu} + \dot{\sigma}_{z,Bu}\left(\frac{E_K + E_e}{E_{\alpha=1,M}} + \frac{E_M}{E_{\alpha=1,K}} + \frac{E_M}{E_{\alpha=1,M}}\right) + \sigma_{z,Bu}\frac{E_M}{E_{\alpha=1,M}}\frac{E_K + E_e}{E_{\alpha=1,K}} = \frac{E_K + E_e E_M}{E_{\alpha=1,K}}\dot{\varepsilon}_{z,Bu} + E_M\dddot{\varepsilon}_{z,Bu} \tag{95}$$

5.7.2. New Rheological Complex Burgers–Faraday Model of a Fractional-Type Viscoelastic Fluid Material

The rheological complex Burgers–Faraday model $\boldsymbol{B}_{u,\alpha}FY$ of an ideal viscoelastic fluid material is shown in Figure 8b, and represents, as we explain, a series connection of the rheological basic complex Maxwell viscoelastic fluid material model and the rheological basic complex Kelvin–Voight–Faraday elastoviscous solid material model (with a Faraday piezoelectric element connected in parallel). Both rheological basic complex models are of the fractional type, and utilize ideal viscoelastic fluids as well as elastoviscous solid materials. The constitutive relations are differential equations of the fractional order of coupled mechanical normal stress and axial expansions. The structural formula of this rheological complex material model is expressed in the following form: $\boldsymbol{B}_{u,\alpha} - \boldsymbol{K}/FY = \boldsymbol{K}/FY - M_\alpha$, $\boldsymbol{B}_{u,\alpha}\boldsymbol{K}/FY = (\boldsymbol{H}/\boldsymbol{N}_\alpha/FY) - (\boldsymbol{H} - \boldsymbol{N}_\alpha)$.

The constitutive relations (equations of relation between normal stress and axial dilatation) of this complex material model, a modified Burgers–Faraday model $\boldsymbol{B}_{u,\alpha}FY$ of an ideal fractional-type material with piezoelectric properties, contain derivatives of the fractional-order exponent α, where $0 < \alpha \leq 1$, by time.

The total axial dilatation of the rheological complex Burgers–Faraday $\boldsymbol{B}_{u,\alpha}FY$ ideal fractional-type viscoelastic fluid material model $\boldsymbol{B}_{u,\alpha}FY$ with the piezoelectric properties of an ideal material is equal to the sum of the component axial dilatations $\varepsilon_{z,M}$, $\varepsilon_{z,K}$, and $\varepsilon_{z,K}$ of the component substructure, as well as the rheological complex basic models: the rheological basic complex Maxwell and the rheological basic complex Kelvin–Voigt–Faraday models (complex model with a parallel-connected Faraday ideal elastic element with piezoelectric properties). Mechanical normal stresses in all cross-sections of the component substructure of the basic complex models are equal throughout the entire rheological complex Burgers–Faraday viscoelastic fluid model: $\sigma_{z,K1} = \sigma_{z,M} = \sigma_{z,Bu}$. Based on this analysis and the derived conclusions, we can determine the following relations:

$$\varepsilon_{z,Bu} = \varepsilon_{z,M} + \varepsilon_{z,K}, \;\; \mathrm{D}_t^\alpha[\varepsilon_{z,Bu}] = \mathrm{D}_t^\alpha[\varepsilon_{z,M}] + \mathrm{D}_t^\alpha[\varepsilon_{z,K}], \; 0 < \alpha \leq 1 \tag{96}$$

$$\sigma_{z,K1} = (\mathbf{E}_K + \mathbf{E}_e)\varepsilon_{z,K} + \mathbf{E}_{\alpha=1,K}\mathrm{D}_t^{\alpha}[\varepsilon_{z,K}],\ 0 < \alpha \leq 1 \tag{97}$$

$$\mathrm{D}_t^{\alpha}[\varepsilon_{z,M}] = \frac{\mathrm{D}_t^{\alpha}[\sigma_{z,M}]}{\mathbf{E}_M} + \frac{\sigma_{z,M}}{\mathbf{E}_{\alpha=1,M}},\ 0 < \alpha \leq 1 \tag{98}$$

Let us differentiate the first constitutive relation using the differential operator of fractional-order exponent α, $\mathrm{D}_t^{\alpha}[\varepsilon_{z,K}]$, from the previous system, as shown in Equation (98), and replace the terms from the third constitutive formula in Equation (99) of the previous system; based on that, we could write the constitutive relation for the rheological complex Burgers–Faraday model $\boldsymbol{B}_{u,\alpha}\boldsymbol{F}Y$ of an ideal viscoelastic fluid material in the following form:

$$\mathrm{D}_t^{\alpha}[\varepsilon_{z,Bu}] = \mathrm{D}_t^{\alpha}[\varepsilon_{z,M}] + \mathrm{D}_t^{\alpha}[\varepsilon_{z,K}] = \frac{\mathrm{D}_t^{\alpha}[\sigma_{z,M}]}{\mathbf{E}_M} + \frac{\sigma_{z,M}}{\mathbf{E}_{\alpha=1,M}} + \mathrm{D}_t^{\alpha}[\varepsilon_{z,K}]$$

or

$$\frac{\mathrm{D}_t^{\alpha}[\sigma_{z,M}]}{\mathbf{E}_M} + \frac{\sigma_{z,M}}{\mathbf{E}_{\alpha=1,M}} = \mathrm{D}_t^{\alpha}[\varepsilon_{z,Bu}] - \mathrm{D}_t^{\alpha}[\varepsilon_{z,K}],\ 0 < \alpha \leq 1 \tag{99}$$

$$\sigma_{z,K1} = (\mathbf{E}_K + \mathbf{E}_e)\varepsilon_{z,K} + \mathbf{E}_{\alpha=1,K}\mathrm{D}_t^{\alpha}[\varepsilon_{z,K}] = \sigma_{z,M} = \sigma_{z,Bu},\ 0 < \alpha \leq 1 \tag{100}$$

As throughout the viscoelastic fluid model structure $\boldsymbol{B}_{u,\alpha}\boldsymbol{F}Y$, the normal stress is equal to $\sigma_{z,K1} = \sigma_{z,M} = \sigma_{z,bu}$, the previous two equations of the fractional order can be expressed as follows:

$$\frac{\mathrm{D}_t^{\alpha}[\sigma_{z,Bu}]}{\mathbf{E}_M} + \frac{\sigma_{z,Bu}}{\mathbf{E}_{\alpha=1,M}} = \mathrm{D}_t^{\alpha}[\varepsilon_{z,Bu}] - \mathrm{D}_t^{\alpha}[\varepsilon_{z,K}],\ 0 < \alpha \leq 1 \tag{101}$$

$$\sigma_{z,Bu} = (\mathbf{E}_K + \mathbf{E}_e)\varepsilon_{z,K} + \mathbf{E}_{\alpha=1,K}\mathrm{D}_t^{\alpha}[\varepsilon_{z,K}],\ 0 < \alpha \leq 1 \tag{102}$$

These last two relations between normal stress $\sigma_{z,Bu}$ and axial dilatation $\varepsilon_{z,Bu}$ are coupled differential constitutive relations of the fractional-order exponent α of the structure model $\boldsymbol{B}_{u,\alpha}\boldsymbol{F}Y$ of the ideal rheological viscoelastic fluid material model, which is shown in Figure 8b.

To repeat, $\boldsymbol{B}_{u,\alpha}\boldsymbol{F}Y$ of the ideal viscoelastic fluid material with piezoelectric properties, with the fractional-derivative-order exponent α, where $0 < \alpha \leq 1$, represents the regular serial connection of the Maxwell and Kelvin–Voight–Faraday models, both rheological complex fractional-type models of an ideal material with piezoelectric properties, one utilizing a viscoelastic fluid and the second an elastoviscous solid, and in regular sequential conection gives the final results for the viscoelastic fluid material model. And under certain conditions, $\boldsymbol{B}_{u,\alpha}\boldsymbol{F}Y$ of the ideal viscoelastic fluid material with piezoelectric properties, with fractional-derivative-order exponent α, where $0 < \alpha \leq 1$, has properties of subsequent elasticity and/or relaxation of normal stress in its substructure.

From this system, expressed in Equations (102) and (103), of differential constitutive relations of the fractional-order exponent α, where $0 < \alpha \leq 1$, we can eliminate the velocity of dilatation of this fractional type and obtain only one differential constitutive relation highlighting the connection between the normal stress and axial dilatation of the structure of the rheological complex Burgers–Faraday model $\boldsymbol{B}_{u,\alpha}\boldsymbol{F}Y$ of an ideal fractional-type viscoelastic fluid material with piezoelectric properties in the domain of the Laplace transform, as follows:

$$\mathrm{L}\{\sigma_{z,Bu}\}\left\langle p^{\alpha} + \frac{\mathbf{E}_M}{\mathbf{E}_{\alpha=1,M}}\right\rangle = \mathbf{E}_M p^{\alpha}\langle \mathrm{L}\{\varepsilon_{z,Bu}\} - \mathrm{L}\{\varepsilon_{z,K}\}\rangle,\ 0 < \alpha \leq 1 \tag{103}$$

$$\mathrm{L}\{\varepsilon_{z,K}\} = \frac{1}{((\mathbf{E}_K + \mathbf{E}_e) + p^{\alpha})}\mathrm{L}\{\sigma_{z,Bu}\},\ 0 < \alpha \leq 1 \tag{104}$$

Next, let us integrate the second equation, Equation (105), into the first equation, Equation (104), to obtain one relation:

$$\mathrm{L}\{\sigma_{z,Bu}\} = \mathbf{E}_M \mathrm{L}\{\varepsilon_{z,Bu}\} \frac{((\mathbf{E}_K + \mathbf{E}_e) + p^\alpha)p^\alpha}{\mathbf{E}_M \left\langle \left(\frac{(\mathbf{E}_K+\mathbf{E}_e)+p^\alpha}{\mathbf{E}_M} \right) p^\alpha + p^\alpha + \frac{(\mathbf{E}_K+\mathbf{E}_e)+p^\alpha}{\mathbf{E}_{\alpha=1,M}} \right\rangle}, 0 < \alpha \leq 1 \quad (105)$$

And next, by applying the inverse Laplace transform in Equation (106), it is possible to obtain the convolutional integral and the time function of the normal stress $\sigma_{z,Bu}$ from the axial dilatation $\varepsilon_{z,Bu}$ of the structure for the rheological complex Burgers–Faraday model of an ideal fractional-type material with piezoelectric properties.

This rheological model, the second rheological complex Burgers–Faraday-F model of ideal viscoelastic fluid material, belongs to a group of rheological viscoelastic creepers.

The second new rheological complex Burgers–Faraday model of a fractional-type viscoelastic fluid material with piezoelectric properties has two internal degrees of freedom of mobility at the points of regular connection in its substructure.

5.8. Second New Rheological Complex Burgers–Faraday-F Model of an Elastoviscous Solid Material

Next, we will analyze the constitutive relations of the substructure of the second new complex Burgers–Faraday-F model of an elastoviscous solid material, when a Faraday element is connected in parallel to the substructure of a basic complex Maxwell model.

Along the entire substructure of the complex Maxwell model, the normal stress is the same, and the velocity of axial dilatation in individual regularly connected elements can be expressed as follows: in the Hooke element, it is $\varepsilon_{z,H} = \frac{\sigma_{z,H}}{\mathbf{E}_H}$, i.e., $\mathrm{D}_t^\alpha[\varepsilon_{z,H}] = \frac{\mathrm{D}_t^\alpha[\sigma_{z,H}]}{\mathbf{E}_H}$, while in the Newton element of a fractional-type fluid, it is $\mathrm{D}_t^\alpha[\varepsilon_{z,M}] = \frac{\sigma_{z,M}}{\mathbf{E}_{\alpha=1,M}}$. The total velocity of axial dilatation in the substructure of the Maxwell viscoelastic material can now be expressed in the following form:

$$\varepsilon_{z,Mu} = \varepsilon_{z,H} + \varepsilon_{z,n} \text{ regardless } \mathrm{D}_t^\alpha[\varepsilon_{z,M}] = \mathrm{D}_t^\alpha[\varepsilon_{z,H}] + \mathrm{D}_t^\alpha[\varepsilon_{z,N}] \quad (106)$$

$$\mathrm{D}_t^\alpha[\varepsilon_{z,M}] = \frac{\mathrm{D}_t^\alpha[\sigma_{z,M}]}{\mathbf{E}_{H,M}} + \frac{\sigma_{z,M}}{\mathbf{E}_{\alpha\backslash,M}}, \ 0 < \alpha \leq 1 \quad (107)$$

If we apply the Laplace transform to the previous differential constitutive relations expressed in Equations (107) and (119) of the fractional-order exponent α, where $0 < \alpha \leq 1$, we obtain the following:

$$\mathrm{L}\{\mathrm{D}_t^\alpha[\varepsilon_{z,M}]\} = \frac{\mathrm{L}\{\mathrm{D}_t^\alpha[\sigma_{z,M}]\}}{\mathbf{E}_{H,M}} + \frac{\mathrm{L}\{\sigma_{z,M}\}}{\mathbf{E}_{\alpha\backslash,M}}, \ 0 < \alpha \leq 1 \quad (108)$$

$$\mathrm{L}\{\varepsilon_{z,M}\} = \left(\frac{\mathbf{E}_{\alpha\backslash,M} p^\alpha + \mathbf{E}_{H,M}}{\mathbf{E}_{H,M}\mathbf{E}_{\alpha\backslash,M} p^\alpha} \right) \mathrm{L}\{\sigma_{z,M}\}, \ 0 < \alpha \leq 1 \quad (109)$$

We obtained the previous relationship shown in Equation (110) as the relationship between the Laplace transform of the axial dilatation $\mathrm{L}\{\varepsilon_{z,M}\}$ in the Maxwell model and the Laplace transform $\mathrm{L}\{\sigma_{z,M}\}$ of the normal stress in that model, which is a substructure of the complex Burgers–Faraday-F model.

The fractional-type axial dilatation velocity $\mathrm{D}_t^\alpha[\varepsilon_{z,M}]$ in a parallel-connected Faraday element with Maxwell's model is expressed in the following form:

$$\mathrm{D}_t^\alpha[\varepsilon_{z,M}] = \mathrm{D}_t^\alpha[\varepsilon_{z,H,N}] + \mathrm{D}_t^\alpha[\varepsilon_{z,N,M}] = \mathrm{D}_t^\alpha[\varepsilon_{z,F}]$$

$$\mathrm{D}_t^\alpha[\varepsilon_{z,M}] = \frac{\mathrm{D}_t^\alpha[\sigma_{z,M}]}{\mathbf{E}_{H,M}} + \frac{\sigma_{z,M}}{\mathbf{E}_{\alpha\backslash,M}} = \mathrm{D}_t^\alpha[\varepsilon_{z,F}] = \frac{\mathrm{D}_t^\alpha[\sigma_e]}{\mathbf{E}_e},\ 0 < \alpha \leq 1 \quad (110)$$

Next, using the previous differential constitutive relationship demonstrated in Equation (111), of the fractional-order exponent α, where $0 < \alpha \leq 1$, it can be determined that $\mathrm{D}_t^\alpha[\sigma_{z,F}]$, in a substructure consisting of a Faraday element connected in parallel with a Maxwell model, which together form the substructure of the complex Burgers–Faraday-F model, is equal to

$$D_t^\alpha[\sigma_{z,F}] = \frac{\mathbf{E}_e}{\mathbf{E}_{H,M}} D_t^\alpha[\sigma_{z,M}] + \frac{\mathbf{E}_e}{\mathbf{E}_{\alpha\backslash,M}} \sigma_{z,M},\ 0 < \alpha \leq 1 \quad (111)$$

If we apply the Laplace transform to the previous constitutive relation of the fractional order, we obtain the following:

$$L\{\sigma_{z,F}\} = \left(\frac{\mathbf{E}_e \mathbf{E}_{\alpha\backslash,M} p^\alpha + \mathbf{E}_e \mathbf{E}_{H,M}}{\mathbf{E}_{H,M} \mathbf{E}_{\alpha\backslash,M} p^\alpha} \right) L\{\sigma_{z,M}\},\ 0 < \alpha \leq 1 \quad (112)$$

We obtained the previous expression as the relationship between the Laplace transform $\mathrm{L}\{\sigma_{z,F}\}$ of the normal stress $\sigma_{z,F}$ in a Faraday element with piezoelectric properties, connected in parallel with the rheological basic complex Maxwell model of the fractional type, and the Laplace transform of the normal stress in the Maxwell model, which is a substructure of the complex Burgers–Faraday-F model.

The total normal stress $\mathrm{D}_t^\alpha[\sigma_{z,M,F}]$ in the Maxwell–Faraday model, which contains a parallel-connected Faraday element, which is a substructure of the complex Burgers–Faraday-F model, can be expressed as follows:

$$D_t^\alpha[\sigma_{z,M,F}] = D_t^\alpha[\sigma_{z,M}] + D_t^\alpha[\sigma_{z,F}] = D_t^\alpha[\sigma_{z,M}] + \frac{\mathbf{E}_e}{\mathbf{E}_{H,M}} D_t^\alpha[\sigma_{z,M}] + \frac{\mathbf{E}_e}{\mathbf{E}_{\alpha\backslash,M}} \sigma_{z,M}$$

$$D_t^\alpha[\sigma_{z,M,F}] = \left(1 + \frac{\mathbf{E}_e}{\mathbf{E}_{H,M}}\right) D_t^\alpha[\sigma_{z,M}] + \frac{\mathbf{E}_e}{\mathbf{E}_{\alpha\backslash,M}} \sigma_{z,M},\ 0 < \alpha \leq 1 \quad (113)$$

If we apply the Laplace transform to the previous constitutive relationship expressed in Equation (114), using the fractional-order exponent α, where $0 < \alpha \leq 1$, we obtain the following:

$$L\{\sigma_{z,M,F}\} = \left(1 + \frac{\mathbf{E}_e}{\mathbf{E}_{H,M}} + \frac{\mathbf{E}_e}{\mathbf{E}_{\alpha\backslash,M} p^\alpha}\right) L\{\sigma_{z,M}\},\ 0 < \alpha \leq 1 \quad (114)$$

We obtained the previous expression as the relationship between the Laplace transform $\mathrm{L}\{\sigma_{z,M,F}\}$ of $\sigma_{z,M,F}$ in the basic complex Maxwell–Faraday elastoviscous solid model, which contains a parallel-connected Faraday element, which is a substructure of the complex Burgers–Faraday-F model, and the Laplace transform $\mathrm{L}\{\sigma_{z,M}\}$ of $\sigma_{z,M}$ in the basic Maxwell–Faraday model.

Next, we use the knowledge that the substructure of the complex Burgers–Faraday-F elastoviscous solid material consists of the order of two substructures—the structure of the basic complex Maxwell–Faraday elastoviscous solid material model and the substructure consisting of the solid material—and we write the following differential constitutive relations of fractional-order exponent α, where $0 < \alpha \leq 1$:

$$D_t^\alpha[\sigma_{z,M,F}] = \left(1 + \frac{\mathbf{E}_e}{\mathbf{E}_{H,M}}\right) D_t^\alpha[\sigma_{z,M}] + \frac{\mathbf{E}_e}{\mathbf{E}_{\alpha\backslash,M}} \sigma_{z,M},\ 0 < \alpha \leq 1 \quad (115)$$

$$\mathrm{D}_t^\alpha\left[\varepsilon_{z,Bugam,F}\right] = \mathrm{D}_t^\alpha[\varepsilon_{z,M,F}] + \mathrm{D}_t^\alpha[\varepsilon_{z,K}],\ 0 < \alpha \leq 1 \quad (116)$$

$$\mathrm{D}_t^{\alpha}[\sigma_{z,K1}] = \mathbf{E}_K \mathrm{D}_t^{\alpha}[\varepsilon_{z,K}] + \mathbf{E}_{\alpha,K} \mathrm{D}_t^{\alpha}[\mathrm{D}_t^{\alpha}[\varepsilon_{z,K}]],\ 0 < \alpha \leq 1 \tag{117}$$

Next, we establish the following system, including the differential constitutive relations of the fractional-order exponent α, where $0 < \alpha \leq 1$, of the complex Burgers–Faraday-F elastoviscous solid material model in the following form:

$$\mathrm{D}_t^{\alpha}\left[\varepsilon_{z,Bugam,F}\right] = \mathrm{D}_t^{\alpha}[\varepsilon_{z,M,F}] + \mathrm{D}_t^{\alpha}[\varepsilon_{z,K}],\ 0 < \alpha \leq 1 \tag{118}$$

$$D_t^{\alpha}\left[\sigma_{z,Birgan,,F}\right] = D_t^{\alpha}[\sigma_{z,M,F}] = \left(1 + \frac{E_e}{E_{H,M}}\right) D_t^{\alpha}[\sigma_{z,M}] + \frac{E_e}{\mathbf{E}_{\alpha\backslash,M}} \sigma_{z,M},\ 0 < \alpha \leq 1 \tag{119}$$

$$\mathrm{D}_t^{\alpha}\left[\sigma_{z,Birgan,,F}\right] = \mathrm{D}_t^{\alpha}[\sigma_{z,K1}] = \mathbf{E}_K \mathrm{D}_t^{\alpha}[\varepsilon_{z,K}] + \mathbf{E}_{\alpha,K} \mathrm{D}_t^{\alpha}[\mathrm{D}_t^{\alpha}[\varepsilon_{z,K}]],\ 0 < \alpha \leq 1 \tag{120}$$

$$\sigma_{z,F} = \mathbf{E}_e \varepsilon_{z,F} \tag{121}$$

$$\mathbf{V}_{z,F}(t) = -g\sigma_{z,F}(t) \tag{122}$$

$$D_z(t) = b\sigma_{z,F}(t) \text{ and } D_z(t) = e\varepsilon_{z,F}(t) \tag{123}$$

These differential constitutive relations of fractional-order exponent α, where $0 < \alpha \leq 1$, as shown in Equations (119)–(124), give the relationships of axial dilatation $\varepsilon_{z,Bugam,F}$ and normal stress $\sigma_{z,Birgan,,F}$ for the complex Burgers–Faraday-F elastoviscous solid material, as well as the normal stresses and axial dilatations in the substructures of the basic complex Kelvin–Voigt elastoviscous solid material and the basic complex Maxwell–Faraday elastoviscous solid material.

If we apply the Laplace transform to the previous two differential constitutive relations of fractional-order exponent α, where $0 < \alpha \leq 1$, as shown in Equations (129)–(124), we obtain the following relations:

$$L\{\sigma_{z,Birgan,,F}\} = L\{\sigma_{z,M,F}\} = \left(1 + \frac{E_e}{E_{H,M}} + \frac{E_e}{\mathbf{E}_{\alpha\backslash,M} p^{\alpha}}\right) L\{\sigma_{z,M}\},\ 0 < \alpha \leq 1 \tag{124}$$

$$\mathrm{L}\{\sigma_{z,Birgan,,F}\} = \mathrm{L}\{\sigma_{z,K1}\} = (\mathbf{E}_K + \mathbf{E}_{\alpha,K} p^{\alpha}) \mathrm{L}\{\varepsilon_{z,K}\},\ 0 < \alpha \leq 1 \tag{125}$$

$$\mathrm{L}\{\varepsilon_{z,Birgan,,F}\} = \mathrm{L}\{\varepsilon_{z,M,F}\} + \mathrm{L}\{\varepsilon_{z,K}\}, 0 < \alpha \leq 1 \tag{126}$$

These differential constitutive relations of the fractional-order exponent α, where $0 < \alpha \leq 1$, give the connections between the Laplace transformations $\mathrm{L}\{\sigma_{z,Birgan,,F}\}$ of the normal stress $\sigma_{z,Birgan,,F}$ and the Laplace transformations $\mathrm{L}\{\varepsilon_{z,Birgan,,F}\}$ of the axial dilatation $\varepsilon_{z,Birgan,,F}$ of the complex Burgers–Faraday-F elastoviscous solid material, and the axial dilatations $\mathrm{L}\{\varepsilon_{z,M,F}\}$, namely $\mathrm{L}\{\varepsilon_{z,K}\}$, and the normal stresses $\mathrm{L}\{\sigma_{z,K1}\}$, namely $\mathrm{L}\{\sigma_{z,M,F}\}$, in the substructures of the basic complex Kelvin–Voigt elastoviscous solid material and the basic complex Maxwell–Faraday elastoviscous solid material.

This new model, the second complex Burgers–Faraday-F model of an ideal elastoviscous solid material, belongs to a group of rheological elastoviscous oscillators.

The second new complex Burgers–Faraday-F model, has two internal degrees of freedom of mobility at the points of regular connections in its substructures.

6. Discussion

Based on the derived differential constitutive relations, differential equations, fractional-order calculations, Laplace transformations, dynamics of the rheological complex material models, and approximate analytical solutions, as well as the attached properties of the structures and models and our analysis of them, in our final considerations, we define a number of conclusions in the form of theorems. These theorems are as follows:

Theorem 1. *From the structural scheme of the rheological complex models, we can identify the differences between the types of models, and it is therefore possible to divide the rheological complex models into two groups. The first group is a group of rheological elastoviscous solid bodies with the potential to oscillate and the other is a group of fractional-type rheological viscoelastic fluid materials with the potential to creep.*

Theorem 2. *If at least one of Newton's viscous fluid elements, of the fractional type, is regularly serially connected in the structure independently, and is not in parallel connection or part of another parallel connection with any Hooke ideal elastic elements or Faraday ideal elastic piezoelectric elements in a complex rheological model, then it has the model and structure of a viscoelastic fluid material. In this case, the electrical voltage of the Faraday element changes according to the creep dynamics.*

Theorem 3. *If each of Newton's viscous fluid elements, of the fractional type, is connected in a parallel or intra-parallel connection with one of Hooke's ideal elastic elements or Faraday's ideal elastic and piezoelectric elements, then the rheological complex material model is an elastoviscous solid material model, with the potential to oscillate. In this case, the electric voltage of the Faraday element oscillates.*

Theorem 4. *Each regular connection of one of Newton's fluid elements, of the fractional type, introduces one internal degree of freedom of movement in the complex rheological model, in addition to the external degrees of freedom of movement present in complex rheological models.*

Theorem 5. *Basic rheological complex models are constructed from at least two rheological models connected in parallel or in series. These are basic complex models that belong to the class of fractional-type models and have piezoelectric properties, and include the rheological basic complex Kelvin–Voigt–Faraday model in parallel connection with three rheological elements and the rheological basic complex Maxwell–Faraday model in series connection with three serially connected rheological elements.*

Theorem 6. *The rheological basic complex Kelvin–Voigt–Faraday model, which is in parallel connection with three rheological elements, is a fractional-type model of an elastoviscous solid material with piezoelectric properties and the property of subsequent elasticity.*

The rheological basic complex Maxwell–Faraday model, which is in series connection with three serially connected rheological elements, is a fractional-type model of a viscoelastic fluid material with piezoelectric properties and the property of normal stress relaxation.

Table 1 shows a tabular comparative overview of this new class of complex rheological models of the fractional type of ideal materials with piezoelectric properties. In the vertical columns of Table 1, rheological complex models of elastoviscous solid materials and rheological complex models of fractional-type viscoelastic fluid materials with piezoelectric properties are compared. In the first row of Table 1, the basic rheological complex Kelvin–Voigt–Faraday and Maxwell–Faraday models are shown, which contain the same three basic rheological elements: in the first model, they are all in a parallel coupling, and in the second model, they are all in a series coupling. In the other horizontal rows of Table 1, other rheological complex models are compared in pairs containing the same rheological elements in terms of number and properties, but in which the type of material model is changed by parallel attachment of the Faraday element to another substructure in the model, from elastoviscous solid to viscoelastic fluid materials.

Table 1. Tabular comparative overview of a new class of complex rheological models of the fractional type of ideal materials with piezoelectric properties.

	Solid Elastoviscous fractional-type material with piezoelectric properties	Fluid Viscoelastic fractional-type material with piezoelectric properties
Rheological basic complex models of the fractional type with piezoelectric properties	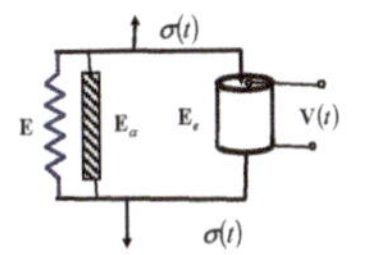 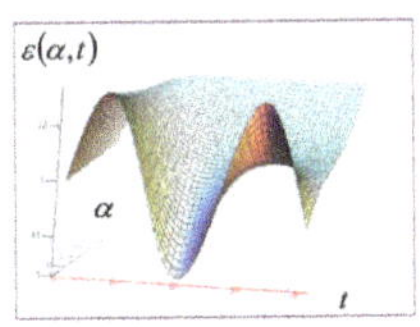 $\mathbf{K}_\alpha = (\mathbf{H}/\mathbf{N}_\alpha)$ FY Faraday $\mathbf{K}_\alpha/\mathbf{F}Y = (\mathbf{H}/\mathbf{N}_\alpha)/\mathbf{F}Y$ Kelvin–Voigt–Faraday model	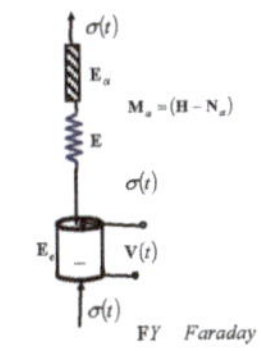 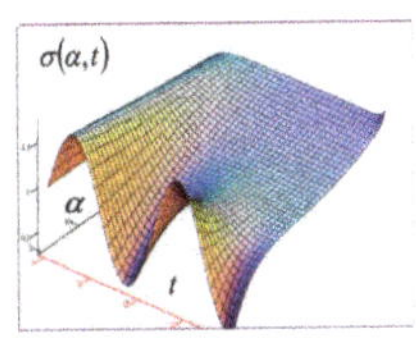 $\mathbf{M}_\alpha = (\mathbf{H} - \mathbf{N}_\alpha)$ FY Faraday $\mathbf{M}_\alpha - \mathbf{F}Y = (\mathbf{H} - \mathbf{N}_\alpha) - \mathbf{F}Y$ Maxwell–Faraday model
Two rheological complex models of the fractional type with piezoelectric properties	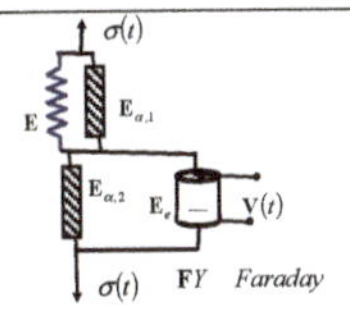 FY Faraday $\mathbf{L}_\alpha = \mathbf{H}/\mathbf{N}_\alpha - \mathbf{N}_\alpha$ $\mathbf{L}_\alpha/\mathbf{F}Y = \mathbf{H}/\mathbf{N}_\alpha - \mathbf{N}_\alpha/\mathbf{F}Y$ Lethersich–Faraday-F model	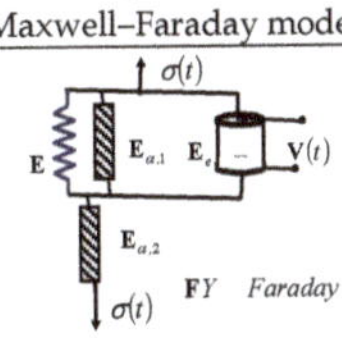 FY Faraday $\mathbf{L}_\alpha = \mathbf{H}/\mathbf{N}_\alpha - \mathbf{N}_\alpha$ $\mathbf{L}_\alpha/\mathbf{F}Y = \mathbf{H}/\mathbf{N}_\alpha/\mathbf{F}Y - \mathbf{N}_\alpha$ Lethersich–Faraday model

Table 1. *Cont.*

Two rheological complex models of the fractional type with piezoelectric properties	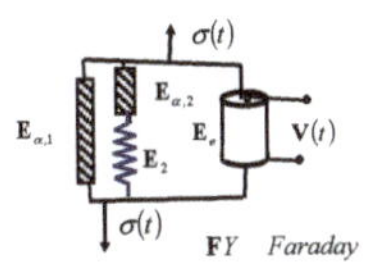 FY Faraday $\mathbf{J}_\alpha/\mathbf{F}Y = \mathbf{N}_{\alpha,1}/(\mathbf{H} - \mathbf{N}_{\alpha,2})/\mathbf{F}Y$ Jeffrey–Faraday-F model	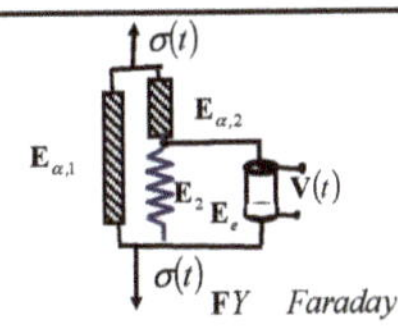 FY Faraday $\mathbf{J}_\alpha/\mathbf{F}Y = \mathbf{N}_{\alpha,1}/(\mathbf{H}/\mathbf{F}Y - \mathbf{N}_{\alpha,2})$ Jeffrey–Faraday model
Two rheological complex models of the fractional type with piezoelectric properties	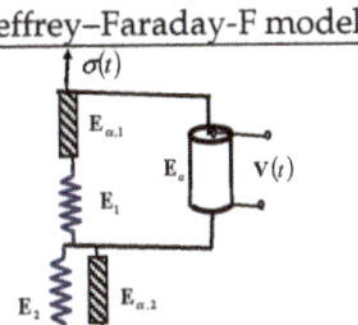 FY Faraday $\mathbf{B}_{u,\alpha} - \mathbf{M}_\alpha/\mathbf{F}Y = \mathbf{K}_\alpha - \mathbf{M}_\alpha/\mathbf{F}Y$ $\mathbf{B}_{u,\alpha-} - \mathbf{M}_\alpha/\mathbf{F}Y = (\mathbf{H}/\mathbf{N}_\alpha) - (\mathbf{H} - \mathbf{N}_\alpha)/$ Burgers–Faraday-F model	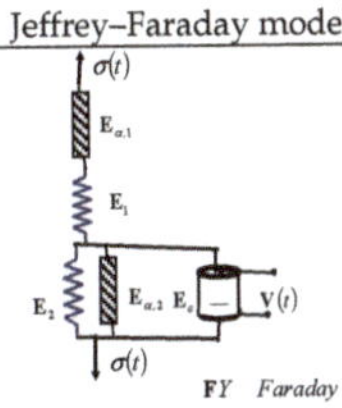 FY Faraday $\mathbf{B}_{Bu,\alpha}/\mathbf{F}Y = \mathbf{K}/\mathbf{F}Y - M_\alpha$ $\mathbf{B}_{Bu,\alpha}\mathbf{K}/\mathbf{F}Y = (\mathbf{H}/\mathbf{N}_\alpha/\mathbf{F}Y) - (\mathbf{H} - \mathbf{N}_\alpha$ Burgers–Faraday model

The letter "F" denotes the second rheological complex fractional-type model with piezoelectric properties, in which the Faraday element is connected in parallel with the second substructure, and thus the model, which was a viscoelastic fluid material, became an elastoviscous solid material, as can be seen in the second column of Table 1.

7. Concluding Considerations

For each rheological model from the newly introduced class of rheological complex fractional-type material models with piezoelectric polarization properties, whose dynamics we have studied and presented in the previous sections, we can introduce the assumption that these are standard light models, which are of negligible mass, but with the properties of possessing potential energy and polarization during mechanical deformations and dissipating mechanical energy due to the fractional-type axial dilatation rate. Then, we can use these standard light rheological models of the fractional type with piezoelectric properties as models of rigid body binding in rheological discrete dynamic systems and consider the dynamics of newly created rheological discrete dynamic systems, which will be explained in more detail in the following works (see References [1–3]).

Rheological complex models of elastoviscous and viscoelastic fractional-type materials with polarized piezoelectric properties of various substances are of interest due to the widespread use of viscoelastic–plastic bodies under loading.

In this paper, new standard light complex rheological models of ideal fractional-type materials with piezoelectric properties are obtained by parallel or serial binding of basic complex rheological fractional-type models with rheological ideal elastic Faraday elements with piezoelectric properties.

The rheological Faraday element, which is an ideal elastic element and has ideal piezoelectric properties, is a rheological element with a coupled mechanical and electric field, and has the properties of polarization when it is deformed in the area of elastic deformation under the external action of load.

In this paper, we presented a large number of completely new scientific results about rheological complex material models and gave important ideas and theoretical foundations for further research into the properties of these rheological discrete dynamic systems of the fractional order with piezoelectric properties.

In addition, we have opened a wide field for further research into the properties of rheological discrete dynamic systems with many degrees of freedom of movement, both discrete and continuous systems of the fractional type and with coupled mechanical and piezoelectric fields. We have laid the fundamental foundations and presented ideas for those studies.

In the end, we can emphasize that all structural formulas of rheological complex models of substances are assembled analogously, like those in chemistry or those of complex electric circuits. Analogies, written by the founder of the Serbian School of Mathematics, Mihailo Pćetrović, one of the three doctoral students of well-known French scientist Julius Henri Poicare in References [67–71], enabled the transfer of acquired knowledge from one scientific field to another.

A new direction of research into the dynamics of the newly introduced class of rheological models of fractional-type materials with piezoelectric properties in non-isothermal conditions has been suggested. This is a very important direction of research for future projects.

In this work, we used analytical methods and analytical approaches, but researchers have access to new modern numerical methods and commercial software that can be used to study the dynamics of rheological discrete dynamic systems with a finite number of degrees. These can be used to solve systems of differential equations of the fractional order, including those with nonlinearities, and to study the phenomena of nonlinear rheological oscillations of the fractional type with piezoelectric properties, or nonlinear rheological creepers of the fractional type with piezoelectric properties.

The manuscript presents the differential constitutive relations of the fractional type for each of the new rheological complex models of materials of the fractional type with piezoelectric properties. Both of them present a mathematical description and represent the validation of each of the models. Validation can also be experimental, and the author is convinced that the theoretical results presented in the paper will inspire experimenters to experimentally validate the theoretical results.

At the end, the paper presents the basic principles of connecting rheological elements into basic complex and more complex material models. It is shown that rheological models can be connected in parallel and in series. It is also shown by decomposition of basic complex models that differential constitutive relations of the fractional order can be composed using the sum of component normal stresses for parallel-connected elements or the sum of axial dilatations for regularly connected elements. These two approaches can be used to construct more complex hybrid rheological material models.

Funding: This research received no external funding.

Data Availability Statement: The original contributions presented in this study are included in the article. Further inquiries can be directed to the corresponding author.

Acknowledgments: The author would like to thank the reviewers and the Assistant Editor for their useful comments and suggestions that improved the quality of the manuscript.

Conflicts of Interest: The author declares no conflicts of interest.

References

1. Hedrih, R.K. *Izabrana Poglavlja Teorije Elastičnosti (Selected Chapters of Theory of Elasticity)*; Prošireno i Dopunjeno izdanje; Mašinski Fakultet u Nišu: Niš, Serbia, 1988; p. 425. Available online: http://elibrary.matf.bg.ac.rs/handle/123456789/3766?show=full (accessed on 5 December 2024).
2. Hedrih, K.S.; Machado, J.T. Discrete fractional order system vibrations. *Int. J. Non-Linear Mech.* **2015**, *73*, 2–11. [CrossRef]
3. Hedrih, K.R.; Hedrih, A.N. The Kelvin–Voigt visco-elastic model involving a fractional-order time derivative for modelling torsional oscillations of a complex discrete biodynamical system. *Acta Mech.* **2023**, *234*, 1923–1942. [CrossRef]
4. Hedrih, K.R.; Milovanovic, G.V. Elements of mathematical phenomenology and analogies of electrical and mechanical oscillators of the fractional type with finite number of degrees of freedom of oscillations: Linear and nonlinear modes. *Commun. Anal. Mech.* **2024**, *16*, 738–785. [CrossRef]
5. Hedrih, K.R.; Hedrih, A.N. Rheological Burgers–Faraday Models and Rheological Dynamical Systems with Fractional Derivatives and Their Application in Biomechanics. *Fractal Fract.* **2024**, *8*, 742. [CrossRef]
6. Zorica, D.M.; Cveticanin, S.M. Dissipative and generative fractional RLC circuits in the transient regime. *Appl. Math. Comput.* **2023**, *459*, 128227. [CrossRef]
7. Jelic, S.Z.; Zorica, D.M. Energy balance for fractional anti-Zener and Zener models in terms of relaxation modulus and creep compliance. *Appl. Math. Model.* **2023**, *123*, 688–728. [CrossRef]
8. Zorica, D.; Oparnica, L. Energy dissipation for hereditary and energy conservation for non-local fractional wave equations. *Philos. Trans. R. Soc. A-Math. Phys. Eng. Sci.* **2020**, *378*, 20190295. [CrossRef] [PubMed]
9. Zorica, D.M.; Atanackovic, T.M.; Vrcelj, Z.; Novakovic, B. Dynamic Stability of Axially Loaded Nonlocal Rod on Generalized Pasternak Foundation. *J. Eng. Mech.* **2017**, *143*, D4016003. [CrossRef]
10. Rabotnov, Y.N. *Creep Problems in Structural Members*; Series in Applied Mathematics and Mechanics; North-Holland Publishing: Amsterdam, The Netherlands, 1969.
11. Escalante-Martínez, J.E.; Gómez-Aguilar, J.F.; Calderón-Ramón, C.; Morales-Mendoza, L.J.; Cruz-Orduna, I.; Laguna-Camacho, J.R. Experimental evaluation of viscous damping coefficient in the fractional underdamped oscillator. *Adv. Mech. Eng.* **2016**, *8*, 1687814016643068. [CrossRef]
12. Gómez-Aguilar, J.F.; Yépez-Martínez, H.; Calderón-Ramón, C.; Cruz-Orduña, I.; Escobar-Jiménez, R.F.; Olivares-Peregrino, V.H. Modeling of a mass-spring-damper system by fractional derivatives with and without a singular kernel. *Entropy* **2015**, *17*, 6289–6303. [CrossRef]
13. Gómez-Aguilar, J.F. Analytic solutions and numerical simulations of mass-spring and damperspring systems described by fractional differential equations. *Rom. J. Phys.* **2015**, *60*, 311–323.
14. Gómez-Aguilar, J.F.; Rosales, J.J.; Bernal, J.J. Mathematical modelling of the massspring-damper system—A fractional calculus approach. *Acta Univ.* **2012**, *22*, 5–11. [CrossRef]
15. Gómez-Aguilar, J.F.; Rosales-García, J.J.; Bernal-Alvarado, J.J.; Córdova-Fraga, T.; Guzmán-Cabrera, R. Fractional mechanical oscillators. *Rev. Mex. FCA* **2012**, *58*, 348–352.
16. Miličić, I.M.; Vlajić, L.M. Models of Civil Engineering–Classification and Definition, Conference Paper, Conference DQM-2006, Belgrade. Available online: https://www.researchgate.net/publication/289098053/ (accessed on 5 December 2024).
17. Tomović, Z. Reološki model puzanja matriksa meke stijene (Rheologica model od of soft rocks of creep). *Mater. I Konstr.* **2007**, *50*, 3–19.
18. Oldham, K.B.; Spanier, J. *The Fractional Calculus*; Academic Press: New York, NY, USA, 1974.

19. Ross, B. A brief history and exposition of the fundamental theory of fractional calculus. In *Fractional Calculus and Its Applications: Proceedings of the International Conference Held at the University of New Haven, June 1974*; Springer: Berlin/Heidelberg, Germany, 2006; pp. 1–36. [CrossRef]
20. Miller, K.S.; Ross, B. *An Introduction to the Fractional Calculus and Fractional Differential Equations*; Wiley: New York, NY, USA, 1993.
21. Letnikov, A.V. Theory of differentiation with an arbitrary index. *Mat. Sb.* **1868**, *3*, 1–66.
22. Letnikov, A.V. An explanation of the concepts of the theory of differentiation of arbitrary index. *Mat. Sb.* **1872**, *6*, 413–445.
23. Samko, S.G.; Kilbas, A.A.; Marichev, O.I. *Fractional Integrals and Derivatives–Theory and Applications*; Gordon and Breach Science Publishers: Amsterdam, The Netherlands, 1993.
24. Das, S. *Functional Fractional Calculus*; Springer: Berlin/Heidelberg, Germany, 2011. [CrossRef]
25. Debnath, L. A brief historical introduction to fractional calculus. *Int. J. Math. Educ. Sci. Technol.* **2004**, *35*, 487–501. [CrossRef]
26. Machado, J.T.; Kiryakova, V.; Mainardi, F. Recent history of fractional calculus. *Commun. Nonlinear Sci. Numer. Simulat.* **2011**, *16*, 1140–1153. [CrossRef]
27. Kilbas, A.A.; Srivastava, H.M.; Trujillo, J.J. *Theory and Applications of Fractional Differential Equations*; Elsevier: Amsterdam, The Netherlands, 2006.
28. Mainardi, F. *Fractional Calculus and Waves in Linear Viscoelasticity. An Introduction to Mathematical Models*; Imperial College Press: London, UK, 2010. [CrossRef]
29. Podlubny, I. *Fractional Differential Equations*; Academic Press: New York, NY, USA, 1999.
30. Kiryakova, V. A brief story about the operators of generalized fractional calculus. *Fract. Calc. Appl. Anal.* **2008**, *11*, 203–220.
31. Herrmann, R. *Fractional Calculus—An Introduction for Physicists*; World Scientific: Singapore, 2014. [CrossRef]
32. Kiryakova, V. *Generalized Fractional Calculus and Applications*; Pitman Research Notes I Mathematics Series, 301; Longman Scientific & Technical: Harlow, UK, 1994.
33. Diethelm, K. *The Analysis of Fractional Differential Equations*; Springer: Berlin/Heidelberg, Germany, 2010. [CrossRef]
34. Sandev, T.; Tomovski, Ž. *Fractional Equations and Models. Theory and Applications*; Springer: Cham, Switzerland, 2019. [CrossRef]
35. Li, C.; Zeng, F. *Numerical Methods for Fractional Calculus*; CRC Press: Boca Raton, FL, USA, 2015. [CrossRef]
36. Baleanu, D.; Diethelm, K.; Scalas, E.; Trujillo, J.J. *Fractional Calculus: Models and Numerical Methods*; World Scientific: Singapore, 2012.
37. Wolfram, S. *The Mathematica Book*; Wolfram Media, Inc.: Champaign, IL, USA, 2003.
38. Esmaeili, S.; Shamsi, M.; Luchko, Y. Numerical solution of fractional differential equations with a collocation method based on M¨untz polynomials. *Comput. Math. Appl.* **2011**, *62*, 918–929. [CrossRef]
39. Atanacković, T.; Pilipović, S.; Stanković, B.; Zorica, D. *Fractional Calculus with Applications in Mechanics: Vibrations and Diffusion Processes*; Wiley-ISTE: London, UK, 2014.
40. Atanacković, T.; Pilipović, S.; Stanković, B.; Zorica, D. *Fractional Calculus with Applications in Mechanics: Wave Propagation, Impact and Variational Principles*; Wiley-ISTE: London, UK, 2014.
41. Garrappa, R.; Popolizio, M. Evaluation of generalized Mittag-Leffler functions on the real line. *Adv. Comput. Math.* **2013**, *39*, 205–225. [CrossRef]
42. Gorenflo, R.; Loutchko, J.; Luchko, Y. Computation of the Mittag-Leffler function and its derivatives. *Fract. Calc. Appl. Anal.* **2002**, *5*, 491–518.
43. Luo, M.J.; Milovanovi´c, G.V.; Agarwal, P. Some results on the extended beta and extended hypergeometric functions. *Appl. Math. Comput.* **2014**, *248*, 631–651. [CrossRef]
44. Mitrinović, D.S.; Djoković, D.Ž. *Special Functions (Specijalne Funkcije)*; Gradjevinska Knjiga: Beograd, Serbia, 1964; p. 267.
45. Novati, P. Numerical approximation to the fractional derivative operator. *Numer. Math.* **2014**, *127*, 539–566. [CrossRef]
46. Milovanovic, G.V.; Rathie, A.K. On a quadratic transformation due to Exton and its generalization. *Hacet. J. Math. Stat.* **2019**, *48*, 1706–1711. [CrossRef]
47. Milovanović, G.V.; Rathie, A.K.; Vasović, N.M. Summation identities for the Kummer confluent hypergeometric function 1F1(a; b; z). *Kuwait J. Sci.* **2023**, *50*, 190–193. [CrossRef]
48. Perić, L. Spregnuti Tenzori Stanja Piezoeletričnih Materijala (Coupled Tensors of the Piesoelectric Material States). Ph.D. Thesis, Faculty of Mechanical Engineering in Niš, Niš, Serbia, 2005. (In Serbian)
49. Hedrih, K.S.; Babović, V.; Šarković, D. An auxi liary size distribution model for the ultrasonically produced water droplets. In *Experimental Thermal and Fluid Science–ETF*; Elsevier: Amsterdam, The Netherlands, 2006; Volume 30, pp. 559–564. [CrossRef]
50. Thomas, J.M. *Michael Faraday and The Royal Institution: The Genius of Man and Place (PBK)*; CRC Press: Boca Raton, FL, USA, 1991; ISBN 978-0-7503-0145-9.
51. Thompson, S. *Michael Faraday, His Life and Work*; Cassell and Company: London, UK, 1901; ISBN 978-1-4179-7036-0.
52. Đurić, M. *Teorija Spregnutih i Prethodno Napregnutih Konstrukcija, SANU, (Theory of Coupled and Prestressed Construction)*; Serbian Academy of Science and Arts, Bool (SANU): Beograd, Serbia, 1963.
53. Mihailović, V.; Landović, A. *The Relation Properties of Concrete and Their Characteristic in Rheological Models*; ZBORNIK RADOVA 19; Univerzitet u Novom Sadu, GraČevinski Fakultet Subotici: Subotica, Serbia, 2010.

54. Stoiljkoic, D.T. Rheological modeling of yarn elongation. *Tekstil* **2007**, *56*, 554–561.
55. Stoiljkoic, D.T. Dinamicko Ponasanje Sistema Mehanizam–Radni Objekat Tkackog Procesa. Ph.D. Thesis, Masinski Fakultet u Nišu, Niš, Serbia, 1992.
56. Yang, X.-J. New rheological problems involving general fractional Derivatives with nonsingular power-law kernels. *Proc. Rom. Acad. Ser. A* **2018**, *19*, 45–52.
57. Yang, X.; Chen, W.; Xiao, R.; Ling, L. A Fractional Model for Time-Variant Non-Newtonian Flow. *Therm. Sci.* **2017**, *21*, 61–68. [CrossRef]
58. Verdier, C. Review: "Rheological properties of living materials. From cells to tissues". *J. Theor. Med.* **2003**, *5*, 67–91.
59. Bonfanti, A.; Fouchard, J.; Khalilgharibi, N.; Charras, G.; Kabla, A. A unified rheological model for cells and cellularised materials. *R. Soc. Open Sci.* **2020**, *7*, 190920. [CrossRef] [PubMed]
60. Dabiri, D.; Saadat, M.; Mangal, D.; Jamali, S. Fractional rheology-informed neural networks for data-driven identification of viscoelastic constitutive models. *Rheol. Acta* **2023**, *62*, 557–568. [CrossRef]
61. Fabrizio, M. Fractional rheological models for thermomechanical systems. Dissipation and free energies. *Fract. Calc.* **2014**, *17*, 206–223. [CrossRef]
62. Goroško, O.A.; Hedrih, K. *Analitička Dinamika (Mehanika) Diskretnih Naslednih Sistema, (Analytical Dynamics (Mechanics) of Discrete Hereditary Systems)*; University of Niš: Niš, Serbia, 2001; p. 426, ISBN 86-7181-054-2. (In Serbian)
63. Hedrih, K.R. *Generalized Function of Fractional Order Dissipation of System Energy and Extended LAGRANGE Differential Lagrange Equation in Matrix Form*; Dedicated to 86th Anniversary of Radu MIRON'S Birth; Kawaguchi Institute of Mathematics Society: Kawaguchi, Japan, 2014; Volume 75, pp. 35–51.
64. Bačlić, B.S.; Atanacković, T.M. Stability and creep of a fractional derivative order viscoelastic Rod. In *Bulletin T, CXXI de L'Academie Serbe des Sciences st de Arts-2000*; Class des Sciences Mathematques et Naturelles Sciences Mathematiques; L'Academie Serbe des Sciences st de Arts: Belgrade, Serbia, 2000; pp. 115–131.
65. Rašković, D. *Teorija Oscilacija (Theory of Oscillatins)*, 2nd ed.; Naućna Knjiga: Beograd, Serbia, 1965. Available online: http://elibrary.matf.bg.ac.rs/handle/123456789/4754 (accessed on 5 December 2024).
66. Rašković, D. Analitička Mehanika (Analytical Mechanics), Mašinski Fakultet Kragujevac. 1974. Available online: http://elibrary.matf.bg.ac.rs/handle/123456789/3778 (accessed on 5 December 2024).
67. Rašković, D. *Teorija Elastičnosti (Theory of Elasticity)*; Naućna knjiga: Beograd, Serbia, 1985; Preface and Index Notation: Hedrih (Stevanović) K.R. Available online: http://elibrary.matf.bg.ac.rs/handle/123456789/37656 (accessed on 5 December 2024).
68. Petrović, M. *Elements of Mathematical Phenomenology*; Serbian Royal Academy: Belgrade, Serbia, 1911.
69. Petrović, M. *Mecanismes Communs Aux Phenomenes Disparames, Nouvelle Collection Scientifique*; F ́elix Alcan: Paris, France, 1921.
70. Petrović, M. *Phenomenological Mapping*; Serbian Royal Academy: Belgrade, Serbia, 1933.
71. Pilipović, S.; Milovanović, G.; Mijajlovič, Ž.; Ćosović, T.; Stepanović, N.; Ivanović, T.R.; Radovanov, Ž.; Seleši, D. *Mihailo Petrović Alas: Life, Work, Times–On the Occasion of the 150th Anniversary of his Birth*; Serbian Academy of Sciences and Arts: Belgrade, Serbia, 2019.

fractal and fractional

MDPI

Article

Rheological Burgers–Faraday Models and Rheological Dynamical Systems with Fractional Derivatives and Their Application in Biomechanics

Katica R. (Stevanović) Hedrih [1,2,*] and Andjelka N. Hedrih [1]

[1] Department of Mechanics, Mathematical Institute of Serbian Academy of Science and Arts, 11000 Belgrade, Serbia
[2] Faculty of Mechanical Engineering, University of Niš, 18000 Nis, Serbia
* Correspondence: khedrih@sbb.rs or katicah@mi.sanu.ac.rs

Abstract: Two rheological Burgers–Faraday models and rheological dynamical systems were created by using two new rheological models: Kelvin–Voigt–Faraday fractional-type model and Maxwell–Faraday fractional-type model. The Burgers–Faraday models described in the paper are new models that examine the dynamical behavior of materials with coupled fields: mechanical stress and strain and the electric field of polarization through the Faraday element. The analysis of the constitutive relation of the fractional order for Burgers–Faraday models is given. Two Burgers–Faraday fractional-type dynamical systems were created under certain approximations. Both rheological Burgers-Faraday dynamic systems have two internal degrees of freedom, which are introduced into the system by each standard light Burgers-Faraday bonding element. It is shown that the sequence of bonding elements in the structure of the standard light Burgers-Faraday bonding element changes the dynamic properties of the rheological dynamic system, so that in one case the system behaves as a fractional-type oscillator, while in the other case, it exhibits a creeping or pulsating behavior under the influence of an external periodic force. These models of rheological dynamic systems can be used to model new natural and synthetic biomaterials that possess both viscoelastic/viscoplastic and piezoelectric properties and have dynamical properties of stress relaxation.

Keywords: rheological models of fractional type with piezo-electrical properties; viscous fluid; Burgers–Faraday fractional-type model; rheological Burgers–Faraday dynamical system; oscillator of fractional type with piezoelectric properties; creeper of fractional type with piezoelectric properties; stress relaxation; inner degree of freedom; biomaterials

1. Introduction

Numerous natural and synthetic materials exhibit viscoelastic/viscoplastic properties and those with purely piezoelectric properties. However, materials that possess both properties exhibit the most intriguing dynamic. Modeling such complex behavior is a real challenge.

The stress problems of piezoceramic plates were studied in [1–4]. Additionally, rheological models exist for various materials [5], including construction materials [6,7], textiles [8], living materials [9–11], and thermomechanical systems [12]. Among the most commonly used models for representing the viscoelastic and viscoplastic properties of materials are the Maxwell and Kelvin–Voigt models, often enhanced with fractional calculus, as well as the Zener model (also known as the Standard Linear Solid (SLS) model) [13]. Materials exhibiting both viscoelastic/viscoplastic and piezoelectric properties include elastomers, certain types of polymers and some composites [14,15], metals at high temperatures and biomaterials. It is known for a long time that hard tissues of living organisms can generate electrical potentials in response to mechanical stress- or any stress deforming their structure [16]. Biological materials with such properties include bones [17,18] tendons, cartilage, hairs, silk, paper, natural polymers such as cellulose, fibroin, keratin, collagen, DNA, RNA, myosin, as well as artificial polymers like acetylcellulose, polycaprolactane and polymethyl-l-glutamate. Bones, for instance, exhibit stress-induced electrical effects in both bending and compression modes. These piezoelectric properties of the bones were first studied decades ago [19]. At that time, it was hypothesized that surface charges on stressed bone may be the controlling factor in bone formation which was proven in other studies [20–23]. Fractional order derivatives have been widely used in modeling the dynamical responses of various structures [24,25]. For example, fractional Maxwell models have been used to describe small strains in porcine urinary bladders during initial stages [26]. For multi-step relaxation under large strains, a fractional-type quasi-linear viscoelastic model combining a Scott–Blair relaxation function and an exponential instantaneous stress response was used [26]; a class of return mapping algorithms for fractional-type visco-elasto-plasticity was developed by using canonical combinations of Scott–Blair elements to construct a series of well-known fractional linear viscoelastic models, such as Kelvin–Voigt, Maxwell, Kelvin–Zener, and Poynting–Thomson [27]. Other applications include modeling relaxation and creep properties in materials such as fractal ladders and [28] for bio-thermomechanical problems in functionally graded anisotropic nonlinear viscoelastic soft tissues [29].

For studying thermo-mechanical interactions in living tissues during hyperthermia treatment by using fractional time derivatives and Laplace transform techniques to the generalized bio-thermo-elastic model and eigenvalue approach [30]. For 3D printed material with creep properties fractional models have also been utilized [31]. A novel AEF–Zener model of viscoelastic dampers incorporating temperature effects and the fractional-order equivalence principle was proposed in [13]. Fractional-order iterative methods were used to model the viscoelasticity and stiffening effects of dielectric elastomer considering both the strain-stiffening and viscoelasticity effects within electromechanical coupling in dielectric elastomer [32]. Recently, Xu et al. [33] proposed a high-accuracy unique fractional-order model that can capture hysteresis and creep nonlinear characteristics such as piezoelectric lag, non-local memory, peak transition, and creep amplitude–frequency features in piezoelectric actuators. A comprehensive and unified theory of analytical dynamics for discrete hereditary systems is presented in [34], along with experimental methods to determine the kernel of rheology for various hereditary properties of rheological materials. Furthermore, a generalized fractional-type dissipation function for system energy and an extended Lagrangian differential equation in matrix form for fractional-type discrete dynamical systems are introduced in [24,35].

Finally, an important question posed in [36] remains highly relevant: "Does a Fractal Microstructure Require a Fractional Viscoelastic Model?" [36].

The aim of this work is to create new rheological models using fractional order derivatives that can be used to model the behavior of biomaterial with piezo-electrical and viscoelastic properties by integrating the Maxwell or Kelvin–Voigt element both with fractional-type properties with the Faraday element. In the era of synthesizing new materials for modern industry and robotics, materials with such properties will be increasingly synthesized and used, so it is necessary to understand their mechanical and electrical properties as well as the coupled fields and interactions of these future materials. In the following chapters, we will first describe the simpler Kelvin–Voigt–Faraday fractional-type model and its behavior in a special case, followed by the Maxwell–Faraday fractional-type model and its behavior in a special case, and then the two complex Burgers–Faraday models as well as Burgers-Faraday dynamic systems composed of the corresponding types of Burgers–Faraday models. We will also examine the dynamics of these dynamic systems depending on the order of the element connections in the system. A current trend in science is to create complex materials alongside their mathematical and mechanical models which can describe their complex behavior that depends on coupled fields. In this paper, we will present new models that can address this problem.

2. Methodology

2.1. Complex Faraday Fractional-Type Models

In this section, two complex rheological Burgers–Faraday fractional-type models are presented, and their differential constitutive relation of fractional order as well as the dynamics of both models for some special cases.

By connecting a Faraday element, which represents a material with ideal elastic and piezoelectric properties, in parallel with a Kelvin–Voigt fractional-type element, we obtain the Kelvin–Voigt–Faraday fractional-type model (KVFYF). If the Faraday element is connected to a series with the Maxwell fractional-type model, we obtain the Maxwell–Faraday fractional-type model (MFYF), as shown in Figure 1.

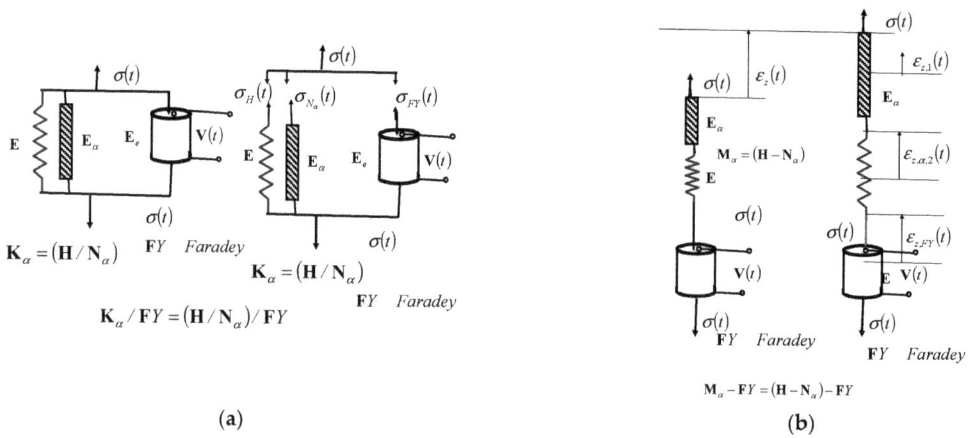

Figure 1. (**a**) Kelvin–Voigt–Faraday fractional-type model. (**b**) Maxwell–Faraday fractional-type model. H—Hook ideally elastic element. N—Newton ideally viscous fluid (fractional derivative is introduced in this element to describe viscoelastic nature of the material). FY—Faraday element with ideally elastic and piezoelectric properties. K—Kelvin–Voigt element. M—Maxwell element.

2.1.1. The Dynamical Properties of the Kelvin–Voigt–Faraday Fractional-Type Model

Kelvin–Voigt–Faraday fractional-type model represents a rheological model of the solids. The Kelvin–Voigt fractional-type model is connected in parallel with the Faraday model. In the Kelvin–Voigt fractional-type model Hook element is represented by the ideally elastic spring and the Newton element is presented as an ideally viscous fluid where a fractional order derivative is introduced to describe the viscoelastic nature of the material. Figure 1a represents a fictive cross-section of the model with component normal stresses of each consecutive element in parallel in the model.

The resultant normal stress at the end of the Kelvin–Voigt–Faraday fractional-type model is as follows:

$$\sigma_z = \sigma_{z,} + \sigma_{z.\alpha,2} + \sigma_{z,12} = \mathbf{E}\varepsilon_z + \mathbf{E}_\alpha \mathrm{D}_t^\alpha[\varepsilon_z] + \mathbf{E}_e\varepsilon_z,\ 0 < \alpha \le 1 \tag{1}$$

where $\sigma_{z,1} = \mathbf{E}\varepsilon_z$ is the normal stress in the Hook element; $\sigma_{z,\alpha.2} = \mathbf{E}_\alpha \mathrm{D}_t^\alpha[\varepsilon_z]$ is the normal stress in the Newton ideally viscous fluid with fractional type properties; $\sigma_{z,12} = \mathbf{E}_e\varepsilon_z$ is the normal stress in the Faraday element, $\mathrm{D}_t^\alpha[\bullet]$ is a differential operator of Caputo type, as shown in Equation (2).

$$\mathrm{D}_t^\alpha[\varepsilon_z(t)] = \frac{d^\alpha \varepsilon_z(t)}{dt^\alpha} = {\varepsilon_z}^{(\alpha)}(t) = \frac{1}{\Gamma(1-\alpha)}\frac{d}{dt}\int_0^t \frac{\varepsilon_z(\tau)}{(t-\tau)^\alpha}d\tau,\ for\ 0 < \alpha \le 1 \tag{2}$$

where $\Gamma(x)$ is Gamma function as follows:

$$\Gamma(x) = \int_0^{+\infty} e^{-t} t^{x-1} dt,\ x > 0\, \Gamma(x+1) = x\Gamma(x),\ x > 0 \quad (3)$$

where α is determined experimentally. When exponent α of the fractional order differentiation is $\alpha = 0$, the application of the fractional order derivative gives the time function $\varepsilon_z(t)$ which represents dilatation.

When $\alpha = 1$, the application of the fractional order derivative gives the first derivative of $\varepsilon_z(t)$ time function. These properties of the differential operator $D_t^\alpha[\bullet]$ of the fractional order, when its fractional exponent α takes values as rational numbers within an interval $0 < \alpha < 1$, including its boundary values, allow us to define both integer-order derivatives and fractional-order derivatives with a single expression. This provides a useful mathematical description in various applications.

Equation (1) represents a differential constitutive fractional-type relation that connect normal stress σ_z and axial dilatation ε_z, and axial dilatation rate $D_t^\alpha[\varepsilon_z]$ in the Kelvin–Voigt–Faraday fractional-type model and can be rewritten as follows:

$$\varepsilon_z + \frac{\mathbf{E}_\alpha}{\mathbf{E}+\mathbf{E}_e} D_t^\alpha[\varepsilon_z] = \frac{\sigma_z(t)}{\mathbf{E}+\mathbf{E}_e} \quad (4)$$

The electric voltage in the Faraday element that is generated as a result of polarization closed by mechanical loading in the Faraday element.

$$\mathbf{V}_z(t) = -g\sigma_z(t) \quad (5)$$

Dielectric displacement in Faraday element is in linear relation with normal stress and axial dilatation: $D_z(t) = b\sigma_z(t)$ and $D_z(t) = e\varepsilon_z(t)$.

2.1.2. The Dynamical Behavior of the Kelvin–Voigt–Faraday Fractional-Type Model in a Special Case

We will study the behavior of the Kelvin–Voigt–Faraday fractional-type model in the special case when the model is in the steady state or under very slow change in the dynamical load. Then, the axial dilatation rate of the fractional-type tends to be zero $D_t^\alpha[\varepsilon_z] \to 0$ and the material behaves as a basic ideally elastic material, and the normal stress of the material is almost proportional to the axial dilatation $\sigma_{z\backslash} \to \mathbf{E}\varepsilon_z$. In that case Equation (1) becomes

$$\sigma_{z\backslash} \to \mathbf{E}\varepsilon_z + \mathbf{E}_e\varepsilon_z \quad (6)$$

If the normal stress σ_z at the end of the Kelvin–Voigt–Faraday fractional-type model suddenly increases from zero to some finite value $\sigma_{z,0} = const$, and remains constant during the subsequent time interval, than $\mathbf{E}\varepsilon_z + \mathbf{E}_e\varepsilon_z + \mathbf{E}_\alpha D_t^\alpha[\varepsilon_z] = \sigma_{z,0} = const$.

In that case to solve/define axial dilatation $\varepsilon_z(t)$ as a time function in the Kelvin–Voigt–Faraday fractional-type model we applied Laplace transform on $\mathbf{E}\varepsilon_z + \mathbf{E}_e\varepsilon_z + \mathbf{E}_\alpha D_t^\alpha[\varepsilon_z] = \sigma_{z,0} = const$, and obtained the following:

$$(\mathbf{E}+\mathbf{E}_e)\mathrm{L}\{\varepsilon_z\} + \mathbf{E}_\alpha \mathrm{L}\{D_t^\alpha[\varepsilon_z]\} = \mathrm{L}\{\sigma_{z,0}\} \quad (7)$$

As $\mathrm{L}\{1\} = \frac{1}{p}, \mathrm{L}\left\{\frac{d^\alpha x}{dt^\alpha}\right\} = p^\alpha \mathrm{L}\{x\} - \left.\frac{d^{\alpha-1}x}{dt^{\alpha-1}}\right|_{t=0} = p^\alpha \mathrm{L}\{x\}$, and, $\left.\frac{d^{\alpha-1}x}{dt^{\alpha-1}}\right|_{t=0} = 0$,

It follows:

$$\mathrm{L}\{\varepsilon_z\} = \frac{\sigma_{z,0}}{p}\frac{1}{\langle(\mathbf{E}+\mathbf{E}_e) + \mathbf{E}_\alpha p^\alpha\rangle} \quad (8)$$

The axial dilatation $\varepsilon_z(t)$ of the Kelvin–Voigt–Faraday fractional-type model (KVFYF) as a time function is then inverse Laplace transform of algebra Equation (8):

$$\varepsilon_z(t) = \mathrm{L}^{-1}\mathrm{L}\{\varepsilon_z\} = \mathrm{L}^{-1}\left\{\frac{\sigma_{z,0}}{(\mathbf{E}+\mathbf{E}_e)} \cdot \frac{1}{p} \cdot \frac{1}{\left\langle 1+\frac{\mathbf{E}_\alpha}{(\mathbf{E}+\mathbf{E}_e)}p^\alpha \right\rangle}\right\} \tag{9}$$

To find the time domain of the inverse Laplace transform of algebra Equation (8) which represents an approximatively analytical expression for axial dilatation of KVFYF as a time function, it is necessary to expand expression $\frac{\sigma_{z,0}}{(\mathbf{E}+\mathbf{E}_e)} \cdot \frac{1}{p} \cdot \frac{1}{\left\langle 1+\frac{\mathbf{E}_\alpha}{(\mathbf{E}+\mathbf{E}_e)}p^\alpha \right\rangle}$ into a series in powers of p, which is a complex number, using the formula for approximate series expansion (see Ref. [35]):

$$\varepsilon_z(t) = \mathrm{L}^{-1}\mathrm{L}\{\varepsilon_z\} = \frac{\sigma_{z,0}}{(\mathbf{E}+\mathbf{E}_e)} \cdot \cdot \mathrm{L}^{-1}\left\{\frac{1}{p} \cdot \left\langle 1+\sum_{k=1}^{\propto}(-1)^k\left(\frac{\mathbf{E}_\alpha}{(\mathbf{E}+\mathbf{E}_e)}\right)^k p^{k\alpha-1}\right\rangle\right\} \tag{10}$$

As

$$\frac{\sigma_{z,0}}{(\mathbf{E}+\mathbf{E}_e)} \cdot \frac{1}{p} \cdot \frac{1}{\left\langle 1+\frac{\mathbf{E}_\alpha}{(\mathbf{E}+\mathbf{E}_e)}p^\alpha \right\rangle} = \frac{\sigma_{z,0}}{(\mathbf{E}+\mathbf{E}_e)} \cdot \frac{1}{p} \cdot \left\langle 1+\sum_{k=1}^{\propto}(-1)^k\left(\frac{\mathbf{E}_\alpha}{(\mathbf{E}+\mathbf{E}_e)}p^\alpha\right)^k\right\rangle \tag{11}$$

The inverse Laplace transform of expression (10) is as follows:

$$\varepsilon_z(t) = \mathrm{L}^{-1}\mathrm{L}\{\varepsilon_z\} = \frac{\sigma_{z,0}}{(\mathbf{E}+\mathbf{E}_e)} \cdot \left\langle 1+\sum_{k=1}^{\propto}(-1)^k\left(\frac{\mathbf{E}_\alpha}{(\mathbf{E}+\mathbf{E}_e)}\right)^k \frac{t^{(2-\alpha)k+1}}{\Gamma(2k+2-\alpha k)}\right\rangle \tag{12}$$

and is related to axial dilatation in time

Dielectric displacement D, $D_z(t) = b\sigma_z(t)$ and $D_z(t) = e\varepsilon_z(t)$, for the special case of constant normal stress $\sigma_z = \sigma_{z,0} = const$, in Faraday-element is:

$$D_z(t) = e\varepsilon_z(t) = e\frac{\sigma_{z,0}}{(\mathbf{E}+\mathbf{E}_e)} \cdot \cdot \left\langle 1+\sum_{k=1}^{\propto}(-1)^k\left(\frac{\mathbf{E}_\alpha}{(\mathbf{E}+\mathbf{E}_e)}\right)^k \frac{t^{(2-\alpha)k+1}}{\Gamma(2k+2-\alpha k)}\right\rangle \tag{13}$$

In the case of constant normal stress $\sigma_z = \sigma_{z,0} = const$ the Kelvin–Voigt–Faraday fractional-type model exhibits the property of delayed elasticity, where axial dilatation lags behind the stress (Figure 2a).

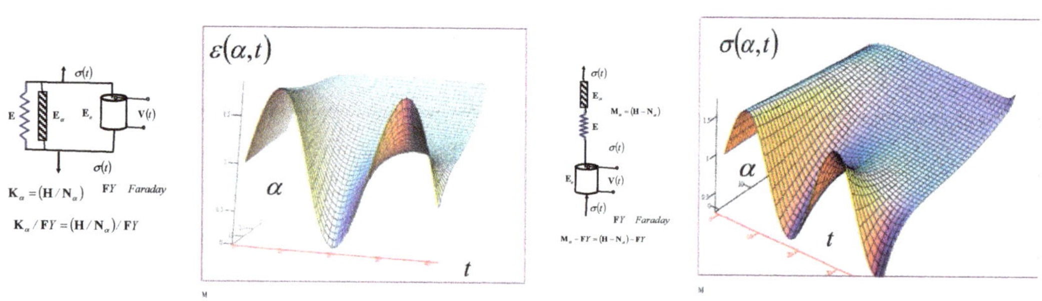

(a) (b)

Figure 2. (**a**) The surface of the delayed elasticity of the Kelvin–Voigt–Faraday fractional-type model, (**b**) the surface of normal stress relaxation in the Maxwell–Faraday fractional-type model. Both models exhibit a piezoelectric property.

If we apply the Laplace transform to differential Equation (4) of the fractional order we obtain the following:

$$L\{\varepsilon_z\} = \frac{L\{\sigma_z(t)\}}{(\mathbf{E}+\mathbf{E}_e)} \cdot \frac{1}{1+\frac{\mathbf{E}_\alpha}{\mathbf{E}+\mathbf{E}_e}p^\varepsilon} \tag{14}$$

Expression (14) is an algebra equation, and represents the product of two Laplace transforms: one Laplace transform of the normal stress $L\{\sigma_z(t)\}$ and the other in the form of $L\{f(t)\} = \frac{1}{1+\frac{\mathbf{E}_\alpha}{\mathbf{E}+\mathbf{E}_e}p^\varepsilon}$, from which it is concluded that these two functions are also in convolution with the axial dilatation function $\varepsilon_z(t)$, which leads to the following:

$$L\{\varepsilon_z(t)\} = \frac{L\{\sigma_z(t)\}}{(\mathbf{E}+\mathbf{E}_e)} \cdot \frac{1}{1+\frac{\mathbf{E}_\alpha}{\mathbf{E}+\mathbf{E}_e}p^\varepsilon} = \frac{L\{\sigma_z(t)\}}{(\mathbf{E}+\mathbf{E}_e)} \cdot L\{f(t)\} \tag{15}$$

As $\frac{\mathbf{E}_\alpha}{\mathbf{E}+\mathbf{E}_e}p^\varepsilon << 1$, the expression $\frac{1}{1+\frac{\mathbf{E}_\alpha}{\mathbf{E}+\mathbf{E}_e}p^\varepsilon}$ can be expand into a series (see Ref. [35]) and written as follows:

$$\frac{1}{1+\dfrac{\mathbf{E}_\alpha}{\mathbf{E}+\mathbf{E}_e}p^\varepsilon} \approx \left\langle 1+1\sum_{k=1}^{\infty}(-1)^k\left(\frac{\mathbf{E}_\alpha}{(\mathbf{E}+\mathbf{E}_e)}\right)^k p^{k\alpha}\right\rangle \tag{16}$$

Inverse Laplace transform of (16) is as follows:

$$L^{-1}\left\{\frac{1}{1+\dfrac{\mathbf{E}_\alpha}{\mathbf{E}+\mathbf{E}_e}p^\varepsilon}\right\} \approx L^{-1}\left\{1+\sum_{k=1}^{\infty}(-1)^k\left(\frac{\mathbf{E}_\alpha}{(\mathbf{E}+\mathbf{E}_e)}\right)^k p^{k\alpha}\right\} = \sum_{k=0}^{\infty}(-1)^k\left(\frac{\mathbf{E}_\alpha}{\mathbf{E}+\mathbf{E}_e}\right)^k \frac{t^{(2-\alpha)k}}{\Gamma(2k+1-\alpha k)} \tag{17}$$

Based on the convolution of these three functions, and for which the following holds:

$$L\{\varepsilon_z(t)\} = \frac{L\{\sigma_z(t)\}}{(\mathbf{E}+\mathbf{E}_e)} \cdot \frac{1}{1+\frac{\mathbf{E}_\alpha}{\mathbf{E}+\mathbf{E}_e}p^\varepsilon} = \frac{L\{\sigma_z(t)\}}{(\mathbf{E}+\mathbf{E}_e)} \cdot L\{f(t)\} \tag{18}$$

Convolution integral has a following form:

$$\varepsilon_z(t) \approx \frac{1}{(\mathbf{E}+\mathbf{E}_e)}\int_0^t \sigma_z(t-\tau)\left\langle\sum_{k=0}^{\infty}(-1)^k\left(\frac{\mathbf{E}_\alpha}{\mathbf{E}+\mathbf{E}_e}\right)^k \frac{\tau^{(2-\alpha)k}}{\Gamma(2k+1-\alpha k)}\right\rangle d\tau \tag{19}$$

Expression (19) is a constitutive equation related to axial dilatation and normal stress in the Kelvin–Voigt–Faraday fractional-type model.

Electric voltage in Faraday element in the Kelvin–Voigt–Faraday fractional-type model is in the following form:

$$\mathbf{V}_z(t) = -g\sigma_z(t) \approx -\frac{g}{(\mathbf{E}+\mathbf{E}_e)}\int_0^t \sigma_z(t-\tau)\left\langle\sum_{k=0}^{\infty}(-1)^k\left(\frac{\mathbf{E}_\alpha}{\mathbf{E}+\mathbf{E}_e}\right)^k \frac{\tau^{(2-\alpha)k}}{\Gamma(2k+1-\alpha k)}\right\rangle d\tau \tag{20}$$

2.1.3. The Dynamical Properties of the Maxwell–Faraday Fractional-Type Model

The Maxwell–Faraday fractional-type model with structural formula $\mathbf{M}_\alpha - \mathbf{F}Y = (\mathbf{H} - \mathbf{N}_\alpha) - \mathbf{F}Y$ consist of the Newton viscous fractional-type element, the Hooke ideal elastic element, the Faraday ideally elastic, and the piezoelectric element all connected in series (Figure 1b). This Maxwell–Faraday fractional-type model properties are that the axial dilatation ratio of fractional type $D_t^\alpha[\varepsilon_z]$ thought all the model is equal to sum of the axial dilatation ratio of each element $D_t^\alpha[\varepsilon_{z,1}]$ (Newton viscous fractional type element), $D_t^\alpha[\varepsilon_{z,2}]$ (Hooke ideal elastic element) and $D_t^\alpha[\varepsilon_{z,e}]$ (Faraday ideally elastic and piezoelectric element) in series.

Resultant axial dilatation velocity of the Maxwell–Faraday fractional-type model is equal to the following:

$$\mathrm{D}_t^{\alpha}[\varepsilon_z] = \mathrm{D}_t^{\alpha}[\varepsilon_{z,1}] + \mathrm{D}_t^{\alpha}[\varepsilon_{z,2}] + \mathrm{D}_t^{\alpha}[\varepsilon_{z,e}] \tag{21}$$

Or in the the following form:

$$\mathrm{D}_t^{\alpha}[\varepsilon_z] = \frac{1}{\mathbf{E}}\mathrm{D}_t^{\alpha}[\sigma_z] + \frac{\sigma_z}{\mathbf{E}_\alpha} + \frac{1}{\mathbf{E}_e}\mathrm{D}_t^{\alpha}[\sigma_z] \tag{22}$$

Expression (22) represents an inhomogeneous ordinary differential constitutive relation of the fractional order of the Maxwell–Faraday fractional-type model. The following relation is valid:

$$\left(\frac{1}{\mathbf{E}} + \frac{1}{\mathbf{E}_e}\right)\mathrm{D}_t^{\alpha}[\sigma_z(t)] + \frac{\sigma_z(t)}{\mathbf{E}_\alpha} = \{\mathrm{D}_t^{\alpha}[\varepsilon_z]\} \neq const \tag{23}$$

2.1.4. The Dynamical Behavior of the Maxwell–Faraday Fractional-Type Model in Special Case

For the special case when $\mathrm{D}_t^{\alpha}[\sigma_z] \to 0$ normal stress is proportional to the dilatation ratio of fractional type:

$$\mathrm{D}_t^{\alpha}[\sigma_z] \to 0 \Rightarrow \sigma_z \to \mathbf{E}_\alpha \mathrm{D}_t^{\alpha}[\varepsilon_z] \tag{24}$$

The material described by the Maxwell–Faraday fractional-type model behaves as a viscoelastic fluid: deformation/axial dilatation increases unlimitedly. Upon unloading of material, axial deformation exists only in the Newton viscous fractional-type element.

If this material is suddenly loaded to a certain value of normal stress, it undergoes elastic deformation, $\varepsilon_{z,0} = \frac{\sigma_{z,0}}{\mathbf{E}+\mathbf{E}_e}$ which occurs instantaneously in the Hooke ideally elastic element and the Faraday ideal elastic piezoelectric element. Due to the sudden loading, the flow in the serially connected Newton viscous element of fractional type does not come into effect at the initial moment of observation.

If we prevent the development of deformation/axial dilatation, assuming that the rate of axial dilatation, of fractional type, tends to be zero $\mathrm{D}_t^{\alpha}[\varepsilon_z] \to 0$, then, the normal stress becomes a function of time, which needs to be determined.

To express the normal stress as a time function using approximate analytical expressions when the axial dilatation ratio of the fractional type is constant $\left\{\mathrm{D}_t^{\alpha}[\varepsilon_z]_{z,,0}\right\} = const$ Laplace transform on expression (23 is performed and then the inverse Laplace using the same procedure that is described previously for finding the approximate analytical expressions for normal stress as a time function in the Kelvin–Voigt–Faraday fractional-type model. The approximate analytical expression for normal stress as a time function in the Maxwell–Faraday fractional-type model for the case when axial dilatation ratio of the fractional type is constant $\left\{\mathrm{D}_t^{\alpha}[\varepsilon_z]_{z,,0}\right\} = const$, is in the following form:

$$\sigma_z(t) = \mathrm{L}^{-1}\mathrm{L}\{\sigma_z\} \approx \mathbf{E}_\alpha\left\{\mathrm{D}_t^{\alpha}[\varepsilon_z]_{z,,0}\right\} \cdot \left\{1 + \sum_{k=1}^{\infty}(-1)^k\left(\frac{\mathbf{E}_\alpha}{\mathbf{E}_e} + \frac{\mathbf{E}_\alpha}{\mathbf{E}}p\right)^k \frac{t^{(2-\alpha)k+1}}{\Gamma(2k+2-\alpha k)}\right\} \tag{25}$$

The electrical voltage that is induced by stress and polarization in the Faraday element in Maxwell–Faraday fractional-type model is as follows:

$$\mathbf{V}_z(t) = -g\sigma_z(t) \approx -g\mathbf{E}_\alpha\left\{\mathrm{D}_t^{\alpha}[\varepsilon_z]_{z,,0}\right\} \cdot \left\{1 + \sum_{k=1}^{\infty}(-1)^k\left(\frac{\mathbf{E}_\alpha}{\mathbf{E}_e} + \frac{\mathbf{E}_\alpha}{\mathbf{E}}p\right)^k \frac{t^{(2-\alpha)k+1}}{\Gamma(2k+2-\alpha k)}\right\} \tag{26}$$

Dielectric displacement is as follows:

$$D_z(t) = b\sigma_z(t) \approx b\mathbf{E}_\alpha\left\{\mathrm{D}_t^{\alpha}[\varepsilon_z]_{z,,0}\right\} \cdot \left\{1 + \sum_{k=1}^{\infty}(-1)^k\left(\frac{\mathbf{E}_\alpha}{\mathbf{E}_e} + \frac{\mathbf{E}_\alpha}{\mathbf{E}}p\right)^k \frac{t^{(2-\alpha)k+1}}{\Gamma(2k+2-\alpha k)}\right\} \tag{27}$$

2.1.5. The Maxwell–Faraday Fractional-Type Model Material Properties

Expression (25) indicates the material properties of normal stress relaxation. In this model, normal stress relaxation is reflected in the decrease in normal stress over time, when the axial strain remains constant over time. The surface of normal stress relaxation for the Maxwell–Faraday fractional-type model is presented in Figure 2b. The studied material, based on a Maxwell–Faraday fractional-type model is a viscoelastic fluid with piezoelectric properties. This model can be used to describe the properties of metals at very high temperatures, while also exhibiting piezoelectric characteristics.

Differential constitutive relation of fractional order (23) can be solved by applying the Laplace transform and then, by expanding into a series by the powers of the complex parameter we obtain the following:

$$\frac{p^{\alpha}}{\left\langle 1+\left(\frac{\mathbf{E}_{\alpha}}{\mathbf{E}_{e}}+\frac{\mathbf{E}_{\alpha}}{\mathbf{E}}\right)p^{\alpha}\right\rangle}=p^{\alpha}\frac{1}{\left\langle 1+\left(\frac{\mathbf{E}_{\alpha}}{\mathbf{E}_{e}}+\frac{\mathbf{E}_{\alpha}}{\mathbf{E}}\right)p^{\alpha}\right\rangle}\approx p^{\alpha}\cdot\left\langle 1+\sum_{k=1}^{\propto}(-1)^{k}\left(\frac{\mathbf{E}_{\alpha}}{\mathbf{E}_{e}}+\frac{\mathbf{E}_{\alpha}}{\mathbf{E}}\right)^{k}p^{k\alpha}\right\rangle \tag{28}$$

Using the property of three functions that are in convolution, as well as the relationships of their Laplace transforms and the convolution integral, in a similar way as it was described for the Kelvin–Voigt–Faraday fractional-type model we can obtain a constitutive integral equation of the Maxwell–Faraday fractional-type model in the form of integral of convolution:

$$\sigma_{z}(t)=\mathbf{E}_{\alpha}\int_{0}^{t}\varepsilon_{z}(t-\tau)\left\langle \mathrm{L}^{-1}\left\{p^{\alpha}+\sum_{k=1}^{\propto}(-1)^{k}\left(\frac{\mathbf{E}_{\alpha}}{\mathbf{E}_{e}}+\frac{\mathbf{E}_{\alpha}}{\mathbf{E}}\right)^{k}p^{(k+1)\alpha}\right\}\right\rangle_{t=\tau}d\tau \tag{29}$$

3. Complex Burgers–Faraday Fractional-Type Models

In this section, we describe complex Burgers–Faraday fractional-type models and their dynamical behavior. The schematic of the Burgers fractional-type model (Figure 3a) and Burgers–Faraday fractional-type models are shown in Figure 3b,c. The Burgers–Faraday fractional-type model presented in Figure 3b is obtained by introducing the Faraday element in parallel connection with the Kelvin–Voigt fractional type element of the Burgers fractional-type model. The Burgers–Faraday fractional-type model presented in Figure 3c is obtained by introducing the Faraday element in parallel connection with the Maxwell fractional-type element of the Burgers fractional-type model. The Burgers fractional-type model (Figure 3a) represents a series of connections between a Maxwell fractional-type element and the Kelvin–Voigt fractional-type element.

3.1. *Burgers–Faraday Fractional-Type Model–Viscous Elastic Fluid with Piezoelectric Properties (BFYF CF Model)*

The constitutive relation for the Burgers–Faraday fractional-type model (BFYF CF model) is as follows:

$$\dot{\varepsilon}_{z,Bu}=\dot{\varepsilon}_{z,M}+\dot{\varepsilon}_{z,K}+\dot{\varepsilon}_{z,FY}=\frac{\dot{\sigma}_{z,M}}{\mathbf{E}_{M}}+\frac{\sigma_{z,M}}{\mathbf{E}_{\alpha=1,M}}+\dot{\varepsilon}_{z,K}+\dot{\varepsilon}_{z,FY} \tag{30}$$

$$\dot{\varepsilon}_{z,Bu}=\dot{\varepsilon}_{z,M}+\dot{\varepsilon}_{z,K}+\dot{\varepsilon}_{z,FY}=\frac{\dot{\sigma}_{z,M}}{\mathbf{E}_{M}}+\frac{\sigma_{z,M}}{\mathbf{E}_{\alpha=1,M}}+\dot{\varepsilon}_{z,K}+\dot{\varepsilon}_{z,FY},\ \ddot{\varepsilon}_{z,Bu}=\frac{\ddot{\sigma}_{z,M}}{\mathbf{E}_{M}}+\frac{\dot{\sigma}_{z,M}}{\mathbf{E}_{\alpha=1,M}}+\ddot{\varepsilon}_{z,K1}+\ddot{\varepsilon}_{z,FY} \tag{31}$$

$$\sigma_{z,K1}=\mathbf{E}_{K}\varepsilon_{z,K}+\mathbf{E}_{\alpha=1,K}\dot{\varepsilon}_{z,K}+\mathbf{E}_{e}\varepsilon_{z,K}\ \ \mathbf{E}_{K}$$

$$\ddot{\varepsilon}_{z,Bu}=\frac{\ddot{\sigma}_{z,M}}{\mathbf{E}_{M}}+\frac{\dot{\sigma}_{z,M}}{\mathbf{E}_{\alpha=1,M}}+\ddot{\varepsilon}_{z,K1}+\ddot{\varepsilon}_{z,FY}\ \mathbf{E}_{\alpha=1,M} \tag{32}$$

$$\dot{\sigma}_{z,K}=(\mathbf{E}_{K}+\mathbf{E}_{e})\dot{\varepsilon}_{1z,K}+\mathbf{E}_{\alpha=1,K}\ddot{\varepsilon}_{z,K}$$

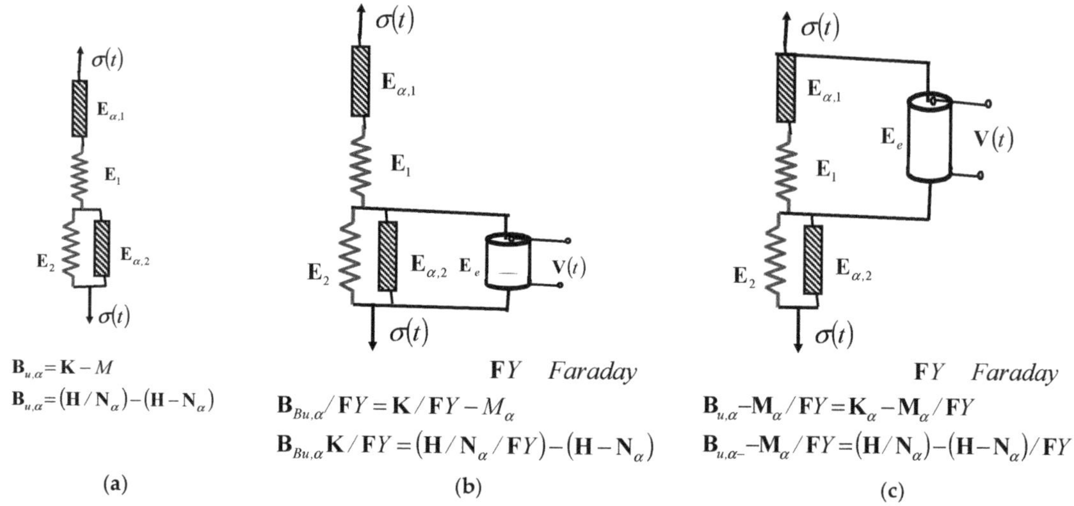

Figure 3. (**a**) Burgers fractional-type model. (**b**) Burgers–Faraday fractional-type model—viscous fluid with piezoelectric properties (BFYF VF model) (**c**) Burgers–Faraday fractional-type model—viscoelastic solid with piezoelectric properties (BFYF VES model). H- Hook ideally elastic element. N—Newton ideally viscous fluid (fractional derivative is introduced in this element to describe viscous nature and fractional-type dissipation energy of the material). FY—Faraday element with ideally elastic and piezoelectric properties. K—Kelvin–Voigt fractional-type element. M-Maxwell fractional-type element. B—Burgers fractional-type element.

The relationship between normal stress and axial strain in BFYF VF classic model is as follows:

$$\ddot{\sigma}_{z,Bu}+\dot{\sigma}_{z,Bu}\left(\frac{\mathbf{E}_K+\mathbf{E}_e}{\mathbf{E}_{\alpha=1,M}}+\frac{\mathbf{E}_M}{\mathbf{E}_{\alpha=1,K}}+\frac{\mathbf{E}_M}{\mathbf{E}_{\alpha=1,M}}\right)+\sigma_{z,Bu}\frac{\mathbf{E}_M}{\mathbf{E}_{\alpha=1,M}}\frac{\mathbf{E}_K+\mathbf{E}_e}{\mathbf{E}_{\alpha=1,K}}=\frac{\mathbf{E}_K+\mathbf{E}_e\mathbf{E}_M}{\mathbf{E}_{\alpha=1,K}}\dot{\varepsilon}_{z,Bu}+\mathbf{E}_M\,\dddot{\varepsilon}_{z,Bu} \tag{33}$$

For the analogy of the details of the mathematical description and the derivation of the differential constitutive equation, see Reference [37].

The constitutive relations of the BFYF VF model contains time derivatives of fractional order as well as higher-order derivatives. The total axial strain in the $\mathbf{B}_{u,\alpha}FY$ CF model is equal to the sum of the component axial strains $\varepsilon_{z,M}$ and $\varepsilon_{z,K}$ of its constituent elements: the Maxwell fractional-type element and the Kelvin–Voigt–Faraday fractional-type element $\varepsilon_{z,Bu}=\varepsilon_{z,M}+\varepsilon_{z,K}$, while the normal stress is the same across all cross-sections of the model's components $\sigma_{z,K1}=\sigma_{z,M}=\sigma_{z,Bu}$. Based on this analysis and the derived conclusions, we can write the following relations:

$$\mathrm{D}_t^\alpha[\varepsilon_{z,Bu}]=\mathrm{D}_t^\alpha[\varepsilon_{z,M}]+\mathrm{D}_t^\alpha[\varepsilon_{z,K}] \tag{34}$$

$$\sigma_{z,K1}=(\mathbf{E}_K+\mathbf{E}_e)\varepsilon_{z,K}+\mathbf{E}_{\alpha=1,K}\mathrm{D}_t^\alpha[\varepsilon_{z,K}] \tag{35}$$

$$\mathrm{D}_t^\alpha[\varepsilon_{z,M}]=\frac{\mathrm{D}_t^\alpha[\sigma_{z,M}]}{\mathbf{E}_M}+\frac{\sigma_{z,M}}{\mathbf{E}_{\alpha=1,M}} \tag{36}$$

After differentiating (34) according to $\mathrm{D}_t^\alpha[\varepsilon_{z,K}]$ from (35) and substitution of terms from (36) constitutive relation of the BFYF VF model is in the following form:

$$\mathrm{D}_t^\alpha[\varepsilon_{z,Bu}]=\mathrm{D}_t^\alpha[\varepsilon_{z,M}]+\mathrm{D}_t^\alpha[\varepsilon_{z,K}]=\frac{\mathrm{D}_t^\alpha[\sigma_{z,M}]}{\mathbf{E}_M}+\frac{\sigma_{z,M}}{\mathbf{E}_{\alpha=1,M}}+\mathrm{D}_t^\alpha[\varepsilon_{z,K}] \tag{37}$$

Or

$$\frac{D_t^\alpha[\sigma_{z,M}]}{\mathbf{E}_M} + \frac{\sigma_{z,M}}{\mathbf{E}_{\alpha=1,M}} = D_t^\alpha[\varepsilon_{z,Bu}] - D_t^\alpha[\varepsilon_{z,K}] \tag{38}$$

$$\sigma_{z,K1} = (\mathbf{E}_K + \mathbf{E}_e)\varepsilon_{z,K} + \mathbf{E}_{\alpha=1,K}D_t^\alpha[\varepsilon_{z,K}] = \sigma_{z,M} = \sigma_{z,Bu} \tag{39}$$

As relation $\sigma_{z,K1} = \sigma_{z,M} = \sigma_{z,bu}$ is valid for each part of the BFYF VF model Equations (38) and (39) can be rewritten in the following form:

$$\frac{D_t^\alpha[\sigma_{z,Bu}]}{\mathbf{E}_M} + \frac{\sigma_{z,Bu}}{\mathbf{E}_{\alpha=1,M}} = D_t^\alpha[\varepsilon_{z,Bu}] - D_t^\alpha[\varepsilon_{z,K}] \tag{40}$$

$$\sigma_{z,Bu} = (\mathbf{E}_K + \mathbf{E}_e)\varepsilon_{z,K} + \mathbf{E}_{\alpha=1,K}D_t^\alpha[\varepsilon_{z,K}] \tag{41}$$

These last two Relations (40) and (41) between normal stress $\sigma_{z,Bu}$ and axial strain $\varepsilon_{z,Bu}$, and their corresponding fractional-order derivatives, are coupled differential constitutive relations of fractional order for the BFYF VF model. Under certain conditions, the model exhibits properties of delayed elasticity and/or normal stress relaxation. From this system of fractional-order differential constitutive Relations (40) and (41), we can eliminate the axial strain rate, fractional order, and obtain a single relation linking normal stress and axial strain in this complex rheological structure by transitioning to the domain of the Laplace transform in the following form:

$$L\{D_t^\alpha[\sigma_{z,Bu}]\} + \frac{\mathbf{E}_M}{\mathbf{E}_{\alpha=1,M}}L\{\sigma_{z,Bu}\} = \mathbf{E}_M L\{D_t^\alpha[\varepsilon_{z,Bu}]\} - \mathbf{E}_M L\{D_t^\alpha[\varepsilon_{z,K}]\} \tag{42}$$

$$L\{\sigma_{z,Bu}\} = (\mathbf{E}_K + \mathbf{E}_e)L\{\varepsilon_{z,K}\} + L\{D_t^\alpha[\varepsilon_{z,K}]\} \tag{43}$$

or

$$L\{\sigma_{z,Bu}\}\left\langle p^\alpha + \frac{\mathbf{E}_M}{\mathbf{E}_{\alpha=1,M}}\right\rangle = \mathbf{E}_M\, p^\alpha \langle L\{\varepsilon_{z,Bu}\} - L\{\varepsilon_{z,K}\}\rangle \tag{44}$$

$$L\{\varepsilon_{z,K}\} = \frac{1}{((\mathbf{E}_K + \mathbf{E}_e) + p^\alpha)}L\{\sigma_{z,Bu}\} \tag{45}$$

After substituting (45) in (44) we obtain the following:

$$L\{\sigma_{z,Bu}\}\left\langle p^\alpha + \frac{\mathbf{E}_M}{\mathbf{E}_{\alpha=1,M}}\right\rangle = \mathbf{E}_M\, p^\alpha \left\langle L\{\varepsilon_{z,Bu}\} - \frac{1}{((\mathbf{E}_K + \mathbf{E}_e) + p^\alpha)}L\{\sigma_{z,Bu}\}\right\rangle \tag{46}$$

At the end we obtain the Laplace transform of the normal stress as a function of the Laplace transform of the axial strain for the complex rheological structure of the BFYF VF model in the following form:

$$L\{\sigma_{z,Bu}\} = \mathbf{E}_M\, L\{\varepsilon_{z,Bu}\}\, \frac{((\mathbf{E}_K + \mathbf{E}_e) + p^\alpha)p^\alpha}{\mathbf{E}_M\left\langle \left(\frac{(\mathbf{E}_K+\mathbf{E}_e)+p^\alpha}{\mathbf{E}_M}\right)p^\alpha + p^\alpha + \frac{(\mathbf{E}_K+\mathbf{E}_e)+p^\alpha}{\mathbf{E}_{\alpha=1,M}}\right\rangle} \tag{47}$$

Now, by applying the inverse Laplace transform to Equation (47), it is possible to obtain the time function of normal stress from the axial strain of the complex rheological structure of the BFYF VF model using the convolution integral. However, the problem of determining the inverse Laplace transform remains unsolved for now.

3.2. The Burgers–Faraday Fractional-Type Model—Elastoviscous Solid with Piezoelectric Properties (BFYS VES Model)

The BFYF VES model presented in Figure 3c consists of a Maxwell–Faraday fractional-type element (a Maxwell fractional-type element connected in parallel with a Faraday element) connected in a series with a Kelvin–Voigt fractional-type element. The stress and strain will be analyzed in elements of the BFYF VES model and the end in the whole BFYF VES model.

The total stress in the Maxwell–Faraday fractional-type element $D_t^\alpha[\sigma_{z,M,F}]$ which is a substructure of the complex BFYF VES model is as follows:

$$D_t^\alpha[\sigma_{z,M,F}] = D_t^\alpha[\sigma_{z,M}] + D_t^\alpha[\sigma_{z,F}] = D_t^\alpha[\sigma_{z,M}] + \frac{\mathbf{E}_e}{\mathbf{E}_{H,M}} D_t^\alpha[\sigma_{z,M}] + \frac{\mathbf{E}_e}{\mathbf{E}_{\alpha\backslash,M}} \sigma_{z,M}$$

$$D_t^\alpha[\sigma_{z,M,F}] = \left(1 + \frac{\mathbf{E}_e}{\mathbf{E}_{H,M}}\right) D_t^\alpha[\sigma_{z,M}] + \frac{\mathbf{E}_e}{\mathbf{E}_{\alpha\backslash,M}} \sigma_{z,M} \quad (48)$$

If we apply the Laplace transform to the previous fractional-order constitutive Relation (48), we obtain the following:

$$L\{\sigma_{z,M,F}\} = \left(1 + \frac{\mathbf{E}_e}{\mathbf{E}_{H,M}} + \frac{\mathbf{E}_e}{\mathbf{E}_{\alpha\backslash,M} p^\alpha}\right) L\{\sigma_{z,M}\} \quad (49)$$

Considering the components of the BFYF VES model, the system of constitutive relations of fractional order of the complete BFYF VES model is in the following form:

$$D_t^\alpha\left[\varepsilon_{z,Bugam,F}\right] = D_t^\alpha[\varepsilon_{z,M,F}] + D_t^\alpha[\varepsilon_{z,K}] \quad (50)$$

$$D_t^\alpha\left[\sigma_{z,Birgan,,F}\right] = D_t^\alpha[\sigma_{z,M,F}] = \left(1 + \frac{\mathbf{E}_e}{\mathbf{E}_{H,M}}\right) D_t^\alpha[\sigma_{z,M}] + \frac{\mathbf{E}_e}{\mathbf{E}_{\alpha\backslash,M}} \sigma_{z,M} \quad (51)$$

$$D_t^\alpha\left[\sigma_{z,Birgan,,F}\right] = D_t^\alpha[\sigma_{z,K1}] = \mathbf{E}_K D_t^\alpha[\varepsilon_{z,K}] + \mathbf{E}_{\alpha,K} D_t^\alpha[D_t^\alpha[\varepsilon_{z,K}]] \quad (52)$$

$$\sigma_{z,F} = \mathbf{E}_e \varepsilon_{z,F} \quad (53)$$

$$\mathbf{V}_{z,F}(t) = -g\sigma_{z,F}(t) \quad (54)$$

$$D_z(t) = b\sigma_{z,F}(t) \text{ и } D_z(t) = e\varepsilon_{z,F}(t) \quad (55)$$

These fractional-order constitutive relations provide the connections between axial strain $\varepsilon_{z,Bugam,F}$ and normal stress $\sigma_{z,Birgan,,F}$ in the complex rheological BFYF VES model, as well as the normal stresses and axial strains in the substructures of the fractional-type Kelvin–Voigt model and the fractional-type Maxwell-Faraday model.

By applying the Laplace transform to the previous two fractional-order constitutive Relations (51) and (52), we obtain the following relations:

$$L\left\{\sigma_{z,Birgan,,F}\right\} = L\{\sigma_{z,M,F}\} = \left(1 + \frac{\mathbf{E}_e}{\mathbf{E}_{H,M}} + \frac{\mathbf{E}_e}{\mathbf{E}_{\alpha\backslash,M} p^\alpha}\right) L\{\sigma_{z,M}\} \quad (56)$$

$$L\left\{\sigma_{z,Birgan,,F}\right\} = L\{\sigma_{z,K1}\} = (\mathbf{E}_K + \mathbf{E}_{\alpha,K} p^\alpha) L\{\varepsilon_{z,K}\} \quad (57)$$

$$L\left\{\varepsilon_{z,Birgan,,F}\right\} = L\{\varepsilon_{z,M,F}\} + L\{\varepsilon_{z,K}\} \quad (58)$$

These previous fractional-order constitutive Relations (56) and (57) provide the connections between the Laplace transforms $L\left\{\sigma_{z,Birgan,,F}\right\}$ of the normal stress $\sigma_{z,Birgan,,F}$ and the Laplace transforms $L\left\{\varepsilon_{z,Birgan,,F}\right\}$ of the axial strain $\varepsilon_{z,Birgan,,F}$ in the complex rheological BFYF VES model, as well as the axial strains $L\{\varepsilon_{z,M,F}\}$ and normal stresses in the substructures of the fractional-type Kelvin–Voigt model $L\{\sigma_{z,K1}\}$ and the fractional-type Maxwell-Faraday model $L\{\sigma_{z,M,F}\}$.

4. Two Rheological Burgers–Faraday Discrete Dynamical Systems of Fractional Type-One Oscillator BFY VES DS and the Other Creeper BFY CF DS Both with Piezoelectric Properties

In this section of the paper, we define two new types of rheological discrete dynamic systems of fractional type and piezoelectric properties, which we have named rheological Burgers–Faraday discrete dynamic systems of fractional type. We introduce the concepts of standard light complex binding elements, and the concept of standard light complex rheological binding elements: the Burgers–Faraday–BFY VES DS and Burgers–Faraday– BFY CF DS standard light binding models. In this part, we will define the rheological Burgers–Faraday discrete dynamic systems consisting of a single material point (rigid body) that moves rectilinearly translatory on a smooth horizontal surface and is connected by one of the standard light rheological Burgers–Faraday (BFY VES DS or BFY CF DS) models to a fixed wall. Such rheological discrete dynamic systems have one external and two internal degrees of freedom. We will study the dynamics of two such rheological Burgers–Faraday discrete dynamic systems: one type is a fractional rheological oscillator with piezoelectric properties (Figure 4), and the other is a creeper of fractional type with piezoelectric properties (Figure 5), each in two variations in the sequence of element connections in the Burgers–Faraday binding models.

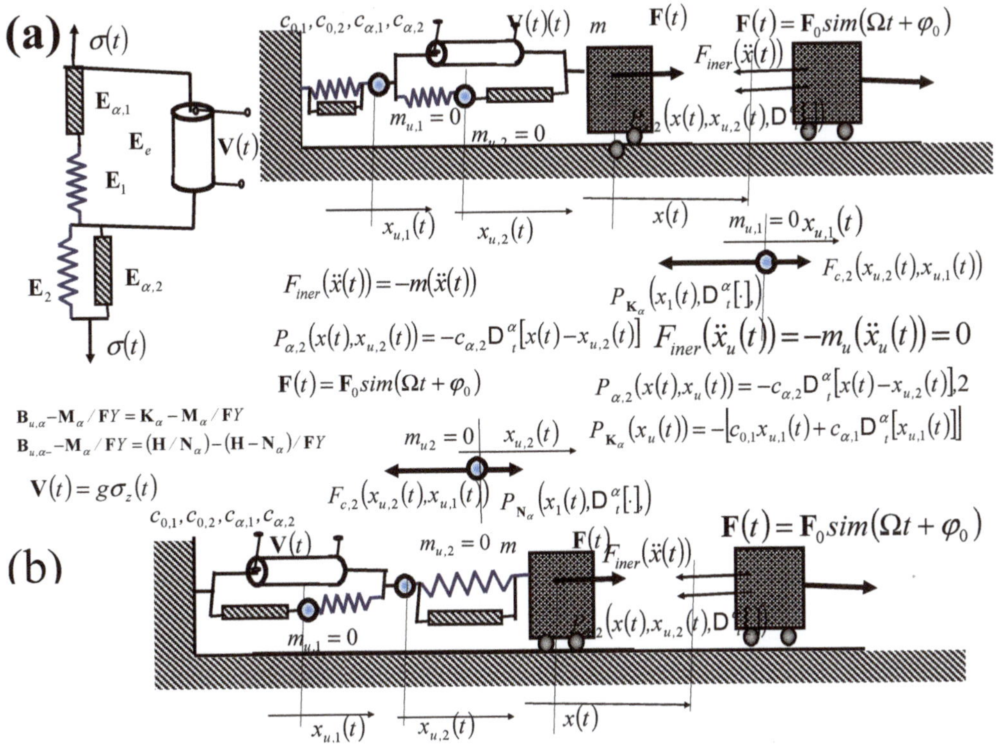

Figure 4. Burgers–Faraday discrete dynamical system of fractional-type BFY VES DS fractional-type oscillator with piezoelectric properties: (**a**) A rheological discrete dynamic system consisting of a single material point (rigid body) with mass *m*, connected by a standard light complex Burgers–Faraday–VES rheological model of the ideal fractional type (BFY VES DS, upper part in figure). The system has one external and two internal degrees of freedom. (**b**) A dynamic rheological system with the reversed sequence of the structure's connections in the standard light complex ideal Burgers–Faraday model of fractional type (BFY VES DSR, lower part in figure).

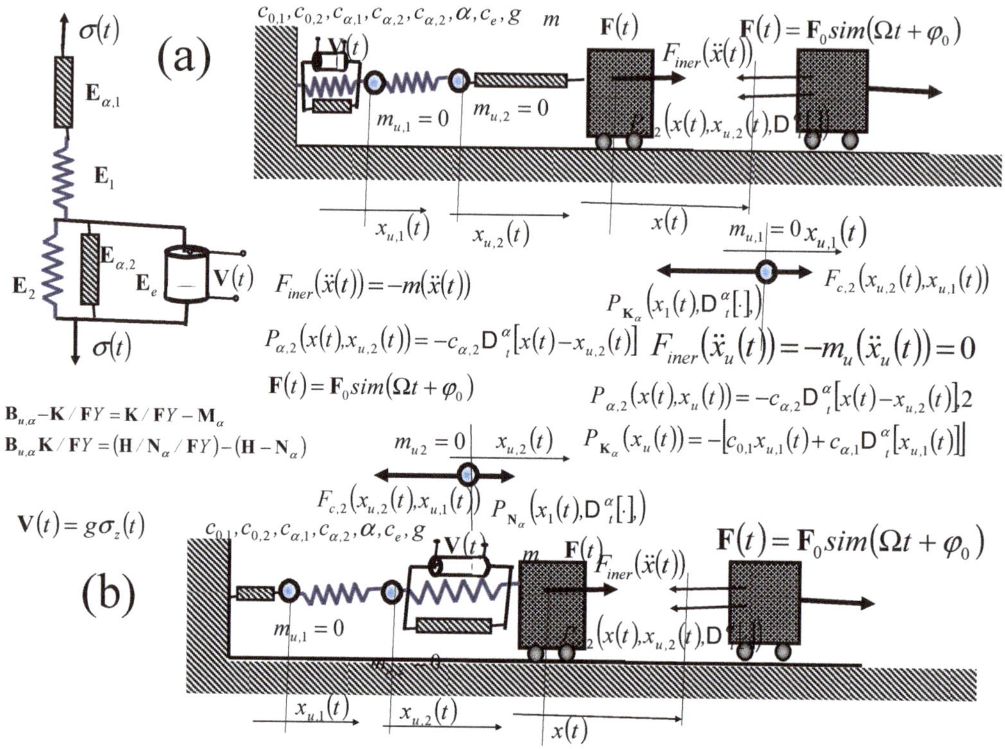

Figure 5. Burgers–Faraday fractional-type dynamical system fractional type creeper with piezoelectric properties—**BFY CF DS**. (**a**) A rheological discrete dynamic system consisting of a single material point (rigid body) with mass m, connected by a standard light complex Burgers–Faraday–VF rheological model of the ideal fractional type (**BFY CF DS**), presented in upper part. The system has one external and two internal degrees of freedom. (**b**) A dynamic rheological system with the reversed sequence of the structure's connections in the standard light complex ideal Burgers–Faraday–VF model of fractional type (**BFY CF DSR**), presented in lower part of (**b**).

4.1. The Burgers–Faraday (BFY VES DS) Rheologic Discrete Dynamical System of Fractional Type—BFY VES DS Fractional Type Oscillator with Piezoelectric Properties

In this section, we will analyze the dynamics of the complex Burgers–Faraday–VES dynamical system of fractional type in two cases depending on the sequence of elements in the dynamical system. BFY VES fractional-type discrete dynamical systems are presented in Figure 4. Both rheological Burgers–Faraday–BFY VF DS dynamic systems are shown in Figure 4. Let us denote by $x(t)$ the independent generalized coordinate corresponding to the external degree of freedom, and $x_{u,1}(t)$ and $x_{u,2}(t)$ the internal independent generalized coordinates corresponding to the internal degrees of freedom of the ideal fractional-type Burgers–Faraday–VES discrete rheological model.

At the points of serial connections of the simple elements and substructure within the structure of the standard light complex rheological Burgers–Faraday–VES model of fractional type, we place a fictitious material point with zero mass, denoted by $m_{u,1} = 0$ and $m_{u,2} = 0$ to set up a system of fractional-order differential equations. Given that the basic mass (rigid body) of the system is m, and the rheological dynamic Burgers–Faraday–BFY VES DS system (Figure 4a, presented in upper part) has three degrees of freedom, the system of fractional-order differential equations takes the following form:

$$m\ddot{x} + c_e(x(t) - x_{u,1}(t)) + c_{\alpha,2}\mathrm{D}_t^\alpha[x(t) - x_{u,2}(t)] = F_0 sin(\Omega t + \varphi_0)$$

$$m_{u,1}\ddot{x}_{u,1} + c_{0,1}x_{u,1}(t) + c_{\alpha,1}D_t^{\alpha}[x_{u,1}(t)] + c_{0,2}(x_{u,2}(t) - x_{u,1}(t)) - c_e(x(t) - x_{u,1}(t)) = 0 \quad (59)$$
$$m_{u,2}\ddot{x}_{u,2} - c_{\alpha,2}D_t^{\alpha}[x(t) - x_{u,2}(t)] + c_{0,2}(x_{u,2}(t) - x_{u,1}(t)) = 0$$

For the second case of the element connection in the structure of the standard light rheological Burgers–Faraday–(BFY VES DS) model of ideal fractional type, as shown in lower part in Figure 4b, the system of fractional-order differential equations is of the following form:

$$m\ddot{x} + c_{0,2}(x(t) - x_{u,2}(t)) + c_{\alpha,2}D_t^{\alpha}[x(t) - x_{u,2}(t)] = F_0 sin(\Omega t + \varphi_0)$$
$$m_{u,1}\ddot{x}_{u,1} + c_{\alpha,1}D_t^{\alpha}[x_{u,1}(t)] - c_{0,1}(x_{u,2}(t) - x_{u,1}(t)) = 0 \quad (60)$$
$$m_{u,2}\ddot{x}_{u,2} + c_e x_{u,2}(t) + c_{0,1}(x_{u,2}(t) - x_{u,1}(t)) - c_{0,2}(x(t) - x_{u,2}(t)) - c_{\alpha,2}D_t^{\alpha}[x(t) - x_{u,2}(t)] = 0$$

Let us now introduce the following notations:

$$\omega_{0,1}^2 = \frac{c_{0,1}}{m}\ \omega_{0,2}^2 = \frac{c_{0,2}}{m}\ \omega_{\alpha,1}^2 = \frac{c_{\alpha,1}}{m}\ \omega_{\alpha,2}^2 = \frac{c_{\alpha,2}}{m}\ \omega_e^2 = \frac{c_e}{m}\ h_0 = \frac{F_0}{m} \quad (61)$$

Now, let us rewrite the previous systems of the fractional-order differential equations in the following forms:

For the first model of the discrete rheological Burgers–Faraday–VES discrete dynamic system, shown in upper part in Figure 4a (BFY VES DS), the system of fractional-order differential equations is now in the following form:

$$\ddot{x} + \omega_e^2(x(t) - x_{u,1}(t)) + \omega_{\alpha,2}^2 D_t^{\alpha}[x(t) - x_{u,2}(t)] = h_0 sin(\Omega t + \varphi_0)$$
$$+\omega_{\alpha,1}^2 D_t^{\alpha}[x_{u,1}(t)] + \omega_{0,2}^2(x_{u,2}(t) - x_{u,1}(t)) - \omega_e^2(x(t) - x_{u,1}(t)) = 0 \quad (62)$$
$$-\omega_{\alpha,2}^2 D_t^{\alpha}[x(t) - x_{u,2}(t)] + \omega_{0,2}^2(x_{u,2}(t) - x_{u,1}(t)) = 0$$

For the second model of the rheological Burgers–Faraday–VES discrete dynamic system, shown in lower part in Figure 4b, (BFY VF DSR) the system of fractional-order differential equations is now in the following form:

$$\ddot{x} + \omega_{0,2}^2(x(t) - x_{u,2}(t)) + \omega_{\alpha,2}^2 D_t^{\alpha}[x(t) - x_{u,2}(t)] = h_0 sin(\Omega t + \varphi_0)$$
$$+\omega_{\alpha,1}^2 D_t^{\alpha}[x_{u,1}(t)] + \omega_{0,2}^2(x_{u,2}(t) - x_{u,1}(t)) - \omega_e^2(x(t) - x_{u,1}(t)) = 0 \quad (63)$$
$$\omega_e^2 x_{u,2}(t) + \omega_{0,1}^2(x_{u,2}(t) - x_{u,1}(t)) - \omega_{0,2}^2(x(t) - x_{u,2}(t)) - \omega_{\alpha,2}^2 D_t^{\alpha}[x(t) - x_{u,2}(t)] = 0$$

4.1.1. The Dynamics of the Rheological Burgers–Faraday–VES Dynamic System

Now, let us apply the Laplace transform to the previous system of fractional-order differential Equation (62), which results in the following (see References [38–40]):

$$L\{x(t)\}\left\langle p^2 + \omega_e^2 + \omega_{\alpha,2}^2 p^{\alpha}\right\rangle - \omega_e^2 L\{x_{u,1}(t)\} - \omega_{\alpha,2}^2 p^{\alpha} L\{x_{u,2}(t)\} = \frac{h_0\Omega}{p^2 + \Omega^2} + (px_0 + \dot{x}_0)$$
$$L\{x_{u,1}(t)\}\left(\omega_{\alpha,1}^2 p^{\alpha} + \omega_e^2 - \omega_{0,2}^2\right) + \omega_{\alpha,2}^2 p^{\alpha} L\{x_{u,2}(t)\} = \omega_e^2 L\{x(t)\} \quad (64)$$
$$\left(\omega_{\alpha,2}^2 p^{\alpha} + \omega_{0,2}^2\right) L\{x_{u,2}(t)\} - \omega_{0,2}^2 L\{x_{u,1}(t)\} = \omega_{\alpha,2}^2 p^{\alpha} L\{x(t)\}\ \left(\omega_{\alpha,1}^2 p^{\alpha} + \omega_e^2 - \omega_{\alpha,2}^2\right)$$

The previous system (64) represents a non-homogeneous system of algebraic equations in terms of the unknown Laplace transforms of the independent generalized coordinates: one external $L\{x(t)\}$ and two internal $L\{x_{u,1}(t)\}$ and $L\{x_{u,2}(t)\}$, and can be solved using

Cramer's rule by employing the determinant of the system and other determinants derived from it by replacing the appropriate column with the column of the free terms of the system.

The determinant of the previous system (64) of non-homogeneous algebraic equations is in the following form:

$$\Delta(p) = \begin{vmatrix} \left\langle p^2 + \omega_e^2 + \omega_{\alpha,2}^2 p^\alpha \right\rangle & -\omega_e^2 & -\omega_{\alpha,2}^2 p^\alpha \\ -\omega_e^2 & \left(\omega_{\alpha,1}^2 p^\alpha + \omega_e^2 - \omega_{0,2}^2\right) & \omega_{\alpha,2}^2 p^\alpha \\ -\omega_{\alpha,2}^2 p^\alpha & -\omega_{0,2}^2 & \left(\omega_{\alpha,2}^2 p^\alpha + \omega_{0,2}^2\right) \end{vmatrix}$$

$$\begin{aligned} \Delta(p) = & \left(p^2 + \omega_e^2 + \omega_{\alpha,2}^2 p^\alpha\right)\left\langle \left(\omega_{\alpha,1}^2 p^\alpha + \omega_e^2 - \omega_{0,2}^2\right)\left(\omega_{\alpha,2}^2 p^\alpha + \omega_{0,2}^2\right) + \omega_{0,2}^2 \omega_{\alpha,2}^2 p^\alpha \right\rangle + \\ & + \omega_e^2 \left\langle \omega_{\alpha,2}^4 p^{2\alpha} - \omega_e^2\left(\omega_{\alpha,2}^2 p^\alpha + \omega_{0,2}^2\right)\right\rangle - \omega_{\alpha,2}^2 p^\alpha \left\langle \omega_e^2 \omega_{0,2}^2 + \omega_{\alpha,2}^2 p^\alpha \left(\omega_{\alpha,1}^2 p^\alpha + \omega_e^2 - \omega_{0,2}^2\right)\right\rangle \end{aligned} \tag{65}$$

While the other determinants obtained by replacing the appropriate column with the column of the free terms from the system (64) are as follows:

$$\Delta_0(p) = \left\langle \frac{h_0 \Omega}{p^2 + \Omega^2} + (p x_0 + \dot{x}_0) \right\rangle \left\langle \left(\omega_{\alpha,1}^2 p^\alpha + \omega_e^2 - \omega_{0,2}^2\right)\left(\omega_{\alpha,2}^2 p^\alpha + \omega_{0,2}^2\right) + \omega_{0,2}^2 \omega_{\alpha,2}^2 p^\alpha \right\rangle \tag{66}$$

$$\Delta_1(p) = \left\langle \frac{h_0 \Omega}{p^2 + \Omega^2} + (p x_0 + \dot{x}_0) \right\rangle \left\langle \omega_e^2 \left(\omega_{\alpha,2}^2 p^\alpha + \omega_{0,2}^2\right) - \omega_{\alpha,2}^4 p^{2\alpha} \right\rangle \tag{67}$$

$$\Delta_2(p) = \left\langle \frac{h_0 \Omega}{p^2 + \Omega^2} + (p x_0 + \dot{x}_0) \right\rangle \left\langle \omega_e^2 \omega_{0,2}^2 + \omega_{\alpha,2}^2 \left(\omega_{\alpha,1}^2 p^\alpha + \omega_e^2 - \omega_{0,2}^2\right) \right\rangle \tag{68}$$

The solution of the system (64) of non-homogeneous algebraic equations in terms of the Laplace transforms of the independent generalized coordinates: one external $\mathrm{L}\{x(t)\}$ and two internal $\mathrm{L}\{x_{u,1}(t)\}$ and $\mathrm{L}\{x_{u,2}(t)\}$ can now be expressed in the following form:

$$\begin{aligned} \mathrm{L}\{x(t)\} &= \frac{\Delta_0(p)}{\Delta(p)} = \frac{1}{\Delta(p)} \left\langle \frac{h_0 \Omega}{p^2 + \Omega^2} + (p x_0 + \dot{x}_0) \right\rangle \left\langle \left(\omega_{\alpha,1}^2 p^\alpha + \omega_e^2 - \omega_{0,2}^2\right)\left(\omega_{\alpha,2}^2 p^\alpha + \omega_{0,2}^2\right) + \omega_{0,2}^2 \omega_{\alpha,2}^2 p^\alpha \right\rangle \\ \mathrm{L}\{x_{u,1}(t)\} &= \frac{\Delta_1(p)}{\Delta(p)} = \frac{1}{\Delta(p)} \left\langle \frac{h_0 \Omega}{p^2 + \Omega^2} + (p x_0 + \dot{x}_0) \right\rangle \left\langle \omega_e^2 \left(\omega_{\alpha,2}^2 p^\alpha + \omega_{0,2}^2\right) - \omega_{\alpha,2}^4 p^{2\alpha} \right\rangle \\ \mathrm{L}\{x_{u,2}(t)\} &= \frac{\Delta_2(p)}{\Delta(p)} = \frac{1}{\Delta(p)} \left\langle \frac{h_0 \Omega}{p^2 + \Omega^2} + (p x_0 + \dot{x}_0) \right\rangle \left\langle \omega_e^2 \omega_{0,2}^2 + \omega_{\alpha,2}^2 \left(\omega_{\alpha,1}^2 p^\alpha + \omega_e^2 - \omega_{0,2}^2\right) \right\rangle \end{aligned} \tag{69}$$

Now, it is necessary to determine the inverse Laplace transforms of the external independent generalized coordinate $\mathrm{L}^{-1}\mathrm{L}\{x(t)\}$ as well as the inverse Laplace transforms of the internal independent generalized coordinates $\mathrm{L}^{-1}\mathrm{L}\{x_{u,1}(t)\}$ and $\mathrm{L}^{-1}\mathrm{L}\{x_{u,2}(t)\}$ to transition to the time domain. Thus, we have the following:

$$\begin{aligned} x(t) &= \mathrm{L}^{-1}\mathrm{L}\{x(t)\} = \mathrm{L}^{-1}\left\{ \frac{1}{\Delta(p)} \left\langle \frac{h_0 \Omega}{p^2 + \Omega^2} + (p x_0 + \dot{x}_0) \right\rangle \left\langle \left(\omega_{\alpha,1}^2 p^\alpha + \omega_e^2 - \omega_{0,2}^2\right)\left(\omega_{\alpha,2}^2 p^\alpha + \omega_{0,2}^2\right) + \omega_{0,2}^2 \omega_{\alpha,2}^2 p^\alpha \right\rangle \right\} \\ x_{u,1}(t) &= \mathrm{L}^{-1}\mathrm{L}\{x_{u,1}(t)\} = \mathrm{L}^{-1}\left\{ \frac{1}{\Delta(p)} \left\langle \frac{h_0 \Omega}{p^2 + \Omega^2} + (p x_0 + \dot{x}_0) \right\rangle \left\langle \omega_e^2 \left(\omega_{\alpha,2}^2 p^\alpha + \omega_{0,2}^2\right) - \omega_{\alpha,2}^4 p^{2\alpha} \right\rangle \right\} \\ x_{u,2}(t) &= \mathrm{L}^{-1}\mathrm{L}\{x_{u,2}(t)\} = \mathrm{L}^{-1}\left\{ \frac{1}{\Delta(p)} \left\langle \frac{h_0 \Omega}{p^2 + \Omega^2} + (p x_0 + \dot{x}_0) \right\rangle \left\langle \omega_e^2 \omega_{0,2}^2 + \omega_{\alpha,2}^2 \left(\omega_{\alpha,1}^2 p^\alpha + \omega_e^2 - \omega_{0,2}^2\right) \right\rangle \right\} \end{aligned} \tag{70}$$

where the system determinant $\Delta(p)$ is defined in (65).

It is necessary to determine the invers Laplace transform $\text{L}^{-1}\text{L}\left\{x_{free}(t)\right\}$ of external independent generalized coordinate $\left\{x_{free}(t)\right\}$, for free eigen fractional type oscillations and transition into the time domain in the following form:

$$x_{free}(t) = \text{L}^{-1}\text{L}\left\{x_{free}(t)\right\} = \text{L}^{-1}\left\{\frac{(px_0 + \dot{x}_0)}{\Delta(p)}\left\langle\left(\omega_{\alpha,1}^2 p^\alpha + \omega_e^2 - \omega_{0,2}^2\right)\left(\omega_{\alpha,2}^2 p^\alpha + \omega_{0,2}^2\right) + \omega_{0,2}^2\omega_{\alpha,2}^2 p^\alpha\right\rangle\right\} \tag{71}$$

Then, it is necessary to determine invers Laplace transform $\text{L}^{-1}\text{L}\{x_{part}(t)\}$ of external independent generalized coordinate $\{x_{part}(t)\}$, for forced fractional type rheological oscillations and transition into the time domain in the following form:

$$x_{Part}(t) = \text{L}^{-1}\text{L}\{x_{Part}(t)\} = \text{L}^{-1}\left\{\frac{h_0}{\Delta(p)}\frac{\Omega}{p^2+\Omega^2}\left\langle\left(\omega_{\alpha,1}^2 p^\alpha + \omega_e^2 - \omega_{0,2}^2\right)\left(\omega_{\alpha,2}^2 p^\alpha + \omega_{0,2}^2\right) + \omega_{0,2}^2\omega_{\alpha,2}^2 p^\alpha\right\rangle\right\} \tag{72}$$

We can then also determine the internal independent generalized coordinates $x_{u,1}(t)$ and $x_{u,2}(t)$ which correspond to the displacements of the points connecting Hooke's ideal elastic element and Newton's ideal viscous element of fractional type, with the parallel-connected with piezoelectric Faraday element in the BFY VES DS dynamical system.

The axial strain (dilation) of the parallel-connected Faraday ideal elastic and piezoelectric element, in the structure of the standard light rheological Burgers–Faraday–BFY VES DS model of fractional type (BFY VES DS) (model shown in the upper part of Figure 4a), is as follows:

$$\varepsilon_z(t) = \frac{x(t) - x_{u,1}(t)}{\updownarrow_0}$$

$$\varepsilon_z(t) = \frac{x(t) - x_{u,1}(t)}{\updownarrow_0} = \frac{1}{\updownarrow_0}\text{L}^{-1}\text{L}\{x(t) - x_{u,1}(t)\}$$

$$\left\langle\omega_e^2\left(\omega_{\alpha,2}^2 p^\alpha + \omega_{0,2}^2\right) - \omega_{\alpha,2}^4 p^{2\alpha}\right\rangle$$

$$\begin{gathered}\{\varepsilon_z(t)\} = \text{L}\{x(t) - x_{u,1}(t)\} = \\ = \frac{1}{\Delta(p)}\left\langle\frac{h^0\Omega}{p^2+\Omega^2} + (px_0 + \dot{x}_0)\right\rangle \\ \left\langle\left(\omega_{\alpha,1}^2 p^\alpha + \omega_e^2 - \omega_{\alpha,2}^2\right)\left(\omega_{\alpha,2}^2 p^\alpha + \omega_{0,2}^2\right) + \omega_{0,2}^2\omega_{\alpha,2}^2 p^\alpha - \omega_e^2\left(\omega_{\alpha,2}^2 p^\alpha + \omega_{0,2}^2\right) + \omega_{\alpha,2}^4 p^{2\alpha}\right\rangle\end{gathered} \tag{73}$$

The normal stress in the parallel-connected Faraday piezoelectric element in the structure of (BFY VES DS) is as follows:

$$\sigma_z(t) = \mathbf{E_e}\varepsilon_z(t) = \mathbf{E_e}\frac{x(t) - x_{u,1}(t)}{\updownarrow_0} \tag{74}$$

The electric voltage of the electrical polarization in the parallel-connected Faraday element in the structure of (BFY VES DS) is as follows:

$$\mathbf{V}_z(t) = -g\sigma_z(t) = g\mathbf{E_e}\frac{x(t) - x_{u,1}(t)}{\updownarrow_0} = \frac{g\mathbf{E_e}}{\updownarrow_0}\text{L}^{-1}\text{L}\{x(t) - x_{u,1}(t)\} \tag{75}$$

and the dielectric displacements in the parallel-connected Faraday element are as follows:

$$D_z(t) = b\sigma_z(t) = \frac{b\mathbf{E_e}}{\updownarrow_0}\text{L}^{-1}\text{L}\{x(t) - x_{u,1}(t)\} \text{ and } D_z(t) = e\varepsilon_z(t) = \frac{e}{\updownarrow_0}\text{L}^{-1}\text{L}\{x(t) - x_{u,1}(t)\} \tag{76}$$

4.1.2. Dynamics of the Reverse Rheological Burgers–Faraday Discrete Dynamic System (BFY VES DSR)

Let us now consider the dynamics of the reverse rheological Burgers–Faraday–VES discrete dynamic system (BFY VES DSR) (model presented in lower part of Figure 4), which is described by the system (63) of three fractional-order differential equations. For the reverse order of element connections in the structure of the standard light rheological Burgers–Faraday–(BFY VES DSR) model of fractional type, we apply the same procedure as in Section 4.1.1, which we will not repeat here. However, we will present the system of non-homogeneous algebraic equations for the unknown Laplace transformations of the independent generalized coordinates, one external coordinate $L\{x(t)\}$ and two internal independent generalized coordinates $L\{x_{u,1}(t)\}$ and $L\{x_{u,2}(t)\}$ describing the dynamics of the rheological system, in the following form:

$$\begin{gathered}L\{x\}\left\langle p^2+\omega_{0,2}^2+\omega_{\alpha,2}^2p^\alpha\right\rangle-\left(\omega_{0,2}^2+\omega_{\alpha,2}^2p^\alpha\right)L\{x_{u,2}(t)\}=\tfrac{h_0\Omega}{p^2+\Omega^2}+(px_0+\dot{x}_0)\\ -\omega_e^2L\{x(t)\}+\left(\omega_e^2-\omega_{0,2}^2+\omega_{\alpha,1}^2p^\alpha\right)L\{x_{u,1}(t)\}+\omega_{0,2}^2L\{x_{u,2}(t)\}=0\\ -\left(\omega_{0,2}^2+\omega_{\alpha,2}^2p^\alpha\right)L\{x(t)\}-\omega_{0,1}^2L\{x_{u,1}(t)\}+\left(\omega_{0,1}^2+\omega_{0,2}^2+\omega_{\alpha,2}^2p^\alpha\right)L\{x_{u,2}(t)\}=0\end{gathered} \tag{77}$$

Starting from the system of three fractional-order differential Equation (63), and applying the Laplace transformation, we derived a non-homogeneous system of algebraic Equation (77). By applying Cramer's rule and using the determinants we obtain the solutions for the Laplace transforms of all three independent generalized coordinates, expressed in the following form:

$$\begin{gathered}L\{x(t)\}=\frac{\Delta_0(p)}{\Delta(p)}=\frac{1}{\Delta(p)}\left\langle\frac{h_0\Omega}{p^2+\Omega^2}+(px_0+\dot{x}_0)\right\rangle\left\langle\left(\omega_e^2-\omega_{0,2}^2+\omega_{\alpha,1}^2p^\alpha\right)\left(\omega_{0,1}^2+\omega_{0,2}^2+\omega_{\alpha,2}^2p^\alpha\right)+\omega_{0,2}^2\omega_{0,1}^2\right\rangle\\ L\{x_{u,1}(t)\}=\frac{\Delta_1(p)}{\Delta(p)}=\frac{1}{\Delta(p)}\left\langle\frac{h_0\Omega}{p^2+\Omega^2}+(px_0+\dot{x}_0)\right\rangle\left\langle\omega_{02}^2\left(\omega_{0,2}^2+\omega_{\alpha,2}^2p^\alpha\right)-\omega_e^2\left(-\omega_{0,1}^2+\omega_{0,2}^2+\omega_{\alpha,2}^2p^\alpha\right)\right\rangle\\ L\{x_{u,2}(t)\}==\frac{\Delta_2(p)}{\Delta(p)}=\frac{1}{\Delta(p)}\left\langle\frac{h_0\Omega}{p^2+\Omega^2}+(px_0+\dot{x}_0)\right\rangle\left\langle\omega_e^2\omega_{0,1}^2+\left(\omega_e^2-\omega_{0,2}^2+\omega_{\alpha,1}^2p^\alpha\right)\left(\omega_{0,2}^2\}\omega_{\alpha,2}^2p^\alpha\right)\right\rangle\end{gathered} \tag{78}$$

where system determinant is in the following form:

$$\begin{gathered}\Delta(p)=\left(p^2+\omega_{0,2}^2+\omega_{\alpha,2}^2p^\alpha\right)\left\langle\left(\omega_e^2-\omega_{0,2}^2+\omega_{\alpha,1}^2p^\alpha\right)\left(\omega_{0,1}^2+\omega_{0,2}^2+\omega_{\alpha,2}^2p^\alpha\right)+\omega_{0,1}^2\omega_{0,2}^2\right\rangle-\\ -\left(\omega_{0,2}^2+\omega_{\alpha,2}^2p^\alpha\right)\left\langle\omega_e^2\omega_{0,1}^2+\left(\omega_{0,2}^2+\omega_{\alpha,2}^2p^\alpha\right)\left(\omega_e^2-\omega_{0,2}^2+\omega_{\alpha,1}^2p^\alpha\right)\right\rangle\end{gathered} \tag{79}$$

The inverse Laplace transform is performed for all three independent generalized coordinates in order to transfer into the time domain:

$$\begin{gathered}x(t)=L^{-1}L\{x(t)\}=L^{-1}\left\{\frac{1}{\Delta(p)}\left\langle\frac{h_0\Omega}{p^2+\Omega^2}+(px_0+\dot{x}_0)\right\rangle\left\langle\left(\omega_e^2-\omega_{0,2}^2+\omega_{\alpha,1}^2p^\alpha\right)\left(\omega_{0,1}^2+\omega_{0,2}^2+\omega_{\alpha,2}^2p^\alpha\right)+\omega_{0,2}^2\omega_{0,1}^2\right\rangle\right\}\\ x_{u,1}(t)=L^{-1}L\{x_{u,1}(t)\}=L^{-1}\left\{\frac{1}{\Delta(p)}\left\langle\frac{h_0\Omega}{p^2+\Omega^2}+(px_0+\dot{x}_0)\right\rangle\left\langle\omega_{02}^2\left(\omega_{0,2}^2+\omega_{\alpha,2}^2p^\alpha\right)-\omega_e^2\left(-\omega_{0,1}^2+\omega_{0,2}^2+\omega_{\alpha,2}^2p^\alpha\right)\right\rangle\right\}\\ x_{u,2}(t)=L^{-1}L\{x_{u,2}(t)\}=L^{-1}\left\{\frac{1}{\Delta(p)}\left\langle\frac{h_0\Omega}{p^2+\Omega^2}+(px_0+\dot{x}_0)\right\rangle\left\langle\omega_e^2\omega_{0,1}^2+\left(\omega_e^2-\omega_{0,2}^2+\omega_{\alpha,1}^2p^\alpha\right)\left(\omega_{0,2}^2\}\omega_{\alpha,2}^2p^\alpha\right)\right\rangle\right\}\end{gathered} \tag{80}$$

The inverse Laplace transform for the external independent generalized coordinate $L\{x(t)\}$ for free eigen rheological oscillations of fractional type is as follows:

$$x_{free}(t)=L^{-1}L\left\{x_{free}(t)\right\}=L^{-1}\left\{\frac{(px_0+\dot{x}_0)}{\Delta(p)}\left\langle\left(\omega_e^2-\omega_{0,2}^2+\omega_{\alpha,1}^2p^\alpha\right)\left(\omega_{0,1}^2+\omega_{0,2}^2+\omega_{\alpha,2}^2p^\alpha\right)+\omega_{0,2}^2\omega_{0,1}^2\right\rangle\right\} \tag{81}$$

Then, using convolution integral and inverse Laplace transform for the following: $L^{-1}\left\{\frac{1}{\Delta(p)}\left\langle\left(\omega_e^2-\omega_{0,2}^2+\omega_{\alpha,1}^2p^\alpha\right)\left(\omega_{0,1}^2+\omega_{0,2}^2+\omega_{\alpha,2}^2p^\alpha\right)+\omega_{0,2}^2\omega_{0,1}^2\right\rangle\right\}$ and $L^{-1}\left\{\frac{h_0\Omega}{p^2+\Omega^2}\right\}$, we determine the external independent generalized coordinate $L^{-1}L\{x_{part}(t)\}$, for forced rheological oscillation $\{x_{part}(t)\}$ in time domain in the form:

$$x_{part}(t)=L^{-1}L\{x_{part}(t)\}=L^{-1}\left\{\frac{1}{\Delta(p)}\left\langle\left(\omega_e^2-\omega_{0,2}^2+\omega_{\alpha,1}^2p^\alpha\right)\left(\omega_{0,1}^2+\omega_{0,2}^2+\omega_{\alpha,2}^2p^\alpha\right)+\omega_{0,2}^2\omega_{0,1}^2\right\rangle\right\}*L^{-1}\left\{\frac{h_0\Omega}{p^2+\Omega^2}\right\} \tag{82}$$

We can then determine the internal independent generalized coordinates $x_{u,1}(t)$ and $x_{u,2}(t)$ along with the displacements at the points of sequential connections between the basic Hooke ideal elastic element, the Newton ideal viscous element of fractional type, and the piezoelectric Faraday element in the modified Maxwell rheological fractional-type model which incorporates in parallel piezoelectric properties. This can be expressed via the convolution integral as follows:

$$xu,1(t) = \mathrm{L}^{-1}\mathrm{L}\{x_{u,1}(t)\} = \mathrm{L}^{-1}\left\{\frac{p}{\Delta(p)}\left\langle\omega_{02}^2\left(\omega_{0,2}^2+\omega_{\alpha,2}^2p^\alpha\right)-\omega_e^2\left(-\omega_{0,1}^2+\omega_{0,2}^2+\omega_{\alpha,2}^2p^\alpha\right)\right\rangle\right\} * \mathrm{L}^{-1}\mathrm{L}\{x(t)\}$$

$$x_{u,2}(t) = \mathrm{L}^{-1}\mathrm{L}\{x_{u,2}(t)\} = \mathrm{L}^{-1}\left\{\frac{p}{\Delta(p)}\left\langle\omega_e^2\omega_{0,1}^2+\left(\omega_e^2-\omega_{0,2}^2+\omega_{\alpha,1}^2p^\alpha\right)\left(\omega_{0,2}^2\right\}\omega_{\alpha,2}^2p^\alpha\right)\right\rangle\right\} * \mathrm{L}^{-1}\mathrm{L}\{x(t)\} \tag{83}$$

The dilation of the parallel connected Faraday ideal elastic and piezoelectric element is as follows:

$$\varepsilon_z(t) = \frac{x_{u,1}(t)}{\updownarrow_0} = \frac{1}{\updownarrow_0}\mathrm{L}^{-1}\mathrm{L}\{x_{u,1}(t)\}$$

$$\varepsilon_z(t) = \frac{1}{\updownarrow_0}\mathrm{L}^{-1}\left\{\frac{1}{\Delta(p)}\left\langle\frac{h_0\Omega}{p^2+\Omega^2}+(px_0+\dot{x}_0)\right\rangle\left\langle\omega_{02}^2\left(\omega_{0,2}^2+\omega_{\alpha,2}^2p^\alpha\right)-\omega_e^2\left(-\omega_{0,1}^2+\omega_{0,2}^2+\omega_{\alpha,2}^2p^\alpha\right)\right\rangle\right\} \tag{84}$$

The normal stress in the Faraday element is as follows:

$$\sigma_z(t) = \mathbf{E_e}\varepsilon_z(t) = \mathbf{E_e}\frac{x_{u,1}(t)}{\updownarrow_0} \tag{85}$$

The electric voltage of electric polarization in parallel connected to the Faraday element is as follows:

$$\mathbf{V}_z(t) = -g\sigma_z(t) = \frac{g\mathbf{E_e}}{\updownarrow_0}\mathrm{L}^{-1}\mathrm{L}\{x_{u,1}(t)\} \tag{86}$$

And the dielectric displacements in the Faraday element are as follows:

$$D_z(t) = b\sigma_z(t) = \frac{b\mathbf{E_e}}{\updownarrow_0}\mathrm{L}^{-1}\mathrm{L}\{x_{u,1}(t)\} \text{ and } D_z(t) = e\varepsilon_z(t) = \frac{e}{\updownarrow_0}\mathrm{L}^{-1}\mathrm{L}\{x_{u,1}(t)\} \tag{87}$$

4.2. The Burgers–Faraday Discrete Dynamical System of Fractional Type- Fractional Type Creeper with Piezoelectric Properties—BFY CF DS

In this section, we will examine the dynamics of the rheological Burgers–Faraday–discrete dynamic system, of fractional type with piezoelectric properties, BFY CF DS, as presented in Figure 5. This system will be analyzed in two variations based on the sequence of binding in the underlying structure of the standard light complex rheological Burgers–Faraday–BFY CF DS model (presented in Figure 5). This discrete dynamic system is characterized by a standard light complex rheological Burgers–Faraday–BFY CF DS model of ideal, fractional-type material, integrated into the system through parallel binding with a piezoelectric Faraday ideal elastic element and a Kelvin–Voigt structure of fractional type. This rheological discrete dynamic system exhibits both delayed elasticity and normal stress relaxation properties, under specific conditions of constant normal stress or constant axial dilation over time.

Both rheological Burgers–Faraday–BFY CF DS discrete dynamic systems, possess one external degree of freedom related to motion; specifically, the sliding material point (rigid body) and two internal degrees of freedom associated with movement: sliding and flowing of the fractional type. This behavior is inherent within the complex standard light rheological Burgers–Faraday–VF model.

We will establish that, in both cases, it represents a type of fractional order crawler with energy dissipation within the discrete dynamic system.

Let us denote $x(t)$ as the independent generalized coordinate corresponding to the external degree of freedom related to motion; specifically, sliding while $x_{u,1}(t)$ and $x_{u,2}(t)$

represent the internal independent generalized coordinates corresponding to the internal degrees of freedom associated with sliding motion in the fractional-type rheological Burgers–Faraday–VF model.

At the internal connections of the simple elements within the structure of the standard light complex rheological Burgers–Faraday–BFY CF DS model of fractional type, we introduce a fictitious material point with zero mass at each joint, denoted as $m_{u,1} = 0$ and $m_{u,2} = 0$. We then formulate a system of fractional-order differential equations. Given that the basic mass (rigid body) of the system is m and the rheological dynamic BFY CF DS system (as shown in the upper part of Figure 5a) has three degrees of freedom for movement, the resulting system of fractional-order differential equations can be expressed in the following form:

$$\begin{gathered} m\ddot{x} + c_{\alpha,2}\mathrm{D}_t^{\alpha}[x(t) - x_{u,2}(t)] = F_0 sin(\Omega t + \varphi_0) \\ m_{u,1}\ddot{x}_{u,1} + c_{0,1}x_{u,1}(t) + c_e x_{u,1}(t) + c_{\alpha,1}\mathrm{D}_t^{\alpha}[x_{u,1}(t)] - c_{0,2}(x_{u,2}(t) - x_{u,1}(t)) = 0 \\ m_{u,2}\ddot{x}_{u,2} - c_{\alpha,2}\mathrm{D}_t^{\alpha}[x(t) - x_{u,2}(t)] + c_{0,2}(x_{u,2}(t) - x_{u,1}(t)) = 0 \end{gathered} \tag{88}$$

Now, let us introduce the following notations:

$$\omega_{0,1}^2 = \frac{c_{0,1}}{m}\ \omega_{0,2}^2 = \frac{c_{0,2}}{m}\ \omega_{\alpha,1}^2 = \frac{c_{\alpha,1}}{m}\ \omega_{\alpha,2}^2 = \frac{c_{\alpha,2}}{m}\ \omega_e^2 = \frac{c_e}{m}\ h_0 = \frac{F_0}{m} \tag{89}$$

We can then rewrite the previous systems of fractional order differential equations in the following forms:

For the (BFY CF DS) dynamical system, the system of fractional differential equations is now represented as follows:

$$\begin{gathered} \ddot{x} + \omega_{\alpha,2}^2\mathrm{D}_t^{\alpha}[x(t) - x_{u,2}(t)] = h_0 sin(\Omega t + \varphi_0) \\ \omega_{0,1}^2 x_{u,1}(t) + \omega_e^2 x_{u,1}(t) + \omega_{\alpha,1}^2\mathrm{D}_t^{\alpha}[x_{u,1}(t)] - \omega_{0,2}^2(x_{u,2}(t) - x_{u,1}(t)) = 0 \\ -\omega_{\alpha,2}^2\mathrm{D}_t^{\alpha}[x(t) - x_{u,2}(t)] + \omega_{0,2}^2(x_{u,2}(t) - x_{u,1}(t)) = 0 \end{gathered} \tag{90}$$

For the (BFY CF DSR) dynamical system, the system of fractional order differential equations is now expressed as follows:

$$\begin{gathered} \ddot{x} + \omega_{0,2}^2(x(t) - x_{u,2}(t)) + \omega_e^2(x(t) - x_{u,2}(t)) + \omega_{\alpha,2}^2\mathrm{D}_t^{\alpha}[x(t) - x_{u,2}(t)] = h_0 sin(\Omega t + \varphi_0) \\ \omega_{\alpha,1}^2\mathrm{D}_t^{\alpha}[x_{u,1}(t)] + \omega_{0,1}^2(x_{u,2}(t) - x_{u,1}(t)) = 0 \\ -\omega_{0,1}^2(x_{u,2}(t) - x_{u,1}(t)) - \omega_e^2(x(t) - x_{u,2}(t)) - \omega_{0,2}^2(x(t) - x_{u,2}(t)) - \omega_{\alpha,2}^2\mathrm{D}_t^{\alpha}[x(t) - x_{u,2}(t)] = 0 \end{gathered} \tag{91}$$

4.2.1. Dynamics of the Burgers–Faraday Dynamic System–(BFY CF DS)

By applying the identical procedure as described in detail in Section 4.1.1, we use the Laplace transform on the previous system of fractional order differential Equation (90) to obtain a system of non-homogeneous algebraic equations for the unknown Laplace transformations of the independent generalized coordinates. We solve these equations using Cramer's rule, utilizing the determinant of the system and other relevant determinants; subsequently, we determine the inverse Laplace transforms for all three independent generalized coordinates, transitioning to the time domain, yielding the following:

$$\begin{gathered} x(t) = \mathrm{L}^{-1}\mathrm{L}\{x(t)\} = \mathrm{L}^{-1}\left\{\frac{1}{\Delta(p)}\left\langle\frac{h_0\Omega}{p^2+\Omega^2} + (px_0 + \dot{x}_0)\right\rangle\left\langle\omega_{0,2}^4 + \left(\omega_{0,1}^2 + \omega_{0,2}^2 + \omega_e^2 + \omega_{\alpha,1}^2 p^{\alpha}\right)\left(\omega_{\alpha,2}^2 p^{\alpha} + \omega_{0,2}^2\right)\right\rangle\right\} \\ x_{u,1}(t) = \mathrm{L}^{-1}\mathrm{L}\{x_{u,1}(t)\} = \mathrm{L}^{-1}\left\{\frac{\omega_{\alpha,2}^4 p^{2\alpha}}{\Delta(p)}\left\langle\frac{h_0\Omega}{p^2+\Omega^2} + (px_0 + \dot{x}_0)\right\rangle\right\} \end{gathered} \tag{92}$$

$$x_{u,2}(t) = \mathrm{L}^{-1}\mathrm{L}\{x_{u,2}(t)\} = \mathrm{L}^{-1}\left\{\frac{\omega_{\alpha,2}^{2}p^{\alpha}}{\Delta(p)}\left\langle\frac{h_0\Omega}{p^2+\Omega^2} + (px_0+\dot{x}_0)\right\rangle\left(\omega_{0,1}^{2}+\omega_{0,2}^{2}+\omega_{e}^{2}+\omega_{\alpha,1}^{2}p^{\alpha}\right)\right\}$$

where the system determinant is in the following form:

$$\Delta(p) = \left(p^2+\omega_{\alpha,2}^{2}p^{\alpha}\right)\left\langle\omega_{0,2}^{4}+\left(\omega_{0,1}^{2}+\omega_{0,2}^{2}+\omega_{e}^{2}+\omega_{\alpha,1}^{2}p^{\alpha}\right)\left(\omega_{\alpha,2}^{2}p^{\alpha}+\omega_{0,2}^{2}\right)\right\rangle - \\ -\omega_{\alpha,2}^{4}p^{2\alpha}\left(\omega_{0,1}^{2}+\omega_{0,2}^{2}+\omega_{e}^{2}+\omega_{\alpha,1}^{2}p^{\alpha}\right) \quad (93)$$

First, it is necessary to determine inverse Laplace transform of the external independent coordinate $\mathrm{L}^{-1}\mathrm{L}\left\{x_{free}(t)\right\}$ for **eigen free sliding-flow** $\left\{x_{free}(t)\right\}$, of fractional type with piezoelectric and transition to the time domain in the following form:

$$x_{free}(t) = \mathrm{L}^{-1}\mathrm{L}\left\{x_{free}(t)\right\} = \mathrm{L}^{-1}\left\{\frac{(px_0+\dot{x}_0)}{\Delta(p)}\left\langle\omega_{0,2}^{4}+\left(\omega_{0,1}^{2}+\omega_{0,2}^{2}+\omega_{e}^{2}+\omega_{\alpha,1}^{2}p^{\alpha}\right)\left(\omega_{\alpha,2}^{2}p^{\alpha}+\omega_{0,2}^{2}\right)\right\rangle\right\} \quad (94)$$

Next, it is necessary to determine the inverse Laplace transformation of the external independent generalized coordinate $\mathrm{L}^{-1}\mathrm{L}\{x_{part}(t)\}$ **for forced sliding-flow** movements of fractional type $\{x_{part}(t)\}$ with piezoelectric properties, or pulsing under the influence of an external periodic one frequency force, and transition to the time domain in the following form:

$$x_{part}(t) = \mathrm{L}^{-1}\mathrm{L}\{x_{part}(t)\} = \mathrm{L}^{-1}\left\{\frac{1}{\Delta(p)}\left\langle\omega_{0,2}^{4}+\left(\omega_{0,1}^{2}+\omega_{0,2}^{2}+\omega_{e}^{2}+\omega_{\alpha,1}^{2}p^{\alpha}\right)\left(\omega_{\alpha,2}^{2}p^{\alpha}+\omega_{0,2}^{2}\right)\right\rangle\right\} * \mathrm{L}^{-1}\left\{\frac{h_0\Omega}{p^2+\Omega^2}\right\} \quad (95)$$

The preceding expression (97) is derived based on the convolution integral and the individual inverse Laplace transformations of the expressions: $\mathrm{L}^{-1}\left\{\frac{1}{\Delta(p)}\left\langle\omega_{0,2}^{4}+\left(\omega_{0,1}^{2}+\omega_{0,2}^{2}+\omega_{e}^{2}+\omega_{\alpha,1}^{2}p^{\alpha}\right)\left(\omega_{\alpha,2}^{2}p^{\alpha}+\omega_{0,2}^{2}\right)\right\rangle\right\}$ and $\mathrm{L}^{-1}\left\{\frac{h_0\Omega}{p^2+\Omega^2}\right\}$.

For eigen creeping of the intrinsic points $x_{u,1,free}(t)$ and $x_{u,2,free}(t)$ of the internal structure of the standard BFY CF DS we obtain the following expressions:

$$x_{u,1,free}(t) = \mathrm{L}^{-1}\mathrm{L}\{x_{u,1}(t)\} = \mathrm{L}^{-1}\left\{\frac{\omega_{\alpha,2}^{4}p^{2\alpha}(px_0+\dot{x}_0)}{\Delta(p)}\right\} \quad (96)$$

$$x_{u,2,free}(t) = \mathrm{L}^{-1}\mathrm{L}\{x_{u,2}(t)\} = \mathrm{L}^{-1}\left\{\frac{\omega_{\alpha,2}^{2}p^{\alpha}(px_0+\dot{x}_0)}{\Delta(p)}\left(\omega_{0,1}^{2}+\omega_{0,2}^{2}+\omega_{e}^{2}+\omega_{\alpha,1}^{2}p^{\alpha}\right)\right\} \quad (97)$$

For force creeping, $x_{u,1,Forced}(t)$ and $x_{u,2,Forced}(t)$ of the internal structure of the standard BFY VF DS, we obtain the following expressions:

$$x_{u,1,Forced}(t) = \mathrm{L}^{-1}\mathrm{L}\{x_{u,1}(t)\} = \mathrm{L}^{-1}\left\{\frac{\omega_{\alpha,2}^{4}p^{2\alpha}}{\Delta(p)}\right\} * \mathrm{L}^{-1}\left\{\frac{h_0\Omega}{p^2+\Omega^2}\right\} \quad (98)$$

$$x_{u,2}(t) = \mathrm{L}^{-1}\mathrm{L}\{x_{u,2}(t)\} = \mathrm{L}^{-1}\left\{\frac{\omega_{\alpha,2}^{2}p^{\alpha}}{\Delta(p)}\left(\omega_{0,1}^{2}+\omega_{0,2}^{2}+\omega_{e}^{2}+\omega_{\alpha,1}^{2}p^{\alpha}\right)\right\} * \mathrm{L}^{-1}\left\{\frac{h_0\Omega}{p^2+\Omega^2}\right\} \quad (99)$$

Using the convolution integral and the property of three functions $f_1(t)$, $f_2(t)$, and $f_3(t)$ in convolution, the Laplace transform $\mathrm{L}\{f_3(t)\} = \mathrm{L}\{x_{u,1}(t)\}$ can be expressed by multiplying of the Laplace transforms of these two functions $\mathrm{L}\{f_{1,1}(t)\}$, i.e.,$\mathrm{L}\{f_{1,2}(t)\}$ and $\mathrm{L}\{f_2(t)\} == \mathrm{L}\{x(t)\}$.

The axial dilatation of the Faraday element connected in parallel in the BFY VF DS discrete dynamical system is as follows:

$$\varepsilon_z(t) = \frac{x_{u,1}(t)}{\updownarrow_0} \quad \varepsilon_z(t) = \frac{x_{u,1}(t)}{\updownarrow_0} = \frac{1}{\updownarrow_0}\mathrm{L}^{-1}\mathrm{L}\{x_{u,1}(t)\}$$

$$\varepsilon_z(t) = \frac{1}{\updownarrow_0}\mathrm{L}^{-1}\left\{\frac{\omega_{\alpha,2}^4 p^{2\alpha}}{\Delta(p)}\left\langle\frac{h_0\Omega}{p^2+\Omega^2} + (px_0 + \dot{x}_0)\right\rangle\right\} \tag{100}$$

The expression for normal stress in the Faraday element connected in parallel in the BFY VF DS discrete dynamical system is equivalent (formally same as) to Equation (85). The electric voltage of the electric polarization in the Faraday element in BFY DS2 is equivalent (formally same as) to Equation (86). And, the dielectric displacements in the Faraday element in the BFY DS2 dynamical system are equivalent (formally same as) to Equation (87).

4.2.2. Dynamics of the Rheological Reverse Burgers–Faraday–CF Dynamic System—BFY CF DSR Crawler

For studying the dynamical behavior for the reverse Burgers–Faraday fractional type system—BFY CF DSR (shown in the lower part of Figure 5b) we applied an identical procedure as described in detail in Sections 4.1.1 and 4.1.2: we use the Laplace transform on the previous system of fractional differential Equation (91) to obtain a system of non-homogeneous algebraic equations for the unknown Laplace transforms of the independent generalized coordinates. We solve these equations using Cramer's rule, utilizing the determinant of the system and other relevant determinants; subsequently, we determine the inverse Laplace transforms for all three independent generalized coordinates, transitioning to the time domain, yielding the following:

$$\begin{aligned}
x(t) &= \mathrm{L}^{-1}\mathrm{L}\{x(t)\} = \mathrm{L}^{-1}\left\{\frac{1}{\Delta(p)}\left\langle\frac{h_0\Omega}{p^2+\Omega^2} + (px_0+\dot{x}_0)\right\rangle\left\langle\left(\omega_{\alpha,1}^2 p^\alpha - \omega_{0,1}^2\right)\left(\omega_e^2+\omega_{0,2}^2+\omega_{\alpha,2}^2 p^\alpha - \omega_{0,1}^2\right)+\omega_{0,1}^4\right\rangle\right\} \\
x_{u,1}(t) &= \mathrm{L}^{-1}\mathrm{L}\{x_{u,1}(t)\} = \mathrm{L}^{-1}\left\{-\frac{\omega_{0,1}^2}{\Delta(p)}\left\langle\frac{h_0\Omega}{p^2+\Omega^2} + (px_0+\dot{x}_0)\right\rangle\left(\omega_{\alpha,2}^2 p^\alpha + \omega_e^2 + \omega_{0,2}^2\right)\right\} \\
x_{u,2}(t) &= \mathrm{L}^{-1}\mathrm{L}\{x_{u,2}(t)\} = \mathrm{L}^{-1}\left\{-\frac{1}{\Delta(p)}\left\langle\frac{h_0\Omega}{p^2+\Omega^2} + (px_0+\dot{x}_0)\right\rangle\left(\omega_{\alpha,1}^2 p^\alpha - \omega_{0,1}^2\right)\left(\omega_{\alpha,2}^2 p^\alpha + \omega_e^2 + \omega_{0,2}^2\right)\right\}
\end{aligned} \tag{101}$$

where system determinant is in the following form:

$$\begin{aligned}
\Delta(p) = &\left(p^2+\omega_{0,2}^2+\omega_e^2+\omega_{\alpha,2}^2 p^\alpha\right)\left\langle\left(\omega_{\alpha,1}^2 p^\alpha - \omega_{0,1}^2\right)\left(\omega_e^2+\omega_{0,2}^2+\omega_{\alpha,2}^2 p^\alpha - \omega_{0,1}^2\right)+\omega_{0,1}^4\right\rangle - \\
&-\left(\omega_{0,2}^2+\omega_e^2+\omega_{\alpha,2}^2 p^\alpha\right)\left(\omega_{\alpha,1}^2 p^\alpha - \omega_{0,1}^2\right)\left(\omega_{\alpha,2}^2 p^\alpha + \omega_e^2 + \omega_{0,2}^2\right)
\end{aligned} \tag{102}$$

First, it is necessary to determine the inverse Laplace-transform of the external independent coordinate $\mathrm{L}^{-1}\mathrm{L}\left\{x_{free}(t)\right\}$ for **eigen free sliding-flow** $\left\{x_{free}(t)\right\}$, and transition to the time domain in the following form:

$$x_{free}(t) = \mathrm{L}^{-1}\mathrm{L}\left\{x_{free}(t)\right\} = \mathrm{L}^{-1}\left\{\frac{(px_0+\dot{x}_0)}{\Delta(p)}\left\langle\left(\omega_{\alpha,1}^2 p^\alpha - \omega_{0,1}^2\right)\left(\omega_e^2+\omega_{0,2}^2+\omega_{\alpha,2}^2 p^\alpha - \omega_{0,1}^2\right)+\omega_{0,1}^4\right\rangle\right\} \tag{103}$$

Next, it is necessary to determine the external independent generalized coordinate $\mathrm{L}^{-1}\mathrm{L}\{x_{part}(t)\}$ **for forced sliding-flow** movements of fractional type $\{x_{part}(t)\}$ under the influence of an external periodic one frequency force by using the integral of convolution and the inverse Laplace transformation of the expressions $\mathrm{L}^{-1}\left\{\frac{1}{\Delta(p)}\left\langle\left(\omega_{\alpha,1}^2 p^\alpha - \omega_{0,1}^2\right)\left(\omega_e^2+\omega_{0,2}^2+\omega_{\alpha,2}^2 p^\alpha - \omega_{0,1}^2\right)+\omega_{0,1}^4\right\rangle\right\}$ and $\mathrm{L}^{-1}\left\{\frac{h_0\Omega}{p^2+\Omega^2}\right\}$ in the form:

$$x_{part}(t) = \mathrm{L}^{-1}\mathrm{L}\{x_{part}(t)\} = \mathrm{L}^{-1}\left\{\frac{1}{\Delta(p)}\left\langle\left(\omega_{\alpha,1}^2 p^\alpha - \omega_{0,1}^2\right)\left(\omega_e^2 + \omega_{0,2}^2 + \omega_{\alpha,2}^2 p^\alpha - \omega_{0,1}^2\right) + \omega_{0,1}^4\right\rangle\right\} * \mathrm{L}^{-1}\left\{\frac{h_0\Omega}{p^2+\Omega^2}\right\}. \quad (104)$$

Also, it is possible to determine the internal independent generalized coordinates $x_{u,1}(t)$ of the BFY VF DSR dynamical system:

$$x_{u,1,free}(t) = \mathrm{L}^{-1}\mathrm{L}\{x_{u,1}(t)\} = \mathrm{L}^{-1}\left\{-\frac{\omega_{0,1}^2(px_0 + \dot{x}_0)}{\Delta(p)}\left(\omega_{\alpha,2}^2 p^\alpha + \omega_e^2 + \omega_{0,2}^2\right)\right\} \quad (105)$$

$$x_{u,2,free}(t) = \mathrm{L}^{-1}\mathrm{L}\{x_{u,2}(t)\} = \mathrm{L}^{-1}\left\{-\frac{(px_0 + \dot{x}_0)}{\Delta(p)}\left(\omega_{\alpha,1}^2 p^\alpha - \omega_{0,1}^2\right)\left(\omega_{\alpha,2}^2 p^\alpha + \omega_e^2 + \omega_{0,2}^2\right)\right\} \quad (106)$$

For **forced creeping**, $x_{u,1,Forced}(t)$ and $x_{u,2,Forced}(t)$ in the BFY CF DSR dynamical system we obtain:

$$x_{u,1,Forced}(t) = \mathrm{L}^{-1}\mathrm{L}\{x_{u,1}(t)\} = \mathrm{L}^{-1}\left\{-\frac{\omega_{0,1}^2}{\Delta(p)}\left(\omega_{\alpha,2}^2 p^\alpha + \omega_e^2 + \omega_{0,2}^2\right)\right\} * \mathrm{L}^{-1}\left\{\frac{h_0\Omega}{p^2+\Omega^2}\right\} \quad (107)$$

$$x_{u,2}(t) = \mathrm{L}^{-1}\mathrm{L}\{x_{u,2}(t)\} = \mathrm{L}^{-1}\left\{-\frac{1}{\Delta(p)}\left(\omega_{\alpha,1}^2 p^\alpha - \omega_{0,1}^2\right)\left(\omega_{\alpha,2}^2 p^\alpha + \omega_e^2 + \omega_{0,2}^2\right)\right\} * \mathrm{L}^{-1}\left\{\frac{h_0\Omega}{p^2+\Omega^2}\right\} \quad (108)$$

The axial dilatation of the Faraday element connected in parallel in BFY CF DSR discrete dynamical system is as follows:

$$\varepsilon_z(t) = \frac{1}{\updownarrow_0}\mathrm{L}^{-1}\left\{\begin{array}{l}\frac{1}{\Delta(p)}\left\langle\frac{h_0\Omega}{p^2+\Omega^2} + (px_0 + \dot{x}_0)\right\rangle\cdot \\ \left\langle\left(\omega_{\alpha,1}^2 p^\alpha - \omega_{0,1}^2\right)\left(\omega_e^2 + \omega_{0,2}^2 + \omega_{\alpha,2}^2 p^\alpha - \omega_{0,1}^2\right) + \omega_{0,1}^4 + \left(\omega_{\alpha,1}^2 p^\alpha - \omega_{0,1}^2\right)\left(\omega_{\alpha,2}^2 p^\alpha + \omega_e^2 + \omega_{0,2}^2\right)\right\rangle\end{array}\right\} \quad (109)$$

Normal stress in the Faraday element in BFY VF DSR discrete dynamical system is as follows:

$$\sigma_z(t) = \mathrm{L}^{-1}\left\{\begin{array}{l}\frac{\mathbf{E_e}}{\updownarrow_0\Delta(p)}\left\langle\frac{h_0\Omega}{p^2+\Omega^2} + (px_0 + \dot{x}_0)\right\rangle\cdot \\ \left\langle\left(\omega_{\alpha,1}^2 p^\alpha - \omega_{0,1}^2\right)\left(\omega_e^2 + \omega_{0,2}^2 + \omega_{\alpha,2}^2 p^\alpha - \omega_{0,1}^2\right) + \omega_{0,1}^4 + \left(\omega_{\alpha,1}^2 p^\alpha - \omega_{0,1}^2\right)\left(\omega_{\alpha,2}^2 p^\alpha + \omega_e^2 + \omega_{0,2}^2\right)\right\rangle\end{array}\right\} \quad (110)$$

The electric voltage of polarization in the Faraday element in BFY CF DSR discrete dynamical system is as follows:

$$\mathbf{V}_z(t) = \mathrm{L}^{-1}\left\{\begin{array}{l}-\frac{g\mathbf{E_e}}{\updownarrow_0\Delta(p)}\left\langle\frac{h_0\Omega}{p^2+\Omega^2} + (px_0 + \dot{x}_0)\right\rangle\cdot \\ \left\langle\left(\omega_{\alpha,1}^2 p^\alpha - \omega_{0,1}^2\right)\left(\omega_e^2 + \omega_{0,2}^2 + \omega_{\alpha,2}^2 p^\alpha - \omega_{0,1}^2\right) + \omega_{0,1}^4 + \left(\omega_{\alpha,1}^2 p^\alpha - \omega_{0,1}^2\right)\left(\omega_{\alpha,2}^2 p^\alpha + \omega_e^2 + \omega_{0,2}^2\right)\right\rangle\end{array}\right\} \quad (111)$$

5. Numerical Analysis

After conducting extensive numerical experiments on the obtained solutions of Laplace transforms $\mathrm{L}\{x(t)\}$, $\mathrm{L}\{x_{u,1}(t)\}$, and $\mathrm{L}\{x_{u,2}(t)\}$ for all three independent generalized coordinates $x(t)$, $x_{u,1}(t)$, and $x_{u,2}(t)$ of the rheological Burgers–Faraday dynamical systems of fractional type (Figures 4 and 5): BFY VES DS, BFY VES DSR, BFY CF DS, and BFY CF DSR for free and forced movements, we selected only a few characteristic graphs from a multitude of results to present in this work. The Burgers–Faraday–VES rheological models of fractional type are both rheological oscillators of fractional type. The order of binding of the structural elements in the Burgers–Faraday–VES model significantly influences the rheological oscillatory dynamics of the rheological discrete dynamic systems.

In contrast, the Burgers–Faraday–CF discrete dynamic systems represent crawlers with flow behavior, also of fractional type. The dynamics of these two models (BFY CF DS and BFY CF DSR) differ significantly, as the order in which the structural elements are connected in the standard light complex rheological Burgers–Faraday model profoundly influences the system.

We will present the characteristic Laplace transformations of independent generalized coordinate surfaces for the dynamics of rheological discrete dynamic systems (Burgers–Faraday–VES DS and DSR, and Burgers–Faraday–CF DS and DSR). These surfaces will be visualized in coordinate systems defined by the following axes: the elongation of the Laplace transform, the exponent α of the fractional-order differentiation operator within the interval $0 < \alpha < 1$, and the parameter p of the Laplace transform.

This allows for the formation of a series of sets of Laplace transforms of eigen and forced modes of rheological oscillation dynamics of a rheological Burgers–Faraday–VES DS discrete dynamics system of fractional type.

The set of Laplace transforms $L\left\{x_{free,likecos}\right\}$ and $L\left\{x_{free,likesin}\right\}$ of the **eigen modes** of independent generalized coordinate $\{x(t)\}$ **of external degree of freedom,** of dynamics of (BFY CF DS) presented in upper part of Figure 4, is as follows:

$$L\left\{x_{free,like\sin}(t)\right\} = \frac{1}{\Delta(p)}\left\langle\left(\omega_{\alpha,1}^2 p^\alpha + \omega_e^2 - \omega_{0,2}^2\right)\left(\omega_{\alpha,2}^2 p^\alpha + \omega_{0,2}^2\right) + \omega_{0,2}^2\omega_{\alpha,2}^2 p^\alpha\right\rangle \quad (112)$$

$$L\left\{x_{free,like\cos}(t)\right\} = \frac{p}{\Delta(p)}\left\langle\left(\omega_{\alpha,1}^2 p^\alpha + \omega_e^2 - \omega_{0,2}^2\right)\left(\omega_{\alpha,2}^2 p^\alpha + \omega_{0,2}^2\right) + \omega_{0,2}^2\omega_{\alpha,2}^2 p^\alpha\right\rangle \quad (113)$$

where determinant of the system is in the following form:

$$\begin{gathered}\Delta(p) = \left(p^2 + \omega_e^2 + \omega_{\alpha,2}^2 p^\alpha\right)\left\langle\left(\omega_{\alpha,1}^2 p^\alpha + \omega_e^2 - \omega_{0,2}^2\right)\left(\omega_{\alpha,2}^2 p^\alpha + \omega_{0,2}^2\right) + \omega_{0,2}^2\omega_{\alpha,2}^2 p^\alpha\right\rangle + \\ +\omega_e^2\left\langle\omega_{\alpha,2}^4 p^{2\alpha} - \omega_e^2\left(\omega_{\alpha,2}^2 p^\alpha + \omega_{0,2}^2\right)\right\rangle - \omega_{\alpha,2}^2 p^\alpha\left\langle\omega_e^2\omega_{0,2}^2 + \omega_{\alpha,2}^2 p^\alpha\left(\omega_{\alpha,1}^2 p^\alpha + \omega_e^2 - \omega_{0,2}^2\right)\right\rangle\end{gathered} \quad (114)$$

The set of Laplace transforms $L\{x_{Forced,sin}(t)\}$ and $L\{x_{Forced,cos}(t)\}$ of **the forced modes** of independent generalized coordinate $\{x(t)\}$ **of external degree of freedom** of dynamics of the rheological Burgers–Faraday–(BFY CF DS) discrete rheological oscillator presented in upper part of Figure 4, is as follows:

$$L\{x_{Forced,like\sin}(t)\} = \frac{1}{\Delta(p)}\left\langle\frac{\Omega}{p^2+\Omega^2}\right\rangle\left\langle\omega_{0,2}^4 + \left(\omega_{0,1}^2 + \omega_{0,2}^2 + \omega_e^2 + \omega_{\alpha,1}^2 p^\alpha\right)\left(\omega_{\alpha,2}^2 p^\alpha + \omega_{0,2}^2\right)\right\rangle \quad (115)$$

$$L\{x_{Forced,like\cos}(t)\} = \frac{1}{\Delta(p)}\left\langle\frac{p}{p^2+\Omega^2}\right\rangle\left\langle\omega_{0,2}^4 + \left(\omega_{0,1}^2 + \omega_{0,2}^2 + \omega_e^2 + \omega_{\alpha,1}^2 p^\alpha\right)\left(\omega_{\alpha,2}^2 p^\alpha + \omega_{0,2}^2\right)\right\rangle \quad (116)$$

The set of Laplace transforms $L\left\{x_{u,1,free,likesin}(t)\right\}$ and $L\left\{x_{u,1,free,likecos}(t)\right\}$ **of the eigen modes** of independent generalized coordinate $x_u(t)$ **of the internal degree of freedom**, of the dynamics of the rheological Burgers–Faraday–(**BFY VF DS**) discrete rheological oscillatory dynamic system, fractional type with piezoelectric property, presented in upper part of Figure 4, is as follows:

$$L\left\{x_{u,1free,like\sin}(t)\right\} = \frac{1}{\Delta(p)}\left\langle\omega_e^2\left(\omega_{\alpha,2}^2 p^\alpha + \omega_{0,2}^2\right) - \omega_{\alpha,2}^4 p^{2\alpha}\right\rangle \quad (117)$$

$$L\left\{x_{u,1free,like\cos}(t)\right\} = \frac{p}{\Delta(p)}\left\langle\omega_e^2\left(\omega_{\alpha,2}^2 p^\alpha + \omega_{0,2}^2\right) - \omega_{\alpha,2}^4 p^{2\alpha}\right\rangle \quad (118)$$

The set of Laplace transforms $L\left\{x_{u,2free,like\sin}(t)\right\}$ and $L\left\{x_{u,2free,like\cos}(t)\right\}$ of the **eigen modes** of independent generalized coordinate $x_{u,2,free}(t)$ **of the internal degree of freedom**, of dynamics of the rheological Burgers–Faraday–(**BFY CF DS**) discrete rheological oscillatory dynamic system, fractional type with piezoelectric property, presented in upper part of Figure 5, is as follows:

$$\mathrm{L}\left\{x_{u,2free,like\sin}(t)\right\}=\frac{1}{\Delta(p)}\left\langle\omega_e^2\omega_{0,2}^2+\omega_{\alpha,2}^2\left(\omega_{\alpha,1}^2p^\alpha+\omega_e^2-\omega_{0,2}^2\right)\right\rangle \tag{119}$$

$$\mathrm{L}\left\{x_{u,2free,like\cos}(t)\right\}=\frac{p}{\Delta(p)}\left\langle\omega_e^2\omega_{0,2}^2+\omega_{\alpha,2}^2\left(\omega_{\alpha,1}^2p^\alpha+\omega_e^2-\omega_{0,2}^2\right)\right\rangle \tag{120}$$

This allows the formation of a series of sets of Laplace transforms of eigen modes and forced modes of crawler-creep dynamics of a rheological Burgers–Faraday–(**BFY CF DS**) rheological crawler-creep rheological discrete dynamics system, fractional type with piezoelectric property.

The set of Laplace transforms $\mathrm{L}\left\{x_{free,likecos}\right\}$ and $\mathrm{L}\left\{x_{free,likesin}\right\}$ of the **eigen modes** of independent generalized coordinate $\{x(t)\}$ of **external degree of freedom**, of dynamics of the rheological Burgers–Faraday–(BFY CF DS) discrete rheological crawler-creep discrete dynamic system, fractional type with piezoelectric property, presented in upper part of Figure 5, is as follows:

$$\mathrm{L}\left\{x_{free,like\cos}(t)\right\}=\frac{p}{\Delta(p)}\left\langle\omega_{0,2}^4+\left(\omega_{0,1}^2+\omega_{0,2}^2+\omega_e^2+\omega_{\alpha,1}^2p^\alpha\right)\left(\omega_{\alpha,2}^2p^\alpha+\omega_{0,2}^2\right)\right\rangle \tag{121}$$

$$\mathrm{L}\left\{x_{free,like\sin}(t)\right\}=\frac{1}{\Delta(p)}\left\langle\omega_{0,2}^4+\left(\omega_{0,1}^2+\omega_{0,2}^2+\omega_e^2+\omega_{\alpha,1}^2p^\alpha\right)\left(\omega_{\alpha,2}^2p^\alpha+\omega_{0,2}^2\right)\right\rangle \tag{122}$$

where determinant determined by expression in the following form:

$$\begin{aligned}\Delta(p)=&\left(p^2+\omega_{\alpha,2}^2p^\alpha\right)\left\langle\omega_{0,2}^4+\left(\omega_{0,1}^2+\omega_{0,2}^2+\omega_e^2+\omega_{\alpha,1}^2p^\alpha\right)\left(\omega_{\alpha,2}^2p^\alpha+\omega_{0,2}^2\right)\right\rangle-\\&-\omega_{\alpha,2}^4p^{2\alpha}\left(\omega_{0,1}^2+\omega_{0,2}^2+\omega_e^2+\omega_{\alpha,1}^2p^\alpha\right)\end{aligned} \tag{123}$$

The set of Laplace transforms $\mathrm{L}\{x_{Forced,sin}(t)\}$ and $\mathrm{L}\{x_{Forced,cos}(t)\}$ of the **forced modes** of independent generalized coordinate $\{x(t)\}$ of the **external degree of freedom** of dynamics of the rheological Burgers–Faraday–(BFY CF DS) discrete rheological crawler-creep dynamic system, fractional type with piezoelectric property, presented in upper part of Figure 5, is as follows:

$$\mathrm{L}\{x_{Forced,like\sin}(t)\}=\frac{1}{\Delta(p)}\left\langle\frac{\Omega}{p^2+\Omega^2}\right\rangle\left\langle\omega_{0,2}^4+\left(\omega_{0,1}^2+\omega_{0,2}^2+\omega_e^2+\omega_{\alpha,1}^2p^\alpha\right)\left(\omega_{\alpha,2}^2p^\alpha+\omega_{0,2}^2\right)\right\rangle \tag{124}$$

$$\mathrm{L}\{x_{Forced,like\cos}(t)\}=\frac{1}{\Delta(p)}\left\langle\frac{p}{p^2+\Omega^2}\right\rangle\left\langle\omega_{0,2}^4+\left(\omega_{0,1}^2+\omega_{0,2}^2+\omega_e^2+\omega_{\alpha,1}^2p^\alpha\right)\left(\omega_{\alpha,2}^2p^\alpha+\omega_{0,2}^2\right)\right\rangle \tag{125}$$

The set of Laplace transforms $\mathrm{L}\left\{x_{u,1,free,likesin}(t)\right\}$ and $\mathrm{L}\left\{x_{u,1,free,likecos}(t)\right\}$ **of the eigen modes** of independent generalized coordinate $x_{u,1}(t)$ **of the internal degree of freedom**, of dynamics of the rheological Burgers–Faraday–(BFY CF DS) discrete rheological crawler-creep dynamic system, fractional type with piezoelectric property, presented in upper part of Figure 5, is as follows:

$$\mathrm{L}\left\{x_{u,1free,like\sin}(t)\right\}=\frac{\omega_{\alpha,2}^4p^{2\alpha}}{\Delta(p)} \tag{126}$$

$$\mathrm{L}\left\{x_{u,1free,like\cos}(t)\right\}=\frac{\omega_{\alpha,2}^4p^{2\alpha+1}}{\Delta(p)} \tag{127}$$

The set of Laplace transforms $\mathrm{L}\{x_{u,1,Forced,like\sin}(t)\}$ and $\mathrm{L}\{x_{u,1,Force,like\cos}(t)\}$ **of the forced modes** of independent generalized coordinate $x_{u,1}(t)$ **of the internal degree of freedom**, of dynamics of the rheological Burgers–Faraday–(BFY CF DS) rheological crawler-creep discrete dynamic system, fractional type with piezoelectric property, presented in upper part of Figure 5, is as follows:

$$\mathrm{L}\{x_{u,1,Forced,like\sin}(t)\} = \frac{\omega_{\alpha,2}^4 p^{2\alpha}}{\Delta(p)}\left\langle\frac{\Omega}{p^2+\Omega^2}\right\rangle \quad (128)$$

$$\mathrm{L}\{x_{u,1,Force,like\cos}(t)\} = \frac{\omega_{\alpha,2}^4 p^{2\alpha}}{\Delta(p)}\left\langle\frac{p}{p^2+\Omega^2}\right\rangle \quad (129)$$

The set of Laplace transforms $\mathrm{L}\left\{x_{u,2free,like\sin}(t)\right\}$ and $\mathrm{L}\left\{x_{u,2free,like\cos}(t)\right\}$ **of the eigen modes** of independent generalized coordinate $x_{u,2,free}(t)$ **of the internal degree of freedom**, of dynamics of the rheological Burgers–Faraday–(BFY CF DS) discrete rheological crawler-creep dynamic system, fractional type with piezoelectric property, presented in upper part of Figure 5, is as follows:

$$\mathrm{L}\left\{x_{u,2free,like\sin}(t)\right\} = \frac{\omega_{\alpha,2}^2 p^{\alpha}}{\Delta(p)}\left(\omega_{0,1}^2+\omega_{0,2}^2+\omega_e^2+\omega_{\alpha,1}^2 p^{\alpha}\right) \quad (130)$$

$$\mathrm{L}\left\{x_{u,2free,like\cos}(t)\right\} = \frac{\omega_{\alpha,2}^2 p^{\alpha+1}}{\Delta(p)}\left(\omega_{0,1}^2+\omega_{0,2}^2+\omega_e^2+\omega_{\alpha,1}^2 p^{\alpha}\right) \quad (131)$$

Figures 6–8 show the spatial surfaces of Laplace transforms $\mathrm{L}\left\{x_{free,likesin}\right\}$ and $\mathrm{L}\left\{x_{free,likecos}\right\}$ eigenmodes of sine-like and cosine-like type, as well as the Laplace transformation $\mathrm{L}\{x_{Forced,likesin}(t)\}$ of forced mode of the independent generalized coordinate of the external degree of freedom of movement of the rheological Burgers–Faraday–CF DS discrete dynamic system of fractional type with piezoelectric property, crawler type, in the cases of single-frequency periodic force $F(t) = F_0 sin(\Omega t + \varphi_0)$ action, presented in the Laplace transformation space and in coordinate system with coordinate axes: elongation of Laplace transformation, the differentiation exponent α of the fractional order in the interval $0 < \alpha < 1$, and the Laplace transforms parameter p, drawn using analytical Expressions (121), (122) and (124), for different system parameter values.

The space surfaces of the Laplace transforms $\mathrm{L}\left\{x_{free,likesin}\right\}$ and $\mathrm{L}\left\{x_{free,likecos}\right\}$ of the free creep (flow) modes and $\mathrm{L}\{x_{Forced,likesin}(t)\}$, $0 < \alpha < 1$ of the forced creep (flow) mode of the external generalized coordinate of the rheological Burgers–Faraday–BFY CF DS discrete dynamic system of fractional type with piezoelectric property, in the cases of single-frequency periodic force action $F(t) = F_0 sin(\Omega t + \varphi_0)$, for different system parameter values, presented in the Laplace transformation space drawn using analytical Expression (124), for different system parameter value is shown in the Figure 9.

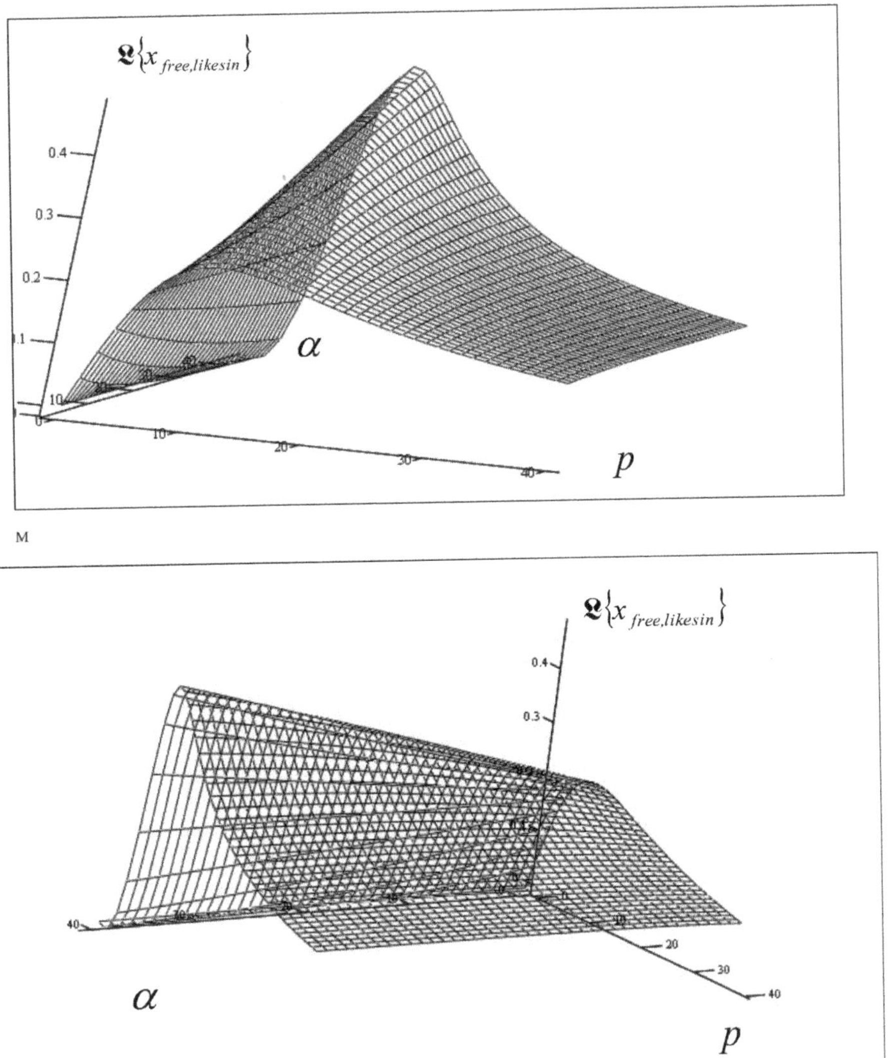

M

M

Figure 6. The space surfaces of the Laplace transform $L\{x_{free,likesin}\}$, $0 < \alpha < 1$ of the **free creep (flow) mode, sine-like type**, of the external generalized coordinate of the rheological Burgers–Faraday–VF DS discrete dynamic system of fractional type with piezoelectric property, presented in the Laplace transformation space and in coordinate system with coordinate axes: elongation of Laplace transformation, the differentiation exponent α of the fractional order in the interval $0 < \alpha < 1$, and the Laplace transforms parameter p, drawn using analytical Expression (121), for different system parameter value.

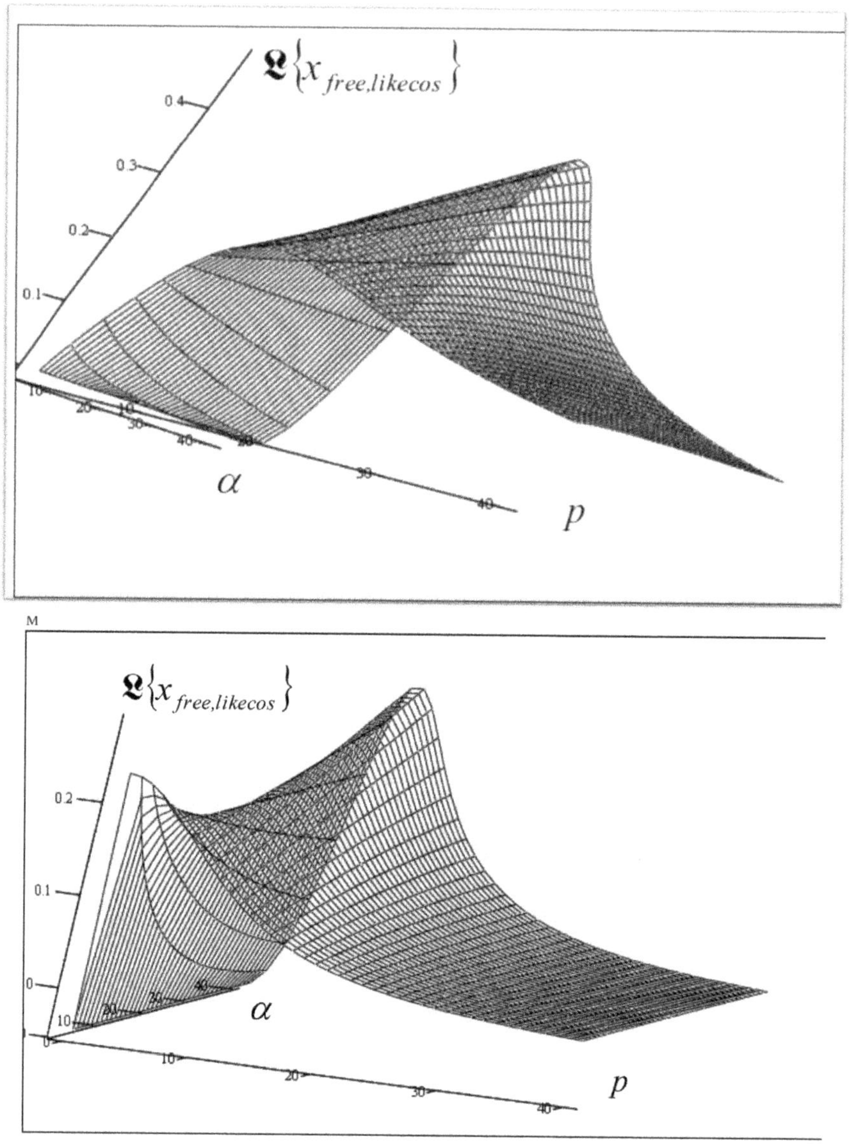

M

Figure 7. The space surfaces of the Laplace transform $L\left\{x_{free,likecos}\right\}$, $0 < \alpha < 1$ of the **free creep (flow) mode, cosine-like type**, of the external generalized coordinate of the rheological Burgers–Faraday–VF DS discrete dynamic system of fractional type with piezoelectric property, presented in the Laplace transformation space and in coordinate system with coordinate axes: elongation of Laplace transformation, the differentiation exponent α of the fractional order in the interval $0 < \alpha < 1$, and the Laplace transforms parameter p, drawn using analytical Expression (122), for different system parameter value.

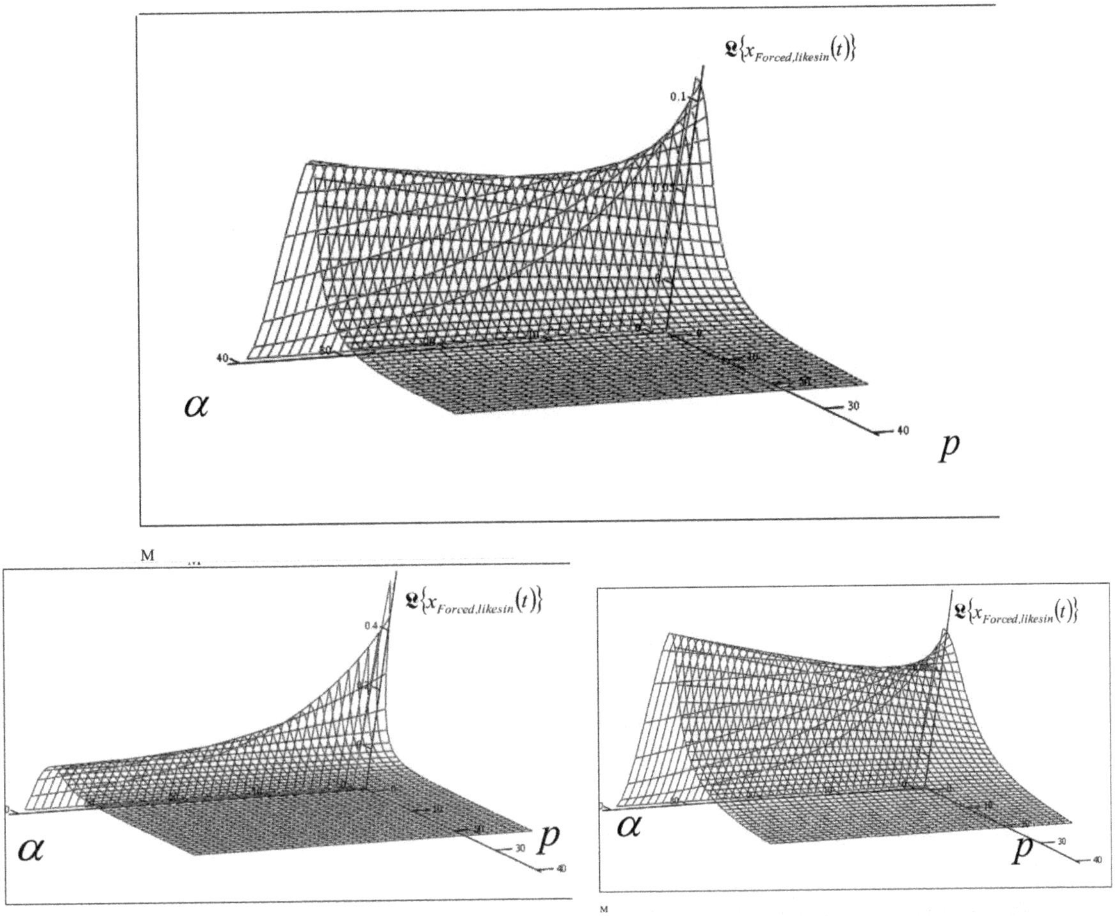

Figure 8. The space surfaces of the Laplace transform $\mathrm{L}\{x_{Forced,likesin}(t)\}$, $0 < \alpha < 1$ of **the forced creep** (flow) mode of the external generalized coordinate of the rheological Burgers–Faraday–VF DS discrete dynamic system of fractional type with piezoelectric property, in the cases of single-frequency periodic force action $F(t) = F_0 sin(\Omega t + \varphi_0)$, presented in the Laplace transformation space and in coordinate system with coordinate axes: elongation of Laplace transformation, the differentiation exponent α of the fractional order in the interval $0 < \alpha < 1$, and the Laplace transforms parameter p, drawn using analytical expression (124), for different system parameter value.

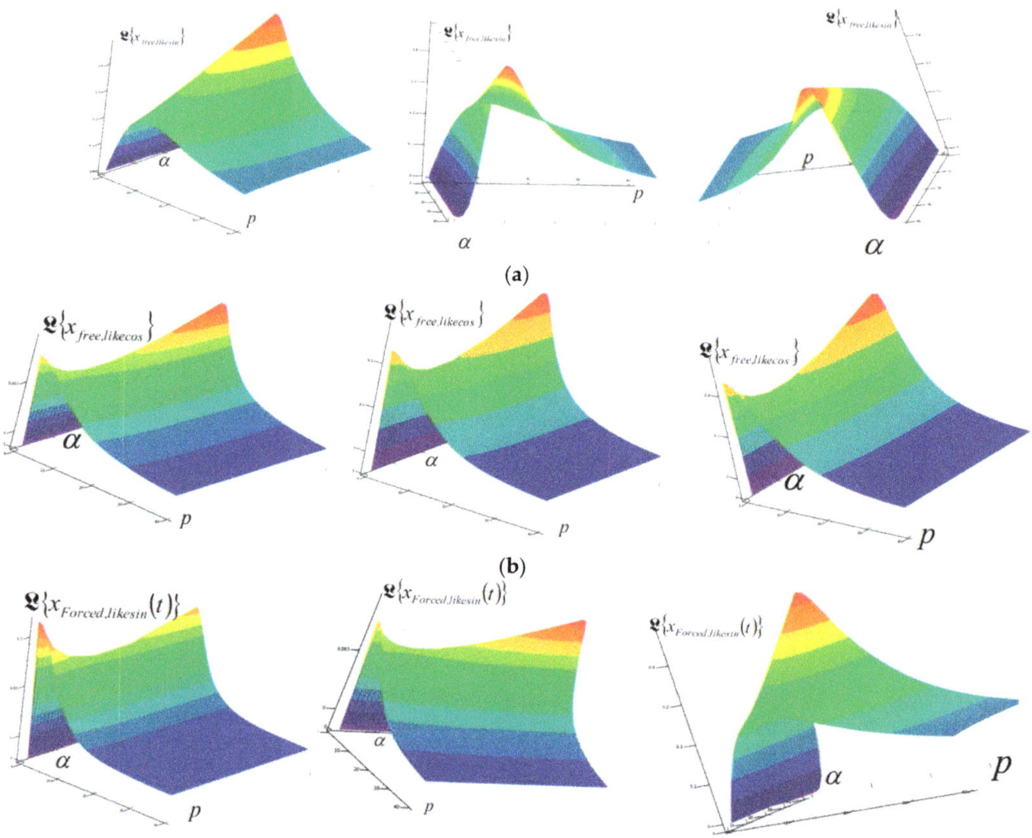

Figure 9. The space surfaces of the Laplace transforms $\mathrm{L}\left\{x_{free,likesin}\right\}$ and $\mathrm{L}\left\{x_{free,likecos}\right\}$ of the free creep (flow) modes and $\mathrm{L}\{x_{Forced,likesin}(t)\}, 0<\alpha<1$ of the forced creep (flow) mode of the external generalized coordinate of the rheological Burgers–Faraday–BFY CF DS discrete dynamic system of fractional type with piezoelectric property, in the cases of single-frequency periodic force action $F(t)=F_0 sin(\Omega t+\varphi_0)$, for different system parameter values, presented in the Laplace transformation space and in coordinate system with coordinate axes: elongation of Laplace transformation, the differentiation exponent α of the fractional order in the interval $0<\alpha<1$, and the Laplace transforms parameter p, drawn using analytical Expression (124), for different system parameter value. (**a**) The space surfaces of the Laplace transform $\mathrm{L}\left\{x_{free,likesin}\right\}, 0<\alpha<1$ of the **free** creep (flow) mode, sine-like type, of the external generalized coordinate of the rheological Burgers–Faraday–BFY CF DS discrete dynamic system of fractional type with piezoelectric property, for different system parameter values. (**b**) The space surfaces of the Laplace transform $\mathrm{L}\left\{x_{free,likecos}\right\}, 0<\alpha<1$ of the free creep (flow) mode, cosine-like type, of the external generalized coordinate of the rheological Burgers–Faraday–BFY CF DS discrete dynamic system of fractional type with piezoelectric property, for different system parameter values. (**c**) The space surfaces of the Laplace transform $\mathrm{L}\{x_{Forced,likesin}(t)\}, 0<\alpha<1$ of the forced creep (flow) mode of the external generalized coordinate of the rheological Burgers–Faraday–BFY CF DS discrete dynamic system of fractional type with piezoelectric property, in the cases of single-frequency periodic force action $F(t)=F_0 sin(\Omega t+\varphi_0)$, for different system parameter values.

6. Discussion

The development of highly efficient engineering and biomaterials with exceptional viscoelastic, fractional, and piezoelectric properties is a challenge in modern materials science. In this study, we introduce novel Burgers–Faraday models designed to characterize the dynamic behavior of fractional-type materials with coupled fields; specifically, the interplay between mechanical stress and strain and the electric polarization field, facilitated by the Faraday element.

These fractional models, integrating piezoelectric properties, offer analysis of complex systems, such as rheological oscillators and creeping materials.

Based on analytical results and their analysis, we define a number of conclusions here in the form of Theorems:

Theorem 1. *From the structural scheme of the standard light rheological complex model, a distinction can be observed between rheological oscillators and rheological sliders (creeper, crawler) of fractional type, which represent the connections within the rheological discrete dynamic system.*

Theorem 2. *If at least one of the Newton viscous fluid elements of fractional type is connected in series within the structure and is not in parallel connection or within parallel connection with any of the Hook ideal elastic elements or Faraday ideal elastic and piezoelectric element, then it is the case of dynamics of the sliding (crawling) elements of the rheological dynamic system.*

Theorem 3. *If each of the Newton viscous fluid elements of fractional type is connected in parallel or within a parallel connection with some of the Hook ideal elastic elements or Faraday ideal elastic and piezoelectric elements, then it presents a rheological dynamic system with elastoviscous damped oscillations of fractional type.*

Theorem 4. *Every series connection of any of the Newton fluid elements of fractional type introduces one internal degree of freedom of motion for the rheological complex element, in addition to the external degrees of freedom of motion of the complex rheological discrete dynamic system.*

Theorem 5. *By comparing the obtained analytical expressions of Laplace transforms for both the free and forced motions of the material point (rigid body in translation), we observed that the order of binding in the standard light structure of the rheological complex Burgers-Faraday-VES discrete dynamic model, DS and DSR, significantly affects the differences in dynamics, but does not change the type of rheological oscillatory dynamics, which remains of fractional and piezoelectric type.*

Theorem 6. *By comparing the obtained analytical expressions of Laplace transforms for both the free and forced motions of the material point (rigid body in translation), we observe that the order of binding in the standard light structure of the complex Burgers–Faraday–VF dynamic model DS and DSR significantly affects the differences in creeping-flow dynamics, but does not change the type of creeping-flow dynamics, which remains of fractional and piezoelectric type.*

7. Concluding Remarks

In this paper, two rheological models of fractional type with piezo-electrical properties are presented. The models can be applied in modeling viscoelastic and elasto-viscous biomaterials with properties of normal stress relaxation and materials where axial dilation lags behind normal stress and serves as the foundation for the construction of more complex structures of ideal biomaterials, with programmed normal stress relaxation properties and subsequent elasticity. These models are suitable for studying the behavior of complex systems such as rheological oscillators or creepers. Complex models have properties related to the occurrence of internal degrees of freedom that must be taken into account when studying rheological oscillators with piezo-electrical properties of a fractional type. We established fundamental principles and opened a broad field for further research into the properties of rheological discrete and continuously dynamic systems, with many degrees of freedom of movement, both in discrete and continuous systems of fractional type with coupled mechanical and piezoelectric fields.

The proposed models are suitable for advanced material design and the verification of modeling hypotheses, enabling the development of next-generation materials whose performance characteristics hinge on their viscoelastic, elastoviscous, or piezoelectric behavior.

In conclusion, we determined the differential constitutive relations of the fractional order, then gave solutions for the cases of basic complex and hybrid complex models of materials; we defined a class of rheological discrete dynamic systems of fractional type and piezoelectric properties and derived the corresponding systems of differential equations of fractional order, which describe the dynamics of these dynamic systems. Then, we determined the Laplace transforms of the corresponding external and internal independent generalized coordinates.

Complex behavior of materials like bones and cartilage that have both mechanical and piezoelectric properties can be described by the models that are presented in the paper.

Our research addresses a highly relevant area of study and demonstrates significant scientific innovation, offering new insights into the field of material dynamics.

We hope that our new Burgers–Faraday models will inspire other researchers to study the complex dynamics of more complex dynamical systems that can be created on the basis of systems that are studied in this paper.

Author Contributions: Conceptualization, K.R.H. and A.N.H.; methodology, K.R.H.; validation, K.R.H.; formal analysis, K.R.H.; writing—original draft preparation K.R.H. and A.N.H.; writing—review and editing K.R.H. and A.N.H.; visualization K.R.H. and A.N.H. All authors have read and agreed to the published version of the manuscript.

Funding: This research received no external funding.

Institutional Review Board Statement: Not applicable.

Informed Consent Statement: Not applicable.

Data Availability Statement: Data sharing is not applicable. Data are contained within the article.

Acknowledgments: The authors gratefully acknowledge support provided by the Ministry of Science, Technological Development, and Innovation of Republic of Serbia trough Mathematical Institute of Serbian Academy of Sciences and Arts. Authors would like to thank the reviewers for useful comments and suggestions that help in improving the quality of the manuscript.

Conflicts of Interest: The authors declare no conflicts of interest.

Abbreviations

$\varepsilon_z(t)$	axial dilatation
σ_z	normal stress
(SLS)	Standard Linear Solid model
$\mathbf{V}_z(t) = -g\sigma_z(t)$	Electric voltage in the Faraday element that is generated as a result of polarization closed by mechanical loading in the Faraday element
(KVFYF)	Kelvin–Voigt–Faraday fractional-type model
(MFYF)	Maxwell–Faraday fractional-type model
$D_t^{\alpha}[\bullet]$	the differential operator of fractional order of Caputo type
α	exponent of fractional order differentiation
$x(t)$	the independent generalized coordinate corresponding to the external degree of freedom,
$x_{u,1}(t)$ and $x_{u,2}(t)$	the internal independent generalized coordinate
BFY VF DS	Burgers–Faraday rheologic discrete dynamical system of fractional type with piezelectric property, viscous fluid
BFY VF DSR	Reverse Burgers–Faraday rheologic discrete dynamical system of fractional type with piezoelectric property, viscous fluid
BFY CF DS	Burgers–Faraday discrete dynamical system of fractional type creeper with piezoelectric properties
BFY CF DSR	Reverse Burgers–Faraday rheologic crawler (creeper) of fractional type with piezoelectric properties

References

1. Hedrih, K.; Perić, L.; Mančić, D.; Radmanović, M. Cross Polarized and Electrode Coated Rectangular Pie-zoceramic Plate Strain Problem. *J. Electrotech. Math. Fac. Tech. Sci. Kos. Mitrovica* **2003**, *8*, 39–54.
2. Perić, L. Prostorna Analiza Stanja Napona i Stanja Deformacije Napregntog Piezokeramičkog Materijala (Space Analysis of Stress and Straon State of Stressed Piezoceramiv Materials) [In Serbian]. Master's Thesis, Faculty of Mechanical Engineering in Niš, Niš, Serbia, 2004.
3. Hedrih, K.; Perić, L. Method of spatial analysis of piezoelectric body with crack using function of complex variable and computer programming in MATLAB. *Int. J. Nonlinear Sci. Num. Simul.* **2003**, *3*, 511–532.
4. Perić, L. Spregnuti tenzori stanja piezoeletričnih materijala (Coupled tensors of the piesoelectric material states). Ph.D. Thesis, Faculty of Mechanical Engineering in Niš, Niš, Serbia, 2005. (In Serbian)
5. Dabiri, D.; Saadat, M.; Mangal, D.; Jamali, S. Fractional rheology-informed neural networks for data-driven identification of viscoelastic constitutive models. *Rheol. Acta* **2023**, *62*, 557–568. [CrossRef]
6. Tomović, Z. Reološki model puzanja matriksa meke stijene (Rheologica model of the soft rocks creep). *Mater. I Konstr.* **2007**, *50*, 3–19.
7. Mihailović, V.; Landović, A. The relation properties of concrete and their characteristic in rheological models. *Zb. Rad.* **2010**, *19*, 115–124.
8. Stoiljkoic, D.T.; Petrović, V.; Đurović-Petrović, M. Rheological modeling of yarn elongation. *Tekstil* **2007**, *56*, 554–561.
9. Verdier, C. Rheological Properties of Living Materials. From Cells to Tissues. *J. Theor. Med.* **2003**, *5*, 67–91. [CrossRef]
10. Hedrih, K.R.; Hedrih, A.N. The Kelvin–Voigt visco-elastic model involving a fractional-order time derivative for modelling torsional oscillations of a complex discrete biodynamical system. *Acta Mech.* **2023**, *234*, 1923–1942. [CrossRef] [PubMed]
11. Bonfanti, A.; Fouchard, J.; Khalilgharibi, N.; Charras, G.; Kabla, A. A unified rheological model for cells and cellularised materials. *R. Soc. Open Sci.* **2020**, *7*, 190920. [CrossRef] [PubMed]
12. Fabrizio, M. Fractional rheological models for thermomechanical systems. Dissipation and free energies. *Fract. Calc. Appl. Anal.* **2013**, *17*, 206–223. [CrossRef]
13. Xu, K.; Chen, L.; Lopes, A.M.; Wang, M.; Wu, R.; Zhu, M. Fractional-Order Zener Model with Temperature-Order Equivalence for Viscoelastic Dampers. *Fractal. Fract.* **2023**, *7*, 714. [CrossRef]
14. Araújo, A.; Soares, C.M.; Herskovits, J.; Pedersen, P. Estimation of piezoelastic and viscoelastic properties in laminated structures. *Compos. Struct.* **2008**, *87*, 168–174. [CrossRef]
15. Zhao, F.; Zhou, B.; Zhu, X.; Wang, H. Constitutive model of piezoelectric/shape memory polymer composite. *J. Phys. Conf. Ser.* **2024**, *2713*, 012037. [CrossRef]
16. Cerquiglini, S.; Cignitti, M.; Marchetti, M.; Salleo, A. On the origin of electrical effects produced by stress in the hard tissues of living organisms. *Life Sci.* **1967**, *6*, 2651–2660. [CrossRef]
17. Reinish, B.G.; Nowick, S.A. Piezoelectric properties of bone as functions of moisture content. *Nature* **1975**, *253*, 626–627. [CrossRef]
18. Kao, F.-C.; Chiu, P.-Y.; Tsai, T.-T.; Lin, Z.-H. The application of nanogenerators and piezoelectricity in osteogenesis. *Sci. Technol. Adv. Mater.* **2019**, *20*, 1103–1117. [CrossRef]
19. Yang, C.; Ji, J.; Lv, Y.; Li, Z.; Luo, D. Application of Piezoelectric Material and Devices in Bone Regeneration. *Nanomaterials* **2022**, *12*, 4386. [CrossRef]
20. Bur, A.J. Measurements of the dynamic piezoelectric properties of bone as a function of temperature and humidity. *J. Biomech.* **1976**, *9*, 495–507. [CrossRef] [PubMed]
21. Shamos, M.H.; Lavine, L.S.; Shamos, M.I. Piezoelectric Effect in Bone. *Nature* **1963**, *197*, 81. [CrossRef]
22. Oladapo, B.I.; Ismail, S.O.; Kayode, J.F.; Omolayo, M. Ikumapayi Piezoelectric effects on bone modeling for enhanced sustainability. *Mater. Chem. Phys.* **2023**, *305*, 127960. [CrossRef]
23. Carter, A.; Popowski, K.; Cheng, K.; Greenbaum, A.; Ligler, F.S.; Moatti, A. Enhancement of Bone Regeneration Through the Converse Piezoelectric Effect, A Novel Approach for Applying Mechanical Stimulation. *Bioelectricity* **2021**, *3*, 255–271. [CrossRef]
24. Hedrih, K.R.; Machado, J.T. Discrete fractional order system vibrations. *Int. J. Non-Linear Mech.* **2015**, *73*, 2–11. [CrossRef]
25. Hedrih, K.R.; Milovanović, G.V. Elements of mathematical phenomenology and analogies of electrical and mechanical oscillators of the fractional type with finite number of degrees of freedom of oscillations: Linear and nonlinear modes. *Commun. Anal. Mech.* **2024**, *16*, 738–785. [CrossRef]
26. Suzuki, J.L.; Tuttle, T.G.; Roccabianca, S.; Zayernouri, M. A Data-Driven Memory-Dependent Modeling Framework for Anomalous Rheology: Application to Urinary Bladder Tissue. *Fractal Fract.* **2021**, *5*, 223. [CrossRef]
27. Suzuki, J.L.; Naghibolhosseini, M.; Zayernouri, M.A. General Return-Mapping Framework for Fractional Visco-Elasto-Plasticity. *Fractal. Fract.* **2022**, *6*, 715. [CrossRef]
28. Yu, X.; Yin, Y. Fractal Operators and Convergence Analysis in Fractional Viscoelastic Theory. *Fractal. Fract.* **2024**, *8*, 200. [CrossRef]
29. Fahmy, M.A.; Almehmadi, M.M. Fractional Dual-Phase-Lag Model for Nonlinear Viscoelastic Soft Tissues. *Fractal. Fract.* **2023**, *7*, 66. [CrossRef]
30. Hobiny, A.; Abbas, I. The Effect of Fractional Derivatives on Thermo-Mechanical Interaction in Biological Tissues during Hyperthermia Treatment Using Eigenvalues Approach. *Fractal. Fract.* **2023**, *7*, 432. [CrossRef]
31. Pascual-Francisco, J.B.; Susarrey-Huerta, O.; Farfan-Cabrera, L.I.; Flores-Hernández, R. Creep Properties of a Viscoelastic 3D Printed Sierpinski Carpet-Based Fractal. *Fractal. Fract.* **2023**, *7*, 568. [CrossRef]

32. Li, Q.; Sun, Z. Dynamic Modeling and Response Analysis of Dielectric Elastomer Incorporating Fractional Viscoelasticity and Gent Function. *Fractal. Fract.* **2023**, *7*, 786. [CrossRef]
33. Xu, Y.; Luo, Y.; Luo, X.; Chen, Y.; Liu, W. Fractional-Order Modeling of Piezoelectric Actuators with Coupled Hysteresis and Creep Effects. *Fractal. Fract.* **2023**, *8*, 3. [CrossRef]
34. Goroško, O.A.; Hedrih, K. *Analitička Dinamika (Mehanika) Diskretnih Naslednih Sistema, (Analytical Dynamics (Mechanics) of Discrete Hereditary Systems)*; University of Niš: Niš, Serbian, 2001; p. 426, ISBN 86-7181-054-2. (In Serbian). Available online: https://link.springer.com/chapter/10.1007/978-1-4020-8778-3_26 (accessed on 24 October 2024).
35. Hedrih, K.R. *Generalized Function of Fractional Order Dissipation of System Energy and Extended Lagrange Differential Lagrange Equation in Matrix Form, Dedicated to 86th Anniversary of Radu Miron's Birth*; Tensor Society: Tokyo, Japan, 2014; Volume 75, pp. 35–51.
36. Ostoja-Starzewski, M.; Zhang, J. Does a Fractal Microstructure Require a Fractional Viscoelastic Model? *Fractal. Fract.* **2018**, *2*, 12. [CrossRef]
37. Mitrinović, D.S.; Djoković, D.Ž. *Special Functions (Specijalne funkcije)*; Gradjevinska Knjiga: Beograd, Serbia, 1964; p. 267.
38. Hedrih, R.K. Izabrana Poglavlja Teorije Elastičnosti (Selected Chapters of Theory of Elasticity), Mašinski fakultet u Nišu. 1988, p. 425. Available online: http://elibrary.matf.bg.ac.rs/handle/123456789/3766 (accessed on 24 October 2024).
39. Rašković, D. *Mehanika III—Dinamika (Mechanics IIII-Dynamics)*, 4th ed.; Naucna Knjiga. 1972. Available online: http://elibrary.matf.bg.ac.rs/handle/123456789/3777 (accessed on 24 October 2024).
40. Rašković, D. *Teorija oscilacija (Theory of oscillatins). Book. Naucna knjiga*, 1st ed.; 1952. Second Edition. 1965. Available online: http://elibrary.matf.bg.ac.rs/handle/123456789/4754 (accessed on 24 October 2024).

fractal and fractional

Article

The Multiscale Principle in Nature (*Principium luxuriæ*): Linking Multiscale Thermodynamics to Living and Non-Living Complex Systems

Patricio Venegas-Aravena [1,*] and Enrique G. Cordaro [2,3]

1 Department of Structural and Geotechnical Engineering, School of Engineering, Pontificia Universidad Católica de Chile, Vicuña Mackenna 4860, Macul, Santiago 8331150, Chile
2 Observatorios de Radiación Cósmica y Geomagnetismo, Departamento de Física, FCFM, Universidad de Chile, Casilla 4873, Santiago 8330015, Chile
3 Facultad de Ingeniería, Universidad Autónoma de Chile, Pedro de Valdivia 425, Santiago 7500912, Chile
* Correspondence: plvenegas@uc.cl

Abstract: Why do fractals appear in so many domains of science? What is the physical principle that generates them? While it is true that fractals naturally appear in many physical systems, it has so far been impossible to derive them from first physical principles. However, a proposed interpretation could shed light on the inherent principle behind the creation of fractals. This is the multiscale thermodynamic perspective, which states that an increase in external energy could initiate energy transport mechanisms that facilitate the dissipation or release of excess energy at different scales. Within this framework, it is revealed that power law patterns, and to a lesser extent, fractals, can emerge as a geometric manifestation to dissipate energy in response to external forces. In this context, the exponent of these power law patterns (thermodynamic fractal dimension D) serves as an indicator of the balance between entropy production at small and large scales. Thus, when a system is more efficient at releasing excess energy at the microscopic (macroscopic) level, D tends to increase (decrease). While this principle, known as *Principium luxuriæ*, may sound promising for describing both multiscale and complex systems, there is still uncertainty about its true applicability. Thus, this work explores different physical, astrophysical, sociological, and biological systems to attempt to describe and interpret them through the lens of the *Principium luxuriæ*. The analyzed physical systems correspond to emergent behaviors, chaos theory, and turbulence. To a lesser extent, the cosmic evolution of the universe and geomorphology are examined. Biological systems such as the geometry of human organs, aging, human brain development and cognition, moral evolution, Natural Selection, and biological death are also analyzed. It is found that these systems can be reinterpreted and described through the thermodynamic fractal dimension. Therefore, it is proposed that the physical principle that could be behind the creation of fractals is the *Principium luxuriæ*, which can be defined as "*Systems that interact with each other can trigger responses at multiple scales as a manner to dissipate the excess energy that comes from this interaction*". That is why this framework has the potential to uncover new discoveries in various fields. For example, it is suggested that the reduction in D in the universe could generate emergent behavior and the proliferation of complexity in numerous fields or the reinterpretation of Natural Selection.

Keywords: thermodynamic fractal dimension; *Principium luxuriæ*; complex systems; multiscale entropy production; power laws; fluctuations; emergent behavior; biological systems; universe; homeostasis; natural selection

1. Introduction

The multiscale properties of a system refer to the existence of multiple scales of organization within the system [1–4], usually during phase transition, where each scale could be characterized by different mathematical physics [5–7], biochemical [8,9], or biological [10–15] properties. A wide range of varied systems, such as cosmology [16], zoology [17], networks [18], cities [19], ecology [20], computational imaging [21], interface physics [22,23], geophysics [24], emergent processes [25], genetic [26], or complex systems [27] often exhibit hierarchical organization [28–30], where smaller-scale components or subsystems interact to create emergent behavior at larger scales. These emergent behaviors are typically described as a type of dynamic that cannot be described as the sum of its parts [31–33]. Often, emergent behaviors may be described by power laws that reflect the distribution of these events across different scales or levels of the system [34–37]. In physical terms, the power laws that characterize complex systems are closely related to entropy production through the concept of scaling [38–44]. This is relevant because systems that can be described by power laws lack a characteristic scale, which implies that each component of the system contributes equally to the global evolution of the system, regardless of its scale [45]. This lack of a characteristic scale is related to the concept of self-similarity, which is a hallmark of many complex systems [46–48]. The relationship between power laws and statistical entropy can be seen in the fact that power law distributions have a high degree of entropy because these systems have many possible configurations when different scales are considered. This means that the system is highly disordered and complex, with many different events occurring at different scales. Thus, the power law distribution reflects the fact that small-scale events are just as important as large-scale events in determining the overall dynamic of the system [49–53]. Despite this, the relation between entropy and complex systems (and fractals) is still not well understood due three reasons. The first reason is related to the incompatible nature of entropy because entropy is a macroscopic property that characterizes the overall evolution of a system [54], while complex systems are characterized by the dynamic of their components at different scales. Additionally, complex systems are often open, which makes it difficult to directly apply traditional thermodynamic concepts and laws, as these were primarily developed for closed systems (in equilibrium). As a result, few attempts to elucidate the relationship between thermodynamics and complex systems have been made [55,56]. A second reason is that complex systems often exhibit emergent behavior that can be difficult to reconcile with traditional thermodynamic approaches that rely on the dynamic of individual particles or molecules. Therefore, few novel representations of emergent behavior have been considered [57]. The final reason is that complex systems can exhibit the effects of heterogeneities in their properties [58], such as their resistivity or fluctuations. These heterogeneities can also make it difficult to apply thermodynamic models that often assume homogeneity.

A recent proposal for a multiscale thermodynamics framework [53,59] addresses the issue of linking multiscale systems and entropy production. The proposed framework incorporates Onsager coefficients and heterogeneous resistivity to provide a more complete understanding of the entropy production and dissipation processes in multiscale systems. In essence, previous works on multiscale thermodynamics reveal that some systems try to dissipate, or release, the excess of external energy, which results in the transport of energy across various scales. In particular, reference [59] establishes a general relationship between power laws and entropy through the thermodynamic fractal dimension D. This can be interpreted as the balance between the large- and small-scale entropy changes in a system. Note that the thermodynamic fractal dimension provides a physical interpretation of complexity in terms of multiscale energy dissipation within a system, resulting in a measure of the system's intricacy or roughness. Therefore, the thermodynamic fractal dimension, while sharing similarities with traditional fractal dimension [60], has the added significance of describing the complexity arising from multiscale energy dissipation and entropy production within a system.

The basic idea that a system can react to the presence of another has been studied using the most basic mechanics [61]. For the thermodynamic case, this principle has been established in terms of thermodynamic forces and fluxes [62,63]. However, the idea of considering that a system can react or dissipate the excess of external energy at different scales is relatively new [53,59]. This implies that more analyses and studies on this multiscale response are needed. An important aspect of this formalism lies in its mathematical generality, implying that it can potentially be applied to any system exhibiting multiscale properties, such as complex systems or fractals. However, one thing is a mathematical description, and another is the physical interpretation of the systems. This implies that if the multiscale dissipation principle is general in mathematical terms, it should be capable of being identified across different systems in a cross-cutting manner. Therefore, this work will seek to determine if this hypothesis of multiscale dissipation can be applied (in general terms) to a large number of diverse multiscale systems so that it can be considered a fundamental principle in nature. That is why Section 2 relates the basic properties of the multiscale transport of energy. Then, Sections 3–6 analyze the basic physical principles of different multiscale physical systems. That is, Section 3 delves into the emergent behavior that prevails in different complex systems, Section 4 analyzes the relationship between multiscale physics and the process associated with dissipative systems, Section 5 establishes a relationship between multiscale physics and chaos theory, and Section 6 considers the particular case of turbulence and its range of applicability across multiples scales. Additionally, Section 7 presents numerous examples of the applicability of the thermodynamic fractal dimension in complex systems, ranging from cosmic evolution and topographical patterns to biology, natural selection, homeostasis, and social sciences. The discussion and conclusions can be found in Sections 8 and 9, respectively.

2. The Multiscale Entropy

The concept of entropy is traditionally defined as a macroscopic property that characterizes the degree of disorder or randomness in a system, which is based on the dynamic of large numbers of particles [64–66]. However, there have been several attempts to extend this definition to the microscopic level, considering the evolution of individual particles or molecules by using the statistical distribution of the positions and velocities of individual particles, rather than on macroscopic properties such as temperature and pressure [67,68]. Recently, a framework has been developed for understanding how the entropy changes as we move between different scales of observation [53,59]. This view proposes a generalization of Onsager's reciprocity relations, which relate the transport coefficients of a system to its thermodynamic forces [62,63] by introducing the concept of multiscale resistance coefficients K_{ij}^{μ}, which describe the response of a system to perturbations at different scales. That is [53]:

$$K_{ij}^{\mu} = \left(\frac{r^{\mu}}{r_0}\right)^{\alpha} K_{ij}^{\prime\mu}, \tag{1}$$

where K_{ij}^{μ} is the local resistance coefficient and r^{μ} is a scaling parameter, which represents the size or scale of each sub-system, while α is a scaling exponent and r_0 is a constant. Here, note that Onsager's coefficients describe the transport of fluxes and forces that allows systems to be in nonequilibrium. Figure 1a shows a schematic representation of an initially closed system that generates different scales of internal structures due to the external forces. This schematic representation corresponds to the generalization of the observed evolution in the cracking process of rock samples, which occurs due to the application of external loads that generate fractally distributed cracks [53,69–78]. Thus, this cracking process is regarded as a release of energy that cannot be held in the system due to external inputs. Then, it was considered that this external force could be described by Onsager's coefficient, which is one of the thermodynamic forces [53]. Here, the thermodynamic fractal dimension D is obtained by the balance between small- and large-scale entropy production, or energy liberation, due to external forces. In other words, D corresponds to the exponent of power laws that rise as a balance between small- and large-scale dissipation of energy when the system cannot hold more external forces. This thermodynamic fractal dimension D is defined as [59]:

$$D = -k_V \ln \Omega_V, \tag{2}$$

where Ω_V is the multiscale entropy change balance and is defined as $\Omega_V = \left(\frac{dS}{dS_0}\right)e^{\left(\frac{1-D_E}{k_V}\right)}$, dS is the macroscopical entropy change, dS_0 is the microscopical entropy change, D_E is the Euclidean dimension, and $k_V = 1/\ln(r/r_0)$, where r is a scaling factor associated with the size of the largest domain and r_0 is a constant that is associated with the dimension of the smallest system. Thus, the thermodynamic fractal dimension (Equation (2)) relates the resistance of a system to the flow of fluxes to the scaling of entropy changes with respect to changes in scale. Therefore, Equation (2) suggests that the fractal properties observed in various physical systems, including the large-scale structure of the universe, may be a consequence of the balance between external forces and the system's ability to dissipate energy at different scales. Note that the thermodynamic fractal dimension could be negative as Mandelbrot [79] noted. In this case, this occurs when the large-scale dissipation is considerably larger compared to the smallest one. Additionally, it is not additive, so the value of D for a system composed of many subsystems with different values of D does not correspond to the mere sum of their D (see Appendix A).

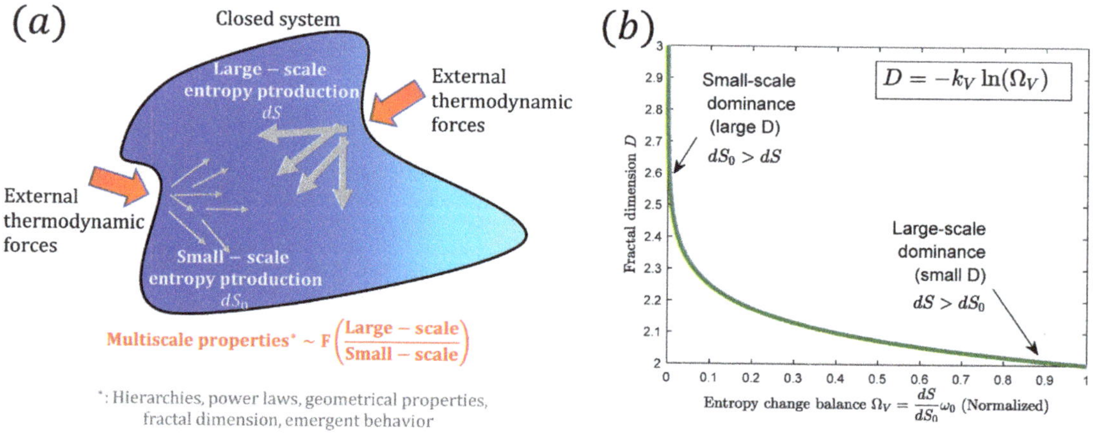

Figure 1. (**a**) Schematic representation of thermodynamics external force that causes a change in the internal thermodynamic gradients, leading to the generation of multiscale thermodynamic forces that result in increased small-scale (left arrow) or large-scale (right arrow) entropy production and a change in its thermodynamic fractal dimension. (**b**) The multiscale entropy production Ω_V is negatively related to the thermodynamic fractal dimension as Equation (2) shows. This means that as the thermodynamic fractal dimension decreases, the large-scale entropy production increases, and vice versa. That is, a higher D implies that the system is more likely to generate entropy at small scales dS_0. On the other hand, a lower thermodynamic fractal dimension means that the system is better at dissipating energy at larger scales.

This multiscale dissipative mechanism could help us to understand the degree of complexity of the system and how it responds to external influences. For example, systems with a higher fractal dimension are more resistant to changes in fluxes because they have a more complex geometrical distribution. This means that these systems are characterized by a greater number of geometric features, such as more irregular surfaces or interfaces. Therefore, the transport of matter, energy, or information in such systems may be hindered, as there are more barriers or pathways to cross [80]. This can result in greater resistance to changes in fluxes or the flow of these quantities in the system. Figure 2 shows the example of the increased relevance of small-scale entropy production by contributing to decreases in the available energy for transport. Note that this figure is created using the algorithm developed by Chen and Yang [81] and Yang [82], which allows for generating fractal surfaces with different smoothness depending on the desired fractal dimension. Also note that in Figure 2, different distributions of thermodynamic resistances are shown, indicating that the opposition to a thermodynamic flow, for example heat, is heterogeneous in space and may vary according to the flow direction. This implies that if the thermodynamic flow encounters a region of higher resistance (red tones in Figure 2), it will generate greater dissipation of energy. In statistical terms, the more complex entropy distribution in a system implies that there are more microstates available to the system. In other words, the more ways there are for the system to arrange its constituents leads to a greater number of microstates and increased entropy [83], which may make the system more resistant to changes. Therefore, systems with higher fractal dimensions may be more stable or robust in the face of perturbations, as they have a greater capacity to distribute and dissipate energy and entropy.

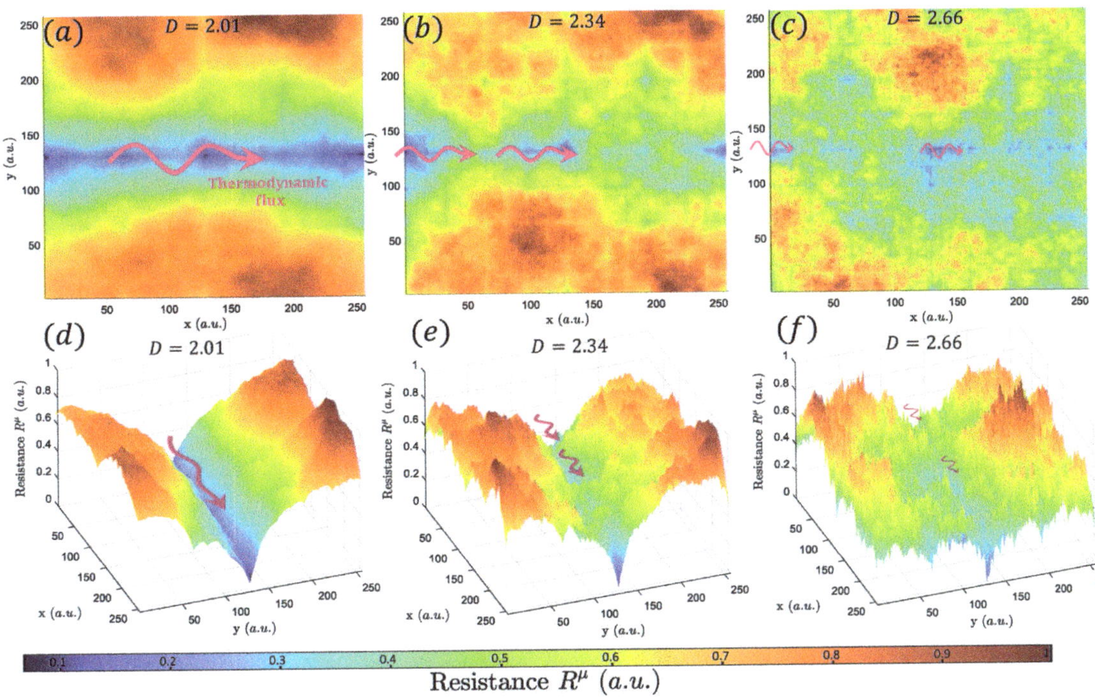

Figure 2. (**a–c**) show examples of randomly distributed resistivities that increase in D (2.01, 2.34, 2.66) generated by the method described in Chen and Yang [81]. Note that it has been constrained by a section of small resistance across the domain (blue colors). This leads to more dominant small-scale entropy production, which is manifested as more irregular surfaces. These increases in the irregular distribution of resistivity can cause the transport of matter, energy, or information (represented by pink arrows) to become more localized and less efficient, with a greater propensity for the formation of bottlenecks or stagnation zones. (**d–f**) show tridimensional views of (**a**), (**b**), and (**c**), respectively.

In terms of the multiscale entropy formulation given by Equation (2), a higher thermodynamic fractal dimension means that Ω_V tends to be small. In other words, the small-scale entropy production dS_0 is larger than the macroscopical one ($dS_0 > dS$). That is, in such systems, dissipation occurs primarily at the small scales due to the large number of these irregular features, which leads to a higher degree of entropy production at those scales. In other words, small-scale entropy production can become dominant when there are strong gradients or fluctuations in the system that affect the evolution of individual components or small groups of components, leading to local entropy production that is not reflected in the large-scale evolution of the system. This multiscale dynamic described by Equation (2) is shown in Figure 1b for $k_V = 1$ and $\omega_0 = e^{(\frac{1-D_E}{k_V})} = 1$.

3. On the Emergent Behavior

Equation (2), which is valid for nonequilibrium thermodynamics, also shows that large-scale entropy production is related to the amount of energy that is dissipated by a system at a macroscopic scale. In general, complex systems tend to dissipate more energy at larger scales, resulting in a larger large-scale entropy production ($dS > dS_0$). This process is related to the self-organization of the system, which leads to the emergence of new properties and evolutions at different scales [84–90]. In the context of multiscale thermodynamics, a low thermodynamic fractal dimension implies that the large-scale entropy production is dominant over small-scale entropy production (Equation (2)). This means that energy dissipation occurs over larger spatial scales and is characterized by smooth geometrical properties, indicating that large parts of the system evolve as a unity or exhibit emergent properties. This description is similar to the interpretation of entropy as the unity of system [91]. In such emergent systems, the macroscopic dynamic of the system can be described by a few effective variables or degrees of freedom, and the evolution of the system is relatively simple and predictable. This is because the interactions between the different parts of the system are strongly correlated and the system is described by a low-dimensional attractor (macroscopic patterns or state that the system tends to settle into overtime), which results in the emergence of coherent macroscopic evolution [92–98]. This description indicates that the large-scale entropy production view is related to the emergence of coherent macroscopic dynamic. This can be seen in the representation that is shown in Figures 3 and 4. Figure 3 shows that large-scale entropy production could produce global coherent behavior. That is, the areas within the black segmented boxes in Figure 3a–c show that different states (represented here as a color palette) are more or less homogeneous depending on the thermodynamic fractal dimension. Large D implies heterogenous states (Figure 3a,d), which are represented by rougher surfaces. Nevertheless, small D indicates that the states within the black segmented box tend to be more homogeneous (represented by smooth surfaces). This is marked as red colors in Figure 3c. Figure 4 shows how a local emergent behavior, similar to that described in Figure 3c,f, can rise in a given area within a system characterized by incoherent states, similar to that described in Figure 3a,d just by changing the thermodynamic fractal dimension. Particularly, Figure 4 is generated by merging Figure 3a,c as $S(c) = c \times S(D=3) + (c-1) \times S(D=2)$ where $S(D)$ is a fractal surface of fractal dimension D and c is a parameter that is interpreted here as a measurement of the total fractal dimension of the surface S. For example, $c = 0.8$ implies that $S(0.8) = 0.8 \times S(D=3) + 0.2 \times S(D=2)$ where the fractal dimension of $S(0.8)$ is assumed to be ~ 2.8 ($D = c+2$) because the geometrical irregularities of $S(D=3)$ are more dominant than that described by $S(D=2)$. Thus, the center region of Figure 4 (red colors) is characterized by small values of c and it linearly increases towards the domain boundaries. These examples show that a low thermodynamic fractal dimension is indicative of (in this local) emergent behavior and cooperative dynamics, suggesting that large-scale entropy production could play a key role in producing the observed macroscopic dynamic. However, systems are not always so evident, as fluctuations that reflect a balance between the different scales of the system may exist.

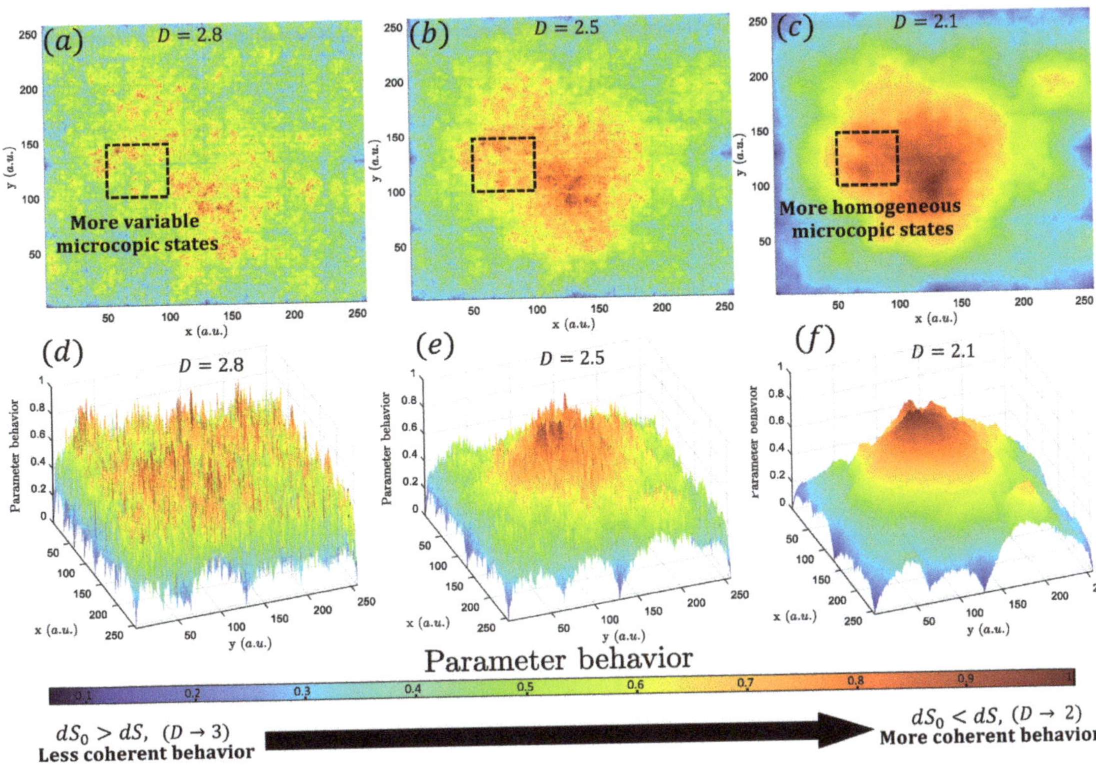

Figure 3. Example of emergent behavior by using the same method used in Figure 2. In this case, the color palette represents different states in terms of location. Thus, similar colors imply similar states. When the thermodynamic fractal dimension decreases (**a–c**), it means that the system becomes less complex and more ordered. This reduction in complexity leads to a decrease in the number of possible states of the system and may cause different small parts of the system to be characterized by similar parameters or states (similar colors). As a result, the system may display emergent behavior, where macroscopic patterns or structures arise from the interactions of the individual components at the microscopic level. The area within the black segmented squared shows how the states become more homogeneous (manly red). (**d–f**) show the tridimensional views of (**a**), (**b**), and (**c**), respectively.

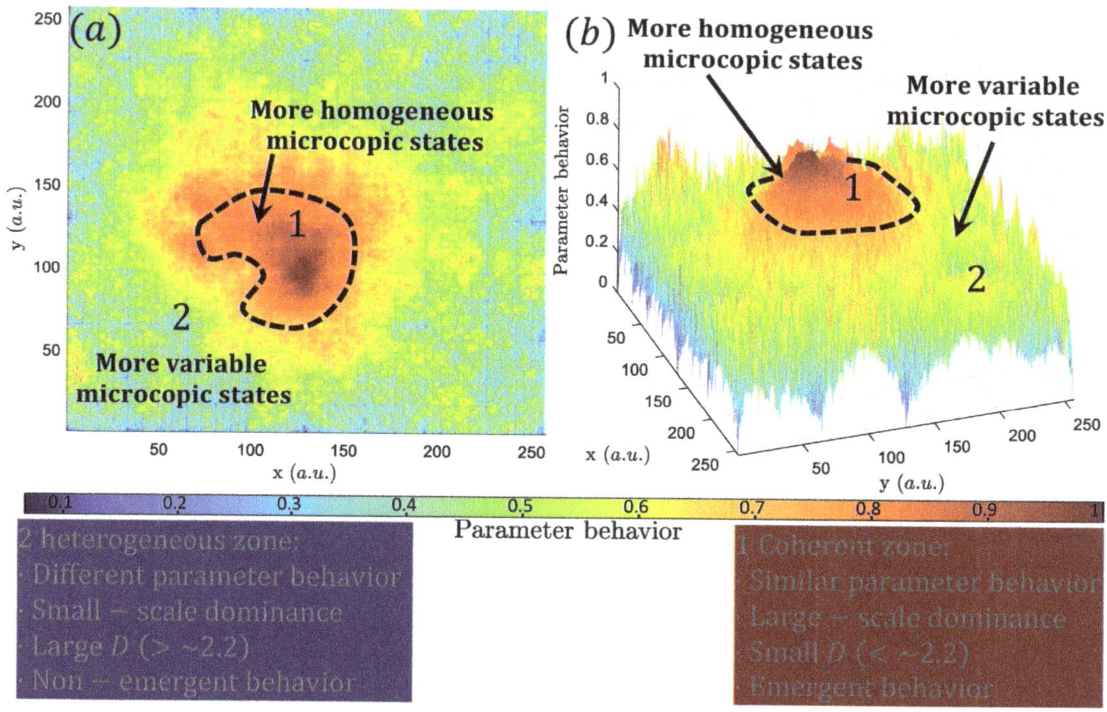

Figure 4. Example of a decrease in the thermodynamic fractal dimension in a certain part of the system that can lead to emergent behavior in that restricted area. Note that here, the color palette and surfaces mean the same as that shown in Figure 3. The method used is the same as that used in Figure 2. This figure shows how the system converges to a limited number of stable states (red colors) in a certain region marked within a black segmented curve ($D = 2.01$), which can be interpreted as an emergent behavior. In contrast, the surrounding regions are characterized by more complex and disordered states ($D = 2.99$). The emergence rises because there is more large-scale entropy production compared to its surrounding regions that are characterized by more small-scale entropy production. This is summarized in the blue and red panels.

4. The Nature of Fluctuations and Dissipation in Multiscale Systems

Fluctuation–dissipation refers to the relationship between the response of a system to an external perturbation and the fluctuations in the system's internal state when it relaxes back to equilibrium [99–101]. The dynamics in this kind of systems arise as responses to external forces, which is a similar characteristic of multiscale systems. In multiscale thermodynamics, D can fluctuate in space and time due to changes in the multiscale entropy generation, indicating that the system's entropy production is not constant at different scales. For example, there could be a change in large-scale entropy production that could lead to an increase or decrease in small-scale entropy production, resulting in a change in D. This change in D can be considered a fluctuation in the system. In mathematical terms, and by using the definition of Ω_V given in Equation (2), this can be written as:

$$dS = \Omega_V(x,t)dS_0 e^{\left(\frac{D_E-1}{k_V}\right)}. \tag{3}$$

Equation (3) indicates that the large-scale entropy change dS influences the small-scale entropy change dS_0, and vice versa, by means of a multiscale balance term $\Omega_V(x,t)$. Thus, Ω_V can be regarded as a function that transfers perturbations across different scales because it determines how dissipations occurs at multiples scales. Therefore, changes in the multiscale balance term Ω_V can cause the thermodynamic fractal dimension to change, which means that the system can exhibit multifractal dynamics and the system's evolution could become even more complex. Thus, D can be used to describe the fluctuation-dissipation properties of the system.

Let us consider a perturbation that increases D at the center of a system characterized by small D values. As the perturbation spreads outward, the dissipation of energy associated with these fluctuations can be described by the fluctuation–dissipation theorem. In this case, as the perturbation spreads outward and the thermodynamic fractal dimension increases, the system is expected to respond with larger fluctuations. The fluctuation–dissipation theorem then predicts that the dissipation of energy associated with these fluctuations will also increase. However, as the perturbation decreases, the thermodynamic fractal dimension will eventually reach a steady state, at which point the fluctuations and dissipation will stabilize. This scenario can be seen in Figure 5 where the system S is characterized by a single thermodynamic fractal dimension $D = c + 2$, which can be described using the same relation used in Figure 4. In this case, the factor c is not linear but Gaussian and is defined as $c = (1 - c_0) \times \exp\left(-c_1(c_i - c_0)^2\right)$, where c_0 and c_1 are constant and c_i is spatial variable. Thus, the state of the system can evolve more macroscopically or microscopically depending on c. This means that $c = 0$ implies that $S = S(2)$ and the system will act more macroscopically because the spatial variation of states is small. In contrast, $c = 1$ implies that $S = S(3)$, which generates large spatial variation among different parts of the system. The factor c_0 determines where the maximum c is found. In other words, if c_0 is moving from the center of the system to its boundaries, it implies that the microscopical dynamic is spreading from the center outward. This can be seen in Figure 5a–f. Particularly, Figure 5a shows a system characterized by a large-scale influence, which implies that the spatial variations of its states (color palette) are smooth. Figure 5b–f reveals the propagation of a disturbance that generates an increase in D (area within the segmented black lines). The white arrows indicate the direction of the disturbance front. The multiscale entropy balance can be expressed using Equation (2) as:

$$\Omega_V = e^{-\frac{D}{k_V}} = e^{-(c+2)}. \tag{4}$$

The spatial distribution of Ω_V can be obtained. Figure 5g–l shows the spatial evolution of Equation (4) for $k_V = 1$. Initially, Ω_V is completely dominated by a large-scale entropy change (red shades in Figure 5g). As the small-scale influence increases (blue shades in Figure 5h), it also propagates outward (Figure 5i–l). In addition, the small-scale influence also tends to decrease as it propagates to the domain's boundaries. This can be seen as blue to light red shades in Figure 5j–l. Thus, this example has shown how the spatial and temporal changes in Ω_V can represent the multiscale fluctuation and dissipation within a system.

The contribution of entropy production at different scales, defined by the multiscale balance term $\Omega_V(x,t)$, could also be used for other diffusive system such as those that incorporate chemical reactions. For example, biological morphogenesis, which corresponds to the process that could generate observable macroscopical patterns in animals, has been regarded because of the interaction between diffusion and reaction processes [102]. As the gradient of chemical potential and chemical reactions can be related to Onsager's coefficients [103,104], it is expected that $\Omega_V(x,t)$ could be useful in characterizing the efficiency of the dissipation of energy at different scales and how it contributes to the emergence of Turing patterns, particularly because many of these interactions and dissipation within a system can form patterns or structures where some features can be distributed as power laws [105–110], which suggests that the physics of pattern formation may be directly associated with the principle of multiscale dissipation. However, more research is needed to fully explore this potential connection.

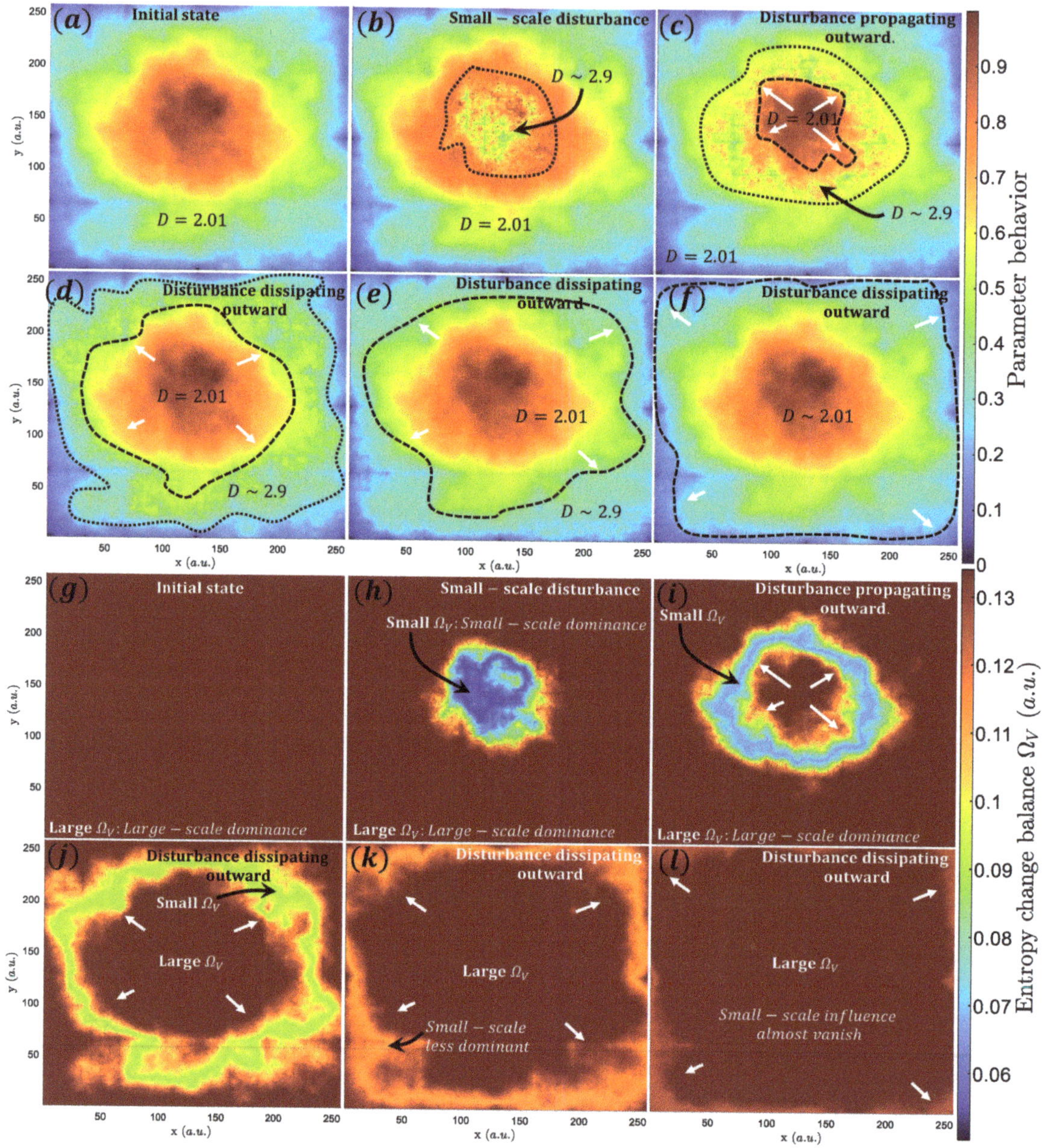

Figure 5. Example of a dissipative effect in system. (**a–f**) show the evolution of a system characterized by a small thermodynamic fractal dimension ($D = 2.01$), which is affected by a perturbation that spread out the system. Note that the method used is the same as that used in Figure 2. This disturbance increases D as it propagates outward (to $D \sim 2.99$) as well as it decreases its influence. (**g–l**) show the multiscale entropy balance Ω_V of the system. Red shades indicate large Ω_V or the influence of large-scale properties. The blue shades indicate zones where the small-scale entropy production dominates. This small-scale dominance is reduced as it spreads outward. That can be seen as a yellow to red shades in (**j–l**).

4.1. Temperature and Critical Phenomena in Biological Systems

Critical phenomena refer to the evolution exhibited by physical systems near a critical point or phase transition [111–115]. A critical point represents the boundary between different phases of a system, such as the transition from a liquid phase to a gas phase [116,117]. Near the critical point, these properties exhibit power law scaling, with critical exponents characterizing the rate at which they change [118]. In terms of temperature, the critical temperature defines the temperature at which a phase transition occurs. When there is an increase in temperature, the particles in a substance gain kinetic energy, resulting in increased movement at the microscopic scale and an enhanced heat capacity [119]. This increased movement enables the system to disperse and distribute the energy input across smaller scales. That is, the small-scale entropy production (dS_0) must increase, which leads to increases in the thermodynamic fractal dimension (Equation (2)) in terms of the increase in temperature. This type of evolution can be observed in some biological systems. For instance, the critical exponent β, which describes the exchange of ions and charges at the cellular level across multiple scales, tends to increase as the system approaches the critical temperature [120]. Consequently, the macroscopic entropy decreases near the critical temperature [121]. In this regard, the principles of multiscale thermodynamics offer a physical interpretation of this phenomenon because β could be directly related to the thermodynamic fractal dimension. This suggests that the system seeks to dissipate energy at the microscopic level rather than at the macroscopic level, resulting in a reduction in macroscopic entropy. This implies that the increase in temperature has a microscopic effect that is relevant to understanding biological processes. For example, this effect is particularly important for the regulation of homeostasis, which will be discussed in Section 7.7. It is also important to add that D is associated with changes in dissipation and not directly with temperature. This means that if there is a system in which the temperature decreases, dS_0 will also decrease, which could cause D to tend toward zero. However, this description is only true if there are no macroscopic changes. Thus, the value of D will depend on how the system dissipates energy macroscopically. This has implications for reaching absolute zero. For example, a lower temperature implies that dS_0 must tend to zero, which could cause both Ω_V and D to diverge. This suggests that one way to achieve this goal is to reduce macroscopic dissipation.

5. Chaos Theory

The relationship between the thermodynamic fractal dimension and chaos theory lies in their shared focus on understanding and describing complex systems and the use of mathematical tools to characterize these dynamics. Particularly, the relationship between chaos theory and power laws arises from the concept of fractal dimension [122]. Fractals are objects or patterns that repeat at different scales, and they are often characterized by power law scaling relationships [60] and self-organization [123,124]. Power laws are closely related to the concept of self-similarity, which is a key characteristic of fractals [125]. In contrast, chaos theory deals with the evolution of dynamic systems that are highly sensitive to initial conditions [126]. This sensitivity and the degree of chaos in the system can be described by the sum of the Lyapunov exponent spectra $\Lambda = \sum_j \lambda_j$ where λ_j is the jth Lyapunov exponent. Thus, a more positive λ_j suggests more chaotic and unpredictable outputs [127–129]. Therefore, to understand the relationship between multiscale entropy production, chaos theory, and sensitivity to initial conditions, it is necessary to analyze the Lyapunov exponent spectra and their relation to the entropy production. A simple relation between entropy production and the Lyapunov exponent spectra is known as the Nose–Hoover relation [130–132]:

$$\frac{dS}{dt} = -\Lambda > 0. \tag{5}$$

Here, this entropy production represents the global macroscopical system and the negative sign represents the irreversibility. This indicates that in a chaotic system, where at least one positive Lyapunov exponent exists, the total sum of Λ should be negative. When the time is reversed, Λ is positive, which implies that the possible trajectories are more unstable, which prevent it from recovering the initial state [130]. Here, positive (negative) Λ means that there are more positive (negative) Lyapunov exponents, and/or the positive (negative) exponents that already exist are larger. In this regard, it could be interpreted that larger positive Λ could represent a more "chaotic system". By using Equations (3) and (4) in Equation (5), the Lyapunov spectrum can be related to the thermodynamic fractal dimension as:

$$\Lambda = -\frac{dS_0}{dt} e^{\left(\frac{D_E - D - 1}{k_V}\right)}. \tag{6}$$

Note that, here, the maximum positive Λ could not necessarily be related to Λ. Equation (6) shows that there is a direct relationship between the sum of Lyapunov exponents and the thermodynamic fractal dimension, where a smaller D is associated with smaller values of the sum of Lyapunov exponents. This can be seen in Figure 6a where $D_E = 3$, $dS_0/dt = dS/dt \exp((D + 1 - D_E)/k_V)$ and $dS/dt = 1$ $(a.u.)$, where a.u. stands for arbitrary units. Equation (6) and Figure 6a also show that smaller D values are associated with smaller values of Λ, implying that emergent behavior could be related to systems that are not too sensitive to initial conditions. Figure 6b shows that the relationship between Λ and the scale of the system r is not linear. At small scales, the sum of Lyapunov exponents increases as the scale increases, indicating that the system becomes more chaotic and sensitive to initial conditions. However, at larger scales, the sum of Lyapunov exponents starts to decrease, indicating that the sensitivity to initial conditions becomes less relevant as the system expands to different scales. This suggests that the emergent behavior of a system may be limited to a specific range of scales, beyond which the influence of small-scale conditions becomes negligible. Figure 6c shows the combined effect of D and r.

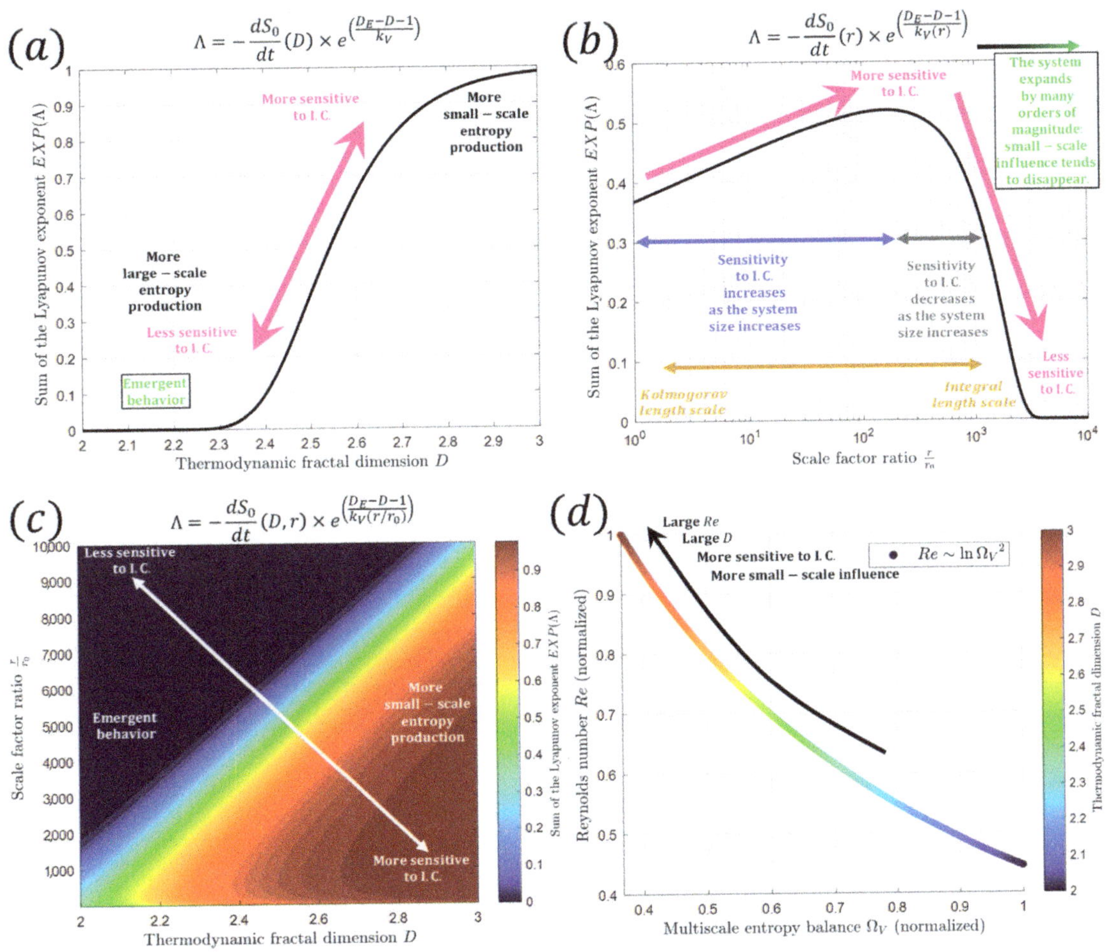

Figure 6. Relation between scale factor r, thermodynamic fractal dimension D, and the sum of the Lyapunov exponent Λ as it is shown in Equation (6). (**a**) Λ vs. D: Systems tends to be characterized by emergent behavior (small D) when the system is less sensitive to initial conditions. (**b**) Λ vs. r: Complex systems are governed by a scale restriction. That is, the influence of small-scale conditions on the behavior of a system is restricted to a certain scale range, and beyond that range, the small-scale conditions have less and less effect on the system. In turbulence, this scale restriction could be related to the Kolmogorov length scale and the Integral length scale. (**c**) Combined effect of D and r on Equation (6). Here it is shown that systems are more sensitive to initial conditions when the small-scale entropy production is large, and the system expands within a certain range of scales (red shades). (**d**) Reynolds number Re and multiscale thermodynamic. Large Re is associated with large D, more small-scale entropy diffusion, and more sensitivity to initial conditions.

6. Turbulence

Turbulence is a type of fluid flow characterized by irregular and chaotic fluctuations in velocity and pressure. These fluctuations occur over a wide range of spatial and temporal scales, making turbulence a multiscale phenomenon. This means that turbulent flows often exhibit power law scaling in their statistical properties, such as velocity fluctuations [133]. Particularly, turbulence occurs in fluid flows at high Reynolds numbers and is characterized by the presence of small-scale vortices and eddies that interact with each other in a nonlinear way [134]. According to Nicolleau [135], the fractal dimension of the fluid can be linked to the Reynolds number Re as:

$$D \sim (Re)^{\frac{1}{2}}. \tag{7}$$

By considering Equations (2) and (7), the Reynolds number can be written as:

$$Re \sim (\ln \Omega_V)^2. \tag{8}$$

Equations (2) and (8) can be useful tools for characterizing turbulence because it captures the multiscale nature of the flow. In particular, a high D could be associated with turbulence because it indicates that the small-scale fluctuations in the flow are dominant. This implies that the Reynolds number is also large (Equation (8)). This can be seen in Figure 6d. Another relation between multiscale thermodynamics and turbulence is the scale restriction shown in Equation (6) and Figure 6b. This scale restriction suggests that the influence of small-scale features on the overall dynamic of the flow is limited to a certain range of scales, beyond which their effect becomes negligible. This is consistent with the idea that turbulence is a phenomenon that is only present within a certain range of scales, and that its effect on the overall evolution of the flow diminishes as the scale of the flow increases [136]. For example, the Kolmogorov length scale represents the smallest length scale at which turbulent energy dissipates into heat due to viscous effects and it is typically several orders of magnitude smaller than the integral scale, which represents the largest-length scale of energy-containing eddies in turbulent flow [137]. In terms of initial conditions, a small difference in the initial conditions of the Kolmogorov length scale can be amplified as the fluid flows and becomes more turbulent. This can lead to significant differences in the dynamic of the flow at larger scales, including the integral scale [138–141]. In other words, small-scale fluctuations at the Kolmogorov length scale can cascade up to larger scales, affecting the flow at those scales. This phenomenon is known as the (inverse) "cascade of energy" in turbulent flow.

The scale-restriction shown in Equation (6) and Figure 6b suggests that the effect of small-scale disturbances on larger scales is limited. This is because the larger scales are less sensitive to small-scale disturbances, which is similar to the idea that a small difference in initial conditions of the Kolmogorov length will not significantly affect the fluid at the scale where the integral turbulence scale is defined. In both cases, the effect of small-scale disturbances is limited to a certain range of scales. Thus, turbulent systems can be seen as an example of this scale restriction (Equation (6)).

7. Other Examples

The universe is composed of systems that go beyond the most basic physical sciences, so this section is dedicated to presenting several examples of multiscale processes present in different systems, such as geophysics, astrophysics, biology, and the social sciences, which could be linked to multiscale dissipation processes. This is because these systems encompass a wide range of scales, from the atomic level to the scale of the universe, and often involve interactions between different scales. The examples presented in this section seek to understand the applicability of Equation (2) in various fields of science.

7.1. Complexity and Cosmic Evolution

According to Chaisson [142], the complexity of the universe has been increasing over time because it creates emergent structures, such as galaxies and clusters of galaxies, which are formed by interactions between smaller structures. Chaisson's perspective is based on the idea that the complexity of the universe is directly related to the ability of matter to store energy per unit volume. He suggests that as new structures are formed throughout cosmic evolution in an expanding universe, they become more efficient at storing energy. As these structures in the universe are commonly multiscale systems governed by power laws [143–154], it is worth analyzing Chaisson's view of complexity in the context of the multiscale phenomenon described by Equation (2). Particularly, some scientists consider that some physical concepts, such as entropy production, should be excluded from the description of the universe's complexity due its lack of strict meaning, which generates misconceptions outside physical sciences [91,155–158].

While some aspects of complexity can be captured by power law distributions, the key aspect is the interpretation associated with the expanding universe. To date, there is no interpretation of the origin of this expansion, which allows us to consider that it could also have an external origin. This would mean that the universe itself could be considered an open system, which is the foundation of the multiscale thermodynamics perspective. This would therefore indicate that the universe itself could be described or characterized by a "universal" or large-scale value of D. In fact, this is observed on a large scale when looking at large structures from the past. For instance, studies have found evidence suggesting that at the beginning of the universe, the structures were characterized by a large fractal dimension (equivalent to $D > 2.6$ in the two-dimension representation) [152,159,160]. In contrast, the large-scale galaxy distributions that we observe today are characterized by a fractal dimension that is lower than that of the early universe ($D < 2.6$) [161]. In the context of the multiscale thermodynamic fractal dimension, this suggests that the early universe was more efficient at dissipating energy at smaller scales. Equivalently, the early universe was dominated by low (microscopic) entropy [162]. Then, the universe became more efficient at dissipating energy at larger scales over time, which led to the emergence of large-scale structures such as galaxy clusters and superclusters. This can be seen schematically in Figure 7, which shows the evolution of the universe's thermodynamic fractal dimension and how it is related to the emergence of large-scale structures over time. Thus, as the universe continues to expand, we may expect to see further evidence of this kind of emergent behavior and the development of larger and more complex structures and patterns. In other words, this is in line with the idea that the expansion of the universe is one of the factors that contribute to the increasing complexity of the universe through emergent behaviors. The ability of a system to self-organize and self-maintain its own organization, such as homeostasis or autopoiesis [163–166], could be a consequence of the decreases in the thermodynamic fractal dimension of the universe. This contradicts the idea that there were some large-scale structures in the early universe, unless these structures were remnants of a prior large-scale universe [167–170]. Note that in this context, the fact that a system is more efficient at storing energy per unit mass could be interpreted as meaning that this storage is actually a useful means of generating dissipation at a larger scale.

7.2. Mountain Range Geomorphology

Jumping to a more human perspective, our experience is linked to the topography of the places we inhabit, which have different roughnesses. In particular, geometrical properties of geological structures have commonly been described as power law [60, 171–175]. That is why D could also be related to geological features. In this multiscale context, the generation of topography can be understood as the result of the balance between macroscopic and microscopic forces that act on the Earth's surface. For example, if energy is dissipated primarily at small scales, this can lead to a rough and jagged landscape. However, if energy is dissipated more efficiently at larger scales, this can lead to smoother and more regular topography at larger scales. The relationship between energy dissipation and topography can also be influenced by external factors such as climate and atmospheric conditions, indicating that topography is an open system. For example, mountains can affect rain conditions because it can block the movement of clouds, which enhance precipitations [176]. As precipitation can generate smooth surfaces [177] by causing the erosion of the most pronounced geometric roughnesses, the generation of topographic smooth surfaces due to climate can be regarded as a macroscopical force. Figure 8a illustrates the relationship between the thermodynamic fractal dimension and the topography of a mountain range. The obstruction of cloud movement by the mountain generates macroscopic dissipation and reduces the thermodynamic fractal dimension, creating smoother surfaces at the bottom or piedmont regions. Figure 8b,c show two views of a random multifractal distribution with a fractal dimension of 2.01 at the bottom and 2.7 at the peak. The decrease in altitude is characterized by smaller values of D, which generates a topography similar to that found in real mountain ranges.

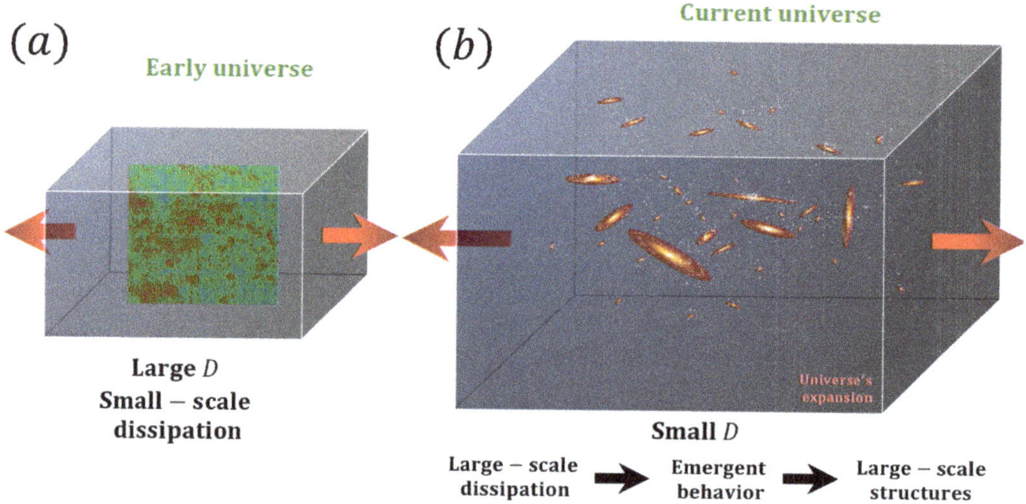

Figure 7. (**a**) A schematic representation of the early universe is shown, which is characterized by a large thermodynamic fractal dimension. This implies that the system was more efficient at dissipating energy at smaller scales, meaning that small-scale entropy production dominated. The figure shows that the structures at smaller scales have a more complex and irregular pattern, which is indicative of a higher degree of small-scale entropy production. At the center is a random fractal distribution with $D = 2.8$ and is a representation of the cosmic microwave background. (**b**) The expansion of the universe over time leads to a decrease in the thermodynamic fractal dimension of the universe, generating emergent behavior and large-scale structures.

7.3. Tree's Transpiration Process and Life System Governed by Power Laws

Some systems that follow power laws ordering are those that exhibit "branching" properties as a result of efficient matter transport. For example, the branching of a tree and plants can follow a self-similar pattern where each branch bifurcates into two, or more, smaller branches, and this pattern repeats at different scales within the tree [29,178]. This can be described using a power law relationship between the diameter or length of a branch and its position within the tree, while the distribution of leaves or needles on a tree can also exhibit fractal patterns, where the distribution is self-similar at different scales [29,179]. These features, along with the tree-shaped design found in nature, allow for efficient transport of fluids or mass from volume/area to point, as facilitated by the pressure generated by the concentration gradient of water from moisture-saturated soil to the dry air [180]. This gradient of water potential between the soil and the atmosphere, which drives the flow of water from the roots to the leaves, is known as transpiration [181,182]. The transpiration process of trees can be seen as an example of an irreversible process in a multiscale system, where external forces generate power laws. In this case, the external force is the gradient concentration of water between the soil and the atmosphere, and the power law arises as a result of the efficient transport of fluids from the water-saturated soil to the dry air through fractal and self-similar structures (roots and branches) [180,183]. As shown in Figure 9, the patterns that form in trees, initially considered a consequence of efficient water transport, can now be viewed as a form of entropy generation across multiple scales. In this context, the design of trees, which arises as a consequence of efficient water transport as described by Bejan [183], can now be seen as a manifestation of a universe striving to evolve toward a more probable state. This process is inherently irreversible, and trees operate under the same principle within this multiscale framework. In other words, this suggests that the fundamental characteristics of a tree, such as its power law scaling, irreversibility, and being affected by external forces, are consistent with the ideas of multiscale thermodynamics.

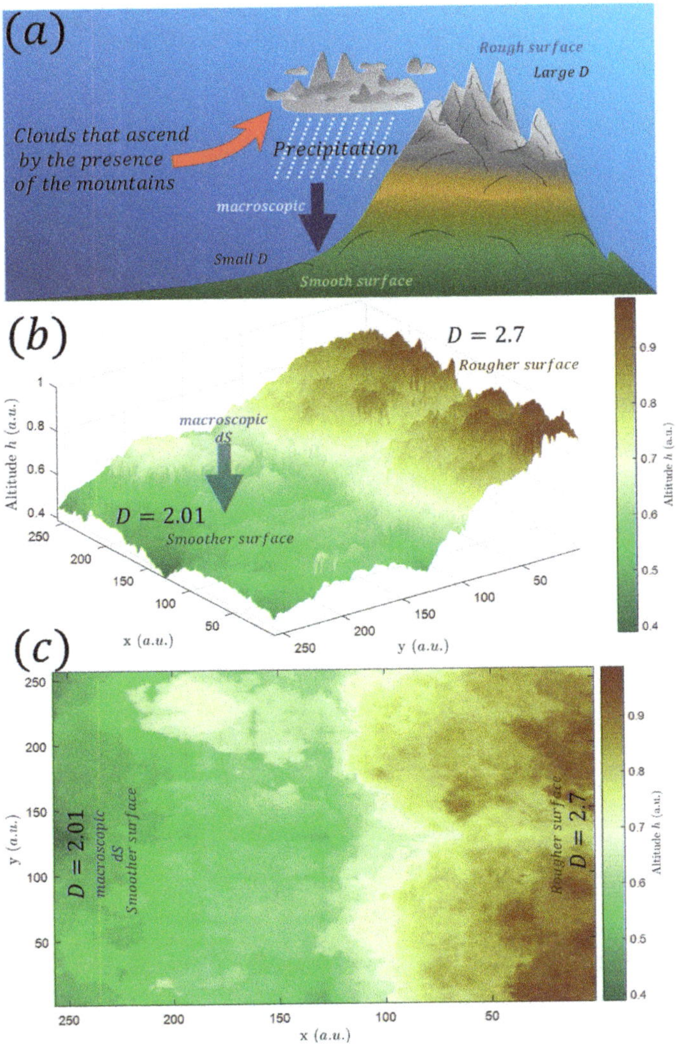

Figure 8. (**a**) The image shows a schematic representation of a mountain range that acts as an obstacle for the movement of clouds. As the clouds move towards the mountain, their altitude increases, and this generates an increase in precipitation. This precipitation can be seen as macroscopic dissipation that reduces the thermodynamic fractal dimension at the bottom of the mountain, generating smoother surfaces. (**b**) The image shows a random multifractal distribution of altitude (same method used in Figure 2), where the bottom is characterized by a thermodynamic fractal dimension of $D = 2.01$, and the peak is characterized by $D = 2.7$. In other words, the increase in altitude is characterized by larger values of D. This random distribution of values generates a topography that is similar to what is found in real mountain ranges. (**c**) The image is the same as the one in (**b**), but it is shown in-plane. It helps to visualize the multifractal distribution of altitude in a different way, making it easier to see the changes in the thermodynamic fractal dimension as altitude increases.

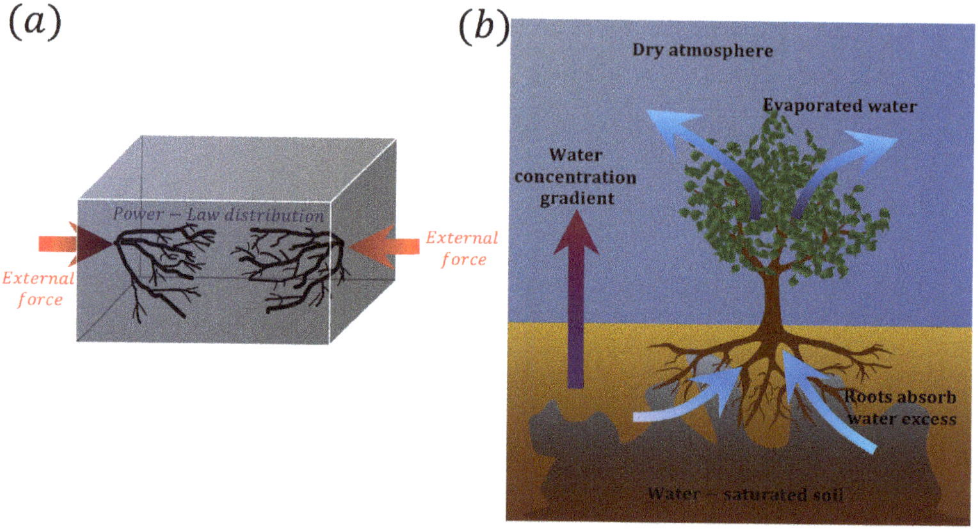

Figure 9. Schematic representation of external forces and their relation to efficient dissipation in natural systems. (**a**) An external force creates a power law distribution, allowing for efficient dissipation of excess energy. (**b**) The transpiration process of a tree can be seen as an external force, with the gradient concentration of water driving an efficient transport of water from soil to atmosphere. The resulting fractal and self-similar structures of the tree are an efficient manner of dissipating the excess energy and maintaining multiscale thermodynamic balance.

As several systems in biology are governed by power laws [184–190], it is possible that some systems in life science are irreversible due to the basic properties of multiscale thermodynamics proposed in this work. This would suggest that open biological systems described by power laws, such as tree branching, circulatory and respiratory systems, or even the body size distribution in ecological communities, could be local manifestations of the dissipation of energy at multiple scales [191–196]. These systems are constantly interacting with their environment and exchanging energy and matter, and thus, are subject to external forces that drive irreversible processes [197]. Thus, the study of multiscale thermodynamics provides a framework to understand the emergence of power laws and irreversibility in complex biological systems.

7.4. Geometry of Human Organs and Aging

As described in Section 7.3, human organs could also exhibit power law and fractal characteristics in their structure and function. For example, the bronchial tree and air sacs in the lungs exhibit a fractal branching pattern that maximizes the surface area available for gas exchange, the blood vessels within the heart exhibit a fractal-like branching pattern that allows for the efficient delivery of oxygen and nutrients to the cardiac tissue, and the dynamics of neural activity also exhibit power law scaling reflecting the complex interactions among neurons [198–202]. That is why the relationship between human organs and power law can be understood in the context of multiscale thermodynamics. In the case of human organs, external forces could be related to the demands of the body for a particular function or the constraints imposed by the physical environment. These external forces create a need for the efficient transport of nutrients, oxygen, and waste products across various scales, ranging from the microscopic capillary networks to the larger vessels and ducts. The fractal organization of human organs, such as the lungs or the circulatory system, can be seen as a response to these external forces, as it allows for the optimal exchange of materials while minimizing the energy required for transportation [9,180]. The fractal organization of human organs can also be seen as an example of how nature utilizes the principles of multiscale thermodynamics to optimize energy consumption and dissipation. In other words, what is interpreted as efficient transport could actually also be interpreted as an efficient form of energy dissipation. Similarly, the increase in the fractal dimension of DNA walks, which refers to the spatial arrangement of the DNA double helix, and human faces during aging [203–205] could be manifestations of the same principles, as the system seeks to dissipate energy in a more efficient manner at smaller scales. For instance, Namazi et al. [205] found that both the fractal dimension of DNA walk and skin rugosity increase with age. Similar findings are obtained in other organs, such as the lung, indicating that the respiration process becomes more complex as we age [206]. This increase in the thermodynamic fractal dimension could be excessive for some organs because this may indicate the presence of intense small-scale dynamics that could lead to tumor proliferation. In fact, the increase in the fractal dimension of tissues is a characteristic of organs affected by cancer, while successful treatment is reflected in a decrease in the fractal dimension [207,208]. This suggests that the human body, including some diseases, can be described as a whole by D. This could be more evident for aging. For example, this perspective suggests that growth could be a macroscopic manifestation of biological forces that dissipate energy. According to the multiscale thermodynamic view, macroscopic dissipation results in smaller thermodynamic fractal dimensions and smoother surfaces, which explains why young humans have smooth skin and less complex DNA sequences. However, as humans age and stop growing, the body cannot dissipate energy at a macroscopic scale, leading to more relevant microscopic dissipation. This results in more complex DNA sequences and greater skin rugosity. This process is schematically described in Figure 10.

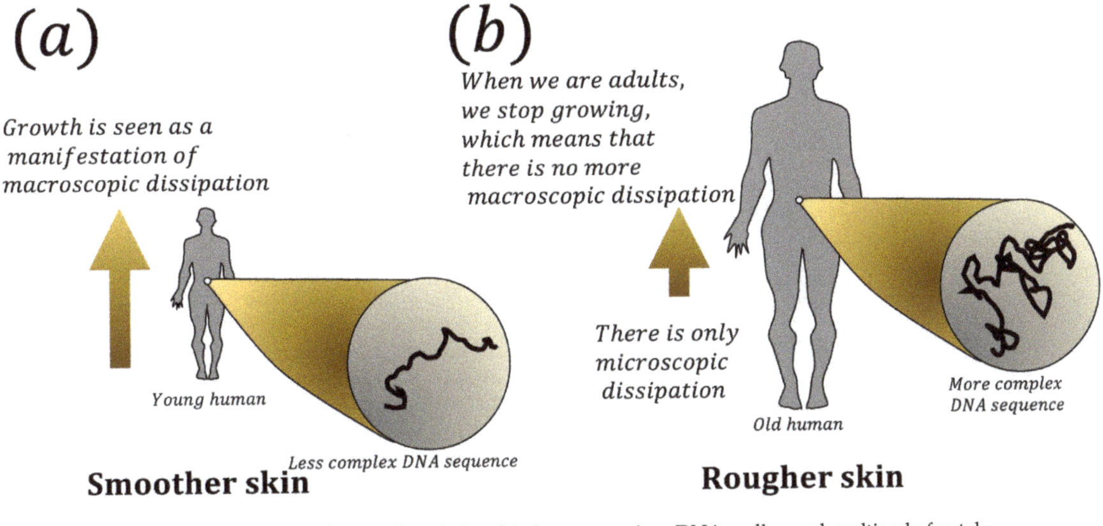

Figure 10. The figure depicts the relationship between aging, DNA walks, and multiscale fractal dimension. (**a**) shows a schematic representation of a young human with a gold arrow indicating growth as a macroscopic dissipation of energy, and less complex DNA sequences. Young human is characterized by smooth skin. (**b**) depicts a schematic representation of an old human where growth has stopped, leading to small-scale dissipation dominating the multiscale entropy production, resulting in more complex DNA sequences and rougher skin.

7.5. Human Brain and Cognition

One of the most interesting organs in the human body is the brain. The brain has a complex structure that can be described using power laws and fractals [209,210]. This means that the structure of the brain is self-similar at different scales and can be characterized by a fractal dimension. The fractal dimension of the brain has been found to be a relevant parameter related to cognition [211]. In other words, the more complex the structure of the brain, the larger the fractal dimension and the better it performs cognitive tasks. This is because a more complex brain structure can support more complex neural connections and information processing [212,213]. It is relevant to highlight that the complexity of the brain, as measured by its fractal dimension, is not constant as we age. Research has shown that the fractal dimension, and thus the network complexity of the brain, tends to increase from young adulthood (<40 years old) to mid-age (40 to 60 years old) and then decrease from mid-age to old age (>60 years old) [214–216]. The latter is due to the gradual degradation of neural connections and the loss of brain tissue, which suggests that age-related changes in brain structure contribute to cognitive decline. External stimuli, such as sensory information from organs like the eyes and skin, can increase the fractal dimension of the brain [217]. This is because external stimuli influence the brain to create new neural connections and processes information in a more complex way [98]. That is, our episodic memory (remembering specific events) and semantic memory (meaning of the world) are also ways to map the state of neural connections given the interaction with the environment [218,219]. Therefore, activities that involve exposure to new sensory information, such as learning a new language or playing a new instrument, can lead to an increase in brain complexity and improved cognitive function [220]. This implies that external stimuli could rewire brain networks in elderly people [221]. The multiscale thermodynamic framework described by Equation (2) suggests that human growth is related to large-scale dissipation (Section 7.4), which occurs during childhood and adolescence. In adulthood, when large-scale dissipation stops, there is a burst of small-scale dissipation that could increase the fractal dimension of the brain's neural networks. This can be seen as increases in the fractal dimension, white matter, and cognitive abilities in young adulthood [222]. Organs, such as the eyes and skin, are at their best performance during this period and provide a steady stream of external stimuli that can drive this small-scale dissipation generating increases in the brain's fractal dimension. Figure 11a,b show a schematic representation of the increases in the thermodynamic fractal dimension at theses ages. Nevertheless, small-scale dissipation could also generate fractal noise, which affects cognition in elderly people [223–225]. However, as the aging process progresses, the channels that connect the brain to the external world may vanish due to the degradation of organs such as the eyes [226]. Besides the increasing brain noise, this can lead to a lack of external stimuli, which in turn generates less small-scale dissipation and lower fractal dimension values. This decline in the fractal dimension could lead to a reduction in plasticity, cognitive abilities, and neural connections. Thus, it can be said that the power law structure of the brain is a consequence of external forces (stimuli), and its efficiency is driven by both the small-scale entropy production due to the stop of macroscopical growth and the degradation of channels that connect the brain and the external world. In other words, the changes that the human brain could experience throughout its development could be strongly influenced by processes similar to those described by multiscale thermodynamics. Key characteristics such as the influence of external forces (stimuli) and the power law distribution (directly associated with cognitive abilities and the fractal dimension) suggest that the brain is another example of the application of multiscale thermodynamics. Note here that this view would imply that the brain, like the rest of the organs described, is dissipative in nature, so its ability to map, understand, or interact with the world could be a secondary process or consequence of dissipation.

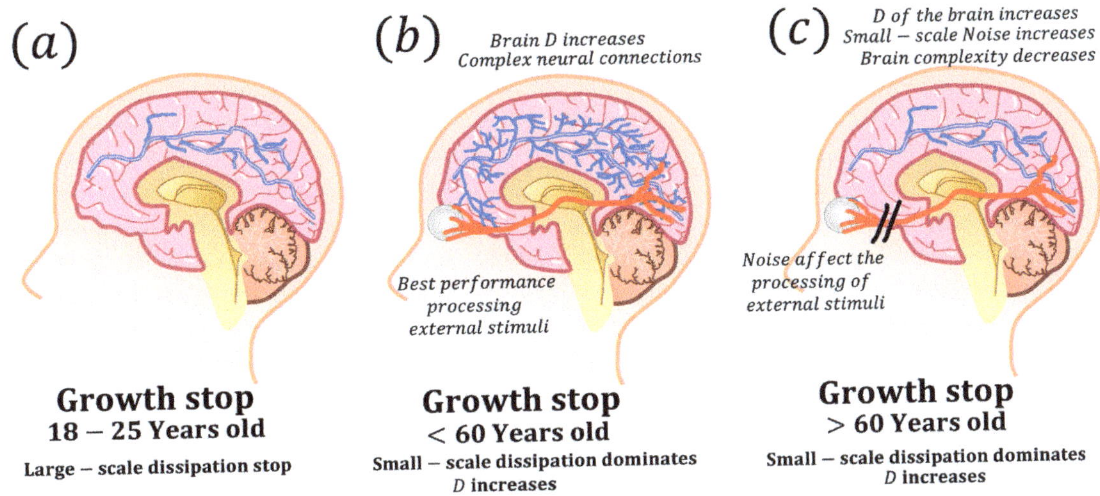

Figure 11. This schematic representation demonstrates the application of multiscale thermodynamics and its thermodynamic fractal dimension (Equation (2)) to the human brain. (**a**) The growth of a young human brain (18 to 25 years old) reaches an arrest point, and macroscopic entropy production ceases. Consequently, microscopic entropy production begins to dominate. Moving on to (**b**), small-scale entropy production increases, leading to a rise in the thermodynamic fractal dimension of the brain. This increase generates more complex neural networks, which, in turn, improve cognitive abilities in mid-age adults (<60 years old). At this stage, external organs are at their prime, making the influence of external stimuli on the brain optimal. Finally, in (**c**), microscopic entropy production also generates a rise in fractal noise in the brain. Similar noise also arises in other organs, such as the eyes, which drive their deterioration, resulting in a lack of external stimuli to the brain. As a consequence, the complexity of neural networks decreases, which is manifested as a drop in the thermodynamic fractal dimension.

7.6. Evolutionary Moral

The brain's structure and function are essential for modeling or influencing the complex social behavior of mammals. In particular, complex systems theory can be applied to study the emergence of social norms, which are unwritten rules of behavior that are enforced through social pressure rather than legal sanctions [227–230]. Social norms can arise through complex interactions between individuals, as people observe and mimic the behavior of others, and can be reinforced or weakened through feedback loops [231]. According to Tomasello [231], the capacity for shared intentionality allows humans to engage in collaborative activities, such as hunting, gathering, and child-rearing, which require individuals to work together and coordinate their actions towards a common goal. This implies that the emergence of morality can give rise to new actions and social structures that are not reducible to the behavior of individual components. Particularly because morality emerges from the interactions and relationships between individuals, it is sustained by social norms, institutions, and practices that are created and maintained by the group. In other words, once cooperation and shared goals become established, they tend to persist and become increasingly complex. This indicates that social norms arise from the interaction between people or groups, as well as with the environment. This also suggests that there is an external force that models human behavior. Nevertheless, the consideration of power laws to explain social interactions may be more diffuse. That is why human morality may be more difficult to identify as a consequence of multiscale thermodynamics. This implies that the concept of emergent behavior [232] is required to link human behavior with multiscale thermodynamics in an indirect manner.

For example, Section 3 suggests that the small values of D indicate that the system acts similarly across different scales, generating macroscopic patterns that persist over time because they are difficult to erase. Therefore, it is possible to interpret the emergence of shared intentionality in human morality as a result of the interactions of individuals in social contexts, similar to how emergent behavior and macroscopic patterns can arise in complex systems through the interactions of individual components at smaller scales. In that line, the moral norms, values, or "union feelings" that make people gather (such as ideologies, nationalism, religions, sports teams' supporters, or patriotism) that emerge in a society that are likely to persist over time (difficult to reverse or undo) could be seen as consequence of the multiscale thermodynamic framework.

7.7. Updating the Perspective of Natural Selection and Biological Death

The evolutionary changes that groups of living beings undergo over long periods of time can make it easier or harder for their members to survive. This is described by natural selection, which is one of the most fundamental principles in evolutionary biology [233]. It states that in a population, individuals with traits that are better adapted to their environment are more likely to survive and reproduce, passing on these advantageous traits to their offspring [234]. Over time, this process leads to changes in the traits of a population, ultimately resulting in the "adaptation" of organisms to their environment. When the multiscale thermodynamic phenomenon is considered, the principles of natural selection undergo an interesting reinterpretation. In traditional Darwinian theory, adaptation is primarily driven by the need to survive and reproduce in a given environment. However, from the multiscale thermodynamic viewpoint, the focus shifts towards the dissipation of energy and the increase in macroscopic entropy, which is a feature of cosmic evolution.

In this context, as the universe reduces its thermodynamic fractal dimension (Section 7.1), it implies that systems tend to dissipate energy more efficiently on a macroscopic scale, leading to emergent behaviors (Section 3). In other words, particles may tend to exhibit similar dynamic, which gives rise to the creation of larger coordinated structures, such as multicellular organisms. It can be said that the evolution of biological systems is a consequence of the efficient dissipation of energy across increasingly macroscopic scales, governed by a reduction in D. However, this description refers to evolutionary changes on timescales of billions of years. In contrast, the Darwinian concept of organisms adapting to their environment can also occur on shorter timescales [235–237]. In the multiscale interpretation applied to a single organism, the environment can play the role of an external force, providing external stimuli. These external forces could drive small-scale changes in biological systems as a means to dissipate excess energy, as shown in Section 7.5 with the example of neuronal changes in response to an external stimulus. Note that this could be reinforced by knowing that there are genes that are related to the interaction with the environment [238]. In other words, multiscale thermodynamics establishes a direct link between molecular or genetic variations (or mutations) and changes in the environment as a mechanism of energy dissipation. This perspective contrasts with the Fundamental Theorem of Natural Selection [239,240] because it requires small-scale changes that can be considered mutations [241,242]. This leads to the fact that mutations are also changes given by the environment, and as these can be varied, it can be thought that their effect at small scales generates mutations that could be perceived as random without the multiscale perspective. If an environment has a type of persistent stimulus, it implies that the small-scale reaction focuses on a few molecular changes to the detriment of others [243]. This external effect can cause small-scale effects such as biochemical imbalances associated with stress or addictions that can lead to changes in individual behavior and health, which could correspond to a macroscopic manifestation in some cases [244–248]. A schematic representation can be seen in Figure 12a.

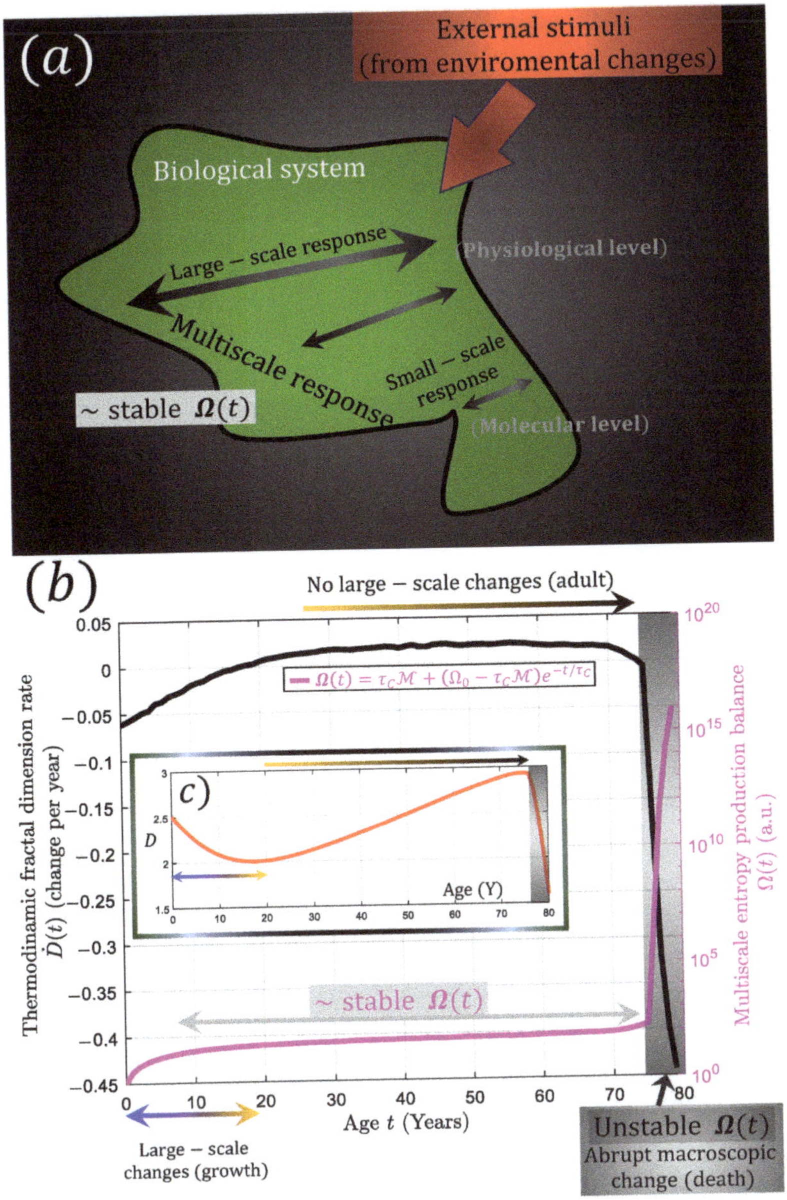

Figure 12. (**a**) A schematic representation of a biological system responding to different scales due to an external perturbation (environment). The living being has a stable balance of entropy production Ω. Panels (**b**,**c**) show the effect of changing the thermodynamic fractal dimension, D, as an organism evolves from birth, grows in size, and subsequently dies. The red curve in panel (**c**) shows that as an organism grows in size, its D decreases. In contrast, D increases for an adult organism. The time derivative of D (black curve in panel (**c**)) is the function that is needed to calculate Ω (magenta curve) according to Equation (10). When an organism dies, it is considered to be a large-scale manifestation, which causes D to decrease and Ω to increase abruptly. Note that the time for panels (**b**,**c**) is shown in years, assuming the typical human evolution and lifespan.

Consider the case of the regulation of the dynamic equilibrium state of an organism, known as homeostasis [249–251]. In general, when a system is exposed to changes in the environment, it reacts through biochemical changes, so it can be considered a small-scale response. Changes, such as temperature, affect the small scale (Section 4.1). However, these alterations can trigger larger-scale effects such as changes in behavior, diseases, or even the death of the organism. This is particularly true when there are, for instance, heat waves [252–254]. Currently, there are authors who do not consider homeostasis as a "search for equilibrium" at a fundamental level because, from a thermodynamic point of view, equilibrium suggests that the organism tends to lose its dynamics since there are no temperature gradients inside the body mass that trigger the biochemical flows that allow metabolism [255]. This means that homeostasis, and likely life itself, is a state of imbalance that is maintained relatively constantly throughout the life of the organism [256,257]. One way to maintain an imbalance is to keep different regions of an organism with different dissipation rates. This can also apply to dissipations between different scales. From the multiscale perspective, this means that, in order to maintain a similar imbalance, the balance term $\Omega = dS/dS_0$ must try to remain stable (constant) throughout the life of the organism. In terms of equations, a quantity X, representing some subsystem of a biological organism, must be homeostatically governed by the relationship of the type: $dX/dt \sim -X$ [164]. This type of equation, in terms of Ω, can be obtained directly from Equation (2) (Appendix B). That is:

$$\dot{\Omega} = -\frac{\dot{D}}{k_V}\Omega + \mathcal{M}, \tag{9}$$

where $\mathcal{M}$ can be interpreted as the rate of energy from the environment that interacts with the biological system and $\dot{D}$ is the temporal change in the thermodynamic fractal dimension. The solution of Equation (9) is (Appendix B):

$$\Omega(t) = \tau_C\mathcal{M} + (\Omega_0 - \tau_C\mathcal{M})e^{-\frac{t}{\tau_C}}, \tag{10}$$

where $\tau_C = k_V/\dot{D}$ and for $\Omega(0) = \Omega_0$. Then, Equation (10) can be considered the one that describes the homeostatic imbalance across different scales. Note that in a growing biological organism, D tends to have small values since there is a macroscopic manifestation of physiological changes (Sections 7.4 and 7.5), which implies that during this growth period (0–18 years if we consider human life), $\dot{D}$ is negative. However, when the organism reaches adulthood, there are no longer macroscopic changes, so D tends to be large, implying that $\dot{D}$ is positive. Since $\dot{D}$ has a direct effect on Equation (10), it would be expected that the balance term Ω would be different throughout the organism's life. This can be seen in Figure 12b,c. For example, the red curve in Figure 12c shows how D falls until 18 years (here represented by a quadratic function, although note that this is only a simple approximation as there may be infinitely many decreasing curves that fit the above for D) and then increases (linearly). The black curve in Figure 12b shows the change in D per year, while the magenta curve shows that Ω is relatively stable throughout life.

On a macroscopic scale, diseases often cause an increase in entropy in biological systems, as they disrupt the organization and functioning of biological systems through damage and "disorder" [258,259]. Thus, diseases that affect the entire system can be considered as cases where D decreases (macroscopically) and $\dot{D}$ is negative. The case of a disease that affects the organism at the end of human life (let us say ~74 years and beyond) manifests as a drop in the red curve shown in Figure 12c (black area). This abrupt change in D has a profound impact on $\dot{D}$, as well as on Ω (black area in Figure 12b). In particular, a disease that affects a large part of the biological system implies an increase in the Ω imbalance of several orders of magnitude. This implies that the death of the organism can also be considered an extreme change in $\dot{D}$.

Additionally, the multiscale perspective, where small-scale dynamics can exist without appreciable macroscopic changes, could explain why life can have changes at the genetic scale without instantly affecting the macroscopic, or robust, structure of organisms [260]. This is supported by the fact that multiscale systems, which dissipate energy more efficiently at the macroscopic scale, are less sensitive to initial conditions, as shown in Figure 6a,b in the context of chaos theory. Any biological system, which is also multiscale, could be considered more stable or "robust" at the macroscopic scale. This means that larger (smaller) animals may be less (more) affected by small-scale changes such as DNA replication errors, which could explain why the probability of developing cancer is not correlated with the size of animals [261–268]. Thus, the environment acting as an external force could generate a response from organisms at different scales, either small (molecules, cells, and temperature) or large (behavior and physiological), as a way to dissipate energy (adaptation). Then, each time an organism "adapts in an environment", what could happen is that a biological system managed to dissipate energy at different scales given an external force.

When an organism dies, it cannot increase the macroscopic entropy of the universe (or equivalently, reduce D). In other words, it cannot reduce either the value of D nor dissipate energy from its environment. That is why only organisms that can reduce the value of D could survive. In the case of the human species, we have created coordinated or emergent hierarchical structures (Section 7.6) as a means to achieve common goals. This has allowed us to increase energy dissipation on increasingly macroscopic scales. For example, it can be considered that global warming could be a way to release trapped energy (heat) within the Earth. Therefore, human adaptation through cooperation towards common objectives is a way to generate energy dissipation (heat) on a large scale. Then, it can be said that this updated perspective on natural selection aligns with the concept that life and biological systems are part of (and connected to) the broader universe's drive to increase entropy and dissipate energy [269,270]. As organisms evolve and adapt, they are not only seeking to survive and reproduce as it is commonly thought but also to contribute to the larger goal of energy dissipation in the context of the universe's evolving thermodynamic landscape.

8. Summary and Discussion

The idea that the universe could be made up of multiple systems that interact with each other, and at different scales, may sound like an obvious idea. Especially when we consider that a particular system will react to the influence of other systems. However, the problem with this is that we might interpret the "systems" as macroscopic domains, forgetting that they could also react to other smaller scales. This leads to the transport and release of excess energy to smaller scales. In other words, a microscopic-scale dynamic could exist as a mechanism for energy release without the need to express large changes macroscopically. The lack of clarity regarding the multiscale influence of one system on another leads to the idea that very different disciplines (such as physics, life sciences, and humanities, among others) are in separate fields and their unification is seen as unthinkable or improbable [271,272]. However, new developments in the field of thermodynamics have questioned this separation, so recent efforts seek to unify the sciences under the lens of thermodynamics, stability, and dissipation [273–283]. The way in which excess external energy is dissipated at different scales can be seen as a description that aligns with the perspective of unifying different scientific fields through thermodynamics as parts of a "big history". Therefore, a global parameter of the multiscale thermodynamics' lens, such as the thermodynamic fractal dimension, could first exist and, second, have different interpretations in different fields and subfields. This could suggest that multiscale thermodynamics can provide a common foundation for understanding complex systems, regardless of their nature. This is why this work explores the use of multiscale thermodynamic fractal dimensions D in various fields and how this framework can be applied to describe complex systems.

The multiscale thermodynamics concept was described in Equation (2). This explained how external forces generate power laws and geometrical features that can be linked to the balance between small-scale and large-scale entropy production (Section 2). Despite the fact that there have been some works dealing with the fractal dimension and entropy [284,285] or entropy and geometry [286,287], Equation (2) incorporates more general properties than the multiscale description of Onsager's coefficients and heterogeneous resistivity to understand the relationship between the hierarchies of complex systems, emergent behavior, power laws, and fractal thermodynamics [59]. That is, Equation (2) can be seen as providing a theoretical foundation for the study of multiscale entropy, by linking the dynamic of complex systems across different scales to the concept of entropy production.

The generation of D in terms of multiscale entropy production balance means that the smaller the D, the more efficient the system is at dissipating energy at larger scales, which can be observed as macroscopic or emergent behavior in complex systems. In contrast, larger D means that the systems are more efficient at dissipating energy at smaller scales, which, in turn, generates rougher surfaces and networks that fill more the space. For example, in a system of interacting particles, the decrease in D may cause the particles to become more ordered and form patterns, such as crystals [288]. Similarly, in a complex system of organisms, this decreases in D may cause the emergence of ordered patterns of behavior or collective movements, such as flocks of birds or schools of fish. In both cases, it leads to the emergence of macroscopic patterns that cannot be explained by looking at the individual components alone. For example, emergent behaviors are often associated with the formation of a large number of chemical bonds, which are processes that release or dissipate energy. That is, the formation of a crystal is an emergent behavior that occurs when molecules in a liquid come together to form a solid. This process releases energy on a large scale because (almost) all of the molecules in the crystal have a lower free energy than the molecules in the liquid [289]. Similarly, the formation of a cell is another emergent behavior that occurs when molecules in a liquid come together to form an organized structure. For example, DNA has an electric charge, so its dynamics are associated with the search for electrical neutrality [290,291]. This process also releases energy since the molecules in the cell have a lower energy than the molecules in the liquid. This leads to the formation of a living organism being the most complex emergent behavior in the known universe. This is because this process releases a large amount of energy due to the formation of many chemical bonds that release and produce entropy. Thus, the emergent behavior that rises in complex systems can be seen because of the relationship between smaller thermodynamic fractal dimensions and more efficient energy dissipation at larger scales (Section 3). That is why this multiscale perspective could be the key point to understanding a stable complex network [292]. Despite the focus on emergent and macroscopic features, systems could also experience disturbances that affect multiple scales or involve interactions between different scales. For example, Section 4 shows the relationship between D and the fluctuation–dissipation theorem. This theorem describes the (multiscale) spontaneous fluctuations (response) of a system to an external perturbation and, as a consequence, could generate macroscopic patterns. In simple words, the variation of the dissipation could lead to fractal properties [293–295]. Here, the multiscale entropy production balance Ω_V can capture this dynamic by describing the fluctuations and dissipation of energy in both space and time. In particular, the spatial and temporal properties of Ω_V could reveal how energy is dissipated at different scales and how the system responds to external perturbations, such as Figure 5 shows. In other words, Ω_V is the factor that relates the interaction of one scale to another within the same system.

Certain systems may not efficiently dissipate the energy that is being injected and instead respond to external inputs by generating multiple losses that amplify the perturbation across multiple scales. That is why Section 5 relates multiscale thermodynamics to chaos theory. This section shows that the D can be linked to the sum of Lyapunov exponents (Equation (6)), which are used to quantify the degree of chaos in a system. This allows one to use D to describe the emergence of chaos in complex systems. In the context of multiscale thermodynamics, it can be observed that the system's sensitivity to initial conditions is influenced by the dominance of small-scale entropy production, as depicted in Figure 6a,c. However, the effect of initial conditions is limited to specific scales, as illustrated in Figure 6b. This could suggest that chaotic systems are limited to very specific subdomains and that tiny changes could never affect the stability of a system large enough (composed of many scales). In a very broad sense, the fact that the classical world is not directly affected by the variations of the quantum world could be a consequence of the multiscale properties of the universe. In contrast, only systems that are not too sensitive to initial conditions could lead to emergent behavior. One specific manifestation of chaos theory is observed in the phenomenon of turbulence, which can be characterized by self-similar evolution [296]. In this case, Section 6 discusses the relationship between D and the turbulence phenomenon by means of the Equations (7) and (8). The relationship between larger D and larger Reynolds numbers associated with more turbulent regimes is revealed by this analysis because turbulence could emerge in systems that exhibit greater sensitivity to initial conditions as is shown in Figure 6d.

This study further explores other applications of multiscale thermodynamics beyond fundamental physics. As a result, Section 7 provides specific examples of how this theory can be utilized in various systems. One example discussed in Section 7.1 suggests that the expansion of the entire universe can be viewed as an external force that drives the emergence of macroscopic patterns and increased complexity. Equation (2) supports this idea by indicating that as the universe continues to expand, it will generate more complex structures and emergent behavior due to the drop in D, in line with Chaisson's theory of increasing complexity [142]. In terms of geometry, the fractal dimension tends to be interpreted as a measure of how much an object fills the space it contains. For example, an object with a fractal dimension close to 2 will tend to be one that resembles an area, while one close to 1 will approximate a line [297]. Therefore, if the early universe had high values of D, it could mean that mass was spread out over space. However, as the universe evolves, D apparently decreases, meaning that the structures that form in the universe will tend to fill less space, or in other words, be more compact to satisfy lower values of D. This means that gravity could be interpreted as the mechanism that aggregates mass to prevent it from spreading out over space, while both biological organisms and emergent behaviors could be ways of compacting matter and preventing it from spreading out over the universe. As mass is intimately related to energy [298], this compaction of matter could also imply that energy is stored in a more compact way, which could explain Chaisson's description that matter stores (compacts) more and more energy as the universe progresses (D decreases). Hence, physical phenomena such as complexity, gravity, or the absence of quantum effects at large scales could be a direct consequence of multiscale thermodynamics. This ongoing emergence, or collaboration, of complex dynamic is also relevant to other theories, such as geology or the evolution of life, which can be seen as a multiscale phenomenon involving biological systems interacting at various levels of organization, from molecular to ecosystem scales and shaped by environmental influences [299–301]. In that line, Section 7.2 provides an example of how topography, which refers to the physical characteristics of a landscape, is linked to the fractal dimension of multiscale thermodynamics. This connection is established through the process of energy dissipation and erosion. As an illustration, mountain topography can trap clouds and produce macroscopic rain, leading to smoother surfaces at the mountain base due to erosion (Figure 8). This effect on geological surfaces also impacts other systems such as the process of generating subduction earthquakes. For instance, seafloor irregularities tend to be polished or smoothed when one tectonic plate is subducted beneath another plate [302]. This implies that the deeper zones of faults can become smoother, potentially making them more susceptible to larger earthquakes and precursor activity [302–305]. In this regard, the non-subducting plate acts as a macroscopic force, which reduces the D of the system by increasing fault smoothness and reducing the resistance to rupture. Furthermore, since D is a global parameter, its decrease not only affects the rupture process [306] but it also increases the generation of microcracks that could lead to fluid migration, emissions of electromagnetic signals, or precursor seismicity [302,307].

Section 7.3 presents another example of Equation (2), which is the transpiration phenomenon in trees. The effective transport of fluids by trees to the atmosphere is an illustration of an external force attempting to establish equilibrium. The self-similar branches of trees signify the effect of external forces, indicating that trees can be viewed as a mechanism to restore the water balance between the soil and the lower atmosphere (Figure 9).

The human body is also a multiscale system, and its macroscopic energy dissipation during growth could also lead to the development of organs characterized by smaller D [308,309]. However, once growth stops in adulthood, macroscopic dissipation ceases, and humans only dissipate energy at the microscopic scale, resulting in an increase in D. That is why Sections 7.4 and 7.5 provide examples of this process. For instance, changes in the DNA structure, which increase with age, reflect small-scale dissipation. The external manifestation of this small-scale dissipation can also be seen in changes in skin surface texture, with smoother skin during growth (macroscopic dissipation dominance) and rougher skin after adulthood (microscopic dissipation dominance). Section 7.5 focuses specifically on the structure of the brain. When growth stops, the increase in D also affects the brain, causing the neural networks to become more complex as one ages, resulting in an improvement in the ability to process information or cognition. However, these small-scale structures can also lead to the generation of fractal noise that may disrupt neural patterns, leading to a decrease in D and a decline in cognitive abilities (as illustrated in Figure 11). In this context, the fractal structure of the brain is considered a result of external stimuli. According to Sloman and Fernbach [310], the thinking process is a means to navigate and respond to the external world, which can increase our chances of survival. This cognitive perspective suggests that the brain and its processes are intimately tied to the environment and that they emerge in response to external factors [311]. Then, the primary function of thinking and the brain increases the external influence as described in Section 7.5. In a similar vein, when a system is uncertain about its environment, a fundamental parameter is its free energy. In the context of the free energy principle, a reduction in free energy could mean that the system is reducing its uncertainty and becoming more efficient at representing and anticipating its surroundings [312–314]. Therefore, cognitive capacity increases [315]. In the context of multiscale thermodynamics, a reduction in free energy is aligned with an increase in D. Thus, the free energy principle can be seen as a special case of the multiscale dissipation principle. It is important to consider that, as the cooperation process is also linked to brain activity [316], Section 7.6 deals with the evolution of moral rising due to shared goals, which could be regarded as a manifestation of emergent processes that satisfy the increased complexity of the universe. This idea can be applied to this paper itself as it could be viewed as an example of decreasing thermodynamic fractal dimension, as it organizes various topics into a coherent macroscopic theoretical framework.

Section 7.7 leads to the reinterpretation of natural selection in terms of the multiscale thermodynamic principles. For example, organisms evolve through two processes. The first one is the assembly of macroscopic or emergent structures due to the universe's inherent tendency to decrease the value of D. That is, the universe tends to construct larger-scale elements from smaller constituents (emergent behavior) as a means to increase the macroscopic entropy of the universe (Sections 7.1 and 7.4). The second one come from the fact that this large-scale evolution can be slightly different when considering individual organisms or local environments. For instance, in nature, organisms influence each other [317], which can be seen as external forces from the environment (not external from the universe). This is similar to what is demonstrated regarding the effect of external stimuli at the cellular level in Section 7.5. This implies that an organism's adaptation directly stems from molecular or cellular changes in response to an environmental force. In other words, an external force (the environment) prompts the organism to release excess energy at both microscopic (molecular or cellular changes) and macroscopic (physiological or behavioral) levels. Therefore, the concept known as adaptation is, in this perspective, the multiscale response to an external force. Put differently, adaptation is the energy dissipation mechanism across different scales that an organism employs to continue reducing the thermodynamic fractal dimension of the universe under local conditions.

This perspective leads to the equation for multiscale homeostatic imbalance shown in Equation (10). This equation describes how energy dissipation can occur differently at different scales within an organism, leading to flow and dynamics within the organism. Figure 12b,c show that an organism can survive because the "imbalance" Ω remains relatively constant throughout life. This is, in part, justified by the fact that chaotic systems (if we consider an organism to be chaotic) are sensitive to initial conditions but their effects do not extend to all scales, which allows for macroscopic stability or "robustness" (Sections 5 and 7.7). However, as an organism dies, its effect can manifest as a drastic change in D. For example, D will tend to decrease dramatically if a generalized system-wide death mechanism, such as apoptosis or necrosis, is taking place. That is, D will influence Ω in such a way that Ω will cease to be constant and diverge (black area in Figure 12b). Then, the concept of considering that a system can respond to different scales given an external force also seems to be applicable to biological systems, since it allows us to describe fundamental processes in the same way that it can describe physical or social systems. For this reason, the multiscale formalism seems to be a prevalent principle in nature. Note that the explanation (or reinterpretation) of complex processes such as life, death, aging, topography, chaos, cosmic evolution, or turbulence are based on systems with many components and scales. Therefore, we have not considered the effects of only one particular scale. This means that we have not described the evolution of individual particles, which would lead to the description of fundamental forces or quantum level. Therefore, the multiscale principle cannot be considered a "theory of everything," but rather a principle that is applicable to systems with many constituents with irreversible or dissipative properties. That is, the theory is only applicable to multiscale systems and could be considered a direct application of Newton's second and third laws.

Lastly, it is important to remember that what we present in this work aligns more with a principle than a method. This is because a principle refers to a fundamental rule that serves as a broad foundation within a field, integrating existing knowledge. On the other hand, methods aim to solve specific problems through a series of actions. Additionally, this multiscale principle could be called luxuriæ, which is a Latin word that means "out of place." We interpret this as a way of saying that a system expels or dissipates energy. A specific application of the luxuriæ principle in a methodology can be found in solid mechanics. For instance, the generation, localization, and coalescence of cracks before macroscopic failure in a rock sample has been a phenomenon lacking a complete explanation due to the complexity of the involved mechanisms. Nevertheless, multiscale thermodynamics have offered a tool that elucidates this process [53,59]. For instance, this perspective is based on the heterogeneous resistivity of the rock material, which generates differential stresses and microcracks to dissipate energy at a smaller scale. As stresses increase without causing macroscopic deformation, these microcracks interact, creating pathways for fluids and chemical changes, allowing the formation of larger cracks and, ultimately, macroscopic failure. Subsequently, the parameter of the thermodynamic fractal dimension (D) is employed to describe the relationship between large-scale energy release and macroscopic failure by establishing analytical relationships between the fault area A and D ($A = A(D)$). In the case of a rupture in a pre-existing macroscopic fault, analytical relationships with changes in fault geometry can also be found. This implies that the luxuriæ principle applied to solid failure is capable of fully explaining the failure process as it posits that a decrease in D leads to crack localization, while the contact area in pre-existing faults becomes smoother, resulting in reduced rupture resistance. Thus, it quantitatively links effects and parameters that other descriptions are unable to achieve. This example could inspire other areas that have not been covered in this work to use the luxuriæ principle as a tool for future development and research.

9. Conclusions

Multiscale thermodynamics is a framework that could be used to study systems with a wide range of scales. Its application to various systems, including trees, turbulence, emergent behavior, chaos theory, human organs, aging, DNA structural evolution, topographical structures, the universe expansion, and the generation of complexity, could generate significant consequences.

First, the universe is full of systems that are composed of many scales. This implies that interactions between these systems could generate responses at scales that are not necessarily evidently macroscopically. This could be a common characteristic of many systems, which could allow us to describe them based on this fact.

Second, many complex (open) systems are characterized by the coordinated dynamic of many of their constituents, which indicates that they have energetic constraints that lead to similar evolution known as emergent behavior. This can be described as the dissipation of energy at the macroscopic scale, which leads to low values of D. In other words, emergent behaviors could occur when systems are more efficient at releasing excess energy in a macroscopic way. Additionally, multiscale systems can also have medium or high values of D, which would imply that the dissipation of energy at small scales could also be relevant in these systems. In this way, systems that are described by power laws could be the consequence of a balance of energy dissipation at different scales against an external force that generates an excess of energy.

Third, chaotic systems could be restricted to certain subdomains. This is because small perturbations in the initial conditions could be smoothed out at larger scales, indicating that when a system is composed of a wide range of scales, changes at small scales would not affect the macroscopic structure of the system. This could explain why many biological systems do not undergo rapid macroscopic changes despite the existence of a vigorous molecular or cellular dynamic. In other words, multiscale thermodynamics allows us to define the macroscopic stability of systems. In the extreme case, it could explain why the classical world is not affected by fluctuations or changes at the quantum level.

Fourth, the universe appears to be decreasing its D, which would indicate that it is more efficient at releasing energy at increasingly larger scales. This implies three things. First, the universe could be affected by an unknown external force. More studies are needed to understand the meaning of the word "external" in this context. Second, all subsystems should tend to have a lower D. This means that systems should have more emergent behaviors as the universe progresses. This can also be seen in surfaces that tend to be smoother. Thus, it could physically explain the role of erosion in nature. Finally, a universe with a lower D also implies, in geometric terms, that matter must occupy less space in the universe. This could directly link the force of gravity to macroscopic dissipation. That is, gravity could be regarded a dissipative force. Since this compaction of mass could also generate the compaction of energy, the fact that mass is storing more and more energy could mean that the complexity of the universe is a direct manifestation of an expanding universe that produces low D values.

Fifth, the multiscale description of the universe allows us to redefine theories associated with life, such as evolution or natural selection. As the universe could foster emergent structures in irreversible conditions, it could be that life itself is a consequence of an expanding universe. Locally, organisms are affected by environmental conditions, which can be reinterpreted as external forces that affect the most microscopic scales of the organism (genes and cells), which could generate macroscopic changes only over long periods of time to overcome the scale restriction described for chaotic systems (point three). As the universe also encourages the dissipation of energy, only those organisms that are better at dissipating macroscopic energy will be able to survive (the proper macroscopic changes). In this way, microscopic changes due to external forces (stimuli) promote physical or behavioral changes only when they are more efficient at dissipating macroscopic energy. Thus, natural selection and evolution could be a consequence, or one form, of multiscale dissipation.

Sixth, organisms also undergo macroscopic changes during growth, which defines the structure of their organs. In this way, during growth, D is small, which implies that the organs (skin, brain, lungs, etc.) act in an emergent and collaborative manner. This manifests itself in smoother skin and brains with lower cognitive abilities. When an organism reaches maturity, D increases, which generates an increase in cognitive abilities, health problems, and eventually the death of the organism. Therefore, the theory of multiscale thermodynamics could clarify why biological systems tend to emerge, grow, and eventually perish. In this way, life can be seen as a dissipative process that can be studied from the equation of homeostasis (Equation (10)). In less scientific words, life could just be a form of "disorder".

Finally, in view of the wide range of applications in which multiscale thermodynamics is found, as was shown in this work by transcribing and reinterpreting several and different systems under the lens of multiscale thermodynamics, it can be concluded that there are indications of a new principle in nature that can be described in a general manner as:

"Systems that interact with each other can trigger responses at multiple scales as a manner to dissipate the excess energy that comes from this interaction".

This *principium luxuriæ* (from the Latin word *'Luxus'*, which means 'out of place' in the sense that the energy tends to be spread out, and *'principium'*, which means principle), through an open system, allows us to explain the internal dynamics of complex systems that generate high complexity, as well as the emergent behaviors, self-organization, and adaptation of systems. The future challenges of multiscale thermodynamics include developing a more complete understanding of how the fractal dimension of complex systems changes over time, as well as exploring new applications of this theory to other scientific fields. A special point is associated to keep studying the mathematical properties of the thermodynamic fractal dimension as well the quantification of the entropy production balance described by Equation (2). Additionally, the development of new mathematical tools and techniques will be necessary to make predictions about their future outputs. Ultimately, the multiscale thermodynamics fractal dimension theory holds great promise for advancing our understanding of multiscale complex systems, fractals, and life processes and for unlocking new insights into the behavior of the universe as a whole.

Author Contributions: P.V.-A. proposed the core idea, mathematical development, literature review, generation of figures, initial draft of the project, and revisions. E.G.C. contributed to the funding of the work. P.V.-A. and E.G.C. contributed to the scientific discussion. All authors have read and agreed to the published version of the manuscript.

Funding: This research received no external funding.

Data Availability Statement: Data is contained within the article.

Acknowledgments: P.V.-A. acknowledges Alejandro Franklin, Patricia Aravena, Valeria Becerra-Carreño, Patricia A. Venegas, and Richard Sandoval for their continuous support. E.G.C. acknowledges Marcela Larenas Clerc for her everlasting support and Francesca Cordaro for her technical support. We also thank referees and editor for their job improving the quality of our manuscript.

Conflicts of Interest: Authors declare no conflict of interest.

Appendix A The Nonadditive Multiscale Thermodynamics

The thermodynamic fractal dimension described by Equation (2) is nonadditive. This nonadditivity arises from the fundamental idea that complex systems cannot be understood as a simple sum of their parts. Instead, D captures the interactions and behaviors that emerge at different scales within a system. As a result, attempting to add or sum the D of individual components may not accurately represent the behavior of the entire system. In order to exemplify this point, let us consider a straightforward scenario involving a system comprising n distinct noninteracting multiscale subsystems. As stated by reference [53], the entropy production of the system can be expressed as follows.

$$\frac{dS_T}{dt} = \frac{dS_1}{dt} + \frac{dS_2}{dt} + \ldots + \frac{dS_i}{dt} + \ldots + \frac{dS_n}{dt} \geq 0. \quad \text{(A1)}$$

In general terms, the definition of the entropy production of a multiscale system in terms of the thermodynamic flux J and the resistance coefficient K is: $\frac{dS_i}{dt} = r^{\alpha}\Sigma K^i_{kl} J^i_k J^i_l$. This applied to Equation (A1) implies that:

$$\frac{dS_T}{dt} = \left(\frac{r}{r_0}\right)^{\alpha_1} \sum_{kl} K^1_{kl} J^1_k J^1_l + \left(\frac{r}{r_0}\right)^{\alpha_2} \sum_{kl} K^2_{kl} J^2_k J^2_l + \ldots + \left(\frac{r}{r_0}\right)^{\alpha_i} \sum_{kl} K^i_{kl} J^i_k J^i_l + \ldots + \left(\frac{r}{r_0}\right)^{\alpha_n} \sum_{kl} K^n_{kl} J^n_k J^n_l. \tag{A2}$$

As these are scaling entropy productions, there must be an original non-scaled or small-scale version of the system denoted by $\frac{dS_i}{dt} = \left(\frac{r}{r_0}\right)^{\beta} \frac{dS_{0i}}{dt}$, which leads to a more compact version of Equation (A2):

$$\frac{dS_T}{dt} = \left(\frac{r}{r_0}\right)^{\alpha_1} \frac{dS_{01}}{dt} + \left(\frac{r}{r_0}\right)^{\alpha_2} \frac{dS_{02}}{dt} + \ldots + \left(\frac{r}{r_0}\right)^{\alpha_i} \frac{dS_{0i}}{dt} + \ldots + \left(\frac{r}{r_0}\right)^{\alpha_n} \frac{dS_{0n}}{dt}, \tag{A3}$$

and

$$\frac{dS_T}{dt} = \sum_i \left(\frac{r}{r_0}\right)^{\alpha_i} \frac{dS_{0i}}{dt}. \tag{A4}$$

As shown by Equation (A3), the macroscopic entropy production corresponds to a sum of different scaling defined by various values of alpha, as demonstrated in Equation (A4). Thus, the only way a unique value of thermodynamic fractal dimension can exist for the entire system is by assuming the presence of a non-scaled version of the right-hand side of Equations (A3) and (A4), as indicated in Equation (A5):

$$\frac{dS_T}{dt} = \left(\frac{r}{r_0}\right)^{\alpha_T} \frac{dS_{0T}}{dt} \tag{A5}$$

When Equation (A5) is used in Equation (A4), it leads to:

$$\left(\frac{r}{r_0}\right)^{\alpha_T} \frac{dS_{0T}}{dt} = \sum_i \left(\frac{r}{r_0}\right)^{\alpha_i} \frac{dS_{0i}}{dt},$$

And:

$$\left(\frac{r}{r_0}\right)^{\alpha_T} = \sum_i \left(\frac{r}{r_0}\right)^{\alpha_i} \frac{dS_{0i}}{dS_{0T}} \tag{A6}$$

The application of the log function implies that the exponent α_T is:

$$\alpha_T = k_V \log\left\{ \sum_i \left(\frac{r}{r_0}\right)^{\alpha_i} \frac{dS_{0i}}{dS_{0T}} \right\}, \tag{A7}$$

where k_V is the same that is used in Equation (2). The definition of the exponent in terms of the thermodynamic fractal dimension is: $\alpha = D_E - D - 1$. This definition is applied to Equation (A7):

$$D_T = (D_E - 1) - k_V \log\left\{ \left(\frac{r}{r_0}\right)^{(D_E-1)} \sum_i \left(\frac{r}{r_0}\right)^{-D_i} \frac{dS_{0i}}{dS_{0T}} \right\}, \tag{A8}$$

Note that $\alpha_i = D_E - D_i - 1$. And equivalently:

$$D_T = -k_V \log\left\{ e^{(1-D_E)/k_V} \left(\frac{r}{r_0}\right)^{(D_E-1)} \sum_i \left(\frac{r}{r_0}\right)^{-D_i} \frac{dS_{0i}}{dS_{0T}} \right\}$$

By definition, $k_V = 1/\ln(r/r_0)$, which is equivalent to $r/r_0 = e^{1/k_V}$ and $(r/r_0)^{1-D_E} = e^{(1-D_E)/k_V}$. This leads to $e^{(1-D_E)/k_V}(r/r_0)^{(D_E-1)} = (r/r_0)^{1-D_E}(r/r_0)^{(D_E-1)}$ $= (r/r_0)^{(1-D_E+D_E-1)} = 1$. Then, Equation (A8) leads to:

$$D_T = -k_V \log\left\{\sum_i \left(\frac{r}{r_0}\right)^{-D_i} \frac{dS_{0i}}{dS_{0T}}\right\}. \tag{A9}$$

Equation (A9) implies that D_T is of the shape:

$$D_T \sim \log\left(a_1 r^{D_1} + a_2 r^{D_2} + \ldots + a_i r^{D_i} + \ldots + a_n r^{D_n}\right), \tag{A10}$$

which is different to $D_T = D_1 + D_2 + \ldots$. Therefore, the total thermodynamic fractal dimension of a system composed of n multiscale subsystems cannot be considered equivalent to the sum of the thermodynamic fractal dimensions of each subsystem. Additionally, note that Equations (A8)–(A10) arise from assuming that the total system maintains self-similarity in entropy production. Otherwise, a D_T for the entire system could not be defined uniformly but would have varying values depending on the considered subsystem. This implies that D would be defined by volumes, as illustrated by Equation (A11):

$$D(x) = \begin{cases} D_1, \ if\ x \in \text{domain } 1 \\ D_2, \ if\ x \in \text{domain } 2. \\ \quad \ldots \end{cases} \tag{A11}$$

Appendix B Homeostasis

Consider a system that consists of a multiscale system that produces macroscopic entropy dS, along with another subsystem that has a macroscopic entropy production dM, as shown in Equation (B1):

$$\frac{dS_T}{dt} = \frac{dS}{dt} + \frac{dM}{dt}, \tag{A12}$$

where the term dM/dt corresponds to the rate of entropy production of the environment when interacting with the multiscale system, and dS_T/dt is the total entropy production. Note that, in this case, we consider a multiscale system one that can refer to a biological system along with the interaction it has with the environment around it, in order to highlight the physics from the point of view of living systems. That is, the total entropy production of the environment might be too large in comparison to the one of a single biological system, so the analysis carried out here might be negligible if the total environment is considered. Then, considering the environment interaction as a macroscopic effect, the total small-scale entropy production of the system dS_{T_0} is equivalent to that of the multiscale system dS_0, so $dS_{T_0} = dS_0$. Applying this along with Equation (A5)–(A12) gives us:

$$\left(\frac{r}{r_0}\right)^{\alpha} = \frac{dS}{dS_0} + \frac{dM}{dS_0} = \Omega + M', \tag{A13}$$

where $M' = dM/dS_0$ and $\Omega = dS/dS_0$, of which the latter corresponds to the balance of entropy production. Equivalently, Equation (A13) in terms of a logarithmic expression leads to:

$$\alpha = k_V \log\{\Omega + M\prime\}. \tag{A14}$$

The time derivative Equation (A14) is:

$$\dot{\Omega} = \frac{\dot{\alpha}}{k_V}(\Omega + M'). \tag{A15}$$

As $\alpha = D_E - D - 1$, the derivative is $\dot{\alpha} = -\dot{D}$ and leads to:

$$\dot{\Omega} = -\frac{\dot{D}}{k_V}\Omega + \mathcal{M}, \tag{A16}$$

where $\mathcal{M} = -\dot{D}M'/k_V$. Note that the expression shown in Equation (A16) has the same form as the equation that is commonly used to describe the homeostatic process ($dx/dt = -x$) [164]. Thus, the solution for this equation is given by:

$$\Omega(t) = \tau_C\mathcal{M} + c_1 e^{-\frac{t}{\tau_C}}, \tag{A17}$$

where $k_V/\dot{D} = \tau_C$. When $\Omega(0) = \Omega_0$, Equation (A17) becomes:

$$\Omega(t) = \tau_C\mathcal{M} + (\Omega_0 - \tau_C\mathcal{M})e^{-\frac{t}{\tau_C}}. \tag{A18}$$

References

1. Bar-Yam, Y. *Dynamics of Complex Systems*; Westview Press: Boulder, CO, USA, 2003.
2. Boccara, N. *Modeling Complex Systems*; Springer: New York, NY, USA, 2010.
3. West, G.B. *Scale: The Universal Laws of Growth, Innovation, Sustainability, and the Pace of Life in Organisms, Cities, Economies, and Companies*; Penguin Press: London, UK, 2017.
4. Ladyman, J.; Wiesner, K. What is a Complex System? Yale University Press: New Haven, CT, USA, 2020. [CrossRef]
5. Vitiello, G. Fractals, coherent states and self-similarity induced noncommutative geometry. *Phys. Lett. A* **2012**, *376*, 2527–2532. [CrossRef]
6. Nigmatullin, R.R.; Chen, Y. Self-Similarity Principle and the General Theory of Fractal Elements: How to Fit a Random Curve with a Clearly Expressed Trend? *Mathematics* **2023**, *11*, 2781. [CrossRef]
7. Pinto, C.M.; Lopes, A.M.; Machado, J.T. Double power laws, fractals and self-similarity. *Appl. Math. Model.* **2014**, *38*, 4019–4026. [CrossRef]
8. Ziepke, A.; Maryshev, I.; Aranson, I.S.; Frey, E. Multi-scale organization in communicating active matter. *Nat. Commun.* **2022**, *13*, 6727. [CrossRef] [PubMed]
9. Yao, Z.; Lundqvist, E.; Kuang, Y.; Ardoña, H.A.M. Engineering Multi-Scale Organization for Biotic and Organic Abiotic Electroactive Systems. *Adv. Sci.* **2023**, *10*, 2205381. [CrossRef] [PubMed]
10. An, G. Introduction of an agent-based multi-scale modular architecture for dynamic knowledge representation of acute inflammation. *Theor. Biol. Med. Model.* **2008**, *5*, 11. [CrossRef] [PubMed]
11. Buizer, M.; Arts, B.; Kok, K. Governance, Scale and the Environment: The Importance of Recognizing Knowledge Claims in Transdisciplinary Arenas. *Ecol. Soc.* **2011**, *16*, 21. [CrossRef]
12. del Castillo, L.F.; Vera-Cruz, P. Thermodynamic Formulation of Living Systems and Their Evolution. *J. Mod. Phys.* **2011**, *02*, 379–391. [CrossRef]
13. Gatti, R.C. The fractal nature of the latitudinal biodiversity gradient. *Biologia* **2016**, *71*, 669–672. [CrossRef]
14. Yu, J.S.; Bagheri, N. Multi-class and multi-scale models of complex biological phenomena. *Curr. Opin. Biotechnol.* **2016**, *39*, 167–173. [CrossRef]
15. Schaffer, L.V.; Ideker, T. Mapping the multiscale structure of biological systems. *Cell Syst.* **2021**, *12*, 622–635. [CrossRef] [PubMed]
16. Einstein, A. Bemerkung zu der Franz Seletyschen Arbeit "Beiträge zum kosmologischen System". *Ann. Phys.* **1922**, *374*, 436–438. [CrossRef]
17. Bremer, K.; Wanntorp, H.-E. Hierarchy and Reticulation in Systematics. *Syst. Zool.* **1979**, *28*, 624. [CrossRef]
18. Cilliers, P. Boundaries, Hierarchies and Networks in Complex Systems. *Int. J. Innov. Manag.* **2001**, *5*, 135–147. [CrossRef]
19. Chen, Y.; Zhou, Y. The Rank-Size Rule and Fractal Hierarchies of Cities: Mathematical Models and Empirical Analyses. *Environ. Plan. B Plan. Des.* **2003**, *30*, 799–818. [CrossRef]
20. Pavé, A. Biological and Ecological Systems Hierarchical Organisation. In *Hierarchy in Natural and Social Sciences Methodos Series*; Pumain, D., Ed.; Springer: Dordrecht, The Netherlands, 2006. [CrossRef]
21. Beck, F.; Burch, M.; Munz, T.; Di Silvestro, L.; Weiskopf, D. Generalized Pythagoras Trees: A Fractal Approach to Hierarchy Visualization. In *Computer Vision, Imaging and Computer Graphics—Theory and Applications*; VISIGRAPP Communications in Computer and Information Science; Battiato, S., Coquillart, S., Pettré, J., Laramee, R., Kerren, A., Braz, J., Eds.; Springer: Cham, Switzerland, 2015. [CrossRef]
22. Komvopoulos, K. A Multiscale Theoretical Analysis of the Mechanical, Thermal, and Electrical Characteristics of Rough Contact Interfaces Demonstrating Fractal Behavior. *Front. Mech. Eng.* **2020**, *6*, 36. [CrossRef]
23. Dos Anjos, P.H.R.; Gomes-Filho, M.S.; Alves, W.S.; Azevedo, D.L.; Oliveira, F.A. The Fractal Geometry of Growth: Fluctuation–Dissipation Theorem and Hidden Symmetry. *Front. Phys.* **2021**, *9*, 741590. [CrossRef]

24. Dublanchet, P. Shear Stress and b-value Fluctuations in a Hierarchical Rate-and-State Asperity Model. *Pure Appl. Geophys.* **2022**, *179*, 2423–2435. [CrossRef]
25. Kovchegov, Y.; Zaliapin, I.; Foufoula-Georgiou, E. Random Self-Similar Trees: Emergence of Scaling Laws. *Surv. Geophys.* **2022**, *43*, 353–421. [CrossRef]
26. Mohanty, V.; Greenbury, S.F.; Sarkany, T.; Narayanan, S.; Dingle, K.; Ahnert, S.E.; Louis, A.A. Maximum mutational robustness in genotype–phenotype maps follows a self-similar blancmange-like curve. *J. R. Soc. Interface* **2023**, *20*, 20230169. [CrossRef]
27. Brown, J.H.; Gupta, V.K.; Li, B.-L.; Milne, B.T.; Restrepo, C.; West, G.B. The fractal nature of nature: Power laws, ecological complexity and biodiversity. *Philos. Trans. R. Soc. B Biol. Sci.* **2002**, *357*, 619–626. [CrossRef] [PubMed]
28. West, G.B. Size, Scale and the Boat Race; Conceptions, Connections and Misconceptions. In *Hierarchy in Natural and Social Sciences*; Methodos Series; Pumain, D., Ed.; Springer: Dordrecht, The Netherlands, 2006. [CrossRef]
29. Sales-Pardo, M.; Guimerà, R.; Moreira, A.A.; Amaral, L.A.N. Extracting the hierarchical organization of complex systems. *Proc. Natl. Acad. Sci. USA* **2007**, *104*, 15224–15229. [CrossRef] [PubMed]
30. Corominas-Murtra, B.; Goñi, J.; Solé, R.V.; Rodríguez-Caso, C. On the origins of hierarchy in complex networks. *Proc. Natl. Acad. Sci. USA* **2013**, *110*, 13316–13321. [CrossRef] [PubMed]
31. Johnson, C.W. What are emergent properties and how do they affect the engineering of complex systems? *Reliab. Eng. Syst. Saf.* **2006**, *91*, 1475–1481. [CrossRef]
32. Luo, J.; Magee, C.L. Detecting evolving patterns of self-organizing networks by flow hierarchy measurement. *Complexity* **2011**, *16*, 53–61. [CrossRef]
33. San Martin, D. *Clarity: Un Modelo Unificador de las Ciencias...y un Relato del Todo*; Planeta Editor: Barcelona, Spain, 2021. (In Spanish)
34. Marković, D.; Gros, C. Power laws and self-organized criticality in theory and nature. *Phys. Rep.* **2014**, *536*, 41–74. [CrossRef]
35. Bejan, A.; Lorente, S. Constructal law of design and evolution: Physics, biology, technology, and society. *J. Appl. Phys.* **2013**, *113*, 151301. [CrossRef]
36. Lopes, A.M.; Machado, J.A.T. Power Law Behaviour in Complex Systems. *Entropy* **2018**, *20*, 671. [CrossRef]
37. Ortman, S.G.; Lobo, J.; Smith, M.E. Cities: Complexity, theory and history. *PLoS ONE* **2020**, *15*, e0243621. [CrossRef]
38. Bashkirov, A.; Vityazev, A. Information entropy and power-law distributions for chaotic systems. *Phys. A Stat. Mech. Its Appl.* **1998**, *277*, 136–145. [CrossRef]
39. Chen, Y. The rank-size scaling law and entropy-maximizing principle. *Phys. A Stat. Mech. Its Appl.* **2012**, *391*, 767–778. [CrossRef]
40. Curado, E.M.F.; Nobre, F.D.; Plastino, A. Associating an Entropy with Power-Law Frequency of Events. *Entropy* **2018**, *20*, 940. [CrossRef] [PubMed]
41. Jin, C.; Song, C.; Bjelland, J.; Canright, G.; Wang, D. Emergence of scaling in complex substitutive systems. *Nat. Hum. Behav.* **2019**, *3*, 837–846. [CrossRef]
42. Nosonovsky, M.; Roy, P. Scaling in Colloidal and Biological Networks. *Entropy* **2020**, *22*, 622. [CrossRef] [PubMed]
43. Jahanmiri, F.; Parker, D.C. An Overview of Fractal Geometry Applied to Urban Planning. *Land* **2022**, *11*, 475. [CrossRef]
44. Wawrzaszek, A.; Modzelewska, R.; Krasińska, A.; Gil, A.; Glavan, V. Fractal Dimension Analysis of Earth Magnetic Field during 26 August 2018 Geomagnetic Storm. *Entropy* **2022**, *24*, 699. [CrossRef]
45. Newman, M.E.J. Power laws, Pareto distributions and Zipf's law. *Contemp. Phys.* **2005**, *46*, 323–351. [CrossRef]
46. Abe, S.; Suzuki, N. Scale-free network of earthquakes. *EPL* **2004**, *65*, 581–586. [CrossRef]
47. Song, C.; Havlin, S.; Makse, H.A. Self-similarity of complex networks. *Nature* **2005**, *433*, 392–395. [CrossRef]
48. Wang, B.; Zhu, J.; Wei, D. The self-similarity of complex networks: From the view of degree–degree distance. *Mod. Phys. Lett. B* **2021**, *35*, 2150331. [CrossRef]
49. Pastor-Satorras, R.; Wagensberg, J. The maximum entropy principle and the nature of fractals. *Phys. A Stat. Mech. Its Appl.* **1998**, *251*, 291–302. [CrossRef]
50. Tate, N.J. Maximum entropy spectral analysis for the estimation of fractals in topography. *Earth Surf. Process. Landf.* **1999**, *23*, 1197–1217. [CrossRef]
51. Dover, Y. A short account of a connection of power laws to the information entropy. *Phys. A Stat. Mech. Its Appl.* **2004**, *334*, 591–599. [CrossRef]
52. Grmela, M. Multiscale Thermodynamics. *Entropy* **2021**, *23*, 165. [CrossRef] [PubMed]
53. Venegas-Aravena, P.; Cordaro, E.G.; Laroze, D. Natural Fractals as Irreversible Disorder: Entropy Approach from Cracks in the Semi Brittle-Ductile Lithosphere and Generalization. *Entropy* **2022**, *24*, 1337. [CrossRef]
54. Gokcen, N.A.; Reddy, R.G. Entropy and Related Functions. In *Thermodynamics*; Springer: Boston, MA, USA, 1996. [CrossRef]
55. Lebowitz, J.L. Emergent phenomena. *Phys. J.* **2007**, *6*, 41.
56. Atmanspacher, H. On Macrostates in Complex Multi-Scale Systems. *Entropy* **2016**, *18*, 426. [CrossRef]
57. Adams, A.M. A graph-theoretic approach to understanding emergent behavior in physical systems. In Proceedings of the ALIFE 2021: The 2021 Conference on Artificial Life, Online, 18–22 July 2021; ASME: New York, NY, USA, 2021; p. 63. [CrossRef]
58. Redondo, J.M.; Garcia, J.S.; Bustamante-Zamudio, C.; Pereira, M.F.; Trujillo, H.F. Heterogeneity: Method and applications for complex systems analysis. *J. Physics Conf. Ser.* **2022**, *2159*, 012013. [CrossRef]
59. Venegas-Aravena, P.; Cordaro, E.; Laroze, D. Fractal Clustering as Spatial Variability of Magnetic Anomalies Measurements for Impending Earthquakes and the Thermodynamic Fractal Dimension. *Fractal Fract.* **2022**, *6*, 624. [CrossRef]

60. Mandelbrot, B.B. *The Fractal Geometry of Nature*; W. H. Freeman and Company: New York, NY, USA, 1982.
61. Newton, I. *Philosophiae Naturalis Principia Mathematica*; Smithsonian Institution: Washington, DC, USA, 1687.
62. Onsager, L. Reciprocal Relations in Irreversible Processes. I. *Phys. Rev.* **1931**, *37*, 405–426. [CrossRef]
63. Onsager, L. Reciprocal Relations in Irreversible Processes. II. *Phys. Rev. B* **1931**, *38*, 2265–2279. [CrossRef]
64. Boltzmann, L. "Über die Mechanische Bedeutung des Zweiten Hauptsatzes der Wärmetheorie" (german). *Wien. Berichte* **1866**, *53*, 195–220.
65. Callen, H.B. *Thermodynamics and an Introduction to Thermostatistics*; Wiley: New York, NY, USA, 1960.
66. De Groot, S.R.; Mazur, P. *Nonequilibrium Thermodynamics*; North-Holland Pub. Co.: Amsterdam, The Netherlands, 1962.
67. Frisch, D.H. The Microscopic Interpretation of Entropy. *Am. J. Phys.* **1966**, *34*, 1171–1173. [CrossRef]
68. Riek, R. A Derivation of a Microscopic Entropy and Time Irreversibility from the Discreteness of Time. *Entropy* **2014**, *16*, 3149–3172. [CrossRef]
69. Sahimi, M.; Arbabi, S. Scaling Laws for Fracture of Heterogeneous Materials and Rock. *Phys. Rev. Lett.* **1996**, *77*, 3689–3692. [CrossRef]
70. Vallianatos, F.; Tzanis, A. On the nature, scaling and spectral properties of pre-seismic ULF signals. *Nat. Hazards Earth Syst. Sci.* **2003**, *3*, 237–242. [CrossRef]
71. Anastasiadis, C.; Triantis, D.; Stavrakas, I.; Vallianatos, F. Pressure Stimulated Currents (PSC) in marble samples. *Ann. Geophys.* **2009**, *47*, 21–28. [CrossRef]
72. Kuksenko, V.; Tomilin, N.; Chmel, A. The role of driving rate in scaling characteristics of rock fracture. *J. Stat. Mech. Theory Exp.* **2005**, *2005*, P06012. [CrossRef]
73. Malakhovsky, I.; Michels, M.A.J. Scaling and localization in fracture of disordered central-force spring lattices: Comparison with random damage percolation. *Phys. Rev. B* **2006**, *74*, 014206. [CrossRef]
74. Triantis, D.; Vallianatos, F.; Stavrakas, I.; Hloupis, G. Relaxation phenomena of electrical signal emissions from rock following application of abrupt mechanical stress. *Ann. Geophys.* **2012**, *55*, 207–212. [CrossRef]
75. Venegas-Aravena, P.; Cordaro, E.G.; Laroze, D. A review and upgrade of the lithospheric dynamics in context of the seismo-electromagnetic theory. *Nat. Hazards Earth Syst. Sci.* **2019**, *19*, 1639–1651. [CrossRef]
76. Potirakis, S.M.; Contoyiannis, Y.; Eftaxias, K.; Melis, N.S.; Nomicos, C. Post-spontaneous-symmetry-breaking power-laws after a very strong earthquake: Indication for the preparation of a new strong earthquake or not? *Phys. A Stat. Mech. Its Appl.* **2021**, *589*, 126607. [CrossRef]
77. Loukidis, A.; Tzagkarakis, D.; Kyriazopoulos, A.; Stavrakas, I.; Triantis, D. Correlation of Acoustic Emissions with Electrical Signals in the Vicinity of Fracture in Cement Mortars Subjected to Uniaxial Compressive Loading. *Appl. Sci.* **2022**, *13*, 365. [CrossRef]
78. Yang, C.; Wu, Z.; Wang, W.; Qu, H.; Ren, N.; Li, H. Study on the influence of natural cracks on the mechanical properties and fracture mode for shale at the microscale: An example from the Lower Cambrian Niutitang Formation in northern Guizhou. *Front. Earth Sci.* **2023**, *10*, 1032817. [CrossRef]
79. Mandelbrot, B.B. Negative fractal dimensions and multifractals. *Phys. A Stat. Mech. Its Appl.* **1990**, *163*, 306–315. [CrossRef]
80. Dvoretskaya, O.A.; Kondratenko, P.S. Anomalous transport in fractal media with randomly inhomogeneous diffusion barrier. *Cond-Mat. Soft* **2013**, *103*, 325–339. [CrossRef]
81. Chen, Y.; Yang, H. Numerical simulation and pattern characterization of nonlinear spatiotemporal dynamics on fractal surfaces for the whole-heart modeling applications. *Eur. Phys. J. B* **2016**, *89*, 181. [CrossRef]
82. Yang, H. The Generator of Fractal Surfaces or Images, MATLAB Central File Exchange. Available online: https://www.mathworks.com/matlabcentral/fileexchange/78179-the-generator-of-fractal-surfaces-or-images (accessed on 30 August 2023).
83. Greiner, W.; Neise, L.; Stöcker, H. Number of Microstates Ω and Entropy S. In *Thermodynamics and Statistical Mechanics. Classical Theoretical Physics*; Springer: New York, NY, USA, 1995. [CrossRef]
84. Nicolis, G.; Prigogine, I. *Self-Organization in Nonequilibrium Systems: From Dissipative Structures to Order through Fluctuations*, 1st ed.; Wiley: Hoboken, NJ, USA, 1977.
85. Heylighen, F. The science of self-organization and adaptivity. *Encycl. Life Support Syst.* **2001**, *5*, 253–280.
86. De Wolf, T.; Holvoet, T. Emergence Versus Self-Organisation: Different Concepts but Promising When Combined. In *Engineering Self-Organising Systems. ESOA Lecture Notes in Computer Science*; Brueckner, S.A., Di Marzo Serugendo, G., Karageorgos, A., Nagpal, R., Eds.; Springer: Berlin/Heidelberg, Germany, 2005. [CrossRef]
87. Addiscott, T. Entropy, non-linearity and hierarchy in ecosystems. *Geoderma* **2010**, *160*, 57–63. [CrossRef]
88. Cavagna, A.; Cimarelli, A.; Giardina, I.; Parisi, G.; Santagati, R.; Stefanini, F.; Viale, M. Scale-free correlations in starling flocks. *Proc. Natl. Acad. Sci. USA* **2010**, *107*, 11865–11870. [CrossRef]
89. Gershenson, C.; Polani, D.; Martius, G. Editorial: Complexity and Self-Organization. *Front. Robot. AI* **2021**, *8*, 2021. [CrossRef]
90. Navarrete, Y.; Davis, S. Quantum Mutual Information, Fragile Systems and Emergence. *Entropy* **2022**, *24*, 1676. [CrossRef] [PubMed]
91. Cottam, R.; Vounckx, R. Entropy is better related to unification than to order. *Biosystems* **2023**, *223*, 104815. [CrossRef] [PubMed]
92. Newman, D.V. Emergence and Strange Attractors. *Philos. Sci.* **1996**, *63*, 245–261. [CrossRef]
93. Bedau, M.A. Weak emergence. In *Philosophical Perspectives: Mind, Causation, and World*; Tomberlin, J., Ed.; Blackwell: Malden, MA, USA, 1997; Volume 31, pp. 375–399. [CrossRef]

94. Nolte, D.D. The tangled tale of phase space. *Phys. Today* **2010**, *63*, 33–38. [CrossRef]
95. Oprisan, S.A.; Lynn, P.E.; Tompa, T.; Lavin, A. Low-dimensional attractor for neural activity from local field potentials in optogenetic mice. *Front. Comput. Neurosci.* **2015**, *9*, 125. [CrossRef] [PubMed]
96. Nabika, H.; Itatani, M.; Lagzi, I. Pattern Formation in Precipitation Reactions: The Liesegang Phenomenon. *Langmuir* **2019**, *36*, 481–497. [CrossRef]
97. Medina, M.; Huffaker, R.; Muñoz-Carpena, R.; Kiker, G. An empirical nonlinear dynamics approach to analyzing emergent behavior of agent-based models. *AIP Adv.* **2021**, *11*, 035133. [CrossRef]
98. Jirsa, V.; Sheheitli, H. Entropy, free energy, symmetry and dynamics in the brain. *J. Phys. Complex.* **2022**, *3*, 015007. [CrossRef]
99. Callen, H.B.; Welton, T.A. Irreversibility and Generalized Noise. *Phys. Rev. B* **1951**, *83*, 34–40. [CrossRef]
100. Kubo, R. The fluctuation-dissipation theorem. *Rep. Prog. Phys.* **1966**, *29*, 255–284. [CrossRef]
101. Prost, J.; Joanny, J.-F.; Parrondo, J.M.R. Generalized Fluctuation-Dissipation Theorem for Steady-State Systems. *Phys. Rev. Lett.* **2009**, *103*, 090601. [CrossRef] [PubMed]
102. Turing, A.M. The chemical basis of morphogenesis. *Philos. Trans. Roy Soc. Lond Ser. B* **1952**, *237*, 37–72. [CrossRef]
103. Miller, D.G. Thermodynamics of Irreversible Processes. The Experimental Verification of the Onsager Reciprocal Relations. *Chem. Rev.* **1960**, *60*, 15–37. [CrossRef]
104. De Corato, M.; Pagonabarraga, I. Onsager reciprocal relations and chemo-mechanical coupling for chemically active colloids. *J. Chem. Phys.* **2022**, *157*, 084901. [CrossRef] [PubMed]
105. O'Shaughnessy, B.; Procaccia, I. Analytical Solutions for Diffusion on Fractal Objects. *Phys. Rev. Lett.* **1985**, *54*, 455–458. [CrossRef] [PubMed]
106. Qian, L.H.; Chen, M.W. Ultrafine nanoporous gold by low-temperature dealloying and kinetics of nanopore formation. *Appl. Phys. Lett.* **2007**, *91*, 083105. [CrossRef]
107. Erlebacher, J. Mechanism of Coarsening and Bubble Formation in High-Genus Nanoporous Metals. *Phys. Rev. Lett.* **2011**, *106*, 225504. [CrossRef]
108. Wada, T.; Kato, H. Three-dimensional open-cell macroporous iron, chromium and ferritic stainless steel. *Scr. Mater.* **2013**, *68*, 723–726. [CrossRef]
109. Geslin, P.-A.; McCue, I.; Gaskey, B.; Erlebacher, J.; Karma, A. Topology-generating interfacial pattern formation during liquid metal dealloying. *Nat. Commun.* **2015**, *6*, 8887. [CrossRef]
110. Olsen, K.S.; Campbell, J.M. Diffusion Entropy and the Path Dimension of Frictional Finger Patterns. *Front. Phys.* **2020**, *8*, 83. [CrossRef]
111. Heller, P. Experimental investigations of critical phenomena. *Rep. Prog. Phys.* **1967**, *30*, 731. [CrossRef]
112. Hohenberg, P.C.; Halperin, B.I. Theory of dynamic critical phenomena. *Rev. Mod. Phys.* **1977**, *49*, 435–479. [CrossRef]
113. Dorogovtsev, S.N.; Goltsev, A.V.; Mendes, J.F.F. Critical phenomena in complex networks. *Rev. Mod. Phys.* **2008**, *80*, 1275–1335. [CrossRef]
114. Dorogovtsev, S.N.; Mendes, J.F.F. *The Nature of Complex Networks*; Oxford University Press (OUP): Oxford, UK, 2022; ISBN 0199695113.
115. Potirakis, S.M.; Papadopoulos, P.; Matiadou, N.-L.; Hanias, M.P.; Stavrinides, S.G.; Balasis, G.; Contoyiannis, Y. Spontaneous Symmetry Breaking in Systems Obeying the Dynamics of On–Off Intermittency and Presenting Bimodal Amplitude Distributions. *Symmetry* **2023**, *15*, 1448. [CrossRef]
116. Nishimori, H.; Ortiz, G. *Elements of Phase Transitions and Critical Phenomena*; Oxford University Press (OUP): Oxford, UK, 2010; ISBN 9780199577224.
117. Halperin, B.I. Theory of dynamic critical phenomena. *Phys. Today* **2019**, *72*, 42–43. [CrossRef]
118. Fisher, M.E. *Critical Phenomena: Proceedings, Stellenbosch, South Africa, 1982*; Hahne, F.J.W., Ed.; Springer: Berlin/Heidelberg, Germany, 1983.
119. Chen, H.; Yue, Z.; Ren, D.; Zeng, H.; Wei, T.; Zhao, K.; Yang, R.; Qiu, P.; Chen, L.; Shi, X. Thermal Conductivity during Phase Transitions. *Adv. Mater.* **2018**, *31*, e1806518. [CrossRef]
120. Pietruszka, M.; Olszewska, M. Extracellular ionic fluxes suggest the basis for cellular life at the 1/f ridge of extended criticality. *Eur. Biophys. J.* **2020**, *49*, 239–252. [CrossRef]
121. Pietruszka, M.A. Non-equilibrium phase transition at a critical point of human blood. *Sci. Rep.* **2021**, *11*, 1–8. [CrossRef]
122. Schroeder, M. *Fractals, Chaos, Power Laws: Minutes from an Infinite Paradise*; W.H. Freeman and Company: New York, NY, USA, 1991.
123. Moore, B.J. Chaos Theory: Unpredictable Order in Chaos. In *Shaking the Invisible Hand*; Palgrave Macmillan: London, UK, 2006. [CrossRef]
124. Eppel-Meichlinger, J.; Kobleder, A.; Mayer, H. Developing a theoretical definition of self-organization: A principle-based concept analysis in the context of uncertainty in chronic illness. *Nurs. Forum* **2022**, *57*, 954–962. [CrossRef]
125. Ottino, J.M.; Muzzio, F.J.; Tjahjadi, M.; Franjione, J.G.; Jana, S.C.; Kusch, H.A. Chaos, Symmetry, and Self-Similarity: Exploiting Order and Disorder in Mixing Processes. *Science* **1992**, *257*, 754–760. [CrossRef]
126. Lorenz, E. *The Essence of Chaos*; University of Washington Press: Seattle, DA, USA, 1993; pp. 181–206.
127. Ruelle, D. *Chaotic Evolution and Strange Attractors*; Cambridge University: New York, NY, USA, 1983.
128. Lichtenberg, A.J.; Lieberman, M.A. *Regular and Stochastic Motion*; Springer: New York, NY, USA, 1983; ISBN 9780387097237.

129. Tabor, M. *Chaos and Integrability in Nonlinear Dynamics*; Wiley: New York, NY, USA, 1989.
130. Hoover, W.G.; Posch, H.A. Second-law irreversibility and phase-space dimensionality loss from time-reversible nonequilibrium steady-state Lyapunov spectra. *Phys. Rev. E* **1994**, *49*, 1913–1920. [CrossRef]
131. Gaspard, P. Time Asymmetry in Nonequilibrium Statistical Mechanics. *Spec. Vol. Mem. Ilya Prigogine Adv. Chem. Phys.* **2007**, *135*, 83–133. [CrossRef]
132. Betancourt-Mar, J.A.; Rodríguez-Ricard, M.; Mansilla, R.; Cocho, G.; Nieto-Villar, J.M. Entropy production: Evolution criteria, robustness and fractal dimension. *Rev. Mex. Fis.* **2016**, *62*, 164–167.
133. Benzi, R.; Paladin, P.; Parisi, G.; Vulpiani, A. On the multifractal nature of fully developed turbulence and chaotic systems. *J. Phys. A Math. Gen.* **1984**, *17*, 3521. [CrossRef]
134. Menon, E.S. Chapter Five—Fluid Flow in Pipes. In *Transmission Pipeline Calculations and Simulations Manual 2015*; Gulf Professional Publishing: Woburn, MA, USA, 2015; pp. 149–234. [CrossRef]
135. Nicolleau, F. Numerical determination of turbulent fractal dimensions. *Phys. Fluids* **1996**, *8*, 2661–2670. [CrossRef]
136. Makris, C.V.; Memos, C.D.; Krestenitis, Y.N. Numerical modeling of surf zone dynamics under weakly plunging breakers with SPH method. *Ocean Model.* **2016**, *98*, 12–35. [CrossRef]
137. Landahl, M.T.; Mollo-Christensen, E. *Turbulence and Random Processes in Fluid Mechanics*, 2nd ed.; Cambridge University Press, (CUP): Cambridge, UK, 1992; ISBN 978-0521422130.
138. Kraichnan, R.H. Inertial Ranges in Two-Dimensional Turbulence. *Phys. Fluids* **1967**, *10*, 1417–1423. [CrossRef]
139. Lorenz, E.N. The predictability of a flow which possesses many scales of motion. *Tellus* **1969**, *21*, 289–307. [CrossRef]
140. Siggia, E.D.; Aref, H. Point-vortex simulation of the inverse energy cascade in two-dimensional turbulence. *Phys. Fluids* **1981**, *24*, 171–173. [CrossRef]
141. Frisch, U.; Sulem, P.-L. Numerical simulation of the inverse cascade in two-dimensional turbulence. *Phys. Fluids* **1984**, *27*, 1921–1923. [CrossRef]
142. Chaisson, E.J. *Cosmic Evolution: The Rise of Complexity in Nature*; Harvard University Press: Cambridge, MA, USA, 2001; ISBN 9780674003422.
143. Coleman, P.H.; Pietronero, L. The fractal structure of the universe. *Phys. Rep.* **1992**, *213*, 311–389. [CrossRef]
144. Evans, N.W. The power-law galaxies. *Mon. Not. R. Astron. Soc.* **1994**, *267*, 333–360. [CrossRef]
145. Joyce, M.; Anderson, P.W.; Montuori, M.; Pietronero, L.; Labini, F.S. Fractal cosmology in an open universe. *Lett. J. Explor. Front. Phys.* **2000**, *50*, 416–422. [CrossRef]
146. Boutloukos, S.G.; Lamers, H.J.G.L.M. Star cluster formation and disruption time-scales—I. An empirical determination of the disruption time of star clusters in four galaxies. *Mon. Not. R. Astron. Soc.* **2003**, *338*, 717–732. [CrossRef]
147. Iovane, G.; Laserra, E.; Tortoriello, F. Stochastic self-similar and fractal universe. *Chaos Solitons Fractals* **2004**, *20*, 415–426. [CrossRef]
148. Labini, F.S.; Vasilyev, N.L.; Baryshev, Y.V. Power law correlations in galaxy distribution and finite volume effects from the Sloan Digital Sky Survey Data Release Four. *Astron. Astrophys.* **2007**, *465*, 23–33. [CrossRef]
149. Watson, D.F.; Berlind, A.A.; Zentner, A.R. A cosmic coincidence: The power-law galaxy correlation function. *Astrophys. J.* **2011**, *738*, 22. [CrossRef]
150. Hogan, M.T.; McNamara, B.R.; Pulido, F.; Nulsen, P.E.J.; Russell, H.R.; Vantyghem, A.N.; Edge, A.C.; Main, R.A. Mass Distribution in Galaxy Cluster Cores. *Astrophys. J.* **2017**, *837*, 51. [CrossRef]
151. Gaite, J. The Fractal Geometry of the Cosmic Web and Its Formation. *Adv. Astron.* **2019**, *2019*, 6587138. [CrossRef]
152. Tarakanov, P.A.; Yezhkov, M.Y.; Kostina, M.V. Fractal Dimension of the Cosmic Microwave Background as a Test of "Planck" Spacecraft Data. *Astrophysics* **2020**, *63*, 288–295. [CrossRef]
153. Gaite, J. Scaling Laws in the Stellar Mass Distribution and the Transition to Homogeneity. *Adv. Astron.* **2021**, *2021*, 6680938. [CrossRef]
154. Kirillov, A.A.; Savelova, E.P.; Vladykina, P.O. Exact fractal model of the universe and possible machine learning methods for the verification of the fractality. In Proceedings of the Sixteenth Marcel Grossmann Meeting 2023, Virtual, 5–10 July 2023; pp. 352–367. [CrossRef]
155. McShea, D.W. Unnecessary Complexity. *Science* **2013**, *342*, 1319–1320. [CrossRef]
156. Chaisson, E.J. Energy Flows in Low-Entropy Complex Systems. *Entropy* **2015**, *17*, 8007–8018. [CrossRef]
157. Bejan, A. Discipline in Thermodynamics. *Energies* **2020**, *13*, 2487. [CrossRef]
158. Barsky, E. *Entropy of Complex Processes and Systems*; Elsevier: Amsterdam, The Netherlands, 2020; ISBN 9780128216620.
159. Kobayashi, N.; Yamazaki, Y.; Kuninaka, H.; Katori, M.; Matsushita, M.; Matsushita, S.; Chiang, L.-Y. Fractal Structure of Isothermal Lines and Loops on the Cosmic Microwave Background. *J. Phys. Soc. Jpn.* **2011**, *80*, 074003. [CrossRef]
160. Mylläri, A.A.; Raikov, A.A.; Orlov, V.V.; Tarakanov, P.A.; Yershov, V.N.; Yezhkov, M.Y. Fractality of Isotherms of the Cosmic Microwave Background Based on Data from the Planck Spacecraft. *Astrophysics* **2016**, *59*, 31–37. [CrossRef]
161. Teles, S.; Lopes, A.R.; Ribeiro, M.B. Galaxy distributions as fractal systems. *Eur. Phys. J. C* **2022**, *82*, 896. [CrossRef]
162. Rovelli, C. Where Was Past Low-Entropy? *Entropy* **2019**, *21*, 466. [CrossRef]
163. Maturana, H.R. Autopoiesis: Reproduction, heredity and evolution. In *Autopoiesis, Dissipative Structures and Spontaneous Social Orders, AAAS Selected Symposium 55 (AAAS National Annual Meeting, Houston, TX, USA, 3–8 January 1979)*; Zeleny, M., Ed.; Westview Press: Boulder, CO, USA, 1980; pp. 45–79. Available online: https://cepa.info/552 (accessed on 27 December 2023).

164. Kryazhimskii, F.V. Homeostasis and self-similarity of biological system dynamics. *Dokl. Biol. Sci.* **2007**, *413*, 156–158. [CrossRef]
165. Rivera, A.L.; Toledo-Roy, J.C.; Frank, A. Symmetry and Signs of Self-Organized Criticality in Living Organisms. *J. Physics Conf. Ser.* **2020**, *1612*, 012024. [CrossRef]
166. Rubin, S.; Veloz, T.; Maldonado, P. Beyond planetary-scale feedback self-regulation: Gaia as an autopoietic system. *Biosystems* **2021**, *199*, 104314. [CrossRef] [PubMed]
167. Penrose, R. *Cycles of Time: An Extraordinary New View of the Universe*; The Bodley Head: London, UK, 2010.
168. Rovelli, C.; Vidotto, F. Pre-Big-Bang Black-Hole Remnants and Past Low Entropy. *Universe* **2018**, *4*, 129. [CrossRef]
169. An, D.; A Meissner, K.; Nurowski, P.; Penrose, R. Apparent evidence for Hawking points in the CMB Sky. *Mon. Not. R. Astron. Soc.* **2020**, *495*, 3403–3408. [CrossRef]
170. Eckstein, M. Conformal Cyclic Cosmology, gravitational entropy and quantum information. *Gen. Relativ. Gravit.* **2023**, *55*, 26. [CrossRef]
171. Richardson, L. The problem of contiguity: An appendix of statistics of deadly quarrels. *Gen. Syst.* **1961**, *6*, 139–187.
172. Mandelbrot, B. How Long Is the Coast of Britain? Statistical Self-Similarity and Fractional Dimension. *Science* **1967**, *156*, 636–638. [CrossRef]
173. Barnsley, M.F. *Fractals Everywhere*; Elsevier Inc.: Amsterdam, The Netherlands; Academic Press: Cambridge, MA, USA, 1993.
174. Turcotte, D.L. *Fractals and Chaos in Geology and Geophysics*, 2nd ed.; Cambridge University Press: Cambridge, UK, 1997; pp. 231–244.
175. Husain, A.; Reddy, J.; Bisht, D.; Sajid, M. Fractal dimension of coastline of Australia. *Sci. Rep.* **2021**, *11*, 6304. [CrossRef]
176. Houze, R.A., Jr. Chapter 12—Clouds and Precipitation Associated with Hills and Mountains. *Int. Geophys.* **2014**, *104*, 369. [CrossRef]
177. Chase, C.G. Fluvial landsculpting and the fractal dimension of topography. *Geomorphology* **1992**, *5*, 39–57. [CrossRef]
178. Ferraro, P.; Godin, C.; Prusinkiewicz, P. Toward a quantification of self-similarity in plants. *Fractals* **2005**, *13*, 91–109. [CrossRef]
179. Hellström, L.; Carlsson, L.; Falster, D.S.; Westoby, M.; Brännström, Å. Branch Thinning and the Large-Scale, Self-Similar Structure of Trees. *Am. Nat.* **2018**, *192*, E37–E47. [CrossRef] [PubMed]
180. Bejan, A.; Zane, J.P. *Design in Nature: How the Constructal Law Governs Evolution in Biology, Physics, Technology, and Social Organizations*; Anchor Publisher: New York, NY, USA, 2013.
181. Granier, A.; Biron, P.; Bréda, N.; Pontailler, J.; Saugier, B. Transpiration of trees and forest stands: Short and long-term monitoring using sapflow methods. *Glob. Chang. Biol.* **1996**, *2*, 265–274. [CrossRef]
182. Tyree, M.T. Hydraulic limits on tree performance: Transpiration, carbon gain and growth of trees. *Trees* **2003**, *17*, 95–100. [CrossRef]
183. Bejan, A.; Lorente, S.; Lee, J. Unifying constructal theory of tree roots, canopies and forests. *J. Theor. Biol.* **2008**, *254*, 529–540. [CrossRef]
184. Shingleton, A. Allometry: The Study of Biological Scaling. *Nat. Educ. Knowl.* **2010**, *3*, 2.
185. Rowland, M.; Dedrick, R.L. Chapter 32—Preclinical Prediction of Human Pharmacokinetics. In *Principles of Clinical Pharmacology*, 3rd ed.; Academic Press: Cambridge, MA, USA, 2012; pp. 531–540. [CrossRef]
186. Pélabon, C.; Firmat, C.; Bolstad, G.H.; Voje, K.L.; Houle, D.; Cassara, J.; Le Rouzic, A.; Hansen, T.F. Evolution of morphological allometry. *Ann. N. Y. Acad. Sci.* **2014**, *1320*, 58–75. [CrossRef] [PubMed]
187. Hallgrimsson, B.; Percival, C.J.; Green, R.; Young, N.M.; Mio, W.; Marcucio, R. Chapter Twenty—Morphometrics, 3D Imaging, and Craniofacial Development. *Curr. Top. Dev. Biol.* **2015**, *115*, 561–597. [CrossRef]
188. Escala, A. The principle of similitude in biology. *Theor. Ecol.* **2019**, *12*, 415–425. [CrossRef]
189. Cloyed, C.S.; Grady, J.M.; Savage, V.M.; Uyeda, J.C.; Dell, A.I. The allometry of locomotion. *Ecology* **2021**, *102*, e03369. [CrossRef]
190. Escala, A. Universal ontogenetic growth without fitted parameters: Implications for life history invariants and population growth. *Theor. Ecol.* **2023**, *16*, 315–325. [CrossRef]
191. Kleiber, M. Body size and metabolic rate. *Physiol. Rev.* **1947**, *27*, 511–541. [CrossRef] [PubMed]
192. Fenchel, T. Intrinsic rate of natural increase: The relationship with body size. *Oecologia* **1974**, *14*, 317–326. [CrossRef] [PubMed]
193. West, G.B.; Savage, V.M.; Gillooly, J.; Enquist, B.J.; Woodruff, W.H.; Brown, J.H. Why does metabolic rate scale with body size? *Nature* **2003**, *421*, 713. [CrossRef]
194. Woodward, G.; Ebenman, B.; Emmerson, M.; Montoya, J.M.; Olesen, J.M.; Valido, A.; Warren, P.H.; Woodward, G.; Ebenman, B.; Emmerson, M.; et al. Body size in ecological networks. *Trends Ecol. Evol.* **2005**, *20*, 402–409. [CrossRef]
195. Guidolin, D.; Crivellato, E.; Ribatti, D. The "self-similarity logic" applied to the development of the vascular system. *Dev. Biol.* **2011**, *351*, 156–162. [CrossRef]
196. Chen, Y. Fractals and Fractal Dimension of Systems of Blood Vessels: An Analogy between Artery Trees, River Networks, and Urban Hierarchies. *Fractal Geom. Nonlinear Anal. Med. Biol.* **2015**, *1*, 8. [CrossRef]
197. Schimpf, K. The Human Body as an Energy System. *AJN Am. J. Nurs.* **1971**, *71*, 117. [CrossRef]
198. Bullmore, E.; Brammer, M.; Harvey, I.; Persaud, R.; Murray, R.; Ron, M. Fractal analysis of the boundary between white matter and cerebral cortex in magnetic resonance images: A controlled study of schizophrenic and manic-depressive patients. *Psychol. Med.* **1994**, *24*, 771–781. [CrossRef]
199. Kenkel, N.C.; Walker, D.J. Fractals in the biological sciences. *Coenoses* **1996**, *11*, 77–100.

200. Masters, B.R. Fractal Analysis of the Vascular Tree in the Human Retina. *Annu. Rev. Biomed. Eng.* **2004**, *6*, 427–452. [CrossRef] [PubMed]
201. Gabryś, E.; Rybaczuk, M.; Kędzia, A. Blood flow simulation through fractal models of circulatory system. *Chaos Solitons Fractals* **2006**, *27*, 1–7. [CrossRef]
202. Tanabe, N.; Sato, S.; Suki, B.; Hirai, T. Fractal Analysis of Lung Structure in Chronic Obstructive Pulmonary Disease. *Front. Physiol.* **2020**, *11*, 1661. [CrossRef]
203. Honda, H.; Imayama, S.; Tanemura, M. A Fractal-Like Structure in the Skin. *Fractals* **1996**, *4*, 139–147. [CrossRef]
204. Cattani, C. Fractals and Hidden Symmetries in DNA. *Math. Probl. Eng.* **2010**, *2010*, 507056. [CrossRef]
205. Namazi, H.; Akrami, A.; Hussaini, J.; Silva, O.N.; Wong, A.; Kulish, V.V. The fractal based analysis of human face and DNA variations during aging. *Biosci. Trends* **2016**, *10*, 477–481. [CrossRef]
206. Peng, C.-K.; Mietus, J.E.; Liu, Y.; Lee, C.; Hausdorff, J.M.; Stanley, H.E.; Goldberger, A.L.; Lipsitz, L.A. Quantifying Fractal Dynamics of Human Respiration: Age and Gender Effects. *Ann. Biomed. Eng.* **2002**, *30*, 683–692. [CrossRef]
207. Hayano, K.; Yoshida, H.; Zhu, A.X.; Sahani, D.V. Fractal Analysis of Contrast-Enhanced CT Images to Predict Survival of Patients with Hepatocellular Carcinoma Treated with Sunitinib. *Dig. Dis. Sci.* **2014**, *59*, 1996–2003. [CrossRef]
208. Lennon, F.E.; Cianci, G.C.; Cipriani, N.A.; Hensing, T.A.; Zhang, H.J.; Chen, C.-T.; Murgu, S.D.; Vokes, E.E.; Vannier, M.W.; Salgia, R. Lung cancer—A fractal viewpoint. *Nat. Rev. Clin. Oncol.* **2015**, *12*, 664–675. [CrossRef]
209. Fernández, E.; Bolea, J.; Ortega, G.; Louis, E. Are neurons multifractals? *J. Neurosci. Methods* **1999**, *89*, 151–157. [CrossRef]
210. Milošević, N.T.; Ristanović, D.; Stanković, J. Fractal analysis of the laminar organization of spinal cord neurons. *J. Neurosci. Methods* **2005**, *146*, 198–204. [CrossRef] [PubMed]
211. Im, K.; Lee, J.; Yoon, U.; Shin, Y.; Hong, S.B.; Kim, I.Y.; Kwon, J.S.; Kim, S.I. Fractal dimension in human cortical surface: Multiple regression analysis with cortical thickness, sulcal depth, and folding area. *Hum. Brain Mapp.* **2006**, *27*, 994–1003. [CrossRef] [PubMed]
212. Smith, J.H.; Rowland, C.; Harland, B.; Moslehi, S.; Montgomery, R.D.; Schobert, K.; Watterson, W.J.; Dalrymple-Alford, J.; Taylor, R.P. How neurons exploit fractal geometry to optimize their network connectivity. *Sci. Rep.* **2021**, *11*, 2332. [CrossRef] [PubMed]
213. Grosu, G.F.; Hopp, A.V.; Moca, V.V.; Bârzan, H.; Ciuparu, A.; Ercsey-Ravasz, M.; Winkel, M.; Linde, H.; Mureșan, R.C. The fractal brain: Scale-invariance in structure and dynamics. *Cereb. Cortex* **2022**, *33*, 4574–4605. [CrossRef]
214. Fernández, A.; Zuluaga, P.; Abásolo, D.; Gómez, C.; Serra, A.; Méndez, M.A.; Hornero, R. Brain oscillatory complexity across the life span. *Clin. Neurophysiol.* **2012**, *123*, 2154–2162. [CrossRef] [PubMed]
215. Wu, K.; Taki, Y.; Sato, K.; Kinomura, S.; Goto, R.; Okada, K.; Kawashima, R.; He, Y.; Evans, A.C.; Fukuda, H. Age-related changes in topological organization of structural brain networks in healthy individuals. *Hum. Brain Mapp.* **2011**, *33*, 552–568. [CrossRef] [PubMed]
216. Farahibozorg, S.; Hashemi-Golpayegani, S.M.; Ashburner, J. Age- and Sex-Related Variations in the Brain White Matter Fractal Dimension Throughout Adulthood: An MRI Study. *Clin. Neuroradiol.* **2014**, *25*, 19–32. [CrossRef]
217. Alain, C.; Zendel, B.R.; Hutka, S.; Bidelman, G.M. Turning down the noise: The benefit of musical training on the aging auditory brain. *Hear. Res.* **2014**, *308*, 162–173. [CrossRef]
218. Tulving, E. Episodic and semantic memory. In *Organization of Memory*; Tulving, E., Donaldson, W., Eds.; Academic: New York, NY, USA, 1972; pp. 381–403.
219. Tulving, E. Episodic Memory: From Mind to Brain. *Annu. Rev. Psychol.* **2002**, *53*, 1–25. [CrossRef]
220. Takahashi, T.; Murata, T.; Omori, M.; Kosaka, H.; Takahashi, K.; Yonekura, Y.; Wada, Y. Quantitative evaluation of age-related white matter microstructural changes on MRI by multifractal analysis. *J. Neurol. Sci.* **2004**, *225*, 33–37. [CrossRef]
221. Zueva, M.V. Fractality of sensations and the brain health: The theory linking neurodegenerative disorder with distortion of spatial and temporal scale-invariance and fractal complexity of the visible world. *Front. Aging Neurosci.* **2015**, *7*, 135. [CrossRef]
222. Mustafa, N.; Ahearn, T.S.; Waiter, G.D.; Murray, A.D.; Whalley, L.J.; Staff, R.T. Brain structural complexity and life course cognitive change. *NeuroImage* **2012**, *61*, 694–701. [CrossRef] [PubMed]
223. Li, S.-C.; von Oertzen, T.; Lindenberger, U. A neurocomputational model of stochastic resonance and aging. *Neurocomputing* **2006**, *69*, 1553–1560. [CrossRef]
224. Söderlund, G.; Sikström, S.; Smart, A. Listen to the noise: Noise is beneficial for cognitive performance in ADHD. *J. Child Psychol. Psychiatry* **2007**, *48*, 840–847. [CrossRef] [PubMed]
225. Stadnitski, T. Tenets and Methods of Fractal Analysis (1/f Noise). In *The Fractal Geometry of the Brain*; Di Ieva, A., Ed.; Springer Series in Computational Neuroscience; Springer: New York, NY, USA, 2016. [CrossRef]
226. Jonas, J.B. Global prevalence of age-related macular degeneration. *Lancet Glob. Heal.* **2014**, *2*, e65–e66. [CrossRef] [PubMed]
227. MacLennan, B. Evolutionary Psychology, Complex Systems, and Social Theory. *Sound. Interdiscip. J.* **2007**, *90*, 169–189. [CrossRef]
228. Lazer, D.; Pentland, A.; Adamic, L.; Aral, S.; Barabási, A.-L.; Brewer, D.; Christakis, N.; Contractor, N.; Fowler, J.; Gutmann, M.; et al. Computational social science. *Science* **2009**, *323*, 721–723. [CrossRef] [PubMed]
229. Hudson, C.G. *Complex Systems and Human Behavior*, 1st ed.; Oxford University Press: Oxford, UK, 2010.
230. Miguel, M.S. Frontiers in Complex Systems. *Front. Complex Syst.* **2023**, *1*, 1080801. [CrossRef]
231. Tomasello, M. *A Natural History of Human Morality*; Harvard University Press: Cambridge, MA, USA, 2016.
232. Suki, B.; Bates, J.H.T.; Frey, U. Complexity and emergent phenomena. *Compr. Physiol.* **2011**, *1*, 995–1029. [CrossRef]

233. Darwin, C. *The Origin of Species, by Means of Natural Selection, or the Preservation of Favoured Races in the Struggle for Life*; Cambridge University Press (CUP): Cambridge, UK, 2009; ISBN 9780511694295.
234. Spencer, H. *The Principles of Biology*; William and Norgate: London, UK, 1864; Volume 1.
235. Gingerich, P.D. Rates of evolution on the time scale of the evolutionary process. *Genetica* **2001**, *112*, 127–144. [CrossRef]
236. Bryson, B. *A Short History of Nearly Everything*; Broadway Books: New York, NY, USA, 2003.
237. Dartnell, L. *Origins: How Earth's History Shaped Human History*; Penguin Random House: New York, NY, USA, 2019.
238. Andrews, G.; Fan, K.; Pratt, H.E.; Phalke, N.; Karlsson, E.K.; Lindblad-Toh, K.; Gazal, S.; Moore, J.E.; Weng, Z.; Armstrong, J.C.; et al. Mammalian evolution of human cis-regulatory elements and transcription factor binding sites. *Science* **2023**, *380*, eabn7930. [CrossRef] [PubMed]
239. Fisher, R.A. *The Genetical Theory of Natural Selection*; Clarendon Press: Oxford, UK; Dover: New York, NY, USA, 1930.
240. Price, G.R. Fisher's 'fundamental theorem' made clear. *Ann. Hum. Genet.* **1972**, *36*, 129–140. [CrossRef] [PubMed]
241. Basener, W.F.; Sanford, J.C. The fundamental theorem of natural selection with mutations. *J. Math. Biol.* **2017**, *76*, 1589–1622. [CrossRef] [PubMed]
242. Basener, W.; Cordova, S.; Hössjer, O.; Sanford, J. Dynamical Systems and Fitness Maximization in Evolutionary Biology. In *Handbook of the Mathematics of the Arts and Sciences*; Sriraman, B., Ed.; Springer: Cham, Switzerland, 2022. [CrossRef]
243. Elena, S.F.; de Visser, J.A.G. Environmental stress and the effects of mutation. *J. Biol.* **2003**, *2*, 12. [CrossRef]
244. Raine, A. *The Anatomy of Violence: The Biological Roots of Crime*; Vintage Books: New York, NY, USA, 2014.
245. Eagleman, D. *The Brain: The Story of You*; Penguin Random House: New York, NY, USA, 2015.
246. Lewis, M. *The Biology of Desire: Why Addiction Is Not a Disease*; PublicAffairs: New York, NY, USA, 2015.
247. Feldman Barret, L. *How Emotions Are Made: The Secret Life of the Brain*; Houghton Mifflin Harcourt: New York, NY, USA, 2017.
248. Sapolsky, R.M. *Behave: The Biology of Humans at Out Best and Worst*; Penguin Press: New York, NY, USA, 2017.
249. Bernard, C. *Leçons sur les Phénomènes de la vie, Communs aux Animaux et aux Végétaux*; Librairie, J.B., Ed.; Baillière et Fils: Paris, France, 1878.
250. Cannon, W.B. Organization for Physiological Homeostasis. *Physiol. Rev.* **1929**, *9*, 399–431. [CrossRef]
251. Billman, G.E. Homeostasis: The Underappreciated and Far Too Often Ignored Central Organizing Principle of Physiology. *Front. Physiol.* **2020**, *11*, 200. [CrossRef]
252. Butke, P.; Sheridan, S.C. An Analysis of the Relationship between Weather and Aggressive Crime in Cleveland, Ohio. *Weather. Clim. Soc.* **2010**, *2*, 127–139. [CrossRef]
253. Kotas, M.E.; Medzhitov, R. Homeostasis, Inflammation, and Disease Susceptibility. *Cell* **2015**, *160*, 816–827. [CrossRef]
254. Zivin, J.G.; Hsiang, S.M.; Neidell, M. Temperature and Human Capital in the Short and Long Run. *J. Assoc. Environ. Resour. Econ.* **2018**, *5*, 77–105. [CrossRef]
255. Damasio, A. *The Strange Order of Things: Life, Feeling, and the Making of Cultures*; Pantheon: New York, NY, USA, 2018; 336p.
256. McEwen, B.S. Stress, Adaptation, and Disease: Allostasis and Allostatic Load. *Ann. N. Y. Acad. Sci.* **1998**, *840*, 33–44. [CrossRef]
257. Torday, J.S. A Central Theory of Biology. *Med. Hypotheses* **2015**, *85*, 49–57. [CrossRef] [PubMed]
258. Riggs, J.E. Aging, Increasing Genomic Entropy, and Neurodegenerative Disease. *Neurol. Clin.* **1998**, *16*, 757–770. [CrossRef] [PubMed]
259. Houck, P.D. Should negative entropy be included in the fundamental laws of biology? *OA Biol.* **2014**, *2*, 7.
260. Poudel, R.C. A unified science of matter, life and evolution. *Philos. Trans. R. Soc. A Math. Phys. Eng. Sci.* **2023**, *381*, 20220291. [CrossRef] [PubMed]
261. Peto, R.; Roe, F.J.; Lee, P.N.; Levy, L.; Clack, J. Cancer and ageing in mice and men. *Br. J. Cancer* **1975**, *32*, 411–426. [CrossRef] [PubMed]
262. Peto, R. Epidemiology, multistage models, and short-term mutagenicity tests. In *The Origins of Human Cancer*; Cold Spring Harbor Conferences on Cell Proliferation; Hiatt, H.H., Watson, J.D., Winsten, J.A., Eds.; Cold Spring Harbor Laboratory: New York, NY, USA, 1977; Volume 4, pp. 1403–1428.
263. Trifunovic, A.; Wredenberg, A.; Falkenberg, M.; Spelbrink, J.N.; Rovio, A.T.; Bruder, C.E.; Bohlooly-Y, M.; Gidlöf, S.; Oldfors, A.; Wibom, R.; et al. Premature ageing in mice expressing defective mitochondrial DNA polymerase. *Nature* **2004**, *429*, 417–423. [CrossRef] [PubMed]
264. Caulin, A.F.; Maley, C.C. Peto's Paradox: Evolution's prescription for cancer prevention. *Trends Ecol. Evol.* **2011**, *26*, 175–182. [CrossRef] [PubMed]
265. Nunney, L. The real war on cancer: The evolutionary dynamics of cancer suppression. *Evol. Appl.* **2012**, *6*, 11–19. [CrossRef]
266. Seluanov, A.; Gladyshev, V.N.; Vijg, J.; Gorbunova, V. Mechanisms of cancer resistance in long-lived mammals. *Nat. Rev. Cancer* **2018**, *18*, 433–441. [CrossRef]
267. Boddy, A.M.; Abegglen, L.M.; Pessier, A.P.; Aktipis, A.; Schiffman, J.D.; Maley, C.C.; Witte, C. Lifetime cancer prevalence and life history traits in mammals. *Evol. Med. Public Health* **2020**, *2020*, 187–195. [CrossRef]
268. Vincze, O.; Colchero, F.; Lemaître, J.-F.; Conde, D.A.; Pavard, S.; Bieuville, M.; Urrutia, A.O.; Ujvari, B.; Boddy, A.M.; Maley, C.C.; et al. Cancer risk across mammals. *Nature* **2021**, *601*, 263–267. [CrossRef] [PubMed]
269. Cushman, S.A. Entropy, Ecology and Evolution: Toward a Unified Philosophy of Biology. *Entropy* **2023**, *25*, 405. [CrossRef] [PubMed]

270. Scirè, A.; Annovazzi-Lodi, V. The emergence of dynamic networks from many coupled polar oscillators: A paradigm for artificial life. *Theory Biosci.* **2023**, *142*, 291–299. [CrossRef] [PubMed]
271. Swenson, R.; Turvey, M. Thermodynamic Reasons for Perception-Action Cycles. *Ecol. Psychol.* **1991**, *3*, 317–348. [CrossRef]
272. Swenson, R. Autocatakinetics, Evolution, and the Law of Maximum Entropy Production: A Principled Foundation Towards the Study of Human Ecology. *Adv. Hum. Ecol.* **1997**, *6*, 1–47.
273. Aerts, D.; Argüelles, J.A.; Beltran, L.; Sozzo, S. Development of a thermodynamics of human cognition and human culture. *Philos. Trans. R. Soc. A Math. Phys. Eng. Sci.* **2023**, *381*, 20220378. [CrossRef] [PubMed]
274. Athalye, V.; Haven, E. Causal viewpoint and ensemble interpretation: From physics to the social sciences. *Philos. Trans. R. Soc. A Math. Phys. Eng. Sci.* **2023**, *381*, 20220279. [CrossRef]
275. Bejan, A. The principle underlying all evolution, biological, geophysical, social and technological. *Philos. Trans. R. Soc. A Math. Phys. Eng. Sci.* **2023**, *381*, 20220288. [CrossRef]
276. De Bari, B.; Dixon, J.; Kondepudi, D.; Vaidya, A. Thermodynamics, organisms and behaviour. *Philos. Trans. R. Soc. A Math. Phys. Eng. Sci.* **2023**, *381*, 20220278. [CrossRef]
277. Gay-Balmaz, F.; Yoshimura, H. Systems, variational principles and interconnections in non-equilibrium thermodynamics. *Philos. Trans. R. Soc. A Math. Phys. Eng. Sci.* **2023**, *381*, 20220280. [CrossRef]
278. Hall, C.A.S.; McWhirter, T. Maximum power in evolution, ecology and economics. *Philos. Trans. R. Soc. A Math. Phys. Eng. Sci.* **2023**, *381*, 20220290. [CrossRef] [PubMed]
279. Lanchares, M.; Haddad, W.M. Stochastic thermodynamics: Dissipativity, accumulativity, energy storage and entropy production. *Philos. Trans. R. Soc. A Math. Phys. Eng. Sci.* **2023**, *381*, 20220284. [CrossRef] [PubMed]
280. Martin, J.L. Theories of disorder and order, energy and information, in sociological thought. *Philos. Trans. R. Soc. A Math. Phys. Eng. Sci.* **2023**, *381*, 20220292. [CrossRef] [PubMed]
281. Swenson, R. A grand unified theory for the unification of physics, life, information and cognition (mind). *Philos. Trans. R. Soc. A Math. Phys. Eng. Sci.* **2023**, *381*, 20220277. [CrossRef] [PubMed]
282. Tsallis, C. Non-additive entropies and statistical mechanics at the edge of chaos: A bridge between natural and social sciences. *Philos. Trans. R. Soc. A Math. Phys. Eng. Sci.* **2023**, *381*, 20220293. [CrossRef] [PubMed]
283. Ván, P. Toward a universal theory of stable evolution. *Philos. Trans. R. Soc. A Math. Phys. Eng. Sci.* **2023**, *381*, 20220276. [CrossRef]
284. Sparavigna, A.C. Entropies and fractal dimensions. *Philica* **2016**, *559*, 01377975.
285. Mageed, I.A.; Bhat, A.H. Generalized Z-Entropy (Gze) and Fractal Dimensions. *Appl. Math. Inf. Sci.* **2022**, *16*, 829–834. [CrossRef]
286. Sasa, S.-I.; Yokokura, Y. Thermodynamic Entropy as a Noether Invariant. *Phys. Rev. Lett.* **2016**, *116*, 140601. [CrossRef]
287. Hermann, S.; Schmidt, M. Why Noether's theorem applies to statistical mechanics. *J. Physics Condens. Matter* **2022**, *34*, 213001. [CrossRef]
288. Johari, G. Entropy, enthalpy and volume of perfect crystals at limiting high pressure and the third law of thermodynamics. *Thermochim. Acta* **2021**, *698*, 178891. [CrossRef]
289. Hoffmann, H.-J. Energy and entropy of crystals, melts and glasses or what is wrong in Kauzmann's paradox? (Energie und Entropie von Kristallen, Schmelzen und Gläsern oder wo steckt der Fehler in Kauzmanns Paradoxon?). *Mater. Sci. Eng. Technol.* **2012**, *43*, 528–533. [CrossRef]
290. McFadden, J.; Al-Khalili, J. *Life on the Edge: The Coming of Age of Quantum Biology*; Transworld Publishers: London, UK; Penguin Random House: New York, NY, USA, 2015.
291. Doudna, J.A.; Sternberg, S.H. *A Crack in Creation: Gene Editing and the Unthinkable Power to Control Evolution*; Houghton Mifflin Harcourt Publishing Company: New York, NY, USA, 2017.
292. Meena, C.; Hens, C.; Acharyya, S.; Haber, S.; Boccaletti, S.; Barzel, B. Emergent stability in complex network dynamics. *Nat. Phys.* **2023**, *19*, 1033–1042. [CrossRef]
293. Pavlos, G.; Iliopoulos, A.; Zastenker, G.; Zelenyi, L.; Karakatsanis, L.; Riazantseva, M.; Xenakis, M.; Pavlos, E. Tsallis non-extensive statistics and solar wind plasma complexity. *Phys. A Stat. Mech. Its Appl.* **2015**, *422*, 113–135. [CrossRef]
294. Reis, A.H. Use and validity of principles of extremum of entropy production in the study of complex systems. *Ann. Phys.* **2014**, *346*, 22–27. [CrossRef]
295. Ivanitskii, G.R. Self-organizing dynamic stability of far-from-equilibrium biological systems. *Physics-Uspekhi* **2017**, *60*, 705–730. [CrossRef]
296. Benzi, R.; Ciliberto, S.; Tripiccione, R.; Baudet, C.; Massaioli, F.; Succi, S. Extended self-similarity in turbulent flows. *Phys. Rev. E* **1993**, *48*, R29–R32. [CrossRef]
297. Sagan, H. *Space-Filling Curves*; Springer: Dordrecht, The Netherlands, 1994; ISBN 038720170X.
298. Benitez, F.; Romero-Maltrana, D.; Razeto-Barry, P. (Re)interpreting $E = mc^2$. *Found. Phys.* **2022**, *52*, 1–19. [CrossRef]
299. Torday, J. The cell as the mechanistic basis for evolution. *WIREs Syst. Biol. Med.* **2015**, *7*, 275–284. [CrossRef]
300. Torday, J.S. Life Is Simple—Biologic Complexity Is an Epiphenomenon. *Biology* **2016**, *5*, 17. [CrossRef]
301. Torday, J.S.; Miller, W.B. Life is determined by its environment. *Int. J. Astrobiol.* **2016**, *15*, 345–350. [CrossRef]
302. Venegas-Aravena, P.; Cordaro, E.G. Subduction as a Smoothing Machine: How Multiscale Dissipation Relates Precursor Signals to Fault Geometry. *Geosciences* **2023**, *13*, 243. [CrossRef]
303. Contreras-Reyes, E.; Flueh, E.R.; Grevemeyer, I. Tectonic control on sediment accretion and subduction off south central Chile: Implications for coseismic rupture processes of the 1960 and 2010 megathrust earthquakes. *Tectonics* **2010**, *29*, 1–27. [CrossRef]

304. Zielke, O.; Galis, M.; Mai, P.M. Fault roughness and strength heterogeneity control earthquake size and stress drop. *Geophys. Res. Lett.* **2017**, *44*, 777–783. [CrossRef]
305. Schurr, B.; Moreno, M.; Tréhu, A.M.; Bedford, J.; Kummerow, J.; Li, S.; Oncken, O. Forming a Mogi Doughnut in the Years Prior to and Immediately Before the 2014 *M*8.1 Iquique, Northern Chile, Earthquake. *Geophys. Res. Lett.* **2020**, *47*, e2020GL088351. [CrossRef]
306. Venegas-Aravena, P. Geological earthquake simulations generated by kinematic heterogeneous energy-based method: Self-arrested ruptures and asperity criterion. *Open Geosci.* **2023**, *15*, 20220522. [CrossRef]
307. Venegas-Aravena, P.; Cordaro, E.G. Analytical Relation between b-Value and Electromagnetic Signals in Pre-Macroscopic Failure of Rocks: Insights into the Microdynamics' Physics Prior to Earthquakes. *Geosciences* **2023**, *13*, 169. [CrossRef]
308. Aoki, I. Entropy production in human life span: A thermodynamical measure for aging. *AGE* **1994**, *17*, 29–31. [CrossRef]
309. Sacco, R.G.; Torday, J.S. Systems biology of human aging: A Fibonacci time series model. *Prog. Biophys. Mol. Biol.* **2023**, *177*, 24–33. [CrossRef]
310. Sloman, S.; Fernbach, P. *The Knowledge Illusion: Why We Never Think Alone*; Penguin: New York, NY, USA, 2017.
311. González-Gómez, P.; Razeto-Barry, P.; Araya-Salas, M.; Estades, C. Does Environmental Heterogeneity Promote Cognitive Abilities? *Integr. and Comp. Bio.* **2015**, *55*, 432–443. [CrossRef]
312. Friston, K. The free-energy principle: A rough guide to the brain? *Trends Cogn. Sci.* **2009**, *13*, 293–301. [CrossRef]
313. Andrews, M. The math is not the territory: Navigating the free energy principle. *Biol. Philos.* **2021**, *36*, 30. [CrossRef]
314. Mazzaglia, P.; Verbelen, T.; Çatal, O.; Dhoedt, B. The Free Energy Principle for Perception and Action: A Deep Learning Perspective. *Entropy* **2022**, *24*, 301. [CrossRef] [PubMed]
315. Friston, K.; Friston, K. The free-energy principle: A unified brain theory? *Nat. Rev. Neurosci.* **2010**, *11*, 127–138. [CrossRef] [PubMed]
316. Dodel, S.; Tognoli, E.; Kelso, J.A.S. Degeneracy and Complexity in Neuro-Behavioral Correlates of Team Coordination. *Front. Hum. Neurosci.* **2020**, *14*, 328. [CrossRef] [PubMed]
317. Carroll, S.B. *The Serengeti Rules: The Quest to Discover How Life Works and Why It Matters*; Princeton University: Princeton, NJ, USA, 2016.

MDPI AG
Grosspeteranlage 5
4052 Basel
Switzerland
Tel.: +41 61 683 77 34

Fractal and Fractional Editorial Office
E-mail: fractalfract@mdpi.com
www.mdpi.com/journal/fractalfract

www.ingramcontent.com/pod-product-compliance
Lightning Source LLC
Chambersburg PA
CBHW061815210926
51850CB00006B/708